How to Become a Mac® OS X Power User

Dr. Mac
The OS X Files

Bob LeVitus

Wiley Publishing, Inc.

Dr. Mac: The OS X Files

Copyright © 2002 Wiley Publishing, Inc., Indianapolis, Indiana

Published by
Wiley Publishing, Inc.
909 Third Avenue
New York, NY 10022
www.wiley.com

Published simultaneously in Canada

For general information on our other products and services or to obtain technical support please contact our Customer Care Department within the U.S. at 800-762-2974, outside the U.S. at 317-572-3993 or fax 317-572-4002.

Wiley also publishes its books in a variety of electronic formats. Some content that appears in print may not be available in electronic books.

Library of Congress Cataloging-in-Publication Data:

Manufactured in the United States of America

10 9 8 7 6 5 4 3 2 1

ISBN: 0-7645-1680-9

1O/ST/QV/QS/IN

Credits

Acquisitions Editor
Michael Roney

Editorial Manager
Rev Mengle

Vice President and Executive Group Publisher
Richard Swadley

Vice President and Executive Publisher
Bob Ipsen

Vice President and Publisher
Barry Pruett

Senior Permissions Editor
Carmen Krikorian

Cover Designer
Jesse Dunn

Special Help
Tony Augsburger, Cricket Franklin, Shelley Lea,
Jill Piscitelli, Anna Rohrer, Lindsay Sandman,
Ian Smith, Beth Taylor

For my wife Lisa, who hung in there, even after the going got tough. LYATMATS and EGBOK! And to my kids, who I've seen far too little of lately—I miss you guys. But it's done and I'm back now. I love you both to pieces.

‰

About the Author

Bob LeVitus, often referred to as "Dr. Macintosh," has written 38 popular computer books including this one. He's also written bestsellers including, "Mac OS X For Dummies" for Wiley, "The Little iTunes Book," for Peachpit Press, and "Stupid Mac Tricks" and "Dr. Macintosh," both for Addison-Wesley. His books have sold more than a million copies worldwide.

Bob is one of the world's leading authorities on the Macintosh and its operating systems. From 1989 to 1997 he was a contributing editor/columnist for MacUser magazine, writing the Help Folder, Beating the System, Personal Best, and Game Room columns at various times in his busy career. He was the host of Mac Today, a half-hour television show syndicated in over 100 markets, which aired in late 1992. (While his first love will always be the Mac, he's also written more than half a dozen popular books for Windows users. But it's been a few years since he's had to do that and he's learned his lesson.)

He is presently a newspaper columnist (Dr. Mac) for the Houston Chronicle and other newspapers and has been published in more than two-dozen computer magazines over the past fifteen years.

Prior to giving his life over to computers, he spent almost seven years at Kresser/Craig/D.I.K., a Los Angeles advertising agency and marketing consultancy and its subsidiary L & J Research. He holds a B.S. in Marketing from California State University.

He lives in Austin, Texas with his wife Lisa, children Allison and Jacob, some birds and lizards, and a small pack of Welsh Springer Spaniels and a Vizsla.

Acknowledgments

First and foremost, thank you for buying my book.

This is always the hardest part for me, because, you see, most books are a collaborative effort and this one is no exception. So many people have contributed in so many ways, I just know I'll forget someone. (Takes a deep breath...)

Dennis R. Cohen, who wrote the first drafts of Chapters 4, and 10–13, was an invaluable resource, not only as a writer, but for his encyclopedic knowledge of Mac OS X lore and trivia, his ongoing advice and council, and his technical editing and expertise. I can't thank him enough for delivering all he promised and more.

And a big thank to Apple and all the great people I worked with over the course of writing this book, namely Bill Evans, Ken Bereskin, Nathalie Welch, and Grace Kvamme, with the able assistance of my favorite Apple flack, Jennifer Ackman of Edelman Public Relations.

Thanks also to my agent, Carole "Swifty" McClendon. You're still rocking after 14 years!

This book began its life as a Coriolis Group project; I hope I don't miss anyone, but I'd like to thank Publisher Katherine Hartlove and Acquisitions Editor Charlotte Carpentier, who had faith in my proposal and fought hard to do this book with me and do it the right way. So thanks.

Then, in roughly the order I worked with them: Thanks to my Development Editor, Jessica Choi—it was a pleasure working with you; to the Coriolis PR, Marketing, and Sales people including (but not limited to) Tracy Rooney, Adrienne Dueck, and my Product Marketing Manager, Jeff Johnson—y'all were fabulous.

Next, I have nothing but thanks for both of the editors I worked with, Meredith Brittain and Dan Young. Most editors are idiots; you are not. For that I'm eternally grateful.

Moving right along, after Coriolis closed down unexpectedly, the nice folks at Wiley Publishing jumped in, picked up the ball (or the book, as the case may be) and ran with it.

First and foremost, I want to thank my Acquisitions Editor, Mike Roney. Not only has he believed in me for years, but also he believed in this book from day one. I'd also like to thank the Visual/Graphic Design group's VP and Publisher, Barry Pruett, and Editorial Manager, Rev Mengle, as well as Carmen Krikorian, Marisa Pearman, Cricket Franklin, Beth Taylor, Tony Augsburger, Ian Smith, and Shelley Lea— without their capable assistance you wouldn't be holding this book in your hand.

I'd be remiss if I didn't also thank Brian Little, this book's technical editor, who was always there with an astute observation, superb suggestion, or bad joke. Thanks, Brian. You done good.

I already thanked them once but once is not enough, so thanks to my family for putting up with me working when I should've been playing. Thanks again for your understanding.

We're winding down now but I'd like to thank the late John Wiley for founding this company nearly 200 years ago, and publishing legendary writers such as Herman Melville, Edgar Allan Poe, Nathaniel Hawthorne, Hans Christian Andersen, Victor Hugo, Charles Dickens, and Elizabeth Barrett Browning. Thanks to Mr. Wiley, I can say stuff like, "I'm with the same publisher as Poe, Hugo, Dickens, and Hawthorne...." That's just too cool.

And finally, last but not least, a very special bigger-than-the-sky thanks to all the people who submitted a tip or desktop for Chapters 15 and 16. You are the best. Thanks again.

Contents at a Glance

Table of Contents

Introduction

Thank you for buying *Dr. Mac: The OS X Files.* There are a plethora of books about Mac OS X you could choose; I'm please you've selected this one, and I'll do my best not to disappoint you.

The subtitle of this book is *How to Become a Mac OS X Power User.* But what, exactly, *is* a power user? According to the unpublished *Dr. Mac Dictionary*:

■ **Power User** *(pou'ər yōō'zer) n.* **1.** Someone who uses a Macintosh better, faster, or more elegantly than you do. **2.** Someone who can answer Macintosh-related questions you can't.

Being a power user means finding faster, easier, and better ways of doing things, as well as knowing what to do if an emergency arises. That's what this book is about.

You don't need to know programming to become a Mac OS X power user. In fact, many power users (including yours truly) couldn't program their way out of a paper bag.

NOTE

> Okay, using Unix is a little like coding. And power users know at least a little of that (and if they don't, they should—it's nothing to be afraid of).

The point being: You don't need to know C++ from Carbon or Cocoa (or even Cocoa Puffs, for that matter) to become a Mac OS X power user. Being a power user is about *using* your Mac, not *programming* it!

Though Mac OS X is not hard to use, there are hundreds (or even thousands or maybe even millions) of shortcuts, secrets, hints, tips, utilities, and programs that make using it even better. I know—I've spent the last year working with and writing about Mac OS X almost exclusively. Along the way I've discovered many useful tips, hints, techniques, and programs, which I share with you in upcoming pages.

I've been using Macs exclusively for more than 15 years and writing about them almost as long. Still, I can't tell you how many times I've done something the same way for months, only to have someone show me a better way—one that takes less time or effort. Or how tickled I am when I discover a new timesaving utility or program.

Unlike some authors, I cheerfully admit that, although I know quite a bit about Mac OS X, I *still* don't know everything. (Heck, I don't even know *almost* everything yet!) And so, Chapters 15 is filled with tips, hints, and techniques *other* power users think you should know, and Chapter 16 features lots of pictures of other power users' desktops and favorite programs in action.

The bottom line is: This book is designed to save you from having to reinvent the wheel and to make you more productive each and every time you use Mac OS X.

I live and breathe Macintosh (and Mac OS X). I use a Mac all day, every day, and have for as long as I can remember. And I've been using Mac OS X since long before it was released to the general public.

More than a decade ago, I served as Editor-in-Chief of *MACazine*, one of the first and most outspoken of all Macintosh publications. After it was acquired by *Macworld* magazine, I became a contributing editor for *MacUser*, where I wrote the Help Folder, Game Room, and Beating the System columns at various times. After eight years at *MacUser*, I took to the Web, and moved to MacCentral (**www.maccentral.com**), where I created and wrote the popular "Ask Dr. Mac" question-and-answer column. And for the past five years I've also penned a syndicated newspaper column, *Dr. Mac*, which runs in the Houston Chronicle and other newspapers each and every week.

In my spare time (ha!) I've written 38 books about the Mac, including the first and second editions of *Dr. Macintosh, Mac Answers, The Little iTunes Book,* and a lot of other books (many of which contain the words *Stupid* or *Dummies* in their titles).

So my job for the past 15 years has essentially been to find information that will help other users use their Macs more efficiently.

I'm not complaining. This job has some wonderful perks—I examine more Mac software and hardware in a month than most people will use in a lifetime. (Best of all, I get most of it for free!)

Needless to say, I've spent a good part of the past 15 years hunched in front of one of my Macs from dawn to dusk, and often long into the night.

NOTE

In case you're wondering, I currently have three Macs running in my office: a G4/500 (my main Mac), a G4 Cube, and my PowerBook Titanium (not to mention the two iMacs my wife and kids share).

When I'm not testing new software or hardware, I'm writing, preparing camera-ready copy, editing video, or surfing the Web with my cable modem to gather information and/or keep in touch with friends and business acquaintances.

Because I use my Mac for *everything*—writing, schedules, graphics, communications, household finance, recipes, and more—I like nothing better than discovering a method of doing something better, faster, or more elegantly. And, in the true Macintosh spirit, I love being able to share it with other Macintosh users like you!

If I'm not writing or editing, I tend to spend a lot of time looking for the best or most convenient way of doing something on my Mac. In the big scheme of things, my job is to figure out what is hot and what is not. So I read everything I can about the Macintosh. And I mean *everything*—almost every Mac magazine I know of, not to mention more than a dozen Mac-oriented Web sites every day. I also read half-a-dozen user group newsletters each month, just for good measure.

> **TIP**
>
> Some of the best information, hints, and tips you'll find appear in user group newsletters. User group members join because they want answers. Many of them are already power users. There's good information in Chapter 1 for those of you who don't know about user groups. You really should—they're great!

This book contains the best of what I've picked up over the years, through my experiences as a Macintosh lover, beta-tester, editor, Web-surfer, advice counselor, consultant, author, and general all-around Macaholic.

Is This Book for You?

Dr. Mac: The OS X Files was written with the intermediate or advanced user in mind. Among the topics that are covered, are:

- Mastering the OS X Finder

- Protecting your work

- The power user's guide to the Web

- The Classic environment

- What to do in an emergency

- Customizing Mac OS X

- Shareware/Freeware/Demoware (on this book's companion Web site, **www.boblevitus.com/xfiles.html**)

- What other power users think you should know and much more

ALERT!

This book is *not* an introduction to Mac OS X, nor is it an introduction to the Macintosh. If you're not already familiar with both, I strongly recommend that you read my other X-rated book, namely *Mac OS X For Dummies* from Wiley, first.

So this book does not cover every single aspect of Mac OS X. For example, you won't find information on setting up your Internet connection, but you will find lots of tips and hints for using the Internet to find cool stuff for your Mac. You won't find page after page of descriptions of the programs that come with OS X, but you will find tips on using (some of) them better. You won't find instructions for hooking up Ethernet, but you will find tips for sharing files both locally and remotely. And so on.

How to Use This Book

The best way to use this book would be to read it from cover to cover. If you are an intermediate to advanced Mac user, skim over the things you already know, but read every chapter. There are a lot of good hints and tips scattered throughout. If you read only part of the book, you run the risk of missing something that could save you time or trouble someday. More importantly, you'll miss lots of dated rock-and-roll references, puns, wordplay, and more.

So just read it all, okay?

How This Book Is Organized

The chapters in this book are organized logically by topic. Each begins with a brief introduction and big-picture overview, followed by detailed discussion, step-by-step tutorials, hints, and tips.

We'll start off nice and easy in Part I with the basics—an overview of OS X, mastering the OS X Finder, organizing your files and folders, and protecting your data from harm. In Part II we'll move on to meatier topics like using the Web to save time and effort, dealing with the Classic environment, some hardware you should know about, troubleshooting, and customizing. Then, in Part III, it's on to the geeky stuff, including chapters on Unix, NetInfo, and AppleScript. In Part IV, which I call "The Cool Stuff in the Back," you'll find software recommendations, descriptions of programs, and lots of great advice (and pictures) from other power users.

Most hardware and software mentioned includes a URL (Web address) for its maker.

TIP

And every (or maybe almost-every) URL in the book is in the bookmark file at this book's companion Web site—**www.boblevitus.com/xfiles.html**.

Finally, as you may have already noticed, you'll occasionally see one of three jellybeans in the margin:

TIP

The tip jellybean indicates a tip. Doh. Although there are tips throughout the body of this book, the tips with jellybeans are something special. Usually.

NOTE

The note jellybean indicates that I am about to go "off topic." These items aren't vital, but are almost always interesting and sometimes even useful or fun as well. Ignore them at your own peril.

ALERT!

The alert jellybean means "pay attention—this is of the utmost importance." If you see an alert jellybean, think before you type. There are only a few of them in the whole book, so when you see one, please take it seriously.

This Book's Philosophy

This book's unique format—thorough technical overviews and practical immediate solutions—is structured to help you use your knowledge, solve problems, and quickly master complex technical issues to become a Mac OS X power user. By breaking down complex topics into easily manageable components, this format helps you quickly find what you're lookingfor, and its clear diagrams and step-by-step instructions will help you "get it" painlessly.

I'd truly appreciate your comments. I want your suggestions about how I can make future editions of this book even better. Was there something I left out that you felt I should have covered? Was something unclear? Was there too much or too little information on a particular topic? And, of course, if you've got any hints or tips of your own, I'd love for you to share them with me.

I really do welcome your feedback, so please feel free to send me email any time you like. You can email me directly at **osxfiles@boblevitus.com**.

This book has been a pleasure to write. I hope you have as much fun reading it as I had creating it for you!

Part I

In the Beginning: The Basics

In the Beginning...

The Macintosh is an extremely powerful tool, contained in an easy-to-use wrapper. Even someone who knows almost nothing about the Mac can be productive after just a few minutes of training. But a power user, one who knows tips and shortcuts and a bit about what to do in an emergency, will always be far more productive than a novice.

And that, gentle reader, is what this book is all about. Doing more in less time, finding easier ways of doing things, and knowing what to do in an emergency. So without further ado, let's dig right in.

MacBasics 101

Long, long ago, when I bought my first Mac (circa 1985 if you're interested), I thought it would take me only a few days to master. After all, the manuals were short and the interface intuitive. Within a few days, I had indeed reached some level of proficiency—I could double-click, save, and use the Trash. I knew what a startup disk was. I knew the difference between an application and a document. I knew how the Apple menu and Font/DA Mover worked. (How many of you are old enough to remember the hoary, horrid Font/DA Mover?) That, I thought, was all I needed.

Over the next few months, I came to realize that there are hundreds of ways I can customize my Mac to control the way it does things, thousands of shortcuts, both documented and undocumented, just waiting to be discovered, tens of thousands of cool and reasonably priced programs that make my Mac better and easier to use, not to mention the myriad different techniques I can use when things just aren't working right.

Not long after that, I put my realizations to good use. First, I became Editor-in-Chief of *MACazine* (until *Macworld* magazine bought and buried it) and then was a contributing editor for *MacUser* for more than eight years (until *Macworld* magazine bought and buried *it*). So for the past 13 or 14 years, my job has been discovering and sharing information that helps Macintosh owners use their machines better, faster, and more elegantly. I'm not ashamed to admit that I'm still learning, because it's true, but I have learned an awful lot in those years I've spent hunched in front of a Mac.

But before you run, you have to learn to walk, and before you walk, you have to learn to crawl. So this first chapter covers the very basics of Mac OS X, starting with an introduction to Mac OS X itself and to system software. The reason this material appears in the first chapter should be obvious: Although every reader may not need or want a DVD-R drive or high-powered software, everyone who uses a Mac must use system software.

The information in this chapter, along with its hints and techniques, should give you the background you need to begin coaxing more performance out of *your* Mac.

TIP

This chapter (and indeed, this entire book) assumes that you have installed Mac OS X *and* Mac OS 9.2.x or greater. If you have not yet purchased Mac OS X, go to **http://store. apple.com** and buy it. (When I say "9.2.x or greater," I mean any version of Mac OS 9 above Mac OS 9.2.) If you are using Mac OS 9.0 or 9.1, you should definitely upgrade to version 9.2.1 (or higher), because these are not only regarded as more stable than earlier 9x versions, they're required by the current version of Mac OS X (10.1 as I type this), if you intend to use Classic mode.

ALERT!

Though I won't talk about Classic mode in depth until Chapter 6, if you *don't* have Mac OS 9.2.x or greater *and* Mac OS X *both* installed, Classic won't work. And most of you are going to need Classic, probably long before you get to Chapter 6.

Introducing Your System Software

Mac OS 9.2.x and Mac OS X are your *system software*, sometimes referred to as your *operating system*. But what exactly are they? In a nutshell, your computer's operating system is a collection of special software that makes your Mac work. So, if Mac OS 9 or Mac OS X, or both, aren't properly installed on an available disk when you turn on your Mac, it will just sit there flashing a question mark until a valid operating system is available to it.

System software differs from application software, such as AppleWorks and Microsoft Word, in that it manages memory and communicates with input and output devices, such as printers and scanners.

NOTE

In addition to your operating system software, other operating instructions are stored in *Read-Only Memory (ROM)* that resides on a chip inside your Mac. ROM is non-volatile, which means it can never be erased or changed.

The Finder

The Finder is part of your system software—but it's a special program that starts automatically when you turn on your Mac. The Mac OS X Finder looks different from the OS 9 Finder, as you can see in Figures 1.1 and 1.2.

Figure 1.1
The Mac OS X Finder: Among other things, it's far prettier than the OS 9 Finder (shown in Figure 1.2).

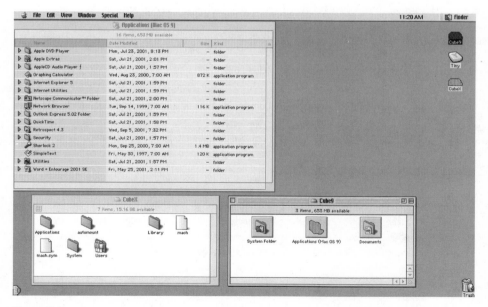

Figure 1.2
The Mac OS 9 Finder: Less pretty, less functional, and less stable than the OS X Finder.

The menus have different names (and different contents, too). Only the OS X Finder has the wonderful Column view (the Cube 9 window in Figure 1.1) and useful Dock (bottom of Figure 1.1), and only OS 9 has the near-useless Button view (the Cube 9 window in Figure 1.2), and so on.

But the OS 9 and OS X Finders are more alike than different. In spite of cosmetic differences, both are in charge of managing your Macintosh desktop, letting you manipulate icons on the desktop; launch applications and utilities and customize them in many ways; organize your files into folders; copy, eject, and erase disks; use menus; and much more.

If you've used Mac OS 9, you'll get accustomed to the Mac OS X Finder in no time at all. If you've never used anything but the OS X Finder, trust me, it's an order of magnitude better than the OS 9 one, if only because it doesn't crash nearly as often, and when it does crash, you can relaunch it and go on with your work. The OS 9 Finder, on the other hand, almost always causes you to restart your Mac when it crashes—which it does all too often.

Think of the Finder as the program you use to *do stuff with your Mac.* Think of most other applications as programs you use to *do stuff* (such as paint, draw, type, and so on).

> **NOTE**
>
> I could talk about the Finder for days, and indeed I will in just a few pages. But this should hold you until you get to Chapter 2, which provides all kinds of tips for mastering the Mac OS X Finder.

The Mac OS X System Folder

Under Mac OS 9, all your system software is stored in a special folder called the System Folder. Under Mac OS X, *most* of your system software is in a special folder called System (note that the X version doesn't contain the word "Folder" in its name), but parts of it are also contained in the Library folder(s), and other parts of it are "invisible."

Figure 1.3 shows a typical Mac OS X System folder.

> **NOTE**
>
> Notice that the title bar says "Library" and not "System." That's because the only thing in the OS X System folder *is* the Library folder, as you can see in Figure 1.3. It's actually the Library folder that contains all those other subfolders.

Unlike Mac OS 9 and earlier, Mac OS X enforces a strict hands-off policy for most of these folders. And so, for the most part, you cannot modify, add to, or delete them. Should you try, you'll receive an error message similar to the ones shown in Figures 1.4 and 1.5.

Figure 1.3
The various subfolders found inside the OS X System folder.

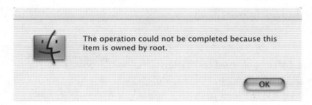

Figure 1.4
OS X doesn't let just anyone mess around with the contents of its System (and Library) folders.

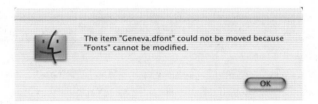

Figure 1.5
Here's another reminder to keep your paws off the OS X System folder and its contents.

Even administrators can't modify, add to, or delete from most of these folders. Power users, of course, not only know how to modify, add to, and delete from these folders, they also know which ones are safe to mess with, and why. You'll know all that, too (and a whole lot more) by the time you finish this book. But I'm getting ahead of myself, so let's move on.

Apple System Software Updates

Every so often, Apple updates Mac OS X to fix bugs and/or add new features, and running the latest and greatest version on your machine is almost always a good idea.

Figure 1.6
This Mac is running OS X 10.1, which was the current version on the day I wrote this.

To find out what version you have, choose About This Mac from the Apple menu, which displays the window shown in Figure 1.6.

You can use this same technique (often referred to as displaying the "About box") to determine the version number of most software. For example, if you are running Microsoft Word, choose About Microsoft Word from the Apple menu to see its version number. This trick will work with 99 percent of your software. (The other 1 percent must have had a forgetful programmer—the About box is where the version number is *supposed* to go.)

Where Did My RAM Usage Information Go?

Unlike earlier versions of Mac OS, the About This Mac window no longer tells you how much RAM each active program is using. There's a good reason for this omission—Mac OS X handles all aspects of RAM allocation for you automatically, so you never have to "give an application more memory" to get it to work right, nor do you have to decide whether to turn virtual memory on—it's always on under OS X and it's much, much faster and more reliable than it was under earlier versions of Mac OS.

If you can't bear the thought of not knowing how your RAM is being used, the Process Viewer application (in the OS X Utilities folder) can provide some information on how much RAM each application or process is currently using. See Chapter 7 for more info. But I rarely use Process Viewer to monitor RAM. The freeware programs MemoryStick and Perfboard, which are covered in Chapters 9 and 14, provide more than enough information most of the time.

1

OS X, like OS 9 before it, can keep track of new and updated versions of itself either automatically or manually. And though you'll learn about this feature in Chapter 2, before you get that far, I need to make an important point right here and now (and it's a point you'll hear more than once in this book):

Back up anything and everything that's important to you before you update.

If you don't understand what this means, read Chapter 4, which contains complete instructions and strategies for backing up your hard disk and files.

There are several reasons this is so important, but the most significant one, at least for this chapter, is that if something doesn't work properly with the new system software, you can go back to the way things were with very little hassle as long as you have a backup of the way things were.

Before I move on to some broad and general hints about using Mac OS X, here are two tips for updating OS X.

TIP

Don't be the first one on your block to update to a new version of OS X (or any program, for that matter). Before installing *any* update, a smart power user will check out the Mac Web sites described in Chapter 5 to determine whether other users are having problems.

If an application or hardware device stops working after you update to a new version of Mac OS X, the manufacturer will often release an update that fixes the problem. So if you're having problems with a specific piece of hardware or software after updating your system software, contact the manufacturer and describe the problem. You'll often learn that a fix is available or will be available soon, and it's usually easier to postpone using that software or hardware until you receive the fix than it is to revert to an earlier version of Mac OS X. The point is, if you *don't* contact the manufacturer, you'll never know.

General Tips, Hints, and Advice for Aspiring Power Users

The following sections provide some *very* general hints that will help you get the most out of your Macintosh. Don't let their general-ness put you off—they can make your life with OS X a whole lot easier.

Read the Fine Manual (a.k.a. R.T.F.M.)

Some folks say, "Power users don't read manuals." That's rubbish. Much of the power and elegance of today's Macintosh software is concealed, and if you don't read the documentation, you will no doubt miss out on powerful features that aren't in the menus.

Read about the Macintosh

You can never stop learning about the Mac, so read everything you have time for. Publications worth investigating include both the print and Web versions of *Macworld* (**www.macworld.com**) and *MacAddict* (**Macaddict.com**), plus all the Web sites covered in Chapter 5.

Reading about the Mac keeps you up to date on your computer, your operating system, and your application and utility software. I find the Web more useful than print, but that shouldn't surprise you because printed magazines can't possibly be as up-to-date as Web sites. Even so, I think you'll find that both the print magazines and the Web sites are packed with useful tips, hints, product reviews, and comparisons.

Improve Your Typing Skills

If you're not typing at least 40 words per minute without looking, you're wasting time. Possibly the easiest way to get more done in less time is to become a better touch-typist. Lots of inexpensive programs can fix you right up in just a few days. I have found the commercial program UltraKey very effective, but almost any typing tutor program— including the excellent shareware program MasterKey, covered in Chapter 14 and available through the link at **www.boblevitus.com/xfiles.html**—will do the trick.

When I bought my first Mac, I couldn't type at all. Now I can type more than 60 words per minute, without looking at the keyboard and with relatively few mistakes.

Customize Your Working Environment

Many users forget that they can change many aspects of the Macintosh work environment with System Preference panes. This is still true with Mac OS X. You can change the desktop picture, sound level, screen resolution, mouse speed, internal clock settings, and much more.

Between them, Chapters 2 and 9 show you many ways to customize your environment, including how to change the sensitivity of your keyboard or mouse, choose a different beep sound, and much more. For now, just keep in mind that you can customize many facets of your everyday work environment. Play around with the different settings until you find the ones that are best for you.

Develop Mouse Independence

Another way to get things done faster is to reduce your dependence on the mouse. Use *command-key equivalents* (sometimes called *keyboard shortcuts*), which are a combination of key-presses usually involving the Command key (a.k.a. cloverleaf/Apple/ pretzel key) and one or more keys that choose commands from menus without using

1

the mouse. For example, when you need to create a new folder in the Finder, get into the habit of using the shortcut Command+Shift+N instead of grabbing the mouse, pulling down the File menu, and selecting New Folder.

Almost every Macintosh program has command-key equivalents for some menu choices. Learn them and use them. Once you get into the habit of using them, grabbing the mouse to pull down a menu will seem archaic.

Unfortunately, many programs don't offer command keys for frequently performed actions. The way around this is to purchase a macro program such as QuicKeys X (**www.quickeys.com**), which is covered in Chapter 9.

Some of the tasks a macro program, such as QuicKeys X, perform can also be done with AppleScript. It's not as simple, but the price—AppleScript is free with OS X— can't be beat. You'll learn about AppleScript in Chapter 13.

Don't Be Afraid to Use Technical Support

When you buy software, you're usually entitled to some kind of technical support from the publisher. Generally, the publisher provides you with a specific telephone number you can call to talk to a technical representative. Many publishers also provide a fax number, a bulletin board, or an email address where you can post questions. Most of the time, these services are free, particularly if you register your software; however, some publishers may charge you for various kinds of extended support.

Nonetheless, if you're having trouble getting something done, or if a feature doesn't seem to work properly, you should call for help. But before making the call, check the manual. There's nothing more embarrassing than calling for help and having the voice on the phone tell you the solution is on page 5 of the manual.

What the Heck Is a Macro?

A *macro* is a sequence of keyboard or mouse actions defined by the user to automate repetitive tasks. With a macro program installed on your Mac, you can do the following with a single keystroke:

- Launch applications or documents
- Open desk accessories
- Scroll, close, or resize windows
- Type any text you like (boilerplate text)
- Type the time and/or date
- Restart/Shut down

... and a whole lot more. You'll learn more about macro programs in Chapters 9 and 14.

Try to be helpful when you call. Know what version of the program you are using and what version of Mac OS X you're running (by checking the About box, as described in the "Apple System Software Updates" section earlier in this chapter).

Explain exactly what happened just before the problem occurred and describe it carefully to the support representative. See if you can duplicate the problem before calling. If it occurs repeatedly, it will be much easier to resolve than if it happens only sporadically.

Being prepared when you call for technical support will save both you and the tech support representative time, and go a long way toward helping the technician solve your problem.

Join a User Group

One of the best ways to learn about the Mac is to join a user group. *User groups* are made up of people just like you—people who want to learn how to use their Mac more effectively. They hold regular meetings, demonstrate the latest software, exchange shareware and public domain software, and publish informative newsletters. There are more than 1,000 user groups in the U.S. alone! If you're not involved with a user group, you're really missing out.

Apple offers an extensive list of *frequently asked questions* (a.k.a. *FAQs*) about user groups. You'll find it at **www.apple.com/usergroups/contact.html**.

Experiment

Don't be afraid to experiment. Try anything and everything. One of my favorites is to hold down the Option key and select items from menus or tools from a palette. Try this in Excel or Adobe Illustrator. You'll be surprised at what pops up. All kinds of hidden dialog boxes and controls are available. Of course, if you read the manual, you'll know all about these "secret" features.

Poke around and try everything. It's nearly impossible to hurt your Mac by merely pulling down a menu or invoking a menu item.

I recommend backing up important files before you begin to play, though, just in case.

Buy What You Need to be Productive

Even though most products I recommend in this book are inexpensive, the question "When should I spend money on something?" has probably crossed your mind already.

1

The items I recommend throughout the book range from shareware that requests a donation of only a few dollars to hard disks and accelerator cards that cost several thousands of dollars.

When faced with any cash outlay, you have to ask yourself: "How much time will it save me each day?" Divide the cost of the product by whatever you think your time is worth.

Performing this calculation for inexpensive software hardly makes sense. But let's assume that you want to justify a *major* purchase, such as a tape backup unit for $600.

Right now, backing up to CD-R discs is taking 20 minutes a day. You have to sit there and swap disks, so it can't be done unattended. If you buy the tape drive, you will be able to perform an incremental backup in less than 10 minutes, unattended. That means you can do something else, like go to lunch or go home for the evening. When you return, the backup is complete. So let's say it saves you the full 20 minutes a day.

If your time is worth $20 an hour, you're saving $6.66 a day. So, assuming that you back up every day (as well you should!), in three months, the tape drive will pay for itself. ($600 divided by $6.66 equals 90 days.)

This approach works beautifully on your boss when you've got your eye on a new piece of hardware or software.

Look at purchases for your Mac as investments in productivity. Evaluate potential purchases based on the amount of time they'll save you. You'll be surprised at how affordable things become when viewed in this light. If that doesn't work, but it's something you can't live without, buy it anyway.

TIP

Before you buy a piece of software, visit the publisher's Web site and look for a trial version. If one is available, download it and give it a try before plunking down your hard-earned cash.

Mastering the OS X Finder

The Finder is the heart and soul of your Mac. It's the all-important program responsible for managing your files, folders, and desktop, and it does lots of other important behind-the-scenes work, too. It's also the one program no Mac user can avoid completely. While you don't ever have to use Photoshop, Word, FileMaker Pro, iTunes, or any other program ever invented, every Mac user uses the Finder.

Power users are in tune with the Finder. They benefit from its strengths and work around its weaknesses. (And most have *fun* doing it.)

I urge you to read this chapter with your mouse in one hand and your keyboard under the other. Try every technique you are not familiar with as soon as you finish reading it. I guarantee that you'll remember it better by doing it than you will by sitting on the couch reading about it.

> **TIP**
>
> It wouldn't hurt to try everything immediately after reading *all* the chapters, but since we're just getting started, I hope that mentioning this here encourages you to adopt a very good habit.

Finder, Window, and Dock Basics

This chapter is chock full of useful information and techniques for using the Finder, Finder windows, and Dock better, faster, and more elegantly. But you have to learn to crawl before you can walk, and you have to learn to walk before you can drive a Porsche at high speed. So, I'll start off nice and easy. This first section covers basic techniques, features, and tips, with an emphasis on stuff that's new, vastly improved since OS 9, or easily overlooked.

Startup Basics

Let's start at the very beginning and look at some of the special keys you can hold down at startup, and what happens when you do:

- *Option*—Hold down the Option key during startup to invoke the Startup Manager and choose a startup disk *before* your Mac boots, as shown in Figure 2.1. The Startup Manager appears before your Mac begins booting, letting you choose a startup disk "on the fly."

> **NOTE**
>
> Not all Macs support this feature. The newer your Mac is, the more likely it will support this nifty feature.

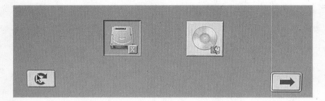

Figure 2.1
The Startup Manager: Click a disk icon to select it, then click the arrow button to start up from that disk.

The timing can be tricky—press and hold Option immediately after you hear the startup sound, then, after the Startup Manager appears, click a disk icon to select the startup disk. The circular button rescans for available startup disks, including a NetBoot server; the right-arrow button tells the computer to go ahead and start up from the selected startup disk. The startup disk selected in the OS 9 Startup Disk control panel or the OS X Startup Disk System Preference pane is always shown on the left.

> **ALERT!**
>
> If both OS X and OS 9 are on the same volume or partition, this trick won't work, which is one of the reasons I prefer having two (or more) volumes-as I'll explain in Chapter 3.

- *C*—Hold down the C key during startup to boot from a CD; the CD, of course, must contain a bootable operating system, either OS 9 or OS X.

> **TIP**
>
> If the C key doesn't work, there are two other techniques that might. The first is to insert the CD *before* you reboot and choose it as the startup disk using the Startup Disk system preference pane, then restart. This should work on any Mac model

capable of running OS X. The second is to hold down the Delete (called "Backspace" on some keyboards), Option, Command, and Shift keys (it's OK to use your nose, if you must) during startup. I use the mnemonic device "DOCS" to remember which keys. Alas, this trick only works on older Macs—not iMacs, blue & white G3 towers, or G4s.

- *Shift*—Hold down the Shift key during startup to close all open Finder windows when the desktop appears.

NOTE

After countless attempts, I never got this to work on *any* of my Macs. But, according to the mothership (Apple), it should. Caveat Mactor.

- *Command+S*—Hold down the Command and S keys to startup in single-user mode.

- *Command+V*—Hold down the Command and V keys to startup in verbose mode.

NOTE

Verbose and single-user modes are only needed when troubleshooting startup issues. We'll talk about them in Chapter 8.

- *Command+Option+P+R*—Hold down the Command, Option, P, and R keys to zap your Mac's Parameter RAM (PRAM).

NOTE

Resetting (zapping) your PRAM is usually only needed when troubleshooting. We'll talk about it in Chapter 8, too.

- *Mouse button*—Hold down the mouse button during startup to eject a disk, CD-ROM, or DVD stuck inside your Mac.

New or Improved Finder Features

OS X 10.1 has several new ways to copy and move files from one place to another, and all the ones you remember from OS 9 and before work in OS X as well. For example, you still hold down the Option key to copy an icon (file or folder) or icons to a new location on the same disk, on the same volume (i.e., different partition on the same disk), or to the desktop.

And you still hold down Command and Option when dragging an icon (or icons) to another location (on the same disk or volume, on another disk or volume, or to the desktop—in this case it doesn't matter) to create an alias (or aliases) of the icon in the new location.

But now, starting with Mac OS X 10.1, there are two great new shortcuts—one to move an icon (or icons) from one disk or volume to another, the other to copy an icon or icons from one location to another without clicking, dragging, or even touching the mouse if you don't want to.

Moving an Icon (File or Folder) from One Disk (or Volume) to Another

In the old days (pre 10.1), there was no way to *move* a file or folder from one volume or disk to another volume or disk. Sure, you could copy a file or folder to another volume or disk, then drag the original to the Trash. But now you can move a file from one disk or volume to another in just one step. Just hold down the Command key when you drag an icon from one volume or disk to another, and the item will be moved instead of copied.

You can tell it's being moved, not copied, by looking at the Copy window, which will say "Moving" instead of "Copying," as shown in Figure 2.2.

Figure 2.2
Notice how the Copy window says "Moving 178 items" and not "Copying 178 items"? Cool, huh?

Once the move is complete, the original file or folder is automatically deleted by Mac OS X, leaving only the "moved" file or folder on the "other" disk or volume.

If you're a long-time Mac user, it kind of makes you wonder why it took so many years for this useful feature to make an appearance in Mac OS.

Copying an Icon (File or Folder) from One Location to Another

The second new shortcut is even neater. In the old days, if you selected an icon and chose Edit|Copy or used the keyboard shortcut Command+C, the name of the icon would be copied to the Clipboard. The old and unintuitive way to copy a file or folder to another location on the same disk was to hold down the Option key as you dragged the file or folder to another location.

The Option-key trick still works, but OS X 10.1 has another, much more handy way to copy files and folders—using good old copy and paste. Doh. These days, OS X lets you copy any icon, then paste it anywhere you like—in another folder on the same volume, or a folder on a different volume, or even the Desktop. First, select the icon(s) by single-clicking it, then choose Edit|Copy "name-of-file-or-folder," as shown in Figure 2.3, where the name of the folder I'm copying is Ch02 Figs.

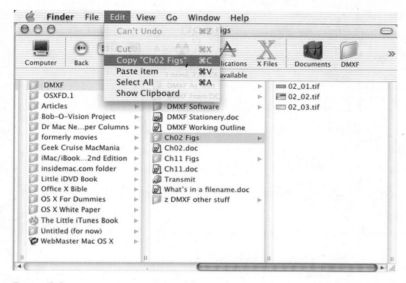

Figure 2.3
Select the icon you want to copy to another location and then choose Edit|Copy.

> **TIP**
>
> You can also use the keyboard shortcut Command+C.

Now, click in the location you want the copy to appear, then choose Edit|Paste Item.

> **TIP**
>
> You can also use the keyboard shortcut Command+V.

You can, of course, still copy an icon's name, the same as always, by first selecting the icon, then pressing Return or Enter to select its name, as shown in Figure 2.4.

Notice the subtle difference between Figures 2.3 and 2.4. In Figure 2.3, the *folder* itself is selected, which is indicated by the fact that the entire folder is highlighted. In Figure 2.4, because I pressed the Enter key after selecting the folder icon, only the *name of the folder* is selected, so only the name is highlighted. Clear as mud, right? Actually, though it takes a little getting used to, you'll soon find this technique is the easiest way to copy something from one place to another.

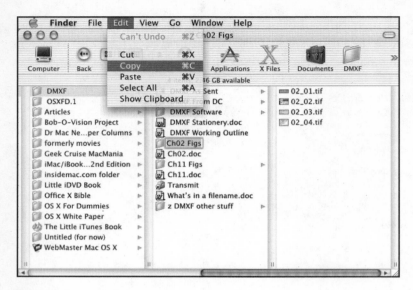

Figure 2.4
The folder's name is highlighted, so only the name is what will be copied (not the icon itself).

NOTE

Two other features got major facelifts and feature-lifts in OS X 10.1. Since not everyone *uses* screen shots or iDisk, the sidebars that follow are self-contained—you can skip them if you wish.

Shooting Screens for Fun and Profit

In Mac OS 10.0.x, there was no built-in keyboard shortcut for creating screen shots—pictures of what appears on your screen. You had exactly one option for screen capture: the Grab utility provided by Apple (which is in the Utilities folder, in the OS X Applications folder). If you ever had to use it, you remember how stinky it was. It's not much better in 10.1, but most of the keyboard shortcuts (for shooting screens) you knew and loved in prior Mac OS releases are back:

■ Command+Shift+3 takes a picture of the whole screen (or screens if you have multiple monitors) and saves it on your desktop as a TIFF file. The first one will be named Picture 1.tiff, the next one named Picture 2.tiff, and so on. Note that the file may not display the .tiff extension, depending on how you've configured the Finder preference for File Extensions (which we'll get to in a few pages).

■ Command+Shift+4 turns the cursor into a "crosshair" you can drag to select any part of the screen (or screens if you have multiple monitors). When you release the mouse button, a picture of the selected area on your desktop is saved as a TIFF file, using the same naming convention as above.

(continued)

2

TIP

You can still use the Grab utility provided with OS X to create screen shots, and it has an added convenience—it lets you create "timed" screen shots. To snap one, launch Grab, choose Capture|Timed Screen or use the keyboard shortcut.

Command+Shift+Z. A little window will appear, as shown in Figure 2.5. Click the Start Timer button and you'll have 10 seconds to set up your screen shot before Grab takes the picture.

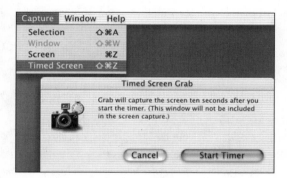

Figure 2.5
Grab's Timed Screen feature gives you 10 seconds to set up your screen before it shoots.

NOTE

The bad news is that Shift+Command+Capslock+4, a useful command in OS 9 that lets you take a picture of a single window by clicking it, isn't in the OS X arsenal. So, it doesn't work when you're in an OS X program. The good news is that all the screen capture shortcuts seem to work in Classic, including the Shift+Command+Capslock+4 for capturing a single window. Furthermore, if you add the Control key to any of the shortcuts described above, the picture is placed on the Mac OS Clipboard rather than saved to a file.

If you have screen-shooting needs beyond what I've just described, you'll love Snapz Pro X, the high-performance screen-shooting utility from Ambrosia Software. It's extremely flexible and much more capable than the built-in OS X stuff, and it's what I used to capture every screen shot in this book. You'll learn more about it in Chapter 14, and find a link to Ambrosia at **www.boblevitus.com/xfiles.html**.

Your New and Improved iDisk

iDisk, for those of you just arriving at the Mac party, is a 20MB virtual disk you access via your Internet connection. Apple provides one to every Mac user absolutely free. Physically, your iDisk is located on an Apple server somewhere in the ether (or maybe Cupertino, CA, where the

(continued)

mothership is based), but it appears on your desktop just like a hard or floppy disk. And if 20MB isn't enough for you, Apple will sell you additional iDisk storage space—up to a gigabyte.

> **TIP**
>
> Additional iDisk space doesn't come cheap. Last time I checked, it was a dollar a megabyte per year, which means, in other words, a gigabyte (1,000MB) of storage will run you $1,000/year. Frankly, I think you'd be better off spending that money on local storage of some sort—another hard disk, a CD-RW, or whatever, and even then, you'd probably have money left over to use for a nice vacation or a huge stack of blank CD-Rs.
>
> On the other hand, since the first 20MB is absolutely free, the only reason I can think of not to use your iDisk is if you don't have Internet access.

Mac OS X makes using your iDisk as easy as pie. Provide your name and password in the iTools tab of the Internet System Preference pane, then choose Go|iDisk or use the keyboard shortcut Command+Option+I. In a few seconds, your iDisk appears on your desktop, acting just like any other disk. You copy files to and from your iDisk the same way you'd copy files to and from any other kind of readable/writable disk. IDisk is totally slick and yet another great Mac-only feature you won't see in Microsoft Windows (or in any other operating system I know of, for that matter).

> **TIP**
>
> If you haven't signed up for your iDisk yet, what are you waiting for? Get your fanny over to **www.itools.mac.com** right away and just do it! iDisk rocks, and you can't beat the price—free.

The three best things I can think to do with an iDisk are:

1. Back up important files.
2. Share files with other users.
3. Build a simple Web page in 5 minutes.

Here's a quick overview of the new or improved features in Mac OS X 10.1's iDisk:

- iDisk no longer bugs you about staying connected. Previous versions nagged you every few minutes if you didn't use it, and often disconnected you abruptly and without warning. The new iDisk has no such restrictions—you can mount it on your desktop and leave it there for days without it hassling you.

- iDisk now uses an advanced networking protocol known as WebDAV, which not only allows you to keep your iDisk mounted all the time, but also lets users with Windows or Linux computers access your iDisk with an appropriate WebDAV client program, something that wasn't possible before.

- iDisk used to choke if you tried to use it in a location with a firewall, like most office networks. It doesn't anymore.

(continued)

2

- It's now simple to connect to another user's iDisk Public folder. Before, you needed to surf to Apple's Web site, find the proper page, and type in the user's address. Now, merely choose Go|Connect to Server and type:

  ```
  http://idisk.mac.com/username/Public
  ```

  The other user's public folder will mount on your desktop almost instantly.

- iDisk is much faster now than ever before. In the past, you could go get coffee (in another city) waiting for an iDisk folder to open. Today, iDisk folders open a lot faster. And they now use an intelligent caching scheme, so they open even faster the second (and third, and fourth, and so on) time you access them in the same session (i.e., without disconnecting).

If you used iDisk in the past—with Mac OS 9 or Mac OS X 10.0—and didn't like it for whatever reason, I urge you to try it again with Mac OS X 10.1. I think you'll be pleasantly surprised with the new and improved features and performance.

OK. You're going to hear a lot more about the Finder in upcoming sections and chapters, so that should be enough to get you started. I can almost hear the little gears turning inside your brains, as you think about how to integrate OS X's fabulous new features into your everyday routine to save you time, effort, and energy.

I've got one last big, broad tip, but it's a good one.

TIP

Get used to the fact that OS X is multithreaded. You can do things you couldn't do in OS 9. Try this: Launch a program. Launch another program. Copy a huge file. Move a huge file. Connect to the Internet. Rummage through folders. Browse the Web. Click a Dock icon or two. Open iTunes. Play music. Send email.

In the past, any one of the above tasks might have "taken over" your Mac for a few seconds, and it would have taken you a few minutes to do everything in that sequence. With OS X, you can do all those things without pausing. And you can keep them all open after launching with little or no performance penalty (RAM permitting, of course—see Chapter 7 for a discussion of how much is enough for what).

Now it's time to drill down and focus on one Finder feature in particular—the window—in a delightful little section I like to call …

Windows (Microsoft Had Nothing to Do with Them)

Trivia point: Did you know that Apple used windows in its operating systems as early as 1983 and probably even before that? Bill Gates was still hawking DOS until he saw Macintosh. (In some versions of the tale, it was until he saw an Apple Lisa, the computer that begat the Macintosh. Either way Bill was in the stone-age, operating system-wise, when Apple introduced its vision of a GUI, or graphical user interface.)

And, so the story goes, Bill pointed out the parts he liked and told his engineers to invent an operating system that did "that" for the Intel boxes that were flooding the market. The rest, as they say, is history.

OK, now back to the meaty beefy content. Let's talk OS X windows and how to get them to work harder for you.

Many OS X power users instinctively attempt to avoid the Finder because of how sluggish it was in earlier releases. In OS X 10.1, the Finder is almost pleasant on most Macs. Still, avoiding the Finder, as I will mention repeatedly throughout this book, is usually a good thing.

About Windows in General

OS X handles windows differently. Since time immemorial, if you clicked any inactive Mac window, the application that owned that window "came to the front" and became active. All its windows and palettes came to the front and became active at the same time.

The OS still works that way for Classic applications, but if you're using native OS X programs, it works differently—when you click a window, only the window you click becomes active, not all the windows that belong to that program. The menu bar switches to the appropriate application for the front most (active) window, but behind that window, Application windows and Finder windows can become interleaved. This is one of those cases in which a picture is worth a thousand words; Figure 2.6 is that picture.

You get the point.

Why does this matter? First—because this feature didn't exist before, and not knowing about it could confuse you. Second—it's a paradigm shift. You can use this new feature to your advantage, but only if you know it's there and how it works. Frankly, I hated this change at first but have gotten used to it.

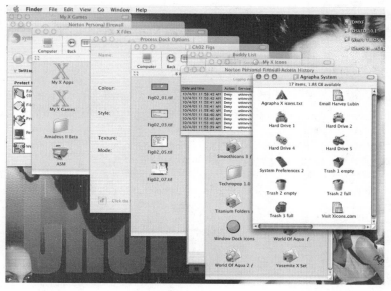

Figure 2.6
How windows may become interwoven. From back to front: a Finder window (My X Games), a Norton Personal Firewall window, another Finder window (X Files), a DragThing window (Process Dock Options), another Finder window (Ch02), a Fire (cool instant messaging client) window (Buddy List), another Finder window (My X Icons), another Norton window, yet another Finder window …

> **TIP**
>
> Most programs and the Finder have a "bring all to front" command, which does just what its name implies—brings all of its windows to the front at once. And when I'm working in a single program for a while, I often use the **Hide Others** command to insure that all the windows I see on screen belong to the task at hand.

This next technique can help you get more use out of the interwoven window scheme. When you *Command+click* an inactive window, you can move that window without making it active or bringing it forward. If you've carefully arranged windows from several applications, this is how to move a window without changing the order of the windows. With the Command key, you preserve the stacking order of other windows and can move any window anywhere on screen without bringing it to the front (i.e., making it active).

Try it. Arrange two or more windows so they overlap. Command+click the title bar of any window except the front one and keep pressing down the mouse button. Now, drag it around. Neat, huh?

Now, here's another little change that may take a bit of getting used to if you were an OS 9 user. In the Finder, to add an icon to your selection, you Command+click. To extend the selection between clicks, you Shift+click.

In OS 9 Shift+click and Command+click, both do the same thing—extend the selection. That's how Command+click works in OS X. But in OS X, Shift+clicking and Command+clicking are two different clicks. Shift+click still works, but it selects all items between the clicks.

Again, it's easier to show you the difference than tell you about it. In Figure 2.7, I clicked *X 2.2B11*, pressed and held the Command key, then clicked *LaunchBar*.

Now, compare that with Figure 2.8. In Figure 2.8, I clicked *FoldersSynchronizer X 2.2B11*, pressed and held the Shift key, then clicked *LaunchBar*.

Figure 2.7
Command+click: Notice that *FoldersSynchronizer* and *LaunchBar* are the only items selected.

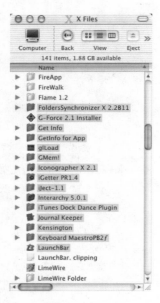

Figure 2.8
Shift+click: Notice that every item between *FoldersSynchronizer* and *LaunchBar* is selected.

To continue, I'll tell you about even more wonderful keyboard shortcuts.

Option Key Magic

I'm a huge fan of keyboard shortcuts because they cost nothing and they save time. Don't get me wrong. I love mousing too (I'm trackball-ing today with the Kensington Turbo Mouse Pro wireless. So far, it rocks, and the software for OS X is the first that actually works well for me. I'll discuss the trackball and lots of other great peripherals in Chapter 7).

As I was saying, I hate to take my hands off the keyboard. So I use shortcuts a lot. Try 'em. Learn 'em. Love 'em.

2

The Option key is often used to activate a shortcut. Depending what you do when you press it, a number of things may happen. For example, if you hold down Option when you:

■ Click a close button (the red gumdrop)

■ Choose File|Close Window

■ Press Command+W (the keyboard shortcut for Close All is Command+Option+W),

the exact same thing happens—Close All—and all open Finder windows close immediately.

The menu and keyboard shortcuts can be seen in Figure 2.9.

Figure 2.9
The File menu both without the Option key (top) and with it (bottom).

TIP

Many of these Finder window shortcuts and tricks work with windows in other OS X programs. Some of them even work in Classic windows.

To minimize all open windows, hold down the Option key when you click a minimize button (yellow gumdrop). All open Finder windows go flying into the Dock.

To maximize a window to show as much of its contents as it can, hold down the Option key when you click its zoom button (green gumdrop).

To hide the active program when you switch to another program, hold down the Option key and do either of the following:

■ Click a window for the program you want to switch to.

■ Click the dock icon for the program you want to switch to.

TIP

My favorite variation of this is Command+Option+clicking a dock icon or window. That will hide all windows from all other applications. I love this one for quickly getting focused when I've got seven or 10 programs running, like I usually do.

Another good shortcut is this one: Command+click the title of a Finder window to see a pop-up menu of the path to where the folder is located, as shown in Figure 2.10.

Because the pop-up is a menu, when I release the mouse button in Figure 2.10, the contents of Number Nine will replace the contents of Agrapha System in this window. So, keep in mind that Command+clicking a folder's title lets you choose any folder that contains that folder. Enough said.

Figure 2.10
I Command+clicked on Agrapha System; a menu popped up displaying the path back to the Computer (500 Tower) level.

Anatomy of a Window

Moving right along, let's look more closely at the Finder's windows and their views. You have three views to choose from for Finder windows—Icon, List, and Column. Each has its own special charm.

To choose a view for the active (frontmost) window, you can:

■ Choose View|as Icons, View|as List, or View|as Columns.

■ Click the appropriate little icon in the toolbar, as shown in Figure 2.11.

Figure 2.11
Choose a view: Icon (top), List (middle), or Column (bottom) in any window's toolbar.

NOTE

If you don't see a set of little icons in your toolbar now, you will in a few pages. We're almost there.

There may be three views but there's only one toolbar, so let's look at it first.

The Taming of the Toolbar

The toolbar appears at the top of every Finder window regardless of view. What's that you say? Your window doesn't have a toolbar? Kind of like the window in Figure 2.12?

Figure 2.12
This poor window has lost its toolbar.

No problem—there are (at least) three ways to get the toolbar back:

1. Choose View|Hide/Show Toolbar.

2. Use the keyboard shortcut for Hide/Show Toolbar, Command+B.

3. Click the Hide/Show Toolbar button (some people call it a "widget") in the upper-right corner of every window (shown in Figure 2.13).

Figure 2.13
The gray gumdrop widget in the upper-right corner is the Hide/Show Toolbar button.

But hiding and showing the toolbar is small potatoes—now, let's soup up the toolbar so it works harder for you. You can see my toolbar in Figure 2.14; I bet it's different from yours.

OK, first the easy stuff. You can add any icon to the toolbar by dragging it onto the toolbar. And you can remove any icon you've installed by dragging it off the toolbar— when you release the mouse button, it will disappear. You can also rearrange icons you've installed by clicking them and dragging them to another location on the toolbar.

NOTE

You notice I keep saying, "to any icon you've installed," and not "to any icon on the toolbar"? That's because the default toolbar icons—the ones that came pre-installed—behave differently from icons you drag onto the toolbar. Think of it as your icons vs. the System's icons.

You can't just drag the System's icons off the toolbar or even move them, which is a good thing because a lot of the icons don't exist in any other window. I mean, where are you going to find a Back Arrow, Eject button, or Burn button in the wild? All of which is my roundabout way of saying, "now choose View|Customize Toolbar... and go to town with your Customize Toolbar window." Mine is shown in Figure 2.14.

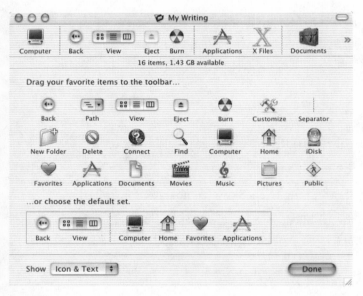

Figure 2.14
The Customize Toolbar window offers a cornucopia of icons.

Just drag any icon from the Customize Toolbar window onto the toolbar. If you drag an icon between two others, they'll politely move aside to make room. I'll leave it to you to discover what all the icons do. Suffice it to say you should absolutely, positively, without question, customize the toolbar. You want your most-used stuff only a click away, no matter what window you're using.

NOTE

If you put too much stuff in the toolbar, it gets truncated.

On the other hand, when the toolbar is too big to fit the window, a little chevron-looking arrow appears in the upper right. Click the little chevron thing to use hidden toolbar icons, as shown in Figure 2.15.

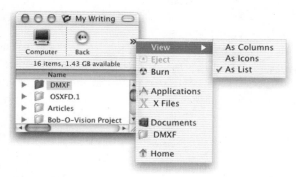

Figure 2.15
This handy pop-up menu (i.e., the menu beneath the little chevron thingie) lets you use hidden toolbar icons easily.

> If you put a little too much stuff in your toolbar, the chevron-thingies are handy. But if you put way too much stuff in your toolbar, even the chevrons won't help. So, use a modicum of restraint. Having every icon in your toolbar is worthless and makes it that much harder to access the icons you actually *do* use.

Now, let's look at the window views and what makes each one unique and useful.

Icon View

Icon view has deservedly earned a reputation among power users as the least useful view. Icons hog screen real estate. While power users may eschew Icon views, some users love big, honking, visual cues. And, in OS X you can have some really big icons.

Even though I use Icon view infrequently, I have found a couple of uses for it. You can use it as a poor person's picture browser to scan a folder full of pictures. It's only useful if the pictures are the kind with thumbnails; this technique relies on the icon looking like what's in the file. You can see what I mean clearly in Figure 2.16.

Now, drag the scroll control up or down (the blueberry-looking globule in the scroll bar I'm pointing to in Figure 2.16).

> Such *scroll controls* were called *scroll boxes* in OS 9 and earlier OSes.

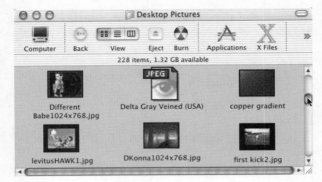

Figure 2.16
Icon view: Use it as a graphics browser; you can't beat the price.

TIP

You can make the icons any size you want (with View Options, which we'll talk about in a few pages).

My other use for Icon view actually involves viewing the icons on your desktop. And while the desktop isn't technically a window, it does use Icon view and relies on the fact that you can make your desktop icons big or tiny using View Options (which we'll cover soon). I like 'em small. I generally keep a handful of aliases of folders with stuff I need to look at on the desktop near my hard disks, as you can see in Figure 2.17.

Figure 2.17
I keep my desktop icons as small as possible.

Some people like big, bountiful, beautiful desktop icons, like the ones in Figure 2.18. If you're a big fan of drag and drop, big desktop icons may be just what the doctor ordered.

Figure 2.18
Big icons make big targets; it's easy to drag and drop onto these big aliases on the desktop.

A Brief Iconic Diversion

While we're on the subject of the Icon view, let's look at the icons themselves 'cause Mac OS X icons are great. They have four times more pixels than OS 9 icons, so they look amazing, even in large sizes like the ones you see in Figure 2.19. And OS X lets you have very large icons if you like (see the upcoming section on View Options to find out how).

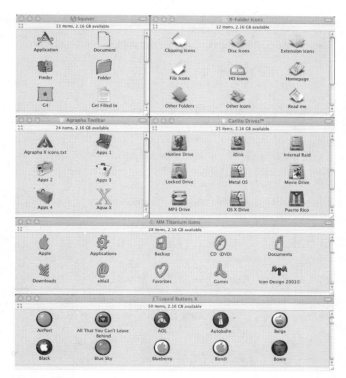

Figure 2.19
Here's a sample from my collection of big, beautiful, high-resolution Made-for-Mac-OS X icons.

I like icons a lot—I download them by the bushel and paste them onto files and folders when I've got time to kill. It's not much more productive than killing a squad of Dwarves or Myrks in multiplayer *Myth*, but it does leave me with a more beautiful Mac. I know at least two fantastic Web sites for connoisseurs of fine OS X icons: **www.iconfactory.com/** and **http://xicons.macnn.com/**. Many icons are free, but even the shareware ones are inexpensive. Also, while it's getting easier to find good made-for-OS X icons in other places on the Net, if you liked any of the icons in Figure 2.19, you'll find them at Iconfactory or Xicons. Almost all my icons come from that pair of sites.

If you knew how to paste a new icon onto a file or folder in OS 9, you know pretty much how to do it in OS X. OS X brings one small new twist to the party: It has a single Show Info (like Get Info in OS 9) window. Show Info is a type of window commonly called an "inspector", which means it stays open until you close it, and its contents update in real time. In OS 9, you would open a separate Get Info window for every file; in OS X, you have a single Show Info window that updates to reflect the currently selected icon. Select another icon, and the Show Info window changes instantly.

The 60-Second Custom Icon Tutorial

To put all I just said above in another way, don't bother closing the Show Info window between steps in the following procedure:

1. Select any cool-looking icon on any file, folder, or recordable disc.
2. Choose File|Show Info or use the keyboard shortcut, which, thankfully, is still Command+I.

ALERT!

Make sure that only one icon is selected. Multiple selections confound the Show Info window.

3. Click the icon in the Show Info window. A narrow border will appear around it to indicate that the icon is selected. Choose Edit|Copy or use the keyboard shortcut Command+C. This step can be seen in Figure 2.20.
4. Select any plain-looking icon on any disk or volume.
5. Click the icon in the Show Info window (the one you weren't supposed to close—if you did, reopen it with the plain-looking icon selected). Choose Edit|Paste or use the keyboard shortcut Command+V. This step can be seen in Figure 2.21. Take a look, also, at Figure 2.22, which follows it.

OK, now do it without peeking. Put the book away and just do it. If you didn't finish in well under a minute, something's wrong. I can change an icon in five seconds (and I do, all too often).

(continued)

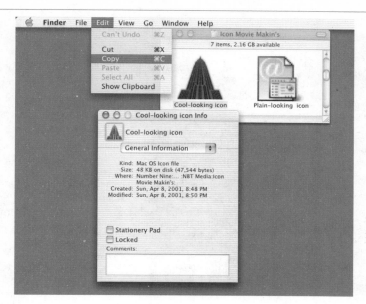

Figure 2.20
Find a cool icon and copy it to the Clipboard.

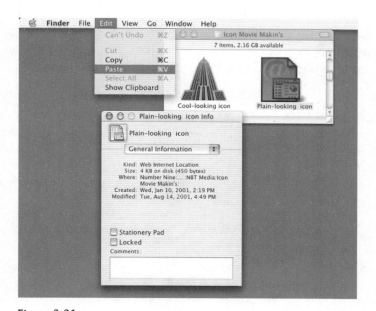

Figure 2.21
This is how you paste a cool-looking icon onto any file, folder, or volume.

(continued)

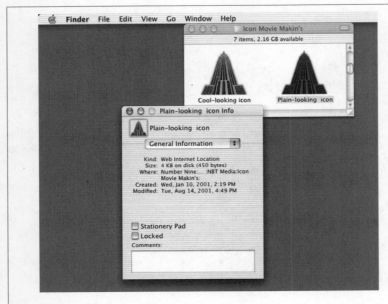

Figure 2.22
And this is how things end up after you paste.

Before we leave the discussion on icons completely, there is one more reason someone might like using the Icon view—it's the only way you can have a picture as a window background (not a desktop background, mind you, but a window background).

NOTE

> Changing desktop pictures and backgrounds will be covered in the section about System Preferences and the Finder. I'll show you exactly how this "picture in a window" trick is done in a few pages, when we discuss View Options.

You can even pick a different picture for every folder if you wish, such as a guy in one window and his dog in another, kind of like in Figure 2.23.

I think we'll end our little tutorial on that stellar note. Next up, the beloved workhorse view we lovingly call…

List View

I'm torn between List and Column views. I use Column view more, but I can't live without List view windows, either. I use a little of each—some windows in List view, others in Column view. I find they compliment each other, and I often use one of each when moving or copying files or folders.

Figure 2.23
Every picture tells a story.

In every view, keyboard shortcuts are a terrific timesaver, but the keyboard is particularly well-suited for List view windows.

> **TIP**
>
> Keyboard shortcuts are very powerful and cost you nothing. Train yourself to use them; you *could* develop worse habits.

I love my keyboard shortcuts. When I use List or Column view, I can pretty much sit back and not touch the mouse—I navigate with the keyboard and I'm at least as fast as with the mouse. If *you* can get there with a mouse, *I* can get there with a keyboard, only faster (and with less stress on my back, shoulders, and wrists).

Try it. The arrow keys—left, right, up, and down—move the selection from icon to icon in any view. But in List view, left-and right-arrow open and close the selected folder or folders. If you use the Option key with left or right arrow, all the subfolders will open or close at once, as shown in Figure 2.24.

> **NOTE**
>
> In the immortal words of my cousin Yogi LeVitus, extolling the virtues of keyboard shortcuts extemporaneously to a crowd at Macworld Expo:
>
> "Use them. Remember them. Remember to use them. Use them to remember them..."
>
> Or something like that.

Figure 2.24
Right-arrow opens one level of subfolders (left). Option+right-arrow opens all of its subfolders at once (right).

OK, for those of you who missed your mice during my little love letter to keyboard shortcuts, here's a shortcut you can do only with a mouse: To change the sort order in a column in List view, click a column header. Figure 2.25 shows how the sort order changes after you click a column's header (i.e., click on its name).

Now, as for those little triangles: they show you which way the sort order is going. To reverse the sort order for that column, click the column header again. The triangle flips over, and the sort order reverses. Look at both "Name" triangles in Figure 2.25 for a graphic illustration.

> **TIP**
> One of my favorite things to use List view for is to show me documents I've used recently. I click the Date Modified column header and the window re-sorts, with the most recently used document on top. (If it's on the bottom, I click Date Modified again to reverse the sort order.)

Moving right along, Mac OS X supports those new, high-falootin, high-tech "ReallyLongFileNames™." Which is both a blessing and a curse.

> **NOTE**
> Read the "What's in a File Name" sidebar later in this chapter for more info on this still-unfolding drama.

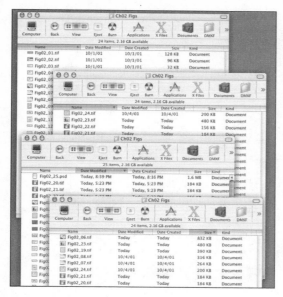

Figure 2.25
From top: Sorted by Name (A first), sorted by Name in reverse order (Z first), sorted by Date Modified (most recent first), and sorted by Size (largest first).

Long file names are mostly a blessing in List view, but only if you know how to resize columns. Just move your cursor over the dividing line between two column headers and hold it there. The cursor will turn into a double-arrowheaded-resizer, as shown in Figure 2.26. Drag the cursor to make the column grow or shrink, and then release the mouse button.

Enough with the List view, already. Explore it at your leisure. You'll almost certainly find something you like about it. Now, let's take a look at my favorite view, the multi-faceted Column view.

Column View

I use Column view more than even List view. It took a while to get used to, but once I "grokked" it, I began to use Column view all the time. In the two other views, Mac OS X default behavior is to open subfolders "in place" when you double-click them. In other words, the contents of the subfolder replace the current contents, all in the same window.

In Column view, things work a bit differently. Column view displays a folder's contents in the column to the right of it when that folder is highlighted (selected). If you navigate to the rightmost column, all columns slide left. Furthermore, double-clicking a folder in Column view may not do anything but give you a sore wrist.

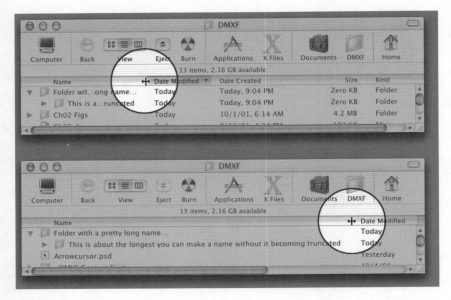

Figure 2.26
Move your cursor over the line between column headers and then click (top). Move your cursor over the line between column headers and then click (top). Now drag right or left and the column will grow (or shrink) until you release the mouse button (bottom).

TIP

> If you check the box that says "Always open folders in a new window" in Finder Preferences (we'll talk about them shortly), folders will do that instead of opening in the same window (i.e., opening "in place"). This applies to the Column view, too. If you can't get used to OS X's new way of managing windows, try checking this checkbox, which makes things a lot more like they used to be.

> If you don't check the preference, you can still force a folder to open in a new window by holding down the Command key when you double-click the folder. To close the current window when the new window opens, hold down Command and Option when you double-click.

I have a window I never close. It's in Column view, with the columns as small as they can be, as shown at the bottom of Figure 2.27. I keep it near the bottom of my screen. I think of it as a panoramic view of the whole shebang. I use this window for most of my file management, usually in conjunction with another window in List view (the DMXF folder on the upper right in Figure 2.27).

Column view and List view complement one another. I tend to use Column view to navigate quickly through large numbers of folders, and List view for folders I'm currently working with. For example, the project I'm working on has a folder for all its "stuff." That folder is almost always open in List view.

Figure 2.27
My "Main" window is the bottom one; the others are examples of Icon (top left) and List (top right) views.

NOTE

> I also have an alias of the folder on my desktop, another alias in my Favorites folder, and I could have one stashed in the Dock. The point is that when I'm working on a project, one or more aliases of its folder are never far from my cursor.

In versions 10.1 or later, columns can be resized individually as well as collectively. With the first releases (OS X 10.0–10.0.4), when you resized one column, you resized them all and that was that. Yuck. In Mac OS X 10.1, resizing columns works the way it should. To resize a single column, Option+drag the column sizer to the right of that column, as shown in Figure 2.28. To resize all columns simultaneously, drag any column sizer without holding the Option key.

Figure 2.28
Hold Option and drag the column sizer to resize a single column; omit the Option key to resize all the columns at once.

Column view has one other extremely nifty feature—a built-in preview pane. If you click a document saved in a format it supports (JPEG, TIFF, QuickTime, and PDF, to name just a few), a preview appears in the rightmost pane. Take a look at Figure 2.29.

Figure 2.29
Column view previews: A QuickTime movie (larger window, "Moovs"); and a TIFF image file (smaller window, "Ch02 Figs").

NOTE

Notice the controller for the movie—you can play a movie right in a Column view window, without launching a program or opening another window. Neat!

Column view is unlike any Macintosh window before it, but once you get the hang of it, I think you'll like it.

NOTE

People say Column view is more NeXT-like than Mac-like. Who cares? As my old marketing professor used to say, "a good idea doesn't care who it happens to." Don't worry about its pedigree—just enjoy it.

View Options

But wait, there's more. To make your enjoyment of views more complete, you can customize Icon and List views globally and on a folder-by-folder basis. To perform this magic, choose View|Show View Options. The View Options window is another one of those "inspector" windows—like Show Info, it reflects the selected (highlighted) icon and updates instantly if you select a different icon.

TIP

> Some people keep View Options open all the time. Or, the keyboard shortcut, Command+J, is a toggle—press it once, and the View Options window appears; press it again, and the View Options window goes away.

The View Options window is context sensitive. If you click the desktop, you get display options for the desktop, as shown in Figure 2.30.

If you click a window using Icon or List view, View Options offers only the appropriate options, as shown in Figure 2.31.

Figure 2.30
View Options for the desktop.

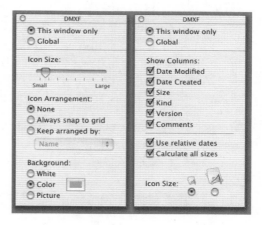

Figure 2.31
View Options for Icon view (left) and List view (right).

Most of these options are self-explanatory. If you click the Global button, the options chosen affect all windows of this type. If you click the "This window only" button, the options chosen only affect your current window.

Finally, if you click a window using Column view while View Options is open, you will be politely informed that no view options exist for Column view.

OK. Let's move on. It's time to discover.

What's Up (with the) Dock: Basics

Maybe this is blasphemy, but I don't like the Dock all that much. It's not the most horrible "improvement" ever foisted on users, but let's just say I don't consider it an improvement on the OS 9 Apple menu.

Don't get me wrong. The Dock has some sweet features, but it's also inflexible and a screen-hog, too. I prefer elegant utilities like DragThing and LaunchBar; both do dock-like stuff and a whole lot more.

> **NOTE**
>
> All the software mentioned in this section will be described in even greater detail in the upcoming section, "Software That Makes the Finder and Dock Even Better." Hang in there—the best is yet to come.

My Dock Is a Very, Very, Very Dry Dock...

My Dock is boring. I only keep a couple of icons there. I'll tell you all about what I do use instead of and in harmony with the Dock later in this chapter and throughout the book. But for now, whenever I install OS X on any of my Macs, the first thing I do is get rid of all the default icons Apple sticks in the Dock. I don't need them today, and if I ever do need them, I know where to find them on my hard disk.

So I get rid of every Dock icon except the Finder and the Trash (which aren't get-rid-able anyway).

> **TIP**
>
> I'm sure you know this already but I'd be remiss if I didn't mention it: To add an icon to the Dock, drag it onto the Dock. To remove an icon from the Dock, drag it off the Dock. It disappears with a satisfying "poof."

I'm partial to a lean, clean Dock, with nothing in it except applications in use and a select few other things. For example, I get a kick out of watching little programs that monitor CPU load and memory use, as shown in Figure 2.32. I'm not sure if they're worth a darn, but it's sure fascinating to observe them; these two are my favorites so far.

> **TIP**
>
> If you like the idea of information displayed in your Dock, you can find lots and lots of other "docklings." There are links to some at **www.boblevitus.com/xfiles.html**, and tons more can be found at **www.versiontracker.com**, Apple.com, America Online (gasp), or wherever fine downloadable OS X shareware is served. Search for "Dock" and/or "dockling."

Figure 2.32
LoadInDock (middle icon; shown with optional translucent movable window) and Memory Monitor (bottom icon) use the Dock to put me in touch with my inner Mac.

Speaking of docklings, another very cool tool for your Dock is Snard, shown in Figure 2.33.

You get the picture—Snard saves steps. With Snard, I don't have to open System Preferences and then choose a pane. No, siree. I just choose the pane I want (Login in Figure 2.33) in the Snard menu and presto—System Preferences opens Login. I use Snard's Frequent Folders menu for fast access to the handful of folders I use every day. And so on.

So that's my Dock in a nutshell. See? In spite of not liking it all that much, I think I've learned to get along famously with the Dock.

I'll tell you more about docklings in the software section at the end of this chapter.

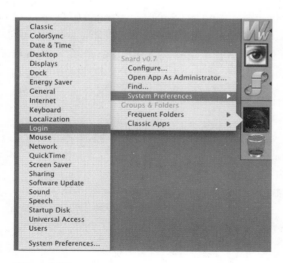

Figure 2.33
Snard saves steps.

More Dock Tips

Here are a few more things you can do with the Dock.

Many users like having a disk, volume, or folder icon in their Dock, which they use to navigate with instead of opening Finder windows. If that suits your style, drag a disk icon to the Dock, then click and hold the icon. A pop-up menu appears and you can navigate to any file on that disk, as shown in Figure 2.34.

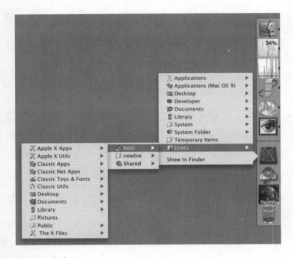

Figure 2.34
The Dock lets you navigate through disks and folders without having to open any of those pesky windows!

If there's a program you use with drag and drop, the Dock is better than the desktop. StuffIt Expander is a perfect example. It's handy to have in the Dock because it can "decode" more than a dozen different file types including .sit, .img, .hqx, .gz, .tgz, .bin, .tar, .uu, .zip, and many others. If you happen upon a file that needs decoding, chances are StuffIt Expander can decode it.

> **TIP**
>
> It's easier to drop a document onto StuffIt Expander when it's in the Dock than when it's buried five folders deep somewhere.

What's that you say? You haven't seen StuffIt Expander in my dock? You're sharp-eyed readers. I use StuffIt so often I upgraded to the commercial-strength version, StuffIt Deluxe. And, among other goodies, it comes with the handy Magic Menu, which you can see in Figure 2.35.

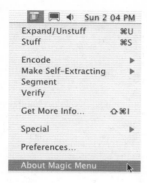

Figure 2.35
The StuffIt Magic Menu. It's free with purchase of StuffIt Deluxe (street price around $80. If you're interested try 831-761-6200 and/or **www.aladinsys.com**).

So, I don't need to waste Dock space on StuffIt Expander. I select any encoded file and press Command+U—if it can be decoded, it will be. It doesn't get much better than that, folks. Of course, I use StuffIt dozens of times a day. The point is, if you have an application you drag documents onto, the Dock may be the best place for it.

Preferences You'll Prefer

We'll be looking at most of the System Preferences here or in other parts of the book.

> **NOTE**
>
> They're called preferences for a reason, which is why I'm not going to try to explain how to use each and every feature in every single one. Not here, not there, and probably not anywhere. For the sake of sanity—mostly my editor's but partly yours and mine—I'm going to make this mercifully brief. I will only comment when I have a strong opinion. No comment means you really ought to try it yourself. After all, only *you* can decide what settings *you* prefer.

Seeing that this is our first encounter with System Preferences and Panes, let's start with a quick overview. To open System Preferences, choose Apple|System Preferences, click its icon in the Dock (if you have one), or open its icon in your Applications folder. The System Preferences window, shown in Figure 2.36, appears. No item is selected and all items are displayed.

> **TIP**
>
> You can drag any frequently used icon into the toolbar for easier access. To remove it, drag it off the toolbar.

Figure 2.36
OS X 10.1's Preferences. Click an icon or choose it from the View menu.

Dock

Since we were discussing it just a moment ago, let's begin with the Dock's Preferences. First things first—I want you to memorize this shortcut: Command+Option+D. Practice it. If you use programs that have windows near the edges of the screen, as most programs do, you'll surely find the Dock in the way. Don't get angry; Command+Option+D is the cure. It hides the Dock instantly and keeps the thing hidden until you move the cursor over where it used to be. Then, the Dock reappears until your cursor leaves the vicinity. When the cursor splits, so does the Dock.

Now as for the rest of the Dock preferences, most of them can be diddled in the Dock System Preferences pane. Open it by clicking the System Preferences icon in the Dock, or, if you've removed yours as I have, open it by choosing Apple|Dock|Dock Preferences or by Control+clicking the divider line in the dock and choosing Dock Preferences from the pop-up menu. Both are shown in Figure 2.37, and my Dock System Preferences pane is shown in Figure 2.38.

Dock preferences are straightforward. Explore them and you'll enjoy a Dock configured to suit the way you work.

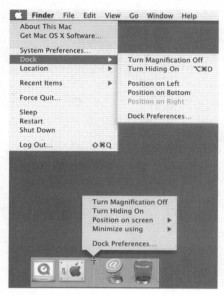

Figure 2.37
Here are two ways to tinker with your Dock preferences—from the Apple menu or the Dock, take your pick.

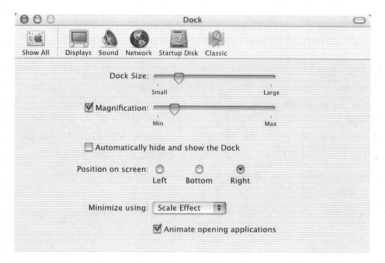

Figure 2.38
This is Dock Preferences. I control "Automatically hide and show the Dock" with that handy keyboard shortcut we just memorized, so I rarely use this checkbox.

Desktop

In this case, I do believe a picture is worth a thousand or more words. Figure 2.39 is a picture of my desktop with the Desktop Preferences pane window.

Figure 2.39
Use Desktop Preferences to beautify your Mac.

Pretty nice, huh? That particular desktop picture, as with most of my 200+ stunning background artworks, came from **www.macdesktops.com**.

> **NOTE**
>
> Let's give some credit where credit is due. Though the picture in Figure 2.39 is like all MacDesktop's pictures, a free download, a real, live person, Per Kristian Grindheim, actually made it. My Mac is a more beautiful place because of the generous talents of Per Kristian Grindheim. I'd like to thank Per Kristian, wherever he or she may be, for this and all the other beautiful MacDesktops that bear the name Per Kristian Grindheim.
>
> As my cousin Yogi LeVitus used to say, "Beauty is a beautiful thing."

I try to visit **MacDesktops.com** at least once a month to pick up fresh pix for my collection.

> **NOTE**
>
> I don't understand why Apple doesn't call the preferences window the "Desktop Picture Preference Pane." I mean, it is a one-trick pony, and that one trick is changing the desktop picture. What ever happened to truth in advertising?

If you like desktop pictures, you'll love a little program called Desktop Randomizer. It's freeware, and you'll find a link for it on this book's companion Web site. Desktop Randomizer changes your desktop picture every time it's launched, or at each login, using pictures from a folder you specify. I'll show you more about it in Chapter 9.

Moving right along, let's look at Login.

Login

Back in Chapter 1, I told you I'd show you how to make OS X act like a single-user operating system, which does not ask you to "log in" when you turn it on. The Login Preference is where you turn the multiuser feature off.

NOTE

But don't forget OS X is *still* a multiuser operating system.

So, if you want your Mac to just start up without asking for a user name or a password, open System Preferences, click Login, then click the Login Window tab near the top. Check the little box next to "Automatically log in," type your name and password in the appropriate text entry fields, then click Save. (See Figure 2.40).

ALERT!

You must be an administrator to use many Preferences panes, including this one. If you're not an administrator (or the sole user of the Mac), you probably shouldn't be poking around the Login Preferences pane anyway. Find the PIC (person-in-charge) and discuss what you're doing before you go any further.

The other cool thing about Login Preferences is its other tab, Login Items. Drag any icon onto the Login Items window or use the Add button. The result is the same—the icon opens automatically whenever you log in, even if you have auto login enabled. I have a bunch of programs I use every day; Login Items starts them all up for me when I log in, as you can see in Figure 2.41.

Mouse, Keyboard, Sound, and Other Preferences

In the last chapter, I said I'd tell you about changing the sensitivity of your keyboard or mouse, choosing a different beep, and some other stuff. The answers can all be found in the appropriate System Preference pane.

NOTE

Preferences panes in OS X are well designed and easy to use. Many of them work in real time, so, unlike many OS 9 Control Panels, you don't have to close them to see results. And also unlike OS 9, you never have to reboot to enable a preference or program. While you may occasionally be required to log out and then log back in to enable a setting or piece of software, OS X never needs to be rebooted.

Well, almost never.

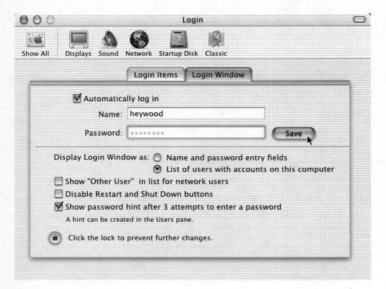

Figure 2.40
This Mac will start right up to Heywood's stuff with no password or user name or other hassle. Kind of like Mac OS 9.

Figure 2.41
Yes, I actually *want* all these programs to open every time I log in.

The point is, experiment with various settings—especially mouse and keyboard—until you find what works best for you.

Finder Preferences

While almost all system preferences are bound together in the single-window System Preferences application, the Finder's preferences are, for some unexplained reason, left all by their lonesome in a window of their own. Choose Finder|Preferences to open it.

> **NOTE**
>
> It could be because the Finder is technically an application and most applications have their own Preferences window. Or not. But it seems to me that Finder Preferences are System Preferences and belong with other System Preferences, not all alone in a window of their own.

These items are straightforward enough that I don't think we need to spend time on them here. I just wanted to make sure you realized they're under Finder Preferences rather than where you'd expect them, and give you a quick look at them (See Figure 2.42).

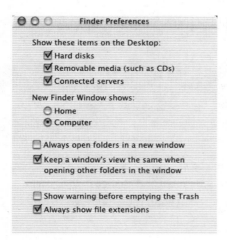

Figure 2.42
The Finder Preferences may be located illogically, but they're still well worth knowing about.

> **TIP**
>
> If you're unclear on anything so far, a lot of good stuff is explained in Mac Help. (Choose Help|Mac Help or use the shortcut Command+Shift+/.) Or just try something—it won't hurt as long as you remember what you just changed so you can change it back if you hate it.

On that high note, let's get this show on the road. It's time to turn to the darker side of OS X, and find out what to do...

When Good Finders Go Bad

Now that you've got the basics down (you're still here, aren't you?), we can roll up our sleeves and get a bit more serious about all this fun stuff. It is time to start learning techniques for troubleshooting Finder "issues."

"Issue" is frequently (but not always) synonymous with "bug."

There's a whole chapter on troubleshooting—Chapter 8—coming up. I'm going to limit the discussion in this chapter to a handful of the most relevant and useful Finder techniques and save the heavy-duty got-your-thing-in-a-sling troubleshooting voodoo for Chapter 8.

If you're experiencing an actual problem, though, you may want to skip to Chapter 8 right about now.

We'll start out with a short treatise on the whole UNIX/multiuser operating system "issue," with a sidebar.

> ## What's This Whole "Administrator" Thing About, Anyway?
>
> I've mentioned several times that OS X is a real multiuser operating system. An administrator is a user authorized to create other user accounts, install new software in the Applications and Library folders, and change global System Preferences.
>
> If you know the name and password of an administrator, you can do many things a non-administrator user can't. You can, for example, click the little locks and change many System Preferences. If you don't have an administrator's name and password, those preferences cannot be changed.
>
> The fewer administrator accounts on your Mac, the better. Of course, having but a single Administrator—you—is ideal. But if you have to have multiple Administrator accounts, think about those awesome Administrator powers. Make sure this person really needs them.
>
> One last thing—you won't be able to accomplish most of what's described in this book without the name and password of an administrator. 'Nuff said.

2

When the Finder Goes Wonky

"Wonky" is an Andy Ihnatko-ism that perfectly describes a Finder meltdown. The good news is that OS X doesn't die if the Finder gets "wonky." The bad news is that you have to restart the Finder. You do that with a little piece of Mac OS X voodoo that rocks when you're in a jam.

Use the Power: Force Quit

One of the great things about OS X is that the whole operating system doesn't go to heck in a handcart when a single program (or even the Classic environment) crashes, locks up, freezes, or does almost anything except work properly.

OS X has a built-in fix for recalcitrant programs. If a program, including the Finder, ever freezes, crashes, or otherwise wonks out on you, invoke the power and use Force Quit.

There are several handy ways to Force Quit:

■ Choose Apple Menu|Force Quit.

Sometimes, though, using the menu is not possible. One alternative is:

■ Use the keyboard shortcut Command+Option+Escape.

Either brings out the Force Quit Applications window, as shown in Figure 2.43, where you just click a program in the list then click Force Quit. The selected program disappears from your screen and from OS X's well-protected memory.

> **NOTE**
>
> The Finder is always running. So if you force the Finder to quit, it will restart itself automatically. The point is, when you select the Finder in the Force Quit Application window, the button changes from "Force Quit" to "Relaunch." And that's just what happens—the Finder quits, than restarts itself.

■ Hold down the Option key when you click on a Dock icon, as shown in Figure 2.44.

This technique quits the program directly and thus avoids the Force Quit Application window completely; which would make it more desirable than the first two.

> **ALERT!**
>
> The Option key technique doesn't work as reliably as the other two for me. Sometimes, I have to do it three times before it "takes." Other times, it doesn't work at all. It can even make things worse, crashing (freezing) my Dock every so many tries.

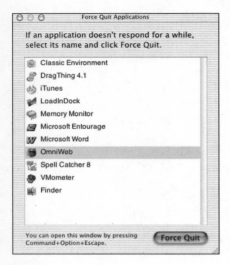

Figure 2.43
I hope you don't see this window often, but when you do, be thankful it's there and works so reliably. Things used to be worse!

Figure 2.44
The "Quit" command changes to "Force Quit" when you press the Option key in the Dock.

Take my warning with however much salt you like—I usually try the keyboard shortcut first, the menu only if the keyboard doesn't work, and the Option+Dock trick as a last resort and only after I've determined that "at this point, it couldn't hurt."

Force Quit can bail you out of jams in a jiffy without breaking a sweat. But what are you going to do the first time you're faced with wonkiness from a so-called "invisible" application like the Dock? The Dock doesn't have a Dock icon. And it doesn't show up in the Force Quit Applications window either. Fortunately, Apple provides a tool that lets you Force Quit the Dock and other invisible applications and UNIX "processes."

But before that, one final warning about "the power".

ALERT!

If you're logged in as an Administrator or your Mac asks for an Administrator password for a task, THINK ABOUT IT. One careless slip of your little Administrator finger, and you could disable your Mac completely. I'm not trying to scare you. I am merely offering you your best chance to avoid pain and suffering at the hands of Mac OS X. Don't use an Administrator account unless you understand the awesome power that comes with it.

2

> **NOTE**
>
> Having said that, I don't follow this good advice. I have to be on an Administrator account or I get all twitchy. If I use my other account, I'm frustrated. I mean, unless you're an Administrator, you can't *really* screw things up properly. And as I'm sure you've figured out by now, screwing up and fixing my Mac is what I live for. So, at least in this case, it might be wise to do as I say, not as I do. That would be prudent. If you choose to ignore me (like me), you can't say I didn't warn you.

Forcing Invisible Programs to Quit

Here's the easy way to Force Quit if you know the name of the invisible program or process you want to quit with a simple six-word AppleScript. I'll use the Dock as an example:

1. Open Script Editor (in the AppleScript folder, in your OS X Applications folder).

> **NOTE**
>
> Script Editor is the program you use to write AppleScripts. You'll get a whole chapter of instruction on it later in the book (Chapter 13), but this little trick is easy and useful enough to make room for it here.

An empty, untitled script appears, as shown in Figure 2.45, top.

2. Type a short description in the upper field. I used "Quit Dock."

3. Type this script in the lower field:

```
tell application "Dock"
        quit
end tell
```

4. Save your script.

It should look like Figure 2.45, bottom.

> **NOTE**
>
> You don't have to bold the words shown in bold above or put space before the word "quit." Script Editor will embolden and indent for you—press the Check Syntax button to have your script formatted automatically. If you've made any typing errors, Script Editor will tell you now.

Run this script the next time you need to kill the Dock. The Dock will disappear briefly, then restart itself automatically.

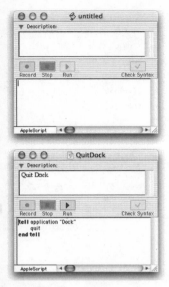

Figure 2.45
The Quit Dock script from start to finish.

Forcing Invisible Programs to Quit v 2.0

This next technique is one of those "be careful what you do…" things administrators need to be awake for. So while there's nothing inherently dangerous in what I'm about to show you, Process Viewer, the program you're about to use, can wreck havoc in an inexperienced administrator's hands.

ALERT!

Don't play around with Process Viewer if you're not confident of what you're doing. If you come to OS X from the OS 9 or earlier generation, you've probably used ResEdit, Apple's Resource Editor. If you know what I'm talking about, you should consider using Process Viewer roughly the same way as using ResEdit. And using Process Viewer the way I'm going to show you is about the same as using ResEdit on the active System file.

It won't be an issue with this particular procedure, but using Process Viewer to force other processes to Quit could very well cause an "unexpected outcome" (i.e., a crash).

That said, Process Viewer is another easy way to force an invisible program or process to quit. Unlike our little script, it gives you a chance to quit, even if you don't know the process's exact name.

I'll continue using the Dock as an example:

1. Open Process Viewer. It's in the Utilities folder, which is in your OS X Applications folder.

NOTE

Process Viewer is a program you use to monitor all running UNIX processes.

2. Find the Dock in the list and double-click it.

3. Click Force Quit, as shown in Figure 2.46.

Figure 2.46
Process Viewer: Another way to force an invisible program to quit.

TIP

If your Mac is still not right after forcing suspected troublemaking-programs to quit, you might want to read Chapter 8 and try some of its troubleshooting tips.

Okey dokey. One more little sidebar, and we're done. Knowing the facts about this one last Finder bugaboo—long file names—can save you hours the next time a long-file-name-related issue occurs.

What's in a (File)name?

Times change—when the Mac first appeared on the scene back in 1984, its support for long, descriptive filenames without a three- (or four-) character extension to tell what kind of file it was showed up as a major advantage in ease-of-use. Microsoft took over a decade (Windows 95) before it concealed the "8.3" DOS filenaming heritage and actually supported long filenames; however, it did the Mac OS one better by supporting names longer than the 31 characters supported by Mac OS on HFS disks. With the release of Mac Extended Format (more commonly known as HFS+), Mac OS once again leapfrogged by having support for 255 character filenames—almost. Unfortunately, Apple didn't provide APIs for these long filenames until Mac OS 9 and then still didn't update the Finder to recognize and display these names (or any of its other applications and utilities, for that matter).

The Mac OS X Finder does recognize and support these names, though, so all is right with the world again, right? Unfortunately, again the answer is "almost." A number of Apple's flagship products still don't support the long name APIs, even in their OS X versions, including AppleWorks, iTunes, and iMovie, culminating in truncated file names like the ones on the right side of Figure 2.47. Hopefully, by the time you read this (or soon thereafter), Apple and other developers will eliminate these shortcomings from their Mac OS X applications.

TIP

That won't completely eliminate the problem, though. Remember that HFS doesn't support long names, so HFS-formatted volumes (like most Zip disks and CDs) won't be able to handle the long names. If you must archive files with long names to CD or Zip, be sure to format them as HFS+ and not plain-vanilla HFS. Know that you'll also see the truncated names when file sharing from a Mac running Mac OS 9 (or from applications running in Classic).

OS X does provide one sweet shortcut for viewing long filenames without actually having to select them. If you hold down the Option key and let the pointer hover over the name, the Finder will display the full name as a "tool tip," as shown in the three pictures on the left of Figure 2.47.

TIP

The tool tip will pop up without the Option key if you hold the cursor over the name for more than a couple of seconds. The Option key makes the tool tip appear immediately.

Here's a quick play-by-play for Figure 2.47:

■ Top—As I attempt to open a file in AppleWorks 6.1 for OS X, the long folder name ("This is my folder...") and file name ("This file has...") are truncated by AppleWorks.

NOTE

I'm pressing Option in the versions on the left, so the tool tip shows. It's easier to see the amputated file name in the version of the picture on the right, without the tool tip in your way.

(continued)

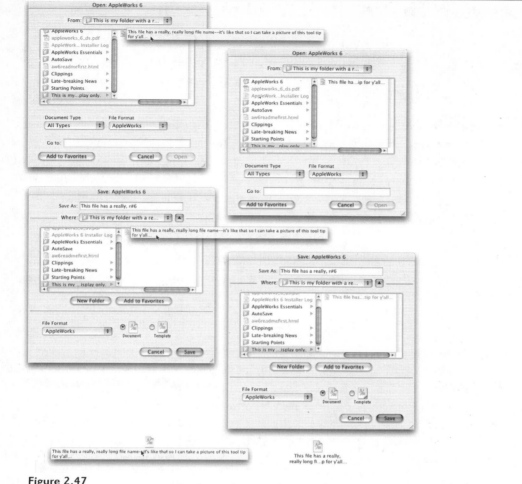

Figure 2.47
What can happen to a long file name in the Finder (bottom) or in an Open (top) or Save (middle) sheet.

- Middle—Saving a file is even worse. You can't save with a long file name—the Save sheet won't let you)—and if you open a file with a long name then try to re-save it, AppleWorks truncates its name, as shown in the Save As field.

- Bottom—Should be self-explanatory. The only difference between the two Finder icons is that the left icon shows the tool tip; the right icon doesn't.

OK, that's it. That's all the Finder, Dock, and toolbar stuff I have room for. It ought to be enough to get you thinking.

Now, let's take a look at the best of the best—a handful of my favorite programs to enhance the Finder and Dock and make them better and easier to use.

Software That Makes the Finder and Dock Even Better

This is the stuff that really tickles my fancy. I love cool utilities, and Mac programmers are famous for inventing elegant ways to work around Apple shortcomings, both real and perceived.

I consider it a big part of my job to ferret out the best OS X software, put it to use, then tell my readers about the best of the best. Yes, it's a tough job, but I love doing it. So, every day I make a point of downloading and checking out a few new programs. But more than that, I spend time every day reading my favorite OS X mailing lists, newsgroups, and message boards (which are discussed at length in Chapter 5), to find out what programs other power users are raving about.

I put links to a lot of great programs for enhancing the Finder and Dock on this book's companion Web site. The programs in this section are the ones I consider the very best of the best—and are the programs I have running at this very moment. I'd hate to be without any of them.

Launchers/Organizers

I've already told you about my proclivity for the keyboard. Most times, I prefer a solution that doesn't require me to reach out and touch the mouse. If I can do something exclusively from the keyboard, without touching the mouse, that's how I'll usually do it. On the other hand, I have a softer, more creative side, one that gets into organizing things—like icons—visually, and enjoys moving them around, rearranging them, and clicking and dragging them. It's that left brain/right brain thing, but I can never remember which one is which.

Which brings me to the point: I use two programs to satisfy both sets of my needs—LaunchBar caters to the part of me in love with keyboard shortcuts; DragThing fulfills my need to be creative and organize things. Between the two of them, I manage to avoid using Finder windows much of the time.

LaunchBar

LaunchBar is one of the best new utilities for the Macintosh. Its name says it all—once installed, LaunchBar lets you browse all your files, applications, Web-bookmarks, and email addresses exclusively from the keyboard. It's intelligent—over time it learns short abbreviations for your most-used files.

To launch a file, press the hotkey that activates LaunchBar (mine is Control+Spacebar), then type the first few letters of the item you wish to launch.

2

So, if I want to launch Internet Explorer, I type "Control+Space" to activate
LaunchBar , then type "int." LaunchBar appears with Internet Explorer selected, as
shown in Figure 2.48.

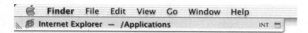

Figure 2.48
Typing Control+Space followed by "i," "n," and "t" activates LaunchBar with Internet Explorer ready to be
launched.

When I press Return or Enter, Internet Explorer will launch. Or, if IE is open already,
it becomes the active application.

But what if I want to launch another program that begins with the letters "int", such
as Internet Connect? I can either keep typing additional letters until the correct
application appears in LaunchBar or press the down-arrow key to display a list of
items that match what I typed "int", as shown in Figure 2.49.

Figure 2.49
Pressing the down arrow key reveals LaunchBar's list of items that begin with the letters "int."

LaunchBar also features an application switcher. Of course you can use the Finder's
built-in shortcut for cycling through running programs, Command+Tab, but
LaunchBar is better because you choose the program from a list, rather than pressing
Command+Tab a dozen times. The application list is shown in Figure 2.50.

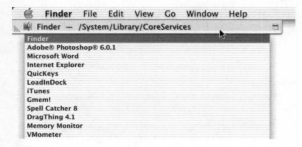

Figure 2.50
Switching from program to program is easy with LaunchBar's handy application-switcher list.

So, it's fewer keystrokes from here to there with LaunchBar. In Figure 2.50, I might have to press Command+Tab six or seven times using Finder to get to the program I want. Choosing it from a LaunchBar list takes fewer keystrokes.

TIP

> While Command+Tab cycles forward to the next open application, Command+Shift+Tab cycles backward to the previous open application. I still find LaunchBar faster and easier.

LaunchBar works everywhere, too—in Finder as well as in any program including Classic apps.

I hate to gush, but I have to mention this: LaunchBar is smart. Very smart. Extremely smart. It actually learns your preferences by watching how you use it. You don't have to do anything special; the program watches what you type and intelligently selects the item it thinks you're most likely to want.

For example, the first time I used LaunchBar, I had to type, "internetex" before Internet Explorer became selected. But the next time I only had to type the first three letters, "int," before it selected Internet Explorer.

Now, that alone would be smart. But LaunchBar is even smarter than that. It has figured out that when I press the "i" key, I almost always launch Internet Explorer and that I've never launched Internet Connect, which comes before Explorer alphabetically. Even so, as soon as I press "i," LaunchBar selects Internet Explorer in spite of the fact that other programs have the same first letter.

So now that we've gotten to know each other a little better, to open my favorite programs, I type Control+Spacebar, then:

- *O, Return (or Enter)*—to open OmniWeb

- *W, Return (or Enter)*—to open Microsoft Word (believe it or not, LaunchBar figured that out, too)

■ *P, Return (or Enter)*—to open Photoshop

and so on.

I am totally addicted to LaunchBar. I use it more times each day than any other program. If you like keyboard control, you're going to become addicted to LaunchBar, too.

2

> **TIP**
>
> The free evaluation copy of LaunchBar available via the link at **www.boblevitus. com/xfiles.html** limits you to seven different items per session. You're going to want more. So once you're addicted, do the right thing and purchase a home user license by sending the author, Norbert, $19.95. You'll love the freedom of the unlimited version—and it would be a bargain at twice the price. (Payment instructions can be found in LaunchBar Help.)

DragThing

I'm not going to gush about DragThing yet. (I intend to do it plenty in the next chapter, though, since that's the one all about organizing your stuff.) DragThing is more than just an organizer—it's a Finder enhancer, Dock enhancer, file launcher, keyboard shortcut-maker, toothpaste, and desert topping all in one, and more.

As I mentioned, I'll give you the complete rundown in Chapter 3. For now, satisfy yourself with this detail of the lower-right corner of my desktop (Figure 2.51), which

Figure 2.51
The silver dock is the "Process" Dock, which displays all currently running apps; the wood-grain Dock is my personal Dock, with all the programs and folders I normally need.

shows the beautiful, space-saving, Dock-enhancing DragThing in action.

> **NOTE**
>
> You can see DragThing with the Docks arranged differently at the bottom of Figure 2.39.

Speaking of Docks, it's time to move on and look at programs designed to work *in* the Dock.

Ladies and Gentlemen: Meet the Docklings

There's been no shortage of programs that augment or enhance the Dock. It seems there's a "dockling" (yes, that's really what they're called) for almost every occasion. Calendar Docklings, volume control docklings, trance music docklings, news ticker docklings, and more, all doing their thing right there in your Dock.

 NOTE

I included links for many cool docklings on this book's companion Web site. You'll learn about some of them here, more of them in upcoming chapters, and the rest of them in Chapter 14.

Snard & LoadInDock

I've already described Snard and LoadInDock, and even shown you what they look like (in Figures 2.32 and 2.33). So, there's not much to add. Snard is most valuable to me for its direct-access-to-individual-preferences-panes menu; LoadInDock is one of the things I keep an eye on for troubleshooting purposes.

More Docklings

If you like LoadInDock, its author, Takashi T. Hamada, has created two other "InDock" docklings—ThermoInDock and NetStatInDock. One tells you the temperature inside your Mac, the other tells you about traffic on your network.

Figure 2.52 shows you all three InDock docklings and a few others good ones, too.

Figure 2.52
So many cool docklings, so little Dock space.

Looking at Figure 2.52 you have, from the top:

- *GMem*—GMem is an OS X memory monitor dockling. It has a display "issue" under OS X 10.1 that hadn't been fixed when I wrote this. It works but is very hard to read, and its preference settings don't help. I've since found a program I like even better-MemoryStick-which, although it's not a dockling, does what GMem does without the "issues." And, like Gmem, it has a warning alarm you can set to notify you when you run out of free RAM. That said, GMem is a neat app-I hope it gets fixed soon.

- *VMometer*—VMometer is a virtual memory activity monitor dockling. I know, it's a horrible name, and you can't help but think "vomit meter" every time you see it. But get over the name, and it's kind of cool. One of the arcs flashes in blue when a virtual memory "page in" occurs; the other arc flashes in red when a virtual memory "page out" occurs. If you're seeing a lot of page outs, your Mac would benefit from a RAM upgrade.

- *MemoryMonitor*—MemoryMonitor is another OS X memory monitor dockling. It's similar to GMem but doesn't have a text display or alarm. It's similar to VMometer, but displays the information differently.

- *LoadInDock*—LoadInDock is a dockling that displays and graphs processor usage.

- *ThermoInDock*—ThermoInDock is a dockling that displays and graphs the temperature inside your Mac.

- *NetStatInDock*—NetStatInDock is a dockling that displays and graphs information about the network your Mac is connected to.

- *DragThing, Snard, and Trash*—Only Snard is actually a dockling. And we've talked about DragThing and Snard already.

NOTE
> Links for all of these docklings are on this book's accompanying Web site.

And that wraps up our discussion of docklings.

Alas, it's said that all good things must come to an end and that includes this chapter. Next, we'll move along to Chapter 3— "Organizing Your Mac".

Hard Disk Organization (and Navigation) Made Easy

When I wrote my first book, *Dr. Macintosh: Tips, Techniques, and Advice on Mastering the Macintosh*, way back in 1989, I began a chapter on a similar topic (which was called "The Care and Feeding of Hard Disks") with these words:

There are at least 20 million reasons to own a hard disk (20 million is the approximate number of bytes in a 20MB hard disk).

I bring this up for two reasons:

■ First, to demonstrate how far we've come since then. In 1989, a hard disk was a very expensive luxury item—few (if any) Macs shipped with one, and fewer Mac users owned one. Most Mac users made do with one (or two) 800K floppy disk drives. Imagine that.

> **NOTE**
>
> My first hard drive, which I bought in 1988 or '89, was a SuperMac DataFrame 40 SCSI drive. It cost a whopping $2,495, which, interestingly, was exactly what I paid for my then state-of-the-art Macintosh Plus with 1MB of RAM and no hard disk. And I thought it was worth every penny.

■ Second, to show how, in 1989 when I got my very first SCSI hard drive, 20MB was considered huge and 40MB was gargantuan. When the DataFrame arrived and I had installed my System Folder and other essentials, I still had more than 30MB of free space and thought to myself, "There's no way I'll ever fill it." Little did I know.

> **NOTE**
>
> In those days, the Macintosh operating system plus one or two applications would fit comfortably on a single 800K floppy disk.

Fast-forward to 2002: My G4/500 *came with* a 30GB hard drive (which is almost full) and can burn CD-Rs and CD-RWs (600+ MB), as well as DVD-R and DVD-RAM discs (4.7+ GB). And in 2002, Mac OS X requires *at least* 1.5GB of free disk space to install, and many of the applications it runs are bigger than my first 40MB hard disk!

The point is, mass quantities of mass storage have become incredibly cheap and totally ubiquitous. But with these huge disks comes what I see as a huge challenge: How to keep all your "stuff" organized so you can find what you need quickly and painlessly.

That, my friends, is what this chapter is all about. In the coming pages, I first show you some of the ways you can organize your files and folders for maximum efficiency; then I share some of my favorite tips, hints, and shortcuts for navigating your disk(s); and last but certainly not least, I show you some great programs that make getting organized, staying organized, and finding what you're looking for even easier.

Tantalized? Let's rock!

Starting with the Basics

Once again, you have to crawl before you walk, and walk before you run, so we start with the basics before we get into details.

In earlier versions of Mac OS, the way you organized your files was quite relaxed. Any user could move or delete any file, and every user had access to every file and folder on every disk.

Mac OS X, being a true multiuser OS, introduces some rules and regulations regarding who can do what to which files and folders, and where certain files and folders must be stored.

So before we talk about getting *your stuff* organized, let's look at how OS X organizes *its stuff* and at some of the rules of the road, so to speak.

How Mac OS X Is Organized

A fresh installation of Mac OS X (including Mac OS 9.2.1) includes seven folders at the top level (a.k.a. root level) of your boot disk.

ALERT!

> The top level in your disk hierarchy—the folders you see when you open a disk's icon— has been known as *root level* since time immemorial. Unfortunately, "root" has an entirely different meaning in Unix (and, as just mentioned, in OS X). You'll learn all about the root account (sometimes referred to as the *super-user* or *god* account) in Chapter 11. For now, just remember that root level on a disk has nothing whatsoever to do with the root account or Unix.

Before we can talk about those folders, let's pause for a brief interlude about "ownership" and how it affects who can do what to which folders.

"Ownership"

Because OS X is a multiuser operating system, each user has access to only the files and folders they "own." For a user to own a file or folder, it needs to either be in the user's Home folder (each user owns everything in their own Home folder) or be a file or folder the user created and stored elsewhere on the disk.

I cover users (and groups) in some detail in Chapter 12, but you need to know at least that much about how this whole ownership thing works now (or instead of getting organized, you'll get into big trouble).

Of course, this ownership rule has at least three exceptions. Administrator and root accounts can access files and folders they don't own. And if you boot under Mac OS 9, all bets are off—any user can modify or delete any file or folder.

The bottom line is that some folders are "off limits" unless you're logged in as an administrator or root. These "protected" folders can't be deleted or modified, nor can you put anything into or take anything out of them.

3

We now return to our regularly scheduled programming.

The Seven Folders at Root Level

OK then. Let's take a look at those seven folders I was talking about before I so rudely interrupted myself:

■ *Applications*—The collection of applications and utilities included with Mac OS X. It can be modified only with an administrator or root account name and password.

■ *Applications (Mac OS 9)*—The collection of applications and utilities included with Mac OS 9. It can be modified only with an administrator or root account name and password.

■ *Documents*—A place for documents. This folder is available to all users.

■ *Library*—Some of the files that OS X requires. Administrators are allowed to modify some of the Library files and folders, but others can be modified only by root.

■ *System*—The rest of the files that OS X requires. Administrators are allowed to modify some of the System files and folders, but others can be modified only by root.

> **NOTE**
> If you are familiar with OS 9, you can think of Library and System as being roughly equivalent to the OS 9 System Folder.

■ *System Folder*—An actual OS 9.2.1 System Folder. You can boot from it to start up your Mac using OS 9, use it to run Classic within OS X, or both.

■ *Users*—Contains a separate Home folder for each user of this Mac.

> **NOTE**
>
> If you installed the Developer Tools included with boxed copies of Mac OS X, you'll also see a folder called Developer at root level. Or, if you upgraded your Mac from OS 9 to OS X, you may see other folders that existed at root level *before* you installed OS X. The point is, if you got a new Mac or installed OS X (and 9.2.1) on a just-initialized disk, you'll see only those seven folders.

Each of these folders has a variety of subfolders and files inside it, but they're not important to this discussion. So we're going to move along and look at the other group of folders you need to be familiar with to organize your disk—the eight folders you'll find in a just-installed Home folder (a.k.a. Home directory).

The Eight Folders of Home

When you create a user account, a Home folder (or directory) is created automatically in the Users folder and populated with the following folders:

■ *Desktop*—Contains the same icons that are on your OS X desktop. (Put another way, every icon on the desktop also appears in this folder.)

> **NOTE**
>
> Why? Because Mac OS X is a multiuser operating system, and every user has their very own desktop.

■ *Documents*—Store your documents here so other users don't see them.

■ *Library*—Contains system and/or application-related files and folders for this user only.

■ *Movies*—Empty folder.

■ *Music*—Empty folder.

■ *Pictures*—Empty folder.

■ *Public*—The only folder in your Home folder other users can see. If you want other users to have access to files or folders, this is a good place for them.

> **TIP**
>
> Inside each Public folder is a folder called Drop Box. Other users can put items in your Drop Box folder, but only you can open it. When you move or copy a file to another user's Drop Box, you'll see an alert that says, "You do not have permission to see the results of this operation. Do you wish to continue?" If you click OK, the file or folder goes into that user's Drop Box, where only its owner can see it.

■ *Sites*—Used by the built-in Apache (Unix) Web server to host a Web site on your Mac. You can browse HTML files in this folder at **http://*your.computer's.IP.address/ ~yourshortname/*** . (You chose your short name when you created your user account. It is the same as the name on your Home directory. Mine, for example, is *bobl*.)

> **TIP**
>
> You can browse HTML files in the root-level Library/WebServer/Documents folder at **http://*your.computer's.IP.address/*** .

You can delete any of the above folders except Desktop.

> **ALERT!**
>
> Although you *can* delete your Library or Public folders, don't. Without the Library folder, OS X will not work properly, and some applications will cease functioning. And re-creating the Public folder requires Unix skills, so it isn't trivial. Just leave those two folders alone and everything will be hunky-dory.

> **TIP**
>
> I wouldn't delete the Documents folder, either, because it's easy to navigate to using the Go menu, and you can select it from the drop-down menu in both Open dialog boxes and Save sheets for OS X applications. In fact, as I'll show you shortly, this is where I recommend you store all your document.

A Tale of Two Libraries

If you've been paying close attention, you've no doubt noticed that there are two different folders called Library, one at root level and another in your Home folder. If you open them, you'll find they both contain folders called Documentation, Favorites, Fonts, Internet Plug-Ins, Internet Search Sites, PreferencePanes, Preferences, Printers, Screen Savers, Voices, and many others.

The difference between these two similar Library folders is this: The root-level Library folder contains files that are available to all users, and the Home folder Library folder is for files used exclusively by the owner of that Home folder.

> **TIP**
>
> Think of the root-level Library as public and the Home folder Library as private.

So, for example, to install a font or screen saver that all users have access to, put it into the appropriate folder within the Library folder at root level. To install a font or screen saver that only you have access to, put it into the appropriate folder within the Library folder in your Home folder.

> Just to make things really confusing, there's a third Library folder inside the System folder at root level. Fortunately, OS X uses this Library folder for its own nefarious purposes, so you rarely have to touch it.

Three Organizational Strategies

Now that you have a basic understanding of the default OS X folder structures and know which folders are "off limits," let's take a look at three different strategies for organizing your files and folders.

Different people organize their hard disks in different ways. There is no one "right" way to do it. And, as long as you keep your folders in your Home folder, you can have as many or as few folders as you like, organized any way you like them.

The following sections offer three general strategies for organizing your hard disk. In each of the strategies, some things are constant. For example, no matter how you decide to organize your folders, you should store frequently used icons in a convenient place, such as the Dock, the desktop, or in one of the utilities we'll look at in a moment. And, I think you'll find it more convenient if you store all your applications (programs) in an Applications folder—at root level if you want everyone to have access to them, or in an Applications folder you create within your Home folder if you don't want others to use them.

> Spreading your applications (and utilities) across dozens of different folders, all over your hard disk, makes finding the right program quickly a chore. If they're all in one or two folders, you always know where to look.

After a brief discussion of the three different strategies, I'll give you a peek at *my* hard disks and tell you a little about how *I* keep my 20GB of stuff organized.

Strategy 1: Organizing by Client/Project

This strategy works best if you are a consultant or other such business professional who works with several different clients or projects simultaneously.

After setting up your Applications folder or folders, organize your work by either client or project—that is, set up a separate folder for each client or for each project. Then, create subfolders inside each client or project folder if you need them, as shown in Figure 3.1.

Figure 3.1
A Home folder organized by client/project.

The advantage of this scheme is that everything that has to do with the project or client is in one folder, where it will be easy to find. If a client calls, or your boss asks about a specific project, you'll be able to find all of the files pertaining to that client or project in their own folder.

If that strategy doesn't ring your chimes, you might prefer Strategy 2.

Strategy 2: Organizing by Task

Another way to organize your hard disk is by task. Documents of the same type go into their own folders. So, for example, you might create one for memos, another for letters, another for proposals, and so on, as shown in Figure 3.2.

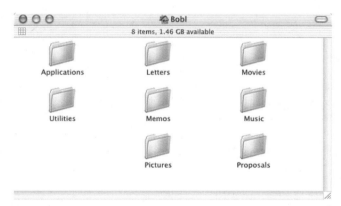

Figure 3.2
A Home folder organized by task.

The advantage here is that if you need to find any letter, regardless of its addressee or purpose, you know that it's stored in your Letters folder.

Finally, here's a third way you might organize your hard disk.

Strategy 3: Organizing by Application

Some people prefer to organize their files and folders by the applications that created the documents. So you'd have a Word folder that contained the Microsoft Word application, all of its associated files (dictionaries, glossary, help file, and so on), and folders containing all the documents created by Word, as shown in Figure 3.3.

Figure 3.3
A Home folder organized by application.

> **TIP**
>
> Notice that the folders within the Word folder are sorted by name. Do you notice anything unusual about the order they're listed in? The reason the Word Programs & Files folder is at the top of the list instead of the bottom is that I put a space before the "W." Because a space comes before an "A" (at least in the Macintosh list-sorting scheme), the folder appears at the top of the list rather than the bottom. So, if you want a particular folder or file to appear at the top of lists in either List or Column view, precede its name with a space.

Your folder for Photoshop (a graphics and illustration application) might contain the application plus folders for logos, drawings, ads, and the like. I don't personally use or recommend this scheme, but I know users who swear by it.

Once again, let me emphasize that there is no "right" way. Maybe some combination of these strategies makes sense to you. Or maybe you have a scheme all your own that you feel comfortable with. Any method that makes it easy for you to find what you're looking for and to back up important files regularly is a good method.

A Look at My Hard Disk(s)

I'm slightly neurotic about keeping track of stuff on my hard disks. I also arrange my desktop obsessively, so the windows that I use frequently don't overlap.

I have several Macs (details are in Appendix A: *Bob's Setup*), but my main everyday Mac has a built-in 25GB hard disk, which I've partitioned into two volumes—a 5GB volume called Das Boot and a 20GB volume called Number Nine.

My philosophy about what goes where is pretty simple. Mac OS X and a Mac OS 9.2.1 System Folder are the only things I keep on Das Boot; everything else, including another Mac OS 9.2.1 System Folder, lives on Number Nine.

I like this arrangement for several reasons, but the big one is that if my operating system ever gets totally hosed, I can either boot into OS 9 from the Number Nine volume and attempt to repair Das Boot, or if that doesn't work, I can initialize Das Boot and reinstall OS X and OS 9.2.1 without losing anything important.

> **NOTE**
>
> This scheme also simplifies my backup regimen, which I'll explain in detail in Chapter 4. The only thing on Das Boot that requires backing up is my Home folder, which, as you're about to see, contains only my Library folder. Everything else in my Home folder is an alias of a folder that is actually stored on Number Nine.

All of my data files (documents) are in the Documents folder on Number Nine. Projects I'm currently working on—like this book, the Mac OS X 10.1 update to *Mac OS X For Dummies*, and my weekly Dr. Mac newspaper columns—are in the Documents folder as well, but also have aliases on the desktop for easy access. All applications, fonts, and games, are in the appropriate folders on Number Nine. Figure 3.4 shows what it all looks like.

The only folders in my Home folder that are *not* aliases are Desktop, Library, and Public. Notice that most of the folders OS X created for me (Pictures, Movies, and so on) are gone—they don't make sense in my organizing scheme, so I got rid of them.

Root level of the Number Nine volume contains folders for every application, game, utility, and font I have, and every document I've ever created.

Root level of Das Boot is a stock Mac OS X installation with nothing added or deleted.

This may not be the most elegant technique in the world, but it works for me. Of course, there are dozens of ways you can organize *your* hard disk. Experiment, and find out what works for you. You may want to set up a combination of more than one way. For example, you could create a folder for each client, and then create folders

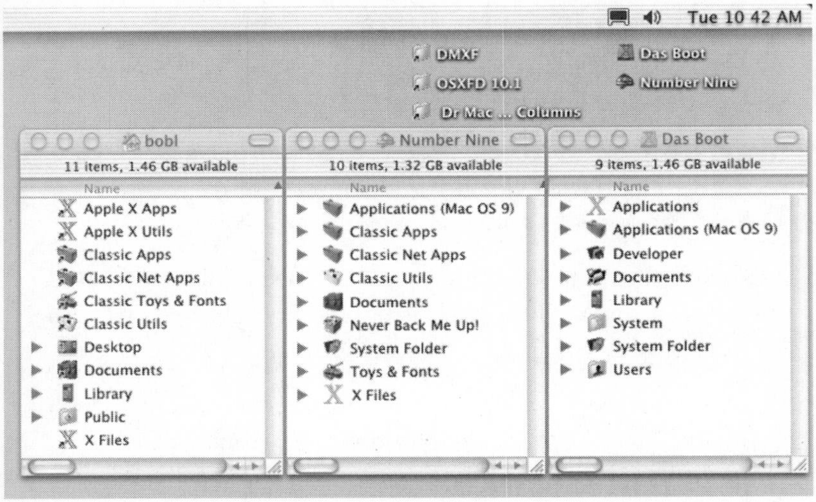

Figure 3.4
Here's my Home folder (bobl) and both hard disk volumes (Number Nine and Das Boot).

within it for letters, memos, proposals, and so on. Another popular way to keep things organized is to use a file for each month. For example, within your Letters, Client/ Project, and Proposals folders, you would have a folder for each month.

Whatever method you use to organize your hard disk, you'll probably find it convenient to put aliases of frequently used icons on the desktop (as I do) or in the Dock (as I don't).

If you're wondering why no application icons are on *my* desktop (or in my Dock, for that matter), it's because I use both LaunchBar and DragThing instead. I'll be telling you more about both at the end of this chapter.

You can see in Figure 3.4 that aliases of projects I am working on are right on the gray desktop, where they're always easy to find and open. (Also notice that the icons for those three folders have little arrows in their lower-left corners to indicate that they are aliases.)

NOTE

My desktop is not gray. I set it up that way only for shooting screenshots for this book. I use a cool little freeware program called Desktop Randomizer to install a new and different picture every time I log in. Desktop Randomizer is covered in Chapters 9 and 14.

Organizational Shortcuts, Tips, Tricks, and Strategies

Having been a Mac user for more than 15 years, I've developed more than my share of shortcuts, tips, tricks, and strategies for organizing my files and folders and for navigating to them. (Hey, with more than 40,000 files and folders on my hard disk, I've got plenty of incentive to make finding what I need as fast and easy as possible.)

TIP

> Of course you can always use Sherlock (File|Find or Command+F) to find a lost file. But that's slow and awkward. Real power users will have everything they use regularly no more than a few clicks away.

So, without further ado, here's some of the stuff I do and/or recommend.

Dealing with Folders and Windows

Because folders and windows are mainstays of the Finder, and you'll be using them every time you use your Mac, I've collected some tips and techniques that may appeal to you. Again, remember that your ultimate goal is to create a system that makes sense to you, so you can find what you need in the least time possible. That said, here are some of my favorite techniques and tips for dealing with folders and their windows.

Open Folders in a New Window or Not: The Sequel

As I mentioned in Chapter 2, one thing that's very different about OS X is that it tries to force you to work in a single window. When you open a folder, its contents fill the current window. When you opened a folder under OS 9, it opened a second window. This can be disconcerting, but don't worry—it's fixable.

If you don't like this behavior, you're welcome to change it back to the "OS 9 way." Here's how:

1. Choose Finder|Preferences.

2. Check the checkbox labeled Always Open Folders In A New Window.

And that's it. Things are back the way they used to be in OS 9. Frankly, I didn't like this feature at first, but now I love it. Give it a little time before you change this setting.

Even when the open in new widnow preference is unchecked, you can open folders in new windows whenever you like. If the toolbar is showing in the current window, Command+double-click to open a folder in a separate window. If the toolbar is not showing in the current window, merely double-clicking a folder opens it in a separate window.

> **TIP**
>
> Don't forget that you can hide or show the toolbar of a window in three different ways—use the menu by choosing View|Hide Toolbar (if it's showing) or View|Show Toolbar (if it's hidden); use the keyboard shortcut Command+B; or click the gray gumdrop in the upper-right corner of the window.

One last thing: If you turn the open in new window preference on, it doesn't matter if the toolbar is showing—opening a folder *always* generates a new window, regardless of whether you press the Command key or whether the toolbar is showing or hidden.

Learn and Use Those Keyboard Shortcuts

Mac OS X makes it easy to navigate through folders using only the keyboard. Once you get the hang of it, using keyboard shortcuts is faster and easier than reaching for the mouse. In all three views, the arrow keys move you from icon to icon. In addition, here are some other arrow-key shortcuts that work in all three Finder views:

■ *Command+down-arrow*—Opens the selected folder

■ *Command+up-arrow*—Opens the parent folder of the active window

■ *Command+Option+down-arrow*—Opens the selected folder in a separate window and closes the active window

■ *Command+Option+up-arrow*—Opens the parent folder of the active window in a separate window and closes the active window

Here are a few more hotkeys specifically for the List view:

■ *Right-arrow*—Reveals the contents of the selected folder

■ *Left-arrow*—Hides the contents of the selected folder

■ *Command+Option+right-arrow*—Reveals the contents of the selected folder and the contents of all its subfolders

■ *Command+Option+left-arrow*—Hides the contents of the selected folder and the contents of all its subfolders

I rarely use the mouse in the Finder. Unless my hand is on the mouse already, I use the keyboard.

Another way you can use the keyboard to navigate is by choosing Go|Go To Folder, which opens a little dialog box where you can type the pathname to any folder on any disk. This dialog box is smart and will try to guess which folder you're looking for. It's easier to show than tell, so look at Figure 3.5.

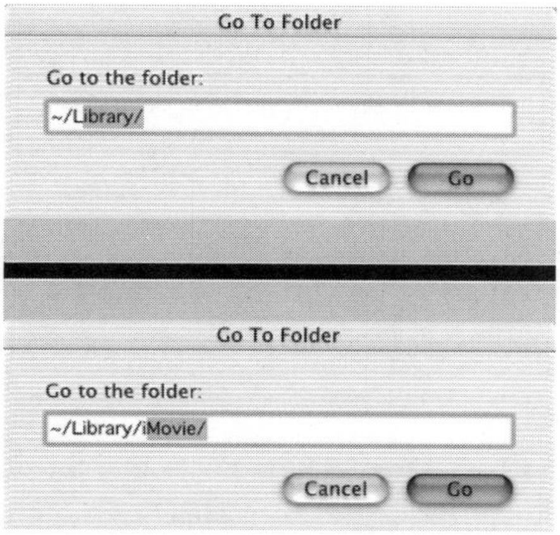

Figure 3.5
The Go To Folder dialog box typed the highlighted letters for me.

> **TIP**
>
> The tilde (~) is Unix shorthand for "Home directory."

Here's what I did (and what the Go To Folder dialog box did for me) in Figure 3.5: First, I typed "~/L," and the dialog box added "ibrary." Then, I pressed the right-arrow key once, to move the cursor to the right of the second slash. Finally, I typed "i" and the dialog box added "Movie."

Although this isn't usually the easiest or fastest way to navigate, it's still worth knowing, especially if you prefer to keep both hands on the keyboard.

Don't Nest Folders Too Deep

Although the Macintosh will allow you to nest folders (that is, place subfolders within folders) as many levels deep as you like, try not to go more than four levels deep. If you have to open four or more folders to get something, it's buried too deep. Create additional folders somewhere else or subfolders within a folder that's four or fewer levels deep.

If you hate having to double-click your way through folders, like I do, several utilities offer alternate methods of organizing and launching files and folders, a method many power users prefer.

The problem is less severe in list or column views, because you can see the contents of all folders within one window without having to double-click their icons to open them. (See Chapter 2 for more information on views.) Even so, files nested more than four levels deep are less convenient.

Use the Toolbar

You can drag any icon—file or folder—into the toolbar, where it's only a click away. Apple starts you out with some icons, but if you're like me, you'll soon be adding your own.

TIP

> Don't forget the menu beneath the little chevron thingy that lets you use hidden toolbar icons easily. It's shown in Figure 2.15, in case you need to refresh your memory.

Open and Save

You can use the arrow keys and letter keys in OS X Open dialog boxes and Save sheets, and you should. And in most Open dialog boxes and Save sheets, typing the first letter or two of the file or folder you seek scrolls to that file or folder.

TIP

> Make sure the list of files is active (i.e., the "focus" is on it, not some other part of the dialog box or sheet), such as the Go To or Save As fields. Whichever item the focus is on will display a little (usually blue) border around it. If the list is not highlighted, you can either click the list once or press the Tab key one or more times until it displays the blue border.

You can also use three other extremely effective techniques for getting to a file or folder quickly, as the following sections demonstrate.

Drag and Drop

I love this one. If you can see the file or folder you want on the desktop or in a Finder window, you can drag it onto the Open dialog box, as shown in Figure 3.6. When you release the mouse, the Open dialog box jumps to that folder, as shown in Figure 3.7.

This same technique works in Save sheets, but only with a folder.

NOTE

> Although you can drag a file *or* folder to the Open dialog box, you can drag only a folder to a Save sheet. Dragging a file to it won't work. Which makes sense when you think about it—you can't save a file in a file, only in a folder.

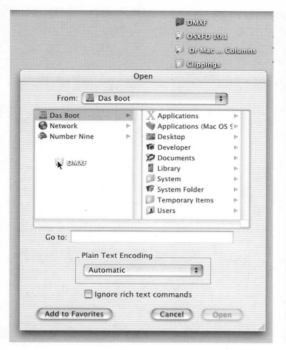

Figure 3.6
I want to open a file that's in the DMXF folder, so I drag that folder onto the Open dialog box.

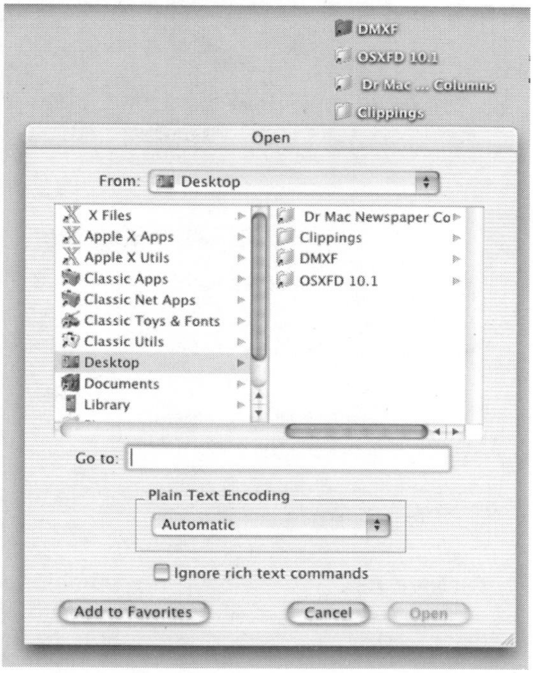

Figure 3.7
Now the DMXF folder is just one click away.

These Are a Few of My Favorite Places

The other nifty way to navigate in both Open dialog boxes and Save sheets is to use your Favorites list, which is available in the pull-down menus (among other places). This menu lets you choose directly from your Favorite folders, without any navigation, as shown in Figure 3.8.

You can add any file or folder to your list of Favorites by using any of the following four methods:

■ In an Open dialog box or expanded Save sheet, click the icon you want to make a Favorite, then click the Add To Favorites button.

> **TIP**
>
> To expand (or contract) the Save sheet, to reveal (or conceal) additional options and choices, click the triangle to the right of the Where menu.

■ In the Finder, select the icon you want to make a Favorite, then choose File|Add To Favorites.

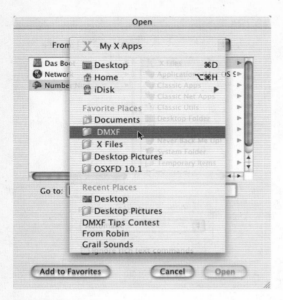

Figure 3.8
When I release the mouse button, I'll be inside the DMXF folder, which would otherwise be four or five clicks away.

- In the Finder, select the icon you want to make a Favorite, then use the keyboard shortcut Command+T.

- Drag an alias of the icon you want to make a Favorite into your Favorites folder, which is located at ~/Library/Favorites (i.e., *YourHardDisk*/Users/*YourHome*/Library/Favorites).

You can also use your Favorites right from the Finder. Choose Go|Favorites, then choose a favorite from the submenu, as shown in Figure 3.9; or use the keyboard shortcut Command+Option+F to open your Favorites folder.

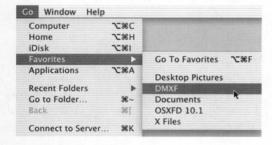

Figure 3.9
When I release the mouse button, the DMXF folder's window will appear instantly in the Finder.

Recent Items Rock, Too

The Recent menus serve a similar purpose, but you can't add your own items—Mac OS X does it for you behind the scenes by remembering which files, folders, and programs you've used lately. If you're trying to navigate to a folder, document, or program you've used recently, one of the Recent menus may be the quickest way.

There are several of them. The drop-down menus in Open dialog boxes and Save sheets have a Recent Places item. In the Finder, Go|Recent Folders has a submenu of folders you've visited lately, and Apple Menu|Recent Items has a submenu of Recent Applications and Recent Documents.

3

> **TIP**
>
> Though you can't specify how many Recent Folders or Recent Places you want OS X to keep track of, you can tell it how many Recent Applications and Recent Documents you want it to remember. Use the General System Preference pane to specify a number—OS X can remember up to 50 applications and 50 documents. Alas, there's no way to delete unwanted folders or places selectively, but if you find these menus cluttered up with folders and places you don't want or need anymore, you can make them all disappear by choosing the Clear Menu item at the bottom of the Recent Items submenu.

Dock It to Me

Before we move on to the cool software for organizing your folders that I use and recommend, I feel obliged to mention one other organizational/navigational tool—the Dock. Now you must understand that I don't use the Dock myself. Although it's pretty, I don't think it's space-efficient. So I use DragThing for most of what the Dock does (and some other stuff, too, as you'll see in the next section). In fact, as I mentioned in Chapter 2, the first thing I do when I install OS X on one of my Macs is to remove everything Apple puts in the Dock. Only the Trash and Finder survive, and that's only because there's no way to get rid of them. I also have Auto-Hide (Command+D) turned on most of the time. Finally, I keep the Dock as small as it can be, and park it in the lower-right corner of my desktop.

> **TIP**
>
> The Dock System preference pane lets you choose Left, Bottom, or Right, but it parks the Dock in the middle of whichever you select. I park mine in the lower-right corner by using an awesome freeware preference pane called TinkerTool, which I will discuss in Chapters 9 and 14.

But using or not using the Dock is a personal thing. You may very well love it. So, here are a few Dock tips.

Figure 3.10
Drag an icon off the Dock and poof—it's gone!

To place an icon in your Dock, drag it onto the Dock; to remove it, drag it off of the Dock, where it'll disappear with a "poof," as shown in Figure 3.10.

If the icon is a disk, folder, or document, you can drag it only to the right of the little white separator line (or below it if your Dock is on the left or right, as mine is). You can drag application and dockling icons anywhere on the Dock.

Your cursor changes into a double-headed arrow when it's over the separator line, and if you Control+click the white dividing line, as shown in Figure 3.11, you can change some of the Dock's preferences from the menu, or open the System Preferences' Dock pane, where you can change any or all of them.

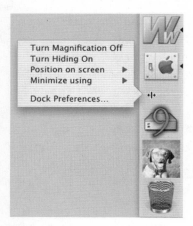

Figure 3.11
The Dock's contextual menu.

Perhaps the most useful thing the Dock can do for you is provide a hierarchical menu for any folder or disk icon in it, as shown in Figure 3.12.

Last but not least, most icons in the Dock—even ones that are not folder or disk icons—have a similar menu. If an icon does have a menu, it will contain at least one item—Show In Finder. Choose it and the window that contains that item will open in the Finder.

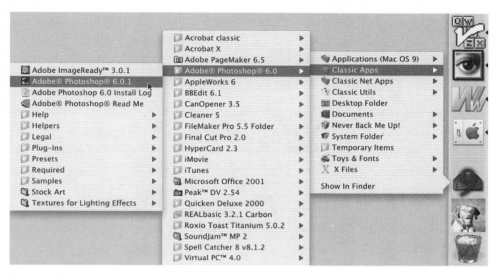

Figure 3.12
Click and hold a disk or folder icon, and you'll see a menu like this—don't release the mouse button until the file or folder you seek is highlighted.

Some icons in the Dock have menus that do other things. For example, when iTunes is running, its Dock icon menu shows the current song, and it lets you pause or select the next or previous song without activating iTunes itself, as shown in Figure 3.13.

Figure 3.13
iTunes icon in the Dock offers more options than many applications.

So when an OS X application is running, click and hold it in the Dock and see what its menu offers—you may get a pleasant surprise!

For what it's worth, the Keep In Dock item appears for any open application in the Dock unless you've dragged that item into the Dock manually. If I were to choose it in Figure 3.13, the iTunes icon would stay in the Dock even after I quit.

Furthermore, all open applications Dock icons also have a Quit command.

As I mentioned in Chapter 2, if you press the Option key, the Quit command turns into to Force Quit, which is useful if an application stops responding or crashes. You can also force a recalcitrant program to Quit by choosing Apple Menu|Force Quit or by using the keyboard shortcut Command+Option+Escape.

Software That Makes Navigating Easier

I use LaunchBar (**www.obdev.at**) instead of the Finder to open most files. But because I spent several pages raving about LaunchBar in the last chapter, here I'll merely say it's one of the best utilities I've ever used, and I use it every time I use my Mac. If you don't install it and try it, you're missing out on something truly blissful. (Don't forget, however, that it's shareware—as mentioned in Chapter 2, and you don't get the full benefit until you pay for it.)

In Chapter 2, I also promised I'd have more to say about DragThing, another fantastic utility I use every day. And so, without further ado, here it is.

DragThing

Another program I use every day is DragThing (**www.dragthing.com**). It's been around for years, serving under Mac OS 8 and 9, but the Mac OS X incarnation is better than ever. James Thomson, DragThing's humble author, refers to it as "the original Dock designed to tidy up your Macintosh desktop." But it's so much more than just a Dock.

Let me give you a quick look at DragThing in action; then, I'll tell you about some of the features I like best and use most. Figure 3.14 shows my two DragThing docks in their "minimized" state in the bottom-right corner, as well as the Switching tab in DragThing's Preferences window above them. As you can see, I've designated the lower-right corner as my "hot spot," to bring DragThing to the front without delay. You can use hot keys to activate DragThing as well, but because I use a trackball, it's easy to just slam the cursor into the lower-right corner, as shown in Figure 3.15, to make my docks expand.

The right dock is my "process" dock, which displays all currently running applications. But the dock I use most is the other one, which I've imaginatively named MyDock. You add items to a DragThing dock the same way you add them to the OS X Dock, just drag them onto it. So far, not much difference, right?

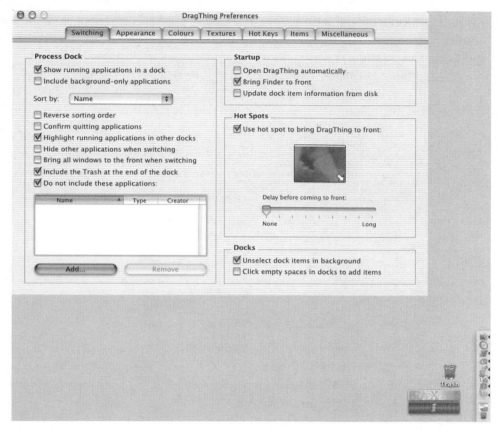

Figure 3.14
DragThing *is unobtrusive when minimized.*

But wait, there's more: DragThing docks can have as many "tabs" as you like, letting you cram much more stuff into much less space. MyDock has five tabs; the X Apps tab is active in Figure 3.15. To use another tab, I click its name. But here's the neat part: If I want to drag and drop a file onto a dock item in one of the inactive tabs, I drag the file over the appropriate tab and the tab becomes active, allowing me to drop the file on the appropriate dock item in that tab.

Figure 3.15
When I move the cursor into the corner as shown, my docks expand and become active immediately.

For example, sometimes I want to look at a picture file that Photoshop created, but I don't need to edit it. So I don't want to open Photoshop, which uses a lot of memory and system resources, and which takes longer than most programs to launch. Preview can't edit pictures, but it can display them, and it launches in less than a second. So I drag the picture file over the X Apps tab (if X Apps isn't already active), then drop it onto the Preview item in the dock and the picture opens in Preview.

Sure, I could do this with the OS X Dock, but I have more than 75 applications and folders in MyDock. The OS X dock would choke if I tried to stuff 75 items into it. And even if it didn't choke, the icons would be so small as to be unusable.

DragThing can do almost everything the OS X Dock can do. No, it doesn't bounce icons when you launch a program, but that's a small price to pay. Instead, it can do many more useful things than the OS X Dock. Here are some more of the reasons I prefer DragThing:

■ Unlike the OS X Dock, DragThing lets you display items as text only, icons only, or both text and icons. I use text only, which lets me fit much more stuff into much less space.

■ DragThing has multiple Undos for most of its functions; the OS X Dock has one Undo, or none.

■ DragThing has an option that lets you put a trashcan on the desktop, as you can see in Figure 3.14. Mac OS X doesn't even offer this feature, which appeals to former OS 9 users like me. Old habits die hard.

■ DragThing lets you assign a keyboard shortcut to any item in it; the OS X Dock does nothing of the sort.

■ You can resize a DragThing dock any way you like; the OS X Dock gives you one choice—long and rectangular.

■ You can move a DragThing dock anywhere on the screen; the OS X Dock is limited to left, right, or bottom.

■ DragThing offers a choice of any font; the OS X Dock offers no choice.

■ DragThing offers a choice of hundreds of color schemes; the OS X Dock offers no color options.

■ DragThing offers a choice of more than a dozen attractive textures; the OS X Dock ... well, you get the picture.

> **NOTE**
>
> MyDock is a brownish gold color with wood texture; my process dock is silver-gray with rock texture. They're quite beautiful, if I do say so myself. I mention this because the black and white pictures on the previous pages don't do the colors and textures justice.

- You can quit DragThing completely if you like. If you try to kill the OS X Dock (using Terminal, ProcessViewer, or AppleScript), it starts right back up.

I could go on and on, but I think you get the idea. Besides, DragThing is available via a link at **www.boblevitus.com/xfiles.html**, so you can give it a try. After you do, I suspect you'll wonder how you ever lived without it.

> **NOTE**
>
> If you fall in love with DragThing, please don't forget to pay James his very reasonable registration fee ($25). Just launch the Register program in the DragThing folder. He's earned every penny.

Prefling

I use System Preferences a dozen or more times each day. But I don't like having to launch the System Preferences program, then click the icon or choose the menu item for the pane I want to use. It's too many steps for me, so I've adopted Prefling (**http://homepage.mac.com/asagoo**), a freeware dockling that does one thing and does it well—it lets me open any Preference pane from its menu, as shown in Figure 3.16.

Figure 3.16
When I release the mouse button, Prefling will open System Preferences with the Classic pane active.

Snard, mentioned in Chapter 2 (and again in Chapter 9), does the same thing and much more but is $10, while Prefling is free. So try them both-they're both on this book's companion Web site **www.boblevitus.com/xfiles.html**. If you use System Preferences often I'm sure you'll fall in love with one or the other.

WindowShade X

If you were a Mac user before OS X came along, surely you remember WindowShade, the built-in feature to "roll up" a window, leaving only its title bar on the screen. And you've probably noticed by now that OS X doesn't have it. Instead, it has "Minimize," which, instead of rolling up the window and leaving the title bar in place, moves the whole window into the Dock. That sucks.

WindowShade was a lot better and more convenient, too. So for the first few months after OS X was released, I missed it terribly. Fortunately, I discovered WindowShade X, a $7 shareware program from Unsanity (**www.unsanity.com**), which gives OS X that wonderful WindowShade functionality you know and love, and a little bit more—an option to make windows semi-transparent, but still fully functional. Neat!

Check it out in Figure 3.17.

> **NOTE**
>
> If you don't register and pay (at **www.unsanity.com**), WindowShade X works for only one hour.

If you liked WindowShade in OS 9, you'll love WindowShade X, and you'll gladly pay the $7 to have it in OS X. Give it a try—it's available via a link at this book's companion Web site.

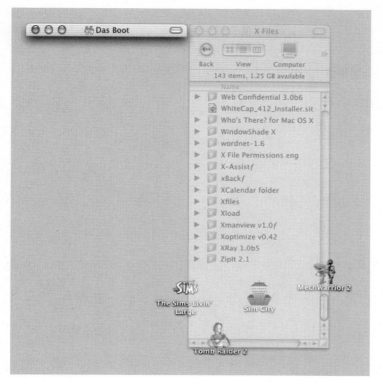

Figure 3.17
You can roll up an OS X window (left) by double-clicking its title bar, or you can make it transparent
(right) by Control+double-clicking its title bar—a nifty feature you won't find in the OS 9 implementation.

Protecting Your Work

Protecting your work involves multiple facets. One is almost a mantra: "Save early and save often." Command+S should be a reflex. When you finish a paragraph: Command+S. When the phone rings: Command+S. When you get up for more coffee: Command+S. In this chapter, however, I'm going to discuss the bigger protection issues: backups, firewalls, and virus protection.

Computer equipment, particularly disks and whatever is on them, can—and will—fail. Removable disks ask to be initialized even when you know there is data on them. Hard disks refuse to display their icons in the Finder, or crash every time you boot from them. Even the Mac itself can fail. I'd say that most computer equipment is 99 percent reliable. Unfortunately, when it breaks, it's always at the most inopportune and unexpected time.

Which is why backing up was invented. Computers (and hard disks) follow their own kind of Murphy's Law—they fail only when you're up against a deadline. Backing up, if you haven't already figured it out, is the process of making copies (backups) of your important files. Restoring, which is the reverse of backing up, is the process of moving files from your backup disk(s) to your working disk or hard disk. Backing up your work protects you from most disasters. Think of backups as file insurance. You wouldn't drive without car insurance, would you? Operating your Mac without a reliable backup of your data is almost as dangerous.

Backing up is one of those chores you must remember to do regularly, like brushing your teeth. Although both may be inconvenient to do regularly, the consequences of not doing either can be extremely unpleasant. If you don't brush your teeth, they'll rot and fall out; if you don't back up your data, your hard disk will crash and you'll have to re-create all your work over again.

This chapter will tell you everything you need to know to insure that your files and disks are safe, no matter what catastrophe should strike.

About Backing Up in General

As usual, we'll start out with some background and big picture information before moving along to strategies and tactics and software that makes backing up easier.

Before we go any further, one of the reasons we do back up is that there are bad things out there—like viruses and intrusion via the Internet. But the issues involved in virus defense and network security under OS X is too big and too important to cover here. So you'll find most of the material on viruses and firewalls in Chapter 8 and the rest elsewhere in this book.

Why Back Up?

You should back up your work for a number of reasons. Here are a few:

■ First, hardware can fail and if the only copy of your masterpiece is on a disk that just went "scr-e-e-e-ch!", you'll be wishing that you had a backup copy somewhere.

■ Second, people make mistakes (even you and me), and we can accidentally delete a file that we still need. A backup copy lets you recover from this sort of pilot error.

■ Third, some sick, twisted personalities create viruses (some pseudo-Latin scholars call them virii) that can damage or wipe out files or disks. Even after you get rid of a virus via virus protection software, you're going to want a clean copy of your file(s) to restore lest the virus be resuscitated.

If you do get a virus, you want clean backups of your documents and applications, because some viruses spread when infected applications run, and others spread when documents are opened.

> **NOTE**
>
> I have a lot of software. More than 4GB, and I use most of the more than 200 programs at least occasionally. Restoring hundreds of programs by downloading and installing from CD would be kind of a drag.

Remember, there are only two kinds of computer users: those who *have* lost data in a crash, and those who *will* lose data in a crash. (I'll probably say that again in future chapters, but it's that important!) Fortunately, losing data in a crash can be almost painless as long as you have a recent backup.

Let's now examine the various backup strategies, as well as the software and hardware available for keeping your work safe and secure.

What to Back Up?

This is a question that has many answers. Almost everybody agrees that your documents (databases, spreadsheets, and so on) should be backed up. Many users also believe that your applications should be backed up, but others argue that you can just reinstall the software if needed. I tend to lean toward backing up my applications, but not that often. The more "updates" I've had to apply to installed software, the more I want a backup because running installer after installer and then running updater after updater can be a real pain in the gluteus maximus. And I back up all software I've downloaded, but not that often. And, in Chapter 8, I'll tell you all about Preference files and why you might want to back them up.

4

At the end of the day, you can back up nothing, or you can back up everything. Each user has a threshold of pain for getting his Mac back up and running. Mine is very low. Because I'm a freelancer, if I'm not working, I'm not making money. And if I lose all my stuff and have to take a few days to set things right, those are "non-revenue" days. So I'm pretty obsessive about having multiple backups of anything remotely important.

My father was the opposite: He backed up his Quicken Data file, FAX phone book, AOL folder, and any Excel or Word files he was working on. He even bought a Zip drive. You see—he lost data once. After that he knew. But only a few files really mattered to him, and he was retired, so time wasn't a problem for him either. His backup regimen took maybe 10 minutes a week.

Which leads me to my next point: There are several different kinds of backups. The first backup, called a *complete backup*, can take quite a while because it will back up everything you tell it to protect. Subsequent backups make use of the original backup to create *incremental backups*, where only new items and changed items are backed up. You can (and this is what I generally recommend) use a commercial backup solution such as BackUp Toolkit or Retrospect, which I describe later in this chapter in the "A Look at the Software" section. These applications take much of the effort out of the backup process.

If you want to ignore this advice, at the very least you should drag important files to some other disk or CD or DVD or Zip cartridge or whatever when you create or modify them. The major downside of this method, of course, is that it requires conscious and regular effort on your part, and it isn't very organized or reliable.

If you're going to ignore my strong recommendation to purchase commercial backup software, here's the cheapskate solution: First, create and save documents in one master folder (your Documents folder comes to mind). Then, on a regular basis, use Sherlock to search for all files in that folder that have been modified since your last backup. Select all those items in Sherlock's window and drag them to your backup medium of choice, such as a Zip disk or a blank CD-R that you've prepared for this purpose. If it was a CD or DVD, don't forget to actually burn the disk.

But What Should I Back Up *To*?

In the dark ages, folks backed up their entire hard disks to floppy disk. But in those ancient times (15 years ago), hard disks were 20MB in size and you could back the whole disk up to 15 or 20 floppies. Today, with 10GB being a small hard disk, you would need well over 1,500 floppies to do the job. This has a lot to do with the demise of the floppy disk when combined with the fact that many (most?) of the files on the typical user's disk won't even fit on a floppy. If you don't believe me, go into Sherlock's Custom search criteria and ask it to find all the files greater than 1,400KB in size. Larger removable media, such as Zip disks and SuperDisks, have even started to falter in this regard. After all, it takes over 100 Zip disks (at a little under 100MB each) or 80 SuperDisks (at 120MB) to back up 10GB of hard disk data. When you factor in the cost of these disks, you'll be looking at a *very* expensive solution. Even at $7/Zip disk, you're talking more than $700 for the slow, antiquated backup media—when you can buy another (FireWire) 60GB disk for about half that price. Unless you back up only very small amounts of data, you'll find using Zip/SuperDisks for major backups way too costly.

The use of CD-R and CD-RW media answers the above complaint. With 650MB–700MB per disk and disks costing less than 50 cents apiece, you can back up a 10GB disk for less than $10. One thing to remember, though, is that because backups are important you probably shouldn't look for bargain-basement media. Purchase quality disks (maybe in bulk). Try different media out and see what brands work well with your CD burner. I use TDK, Verbatim, and Fuji.

> **NOTE**
>
> My father backed up to the cheapest thing he could find at the time—a 100MB Zip drive. I tried to use the media cost argument to interest him in a CD burner, but he countered with, "Why? I have three Zip disks and none of them is anywhere near full." I retorted with an audio CD of his favorite music, all on one CD that I made with iTunes. That was the turning point—he couldn't wait to make his own audio CDs. That it was a better way to back up was a bonus.

One backup medium that has been around since before the days of even the Apple][is magnetic tape. Of course, it no longer comes on great big reels and a tape drive three times the size of an iMac. Now, you'll find Digital Audio Tape (DAT) being used—cassettes smaller, but a little thicker, than the cassette tapes you play in an auto tape deck.

As I mentioned, external hard disks can also be a reasonable solution. One of my backup routines backs up files to a 30GB FireWire drive that weighs less than a pound. (Tiny—you may have seen its picture, and if not, you can in Figure 4.1).

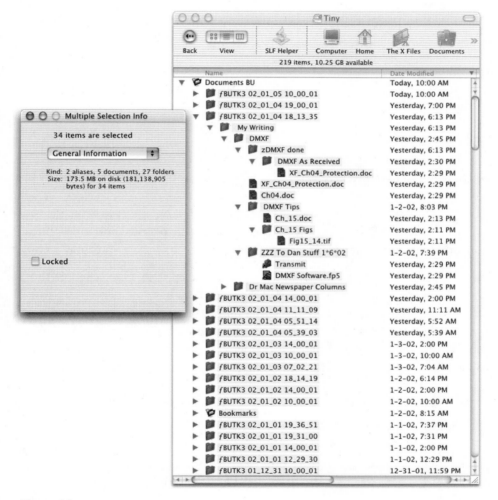

Figure 4.1
This is five days' worth of incremental backup files on Tiny.

In Figure 4.1, you're seeing multiple incremental compressed copies of everything (as denoted by the *f*BUTK3—for BackUp ToolKit—on the folder). If I work on a file for four days, I'll have 10 or 15 copies of it on Tiny. That's important to me. Aside from the safety issue, I like being able to grab a file in the state it was yesterday. Or three hours ago. Sometimes I mess up a document so badly that even multiple undos can't bail me out. When that happens, I just grab one or two of the recent backups, which I remember as being better than what I have in front of me. Then I can copy and paste the best parts of all three versions in to one comprehensible one.

We'll talk more about the software soon, but for now, know that my scripts keep Tiny in a state where no file is more than a month old (mostly apps I haven't used in a month) and important files are no more than three hours old.

Everything of any value to me is backed up on this drive. With that hard disk, which fits into my pocket, I can have a brand new Mac usable, with almost no work lost, in half an hour.

How Often to Back Up?

This question's answer again depends to a great extent on how you use your computer. Do you use it almost exclusively for games, personal email, and browsing the Internet? If so, you can probably get by with backing up once a week or so. After all, you aren't creating many files other than the email and some personal high-score files. However, if you use your Mac to create documents for work or·school, manage personal or business finances, or create other important files, you'll want to backup a lot more often—probably nightly.

The best advice I can offer is to set a schedule and keep to it. That schedule should involve backing up often enough so that if you were to have a disastrous hardware failure, you would be able to recover with a minimum of pain from the backup. I back up my most vital files to Tiny the FireWire hard disk at least every three hours. Because of OS X's delightful multitasking architecture, BUTK runs in the background, and I frequently don't even notice when it runs a script in the background.

How Many Sets of Backups? (Answer: Three, with One Off Site)

If you have a backup utility program (that is, an application designed to assist you in backing up disks—two are discussed in the "A Look at the Software" section later in this chapter), you can use more sophisticated backup strategies. But first, let me define a couple of terms you'll need to understand:

- *Complete backup*—Backup of the entire contents of a disk

- *Incremental backup*—Backup of only files that have been changed since the last complete or incremental backup

■ *Backup-style backup*—Backup that keeps only one copy of each file in the backup set

■ *Archive-style backup*—Backup that stores all changed versions of each file in the backup set

All backup software can perform complete and incremental backups. Beyond that, the program does its work one of two ways, either backup style or archive style. Most modern backup programs, including both of the ones I'm going to demonstrate in a moment, can do all four (and more). Which brings me to an important point: No matter what software (or no software) you use, be sure you understand exactly what you're backing up, check to make sure that what you think is being backed up actually is, and regularly test your ability to restore files successfully.

The backup-style backup creates a complete mirror image of your hard disk the first time you use it. Then, when you perform incremental backups, it replaces files modified since the last backup with the current version. In other words, a backup-style backup set contains only the most recent version of each document. The advantage of this philosophy is that it uses less backup media—usually it means using fewer Zip disks or CD-Rs. The disadvantage is that if you want to retrieve an old version of a document, it won't be in your backup set—only the most recent version will be there. And, if a file gets a virus—that infected document will be the only backup you have.

The backup style is best used in combination with other backups—never use a backup-style backup as your only backup.

The archive-style backup, on the other hand, adds modified files to the backup set without removing earlier versions. The disadvantage is that you'll need more media. The advantage is that if you decide you liked a document better last week, before you edited it extensively, you can easily find and restore that version. Or, if a file becomes damaged, you can restore an earlier version.

You can usually tell the difference between a program that performs backup-style backups and one that performs archive-style backups—if the program asks you to insert old disks from the backup set, it's probably doing a backup-style backup; if the program asks you to insert new, blank disks, it's probably doing an archive-style backup. Read your manual carefully so that you know how your files are being backed up.

ALERT!

I mean that. Using a modern backup program without reading the manual from cover to cover is roughly akin to performing a self-lobotomy or trying to pilot a jet after playing *Fly!* for an hour.

Some programs, such as Retrospect, favor one style over the other. For Retrospect, that's archive style; for BUTK, it's synchronization, which is another form of backup—you don't store multiple copies of files, just the most recent. But both programs will allow you create a script or scripts that do one, both, or a combination.

So it comes down to a choice between safety and convenience. If you're backing up to expensive removable media (Zip disks, Jaz cartridges, and SuperDisks are not cheap), backup style will save you time and money. The downside is that you'll have only one copy of each file in your backup set. If you're only going to have one set of backups, it should be an archive-style backup. It uses more disks (or cartridges, or tapes), but lets you restore the most recent version of a file, or any earlier version you choose.

Both backup-style and archive-style backups will allow you to restore either your entire hard disk exactly as it was the last time you used the software, or to restore a single file. And most programs, including Retrospect and BUTK, let you restore a group of files, by using filters (all files modified since last Monday; all documents; all System files, and so on).

ALERT!

Both Retrospect and BUTK were having a bit of trouble restoring a bootable Mac OS X volume when this book went to press. It appears that the problems will be resolved soon—both products have beta versions that can restore a bootable X disk. Still, you should confirm that the version you're using will indeed allow you to restore a bootable disk. And as I said before, you should try a restore before you rely upon it by restoring an entire OS X disk from a backup and then successfully booting from it.

When you first begin your backup regimen, you'll probably want to perform a complete backup. Then, on subsequent days, you'll perform incremental backups—the software will back up only files that have been changed since the last backup. If you're using a backup-style routine, it will replace earlier versions of files with the most current versions; if you're using an archive-style routine, the most current versions will be added to the backup set (joining all previous versions).

TIP

Whichever you choose, backup style or archive style, one backup set is never enough. If you opt for backup-style, make sure that you have several other backup sets going simultaneously. A single backup-style backup isn't reliable protection. If you choose an archive-style, you still need at least two backup sets to be safe and, again, I recommend a third one to be kept off site.

Three Backup Strategies for Every Occasion

Here are three strategies you can use to provide various degrees of protection for the contents of your hard disk.

Strategy 1—Maximum Safety and Convenience

Start by performing a complete backup with whatever backup software you've selected. On a 20GB hard disk, this should take under an hour, providing that you've initialized all the media you'll need first. Now, at the end of each workday, perform an incremental backup of the entire hard disk—that is, back up files that have been modified since the last backup. Every backup utility I know of can perform complete and incremental backups automatically. Unless you've made a lot of changes to the files on your hard disk, an incremental backup shouldn't take more than 10 minutes a day. Believe me, it's time well spent.

For maximum protection, alternate between at least two sets of media, always keeping one set off site. That way, if your office is destroyed by a fire, flood, theft, or other disaster, you'll have everything you need to start working again immediately. Although you'll probably need a new Mac and hard disk, without an off-site backup, not only would you need new hardware, but you would have to re-create everything on your hard disk from scratch. Not fun.

This strategy is the safest because if your hard disk is damaged in any way, you have two complete backup sets—applications, system files, and documents—that you can use until your main disk is up and running. The chance of your not having a copy of something in one of the two backup sets is remote as long as you remember to perform your incremental backup each day.

You can color-code the sets and back up to a different set each night. Colored labels are available at most computer or office supply stores. The older set should always be taken off site at night. That way, if your office is destroyed, you have a complete copy of your hard disk that's no older than one day.

The safest version of this has three different sets rotated as follows: One set is always stored off site, preferably in a safe deposit box or other fireproof, disaster-resistant place. The off-site set is swapped with one of the other two sets once a week. The other two sets are used as described earlier in this section; taking the day-old set off site with you when you leave the premises. Once a week, you rotate the safe-deposit set with one of the others.

This strategy will take longer than the others, but it insures that, whatever happens, you have a backup set that's a snapshot (no more than one-day old) of your hard disk's contents.

A variation of this strategy is to follow the same regimen but keep only a single backup set. If you elect not to use two backup sets, you might consider taking your backup set with you when you leave the office. Obviously, your level of security is reduced if you keep only one backup set—by a lot. In addition to the reasons I've already stated, there's also the possibility that one or more of the disks in the backup set will become damaged and unusable, which usually renders the ability to restore from that set useless.

Strategy 2—High Safety, Less-Convenient Crash Recovery

This strategy takes less time than the first—it can reduce the time required to make incremental backups by as much as 50 percent. Using your backup software, follow these steps:

1. Create one backup set of system and application files only.

2. Create another backup set and include just your Home directory, including all your documents.

3. To keep both sets current, perform an incremental backup of Home every day, and back up system and application files every week or two.

This strategy will save time, because backup programs decide what to include in an incremental backup based on when the file was last modified. Sometimes certain files—usually applications, system files, or preferences—appear to your backup software as having been modified even if all you did was *use* them. That's because the information in your invisible desktop file, which is what the backup utility uses to decide which files it should back up, reflects a modification date that is later than the date of your last incremental backup. So they may not really have *changed*, even though your backup software thinks they have.

The reason you can get away with backing up system and application files less frequently is that you *should* have copies of your application and system files on the master disks you keep on your shelf, or better still, in a safe place off site. If you had to, you could always restore applications or system files from the master disks. Just remember, if you've made any modifications to your Library folder (such as adding fonts) or to applications (such as applying an update), and you have to restore the system or applications from the master disks, you'll lose the modifications you made.

Although not as secure as Strategy 1, this strategy makes sure that the irreplaceable files—your Home directory, or at least your documents—are backed up daily. For added security, you could create at least two backup sets of each kind—sets of application and system files backups and sets of Home directory backups—rotating and storing one set off site as in Strategy 1. You could then rotate the system and application sets off site once a month and rotates the Home sets daily.

Strategy 3—Better Than No Backup

Set your backup software to include only documents. (Most backup programs allow this.) Do a complete backup (of documents only) to whatever your media choice, then do incremental backups (of documents only) as often as you feel like it.

This strategy assumes that you have copies of a recent OS X install CD and all your applications somewhere on their original CDs. Again, if you've made modifications to your system or applications, you'll lose them if you have to restore from your install CD. But at least you'll have all your documents as of the last time you backed up. And that's better than losing everything.

I don't much recommend this strategy unless you don't have much stuff on your hard disk that you care about.

Whatever strategy you adopt, you *must* back up your work. Though hard disks are, for the most part, reliable beasts, they always choose the worst possible moment to die. And although a hard disk can usually be repaired or recovered, that could take hours. Or days. Trust me: Someday it will happen to you. Backing up your hard disk is like dental hygiene—you should feel guilty when you forget it.

Now, let's take a look at some of the software products that make the bothersome-but-essential task of backing up somewhat less painful.

A Look at the Software

Here's a look at the two leading commercial backup software options for OS X: Retrospect and BackUp ToolKit.

Retrospect Revealed

Long the leader in Macintosh backup software, Dantz's Retrospect for OS X is in beta at the time I'm writing this book. As is almost always the case with beta software, some minor changes will probably take place between now and the time the software is released. Actually, some major changes will take place because a lot of the features are marked as "not yet implemented" in the beta I'm working from.

What Is and What Shall Soon Be

To be honest, when it's done, and Dantz releases the final code, I'll almost certainly move to Retrospect and ditch BUTK. I have nothing but praise for BUTK so far—it's the only thing I found that would do most of what I needed done in OS X. But, I've depended on Retrospect for many years already, and I trust in Dantz—I know they're a company that does the right thing and treats their customers as an asset. (Try their tech support some time—it's superb.)

This is no snub against BUTK. It's reasonably priced, works well, and FWB may have the right stuff, too. But I've depended on Dantz software for more than 10 years (since DiskFit). I've made more than one frantic call to their tech support, and I know that their support reps are top notch and take your pain seriously. And most of all, I know where the founders, the brothers Zulch, live.

I don't really know anyone from FWB, and this is their first backup product. So I have no idea what their level of commitment to the Mac community will be.

Finally, because I'm very used to its interface, I'll feel more comfortable using Retrospect.

And finally (I know I already said that but this time I mean it), because with all the junk I back up and how often I back it up, and how many sets I have, I'm considering going back to a high-speed, high-capacity tape drive for all my backup needs, and Retrospect is the only program I know of that even supports tape drives.

You can use Retrospect as a standalone backup utility, or you can administer it across a network where the various computers to be backed up run the Retrospect client application. I discuss the standalone operation here, but having run the network thing here for months, it's easy to set up and really rocks if you want to back up a small network from a single Mac.

After you've installed Retrospect and launch it, the first thing you'll see is the Retrospect Directory window, shown in Figure 4.2.

If all you want is a quick backup, just click Backup on the Immediate tab. The Immediate Backup window appears (middle of Figure 4.3). Click Sources, and all available volumes are displayed in the Volume Selection window (bottom of Figure 4.3). Select the one(s) you want from the scrolling list or click Subvolume to select a folder or folders. Once you've made your selections, click OK.

Next you'll see the Backup Set Creation window, shown in Figure 4.4. Choose the type of backup set you want and click New to save it.

If you've already created backups, Retrospect will display a choice of your existing backup sets instead of the Backup Set Creation window.

Figure 4.2
The Directory window is Retrospect's virtual control center.

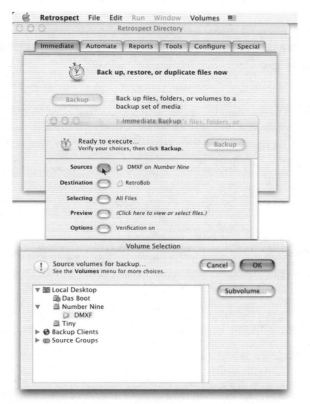

Figure 4.3
The Immediate Backup window (middle) and the Volume Selection window (bottom).

Figure 4.4
The Backup Set Creation window.

The Backup Set Selection window appears—select your newly created set and then click OK.

You'll be returned to the Immediate Backup window. Check to see that everything is set up properly by clicking the five gumdrops (Sources, Destination, Selecting, Preview, and Options).

When you're ready, click Backup. After confirming that you really want to do this, you'll be prompted for the backup media if needed. If you chose another hard disk or mounted network volume, Retrospect will just start the backup. Insert the disk, CD, or tape, if necessary, and then click Proceed.

Retrospect will start writing your backup, and, if necessary, prompt you for more media. Throughout the process, Retrospect keeps you informed of its progress in the Immediate Backup window, as shown in Figure 4.5.

Restoring your files is pretty much the inverse of backing up. You click the Restore button in the Immediate tab, choose the backup set from which you're going to restore, the place to which you are going to restore the file(s), and then (after checking the summary to see that the global settings are correct) select the actual files to be restored from the Restore From Backup Set window shown in Figure 4.6.

There's much more to Retrospect. But I only have room for one more screen shot, so here is Figure 4.7.

You can automate Retrospect using any of five different kinds of scripts (top left of Figure 4.7); you can use filters, called *Selectors*, for both backup and restore (top right). Retrospect supports more types of media and varieties of hardware than any other

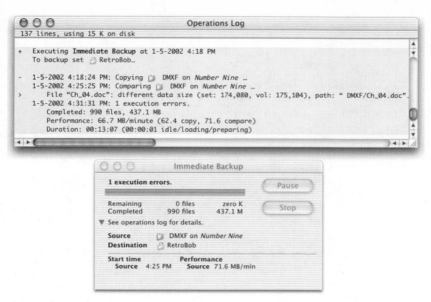

Figure 4.5
I had one error as you can see in both the log and the Immediate Backup window.

Figure 4.6
The Restore From Backup Set window.

program (bottom left), and the OS X version even lets you use Unix permissions as a criteria in your Selectors (bottom right).

Retrospect has features you won't find in BackUp ToolKit or Retrospect Express.

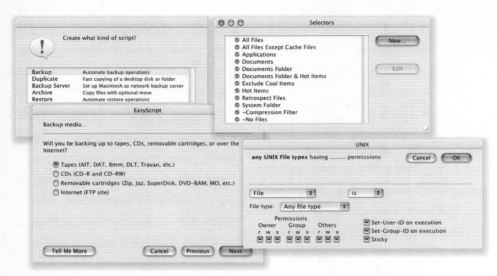

Figure 4.7
Just a quick peek at some of Retrospect's more interesting features.

Retrospect Express is a "lite" version lacking some of the high-end features of Retrospect, including support for tape drives, smart network clients, extensive automation and filtering options, and stuff like that. But you may very well not need those high-end features. Read up on BackUp ToolKit and check the Dantz Web site for news about Retrospect Express for OS X (it wasn't available when I wrote this but should be by now).

You can learn more about Retrospect by visiting the Dantz Development Web site at **www.dantz.com**. Prices were not available at press time, but the previous version of Retrospect was $149, and the previous version of Retrospect Express was $49.

Check Out FWB BackUp ToolKit

I'm going to start with an overview and try to give you a feel for the philosophical similarities and differences between the two programs. Like Retrospect, BUTK offers direct operation (*immediate*) and a scripted operation (*programmed actions*). One advantage that attracts many users to BackUp ToolKit is that the default backup format is not any kind of proprietary archive format (such as that used by Retrospect for most types of backups). I use this format when I back up to Tiny. If I need to restore something, I just drag it from Tiny to Das Boot or Number Nine, and I'm done. No need to use BackUp ToolKit for the restore.

BackUp ToolKit offers four kinds of backups:

- *Incremental backup*—Back up new or modified files

- *Synchronization*—Synchronize folders or volumes

- *Mirror backup*—Copy entire volumes

- *Evolutive Mirror backup*—Save entire contents with recent versions of modified documents

Not only can BackUp ToolKit back up files or disks, it can also *synchronize* folders or disks. Synchronization is keeping pairs of folders or disks in sync with each other so that both have identical contents at any given moment.

Further, both directory structures will have the most recent version of each file. You can use this capability to synchronize the contents of two computers—for example, your desktop Mac and your laptop. If you use this feature, make certain that your system clocks are correctly set (using a Network Time Server is a good idea in this case; you can turn yours on in the Network Time tab of the Date & Time System Preference pane).

BackUp ToolKit's rather limited scripting ability is called Programmed Actions. BackUp ToolKit needs to be running to execute them, so you need to make BackUp ToolKit one of your Login items in the Login System Preferences pane.

You can use BackUp ToolKit to back up onto another disk, a network drive, or external media such as Zip or Jaz disks. The backup consists of making copies of whatever you're backing up, just as if you had used the Finder to copy the files. Because of this, you can access the contents of your backup in the Finder and restore individual files or directories when desired.

The Mirror backup creates an exact copy of the source, and in subsequent backups, that copy is updated to reflect the current state of the source. This is the aforementioned backup-style backup. The Evolutive Mirror backup is similar to the Mirror backup, but it also provides an audit trail by keeping previous versions of updated or removed files (the number of previous versions to be maintained is user-configurable). The Incremental backup writes only files that have been modified or added since the last backup, but each backup gets its own folder.

The advantage of a Mirror backup is that it is the easiest and quickest method, especially when it comes to restoring a file, folder, or volume. The down side is the same as discussed previously—it's best when used in conjunction with another type of backup, because having only one backup copy of important files can be dangerous.

The Evolutive Mirror backup, an archive-style backup, is the most secure method, because you can also recover previous versions and backtrack until you find a copy that's just right for your needs. The down side is that you need more media or disk space to maintain this kind of backup.

The Incremental backup lets you maintain fairly small (in disk space) sets of changed files, thus permitting you to bring (for example) a single day's work home. The down side here is that you can't perform a complete restoration. If you're going to use this method, you should probably employ it as an adjunct to a Mirror backup.

All of the backup strategies allow the optional use of compression technology to save the files in less space, but BackUp ToolKit must be available to decompress a file.

Okay, now we're up to the closer look part. BackUp ToolKit is straightforward and easy to use. Its control center or main window, called—surprisingly enough—BackUp ToolKit 3, is shown in Figure 4.8.

Figure 4.8
The main BackUp ToolKit window.

When BackUp ToolKit is not the active application, it shrinks to a little icon in the corner with a display that tells when the next script is scheduled to run (18:00 in Figure 4.9).

Figure 4.9
Back Up Tool Kit barely takes up any space, but it tells you when it's going to wake up.

To perform an immediate backup, click the Backup button and see the Backup (Immediate) window shown in Figure 4.10. You specify the folders or disks to back up by dragging them from the desktop to the appropriate pane. You can specify various (obvious) options by using the checkboxes below the list box.

Figure 4.10
The Backup (Immediate) window is simple but effective.

If you click the Main window's Restore button, you'll see a window that looks almost exactly like Figure 4.10, but is named Restore (Immediate). Select the file(s) or folder(s) to be restored in the left pane, and, so long as there is a backup containing a folder of the same name in the right pane, the restoration can proceed.

BackUp ToolKit's real power comes from scripting it, though. Using programmed actions, you can automate the backup process, having it back up specified directories at specified times, frequently with no human interaction required (sometimes, you have to be present to swap disks out if the backup is too large for the destination media). Figure 4.11 shows the components of a programmed action.

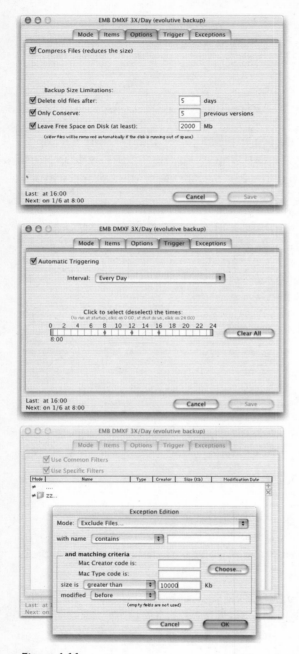

Figure 4.11
The Create New Action window's Options (top), Trigger (middle), and Exceptions (bottom) tabs.

You can specify action-specific options in the Options tab. Each action type has its own set of options. Click the Trigger tab, shown in the middle panel of Figure 4.11, to specify when or how the action is to be invoked.

If you want to exclude specific files or folders from an action, you can specify those on the Exceptions tab, shown in Figure 4.11, bottom.

BackUp ToolKit is made by FWB Software LLC (**www.FWB.com**); it retails for $50.

One last thing: If your budget is tight, but you want backup software, the shareware program FoldersSynchronizer is $30. There's a copy available via the link at **www. boblevitus.com/xfiles.html** and you'll find pictures and a description in Chapter 14.

4

Backup to a miniDV Camcorder? Maybe . . .

It's not ready for prime time, and it runs only from the Unix command line, but another interesting backup solution is coming along. The commands are **dvbackup** and **dvrestore**. You might guess, from the names, that this has something to do with digital video—you would be correct. These commands will back up to, and restore from, digital video tape in a miniDV camcorder over the FireWire connection. If you were to try to import the "movie" you created in iMovie, you would see patterns of colored dots—some of them are actually rather pretty. The current implementations have 2GB limits on files in a session. That's not a limitation imposed by the media, because you can get quite a few sessions on a single tape (one hour of digital video is about 12GB of data). If you want to find out more about this, check the iMovie discussion boards on Apple's Web site.

Part II

On Becoming a Power User

Getting More Out of the Internet

When I first started using a Macintosh, there was no such thing as the World Wide Web. The Internet, browsers, cable modems, DSL, ISDN, Ethernet, and lots of other stuff we take for granted today had not yet been invented. What we did have were big, bulky, expensive, noisy analog modems that ran at 300 bps, or 1200 bps if you could afford it. Online services (ha!) with names like CompuServe and Delphi offered state-of-the-art command-line interfaces accessed by typing commands into a special communications program known as a Terminal Emulator (which, incidentally, makes the OS X Terminal program look almost user-friendly). Graphical interfaces for telecommunication hadn't been invented yet and neither had the instant message. In fact, though America Online was available back then, it was called QuantumLink, and was for Commodore computer users. (Is anyone besides me old enough to remember that?)

Yes, there was email in those days, but you could exchange it only with people on the same service, so if your friend had Delphi and you had CompuServe, well, you communicated the old-fashioned way—by letter or phone call.

Fifteen years later we have high-speed, always-on Internet access 10, 20, or even 100 times faster than analog modems. Email is ubiquitous—everyone from junior high students to grandparents does email these days. And a company without a Web site is a quaint anachronism.

My point is this: We've got a good thing going on. Telecommunicating with a Mac has never been easier, faster, or cheaper. And the content has never been better.

One more time, at the risk of beating my "crawl before you walk; walk before you run" metaphor into the ground, we start with the basics. Think of it as an appetizer before you feast (your eyes) on the really cool stuff later in the chapter.

Internet 101

Mac OS X includes some of the most sophisticated software for communicating with other computers in any operating system, and every Mac comes with the ports you need to connect your Mac to the Internet. Fortunately, you don't need to know much about the software or the ports to get on the Internet.

> **NOTE**
>
> You don't actually connect your computer to the Internet, you connect one of its ports (USB, modem, or Ethernet) to a device that communicates with the Internet: a phone line (or a modem and phone line if your Mac didn't come with an internal modem), a cable modem, a hub, a router, or other device.

There *are* two things neither OS X nor your Mac provide:

- The actual device you connect your Mac to: a telephone line (if your Mac has a modem already), a modem and a telephone line (if it doesn't), a cable modem, a DSL router, or some other means of communicating with the outside world.

- An account with an Internet Service Provider (ISP). Your ISP is the one who sends you a bill (usually each month) for your Internet access.

> **NOTE**
>
> Although OS X comes with application software for email, Web browsing, and other Internet-related stuff, better programs are often available, as you'll see throughout this chapter.

The deal is, you supply those two things, and your Mac and OS X supply the rest. The two go hand in hand. Some ISPs offer only telephone (dial-up or modem) service. A cable television company offers Internet access via cable modem only. Your telephone company may sell access via DSL, frame relay, or T1 line. And so on.

At the end of the day, though, it's all about the bandwidth—how much information you can send and receive through your Internet connection. Bandwidth determines how quickly Web pages appear, how decently (or indecently) streaming media plays, and how fast you can upload or download files.

The more bandwidth you have, the faster all this will be. Ergo, the more you use the Internet, the more you'll want (or need) a high-bandwidth connection.

So let's start with a look at connections and bandwidth.

Telephone Line with Analog Modem

This is the lowest bandwidth connection, but it's also (usually) the least expensive. You need to provide a (Plain Old Telephone Service) POTS line and a modem. Many Macs came with 56KB internal modems—including all those Macs with a little "i" before their names, most PowerBooks, and many G3s and G4s.

TIP

If you're going to be online very often, you may want to have a dedicated phone line for your modem. I have one line that is used by two iMacs with modems and a fax machine. (The iMacs belong to the wife and kids. As you're about to learn, I don't use dial-up much anymore.)

If You Don't Have a Modem Yet

If you don't have a modem, and you do want to connect this way, you can get an external modem that connects to a USB port (and a POTS line) for less than $100.

Don't ask me for a recommendation, though. I've had a cable connection from TimeWarner's RoadRunner service for the past three years, and I had Southwestern Bell's precursor to DSL, (ISDN, the acronym for Integrated Services Digital Network) for five years before that.

How do I know you can buy them for less than $100? Well, with all this bandwidth, lots of RAM, and a fabulous multitasking operating system, I stopped typing for a second, switched to my browser, typed "outpost.com", which took me to one of my favorite online stores, Outpost.com, where I searched for a "USB 56K modem" and found page after page of 'em, mostly under $100.

I was back to work on this chapter in less than a minute.

Higher Bandwidth Connections: Cable Modems, DSL, and the Rest

Or, at least I would have been back to work in a minute, if I hadn't decided I also needed some hard numbers for this section.

So I once again switched to my browser, but this time I used one of my favorite search engines for questions like this, Ask Jeeves (www.ask.com). I like this particular search engine because it understands "natural language" queries. I merely typed, "How fast is DSL compared to cable modem", as you can see in the top picture in Figure 5.1, and Ask Jeeves figured out what I meant and provided me with a list of *hits*, otherwise known as "links to the Web pages it thinks will answer my question."

One of Jeeves' suggestions looked particularly promising—among other things, www.cablemodemhelp.com offers a free online bandwidth test.

I clicked that link, and it was just what I was looking for. So, in just 45 seconds I learned exactly how much bandwidth I was getting on my connection, as well as the average speeds for cable modem, DSL, dialup modem, and T1, to compare with mine.

You can see all of this in the bottom picture in Figure 5.1.

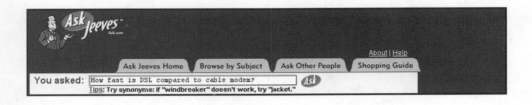

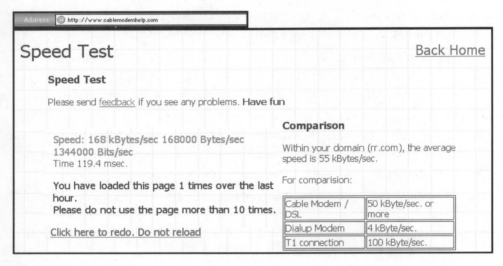

Figure 5.1
Searching for bandwidth comparisons at **www.ask.com** (top), and finding a great one at **www.cablemodemhelp.com** (bottom).

Not bad for less than a minute of work, eh? The Internet makes so many things so much easier, but you have to know *how*. And that, my friends, is the point of this whole chapter: To show you how to get the most out of your Internet connection.

Oh yeah, DSL and cable connections are roughly 12 times faster than analog modems over POTS. And my cable connection appears to be running faster than the average T1 connection right this second!

NOTE

> T1 is an ultra-high bandwidth telephone connection to the Internet, sort of a "DSL-on-steroids" that costs hundreds or even thousands of dollars a month.

You can connect in other ways. Satellite TV is beginning to offer high-bandwidth access without wires. And there are telephone connections for extremely high-usage installations where massive bandwidth is required (such as frame relay and T3, the faster and even more expensive big brother of T1).

NOTE

I don't know much about any of that stuff, so you're on your own if you need to venture there.

The Bottom Line on Buying Bandwidth

Don't buy more bandwidth than you can afford or than you need. If you don't use the Net much, or use it only for a modest amount of email, a dial-up connection may be the most cost-effective solution.

But (and there's always a "but") the bottom line is that if you work with large files, enjoy flashy Web sites and streaming media, or are the type who wants every Web page to appear on your screen in seconds, not minutes, you'll find a cable connection or DSL well worth the $50 a month.

If the rest of this chapter isn't enough to convince you of your need, look at it another way: Time is money. Say you waste 30 minutes a day waiting for stuff on the Net, because you are cheap and choose *Mr. Thrifty's ISP, Laundromat, and Deli BudgetNet Plan*—a 14.4KB dial-up account for just $9.95 a month, though some restrictions apply.

Now do the math. If your time is worth at least $20 an hour; then your pokey-but-cheap connection is costing you at least $50 a week, $200 a month, and $2,500 a year. Is that any way to save money? I think not.

And another thing: If you have a separate phone line for an analog modem, you can probably give it up once you have a cable connection or DSL, which will save you even more.

The point is, if you need it, and you can benefit from it, for heavens sake get a cable connection, DSL, or whatever you can, but get something faster than dial-up. You'll hardly believe how much better it makes the Internet.

At Your Service (Provider)

The other side of the equation is your ISP, or service provider. You should have to think about your ISP only once a month, when you write them a check. Some of the better-known national ISPs are AOL, EarthLink, Prodigy, @Home (a large cable ISP which filed for bankruptcy just as this book went to press), and RoadRunner (another large cable ISP, though this one is part of the newly merged Time-Warner-AOL and isn't likely to go bankrupt any time soon).

NOTE

In some areas in the USA, dial-up is still the only option available. My only advice to you is to keep after your cable operator or telephone company and tell them to "get with the program" and provide you with high-bandwidth access already.

Your choice of an ISP will be based mostly upon who will provide service in your geographic location. Once you have an ISP and can connect to the Internet, Apple will be happy to perform many of your ISP chores for free. The catch is, they don't provide your actual access to the Internet; you have to find yourself an ISP first.

But, once you're actually connected to the Net, Apple will perform most of your ISP-like tasks for you. Their free iTools services host your:

- Web pages, Web picture galleries, and Web streaming movies

- Email accounts (with a prestigious "@mac.com" address)

- iDisk (20MB of free storage; additional storage costs big money)

NOTE

We often curse Apple for their transgressions, but here's something darned nice they do for their users, mostly to make using a Mac a more pleasant experience than using a... well, you know what I mean. Let me put it another way: Do you think Microsoft gives you all that for free when you buy Windows? I doubt it.

Never one to look a gift horse in the mouth, I have taken full advantage of Apple's largesse. Although I find it more convenient to get all my mail at **boblevitus@boblevitus.com** and don't ever check **boblevitus@mac.com**, I do use Apple's free iDisk and streaming video Web hosting.

I don't think I'd have bothered to try making a Web page with a streaming QuickTime video if Apple hadn't made it so easy. I put the movies in a folder on my iDisk, chose a template, and in literally minutes, had constructed nice-looking Web pages with streaming QuickTime movies!

NOTE

I made the movie while I was reviewing Final Cut Pro. Editing the movie took 20 times longer than making this Web page. I used a nice-looking Apple template called "Home," and had the whole thing up and running in three minutes.

You can see the page I made in three minutes at **http://homepage.mac.com/ boblevitus/iMovieTheater1.html**. Figure 5.2 shows what it looks like.

ALERT!

The page contains a 5MB QuickTime movie, so it's only suitable for—you guessed it— high-bandwidth connections.

Never fear. I have friends with low-bandwidth connections, so I made a second page

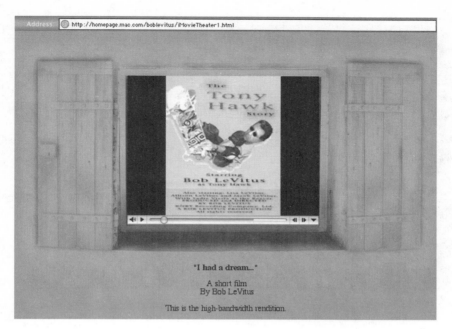

Figure 5.2
A streaming video Web page—just add your own movie—is free with every Mac.

and used a more-compressed copy of the movie—this one is less than 1MB. It plays okay on low-bandwidth connections, but it's nowhere near as clear and pretty as the first one.

This time I used the Apple template, "City," and this page took me only *two* minutes, because I knew what I was doing this time. It came out looking like Figure 5.3.

You can see that low-bandwidth version at **http://homepage.mac.com/boblevitus/ iMovieTheater.html**.

If you don't have any Internet access, you'll have to make do with Figures 5.2 and 5.3. But you should know that the movie version is much better than the screenshots, (mostly because the movie actually moves).

Take advantage of Apple's kindness. After you find an ISP that suits your speed and budgetary needs, use Apple's free iTools to build a Web page. Your Windows-using brethren (and sisteren) will turn green with envy when they see the excellent results you achieve with a minimum of effort.

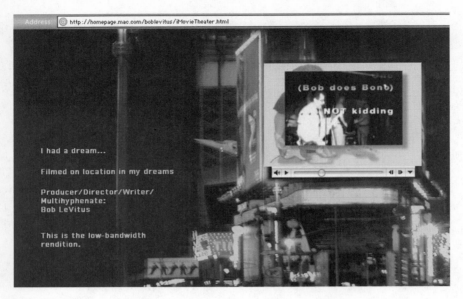

Address ⊙ http://homepage.mac.com/boblevitus/iMovieTheater.html

I had a dream...

Filmed on location in my dreams

Producer/Director/Writer/
Multihyphenate:
Bob LeVitus

This is the low-bandwidth
rendition.

(Bob does Bonb)

NOT kidding

Figure 5.3
Free streaming video hosting courtesy of Apple Computer. Thanks!

See the Sites

I need to know a lot about a lot of Mac stuff so that when I'm writing a book or column I don't stick my foot in my mouth, or at least don't stick it in too often. Which is why I set aside at least 30 or 40 minutes every day for Web surfing and software sleuthing.

There are at least 10 Web sites I hit once a day, and many others I don't visit as often, but that are still worth seeing. But before we begin looking at pages, let me get one thing out of the way.

I discuss browsers later in this chapter, but for now I want to point out one big difference between OmniWeb (shown in Figure 5.4) and Internet Explorer (shown in Figure 5.5).

> **NOTE**
>
> I think OmniWeb is the best-rendering browser I've seen on any platform, and its anti-aliased text (Figure 5.4) is much easier on the eyes than the blocky text Internet Explorer uses (Figure 5.5).

I mention the big difference here for three reasons:

- It's the reason OmniWeb is used in most of my screenshots.

- Now you know the reason when a page looks different on your screen.

- Because I spend a page or two talking about different browsers in the very next section of this chapter.

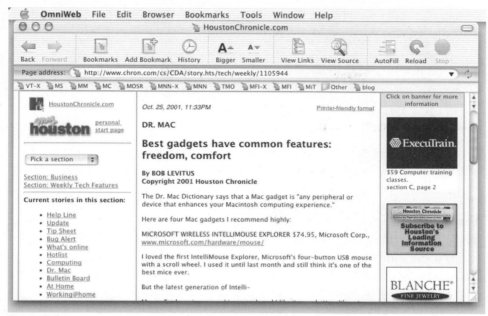

Figure 5.4

This is how OmniWeb displays this page.

Figure 5.5

This is how Internet Explorer displays the same page.

I'm about to tell you about more than a dozen great Web sites. But before I do, I want to single out three that stand far above the rest.

The Envelope, Please

One of the television networks formerly called some of its shows "Must-See-TV." These three Web sites I'm about to introduce you to—VersionTracker, MacFixIt, and MacInTouch—are what I call "Must-Surf-Web."

If you're a Mac enthusiast, you'll want to visit all three each and every day, which is why they get their very own section and an appropriate amount of reverence.

VersionTracker

VersionTracker.com is *the* site for finding new Mac software releases, patches, up-dates, and information. Whether you're interested in commercial software, shareware, freeware, or demoware, the first place to go to find out more about it is VersionTracker. I hit this site several times a day to make sure nothing new and cool has been released without me knowing about it. In Figure 5.6, you see VersionTracker's main page, and today's list of new OS X programs.

Let's see… iTunes Tool 1.0 sounds intriguing. I click its name in the list; the details and a Download Now link appear, as shown in Figure 5.7.

It takes about 30 seconds to download the 664KB file, and it turns out to be a useful little freeware program that provides an iTunes 2.0 controller that floats in front of other applications and windows, as shown in Figure 5.8.

I'm turning the volume down without having to activate iTunes first.

ALERT!

> I can do some of what iTunes Tool does by pressing and holding on the iTunes 2 icon in the dock. The pop-up menu has Pause/Play, Next Song, and Previous Song commands, as well as something iTunes Tool doesn't—the title of the current song. But iTunes Tool has something the iTunes pop-up Dock menu doesn't—a volume control. I guess it's a draw.

Last but not least, VersionTracker has an excellent advanced search engine. Look at all the search options you have in Figure 5.9.

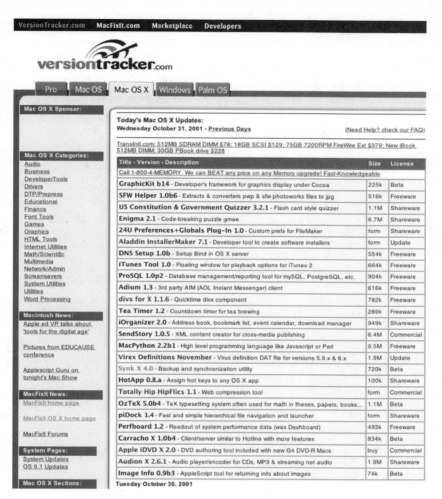

Figure 5.6
VersionTracker's main page for OS X displays all the new software that became available today for your downloading enjoyment.

And, of course, now that I've discovered it, you'll find a copy of iTunes Tool available via a link at **www.boblevitus.com/xfiles.html**.

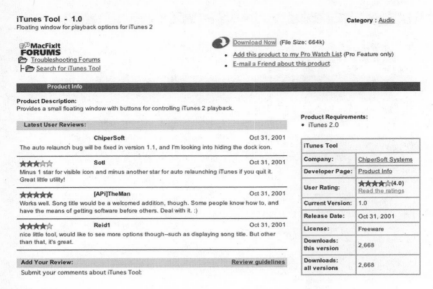

iTunes Tool - 1.0
Floating window for playback options for iTunes 2

Category : Audio

MacFixIt
FORUMS
Troubleshooting Forums
Search for iTunes Tool

Download Now (File Size: 664k)

• Add this product to my Pro Watch List (Pro Feature only)
• E-mail a Friend about this product

Product Info

Product Description:
Provides a small floating window with buttons for controlling iTunes 2 playback.

Product Requirements:
• iTunes 2.0

Latest User Reviews:

ChiperSoft Oct 31, 2001
The auto relaunch bug will be fixed in version 1.1, and I'm looking into hiding the dock icon.

★★★☆☆ **SotI** Oct 31, 2001
Minus 1 star for visible icon and minus another star for auto relaunching iTunes if you quit it.
Great little utility!

★★★★★ **[APi]TheMan** Oct 31, 2001
Works well. Song title would be a welcomed addition, though. Some people know how to, and
have the means of getting software before others. Deal with it. :)

★★★★☆ **Reid1** Oct 31, 2001
nice little tool, would like to see more options though–such as displaying song title. But other
than that, it's great.

Add Your Review: Review guidelines
Submit your comments about iTunes Tool:

iTunes Tool	
Company:	ChiperSoft Systems
Developer Page:	Product Info
User Rating:	★★★★☆(4.0) Read the ratings
Current Version:	1.0
Release Date:	Oct 31, 2001
License:	Freeware
Downloads: this version	2,668
Downloads: all versions	2,668

Figure 5.7
Sounds good to me. I'll click the Download Now link and check it out.

Figure 5.8
The iTunes Tool folder window with the iTunes Tool program floating in front of it.

For VersionTracker for Mac OS X, visit **www.versiontracker.com/macosx/index.shtml**. For VersionTracker for Mac OS 9, visit **www.versiontracker.com/macos/index.shtml**.

MacFixIt

MacFixIt.com is the best Mac troubleshooting site, bar none. Ted Landau is its founder, Webmaster, and proprietor.

Figure 5.9
If you can't find it using VersionTracker's Advanced Search page, it probably doesn't exist.

NOTE

I've known Ted since the late 1980s. (How old does that make *me*?) I may have even, however inadvertently, given him his start in show biz—he wrote for the late, lamented (and demented) *MACazine* while I was Editor-in-Chief. He's a great guy, but that's not important. What is important is that Ted is more knowledgeable about that which ails your Macintosh than any other person I can think of. He's also the author of the classic Mac troubleshooting guide, *Sad Macs, Bombs, and Other Disasters*, now in its fourth edition (and published by Peachpit Press). Unfortunately, the fourth edition has no info on OS X and a fifth edition has yet to be announced.

Rather than make this stuff up, here's how MacFixIt describes itself and its focus (from the About MacFixIt page):

■ Troubleshooting tips, hints, workarounds, and solutions of any sort

■ News about documented bugs, conflicts, and problems with existing versions of popular software and hardware

■ Announcements of new and/or updated products (specifically when the product has direct troubleshooting relevance or fixes significant troubleshooting problems with a previous version of the product)

- Links to other sites that have troubleshooting relevance

- Special emphasis on any aspect of Apple's system software, including news and rumors about future developments when appropriate to troubleshooting

In Figure 5.10, you see MacFixIt's home page.

Notice the navigation bar near the top—those are MacFixIt's departments.

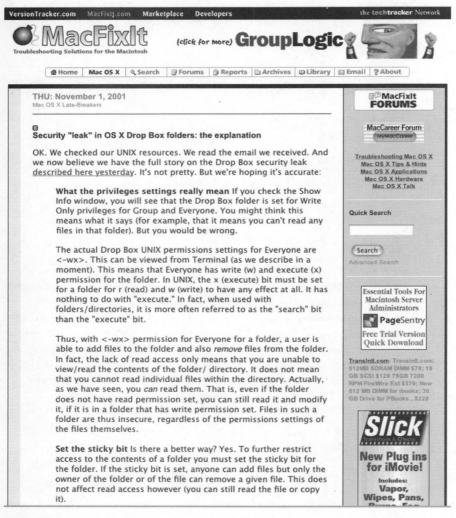

Figure 5.10
The main MacFixIt homepage.

Home (**www.macfixit.com/**) and Mac OS X (**www.macfixit.com/macosx.shtml**) are MacFixIt's two home pages—Home for general Mac info, and Mac OS X devoted exclusively to OS X. Search allows you to search the entire MacFixIt site except for the Forums (which have their own search engine). Forums are message boards, Reports are in-depth "reports" on specific topics, and Library is a well-organized set of links to troubleshooting-related freeware and shareware utilities.

A knowledgeable staff ably assists Ted; the MacFixIt forums are perhaps the best-run message boards on the Net. They are easily among the busiest Mac boards on the Internet (see Figure 5.11)—so you get answers to your questions fast.

Mac OS X	Threads	Posts	Last post	Forum Moderators
Troubleshooting Mac OS X For the release version of Mac OS X (10.0.x and up). Polite unregistered users welcome.	6940	27190	11/01/01 08:57 AM	darkstranger, dmcadmin, Ilene Hoffman, jcwelch, Ted Landau
Mac OS X Applications For troubleshooting non-OS software running in Mac OS X.	1764	6351	11/01/01 09:00 AM	dmcadmin, Ilene Hoffman, Ted Landau
Mac OS X Hardware For problems getting peripheral devices (printers, scanners, CD-RW drives, etc.) to work with Mac OS X.	769	2493	11/01/01 08:41 AM	dmcadmin, Ilene Hoffman, jcwelch, Ted Landau
Mac OS X Tips & Hints Mac OS X tips and hints. DO NOT leave questions here please! Use OS X Troubleshooting. Solutions only please. You may copy/paste solutions from question threads in other forums.	900	3499	11/01/01 04:59 AM	Ilene Hoffman, Ted Landau
Mac OS X Talk For comments and general information about Mac OS X. Registered users only.	2118	20084	11/01/01 07:56 AM	Ilene Hoffman, Ted Landau
Troubleshooting Mac OS X Public Beta This Forum is read-only.	1502	5830	03/24/01 12:53 AM	Ted Landau

Mac OS	Threads	Posts	Last post	Forum Moderators
Troubleshooting Mac OS 9.2.x Covers Mac OS 9.2 and 9.2.1.	1270	5284	11/01/01 08:13 AM	Ted Landau
Troubleshooting Mac OS 9.1 Covers Mac OS 9.1 only. See also: Forums Today Threads & Solutions forum for special report threads.	4114	16299	11/01/01 08:38 AM	David Knuth, Lee, Shawn Platkus
Troubleshooting Mac OS 9 Covers Mac OS 9.0 through 9.04 problems.	3074	10706	11/01/01 07:15 AM	darkstranger, David Knuth, Ilene Hoffman, Shawn Platkus
Troubleshooting Mac OS Covers System 7 through Mac OS 8.6 problems.	1682	6985	11/01/01 06:30 AM	darkstranger, Ilene Hoffman, Voyager

Figure 5.11
You can ask anything you want in the MacFixIt forums.

These forums are one of the best places on the Web to pick up useful Mac information you won't find elsewhere or to ask if someone else is having a problem like yours. If you've never tried forums/message boards, these are good ones to start with.

MacFixIt is now part of the TechTracker support network, which VersionTracker is part of as well. So the two sites work together—stories on MacFixIt and its library are linked to software on VersionTracker, which is good because VersionTracker's servers are usually fast and reliable.

Published Monday through Friday and sometimes Saturday, I read both the Home and Mac OS X pages every single day.

NOTE

I wish it were published earlier in the day, so I could savor it with my morning coffee. But it doesn't usually get updated until 10:00 or 11:00 Central Standard Time.

MacInTouch

MacInTouch (**www.macintouch.com**) is the "original Mac news and information site since 1994"—it says so right there on their home page (shown in Figure 5.12).

Figure 5.12
Clean design and in-depth reporting are hallmarks of MacInTouch.

In this case, it's not hype. Editor-in-chief Ric Ford and his partner editor Rick LePage have been covering Mac news as long as I can remember. It started in 1985 as the *MacInTouch* newsletter. The newsletter evolved into a popular column in *MacWEEK* until that magazine's untimely demise, then morphed into a Web site around 1994.

MacInTouch reads like a well-moderated forum edited by a real pro. With an engaging combination of facts, product announcements, opinion pieces, bugs, and reports from readers each day, MacInTouch makes you feel like you are in touch. It's an excellent barometer of "the way things are" in the Mac community on any given day.

LePage has a new day job—as VP of Content and editor-in-chief of *Macworld* magazine—but Ford continues to manage the Web property, as he's done for years, so I expect things to remain status quo.

MacInTouch is the first site I turn to for Mac news and analysis. It's concise and to the point, its readers and writers are bright and articulate, and every day it's packed with useful and interesting information.

The Best of the Rest

The three sites in the previous section have something for almost every Mac user, almost every day, but there are many, many other Web sites I visit often. Beyond those first three, my choices, like the Ramones or Camembert cheese, are very much a personal preference and may be an acquired taste.

The following sections discuss some other sites that I find tasty.

For the Mac

Now, here are a handful of other interesting and useful Mac sites you may enjoy.

www.macobserver.com

The Mac Observer is a site for news, reviews, editorials, columns, links, and message boards, all delivered with a healthy dose of good old-fashioned Mac-just-plain-better attitude. Often controversial and occasionally cantankerous, the site is guided by editor-in-chief Bryan Chaffin. He and his cohorts post their rants to the site at the speed of Web—The Mac Observer frequently weighs in with the, "Mac Observer Spin" on breaking news before other so-called news sites have even recycled the electrons in the press release.

Figure 5.13 shows what news and views look like at The Mac Observer on a typical day.

I like it. The writing can be uneven, and some days are better than others. But it's a site with a soul, run by real people. And it's rarely boring. I find something worth reading here almost every day.

www.macnn.com, www.macminute.com, www.maccentral.com, www.macsurfer.com

MacNN, MacMinute, MacCentral, and MacSurfer are four of the better Macintosh "news" sites. Each has a slightly different "angle," but they all cover breaking Macintosh news "as it happens," and all are updated frequently throughout the day.

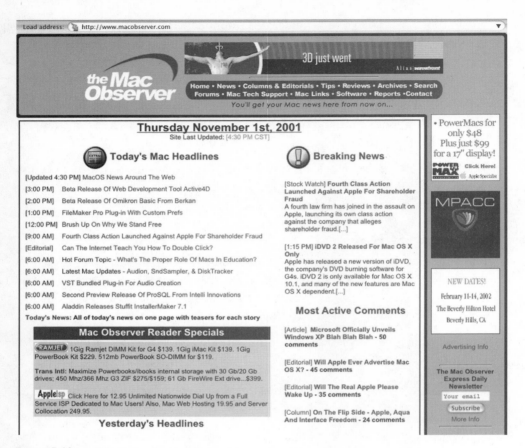

Figure 5.13
News with an attitude at The Mac Observer.

Mac NN and MacMinute, shown in Figures 5.14 and 5.15 respectively, use the old "rewrite and edit the press release and use it as a teaser" approach. MacMinute is more professional and more businesslike, but MacNN is often more interesting and is more likely to carry less mainstream stories than MacMinute. Both have editorial staffs and write their own short news items; most are nothing more than rewrites of press releases.

MacCentral is another news site, but it uses the even older "rewrite the press release's headline and use that as a teaser" approach. Like MacNN and MacMinute, MacCentral uses staff writers to recycle press releases. Unlike MacNN and MacMinute, several of MacCentral's staff writers actually write something original and interesting every so often, and the pieces here are usually longer and more de-

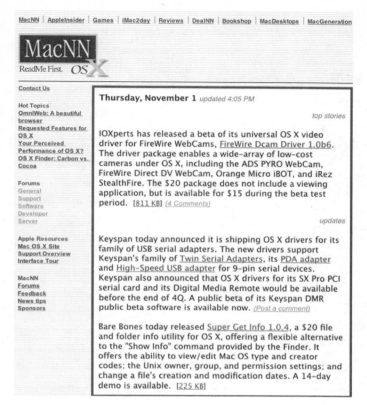

MacNN | AppleInsider | Games | iMac2day | Reviews | DealNN | Bookshop | MacDesktops | MacGeneration

MacNN
ReadMe First. OS X

Contact Us

Hot Topics
OmniWeb: A beautiful browser
Requested Features for OS X
Your Perceived Performance of OS X?
OS X Finder: Carbon vs. Cocoa

Forums
General
Support
Software
Developer
Server

Apple Resources
Mac OS X Site
Support Overview
Interface Tour

MacNN
Forums
Feedback
News tips
Sponsors

Thursday, November 1 *updated 4:05 PM*

top stories

IOXperts has released a beta of its universal OS X video driver for FireWire WebCams, FireWire Dcam Driver 1.0b6. The driver package enables a wide–array of low–cost cameras under OS X, including the ADS PYRO WebCam, FireWire Direct DV WebCam, Orange Micro iBOT, and iRez StealthFire. The $20 package does not include a viewing application, but is available for $15 during the beta test period. [811 KB] *(4 Comments)*

updates

Keyspan today announced it is shipping OS X drivers for its family of USB serial adapters. The new drivers support Keyspan's family of Twin Serial Adapters, its PDA adapter and High–Speed USB adapter for 9-pin serial devices. Keyspan also announced that OS X drivers for its SX Pro PCI serial card and its Digital Media Remote would be available before the end of 4Q. A public beta of its Keyspan DMR public beta software is available now. *(Post a comment)*

Bare Bones today released Super Get Info 1.0.4, a $20 file and folder info utility for OS X, offering a flexible alternative to the "Show Info" command provided by the Finder. It offers the ability to view/edit Mac OS type and creator codes; the Unix owner, group, and permission settings; and change a file's creation and modification dates. A 14–day demo is available. [225 KB]

Figure 5.14
This is the MacNN approach.

tailed. So while MacNN and MacMinute are almost 100 percent recycled press propaganda each day, MacCentral is only 90 percent, with 10 percent original writing. Two MacCentral writers, Dennis Sellers and Peter Cohen, do much of the good writing; I am more likely to read their stories than some of the others. MacCentral's main page is shown in Figure 5.16.

MacSurfer is a different story. It makes no bones about offering no original editorial content. MacSurfer is a news aggregator, pure and simple, with frequently updated links to breaking Mac news stories on other sites. Of the four, MacSurfer is probably the most useful. They offer more links to a wider variety of Mac stories than all three of the others combined. And I appreciate that they don't even attempt to add editorial comments of their own. When a news story is breaking, I often visit MacSurfer a few times a day so I can keep up on what other publications and sites are saying.

MacMinute.com

Up-to-the-minute Mac coverage. Around the clock... around the world.

[Send Your News] [Site Comments] [Reader Café] [Advertising]

Last Updated: Thursday, November 1, 13:21 EDT (17:21 GMT)

WSJ, Business 2.0 review the iPod
November 1 - 13:21 ET: Apple's iPod continues to receive a warm reception from the press. Today's edition of *The Wall Street Journal* features a review of the iPod by Walter Mossberg, who calls the device "the best digital music player I've seen." *Business 2.0* has also published a very in-depth review of the device in its November edition.

www.macuser.co.uk

Please support MacMinute by visiting our Sponsor

Backyard Basketball, Backyard Football 2002 available now
November 1 - 13:04 ET: Infogrames has announced the release of Backyard Basketball and Backyard Football 2002, two new titles in its popular sports series for kids ages 7 and up. Backyard Basketball lets kids play as junior versions of their favorite NBA and WNBA players, while Backyard Football 2002, building on the success of the number one football CD-ROM for kids, features two returning NFL star quarterbacks—Drew Bledsoe and Brett Favre—as well as eight new players including Terrell Davis, Ricky Williams, Junior Seau, Steve McNair, Jevon Kearse, Rich Gannon, Donavan McNabb and Cade McNown. Both titles are available now for US$19.99 each.

Canadian businesses lose millions to piracy
November 1 - 12:58 ET: The Canadian Alliance Against Software Theft (CAAST), in conjunction with the Business Software Alliance (BSA), has released the results of a study conducted by the International Planning & Research Group (IPR) showing that the national software piracy rate in Canada is 38 percent. While software piracy in Canada has declined over the past two years, the Canadian software industry lost a combined C$457 million in retail sales of business software applications, $1.9 billion in wage and salary loss, and more than 32,000 jobs in 2000. Apple is a member of both CAAST and BSA.

In Case You Missed It...
- Up-to-date CDs arriving
- US$799 iMac shipping
- Fuji drops camera prices
- Excite@home bankrupt
- *Money* "iBook is best"
- Apple's new US$799 iMac
- QuickTime Live! postponed
- Seybold: Photo gallery
- Corel Graphics Suite 10
- Mac OS X 10.1 on Saturday
- Seybold: Keynote coverage
- TN Apple store delayed
- Illustrator 10, InDesign 2
- Hotline closes doors
- Two new Olympus cameras
- Nikon 5 megapixel camera
- Palm's new m125
- StuffIt Deluxe 6.5 announced
- Maya for OS X ships
- Office X due in Nov.
- Macworld Expo NY Wrap-up
- **What is MacMinute.com?**

Executive Briefings...
- Saturday, October 27
- Saturday, October 20
- Saturday, October 13
- Saturday, October 6
- Saturday, September 29
- Saturday, September 22
- Older Briefings...

Figure 5.15
This is the MacMinute blurbing.

I visit all four news sites at least once or twice a day. But when a hot news story is breaking, I visit MacSurfer the most—it has more links and is updated more often, so I can find more coverage with more viewpoints in less time.

www.macosrumors.com, www.macrumors.com, www.thinksecret.com
Finally, if you like the *National Enquirer* or the *Star*, or even *People* magazine, you may like MacOSRumors.com, MacRumors.com, and ThinkSecret, a trio of sites that compete to see which can make up the stupidest story.

Yes, they do break a story for real every so often, but mostly their stuff is pure pulp fiction. Rumor sites are like a car wreck—you don't want to look, but sometimes you can't help yourself. I don't read these three all that often, but every once in a while they're good for a laugh.

Figure 5.16
MacCentral uses single-line blurbs as come-ons.

Not Mac-Specific but Still Worthwhile

Even though these URLs are not Mac-specific, they are still very useful and can help out in a pinch.

www.google.com

I told you about Ask Jeeves earlier in the chapter—it's the search engine I use when I have a question I want to ask in "natural language," which is Jeeves' specialty. But when I know the exact words or phrase I'm looking for, I use a search engine called Google.

There are many excellent Internet search engines, but I've found that Google (shown in Figure 5.18) has an uncanny ability to find the most relevant document and display it on the first page of results, and do it much more often than other search engines. In less than half a second, Google found 64,400 pages it considered relevant for the keywords "Mac OS X freeware shareware."

MHN offers a Search Engine for your convenience.

Thursday, November 1, 2001
Updated 6:45 PM CST; 00:45 GMT

Apple Stock | *TechNN* | *WaveLinks* | *Advertising* | *E-Mail* | *Sherlock Plugin*

OS X

- "Suite news for Mac users: The idea might have Apple fanatics steaming out their ears but the single most important application for the mass of Mac users is about to be released by Microsoft. It's Microsoft Office v.X for the Macintosh." The Age
- "Be a webmaster with Mac OS X: OS X is the easiest platform for a personal or SOHO Web site." ComputerUser.com
- "Columnists choose Mac OS X over Windows XP" MacCentral
- "Unix on Apple: Mac OS X Server" Web Techniques
- "Safe and Happy UNIX Hacking with MacOS X" MacGuru HQ
- "An Everyday User Looks at Mac OS X" Low End Mac
- "The Mac Advocacy Fortnight: The Glory that is Mac OS X" Why the Mac is so great.com
- "In the X Zone: The Mac OS X Gaming Scene" MacNETv2
- "Super Get Info for Mac OS X gets updated" MacCentral
- "Fly! II Recognizes Joystick in OS X" Inside Mac Games
- "Public speaking rolls to Mac OS X on the ScrollTrain" MacCentral
- "Keyspan Ships Mac OS X drivers for USB Serial Adapters" MacTech Magazine
- "Keyspan releases OS X drivers for serial adapters" MacCentral
- "WebCam Driver for Mac OS X: IOXperts Delivers on Apple's Digital Hub Promise and Offers Mac Users More Choice by Releasing the First WebCam Driver for Mac OS X" MacTech Magazine
- "Beta version of Mac OS X Webcam driver available" MacCentral
- "ScientificAssistant 0.6.1: Advanced Science Corporation announces the availability of ScientificAssistant 0.6.1 for MacOS X." MacDirectory
- "Umax posts X beta scanner-driver" Macworld UK
- "Time Track 1.0.2 fixes Mac OS X 10.1 glitch" MacCentral
- "Audion 2.6.1 improves stability, OS X performance" MacCentral
- "iOrganizer 2 Carbonized for Mac OS X" MacCentral
- "Grinch – Playstation 2 Emulator for Mac OS X in Development" Go2Mac.com
- "Themes For Mac OS X – X Themination" Go2Mac.com

Figure 5.17
MacSurfer's single-line entries are the actual headlines of the stories they're linked to.

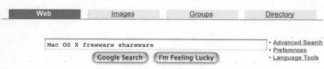

Figure 5.18
Google is fast, clean, and really smart.

But 64,000 is a lot of pages so I tried again, but this time I enclosed "Mac OS X" in quotation marks. That tells Google to interpret whatever is inside the quotes as a phrase, not separate words. In Figure 5.18, Google will select any document with any of the words "Mac," "OS," and "X," as well as "Mac OS X," in any order. By limiting the search to a phrase, "Mac OS X," Google found only pages where the whole phrase appeared, with the words in that exact order. This brought the hit count down to a somewhat more manageable 22,000 pages.

By the way, both searches had VersionTracker as the very first entry on the hit list. And as you already know, that's the site I prefer for finding freeware and shareware for Mac OS X.

If you don't like Google, here are a few other search engines to try:

www.altavista.com ("The Search Company"), www.alltheweb.com ("all the Web, all the time"), www.northernlight.com ("we're all about information"), and www.mamma.com ("the Mother of all Search Engines").

One last thing: Sherlock can search the Web, if that's what you prefer.

TIP

Most search engines and Sherlock offer an advanced search feature, which lets you specify additional search parameters. You'll save a lot of time in the long run if you master this feature and learn to fine tune your searches.

www.live365.com

Live 365 is Internet radio at its best, with thousands of stations that play every type of music imaginable, all for free. iTunes is your radio, but Live 365 makes it better.

A picture is worth a thousand songs, so check out Figure 5.19.

What can I say? I'm a closet metalhead.

That little player window is the best part for me. Since iTunes doesn't display song titles or artists for Internet radio, I keep a player window open as shown. I always know what song is playing (Sweet Leaf), and what the last two songs were (Highway Star and Back in Black). That's sweet, don't you think?

www.sci.tamucc.edu/~pmichaud/toast/

Strawberry Pop-Tart Blow-Torches is an oldie but goodie. This vintage 1994 site posits, "Can Strawberry Pop Tarts be a cheap and inexpensive source of incendiary device?" And more importantly, "Will toasters that fail to eject a Pop Tart cause said Pop Tart to emit flames 10–18 inches in height?"

There's only one way to find out...as shown in Figure 5.20.

Figure 5.19
This is what I've been listening to.

I could probably write a whole book about great things to do with a Web browser, but I have a lot more to cover and only so many pages in my budget.

TIP

> For even more Web entertainment and enlightenment, many more links to sites I like and recommend are only a click away. You'll find a long list on my Links page, on my Web site at **www.boblevitus.com/BLCOM2Pages/Links.html**.

Software for the Surfing Set

So, now that you have destinations in mind, let's talk about software that makes the "Net" experience even better.

The following sections offer a quick look at some Web browsers, followed by some mostly little-known programs I find exceptionally useful.

NOTE

> Most (if not all) of the software discussed in this chapter (and the whole book for that matter) should be available via links at this book's companion Web site. The only reason a program wouldn't appear is that the developer either didn't provide me with a permission form in time for publication, or didn't want his/her program included for one reason or another.

Figure 4. Time Series Photograph of Flaming SPT

As the flames were reaching their maximum height, the toaster abruptly stopped making buzzing noises. We speculate that the flames had by this point shorted the electronics within the toaster. The toaster was quickly disconnected from the primary electrical source to avoid any potential damage to the author's house. At this point, the researchers also realized that the heat could inadvertently melt the adhesive cellophane and cause the flaming SPTs to suddenly eject from the toaster. Unfortunately, this did not occur. The flames continued for several minutes.

At this point there was some slight concern that the flames might take considerable time to diminish. We then enlisted the help of a reluctant research assistant to sprinkle baking soda on the flames. (The reluctance was understandable given the potential for premature SPT ejection described in the above paragraph.) The baking soda quickly extinguished the flames and produced still further smoke (Figure 5a).

Figure 5. Extinguising the SPT

Figure 5.20
The great SPT (Strawberry Pop-Tart) blowtorch experiment.

All about Web Browsers

I kicked off the browser discussion earlier in the chapter, when I explained why I used OmniWeb for most of my screenshots.

NOTE

A more technical description of why OmniWeb renders pages better is beyond the purview of this book. The brutally condensed version is this: OmniWeb was developed exclusively for OS X using Apple's Cocoa development tools. So OmniWeb takes full advantage of Mac OS X's advanced Quartz imaging engine. Internet Explorer was an OS 9 program that's been "Carbonized," or "updated," so it runs natively in either OS 9 or OS X. Though Microsoft could rewrite Internet Explorer to use Quartz, so far they haven't. Which is why, at least so far, OmniWeb renders pages that look better (to me) than Internet Explorer.

I have four or five browsers on my hard disk and I use most of them (though I use some a lot more than others). They each have different features; I use different browsers for different tasks.

For example, sometimes only Internet Explorer will do. Remember Live 365 from a few pages back? For some reason the little player window doesn't work in OmniWeb. Wells Fargo Online banking is another site OmniWeb has problems with.

The point is this: Choosing a browser is a very personal preference. I can't recommend one over the others, and I am not even going to try. What I will do is tell you what I know about each of them. They're all free or have free trial versions available, so try one or try them all. As far as I'm concerned, you can't have too many browsers.

OmniWeb

OmniWeb (**www.omnigroup.com/applications/omniweb/**) is like the little girl with the little curl…when it's good, it's very, very good, but when it's bad, it sucks. It's not for lack of trying—the Omni Group has updated OmniWeb regularly, with major improvements every time. But it still crashes too often, and it chokes on pages Internet Explorer renders with aplomb.

So I can't recommend OmniWeb as your main browser—you will find sites and pages that don't work with OmniWeb at all. So if you want to use OmniWeb, keep a copy of Internet Explorer nearby, just in case.

Internet Explorer

Nothing is inherently wrong with Internet Explorer (downloadable on the Web from **www.mactopia.com/**). It's the default browser for Mac OS X, so you already have a free copy in your Applications folder. In many ways it's a better browser than OmniWeb. It's got many useful and exclusive features—Scrapbook, Page Holder, and Auction Manager are the first that come to mind—and it renders pages somewhat faster than OmniWeb, too. Its support of plug-ins is better, and it seems to have fewer problems with JavaScript than OmniWeb does.

So Internet Explorer is actually a fine browser, with lots of bells and whistles you won't find in OmniWeb (or any other browser, for that matter). I have just one little problem with it—it renders pages that look positively ugly next to OmniWeb's.

I'm not going to waste trees on another picture—Figures 5.4 and 5.5 show both browsers in all their glory.

> **TIP**
>
> One of my favorite tricks with Internet Explorer is to Command+Shift+click on any link. That will open a new window containing the linked page behind the window

you're currently reading. That way the page loads in the background while you go on reading the frontmost page. It's a slick feature and I use it all the time. For what it's worth, Command+click does the same thing in OmniWeb.

I don't know that much about the other browsers. None of them—Netscape, Opera, iCab, and AOL—had a shipping native Mac OS X product as I wrote this; all four were still in public beta testing.

On the other hand, all but one shows promise, so let's take a quick peek before we dive in to the meatier, beefier Internet software.

Netscape

Netscape (**www.netscape.com**) is the granddaddy of all Web browsers, but when Internet Explorer came along a few years back, it (how do I put this delicately?) kicked Netscape's butt all the way to its new home in Virginia (Netscape was acquired by AOL before it merged with Time-Warner). Are you with me so far?

Netscape has been an also-ran on the Mac for years, but their OS X native version 6.2 has made me consider reconsidering. Figure 5.21 shows what the new Netscape looks like along with the revamped Netscape home page.

I haven't used it much, but when I did, nothing about it made me want to shout, "I hate it!"

NOTE

After I wrote this section, the official, final, "shipping" version of Netscape (6.2) for OS X was released. The others were still in public beta but final versions should be available by the time you read this. Check their Web sites for details.

Opera

Opera (**www.opera.com**) is a popular browser on other platforms, and in fact may be the third or fourth most popular browser on the Web. Now, a Mac version is in testing.

Opera calls itself "the fastest browser on Earth." After just a few minutes of testing, I'll give it that—it does open pages fast. At least most of the time—some pages stuttered and took longer to draw than in OmniWeb or Internet Explorer, but only a few. Mostly, it's fast. And as I've surely convinced you by now, fast is good.

It's kind of cute, too, as you can see in Figure 5.22.

Alas, this early beta release (b2) version isn't robust enough to use regularly—it quit unexpectedly twice in five minutes this afternoon, and a few hours later I had to Force Quit.

Figure 5.21
Netscape's latest Mac offering looks kind of tasty.

Don't hold that against them. By the time you read this, a new (or possibly a final) version should be available. When they get it working, I think this may be a browser I could learn to love, at least for some of my surfing.

iCab

iCab (www.icab.de) is another newcomer to the Mac, and again, it's nice looking (see Figure 5.23) and seems to have some features other browsers don't—apparently it can block pop-up ads, among other things.

Another nice touch, and a feature not found in many OS X native programs, are iCab's comprehensive contextual menus, as shown in Figure 5.24.

I've only had time to use this beta copy a little bit, but I'm looking forward to checking out future releases. iCab could be another browser to love when the final version ships.

Figure 5.22
The self-proclaimed fastest browser on Earth.

America Online (AOL)

Last, and least, we have the AOL proprietary browser (**www.aol.com**), the browserlike thing built into their proprietary client program, shown in Figure 5.25.

Yuck. I'm sorry for this outburst. And I know I run the risk of angering AOL lovers (and I know there are legions), but gosh darn it, those AOL graphics and color schemes are disgusting. Mac OS X is so beautiful, so elegant, and so refined; AOL is a freaking insult to Aqua.

I can't help it—AOL grosses me out.

And that's it.

OK, that's not actually "it." I have a little more to say about browsers, mostly tips, but I won't get to them until the section after the excellent section that's about to start.

Figure 5.23
iCab is attractive and has numerous exclusive features.

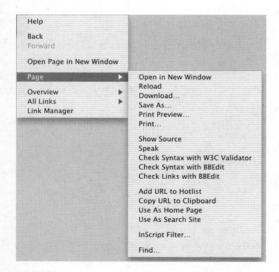

Figure 5.24
Control+click and you can do just about anything in iCab.

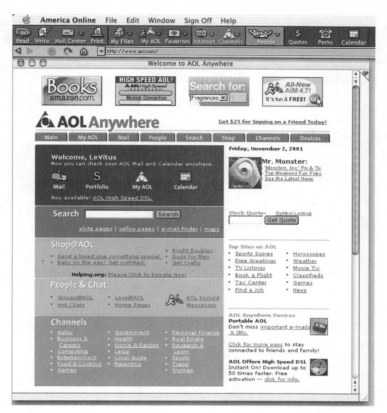

Figure 5.25
AOL's garish colors and retro icons make me want to ... well, do anything but look at them.

More Tools of the Trade

The Internet is more than just the World Wide Web and browsers. It's email, FTP (file transfer protocol—we get to it shortly), secure transactions, and getting (and using) information quickly and easily, among other things.

I spend a lot of time connected, and I've spent a lot of time getting my OS X Internet setup running just right. Considering that so many pieces are still in beta (prerelease) or are version 1.0, I've had only one or two stability issues and a handful of program crashes in OS X 10.1.

Anyway, the upcoming sections cover some tools I'm using today. That doesn't mean there isn't another tool available that might suit your style better. There could be and probably is. But these are the ones I've adopted and use regularly, and so feel comfortable recommending.

An Internet connection means you can swap all kinds of things with users in all kinds of places. Want to trade text with a Texan? No problem? Want to swap files with a fellow in Phoenix? Slice of cake. Want to share your screen with someone? Even that can be easily done if you have the right tools.

Here's some of the stuff I use, and why I use it.

Email: Entourage

Before I talk about my main axe for mail, Microsoft Entourage, let's talk about mail in the broader sense. Many of the things I do with Entourage are easily done in other mail programs with lower price tags: Apple's free Mail program, the advertiser-supported free version of Eudora, and Outlook Express. Those are all perfectly useable mail programs, and I have no quarrel with them.

But Entourage has one killer feature no other program has (nor could they): Entourage lets you link just about anything to anything else. That includes files—Word files, PowerPoint presentations, Excel spreadsheets, or any file on your hard disk. Because Entourage lets me keep everything that's related linked together, it's perfect for a guy like me, who tends toward disorganization. In fact, this feature is crucial, and it's a deal-breaker. I'm lost without it.

Fortunately, Entourage has proved to be a very good email program, handling my sophisticated email needs easily. As for the linking—well, it's just the icing on the cake.

It's probably best if I show before I tell, so look at Figure 5.26.

The list on the left is made up of Entourage folders I created for organizing my email and other stuff. The custom view Carole Messages is selected. This view displays any message to or from my literary agent, Carole. My email message (selected: "Few Things…") had a bunch of questions in it and I didn't want to forget to follow up on any of them. So links were the answer. I linked the message and other relevant items to my "Carole" task, shown in Figure 5.27.

Whenever the task comes due, I have instant access to all the relevant messages, notes, and files from the task's Links window, shown in Figure 5.28.

To me, that's nirvana. I rarely play "where did that email message go" since I adopted Entourage several years ago.

Of course, I have Entourage rigged up to do at least some of the work for me. I have rules for organizing incoming mail automatically. I have rules for deleting junk mail that gets past Entourage's built-in Junk Mail Filter. I have special rules for mailing list

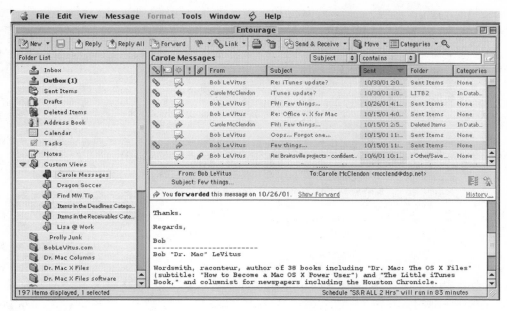

Figure 5.26
This is the main Entourage window, or at least the main one for email.

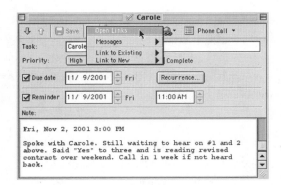

Figure 5.27
My "Carole task", complete with a nagging reminder at 11:00 AM on its due date.

digests that burst them into separate messages and stash them in folders, all unassisted. So overall I'm happy with Entourage as a mail program.

But there's more: It's also a full-blown appointment calendar, contact database, task list manager, and note manager, too, as you can see in Figures 5.29.

Best of all, I can link everything to everything!

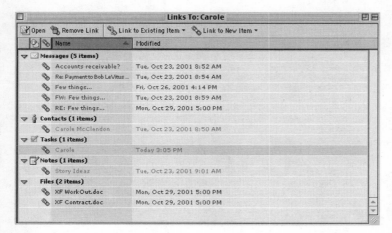

Figure 5.28
These are all the items I've linked to my "Carole" task.

The 2001 Classic edition of Entourage, shown in Figures 5.26 to 5.29, has performed almost flawlessly under OS X in Classic mode. The OS X native version, shown in Figure 5.30, is slated to ship "any day now" and should be available long before you read this.

The only bad thing about Entourage is its price. You can get it only as part of Microsoft Office (at least at this moment), and Office v.X ain't cheap. Even if you need the other programs in the Office suite—Word, Excel, and PowerPoint—it still isn't cheap. The full version of Office v.X (or 2001—they're both available) retails for $499, or $299 to upgrade from a previous version. Ouch. Learn more at **www.mactopia.com**.

FTP: Transmit

FTP is a protocol (set of instructions) used for uploading and downloading files remotely. When you click a link, your Web browser often uses the FTP protocol to download a file to your computer. If you use FTP only occasionally, your Web browser is probably sufficient for the chore. But if you use FTP more often, as I do, you'll need a dedicated FTP program like Transmit (**www.panic.com**).

I use Transmit to transfer files to and from my publisher for editing, and I use it to transfer files to and from my Web site. I also use it in conjunction with my browser (see the tip at the end of this section).

A dedicated FTP program offers several benefits over using a browser for FTP downloading:

■ FTP programs are faster than browsers for downloading.

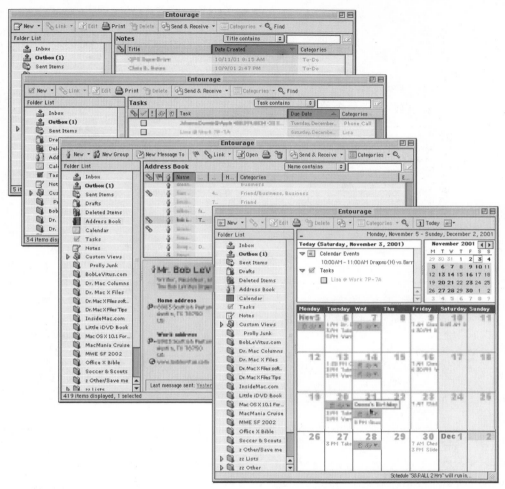

Figure 5.29
Entourage manages email and all this other stuff, too! (Names purposely blurred to protect the innocent.)

- FTP programs are able to handle multiple uploads and downloads simultaneously.

- FTP programs can resume an interrupted download.

- FTP programs let you browse lists of files for downloading and move up or down through the hierarchy of folders.

I've used many FTP programs to perform what should be a simple task—exchanging files with a remote computer. But when it came time to pay for one, Transmit is the one I chose. It's reliable, fast, and has a clean, easy-to-use drag-and-drop interface, shown in Figure 5.31.

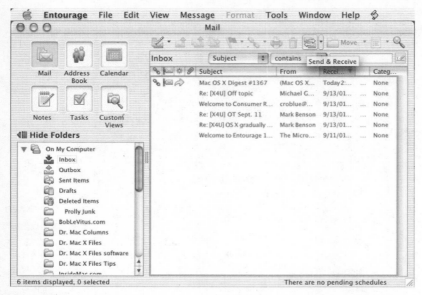

Figure 5.30
Entourage v.X has a better interface than the 2001 Classic release, don't you think?

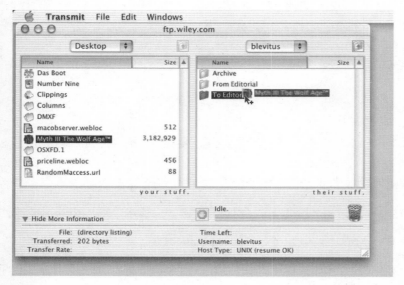

Figure 5.31
Transferring a 3MB file—Myth III The Wolf Age™—from my desktop to my publisher's FTP computer.

After more than a month of heavy use, I have yet to find a single thing to complain about. Transmit just works—and it's fast, easy, and elegant. If you use FTP to upload or download files, Transmit is worth every penny of its $25 shareware fee (which I paid).

TIP

> You can force Internet Explorer to use Transmit when it encounters an FTP link, launching Transmit and downloading the file automatically. In Internet Explorer, choose Preferences, then select the Protocol Helpers item in the list on the left. Edit the Protocol Helper for FTP so it's Transmit, and make sure you do not check the Use Current Application If Possible checkbox. Now, the next time you encounter a link to a file for downloading via FTP, Internet Explorer will hand the job off to Transmit.

Screen Sharing: Timbuktu Pro

Timbuktu Pro (**www.netopia.com**) is remote control for computers. When you control a Timbuktu session, you commandeer a remote computer's mouse and keyboard and operate them with your Mac's mouse and keyboard. Timbuktu also has fast file exchange (faster than built-in file sharing), plus chat and intercom functions. And it works with both Windows boxes and Macintoshes, via the Internet, local area network, wide area network, dial-up, or direct-dial connections. I've used it for years, and the new OS X version works great.

What do I use it for? Two things.

First, I run Timbuktu on two of my office Macs—my everyday Mac and my G4 Cube, which I use to run "beta" software in a controlled environment, without endangering *my* Mac whatsoever. I don't care if software crashes or wonks out my hard disk on my cube. I don't care if all the data goes to heaven. Because with Timbuktu, I can control all programs on another Mac without leaving my comfortable chair!

Take a look at Figure 5.32. Everything inside the black-bordered window is running on the Cube, about 15 feet away; everything outside it is my computer, the 500 Tower.

I sent a chat message, "This is how you change your desktop picture," then clicked the ladybug in the collection, as you can see in Figure 5.32.

The remote computer's desktop changed to the ladybug right before that fictitious user's fictitious eyes. It's like magic.

Figure 5.32
I'm showing a fictitious remote user how to change the desktop picture.

> **NOTE**
>
> They (Netopia, makers of Timbuktu) used to offer a no-frills, easy-as-pie version of Timbuktu called House Call (and Doctor). For around $30 (if I remember correctly), you could remote control one computer via modem. I bought it and installed the doctor on my end and the House Call on my dad's iMac. The next time he screwed up his computer I told him: "Restart, then stand back and watch." I then used House Call to tidy up his desktop, remove some outdated extensions, and fix some ailing aliases. He raved about me "driving his Mac" for months afterwards. I don't think they (Netopia) offer that "mini-Timbuktu" anymore, but you can achieve the same effect, (albeit for more money) with Timbuktu Pro.

Oh, and the second way I use it? When I travel, I have one copy of Timbuktu on my PowerBook and another copy on my Mac back at the office. If I forget something while I'm on the road, I can connect to my home computer and control it. How many times have you been on the road and wished you could do that?

TIP

> Another great trick with Timbuktu is that you can send a Force Quit command to remote OS X machines. So when a program dies on the Cube across the room, I can Force Quit that application from my desk, which means I can go on working (on both Macs) without ever having to leave my chair. Cool, huh?

A Timbuktu twin-pack (for two computers) is less than $200. I use it all the time and recommend it if you would benefit from remote control. If you do tech support for a friend or relative in another city, get them to spring for a copy for each of you. It'll save you a ton of time in the long run.

Windows Emulation: Virtual PC

Virtual PC (**www.connectix.com**) lets you run a Pentium computer, running almost any operating system, including all Windows flavors and Linux. Although it's not speedy enough for twitch games, it is fast enough to use the way I use it.

I don't use it often, but I do use regularly for three things:

■ To view a Web site in a Windows browser without leaving the comfort of my chair, as shown in Figure 5.33.

Figure 5.33
Yes, that is Windows Internet Explorer running on my Mac—we all have to make sacrifices sometimes.

- To run those EXE files PC users send me, thinking a Windows executable will just "work" on my Mac. (Actually, with Virtual PC, they do, but it's still kind of lame to send 'em unsolicited.)

- Every once in a while a program comes along that's Windows-only or Windows-first, and I want to check it out.

Virtual PC is perfect for all those things. You could run a Windows database program at respectable speeds if you had to. Just don't expect real-time, high frame-rate games to work.

Virtual PC is cool mostly because we can do it and they (Windows users) don't even have the option. It's definitely a consideration if you need occasional PC/Windows compatibility but don't want to clutter your desk with an ugly box.

Pervasive Bookmark Manager: URL Manager Pro

Because I change browsers often, it didn't take long for me to get sick of importing and exporting bookmarks. I like to take all my bookmarks with me to use with whichever browser I choose to use. So I have used Alco Blom's inexpensive bookmark manager, URL Manager Pro, for years.

> **NOTE**
>
> I'm going to refer to URL Manager Pro as URLMP, which is easier to type.

URLMP lets me keep my bookmarks in one file, organized just the way I like it, and available from any browser I choose to use. And, as you've just heard, I don't limit myself to just one browser—I like to use them all! So URLMP is particularly valuable to me. Never mind that it's a better bookmark organizer than what's built into any browser; it has other features I love.

Perhaps the best one is the Shared Menu that URLMP adds to most browsers' menu bars, as shown in Figure 5.34.

> **NOTE**
>
> What is that menu thing, anyway, Alco? A jellyfish?

Behind the menu is the result of my choosing Read All—Internet Explorer opened separate windows for all the sites in my Read Daily folder at once. Now scanning and reading all those pages will be much faster—they're all loaded and ready.

The second Favorites menu, the one to the right of the jellyfish, is also a URLMP Shared Menu that contains my whole bookmark file, organized just the way I like it. I can add new bookmarks to any folder at any time from any browser (almost—read on), as you can see in Figure 5.35.

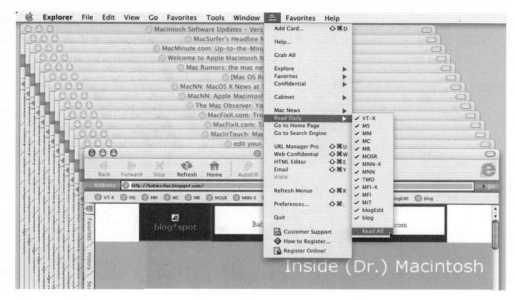

Figure 5.34
The URL Manager Pro's menu in Internet Explorer's menu bar.

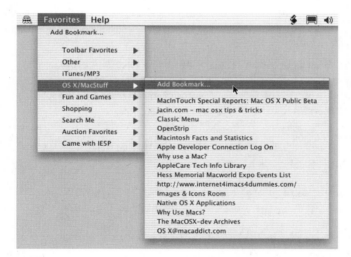

Figure 5.35
Whenever I encounter an OS X–related site worth revisiting, I add it to the OS X/MacStuff folder, like this.

Now the bookmark will be available no matter which browser I'm using the next time I feel the urge to visit that site again.

One last thing: Although the URLMP program doesn't have to be running to use the Shared Menus, when it *is* running, you *also* get your Favorites menu in the Dock, as shown in Figure 5.36.

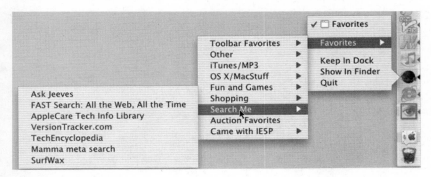

Figure 5.36
Last cool feature: Bookmarks in the Dock!

That's pretty sweet if you're a Dock person.

Alco also makes a companion program that uses the same Shared Menu. It's a password manager called Web Confidential, but because my memory is so razor-sharp, I don't use it.

NOTE

And if you believe that... The reason I don't use this otherwise excellent program is that I adopted another method long ago to keep track of passwords and serial numbers and all that other stuff. In the immortal words of my favorite Apple PR person, "I'd tell you, but then I'd have to kill you."

Many users swear by Web Confidential, which integrates nicely with OS X's Keychain, and URLMB and its Shared Menus.

Both URLMP and Web Confidential are "still in beta," but I've been running the current version (3.0b19) for a few weeks without any problems.

The Shared Menu doesn't work in OmniWeb or Netscape 6, but it works great in Internet Explorer and the iCab and Opera betas. I paid my $10.95 (to upgrade from version 2) anyway. You've got to support good software, you know—and URLMP is another program worth paying for. Visit **http://url-manager.com/** or **www.web-confidential.com/** to check them out.

Don't Forget the Freebies...

Thousands of great, free programs are out there, created by brilliant programmers (usually) for kicks, for their own use, for their own enjoyment, for the joy of giving something to the Mac community, for fame, notoriety, or whatever.

Here are five free Net-savvy programs I think you'll enjoy:

■ *NetStatInDock (Figure 5.37)*—Created by Takashi T. Hamada (check out his Web page at **www.lisai.net/~hamada/**), NetStatInDock shows your Mac's outgoing and incoming network traffic statistics. Notice that the numbers for in and out are elevated (they say zero when there's no traffic). That's because I'm loading Web pages and checking my mail in the background.

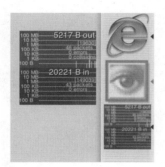

Figure 5.37
The larger box is NetStatInDock's floating semi-transparent movable windoid. The information is also displayed in the Dock icon.

■ *Perfboard (Figure 5.38)*—Created by Pepsan & Associates (**www.pepsan.com**), Perfboard is another performance statistics tool, but with more bells and whistles than NetStatInDock, including CPU, load, memory, and disk I/O stats. Perfboard is one of my login items, and it's always running on my Mac. Sometimes I can even tell from its display that my Mac is about to become (or has already become) wonky.

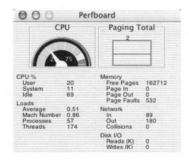

Figure 5.38
Perfboard sure has a lot of info for such a small window. I run it 24/7/365.

■ *Son of Weather Grok (Figure 5.39)*—Written by John Schilling at StimpSoft (**www.stimpsoft.com**), this program connects to the National Oceanic and Atmospheric Administration's (NOAA) data center over the Internet, and looks up the weather for almost any location.

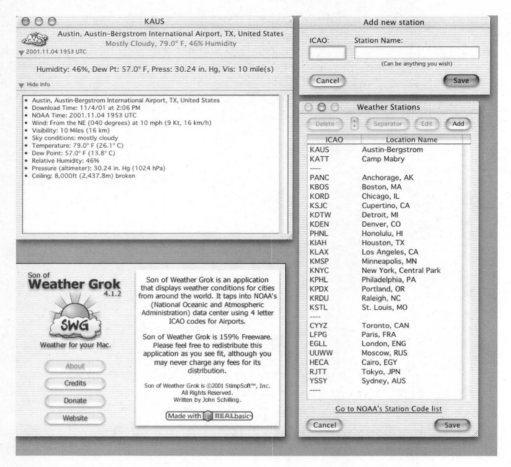

Figure 5.39
Weather? SWG's got your weather right here.

- *Ticker (Figure 5.40)*—From R. Fronabarger/Soporific Software (at **http:// homepage.mac.com/soporific/**), Ticker is a free, configurable stock ticker.

- *Tea Timer (Figure 5.41)*—From Herwig Henseler (at **www.herwig-henseler.de/ teatimer**), this program has only a tangential relationship with the Internet. But it's an important tool, nonetheless. You see, sometimes I get so involved in surfing I forget that I've got food in the oven or on the stove. So I use this clever little freebie to remind me not to burn the house down.

And that'll just about do it for software for now.

You know, an old proverb goes, "if you *give* a man a fish, you feed him for a day, but if you *teach* a man to fish, you feed him for a lifetime." I hope you've picked up a fishing tip or two in this chapter. But, as Steve Jobs is so fond of saying (usually near the end of one of his infamous Macworld Expo keynote addresses), "there is one last thing…"

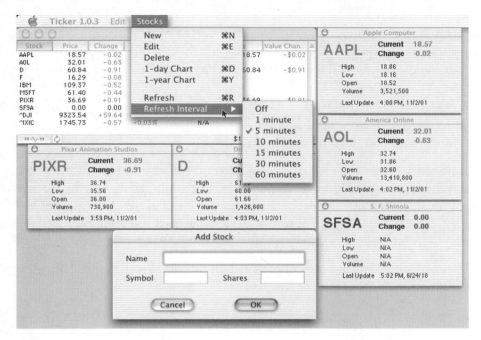

Figure 5.40
All the stocks you want, updated as often as you like.

Figure 5.41
I haven't burnt a single slice of pizza since I started using Tea Timer.

One Last Thing

Everyone talks about tools and sites and Java and Flash and video and Dreamweaver and rollovers, and so on, but the thing you *don't* hear much about is the Web *community*. And, at least for me, community is a huge part of what makes the Web so great. The people you encounter along the way are what make the Internet so wonderful. Heck, it could easily be said that the people you meet on the Internet *are* the Internet.

The Web Community

The Internet is perfect for finding affinity without regard to geography. If you like something, chances are that others like you like it too.

So, although only one or two Vizsla enthusiasts may be in your neck of the woods, thousands of Vizsla people are on the Internet. They run mailing lists for those who enjoy Vizslas. They hang out on the message boards and in the chat rooms of Web sites dedicated to Vizslas. In fact, many Vizsla enthusiasts run their own Web sites devoted to (what else?) Vizslas.

And Google found 591 hits when I searched for "Vizsla Web Ring" including one at **www.blayne.com/v_ring/** (see Figure 5.42).

Figure 5.42
There are Web rings for just about anything you can think of, including Vizslas!

A *Web ring* is a semiformal group of Web sites, all with a similar theme, and all linked together.

What, exactly, is a Vizsla? Glad you asked: Vizsla.—n: Hungarian hunting dog resembling the Weimaraner but having a rich deep red coat [syn: Hungarian pointer].

Instant Definition

What's more interesting is how I *found* the Vizsla definition at **www.dict.org** instantly via the Internet. I'm beta testing something called OmniDictionary (see **www.omnigroup.com/**), which runs as an OS X "Service."

First you put OmniDictionary into the Services folder, in either your personal Library (~/Library; only you will be able to use it) or the main Library in the System folder (/System/Library/Services/; all users of this Mac will be able to use it).

Then, just highlight any word you want to define and type the keyboard shortcut, Command+= (Command+equals). It works in any OS X application that has a Services submenu; I happen to be using OmniWeb in Figure 5.43, and have selected the word "Vizsla."

In a blink of the eye, OmniDictionary popped up with my definition, as shown in Figure 5.44.

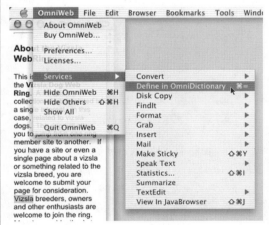

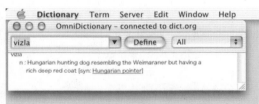

Figure 5.43
"Computer, look up the word 'Vizsla' in the dictionary..."

Figure 5.44
So *that's* what a Vizsla is.

Find a Community You Can Love

That was more than a mere plug for a little-known but still loveable breed of dog—it was proof positive that no matter what your interests are, you'll find many others with that same interest on the Internet.

If troubleshooting the Mac rings your chimes, for example, check out MacFixIt's message boards, or the message boards at any Mac Web site. You'll find a community of helpful and (usually) nice Mac enthusiasts, more than willing to answer a question about what is broken and how to fix it. Give it a try—you'll be pleasantly surprised.

If you're an AOL user, try their message boards—they have plenty. Or, if your interest is more esoteric, try a search engine.

If you want to find others on the Web who share your passion, you now know how.

But there are also connected communities *off* the Web. One is the humble *mailing list*, which is like a message board that you use via email and never have to surf to. It's just what it sounds like—an email list of like-minded people, asking and answering questions and carrying on (usually) civilized discourse.

The good thing about lists is that you can set up a filter for them in your mail program, have them all saved in one folder, then read as much or as little as you like when you have time. Or you can search the messages for a word or phrase.

Since OS X was released, I've archived and read several of the Mac OS X lists run by Eric Prentice, The Macintosh Guy of Portland (**listmom@themacintoshguy.com**).

> **NOTE**
>
> Eric is also CEO of Dr. Bott LLC (**www.drbott.com**), a distributor of unique Mac products and accessories. But he's a pretty good list mom anyway.

There are at least seven OS X lists, for Users, Newbies, Servers, Apps, Hardware, Unix, and Dreams. I read three or four of them and have learned tons. They've answered questions when I had them, and I was able to help other readers with their adoption of OS X. It's been a great resource, and most of the conversation has been genial and constructive.

> **NOTE**
>
> List readers submitted many of the tips you'll find in Chapter 15 in response to my offer—a free book for a good tip or desktop picture!

That said, like most public forums, these lists have had more than their share of loud contrarians (we refer to them as "trolls") who insist on using the list so they can see themselves type. You know the kind—they only want to argue, fight, demean, name-call, and otherwise incite "flame wars." For a while I was pressing the Delete key an awful lot in my OS X Lists folder, though everyone seems to have calmed down a bit.

ALERT!

On mailing lists (or message boards, or any other public forum) emotions often run high, and language and content used will surely offend some readers at some time.

For more information on Eric's lists, visit **www.themacintoshguy.com/lists/X.html**. Or, for other lists, use the search engine of your choice to find "Macintosh email lists." There are a lot of them, some better than others; you may have to shop around to find a community that fits.

The second non-Web community is made up of newsgroups. For newsgroups, you need a program called a *newsreader*.

NOTE

I use Entourage as my newsreader, so you're on your own here. If I were you, I'd search **www.versiontracker.com** for "newsreader." I know you'll find at least half a dozen freeware and shareware newsreaders; try one or all.

Use your newsreader software to filter the list of newsgroups by the word "Mac." When I did that, I got 619 hits—newsgroups that have "Mac" in their names—out of a total of more than 62,000 different newsgroups, as shown in Figure 5.45.

Once you've got newsreader software, the newsgroups work pretty much the same as Web site message boards, except you don't need the Web or a Web browser to participate. Figure 5.46 shows what it looks like in my newsreader program, Entourage.

And that's pretty much it—Newsreaders make it easy to filter or search a message collection, then read, skip, or reply to an existing message, or submit a new message of your own.

NOTE

The company that used to run all the newsgroup feeds (**Deja.com**), was recently acquired by the search engine company **Google.com**. Google offers a great interface for searching for a newsgroup on their Web page at **groups.google.com**. This is probably the best place you could begin looking for a group or community that suits you.

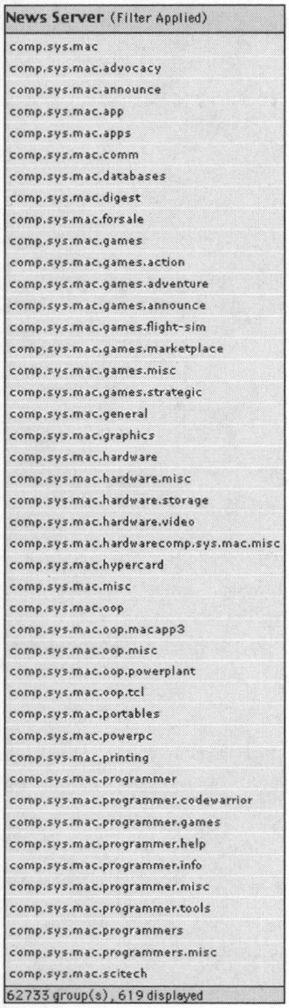

```
News Server (Filter Applied)
comp.sys.mac
comp.sys.mac.advocacy
comp.sys.mac.announce
comp.sys.mac.app
comp.sys.mac.apps
comp.sys.mac.comm
comp.sys.mac.databases
comp.sys.mac.digest
comp.sys.mac.forsale
comp.sys.mac.games
comp.sys.mac.games.action
comp.sys.mac.games.adventure
comp.sys.mac.games.announce
comp.sys.mac.games.flight-sim
comp.sys.mac.games.marketplace
comp.sys.mac.games.misc
comp.sys.mac.games.strategic
comp.sys.mac.general
comp.sys.mac.graphics
comp.sys.mac.hardware
comp.sys.mac.hardware.misc
comp.sys.mac.hardware.storage
comp.sys.mac.hardware.video
comp.sys.mac.hardwarecomp.sys.mac.misc
comp.sys.mac.hypercard
comp.sys.mac.misc
comp.sys.mac.oop
comp.sys.mac.oop.macapp3
comp.sys.mac.oop.misc
comp.sys.mac.oop.powerplant
comp.sys.mac.oop.tcl
comp.sys.mac.portables
comp.sys.mac.powerpc
comp.sys.mac.printing
comp.sys.mac.programmer
comp.sys.mac.programmer.codewarrior
comp.sys.mac.programmer.games
comp.sys.mac.programmer.help
comp.sys.mac.programmer.info
comp.sys.mac.programmer.misc
comp.sys.mac.programmer.tools
comp.sys.mac.programmers
comp.sys.mac.programmers.misc
comp.sys.mac.scitech
62733 group(s) , 619 displayed
```

Figure 5.45
You can only see roughly 40 (out of the 619 total newsgroups with "Mac" in their names) in this picture.

One Final Treat ...

After writing this chapter, I realized that there are a lot of URLs in these pages, and that typing them isn't going to be much fun. And so, as soon as I finished all the writing, I went back and collected every URL in the whole book, then created an HTML page with every link, organized by chapter. You'll find this handy page (it's called X-Files bookmarks.html) at **www.boblevitus. com/xfiles.html**. Just open the file with your favorite browser and click away. Have fun!

Figure 5.46
A newsgroup's message collection (top pane) and a message posted by "Mark" (bottom pane).

5

The Classic Environment

Classic is OS X's built-in Mac OS 9 emulator and the part of OS X that lets you run Mac OS 9 software right in Mac OS X. It's a remarkable feat of engineering and without it, I'm sure Mac OS X would have been a flop. That's the good news. The bad news is that Classic is like the little girl with the curl—when it's good, it's very, very good, but when it's bad, it'll make you want to throw your Mac out the window. Or switch to Windows.

But the news is more good than bad—the latest iterations of both OS X and Classic are much, much better than the 10.0.*x* releases. And, we the power users, have learned a lot about how to tame Classic, how to avoid crashing it, and how to avoid using it.

Even so, I think of Classic as a necessary evil. I'm glad to have it, but I try to launch it as infrequently as possible and can't wait for the day I can delete OS 9 from my disks completely. As of late 2001, I rarely have to use Classic (or OS 9), but I'm not ready to get rid of it, yet. But I hope I will soon.

At present, I can go several days without using Classic, but every so often I need Adobe Photoshop (no OS X version announced yet) or Adobe GoLive (ditto). And when I want to use Final Cut Pro 2 even Classic doesn't cut it—I have to reboot into Mac OS 9 because FCP2 won't even *launch* in Classic. (Fortunately, Final Cut Pro 3, which does run under OS X, is coming out soon.)

So let's get going and look at not only how to use Classic, but how to *avoid* using it as well. As usual, we'll start with a brief overview before we delve into the more interesting stuff.

The Basics of Classic

You can get Classic up and running two different ways. The first is to use the Classic system Preference pane's Start button. The second is to launch any Classic program— if Classic isn't running, it will launch automatically.

What I Have against Classic

What do I have against Classic? And why do I want to avoid Classic as much as possible? I can think of several reasons off the top of my pointy little head:

- Classic programs crash more than native OS X programs.

- The Classic environment itself crashes more than most native OS X programs.

- When Classic programs crash, they often crash the entire Classic environment, bringing down all other Classic applications with them.

- Classic is a resource hog—it uses a lot of memory and consumes an inordinate share of your CPU, which is the brain of your Mac. So running without it is faster, in addition to being more stable.

- If you have to force a Classic application to quit, it often causes all Classic programs and the Classic environment itself to quit.

NOTE
You should restart the whole Classic environment each time you force quit a Classic application. I say "should," because you really ought to. Unlike OS X, Mac OS 9 is left in an unstable state after a force quit. Do *I* do it? Not as often as I should. But then again, it's a well-known fact that I like living dangerously on the edge.

- It's ugly. (OK, that's a very personal preference, but since I met the Aqua interface, I think OS 9's looks flat, lifeless, boring, and just plain ugly. And I really miss OS X's gorgeous drop shadows.)

The Classic System Preference Pane

Let's look at some of the other things you can do in the Classic system Preference pane, shown in Figure 6.1.

The Start/Stop Tab

The list of startup volumes displays any disk or volume with a bootable OS 9 system folder (9.2.1 or later) on it. I have two—Das Boot is the one I use exclusively for Classic; Number Nine is the one I use when I need to actually boot into OS 9. (I explain why I do it this way in the next section.)

Just click the disk or volume you want (or the only one if you have only one) and click Start to start Classic.

NOTE
Well, not quite. It takes a minute or two to start up, depending on the speed of your Mac and the number of extensions and control panels you have enabled.

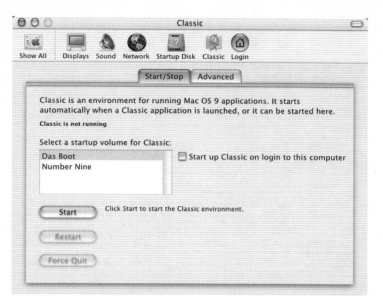

Figure 6.1
The Start/Stop tab of the Classic system Preference pane.

If you use Classic a lot, you may want to check the box next to Start Up Classic On Login To This Computer. If you do, whenever you start, restart, or log onto your Mac, Classic will start itself automatically.

> **TIP**
>
> You can achieve the same effect by making any Classic application one of your login items. This technique is a little bit more useful; the checkbox merely starts Classic without launching any Classic programs.

Either way, if you configure your Mac so Classic is always running, you'll never have to wait the minute or two for it to launch when you need it—it'll already be running. Until recently this is how I did it. Lately, though, because I'm trying to avoid Classic, I've stopped. These days I'm willing to endure a brief wait when Classic starts up, to avoid some of the ickyness I described at the beginning of the chapter. Because I can sometimes go a day or more without Classic, not having Classic running saves me heartache and RAM, and some processor cycles, too.

The Advanced Tab
The Advanced tab of the Classic preferences pane offers three utilities for working with Classic.

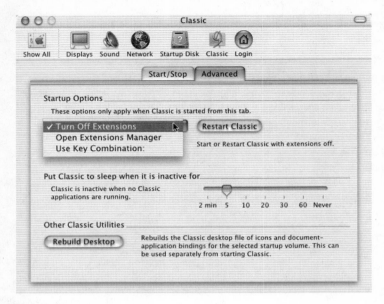

Figure 6.2
The Advanced tab of the Classic system Preference pane.

The top section offers three startup options you choose from a pop-up menu, as shown in Figure 6.2. The pop-up menu offers a choice of Turn Off Extensions, Open Extensions Manager, and Use Key Combination, all of which are used in conjunction with the Restart Classic button.

> **NOTE**
>
> If Classic's not running, the button says "Start Classic" instead of "Restart Classic," as you see in Figure 6.2. Ergo, Classic was running when I took that picture.

Turn Off Extensions is the same as booting into OS 9 while holding down the Shift key. It keeps all your extensions and control panels from loading. Classic will start up much faster without them, but you'll lose some capabilities, and some programs may not work.

Open Extensions Manager is the same booting into OS 9 while holding down the spacebar. The Extensions Manager window will appear, allowing you to turn individual extensions and control panels on or off before Classic loads.

Use Key Combination is for those rare times when you are instructed to hold down a specific key or keys when you start up your Mac. For example, holding down a particular key or keys during startup can change how certain extensions and control

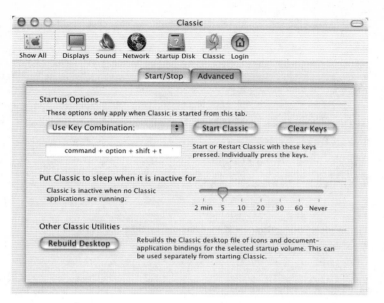

Figure 6.3
Press the Command, Option, Shift, and T keys, then click Start (or Restart) Classic.

panels work. If you ever come across an extension or control panel that has an instruction such as, "to start up in Turbo mode, hold down Command+Option+Shift+T during startup," this is how you would do it, as shown in Figure 6.3. I've only used it once or twice, but knowing it's here and how to use it could come in handy some day.

The Put Classic To Sleep slider lets you put Classic to sleep after a specified period of inactivity. When it's sleeping, Classic uses fewer CPU cycles (but not less RAM), but sleep can occur only if no Classic applications are running. So, the slider controls how long after you quit your last Classic application until Classic sleeps. The down side is that when Classic is sleeping, opening a Classic application may take a little longer than usual.

Finally, the Rebuild Desktop button performs a good old Mac OS 9–style rebuilding of the desktop, but only for the disk or volume that contains the Classic system folder.

TIP

If you want to rebuild the desktop of other disks or volumes, use the key combination option discussed a few paragraphs back, with Command and Option pressed. This will start Classic and rebuild the desktop of any or all mounted disks. Or, restart into OS 9 and do it.

Figure 6.4
A generic icon often indicates that it's time for you to rebuild your desktop.

How do you know if your desktop needs rebuilding? Apple says you should do it monthly whether you need it or not. But if your document icons change mysteriously, or begin looking like blank sheets of paper (see Figure 6.4), a desktop rebuilding is probably just what the doctor ordered.

Another reason for an incorrect document icon is that the wrong application has been chosen to open that document. We'll talk more about this in Chapter 8.

Maximizing Classic Performance

Now that you know a bit about Classic, let's look at a couple of ways to make it perform better. Then, in the next section, we'll look at some tips that make Classic easier to deal with.

The best way to make Classic perform better, of course, is not to launch it. But for various reasons—a program you can't live without that has no OS X equivalent; a program that does have an OS X equivalent that you're too cheap to buy; a control panel or extension that's required to use a peripheral device; or whatever—many users will be launching Classic for many years to come. So here are three ways to make it work better and/or faster.

Speed Up Your Mac

One way to make Classic (and OS X) run faster is to make your Mac faster. Although OS X runs okay on a Mac with a G3 processor, it (and Classic) will run significantly faster on a G4. And if your processor—G3 or G4—runs at 300 MHz, a 500 or 600 MHz processor will run OS X (and Classic) noticeably faster.

So consider these approaches:

- Buy a new, faster Mac

or

- Buy a processor upgrade for your existing Mac.

Which is better? It depends on your budget, your willingness to run OS X on an unsupported system (processor-upgraded Macs are not supported by Apple), and how much more speed you want.

NOTE

> I have a definite opinion on this subject, but you're going to have to wait until you get to Chapter 7 to hear it.

Stock Up on RAM

Another way to make Classic (and OS X) run faster is to give it enough RAM. Apple says 64MB is enough to run Mac OS X without Classic or 128MB with. Technically, that's true—the operating system *will* run, but if you want to use any *other* software, you should have at least twice that—128MB without Classic or 256MB with. And if, like me, you want to run 6 or 9 or 12 programs at once, you need even more than that. Since OS X came along, none of my Macs has less than 384MB of RAM, and my everyday system has 1.2GB of the stuff.

TIP

> RAM has never been cheaper, so buy more if you need it.

If you don't have enough RAM, OS X uses your hard disk as *surrogate RAM*, or, more technically, as *virtual memory*. But because RAM is completely electronic with no moving parts, it is many (many, many) times faster than even the fastest hard disk. So the more programs you run, the more your Mac has to "page out" to hard disk, and the slower things will get.

NOTE

> Because RAM and virtual memory impact much more than just Classic, we'll continue this discussion in more depth in Chapter 7.

Use a Minimal Set of Extensions and Control Panels

Extensions and control panels use at least a little bit of RAM, and some use quite a bit. And because they load at startup, the more you have, the longer Classic takes to start up. Finally, some of them gobble up processor time whether you're using them or not. So to coax better performance out of both Classic and OS X, you should deactivate any extensions and control panels you don't need.

NOTE

> Unlike the previous two suggestions, this one won't cost you a penny.

For example, it's well-known that if you disable all the ATI extensions (you don't need them when you're running OS X), some Classic applications will run faster. But my contention is that if you turn off every one you don't need, almost everything in Classic will run better and Classic will launch faster to boot (another bad pun; intended).

> **TIP**
>
> One pleasant side effect (of loading fewer extensions and control panels) is that Classic will not only launch and run faster, it will crash less often.

To get the job done, you'll need Extensions Manager. You can launch it from your (OS 9/Classic) system folder's Control Panels folder, or you can use the Classic system Preference pane to launch it when you start or restart Classic, as you saw in the previous section. Either way, you're going to need it to do what I'm about to tell you.

> **ALERT!**
>
> I'm going to show you what I've done on my Mac. But be warned that doing it exactly as I did may not work for you. I have no way of knowing what software and hardware you plan to use with Classic, nor what extensions or control panels that software or hardware requires. So you may need to experiment a little to get your set of extensions and control panels configured just right for you.

> **NOTE**
>
> I refer to Mac OS 9.2.1 in this tutorial, because that's the current version of OS 9 as I write this, and the one you'll see in the pictures. If yours has a higher number than that (i.e., Apple updates OS 9 again), mentally replace all occurrences of 9.2.1 with 9.2.2 (or whatever version you're using).

Here's how:

1. Launch Extensions Manager.

2. Choose Mac OS 9.2.1 Base as your Selected Set.

3. Choose File|Duplicate Set, as shown in Figure 6.5.

   This step is necessary because the Mac OS 9.2.1 Base set is locked, meaning you can't modify it. And modify it is just what you're about to do. So. . .

4. Name your duplicate set something meaningful (I named mine Base For Classic).

Now start or restart Classic, and test this set for a while. Do the things you'd normally do in Classic, and use the programs you'd normally use. If something doesn't work properly, enable whichever control panel(s) or extension(s) it requires, restart, and try again.

Now, once you've got a base set that's working for you, if you want to try to improve your performance even further, launch Extensions Manager and disable any *other* control panels or extensions in your Base For Classic set (or whatever you called the set you made a moment ago) you don't think you'll need.

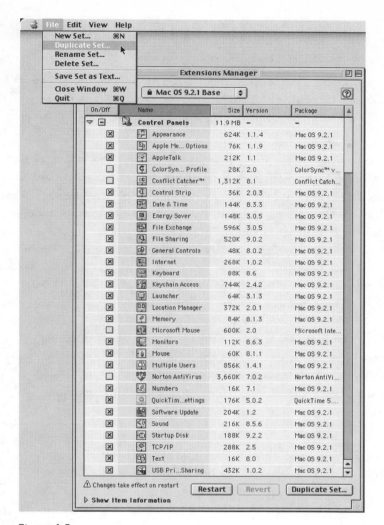

Figure 6.5
Duplicate the Mac OS 9.2.1 Base set.

This will take some trial and error, but it may be worth it. First, disable a few extensions and/or control panels, then restart Classic and try all the Classic programs you use. If they all work, disable a few more extensions and/or control panels, restart Classic, and try the programs again. Repeat this process until you're either sick of doing it or you can't find any more items you can disable without affecting the Classic programs you use.

NOTE

As promised, this is why I keep two OS 9 system folders—one on Das Boot for use with Classic, the other on Number Nine for booting into OS 9 (i.e., without OS X).

Extensions and Control Panels I Disabled in Classic

Just for reference, here are the items I have disabled in my Base For Classic set:

Control Panels: Apple Menu Options, AppleTalk, Control Strip, Date & Time, Energy Saver, File Exchange, File Sharing, Keyboard, Launcher, Location Manager, Memory, Monitors, Mouse, Multiple Users, Numbers, QuickTime Settings, Software Update, TCP/IP, Text, and USB Printer Sharing.

Extensions: Apple Audio Extension, Apple CD/DVD Driver, Apple Photo Access, Apple QD3D HW Driver, Apple QD3D HW Plug-In, AppleShare, Application Switcher, ATI 3D Accelerator, ATI Driver Update, ATI Graphics Accelerator, ATI MPP Manager, ATI Radeon 3D Accelerator, ATI Rage 128 3D Accelerator, ATI Resource Manager, ATI Video Accelerator, Audio CD Access, Authoring Support, Control Strip Extension, Disc Burner Extension, FBC Indexing Scheduler, File Sharing Extension, File Sharing Library, Find, Find By Content, FireWire Authoring Support, FireWire Enabler, FontSync Extension, Foreign File Access, Internal V.90 Modem, Iomega Driver, ISO 9660 File Access, Location Manager Extension, Multi-User Startup, OpenGLEngine, OpenGLLibrary, OpenGLMemory, OpenGLRenderer, OpenGLRendererATI, OpenGLUtility, QD3DCustomElements, QuickDraw 3D, QuickDraw 3D IR, QuickDraw 3D RAVE, QuickDraw 3D Viewer, QuickTime FireWire DV Enabler, QuickTime FireWire DV Support, SDAP Authoring Support, ShareWay IP Personal Bgnd, Software Update Engine, Software Update Scheduler, Sound Manager, System Monitor Plugins, Time Synchronizer, UDF Volume Access, USB Authoring Support, USB Device Extension, USB Printer Sharing Extension, USB Software Locator, and USBAppleMonitorModule.

Keep in mind that I rarely use Classic anymore, and have only a couple of Classic programs—most notably Adobe Photoshop and Adobe GoLive—that I still have to run in Classic. If you're using a lot of Classic programs, you may have to keep some of the items listed in the sidebar enabled. That said, Classic works great for me without them—it starts up much faster, rarely crashes, and the programs I use run fine without them.

TIP

If Adobe GoLive didn't require them, I could also disable QuickTime, QuickTime MPEG Extension, QuickTime Musical Instruments, QuickTime PowerPlug, and QuickTime VR. Sigh.

The bottom line is that the fewer extensions and control panels you enable, the better and faster Classic will run. So go trim yours now if you haven't already—I'll wait.

Consider Conflict Catcher

I have a confession to make. I lied to you in the previous section when I discussed Extensions Manager. I don't use it—instead, I use Conflict Catcher, from Casady & Greene (**www.casadyg.com**). It's a far better extension manager, and it has at least one feature that makes it worth every penny: It can automatically detect whether you're using OS 9 or Classic, and choose a set of extensions based on that. It's a time-saver, because you won't accidentally start up Classic with your "real" OS 9 set, nor will you start up OS 9 with your minimal Classic set.

I talk more about Conflict Catcher and why I prefer it in Chapter 14.

More Classic Tips, Techniques, and Advice

Here are more tips, techniques, scripts, tutorials, and advice I've picked up since I began using OS X more than a year ago.

NOTE

I learned many of these tips and techniques from other sources; you learned about most of those sources in Chapter 5. I've done my best to credit individuals and Web sites when I can remember, but many, including the handy script that leads off the following section, came from *somewhere* other than my head. But they've been on my Mac for so long, I can't for the life of me remember where they originated. It's safe to assume I learned them from a Web page, mailing list, or email from a friend, but I couldn't say which, or who thought of it first. The prose descriptions, however, are entirely my own.

Back and Forth: From OS X to OS 9 and Back

Sometimes you just can't get around having to boot into Mac OS 9 for some reason. One of them, for me, is to use Final Cut Pro 2. Another is to use my old scanner, which balks under Classic.

If you still have to use OS 9, I have two tips for making the round trip from OS X to OS 9 and back more pleasant.

Startup Disk Script

As I just said, I don't remember where I got it, but I have a handy little AppleScript that changes my startup disk to OS X when I'm booted in OS 9, then restarts my Mac with OS X. And it goes like this:

```
tell application "Startup Disk"
    activate
     set startup system folder alias to alias "Das
Boot:System:Library:CoreServices:BootX"
    quit
```

```
end tell
tell application "Finder"
    restart
end tell
```

Of course, you'll need to change *Das Boot* to the name of your OS X startup disk. But it's a handy one-step deal to change boot disks and restart all with a single flick of the wrist.

> If you're familiar with AppleScript, go ahead and try it; if you're not, you might want to read Chapter 13 first.

I tried to figure out how to create the reverse of this script for OS X—that is, open the Startup Disk system Preference pane, choose the OS 9 system folder, then restart. So far I've been unsuccessful. If you figure out how to do it, give me a holler.

Stop Classic before You Restart in OS 9

If you get the warning about your Mac being shut down improperly when you boot OS 9 (from OS X), try stopping Classic before you reboot into 9. Although this particular bugaboo is mostly fixed in version 10.1, it still seems to happen occasionally. If it happens to you, stopping Classic before you reboot into OS 9 should fix it.

Software That Makes Classic Better

Of course, any program, extension, or control panel that works in OS 9 is likely to also work in OS X. So, technically, all your old Classic software is capable of making your use of Classic more enjoyable.

Here are three OS X programs that enhance Classic or bring a desirable OS 9 feature to OS X; you'll find all three via links at **www.boblevitus.com/xfiles.html**.

WindowShade X

Do you miss OS 9's WindowShade feature? I know I did until I discovered WindowShade X, a "haxie" (I think that means it's a little hack for OS X) by "unsanity." It's so good I paid for it ($7 shareware) the second day I had it.

Without WindowShade X, double-clicking a window's title bar minimizes it and stashes it in the Dock. While that's sometimes desirable, I missed the old WindowShade effect of OS 9.

WindowShade X is a system Preference pane. After you install it, you have three choices for minimizing windows: WindowShade, Make Window Transparent, and Hide Application. Figure 6.6 shows my WindowShade X Preference pane.

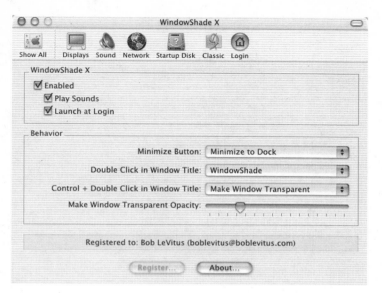

Figure 6.6
My WindowShade X settings.

When I click the yellow gumdrop, the window minimizes the old-fashioned way and goes into the Dock, leaving no part of itself on the screen. But now, if I double-click a window's title bar, it "rolls up" like a window shade, and if I Control+double-click, it makes the window transparent, so I can see what's behind it.

Figure 6.7 shows what happens when I double-click a window's title bar (the bottom WindowShade X folder window) and when I Control+double-click a window's title bar (the bottom WindowShade X ReadMe.rtfd window). The neat part is that the transparent window is totally usable—I can select text, copy, paste, or do anything else I could do with a nontransparent window. This is a great improvement on OS 9's already great WindowShade feature.

I just love this little hack and use it all the time, every day. It's worth every penny of the $7 I paid for it.

classihack

classihack is a little hack that turns on a hidden OS X feature called Classic window buffering. Enable it and your Classic applications windows will redraw one heck of a lot faster. It's almost like magic.

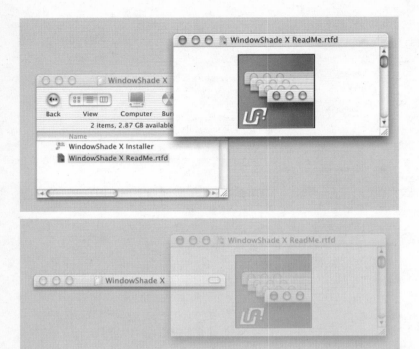

Figure 6.7
Before (top) and after (bottom) using WindowShade X.

ALERT!

With classihack enabled, if you switch monitor color depths (say from thousands to millions) or if you switch monitor resolutions, all your running applications will quit. That's probably why Apple left this feature disabled. I think it makes Classic work much better and it's caused me no problems, but I have to say: Use it at your own risk.

To disable classihack, log out, shut down, or restart.

classihack was written by one of the greatest Mac utility programmers of all time, Andrew Welch of Ambrosia Software, who also wrote the fabulous screen capture utility I've used for every picture in this book, Snapz Pro X.

NOTE

Speaking of screen shots, the effect of classihack doesn't show up well in pictures, so there isn't one here. Give it a try if you want to see what I mean by "a heck of a lot faster."

classihack is entirely free (and entirely unsupported by Andrew).

Classic Menu

Classic Menu is a $10 shareware program from Sig Software that brings back the configurable Apple menu you knew and loved in OS 9. Your Classic Menu replaces the OS X Apple menu, and displays the contents of the Classic Menu Items folder, which you'll find in ~/Library/Preferences.

> **TIP**
>
> If you want your OS X Apple menu instead of Classic Menu, just hold down the modifier key you specified in Classic Menu's Preferences dialog box.

A picture is worth. . . and all that jazz, so see Figure 6.8 for what Classic Menu looks like in action.

I don't use it. It's not that there's anything inherently wrong with Classic Menu, but I've got LaunchBar and DragThing already. So I don't need yet another program to keep my frequently used items handy—they're handy enough as it is. But for those of you who were hooked on OS 9's Apple menu (which I wasn't—DragThing worked in OS 9 for years before becoming an OS X app), you may prefer it to other organizer/launcher programs.

Figure 6.8
It's a classic all right, down to its retro rainbow icon.

If you do prefer it, don't forget to add it to your Login system Preference pane so it's always available.

More Classic Hints and Tips

Here are two more tips I've found helpful when dealing with Classic.

Documents That Keep Trying to Launch a Classic Application

Sooner or later you'll encounter a document that, when you double-click it, wants to launch a Classic program. It's especially vexing when Classic isn't running and you don't want that program to open the file anyway.

Here's a great example: For a long time my main word processor was Microsoft Word 2001, a Classic application. Then, Word v.X came out, and I no longer wanted to use Word 2001. One solution would have been to delete the Word 2001 (Classic) application, but I was afraid I might need it someday. So I found another solution, which is one that you may find helpful for any document you would prefer to open in an application other than the one it currently opens in:

1. Select the recalcitrant document and choose File|Show Info (or use the keyboard shortcut Command+I).

2. Choose Open With Application from the pop-up menu.

3. Click the icon to the left of the application's name. A menu appears with other programs you can choose to open this document, as shown in Figure 6.9.

I choose Microsoft Word 10.0.0 (a.k.a. Word v.X) as shown, and from that moment forward, when I double-click this document, Word 10 opens, not Word 2001 (or Classic).

Furthermore, because I want every Word document to open in Word 10.0.0, I clicked Change All. Now, any time I open a Microsoft Word file, the OS X version launches, not the Classic version.

If the program you want isn't in the menu, choose Other from the menu and select the application you desire.

A Solution for Printers That Aren't Supported in OS X

Here's a tip that will save your bacon if you can't use your printer in OS X. When I first began using OS X, I had an older Epson Stylus Photo 750 printer that wasn't supported by Apple or Epson in OS X, which meant I could not print anything from an OS X application. Printing from Classic, however, worked fine. The solution I

Figure 6.9
Choosing a different program to open a document.

6

quickly figured out was that I could use OS X's built-in PDF support (part of the Quartz graphics layer) to save a PDF file, then open that file in the Classic version of Adobe Acrobat, which printed it quickly and painlessly.

Here's a quick blow-by-blow description of how it's done:

1. In your OS X program (with the document active), choose File|Print (or use the keyboard shortcut Command+P).

2. Choose Output Options from the pop-up menu.

3. Click the Save As File checkbox.

4. Choose PDF from the pop-up Format menu.

Figure 6.10 shows how this looks.

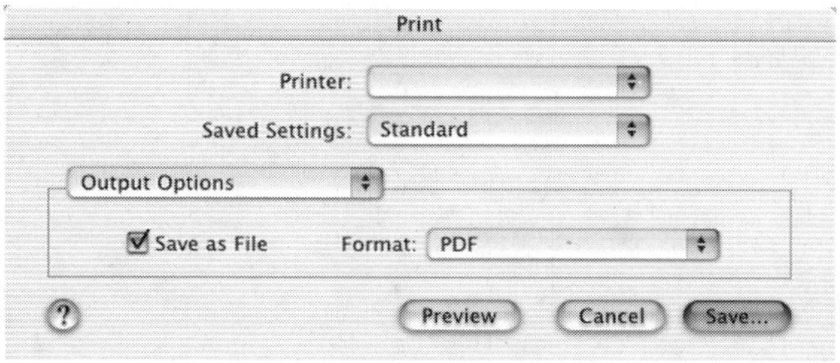

Figure 6.10
Printing a PDF file to disk.

Okay, that's the first half of the equation. The second is to open this PDF in a Classic app to print it. So, find your Classic version of Adobe Acrobat Reader.

TIP

The copy of Acrobat Reader that comes with Mac OS X 10.1 (in the Applications folder) is for OS X only. If you don't have an OS 9 version on your hard disk, download one from Adobe (**www.adobe.com**). It's free.

If you have Adobe Acrobat Reader 4, you're golden. Drag the PDF document you just created onto the Adobe Acrobat Reader 4 icon. Classic will launch (if it's not already running). Now choose File|Print (or use the keyboard shortcut Command+P). And that's it.

If you have Adobe Acrobat Reader 5 (but not the copy that was bundled with OS X, which, as I said, is for OS X only), there's one additional step. Select the Acrobat Reader icon and choose File|Show Info (or use the keyboard shortcut Command+I). In the Show Info window, click the Open In The Classic Environment checkbox, as shown in Figure 6.11.

NOTE

You must have your printer selected in the OS 9 Chooser for this to work.

TIP

Although the Open in The Classic Environment checkbox is a nice feature, not every program has it. It exists only in "Carbonized dual-boot" programs, which are capable of running under both OS 9 and OS X. The only way to find out if you can force a particular program to launch in Classic is to select the application's icon and Show Info (Command+I). If the checkbox is there, bingo; if it's not, then it's "sorry Charlie."

Close the Show Info window (optional), then drag the PDF document you just created onto the Acrobat Reader icon you just Classic-ified, then choose File|Print (or use the keyboard shortcut Command+P).

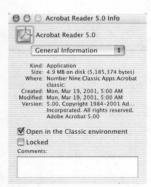

Figure 6.11
Telling Acrobat Reader 5 to open in Classic.

Hardware That Makes Your Mac More Powerful

It's said that, "You can never be too rich or too thin." I don't know if that's true, but as far as I'm concerned, "You can never have too much RAM, too much storage space, or too fast a processor."

There is no such thing as too much RAM, too big a hard disk, or too fast a processor. At least I've never heard anyone complain about it. RAM, disks, and processors may not be sexy, but they are all absolutely essential and the first place to consider spending your hard-earned money. Only after your RAM, storage, and processor are the best that they can be should you think about spending more dough on all those other drool-worthy pieces of hardware.

Some fabulous hardware products are available for the Mac. Some save you time, some save you money, and some are just fun to have. And the best ones, if you're lucky, do all of the above. But hardware usually isn't cheap, and unlike software, you can't usually try hardware before you buy it—there are no downloadable demos, and you won't find RAM or a CD burner on the CD-of-the-month you get from your favorite Mac magazine.

So here's Dr. Mac's immutable law of hardware purchasing: You absolutely and positively must resist the temptation to buy every Mac device you see in *MacAddict* or *Macworld*. Ask any long-time Mac user about hardware purchases they wish they'd never made. The vast majority will let out a long sigh, roll their eyes toward the heavens, and launch into a horror story or two (or three or four).

Of course, I get a lot of hardware to evaluate and review. And, unless it's expensive, the manufacturer usually wants me to keep it (and hopefully, keep using it). So I have a room (actually, two closets and half an attic) full of hardware devices that are so bloody awful I can't bring myself to inflict them on another Mac user.

> **NOTE**
>
> I could give them to people I hate, but there are very few people I hate, and even fewer who use Macs.

This chapter will help you avoid making expensive mistakes. We'll look at a broad spectrum of killer hardware products, but we'll begin with the three I consider most crucial to your powerfulness: RAM, storage, and processors.

RAM Cram

This is relatively simple: If you haven't installed additional Random Access Memory (RAM) in your Mac, you don't have enough. Even Apple's best-equipped Macs, the top-of-the-line models, which come with 256MB, don't have enough. Or at least they don't have enough to take full advantage of Mac OS X's two greatest strengths: Protected memory and preemptive multitasking.

If you don't know how much RAM is in your Mac, choose Apple Menu|About This Mac. The amount of RAM you have appears just below the version number, as shown in Figure 7.1.

Figure 7.1
A gig and a quarter of RAM is about right for my needs.

My Mac came with 256MB of RAM and now has 1.2GB of RAM; the additional gigabyte cost me around $100 and is worth every penny.

If you're a former Mac OS 9 user, you probably noticed that the About This Mac window no longer displays the memory allocation and usage levels for individual programs. That's because Mac OS X automatically manages memory and its usage (YEA!). This is different from earlier incarnations of Mac OS.

If you're into that kind of thing, I'm going to show you where to find memory allocation and usage levels of OS X in a moment.

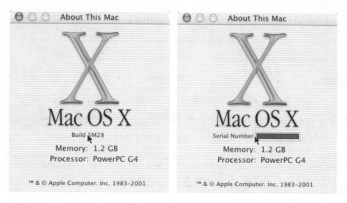

Figure 7.2
Click the version number and you'll see the build number (left); click again and you'll see your Mac's serial number (right).

Though this may be a bit off-topic, as long as you have the About This Mac window open, click the version number, as shown in Figure 7.2, and you'll see the "build" number take its place (left window in Figure 7.2). Click there again and your Mac's serial number takes its place (right window in Figure 7.2). Although this trick is not particularly useful most of the time, there will come a day when you need to know one or both of these bits of information about your Mac. Now you know where to find them.

NOTE

I'm not sure why I bothered, but I obscured my serial number in Figure 7.2. Yours, of course, will not have a dorky gray rectangle—it'll have your Mac's actual serial number.

Memory and Virtual Memory

With Mac OS X, memory (RAM) is good, and virtual memory (VM) is bad. Even though virtual memory is several orders of magnitude better in OS X than it was in OS 9, you still want to avoid it if possible.

As I explained in Chapter 6, when you don't have enough RAM for the operating system and all your open applications, OS X uses your hard disk as a substitute. Hard drives are much slower than RAM; to avoid the slowdown, you need plenty of RAM. I'll show you how to monitor RAM usage in the next section, and how you can tell if your Mac is using VM, but for now, here's a quick overview.

Mac OS X, as I said in Chapter 6, can run on a Mac with 64MB of RAM without Classic, or on a Mac with 128MB with it. But you plan to use your Mac for more than just running OS X, don't you? You do want to use an application or two, don't you? In that case, you need more RAM than what Apple calls the "minimum system requirement."

Mac OS X uses darn close to 64MB (or 128MB if you're using Classic) all by itself. So if that's all the RAM you have, as soon as you begin launching applications, it starts using VM and substituting slow hard disk for the fast RAM you don't have.

When you don't have enough RAM available, the more things you open—programs and documents—the slower your Mac runs. You'll feel a pause when you switch from one program to another, and you'll see the spinning "beach-ball" cursor when you scroll through pages, or search within a document, or do almost anything.

If you have enough RAM, on the other hand, and all your open applications and documents are running in RAM space instead of virtual RAM space, almost every-thing about your Mac will feel faster. Programs will launch faster. Features in your programs—such as find, replace, and formatting in text-oriented programs, or filters and transformations in graphics-oriented programs—will run noticeably faster. Switching between programs will be faster. To sum things up, the more RAM you give it, the better OS X will perform.

Optimizing Your RAM Usage

In order to know if you're using VM, you need to know how much RAM your system software, applications, and processes (i.e., pieces of the system software or programs) are using. Fortunately, a number of tools can help you get a handle on what's going on under the hood, including two you already have (they came with Mac OS X) and several more you'll find links to at **www.boblevitus.com/xfiles.html**.

Here's how to check it out. We'll start with the programs that came with OS X— ProcessViewer and Terminal, then move on to shareware and freeware programs you may like better. In any event, you'll know a lot of different ways to check out what your Mac is doing with your RAM at any given moment.

Using ProcessViewer to View RAM Usage

We'll start with ProcessViewer, because it's a little easier to use and understand than Terminal:

1. Open the ProcessViewer application (which is located in the Utilities folder in your Applications folder, which should be at root level on your boot disk).

2. Look at the right-hand column, "% Memory," which indicates the current per-centage of available RAM that is in use by an application or process.

Figure 7.3 shows what mine looks like as I write this.

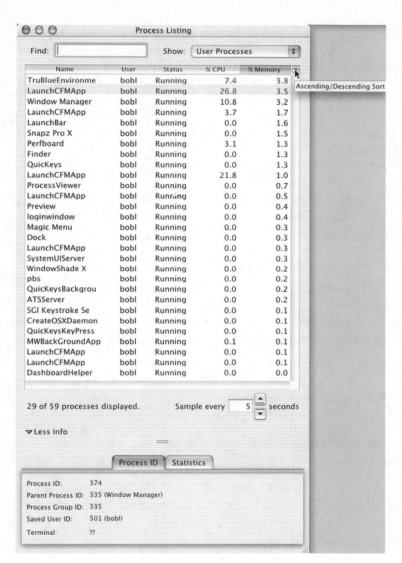

Figure 7.3
My ProcessViewer in all its glory.

Here are some tips and observations about ProcessViewer and Figure 7.3:

■ Some processes use 0.0 percent or 0.1 percent. This is normal.

■ Memory usage will fluctuate, depending on what your applications and processes are doing at the instant ProcessViewer examines (i.e., "samples") them. This is also normal.

- Not all applications display their proper names. For example, the Launch CFM Application item that's highlighted and using 26.8 percent of my processor and 3.5 percent of my RAM, is actually Microsoft Word v.X. This name game drives me batty, but it's a function of Mac OS X's Unix roots and is unlikely to change. Sigh.

> **NOTE**
>
> Although 3.5 percent sounds like a small amount of RAM, remember that my Mac has 1,280MB of RAM. So 3.5 percent translates into 44.8MB of RAM for Word alone. See what I mean about needing a lot of the stuff (RAM)?

- All your Classic applications and the Classic environment itself appear as a single process called TruBlueEnvironme. As you can see, it uses a substantial amount of CPU and RAM.

- ProcessViewer is listed because it is a running application.

- You can sort the list by clicking the header of any column. In Figure 7.3, I've clicked Memory and the list is sorted from highest percentage to lowest. To reverse the sorting order, I would click where you see the arrow cursor (immediately to the left of the tool tip that says Ascending/Descending Sort).

- You can pretty much ignore the Process ID and Statistics tabs at the bottom. They're useful only if you're going to use Terminal to act on a process, something most of you probably won't be doing much.

- You can "kill" a process by choosing Processes|Quit Process or using the keyboard shortcut Command+Shift+Q. A dialog box will appear offering you the choice of quitting, force quitting, or canceling.

In Figure 7.3 you see only my User Processes—29 out of the 59 processes that are currently running. To see the other processes—Administrator (28 processes), NetBoot (2 processes), or All (all 59 processes), make the appropriate selection from the pop-up Show menu. The results appear in Figure 7.4.

> **TIP**
>
> You can't kill processes you don't own. But you can see if an administrator or NetBoot process is sucking up a lot of RAM or CPU.

When you're done looking, choose ProcessViewer|Quit ProcessViewer or use the shortcut Command+Q to quit.

Okay. You now know as much about ProcessViewer as anyone outside of Cupertino.

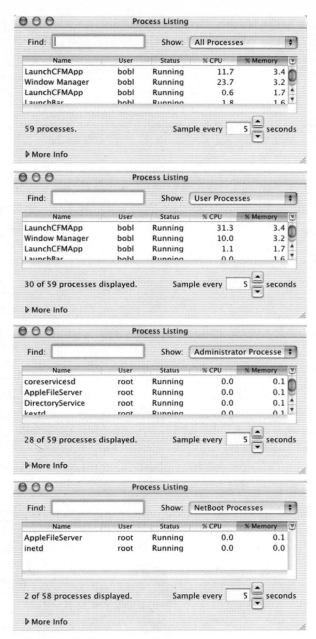

Figure 7.4
View some or all of your processes with the Show menu.

Using Terminal (top) to View RAM Usage

Now let's look at using the Terminal program and the Unix **top** utility, which provides even more detailed information about where your RAM is going.

> **NOTE**
>
> If you've never used Terminal before, don't worry: This process entails typing four keys and won't harm anything. If you're nervous about using the Terminal or Unix, read Chapters 10 and 11, then come back to this. But you don't need to—this is simple and harmless.

1. Open the Terminal application (which is located in the Utilities folder in your Applications folder, which should be at root level on your boot disk).

2. Type "top" then press Return.

That's all there is to it—you've just opened the Unix **top** utility in a Terminal window. Give yourself a pat on the back.

Figure 7.5 shows what mine looks like.

The fifth and sixth rows (from the top of the window) are PhysMem and VM. Those are the two that are most important to you. PhysMem indicates overall physical RAM usage and VM tells you about virtual memory usage.

Below that, you'll see a series of columns. The two columns on the right, RSIZE and VSIZE, tell you about physical and virtual memory usage for each running application or process. RSIZE tells you how much physical RAM is being used by the application or process, in megabytes (M) or kilobytes (K). VSIZE tells you how much virtual memory Mac OS X has assigned for this process or application, in megabytes (M) or gigabytes (G).

Don't worry if it looks like you're using a lot of VM. As you can see, even on my Mac with 1.2GB of physical RAM, most of my programs and processes are using a substantial amount of VM. That's how Unix works, but it's not the part that's important. What is important is whether or not VM is "paging out," which is the part of VM that slows your Mac down. If you look at that sixth row (VM) again, you'll see that while I'm using a ton of VM, there are 0 page outs, which is as good as it gets.

The other important number to notice is the number at the end of the fifth row, which tells you how much physical RAM is still available (free). In my case, I've got 633MB free, which means I can open quite a few additional applications before I begin seeing page outs that will slow things down.

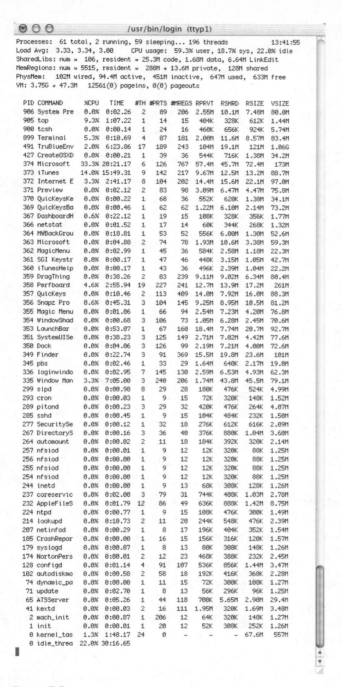

```
● ○ ○                    /usr/bin/login (ttyp1)
Processes:  61 total, 2 running, 59 sleeping... 196 threads          13:41:55
Load Avg:  3.33, 3.34, 3.00    CPU usage: 59.3% user, 18.7% sys, 22.0% idle
SharedLibs: num =  106, resident = 25.3M code, 1.68M data, 6.64M LinkEdit
MemRegions: num = 5515, resident = 288M + 13.6M private, 128M shared
PhysMem:  102M wired, 94.4M active, 451M inactive, 647M used, 633M free
VM: 3.75G + 47.3M  12561(0) pageins, 0(0) pageouts

  PID COMMAND      %CPU   TIME    #TH #PRTS #MREGS RPRVT  RSHRD  RSIZE  VSIZE
  906 System Pre   0.0% 0:02.26    2    89   206  2.55M  10.1M  7.48M  80.0M
  905 top          9.3% 1:07.22    1    14    15   404K   328K   612K  1.44M
  900 tcsh         0.0% 0:00.14    1    24    16   460K   656K   924K  5.74M
  899 Terminal     5.3% 0:10.69    4    87   181  2.00M  11.6M  8.57M  83.4M
  491 TruBlueEnv   2.0% 6:23.86   17   189   243   104M  19.1M   121M  1.06G
  427 CreateOSXD   0.0% 0:00.21    1    39    36   544K   716K  1.38M  34.2M
  374 Microsoft   33.3% 20:21.17   6   126   767  57.4M  45.7M  72.4M   173M
  373 iTunes      14.0% 15:49.31   9   142   217  9.67M  12.5M  13.2M  88.7M
  372 Internet E   3.3% 2:41.17    8   104   202  14.4M  15.6M  22.1M  97.0M
  371 Preview      0.0% 0:02.12    2    83    98  3.09M  6.47M  4.47M  75.8M
  370 QuickKeysKe  0.0% 0:00.22    1    68    36   552K   620K  1.38M  34.1M
  369 QuickKeysBa  0.0% 0:00.46    1    62    62  1.22M  6.10M  2.14M  73.2M
  367 DashboardH   0.6% 0:22.12    1    19    15   108K   328K   356K  1.77M
  366 netstat      0.0% 0:01.52    1    17    14    60K   344K   268K  1.32M
  364 MWBackGrou   0.0% 0:18.81    1    53    52   556K  6.00M  1.30M  52.6M
  363 Microsoft    0.0% 0:04.88    2    74    78  1.93M  10.6M  3.38M  59.3M
  362 MagicMenu    0.0% 0:02.99    1    45    36   584K  2.58M  1.18M  22.3M
  361 SGI Keystr   0.0% 0:00.17    1    47    46   448K  3.15M  1.05M  42.7M
  360 iTunesHelp   0.0% 0:00.17    1    43    36   496K  2.39M  1.04M  22.2M
  359 DragThing    0.0% 0:38.26    2    83   239  9.11M  9.02M  6.34M  80.4M
  358 Perfboard    4.6% 2:55.94   19   227   241  12.7M  13.9M  17.2M   261M
  357 QuickKeys    0.0% 0:10.46    2   113   409  14.0M  7.92M  16.0M  88.3M
  356 Snapz Pro    0.6% 0:45.31    3   104   145  9.25M  8.95M  10.5M  81.2M
  355 Magic Menu   0.0% 0:01.06    1    66    94  2.54M  7.23M  4.20M  76.8M
  354 WindowShad   0.0% 0:00.68    3   106    73  1.05M  6.28M  2.45M  70.6M
  353 LaunchBar    0.0% 0:53.07    1    67   160  18.4M  7.74M  20.7M  92.7M
  351 SystemUISe   0.0% 0:38.23    3   125   149  2.71M  7.02M  4.42M  77.6M
  350 Dock         0.0% 0:04.06    3   126    99  2.19M  7.21M  4.00M  72.6M
  349 Finder       0.0% 0:22.74    3    91   369  15.5M  19.8M  23.6M   101M
  345 pbs          0.0% 0:02.46    1    33    29  1.64M   640K  2.17M  19.0M
  336 loginwindo   0.0% 0:02.95    7   145   130  2.59M  6.53M  4.93M  62.3M
  335 Window Man   3.3% 7:05.00    3   240   206  1.74M  43.8M  45.5M  79.1M
  299 slpd         0.0% 0:00.98    8    29    28   180K   476K   524K  4.99M
  293 cron         0.0% 0:00.03    1     9    15    72K   320K   148K  1.52M
  289 pitond       0.0% 0:00.23    3    29    32   420K   476K   264K  4.07M
  285 sshd         0.0% 0:00.45    1     9    15   104K   484K   232K  1.50M
  277 SecuritySe   0.0% 0:00.12    1    32    18   276K   612K   616K  2.09M
  267 DirectoryS   0.0% 0:00.16    3    36    40   376K   880K  1.04M  3.60M
  264 automount    0.0% 0:00.02    2    11    18   184K   392K   320K  2.14M
  257 nfsiod       0.0% 0:00.01    1     9    12    12K   320K    88K  1.25M
  256 nfsiod       0.0% 0:00.00    1     9    12    12K   320K    88K  1.25M
  255 nfsiod       0.0% 0:00.00    1     9    12    12K   320K    88K  1.25M
  254 nfsiod       0.0% 0:00.00    1     9    12    12K   320K    88K  1.25M
  244 inetd        0.0% 0:00.00    1     9    13    68K   308K   128K  1.26M
  237 coreservic   0.0% 0:02.00    3    79    31   744K   408K  1.03M  2.78M
  232 AppleFileS   0.0% 0:01.79   12    86    49   636K   888K  1.42M  8.75M
  224 ntpd         0.0% 0:00.77    1     9    15   108K   476K   300K  1.49M
  214 lookupd      0.0% 0:10.73    2    11    20   244K   548K   476K  2.39M
  207 netinfod     0.0% 0:00.29    1     8    17   196K   404K   352K  1.54M
  185 CrashRepor   0.0% 0:00.00    1    16    15   156K   316K   120K  1.57M
  179 syslogd      0.0% 0:00.07    1     8    13    80K   308K   148K  1.26M
  174 NortonPers   0.0% 0:00.01    2    12    23   468K   388K   232K  2.45M
  128 configd      0.0% 0:01.14    4    91   107   536K   856K  1.44M  3.47M
  102 autodiskmo   0.0% 0:00.58    2    58    18   192K   416K   368K  2.28M
   74 dynamic_pa   0.0% 0:00.00    1    11    15    72K   300K   108K  1.27M
   71 update       0.0% 0:02.70    1     8    13    56K   296K    96K  1.25M
   65 ATSServer    0.0% 0:05.26    1    44   118   700K  5.65M  2.90M  29.4M
   41 kextd        0.0% 0:00.03    2    16   111  1.95M   320K  1.69M  3.48M
    2 mach_init    0.0% 0:00.87    1   206    12    64K   320K   148K  1.27M
    1 init         0.0% 0:00.01    1    20    12    52K   308K   252K  1.26M
    0 kernel_tas   1.3% 1:48.17   24     0     -      -      -  67.6M   557M
    0 idle_threa  22.0% 30:16.65
```

7

Figure 7.5
Don't be intimidated by all those numbers—it's only the Unix utility called **top**.

When you are finished with **top**, press the *Q* key to exit the **top** utility, then choose Terminal|Quit Terminal, or use the shortcut Command+Q, to quit the Terminal program.

Here are some tips and observations about **top** and Figure 7.5 (if some of this sounds repetitive, it's because top and ProcessViewer are very much alike and gather their information from the same Unix sources):

- Some processes use very little RAM, such as 64K. This is normal.

- Not all applications display their proper names. For example, Microsoft Word v.X appears as just Microsoft. That said, **top** uses somewhat more descriptive names than ProcessViewer for most programs and processes.

- As with ProcessViewer, all your Classic applications and the Classic environment itself appear as a single process called TruBlueEnv. As you can see, it still uses a substantial amount of CPU and RAM.

- **top** is listed because it is a running (Unix) process.

- Type "man top" at the prompt in Terminal for more information on **top**.

> **NOTE**
>
> **man** is a Unix command to display a program or process's user manual. So **man top** will show you the user's manual for the **top** utility. You'll find a discussion of the **man** command (and some software that makes it easier to use—it's not very much fun reading those pages in Terminal) in Chapter 10.

To conclude this little segment, I need to tell you that I learned almost all of what I know about ProcessViewer and **top** from Apple's searchable Knowledge Base (**http://kbase.info.apple.com**). The Knowledge Base is a valuable, free tool that leads you to useful Apple articles using a combination of natural language search (using your own words) and questions. If you haven't tried it before, check it out and bookmark it right this second—it's that good.

Shareware and Freeware RAM Monitoring Utilities

I know of at least three freeware or shareware utilities that, among other things, help you keep an eye on what's going on with RAM and VM. I've used all of them at some time over the past year and they each have something to recommend them (or I wouldn't bother with them here), but I've settled on one of them, Perfboard (formerly Dashboard), as the one I run 24/7. It's in my Login Items, and I never quit it, so it's always there.

Perfboard provides feedback on what's going on under your Mac's proverbial hood: CPU usage (complete with a gauge, no less), loads (how busy Unix is), memory, network, and disk I/O.

TIP

Perfboard includes a manual in PDF form (called, imaginatively enough, Manual.pdf) that explains how each measurement works in some detail. If you're really interested in what Perfboard is measuring and what those measurements mean, it's highly recommended.

Figure 7.6 shows what Perfboard's little window looks like.

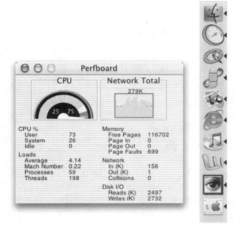

Figure 7.6
Perfboard packs a lot of information into a very small window.

As you can see, I included the Dock in this picture so you can see that I have 10 applications running. (I actually have more than that, but the others, such as Snapz Pro X and StuffIt Deluxe's Magic Menu, don't show up in the dock, so you can't tell from this picture.) From the top, those programs are: Finder, Perfboard, QuicKeys, DragStrip, Preview, Internet Explorer, iTunes, Word, Photoshop (running in Classic), and System Preferences.

So that's how I'm using my Mac as I write this. Now, here's what Perfboard has to say about it and how I interpret it.

(Counterclockwise from CPU in Figure 7.6): The CPU needle is pinned to the redline (all the way to the right) in the gauge. Below that, you can see that 0 percent of my CPU is idle. That basically means I'm using all of my Mac's processing power at this moment.

I'm not sure how to interpret those Loads numbers, so I pretty much ignore them. (I can see that 59 processes are running, as they were last time we looked with ProcessViewer. The manual explains it further, but they still don't mean much to me.)

The Disk I/O (input/output, a.k.a. reads/writes) numbers are high because I'm copying a 200MB folder from one volume to another in the background.

The Network In number is high because I've got a streaming video of Pink Floyd running in the background (in Internet Explorer).

> **NOTE**
>
> If I were sending mail or copying a file to a remote location via FTP, the Out number would be high, too. But I'm not, so it's not.

Finally, the two things I care most about: Free Pages and Page Out. Free Pages is similar to Free RAM in **top**—the closer it gets to zero, the less RAM I have available, and the more page outs I will see. In Figure 7.6, I'm not having any page outs, which tells me I still have free memory. Think of Free Pages and Page Outs as opposite sides of the same coin. When one is high, the other is low, and vice versa.

The Network Total graph above the memory statistics is user-configurable—you can choose any of the statistics below and graph it over time.

Perfboard is freeware; you'll find a link for it on this book's companion Web site.

Two other programs in a similar vein are GMem (also mentioned in Chapter 1), and VMometer. If you're short of screen real estate, both of these display their information right in the Dock, as shown in Figure 7.7.

Figure 7.7
VMometer and GMem use their dock icons to provide feedback about RAM usage.

> **NOTE**
>
> Unfortunately, GMem has a bug that causes the text to display in odd colors, regardless of your choices in GMem Preferences, often making it illegible. Email to the developer asking if a fix was ever going to be posted went unanswered. You might want to check the Web site for an update: **http://g-utilities.com**.

OK, now let's talk about buying more RAM.

How and Where to Buy RAM

The most important thing to remember is that RAM is a commodity. That means it doesn't matter who made it, it's all pretty much the same. If you buy RAM from a reputable dealer, it'll either work when you install it, or it won't. And if it doesn't work, which is rare, a reputable dealer will make it right by either swapping it for new chips or refunding your money.

RAM comes in many different "flavors." You'll hear terms such as, "SDRAM," "EDO," "DRAM," "PC100," "PC133," "ECC," and more. Ignore them. All you need to know is what Mac model you have. RAM vendors will sell you the correct RAM as long as you know what model it's going into.

> **TIP**
>
> If they don't or can't, find another vendor who can, and who understands Macs.

One thing to consider is that some Macs can use RAM that runs at two different speeds, measured in nanoseconds (ns). Here's an example: My Power Mac G4s' (a G4/500 and G4 Cube) manuals specify "PC100" RAM. That means they use 100 ns chips. But both models can also use PC133 RAM, which runs at 133 ns. Faster RAM doesn't make a Mac run faster, but there is a reason to consider it—PC100 chips can't be used in the next-generation G4 models (known as "QuickSilver"), but PC133 chips can.

So when I bought RAM for my G4s, I ordered the PC133 chips. The down side is that my current Macs can't use the extra 33 ns of speed, so I may have paid a little more than I had to. The up side is that when I get a new Mac, I can pull the RAM out of my current Mac(s) and pop it into the new one.

You can find the best prices for RAM at mail-order vendors, mostly via the Internet. Even if you don't plan to buy it on the Internet you should check prices there before you plunk down a penny. Many retail operations, such as CompUSA, price their RAM a lot higher than mail-order vendors. The only storefront operation I know of that offers competitive prices on RAM is Fry's Electronics. So if you're lucky enough to have a Fry's store nearby, it's usually a good bet.

The best place I've found on the Internet to shop for RAM are DealRam (**http://dealram.com**) and RamSeeker (**www.ramseeker.com**). Neither of them actually sells RAM, but both monitor the prices of dozens of mail-order vendors, and display the prices in an easy to read grid, with links to the vendor. Figure 7.8 shows what RamSeeker looks like.

7

Figure 7.8
Comparing RAM prices at **ramseeker.com**.

Here's my RAM buying advice: Visit **ramseeker.com** or **dealram.com** first, then check out some of the low-priced vendors and order from whichever one tickles your fancy. They're all, for the most part, selling the same chips made in the same factories. You'll notice that some of them sell name-brand RAM for more money. I don't buy it. RAM is RAM. If the chip works when you install it, it's going to work until your Mac dies.

I've always bought the lowest priced generic RAM, and I've never had a problem. If you're a name-brand kind of person, go ahead and spend the extra money, but as far as I can tell, the stuff all works the same.

One thing you should avoid at all costs (pun intended) is buying RAM from Apple. Their prices are among the highest on the planet. When you order a new Mac, order it with the least amount of RAM you can, then buy your RAM somewhere else for a lot less money.

Last but certainly not least, always pay with a credit card.

> **NOTE**
>
> This applies to all your hardware purchases, not just RAM. That way, if there's any problem whatsoever, you have some recourse. If you pay by check or cash and later have a dispute, you are likely to be out of luck; with a credit card, you can almost always get your credit card company to fight the battle for you.

An Apology for Being So Longwinded

If you're wondering why I rambled on and on about RAM, and took up half the chapter doing so, here's the answer: Because this is a book about becoming a power user, and understanding how RAM works and how yours is working is something any power user worth his salt should know like the back of his hand. Plus, I wanted to explain how you examine what's happening "under the hood," and what better place could there be than this section? Finally, I'd have felt guilty if I had just said, "You probably need more," and left it at that.

Mass(ive) Storage

This section is shorter than the one about RAM. I happen to know that your Mac almost certainly came with 4GB or more of hard disk storage built in.

> **NOTE**
>
> How did I know? If your Mac is capable of running OS X, your hard disk is at least 4GB. And how did I know *that*? According to the complete database of Apple products (**www.info.apple.com/applespec/applespec.taf**), the smallest hard drive in a G3 model (the earliest models supported by OS X) is 4GB.

For many users, 4GB will last a lifetime without filling up, but for others, even 40GB isn't enough. And, if you work with video, audio, or even high-resolution images, you may need even more than that.

The Many Faces of Mass Storage

Mac users have many options for adding storage to their computer—FireWire versus USB versus SCSI versus ATA, hard drives, removable magnetic media, optical drives, tape drives, and more. My intention here is to discuss the most popular storage options, and help you decide if you need more storage, and if so, which type will best suit your needs.

External vs. Internal

The first choice is whether to add storage internally or externally. If you have an iMac, iBook, or G4 Cube, it's a no-brainer—you can't *add* additional internal storage devices because there's no room for them. You could replace your existing hard disk with a larger one but I don't recommend that unless you don't have FireWire, as I'll explain in a moment.

If you have a PowerBook, you may have a "bay" that allows you to swap internal storage devices. My old PowerBook had a CD-ROM module and a floppy disk module. But modules for PowerBooks are significantly more expensive than external FireWire devices, so you should consider whether having it builtin is worth the extra money.

Finally, if you have a G3 or G4 desktop model, there are internal bays for adding storage. Once again, I don't recommend this unless your desk space is extremely constrained and adding an external device would be a hardship.

I am dead set against adding internal storage devices unless there is no other option. For one thing, if an internal device breaks, you have to disassemble your Mac to have it fixed, which I consider a hassle. But more importantly, if you choose an internal device, you can use it with only that one Mac. On the other hand, you can move an external device from one Mac to another quickly and easily. Or, if you sell your old Mac, you can keep the device and use it with you new Mac.

These days you don't even have to shut down or restart to connect or disconnect most external devices—almost all USB and FireWire drives are "hot swappable."

ALERT!

You do have to dismount (hard disk) or eject the disk or media (most other storage devices) before you disconnect it or you risk damage to the drive or media. See your manual for info on how to properly disconnect your particular device.

So, I never install additional storage devices in my Macs—I always choose an external model.

Alphabet Soup: IEEE 1394 (a.k.a. FireWire) USB, SCSI, ATAPI, and So On

Before we get into the specific storage devices, let's look at how you connect internal and external storage devices to a Macintosh.

Let's start with definitions:

■ *Universal Serial Bus (USB)*—A cross-platform standard for connecting peripheral devices to personal computers. It's best used for less-demanding devices, such as keyboards, mice, drawing tablets, and so on. You can use it for storage, but if you can choose another bus, such as FireWire or SCSI, or any internal bus, it will be much faster. All Macs that are capable of running OS X have USB ports.

■ *FireWire*—Apple's implementation of the IEEE 1394 High Performance Serial Bus standard (which is the same one Sony calls iLINK). It's a cross-platform standard for connecting and using digital peripheral devices (such as DV camcorders) and storage (all types). It's very fast and probably the most popular choice for external storage. Most Macs that are capable of running OS X have FireWire ports.

■ *Small Computer Systems Interface (SCSI)*—The high-speed bus used by Macs prior to FireWire. It can be faster than FireWire, but to use it with a desktop Mac, you'll need a PCI card called a *SCSI controller*. SCSI is no longer standard equipment on any Mac model; it's available only as an aftermarket add-on.

■ *AT Attachment; (often referred to as IDE ATA)*—A family of internal busses that support one or two internal devices. There are a variety of flavors—ATA-2, ATA-3, ATA-4, and ATAPI, each with slightly different features. All desktop Macs have some type of ATA bus internally.

> **NOTE**
>
> All desktop Macs include a printed manual that explains what flavor of ATA you have, and how to install an internal device.

I spent more than an hour looking for a comparison of the various busses and their speeds, but the best I could find was a table in the Apple Knowledge Base that doesn't include any of the ATA varieties. Still, it's better than nothing; it appears as Figure 7.9.

Most users choose FireWire for external and ATA for internal. Although USB can be slightly less expensive for an external device, it's also a lot slower. You can use SCSI internally or externally, but the drives are more expensive than FireWire drives, and you'll have to buy a PCI SCSI controller card, too. Unless you do extremely demanding graphics, audio, or video processing, FireWire is a better and less expensive choice.

Finally, some vendors offer storage devices with both USB and FireWire connections. You can't use them both at once, but this setup does offer additional flexibility and

Below is a comparison of speeds of different technologies, from slowest to fastest. Please note that these are theoretical maximum throughputs of the different technology.

Technology	Theoretical Maximum Throughput
Apple Desktop Bus (ADB)	0.01 Mbps or 10 Kbps
Serial Port	0.23 Mbps or 230 Kbps
Geoport Port	2 Mbps
USB at low data transfer rate	1.5 Mbps
USB at high data transfer rate	12 Mbps
FireWire	400 Mbps
SCSI	1-40 MB/sec
Fast SCSI	8-80 MB/sec
Ultra SCSI-3	18-160 MB/sec

Document Information
Product Area: iMac
Category: USB
Sub Category: Features
Keywords: kimac

Figure 7.9
Transfer speeds of USB, FireWire, and several flavors of SCSI compared.

usually doesn't cost much more than a similar FireWire-only device. These hybrids are worth considering, especially if you have a Mac (or Macs) that don't have FireWire.

Okay, it's time to look at the different types of storage devices.

Hard Disk

As I told you in Chapter 3, in 1989 I paid $2,500 for a 40MB external SCSI hard disk and considered it a bargain at that. Today you can buy a 40GB external FireWire hard disk (that's roughly 1,000 times the size of my first hard drive) for 10 percent ($250) of what I paid for that first one. Or less.

Drive speed is measured in many ways—transfer rate, sustained transfer rate, seek time, revolutions per minute (RPM), and about six others. It is totally confusing and makes it extremely tough to compare apples to apples (pun intended—even though Apple no longer sells any storage products that aren't preinstalled). In my estimation, most users can't tell the difference between a 7,200 RPM drive and a 10,000 RPM drive just by using them, anyway.

So, my advice is to look for an inexpensive, high-capacity FireWire drive from a reputable vendor that runs at either 5,400 RPM or 7,200 RPM. It will almost certainly be fast enough, and a "faster" drive won't make your Mac run that much faster. Spend the extra dough on some additional RAM instead.

The exception is users who do extremely demanding work that requires tremendous I/O throughput, such as opening and saving huge (100MB+) files or working with huge digital media files. If you're such a user, you may benefit from a faster drive. And, of course, if you're one of them, you probably have a ton of RAM in your Mac already.

> **TIP**
>
> Read the upcoming sidebar called "Finding a Reputable Storage Vendor/Finding the Best Drive for the Money." It provides some valuable tips you should consider before you spend a single penny.

Optical

Optical drives—drives that read and write data with a laser—have become the standard for moving large amounts of data from a Mac in one location to a computer in another, as well as for creating discs full of music (audio CDs) and video (DVDs).

> **NOTE**
>
> Recording on any type of optical disc is called *burning*. So you don't say, "I'll record a CD," instead, you say, "I'll burn a CD." At least you will if you don't want to people to make fun of you.

Optical drives are rated using an "X" factor. The X factor represents the theoretical top burning speed. Though you'll use your drive to burn data (files) as well as audio discs that work in audio CD players, visualizing this X factor relationship is easier using an audio CD as an example. And so, for example, a 4X CD-R drive can, theoretically, burn a CD with 60 minutes of music in 15 minutes, which is 4X "real time." An 8X drive will theoretically burn it in 7.5 minutes, and so on. Most drives come close to that theoretical limit; my 8X CD-RW drive burns 60 to 80 minute audio CDs in around 10 minutes. You'll see similar results when you burn discs full of data—a disc with 650 or 700MB of files will take around 20–25 minutes to burn on a 4X drive but only 10–12 minutes on an 8X drive.

Here's a quick overview of the different flavors and their capacities:

- *CD-R*—Short for CD-Recordable. A CD-R drive burns 650 or 700MB CD-R discs. CD-Rs can be burned only once. Once you've burned them, you can't add or remove data from them.

  Not too many CD-R drives are sold anymore; these days most drives have both CD-R and CD-RW in the same device.

- *CD-RW*—Short for CD-Rewritable. A CD-RW drive burns 650 or 700MB CD-R discs just like a CD-R drive, but it can also burn 650 or 700MB CD-RW discs. A CD-RW disc, unlike a CD-R, can be erased and reused over and over again.

7

Here are the major differences between CD-R and CD-RW:

- Burning the same data on a CD-RW disc takes up to twice as long (compared to burning it on a CD-R disc).

- Erasing a CD-RW disc takes several minutes. (You can't erase a CD-R disc.)

- CD-R discs are less expensive than CD-RW discs.

- *DVD-R*—Short for DVD-Recordable. A DVD-R drive burns up to 4.7GB of data on a DVD-R disc, and can also burn video DVDs that play in regular old home DVD video players.

Most drives support two or more of these flavors. And Apple's SuperDrive supports all three—CD-R, CD-RW, and DVD-R discs.

Other flavors include DVD-RAM, which read standard DVD discs and burn 4.7GB rewritable DVD cartridges, and DVD-RW, which burn both 4.7GB DVD-R and 4.7 DVD-RW (rewritable) discs. DVD-RAM seems to be going out of style, so I don't recommend it, and DVD-RW is just becoming available, so I can't tell you much about it.

Mac OS X has built-in support for burning data to CD-R, CD-RW, and DVD-R discs without any additional software. iTunes burns audio CDs that play in your home or car CD audio player, and iDVD burns DVDs that you can view on almost any DVD player. That is the good news. The bad news is that it's only guaranteed to work with Apple internal CD-R, CD-RW, and SuperDrives.

> **ALERT!**
>
> Although most external optical drives support burning data discs in OS X without any additional software, iTunes and/or iDVD may or may not support an external drive. Apple's Web site has information about which external drives are supported; check it before buying any external optical drive.

Always buy brand name media (blank discs), and always buy media rated at or above your drive's maximum speed. Cheap off-brand or no-brand discs often fail, as do 8X discs burned on a 24X drive. In either case, you'll end up with a lot of what those in the know call "coasters."

> **NOTE**
>
> They got that name because the only thing you can do with a disc that fails to burn is use it as a drink coaster.

Media prices tend to fluctuate, but to give you an idea, in late 2001, CD-R discs cost well under $1 a piece in quantities of 30 or more, CD-RW discs are usually less than $2 each in quantity, and DVD-R discs recently dropped from $10 to $6 a piece.

> **NOTE**
>
> All of this stuff is in flux. By the time you read this, there may very well be 1.2GB CD-RW drives and 9GB DVD-RW drives or even something totally new. So don't make a decision based on the brief overview in this section. Read the upcoming sidebar called "Finding a Reputable Storage Vendor/Finding the Best Drive for the Money" and follow its advice and you won't go wrong.

Removable Magnetic Media

Removable magnetic media devices use magnetic technology similar to what's in your hard disk, but the disks are inside removable cartridges. With optical storage becoming more ubiquitous every day, the day of the removable magnetic storage device is rapidly drawing to a close. Although Iomega would like you to believe that their Zip, Jaz, or Peerless drives are a viable alternative to CD-R/CD-RW/DVD-R or other optical storage media, I don't buy it. CD-Rs, CD-RWs, and DVD-Rs can be read by almost any Mac user; removable magnetic media cartridges can be read only if you own the same type of drive. And magnetic media cartridges are a lot more expensive than blank optical discs.

Unless somebody forces you (because it's what they use), or you need a lot more speed than you can get from optical media (magnetic is usually much faster than optical—that may be its only advantage), I'd avoid all of these dinosaurs and spend my money on an optical drive.

Tape

Tape drives are a special type of storage device that write data onto a tape cartridge similar to an audiocassette or digital videotape. Tape drives are relatively expensive ($500 to several thousand dollars) and you can use them only with specialized software like Dantz Development's Retrospect. They have two main advantages over other media. First, you can store 20, 40, or even 80GB of data on a single inexpensive tape. Second, if you have a lot of data to archive or back up, you can use them unattended.

Frankly, with DVD-R discs that hold 4.7GB selling for around $6, a tape drive is overkill for most users. About the only reason I can think of for having one is if you're responsible for backing up several Macs (or more) over a network and don't want to hang around to swap discs.

Finding a Reputable Storage Vendor/Finding the Best Drive for the Money

How do you find a reputable storage vendor and how do you figure out which is the best device for the money? I'll tell you how I do it.

First, I scour the Internet looking for reviews and opinions on the devices I'm considering. *Macworld, MacAddict, MacHome,* and others evaluate hardware regularly and are a good place to start. Search engines, such as Google and Ask Jeeves, are also useful, though somewhat more time-consuming.

Then, I visit DealMac (**http://dealmac.com/**) and see what is available cheap. This site rocks for ferreting out the best deals on Mac merchandise, and their discussion boards, which they call DealChat, are among the best and most active on the Web.

Once I've narrowed down my options, I search the forums and message boards at several Web sites (DealMac, MacFixIt, MacInTouch, MacNN, MacObserver, and so on) for messages posted by people who actually bought the devices. I post a message (or messages) asking if anyone has any experience with the device(s) and if they would they recommend it and/or buy it again.

Finally, I contact tech support for the product and pose a question. This gives me some indication of what kind of response time to expect if I have a problem. If they don't respond, or aren't polite, I don't buy their product.

I rarely make a hardware purchase without doing most or all of these things.

The point is, although reviews and manufacturers' descriptions of a product can be helpful, you'll get much better and less biased information from people who actually plunked down their own hard-earned cash for one and use it every day.

Faster Processors

You have two options for increasing your processor speed—upgrade your existing processor or buy a new Mac. Now, I don't want to disparage the processor upgrade manufacturers, but the truth is, I never upgrade. If I need more speed, I sell my old Mac and buy a new one. I do it about every year or 18 months and I think, for the money, it's the way to go.

Here are some of the reasons I prefer getting a new Mac to upgrading an old one:

- *Upgrades can be temperamental.* Some software and hardware that works on a stock Mac balks if it finds an upgraded processor. I admit this has become somewhat less likely in the past couple of years, but I prefer not to risk it.

■ *An upgrade makes only your processor faster, whereas a new Mac usually makes many components (motherboard bus speed, optical drive, hard disk, and so on) faster.* A Mac is a collection of subsystems. Making one of them faster without making others faster doesn't make sense to me.

■ *New Macs today are much less expensive than they were 10 years ago.* Back then, when a top-of-the-line Mac cost $5,000 or more, processor upgrades and accelerator cards were often the most cost-effective solution. Today, with low-end G4 models starting at around $1,500, it seems more prudent to go that route than to spend hundreds of dollars jury-rigging an old Mac with a new processor.

■ *In order to feel a significant speed-up, you need a much faster processor than the one you have.* For example, if you upgrade from a G3/300 to a G3/400 you may not notice any difference for some (if not most) tasks.

Also, don't forget that iMacs, PowerBooks, and iBooks are harder to upgrade than desktop and minitower models, if they can even *be* upgraded (some models cannot be upgraded at all). Furthermore, if you can find an upgrade for them, they're more expensive than that same upgrade for a desktop model (i.e., G3 or G4).

I've had great luck selling old Macs (and other hardware) on eBay (**www.ebay.com**). I've often gotten more than I expected for old hardware, and it's virtually painless to list a product for sale.

Speaking of eBay, if you're willing to consider a used Mac, you can often pick up a recent vintage Mac (being sold by someone like me) for a reasonable price. And you often see people listing Mac packages that include software, monitors, input devices, and/or other add-ons, at very reasonable prices.

On the other hand, sometimes economics are more important than getting the fastest Mac. If you're on an extremely tight budget, a processor upgrade may be the only option you can afford. If that's the case, just make sure you already have all the RAM you need, because it will do more for you for less money than a processor upgrade.

Other Hardware

OK, those are the big three. But there are plenty of other devices you can spend money on to soup up your Mac. Let's take a look.

Input Devices

I have not been satisfied with Apple's keyboards and mice since the old ADB Apple Extended Keyboard, which was huge (we called it the "battleship Saratoga" keyboard) but felt great. And they've never made a mouse that I loved.

I have to admit that the latest renditions, the crystal clear Pro keyboard and mouse, are the best Apple has ever offered. But I prefer so-called ergonomic keyboards and multibutton mice or trackballs, so I spend more time and money than most users in search of the perfect keyboard and mouse (or trackball)—in the past year alone I have tried more than a dozen of each.

Input devices are very much a personal preference—you have to get your hands on them to know if they're right for you. Bearing that in mind, I discuss some of my preferences and observations in the next few sections.

Keyboards

I could probably get used to the Apple Pro keyboard if I had to. But because I don't have to, I've been trying out keyboards for as long as I've been using a Mac, and I think I've finally found the one that feels perfect to me. It's an ergonomic keyboard called the Natural Keyboard Pro, and it's made, believe it or not, by Microsoft (**www.microsoft.com**).

It's got the best tactile feedback I've found so far. The keys have exactly the right amount of springiness and don't clickety-clack too much. And the split keyboard design and built-in palm rest (see Figure 7.10) fit my hands almost perfectly and make extended use nearly painless.

Figure 7.10
The Natural Keyboard Pro's split design makes typing all day more comfortable for me.

Now for the bad news. As of this writing, there are no drivers for Mac OS X. So, although the keyboard works fine, the Command key and Option key are switched (Option is next to the spacebar, with Command next to it) and none of the useful little buttons you see along the top (Back, Forward, Stop, Refresh, Search, Favorites, Home, Volume +, Volume –, Previous Track, Next Track, and so on) do anything. They don't even work in Classic. Furthermore, the Option key says "Alt" on it, and the Command key has a Windows logo where the Apple or pretzel-thing ought to appear—yuck.

A close second is the Adesso (**www.adessoinc.com/**) Tru-Form keyboard, which is quite similar to the Microsoft model. It doesn't have all the little direct launch buttons (which don't work in OS X yet anyway) and may be a bit less expensive. It's also made for the Mac, so the Command key has a proper pretzel symbol on it, and is in the proper location.

Still, I like the Microsoft Natural Keyboard Pro enough that I'm going to keep using it, warts and all, at least until I find something I like better. I spend an inordinate amount of time with my hands on the keyboard, so comfort tops my list of selection criteria, and this is the most comfortable one I've ever used.

I've looked for over a year, and so far I haven't found anything, except perhaps the Adesso Tru-Form, which even comes close.

Mice and Trackballs

I used to be a rabid trackball user. The Kensington Turbo Mouse ADB was my favorite input device for years and years. Then I discovered a mouse I liked even better, and, like the keyboard I love most, Microsoft makes it. The IntelliMouse Explorer and the Wireless IntelliMouse Explorer (Figure 7.11) are the best mice I've ever used, so good I'd even forsake my trackball for either one.

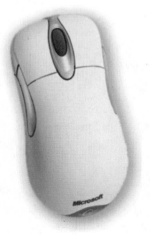

Figure 7.11
The Wireless IntelliMouse Explorer.

The Wireless IntelliMouse Explorer has four buttons, a scroll wheel, silky smooth optical tracking and best of all, no wires.

Alas, Microsoft still hasn't released drivers for Mac OS X. And, unlike the keyboard, the mouse isn't worth using without drivers. The scroll wheel only works in about half of my programs, and two of the four buttons are inoperable. So I've given it up, at least until they come out with OS X drivers for it.

But I'm not complaining. I've found something I like just as well (maybe even better). It's the Kensington Turbo Mouse Pro Wireless (Figure 7.12), an awesome trackball with excellent Mac OS X driver support (**www.Kensington.com**).

Figure 7.12
The Wireless Turbo Mouse Pro.

With five click-buttons, a scroll wheel that works with all my programs, and six way-cool "direct-launch" buttons that launch or activate my six most-used programs (Figure 7.13), it's a dream. And the big ball feels great under my big hand.

If Microsoft ever gets off their duff and releases drivers for the IntelliMouse, I'm going to have a hard time deciding which one to use. Until then, I am perfectly happy with the Kensington Wireless Turbo Mouse Pro.

> **NOTE**
>
> I prefer wireless devices because I tangle up cords faster than anyone I've ever met. If I have two cables on my desk, I'll have them all twisted up in minutes. If I have three or more, well, forget about it. That said, both Microsoft and Kensington offer the same device with a wire for a little lower price.

Figure 7.13
Kensington MouseWorks driver software—these Direct Launch buttons are incredibly convenient.

Tablets

I'm not much of a graphic designer, but I do more than my share of design work. Until last year, I never considered a drawing tablet—they were all too big; I didn't have room for one on my desk. And, of course, they weren't cheap.

But the Graphire2 from Wacom (**www.wacom.com**) is priced for occasional users like me at under $100. And it's small enough—8 inches by 8 inches—that it's not an inconvenience on my desk.

It's an incredible value—for your hundred bucks you get all this:

- The Graphire2 tablet, a removable pen stand, and a transparent overlay for tracing drawings and pictures.

- The Graphire2 Pen, which has a nifty built-in eraser and 512 levels of pressure sensitivity.

- Adobe Photoshop LE and Corel Painter Classic. (The software alone is probably worth a hundred bucks.)

- A three-button cordless mouse with scroll wheel (which I hated—it's stuck in a drawer somewhere).

Figure 7.14 shows what the whole deal looks like.

It's fun, it's cheap, and the two programs that come with it are worth having if you don't already have a copy of (the expensive versions of) Painter or Photoshop.

Figure 7.14
The Wacom Graphire2 tablet, cordless pen (with eraser), and cordless mouse.

Voice

This will be short. I haven't seen the latest version of IBM ViaVoice for OS X, but I've tried every previous version of it, not to mention every version of iListen, PowerSecretary, and several others whose names I can't remember. And the fact of the matter is that voice recognition isn't good enough yet. I've wanted continuous voice dictation for as long as I've been using computers. And every year it gets a little better, but it's still not good enough to use all the time. And, in fact, so far it hasn't even been good enough to keep installed.

And so, my advice is: Save your money. Don't spend your own money on voice recognition software/hardware. Unless you have a disability that prevents you from using a keyboard and mouse, you'll almost certainly be disappointed.

Speakers

I don't know about you, but my Mac has replaced my old stereo system as my primary music listening device. With iTunes and my iPod, I have turned my Mac into, as Apple would say, my "digital hub." I have more than 8GB of music for iTunes on my hard disk, and I carry 4GB of songs around with me on my iPod.

The key to listening to music on a Mac is having good speakers. I have two sets, and I recommend them both wholeheartedly: The Sonigistix Monsoon iM-700 Flat Panel Audio System is by far my favorite (**www.sonigistix.com**), but Harman-Kardon's SoundSticks (**www.harmanmultimedia.com**) are also sweet.

Figure 7.15
The Monsoon iM-700s are the loudest, cleanest computer speakers I've owned.

Figure 7.16
SoundSticks aren't as loud as Monsoons, but they deliver a crisp, clean sound and are gorgeous, too.

Figure 7.15 shows the Monsoons; Figure 7.16 shows the SoundSticks. Both are three-piece systems consisting of a pair of speakers you put on your desk and a subwoofer you can place anywhere you like. The Monsoons are available with either a USB or speaker jack; the SoundSticks are USB-only.

The Monsoons are my absolute favorites because they are louder, have bigger, tighter, more bone-rattling bass response, and sound great even when you're not sitting between the two speakers. They come with a little volume-control/mute remote gizmo on a wire, which is convenient when the phone rings and Led Zeppelin is playing at high volume.

The SoundSticks are quite good, too, and more beautiful than any other speakers on the market today. I call them the jellyfish speakers because that's what they look like. A soft blue glow emanates from the subwoofer, and it's so pretty you'll want to place it where it can be seen. (The Monsoon subwoofer is a plain black box, but it sounds great.) The biggest problem with them, aside from not being loud enough for me, is that they are very location-dependent. If you're not sitting right between them, they don't sound so great. But when the speakers are aimed at your face, they sound excellent. And they are soooo pretty.

You can't go wrong with either one.

MP3 Players

I had pretty much given up on solid-state MP3 players. When I wrote, "The Little iTunes Book," I had the opportunity to try several of them, and in the end decided they weren't for me. Their biggest advantage was size. Sure they were tiny, but they didn't hold enough music (an hour or two), cost too much (at least $100 for the device plus a lot more for 64 or 128MB of solid-state storage), and took too long to load with music via USB.

Then I got my hands on a RioVolt SP250 (**www.riohome.com**), which looks like a personal CD player (e.g., Sony DiscMan) but can, in addition to playing standard audio CDs, play MP3 CDs you burn yourself with iTunes 2.0 or later. This means you can cram more than 20 hours of music onto a single CD-R or CD-RW disc that costs around a buck. Now we're talking. I have the whole Beatles catalog (which I ripped from my boxed set of store-bought CDs—I don't steal music), on a single CD-RW disc. It's freaking awesome. Figure 7.17 shows what a RioVolt looks like.

Figure 7.17
The RioVolt—looks like a Sony DiscMan, but it plays homemade MP3 CDs that can contain more than 100 songs.

These are the features I like best about the RioVolt:

- *A remote control module*—I appreciated being able to use most functions while the device itself was in its (included) carrying case, my backpack, or slung over my shoulder with the (included) shoulder strap. It's not wireless but it's still pretty nifty.

- *Eight minutes of shock protection*—I bounced this puppy around plenty—I walked with it, ran with it, and even took it on a treadmill with me—and never heard it skip once.

- *FM radio*—Not all MP3 players have one (iPod doesn't; more on iPod in a moment). I used it more than I thought I would.

- *Rechargeable batteries*—Again, not all MP3 players have them and trust me, you want them (unless you're very rich).

- *Adjustable EQ*—My ancient ears don't hear high frequencies as well as they used to, so this was a welcome, if slightly difficult-to-use feature.

It also offers repeat and shuffle play modes, programmable playlists, and an LCD display for artist, song title, and preferences.

I have one major complaint and a nit to pick. My complaint is that RioVolt is just not loud enough for my old ears. You'd think they'd use a decent amplifier in a device that's otherwise near-perfect, but they didn't.

The nit is that it doesn't come with CD-burning software or even any information on *how* to burn an MP3 CD. Fortunately, iTunes 2.0 or later makes it easy to do, and you can learn how by choosing Help|iTunes Help (see Figure 7.18).

RioVolt is a good value; it comes with the CD player, two pairs of headphones (one folding, one earbuds), rechargeable batteries, an AC adapter/battery recharger, and a carrying case with strap, all for around $175. I used to recommend it wholeheartedly, but then I got an iPod.

iPod, which, for those of you who've been living in a cave, is Apple's breakthrough MP3 music player, shown in Figure 7.19.

iPod is half the size and weight of the RioVolt, holds 10 times as much music on its 5GB hard disk (which doubles as a portable FireWire hard drive for Macintosh files—a very nice touch), syncs automatically with iTunes 2.0 via FireWire, and recharges its 10-hour lithium polymer battery automatically when you connect it to your Mac via FireWire.

As a music enthusiast who has owned dozens of little personal music-playing devices, I'll say it right up front—it doesn't get much better than this.

7

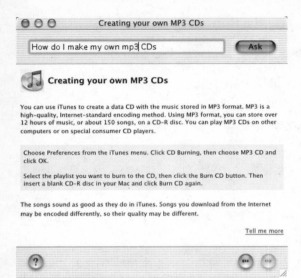

Figure 7.18
Fortunately, Apple's iTunes 2.0 makes up for RioVolt's sin of omission.

Figure 7.19
iPod is beautiful, but it's also the best MP3 player I've ever used. (Photo courtesy of Apple Computer, Inc.)

iPod is amazing. It holds up to 1,000 CD-quality songs, and you can download an entire CD into iPod in less than 10 seconds, or 1,000 songs in around 10 minutes. That's 10 times faster than my old 32MB solid-state Rio, which uses USB instead of FireWire.

iPod integrates seamlessly with iTunes 2.0 (included), so when you plug iPod into your Mac via (included) FireWire cable, it automatically launches iTunes 2.0, and updates your iPod with any new songs or playlists. The whole process takes just seconds unless you have hundreds of new songs.

A tiny, rechargeable lithium polymer battery lasts about 10 hours, and takes just one hour to charge to 80 percent, or three hours to charge to 100 percent.

The 160×128-pixel backlit display is big, bright, and easy on the eyes. And the human interface is the best ever. It has five large buttons and a large scroll wheel. You rotate the wheel with your thumb or finger to navigate your music, which is organized by playlist, artist, and song title. It's a cinch to operate the controls with one hand, and the scroll wheel has this spiffy automatic acceleration, so you get to the song you want in seconds, even if you have to scroll through hundreds of songs to get there.

But wait, there's more: iPod is able to hold so much music because of its ultra-thin 5GB hard drive, which you can also use as a portable FireWire hard disk. So, in addition to being the best music player of all time, it's also a bootable disk I can carry around in my pocket. It's got a complete OS 9.2.1 System Folder, plus all my diagnostic utilities—DiskWarrior, Norton Utilities, Norton Anti-Virus, and TechTool Pro—and even with more than 750 songs loaded, still has more than a gigabyte of free space available.

Finally, it sounds just awesome. It's loud and clear enough to please even me and it's as good or better than anything I've had before.

Gripes? There are no deal-breakers, but I don't like the lower part of the case. The face of the iPod, which is shown in Figure 7.19, is beautiful, but its backside is made from some mirror-like disco ball material that scratches and smudges far too easily and looks oh so '80s. And it doesn't come with a case nor any way to fasten it to your belt.

But iPod sounds better and is easier to use than any music player I've ever tried. And when you consider that you also get a bootable 5GB FireWire hard disk, it's a bargain at $399.

Of all my hardware toys, iPod has to be my very favorite. I don't leave home without it.

On the other hand, if you're on a tight budget, the RioVolt SP250 is pretty darn good, and costs less than half of what an iPod costs.

7

TIP

You can listen to your iPod in any car that has a cassette player. Just buy a CD-to-cassette adapter at Radio Shack for $20, stick it into your car's cassette player, and connect it to the iPod's headphone jack (it's a perfect fit). It's awesome.

A Bit More Hardware

This section is shorter because I don't have nearly as much advice for you about video cards, monitors, printers, digital cameras and camcorders, and/or hubs. But I have a little to say about each. So bear with me—we're almost there.

Video Cards and Displays

This one is easy. The only thing I can tell you about video cards and displays is that desktop Macs are capable of having as many monitors as you have available PCI slots. You need a video card for each monitor, and a monitor to connect to each video card. After installing the cards and connecting the monitors, Mac OS X automatically recognizes them and creates one large virtual desktop that includes all your monitors. You manage multiple monitors in the Arrange tab of the Displays system Preference pane, as shown in Figure 7.20.

NOTE

If you have only one monitor, you won't have an Arrange tab. It comes out only when your Mac detects more than one monitor.

In Figure 7.20, the middle monitor has the menu bar, represented by the white strip at the top of it. If I wanted the menu bar on one of the other monitors, I click the white faux menu bar and drag it onto a different monitor.

So, in Figure 7.20, if I move the cursor all the way to the right, it will appear on the 17-inch monitor, as if the two were connected. Likewise, if I move the cursor all the way to the left, it will appear on the 15-inch monitor.

You can rearrange the monitors' relationship to each other by merely dragging them around the Arrange tab, dropping them where you want them. If I wanted the 17-inch monitor to appear below the 15-inch monitor, I'd just drag it. Then, if my cursor was in the 15-inch monitor and I dragged it downward, it would appear on the 17-inch monitor.

Many power users prefer a dual monitor setup, especially if they use a program such as Photoshop, Dreamweaver, or Final Cut Pro, all of which have numerous palettes. That way you can have most of the palettes on one monitor, and your document full-screen on the other.

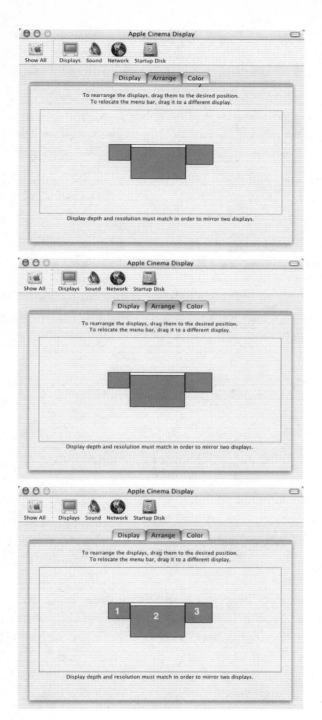

Figure 7.20
This Mac has three monitors—a 15-inch (left), an Apple Cinema 22-inch (center), and a 17-inch (right).

I once saw a setup where a guy had three 22-inch Apple Cinema Displays connected to his G4. Although it was a bit excessive, that didn't stop me from drooling. But a pair of smaller displays—say two 17-inchers—is a cost-effective way to double your screen real estate.

As far as video cards and specific monitors go, I don't have much to say. I've been on a budget so I've been recycling old monitors. The two 17-inchers I use are both CRT (glass picture tubes), not even flat-panels.

I will say that the flat screens are easier on the eyes and use less space than CRTs. My next monitors will be flat, for sure. But my current monitors are still working just fine, and the price is right—I already own them.

I do want to add one comment about the Apple Cinema Display—the one in the middle of Figure 7.20 was here for only a month for a review. I just wish I could afford one. Here's what I said about it in my review: "The Apple Cinema Display, which measures 22-inches diagonally and runs at a dazzling resolution of 1,600×1,024 pixels, is without a doubt the finest computer display I've ever had the pleasure of using. I can't say enough nice things about it—it's a complete and total pleasure. My only complaint: Even with a price drop of more than $1,000 over the past year, it's still expensive."

At $2,499, they're a bargain. Unfortunately, I can't afford any more bargains for a while. I'm still paying off my G4s.

Printers

There are a wide variety of OS X-compatible printers, so I can't give you a whole lot of advice: Your choice depends entirely upon your needs. I find I'm not printing nearly as much as I used to—I send my columns and book chapters via email, and rarely print any of my "real" work. I find most of my printing these days is color pictures, invitations, flyers, and stuff like that. When I had to submit hard copy of the things I wrote, I required a fast monochrome laser printer; these days I'm able to get by with a slower, much cheaper, color inkjet.

I do have two tips. The first is that if you're going to buy a new printer, make sure that OS X supports it. One way to find out is to surf to the Mac Products Guide at **http:// guide.apple.com**, which denotes products that are "made for Mac OS X" with a little "X" icon.

The Products Guide is also an excellent resource for checking whether other hardware or software is "X-ready" or not.

I currently have an Epson Stylus Color 740i, and so far I haven't had a single issue with it under OS X. In fact, my only complaint is that the Epson brand ink cartridges for it are expensive.

Which brings me to my second tip: You don't *have* to buy expensive original equipment manufacturer (OEM) ink cartridges for your inkjet. You can find dozens of aftermarket suppliers on the Web. I've bought cartridges from several of them and had no problems at all. Recently I've been getting them from a company called Ink4Art (**www.ink4art.com**), and they've been excellent.

> **NOTE**
>
> According to the company, their cartridges won't void my warranty. I don't care—the printer is out of warranty anyway, but it's nice to know.

The cartridges I bought cost around a quarter of what Epson gets for theirs, and as far as I can tell, work the same. I suppose if you're a graphic artist and have perfect pitch (or whatever it's called when you can discern similar colors better than normal people), you might find something to complain about. But I've been quite satisfied with everything I've printed.

You can find lots of other aftermarket ink vendors, and I'm sure many of them have good products, too. If you're a bargain hunter, some probably have even lower prices. If you discover a great one, drop me a line—we use a lot of ink here at Rancho de LeVitus.

Hubs

This is a very short section. I just want to mention that if you find yourself with more devices than ports, you can buy hubs for Ethernet, USB, and FireWire. A *hub* is nothing more than a port multiplier. So you plug one end into your Mac's port, and the other end provides two, three, four, five, or even six additional ports. Some require AC power; others don't.

I don't know much about these hubs, and I can't recommend one over another. But I've got a few of each kind laying around the office, and they all seem to work pretty much the same.

If you need a hub, my best advice is to read the "Finding a Reputable Storage Vendor/ Finding the Best Drive for the Money" sidebar earlier in the chapter and do what it suggests to find a vendor and a brand that other OS X users have had good experiences with.

As they say in baseball, that retires the side. Whew.

When Good Macs Go Bad

Eventually something bad will happen to your Mac. I'm sorry, but that's not a threat; it's a promise. You'll turn it on some day and see a flashing question mark, or an application will crash and not be able to restart, or your mouse will stop responding. Or whatever.

I'm not going to be able teach you everything there is to know about troubleshooting Mac OS X in a mere 47 pages. Heck, whole books are no doubt being written on the subject. But never fear—I am going to do the next best thing. Remember back in Chapter 5 when I talked about the proverb that says, "if you *give* a man a fish, you feed him for a day, but if you *teach* a man to fish, you feed him for a lifetime." Because it's unlikely I can cover every possible occurrence in this chapter, I'm going teach you how to fish, by providing you with the tools and techniques to figure out how to deal with almost any problem with your Mac, including ones that aren't mentioned in this chapter at all.

Relax. Don't worry. Ninety-nine percent of the problems you're likely to encounter using Mac OS X can be resolved in just a few minutes, as long as you understand how things work and know what to do. Which happens to be what you'll learn in this chapter—how to prevent problems before they happen and fix them when they do.

In the first section, I give you some background on how things work, and show you some ways to prevent problems before they occur. Then, I show you some specific techniques you can use to fix problems when they do occur.

Preventing Emergencies before They Occur

Before I even start to talk about troubleshooting, there are a bunch of things you should know and do before the fact, things that will keep you from having to trouble-shoot at all if you know them and do them. Mac OS X is so totally different from earlier incarnations of Mac OS that no matter how much you knew about making OS 9 run smoothly and how to fix it when it broke, most of what you know is no longer relevant. For instance, you don't adjust memory for applications anymore. You don't turn virtual memory on or off (it's always on, like it or not). And you don't need to rebuild the desktop for OS X, though it's still necessary for Classic and/or OS 9.

Having used Mac OS X for close to a year already, I would like to believe I've learned a thing or two about what to do and what not to do to keep it running smoothly. So let's start with some tips that will help you avoid problems right up front. If you follow my advice, I assure you you'll do less troubleshooting later.

What Not to Move, Rename, or Delete

If you cut your teeth on Mac OS 9 or earlier flavors of Mac OS, you've become used to storing your files and folders in any folder you like. With the exception of certain special files and folders—control panels, extensions, fonts, and the like, all of which must reside in their proper subfolder inside the OS 9 System folder to function—you could put just about anything just about anywhere. Applications, documents, AppleScripts, clippings, whatever—if it was on some type of disk, and that disk appeared on the Finder's desktop, the thing would just work.

Mac OS X is somewhat less flexible about what goes where. Some files and folders should *never* be moved, renamed, deleted, or changed in any way, shape, or form. Violate this edict and you could easily render Mac OS X totally inoperable. Some applications work properly only when installed in your root-level Applications folder. And don't forget: There are folders installed by Mac OS X that will let you put items into them, but won't let you remove or delete them without performing some fancy power-user voodoo. Furthermore, although almost all of these items are protected by Mac OS X's permissions (more on this shortly) so you can't mess them up, if you boot into Mac OS 9, that protection disappears completely, and you can delete, rename, or move any file or folder without a single warning.

Figure 8.1 shows what happens when you try to drag any of the OS X-installed folders (Applications, Developer, Documents, Library, System, or Users) to the Trash when using Mac OS X.

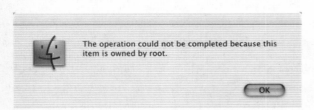

The operation could not be completed because this item is owned by root.

OK

Figure 8.1
Mac OS X takes great pains to protect you from yourself.

But if you restart with Mac OS 9, not only can you drag those particular files or folders to the Trash if you wish, but important files that are invisible under Mac OS X become visible under OS 9, and you can delete them also. Figure 8.2 shows the root level of my boot disk (Das Boot) as seen when running Mac OS X and Mac OS 9.

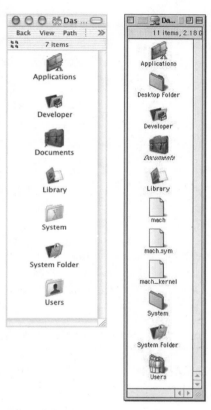

8

Figure 8.2
My boot disk as seen in OS X (left) and OS 9 (right).

Resist the temptation to move, rename, delete, or change these files when you're running OS 9. Although this particular situation can be exploited to great advantage, as you'll see later in this chapter, it can also cause major havoc if you're not careful. You'll only figure out that you've messed something up badly when you reboot into OS X and nothing happens, or you see the infamous flashing question mark, or you're greeted by a screen full of geeky-looking text, instead of the usual, comforting aqua Apple logo and Mac OS X startup screen.

So here's the law: If OS X installed a file or folder and it's not in your Home directory, you should probably keep your paws off of it. If your Mac has multiple user accounts, there are a couple of exceptions to this rule, but if you're the only user of your Mac, there's almost no good reason to touch any of the files or folders installed by Mac OS X, which includes everything at root level on your startup disk or volume except the Documents folder.

Who Can Do What to What?

To take this example further, you need a solid understanding of who can use items stored in a folder at root level, and who can use items stored the Home directory/folder. It's really quite simple, but requires a shift in your thinking if you're used to using OS 9. Here's how it works in a nutshell:

If a file or folder is in any folder at root level, it is available to every user of this Mac. Conversely, if a file or folder is anywhere in your Home folder, it is not available to anyone but you.

So you use the Applications folder at root level to store programs you want every user to have access to, and you use the Applications folder in your Home directory for programs you don't want other users to have access to.

At the (Multiple) Libraries

Another point that deserves some attention is that there are at least four different Library folders installed by OS X, plus an additional one for each user you create. Library folders contain items such as preferences, fonts, screen savers, help files, application plug-ins, and much more. Here's what each library folder is for:

■ *The root level Library folder contains items used by all users of this Mac.* You must be a system administrator to add or remove files from this Library. If you want everyone to have access to a screen saver or font, for example, you'd put it in the Screen Savers or Fonts folder in this Library.

■ *The Library in your Home directory is used for your stuff.* If you want to use a screen saver but don't want everyone else who uses this Mac to be able to use it, you'd put it in the Screen Savers folder in this Library. Access to this Library is limited to administrators or its owner—other users aren't allowed to touch it.

■ *The Library folder in the System folder at root level is used exclusively by Mac OS X.* You will almost never need to do anything to the files or folders in this Library, and even administrators aren't allowed access to this folder without first performing a Unix contortion or two (more on this later in the chapter).

■ *The Library folder in the Network folder contains items used by all users of this Network.* You must be a system administrator to add or remove files from this Library. If you want everyone on the network to have access to a screen saver or font, for example, you'd put it in the Screen Savers or Fonts folder in this Library.

OS X Prefers to Run 24/7

Unix was designed to run 24 hours a day, 7 days a week, and because its creators expected it to do so, it performs a number of "housekeeping" tasks nightly, weekly, and monthly. Mac OS X, having Unix at its core, is no exception. So most Unix fans think it's best to run your Mac 24/7, so these tasks run when they are scheduled (by the OS), which is usually in the middle of the night.

Frankly, I'm not thrilled about this. First, and foremost, I don't like to waste energy. Yes, I know about Energy Saver and sleep, but some days I don't even touch my Mac, and I hate to think it's using even a little power. Second, my office tends to get very warm from all the electronic equipment, including several Macs. Turning them off allows the office to cool down a lot faster. Finally, here in Texas we have frequent thunderstorms. The best defense against lightning damage is to unplug your Mac from the wall (and disconnect any phone lines plugged into it as well—lightning can fry your Mac via phone line almost as easily as through the power cord). The second best defense is a good Uninterruptible Power Supply (UPS). The third best defense, at least in my opinion, is to shut down your Mac when lightning threatens.

So I shut down my Macs at night, and when I'm not planning to use them for eight or more hours. And if I expect thunderstorms, I unplug everything.

Of course, you don't *have* to run it 24/7. But what about those housekeeping tasks Unix wants to run in the middle of the night? Fortunately, ace programmer Brian Hill created a little freeware program called MacJanitor that runs these tasks whenever you ask it to. I just ran all three tasks—daily, weekly, and monthly—which took about five minutes. (Of course, I was able to continue writing while they ran—isn't preemptive multitasking wonderful?) Anyway, Figure 8.3 shows what everything looked like when MacJanitor was done.

8

> **TIP**
>
> I have a repeating reminder (created in Microsoft Entourage v.X) that pops up on my screen every three days. It says, "Have you run MacJanitor today?" So I rarely forget. You could instead add MacJanitor to your Login Items, so it opens up every time you reboot, but I think, at least for me, that that's overkill.

If you remember to use MacJanitor every so often, you can ignore that 24/7 advice completely, which is exactly what I do.

> **NOTE**
>
> You'll find MacJanitor on this book's CD-ROM. If you're interested in what exactly the tasks it runs are, read the text file entitled, "What Is It Doing?.rtf" in the MacJanitor folder, or launch MacJanitor and choose Help|MacJanitor Help.

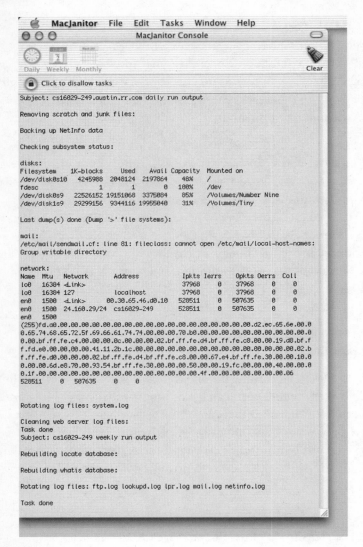

Figure 8.3
MacJanitor performs the daily, weekly, and monthly Unix housekeeping tasks so you don't need to run your Mac 24 hours a day. Sweet!

One last thing: Nothing terrible will happen if you never run these tasks. You'll sacrifice a bit of hard disk space, and some Unix processes may run a tiny bit slower, but nothing horrible is going to happen. That said, performing these housekeeping chores regularly, like brushing your teeth or rebuilding the OS 9 desktop every month or two, is a good habit to get into.

You Can Force Quit with (Almost) Reckless Abandon

In OS 9, you could sometimes force an application to quit if it was acting up or frozen, by invoking the secret Force Quit keyboard shortcut—Command+Option+Esc. Unfortunately, when you forced a program to quit, the system presented a harshly worded alert that said, in effect, "Restart your Mac as soon as possible or face unspeakable consequences." Those consequences were almost always a hard crash or total freeze within a few minutes. So Mac OS 9 users got into the habit of avoiding the Force Quit, and invoked it only as a last resort.

Forget that. OS X lets you Force Quit any program, including the Finder, without any penalty and without rebooting your Mac. If an application acts up, simply press Command+Option+Esc or choose Apple Menu|Force Quit. A little windoid appears, as shown in Figure 8.4.

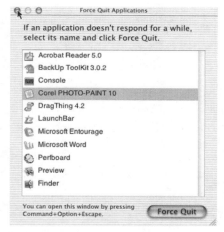

8

Figure 8.4
Choose the recalcitrant program and click Force Quit.

TIP

> If you change your mind and decide that you don't want to force anything to quit, just click the red "close window" gumdrop, as I'm about to do in Figure 8.4.

If you choose the Finder in this windoid, the Force Quit button will say Relaunch instead of Force Quit. That's because whenever you quit the Finder (or it quits on its own, as it occasionally does), it starts right back up again automatically. For all other programs, it will say Force Quit.

If you do click Force Quit, a dialog sheet will appear on top of the Force Quit Applications windoid, as shown in Figure 8.5, giving you a second chance to change your mind.

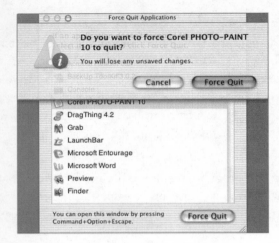

Figure 8.5
This time, if you click Force Quit, the program really will quit.

If you click Force Quit now, you'll lose any changes you've made since your last save and the application will quit. If you click Cancel, the dialog sheet will disappear and you'll be back where you were in Figure 8.4.

If using the windoid doesn't do the trick, and it sometimes doesn't, you can try the alternate method—press the Option key while clicking the program's icon in the Dock, as shown in Figure 8.6.

I find that the windoid method works more often than the Dock method, but if one fails, I always try the other, just in case.

> **TIP**
>
> If neither method works, you can try using ProcessViewer (discussed in Chapter 7) to force an application or process to quit. This is a good tidbit to tuck away in the back of your mind, because some programs and processes that run in the background, including the Dock, can't be forced to quit in either of the ways I just discussed.

I know I've mentioned this topic several times before, and I apologize for repeating myself. But this whole Force Quit thing is so different in OS X, I want to make sure I've convinced you that you can Force Quit with impunity, any time you like in OS X, and that the only ill effect is that you'll lose any changes you've made since your last save. Of course, if you're forcing a program to quit, that program has probably crashed and you'd lose those changes regardless. The point is, you won't have to restart or shut down after a Force Quit, so it's a lot more useful now than ever before. Use it. It works!

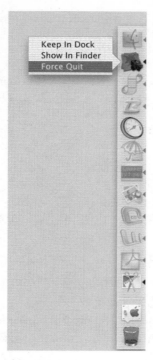

Figure 8.6
Another way to force a program to quit.

8

Avoid Unnecessary Extensions and Control Panels in Classic

I discussed this subject in detail back in Chapter 6 but it bears mentioning here—don't enable extensions and control panels that aren't absolutely vital for something you use or do in Classic. This chapter is about avoiding problems: Following this advice will significantly reduce problems you might have with Classic; ignoring it could cause you hours of pointless troubleshooting.

Two More Tips That Aren't for Everyone

Everything I've mentioned up to this point applies to each and every Mac OS X user. But I still have two more tips that may very well help you avoid future heartache. Alas, these two are not as universal as the ones I've already presented, and they may not appeal to each and every one of you.

The first tip deals with security and networks, and is only important if you're on a network or have broadband Internet access. If you use an analog modem to connect, much of the discussion won't apply to you. Still, I recommend you read it anyway—it's short, sweet, and some of it may be helpful. But I wanted to warn you first, so that if you're a modem user, you don't read it and become confused or upset ("I need a fire what?").

The second tip, which is about the Developer Tools that come with Mac OS X, is somewhat geeky, and installing the tools chews up around a quarter gigabyte of hard disk space. That said, I suggest that you read this section, then decide if installing the 250MB of Developer Tools is worth it to you.

Net Security and Viruses

If you use Mac OS X the way Apple shipped it, you open yourself to only slightly more risk of intrusion than you did under OS 9, even if you have a broadband "always-on" Internet connection such as cable (like me) or DSL. But if you enable certain options, most notably root access (see Chapters 10 and 11), FTP access, Web sharing, file sharing, or remote login (which are all disabled by default when you first install OS X), you increase your susceptibility to malicious attacks.

If you don't intend to connect to your machine remotely ("Allow remote login"), or share files across a network ("File sharing"), or run a Web server ("Web sharing"), or let people use FTP ("Allow FTP access"), make sure these services are disabled in the Sharing System Preference pane. These services take some minimal amount of CPU and RAM, but the scarier part is that they also open potential security holes that you don't need to worry about if you're not using them. On my own machine, I enable and disable them regularly, based on whether I'll be using the services or not.

Although it's generally safe to use any or all of these services if you need them, you should know the potential security issues before you enable any of them.

A complete discussion of hardware and software firewalls, Network Address Translation (NAT), hardware routers, and other security measures is beyond my purview, so here are a few good Web sites you can visit for more information:

- www.macintouch.com/security.html

- http://developer.apple.com/internet/macosx/securityintro.html

- www.securemac.com/

- www.macwrite.com/macsecurity/

Here's the bottom line: If you're connected via cable modem, DSL, or other high-speed, always-on connection, you may be exposed. I don't mean to scare you, but if you use OS X and the Internet, you ought to take the appropriate steps to protect your Mac.

Why I Have a Personal Firewall

After doing my homework, by reading about Mac OS X security and cable modem issues, I became convinced that I wanted/needed a personal firewall. I tried several (a very nice shareware firewall—BrickHouse—is on this book's Web site), but I finally settled on Norton Personal Firewall, which was easiest to configure and use, and has separate versions that protect me under both OS 9 and OS X.

After installing the firewall, I discovered that dozens of unwanted attempts to access my Mac are made each day. Fortunately, they're almost always looking for a susceptible Windows machine, so they do no harm. But having the firewall still makes me feel better.

I suppose I should cover viruses here also, because they're a part of the bigger "security" picture and something not all users need to be concerned about.

First the good news: Only a small fraction of computer viruses affect Macintoshes, and only a small fraction of those affect Mac OS X. Why? Because of the way most viruses are constructed. Some use Visual Basic to deliver their "payload," but because Visual Basic programs don't run on Macs, only PCs running Window's are affected. Other viruses attack by exploiting holes in Windows file sharing. Again, Macs don't have that, so those viruses won't hurt us either. Yet others rely on the victim's using the Microsoft Outlook email client, which (you guessed it) also isn't available for the Mac. (Outlook Express, which is available for the Mac, isn't affected by Windows viruses.)

But that begs the question of whether Macs are vulnerable to viruses at all—the answer is: Yes, they are, absolutely and positively. Although viruses that affect Macs are fewer and farther between than viruses that affect Windows, there are still a number of Mac viruses that can wreck your entire life if they get loose on your hard disk. So, I recommend virus protection if you're at risk of viral infection.

So who is at risk of catching a virus? The first group consists of anyone who uses a disk—floppy disks, SuperDisks, CD-R discs, CD-RW discs, DVD-RAM cartridges, DVD-R discs, Zip disks, Jaz or Orb cartridges, magneto-optical cartridges or any other read/write media—that has *ever* been inserted in another Mac. If that describes you, you should absolutely be running virus protection. Any disk that has ever been inserted into an infected Mac is potentially infected itself. If you insert such disks, you will become infected if you don't have virus protection.

Another group at risk from viral attack are people who download files. Although commercial online services such as America Online, and big popular Web sites such as **Tucows.com, VersionTracker.com,** or **Shareware.com** screen their files carefully and rarely pass along viruses, many Internet Web sites, FTP sites, and other repositories of files aren't so carefully patrolled. So if you download files—from almost anywhere—you should use virus protection.

The final group at risk is people who receive email with attachments. So far, no virus can be spread just by a user *reading* an email, but many viruses can be spread when you open an email enclosure. So, if you receive email with enclosures or attachments, you need virus protection.

Finally, if you use Microsoft Office and ever open documents you didn't create, you should be aware that a type of virus called a "macro" virus infects you by using the built-in macro utilities in the Microsoft Office programs. Although there are a lot more Windows macro viruses than Mac macro viruses (say that three times fast!), you should still be aware of them. Office warns you about this risk when you open a document with embedded macros, but if you're like most users, myself included, you ignore the warning and click OK. So if you open Word, Excel, or PowerPoint documents created by others, understand that those files could possibly inflict a macro virus on your Mac.

> **NOTE**
>
> One down side of not running an anti virus program is that there's a chance you could pass one of these viruses along to another Windows user without even knowing you did. After all, it doesn't affect you. . . A more likely and more embarrassing scenario is when you send your client or boss who uses a Mac an infected Office document and *their* virus detector busts your chops. Nothing brings out my respect for a PR person better than an infected press release. It speaks so highly of the client, too.

I'm quite happy with Norton Antivirus for Macintosh. It has a great "Live Update" feature that lets me download and install the latest virus definition files automatically, which means my Mac is always protected against recently discovered viruses. It protects you when you're running OS X, OS 9, and even Classic. And it automatically scans every file I download and every disk I insert for viruses.

I'm happy to say that in years of using Norton Antivirus, I've never become infected.

Not everyone needs a firewall, virus protection, or a hardware router. But don't be an ostrich with your head buried in the sand. If you need any of these, do the homework, then get it.

Why You Want to Install the Developer Tools

I recommend installing and checking out the Developer Tools that come with OS X (they're on that third CD you probably tossed in a drawer when you saw its name). If you have room on your hard drive (you'll need around 250MB), Developer Tools includes a bunch of good stuff, including several items that may come in handy if things go wrong with your Mac.

The Developer Tools contain both double-clickable "made for Mac OS X" apps (in the /Developer/Applications folder) and Unix tools you use from the command line

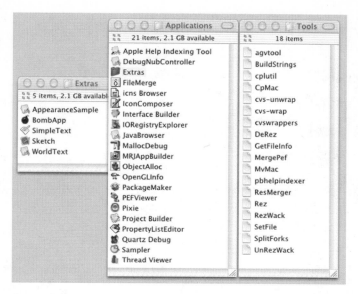

Figure 8.7
Just look at all this free stuff.

(in the /Developer/Tools folder). Because space prohibits me from doing much more than mentioning them, Figure 8.7 shows a picture of both folders.

For example, the PropertyListEditor application lets you look inside preference files, change options (like high scores), and other occasionally handy pref-file diddles; the Unix **SetFile** command lets you change the attributes, creator, creation date, modification date, or type of any file from the Terminal's command line. If you don't install the Developer Tools, you won't have these (as well as a lot of other interesting stuff).

You're going to learn more than you probably want to know about Unix in Chapters 10 and 11, so we'll just leave it at this: If you have the space on your hard drive, install the Developer Tools and check them out. If you don't find them useful, drag them into the Trash and you've lost nothing but a few minutes of time.

NOTE

One last thing before we move on. Although this has nothing to do with troubleshooting, before we leave the subject (free stuff on the Developer Tools CD), I thought I'd toss it in here. One of the items in the /Developer/Applications/Extras folder is a sweet little graphics editor called Sketch, shown in Figure 8.8.

Okay. That's it for tips and hints before the fact. Now let's look at. . . .

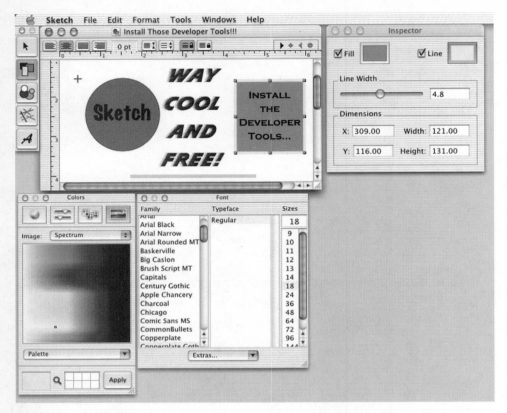

Figure 8.8
The Sketch application. It's not Photoshop, but it's also not $600.

When Good Macs Go Just a Little Bit Bad

In this section, I show you some of the most common problems that occur with Mac OS X, and how to fix them quickly and painlessly.

My first bit of advice is this: Don't panic. If something is wrong with your Mac, chances are very good it's fixable and that you'll be able to fix it if you don't do something dumb first.

Enable Your Crash Logs

My second bit of advice is that you should enable Mac OS X's built-in crash logging system, which is disabled by default. This system tries to capture relevant details when a program or the Finder crashes. It's not a panacea, but it can be helpful in tracking down problems—for you and for the tech support guy on the other end of the phone.

To enable the crash log, open the Console application (/Applications/Utilities) and choose Console|Preferences. Click the Crashes tab, then click the checkbox that says Log Crash Information In ~/Library/Logs/, as shown in Figure 8.9.

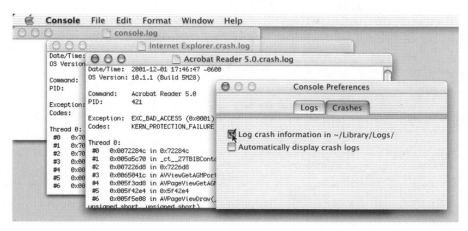

Figure 8.9
Here's how to enable crash logging.

The second checkbox—Automatically Display Crash Logs—displays a program's log on your screen immediately after that program crashes. Because some program crashes don't cause the program to quit or stop responding, having these logs pop onto your screen is a kind of early warning. If you see one, note which program crashed, then immediately save your work in that application (if it's not too late already), and quit and restart the program. I find the automatic log display annoying sometimes, but I leave it enabled anyway.

NOTE

> Many of the so-called crashes the automatic crash log displays don't seem to be hurting anything. After a while, you'll get to know which ones you can safely ignore. Still, every so often it tips me off to a problem that's about to occur, so I put up with it.

NOTE

> If a program crashes every time you do a particular thing—such as open a dialog box, or choose a particular item from a menu—read the upcoming section called "Dealing with Preferences." If that doesn't fix the problem, report the issue to the program's developer and send them the crash logs if they ask.

To examine any log at any time, open your Home/Library/Logs/ folder and open any of the log files it contains. The Console application opens (if it's not already running) and displays the log.

One other trick you might find helpful, especially if your Mac crashes when you're not sitting in front of it to see the automatic display, is to open the Logs folder in List view and sort the logs by modification date. The log with the latest modification date (Acrobat Reader 5.0 in Figure 8.10) is probably the log of the program that crashed.

Name	Date Modified ▼	Size	Kind
Acrobat Reader 5.0.crash.log	Yesterday, 5:46 PM	4 KB	LogFile
Microsoft Word.crash.log	Yesterday, 3:00 PM	20 KB	LogFile
Internet Explorer.crash.log	Yesterday, 12:17 PM	12 KB	LogFile
Corel PHOTO-PAINT 10.crash.log	Yesterday, 10:45 AM	16 KB	LogFile
Create.crash.log	Fri, Nov 30, 2001, 10:37 AM	4 KB	LogFile
LaunchCFMApp.crash.log	Fri, Nov 30, 2001, 10:36 AM	8 KB	LogFile
Finder.crash.log	Fri, Nov 30, 2001, 8:35 AM	4 KB	LogFile
Microsoft Entourage.crash.log	Thu, Nov 29, 2001, 1:46 PM	16 KB	LogFile
console.log	Thu, Nov 29, 2001, 1:05 AM	4 KB	LogFile
Myth III The Wolf Age.crash.log	Wed, Nov 28, 2001, 11:32 PM	4 KB	LogFile
SystemUIServer.crash.log	Wed, Nov 28, 2001, 7:13 PM	Zero KB	LogFile

Logs — 11 items, 2.1 GB available

Figure 8.10
Acrobat Reader 5.0 crashed while I was eating dinner last night.

I won't pretend the information in these log files will be useful to you—it's mostly indecipherable to mere mortals (i.e., nonprogrammers). But it can alert you to problems you might not notice otherwise, and the log files are essential if you are reporting a bug to Apple or another developer.

> **TIP**
>
> You can throw logs in the Trash whenever you like. I clean my Library/Logs folder every couple of weeks. In that time, I usually amass 10 to 20 log files. I sometimes don't realize that a program had crashed until I look in the Logs folder. By cleaning out the folder occasionally I can quickly determine which programs have been crashing behind my back by noting which programs have created logs in this folder. Yet another good reason to keep logging enabled.

Nonfatal Crashes and Other Relatively Minor Inconveniences

Before we get to the serious stuff—crashes that take down your entire computer or otherwise prevent you from working—I'm going to take you through a series of more likely and less-fatal scenarios. My reasoning is simple: If something really bad happens, you should eliminate what I discuss here first, before moving on to more drastic measures discussed in the next section.

I start with a real simple one: What do you do if you forget your password?

Forgot Your Password?

You probably won't forget the password for your main administrator account, but forgetting other users' passwords is easy. Here's how to deal with any or all password-related incidents.

If it's a user other than yourself (i.e., other than the administrator who set up this Mac) with the forgotten password:

1. Log in as usual.

2. Open the Users System Preference pane.

3. Click the user's name, then click Edit User.

4. Click the Password tab.

5. Type and verify a new password.

That's it. But wait, there's more (and a reason I'm covering passwords first in this section), which is this: The Mac OS X installation CD can reset your password.

ALERT!

> Read that sentence again. It says that anyone with a Mac OS X CD can gain total and unrestricted access to your computer.

An OS X install CD is a master key to your Mac. Keep it locked up or hidden if you are concerned about someone breaking into your Mac locally (as opposed to remotely, over a network or the Internet, which can't be done with an OS X install CD but can be done other ways requiring significantly more skill).

So don't forget that a determined burglar could use his own OS X CD and still break into your Mac locally. So if you're extremely concerned about break-ins, the only way to be totally safe is to secure your Mac under lock and key.

NOTE

> You could remove the CD-ROM drive, but that might only slow down a smart break-in artist (he could even bring his own CD-ROM drive) and is more than a little bit inconvenient for you.

Anyway, here's how easy it is to reset the master password on any Mac:

1. Boot from a Mac OS X CD. (Insert the CD, restart or power on, then press the "C" key until the smiley-face icon appears in the middle of the screen.)

2. Choose Installer|Reset Password.

3. When the Reset Password window appears, choose a disk and a user, then type the new password into both fields as requested.

4. Click Save.

5. Choose Reset Password|Quit Reset Password (Command+Q).

6. Choose Installer|Quit Installer (Command+Q).

7. Click Restart.

Last but not least, remember that any malicious person can use this technique not only to break into your Mac, but to change your password so that you can't log in without going through the preceding process.

There. Now you're forewarned of the Mac OS X CD's potential for abuse, and you know what you can do about it.

Dealing with Documents That Launch the Wrong Program

Have you ever encountered a document that, when you opened it, launched an application other than the one you expected (or wanted) it to launch? Or a document that displays the wrong icon? Both of these issues are closely related and easily fixed.

Rather than provide a lengthy text explanation, let me instead relate an illustrated parable. I have used Photoshop for my graphics editing since time immemorial. And for the first six months I had OS X, I ran Photoshop in Classic mode (quite successfully, I might add). But then, several graphics programs came along that were "made for Mac OS X" and didn't require Classic. Because Photoshop was the last Classic application I couldn't live without (Office v.X had shipped a month before), I decided I would switch to a "native" graphics program and avoid Classic completely if I could, and decided to learn Corel PHOTO-PAINT.

> **NOTE**
>
> I tried a bunch of other graphics editors—Canvas 8, GraphicConverter, TIFFany3, Create, Painter 7, and probably a few I've forgotten already—but Corel PHOTO-PAINT came the closest to meeting my needs.

Now for the problem: I have thousands of Photoshop files on my hard disk, and every time I double-clicked one of them, Classic would begin to start up so it could launch Photoshop, which was exactly what I was trying to avoid.

Fortunately, OS X makes the solution painless.

First, I clicked a Photoshop document, chose File|Show Info, and then chose Open With Application from the pop-up menu, as shown in Figure 8.11.

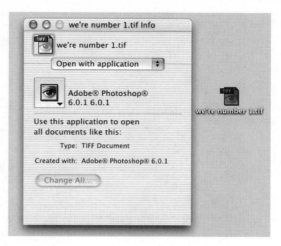

Figure 8.11
This is the "before" picture.

Next, I clicked the Adobe Photoshop icon, which is actually a menu, and selected Corel PHOTO-PAINT 10, as shown in Figure 8.12.

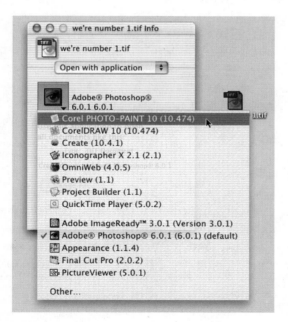

Figure 8.12
The little black triangle (lower-right on the Photoshop icon) indicates that this icon is actually a menu.

If the application I wanted didn't appear in this menu, I could have chosen Other and selected another application in the Choose Other Application dialog box that appears.

ALERT!

It's best to stick with the applications OS X recommends in the Choose Other Application dialog box, but if you know what you're doing, you can choose All Applications from the Show menu and choose a different program. But be careful—not all programs can open all document types. For example, if you try to open a JPEG graphics file with Microsoft Excel (a spreadsheet), you'll end up with a screen covered with garbage, as shown in Figure 8.13.

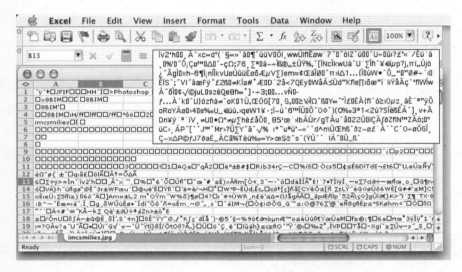

Figure 8.13
Here's what happens when you try to have an inappropriate program (Microsoft Excel) open a document it can't handle (a JPEG graphics file).

Finally, I clicked Change All, to inform Mac OS X that I wanted all files like this to open Corel PHOTO-PAINT 10. A dialog box asked me if I was sure I wanted to do this. I was, so I clicked Continue and the icon magically changed from a Photoshop document to a Corel document, as shown in Figure 8.14. From this moment forward, when I open a TIF graphics file, it launches into Corel PHOTO-PAINT 10 in OS X instead of Photoshop in Classic. Yea!

Because Photoshop and Corel PHOTO-PAINT are both capable of opening many different types of graphics files, I had to repeat this process a few more times for my JPEG, PICT, and GIF files, among others. But within a few days, I had things fixed up so I almost never accidentally launch Classic by opening a graphics document, and so that most graphics documents launched into Corel PHOTO-PAINT.

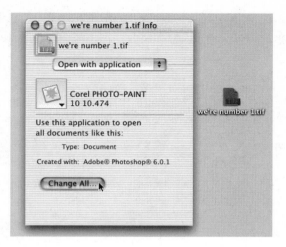

Figure 8.14
The Change All button determines whether this change applies only to this document or to this document and all other documents like it.

> **TIP**
>
> You can also change document–application relationships to substitute a more capable OS X native application for a less capable one, such as having your PDF files launch in Acrobat Reader instead of Preview or text files launch in BBEdit or Microsoft Word v.X instead of TextEdit.

So there you have it—if you ever encounter a document that launches the wrong program, you now know what to do. The longer you use Mac OS X, the less often you'll find yourself performing this trick, and most or all of your documents will eventually open in the program you prefer.

You Don't Have Enough Privileges to Do That

Every so often you'll encounter a file or folder that, when you try to move or delete it, informs you politely that you don't have "sufficient access privileges" for that. Or that the file is "owned by root." Or that you can't empty the Trash because you don't have "sufficient privileges for some of the items."

Welcome to Unix. Although Mac OS X does its best to shield the user from its Unix underpinnings, every so often something gets out of whack, and you get a message like the ones in the previous paragraph for a file or folder that you created and should "own."

A complete discussion of how to deal with this state of affairs is beyond the scope of this chapter, but I can provide some tips and hints that will help you deal with most privilege-related issues painlessly (i.e., I'll teach you to fish).

If you don't mind using the command line in the Terminal program, Chapters 10 and 11 explain the underlying Unix principles behind some of these occurrences and how to fix them from the command line.

But I prefer to avoid Unix whenever I can, so I do it the easy way—with one of the myriads of "made for Mac OS X" applications that can diddle privileges (sometimes referred to as "permissions") without typing (or learning) a single messy Unix command.

I'll illustrate how it works with an example. In Figure 8.15 you can see the Finder's Show Info window for a graphics file I created. In theory, I should be able to open it, but I can't because the stupid file thinks its owner is "newbie" and that nobody else should be allowed to read or write to this file.

Figure 8.15
It's mine! I made it! Give it back!

NOTE

How and why the priveleges are wrong aren't germane to this discussion. Suffice it to say that every so often something like this is going to happen to you. What is important is how to make it right, which is what I'll show you now.

I fire up BareBones Software's Super Get Info ($20 demoware from **www.barebones.com**), open the recalcitrant file, and click the Permissions tab, as shown in Figure 8.16.

I change the owner back to myself, and give the group and world permission to read and write to the file, then click Save. Super Get Info makes sure I'm permitted to make these changes by asking me for an administrator name and password, as shown in Figure 8.17.

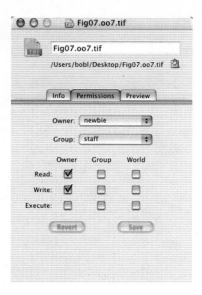

Figure 8.16
Super Get Info is like the Finder's Show Info command on steroids.

8

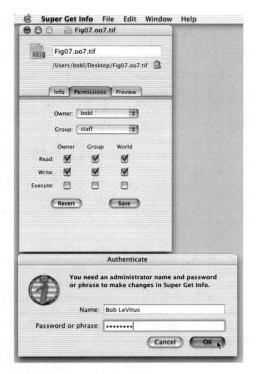

Figure 8.17
Not just anybody can use Super Get Info to change a file's permissions—you have to be an administrator.

And that's it. I quit Super Get Info, and the file is the way it should be. The Finder's Get Info window, which you last saw in Figure 8.15, is shown in Figure 8.18 as it appears after this surgery.

Figure 8.18
Aaaah. That's better.

Super Get Info isn't the only program you can use for this task—not by a long shot. Others include:

■ Renaud Boisjoly's BatChmod (freeware; **http://homepage.mac.com/arbysoft**)

■ Gideon Softworks' Get Info ($10 shareware; **www.gideonsoftworks.com**)

■ Brian R. Hill's xFiles ($20 shareware; **http://personalpages.tds.net/~brian_hill**)

BatChmod has the distinct advantage of being totally free, but each of the other programs offers additional features and is worth exploring.

> **NOTE**
>
> All four programs are available via links at **www.boblevitus.com/xfiles.html**; you can find additional details in Chapter 14.

> **ALERT!**
>
> All of these programs could make changes to your privileges that could cause your system to cease functioning. Make sure you know what you are doing before using them, and make double or triple sure you know what you're doing if you attempt to use any of them on any of the OS X–installed files or folders.

The Trouble with Trash

The most common Trash-related problems may or may not be related to privileges. Sometimes they are; sometimes they aren't. In any case, here are the two most common problems, and how to fix them.

The first issue arises when you drag an item to the Trash and get the dreaded error message shown in Figure 8.19.

Figure 8.19
What do you mean I don't? That's my file and I can Trash it if I want to!

The most common reason for seeing this message is that the file is locked, a situation that's easily remedied right from the Finder. Just click the reluctant file's icon and choose File|Show Info, then choose General Information from the pop-up menu if it's not already selected. If the Locked checkbox in the lower-left corner of the Show Info window has a checkmark in it, click it once to clear it. You should now be able to drag the file into the Trash.

If that doesn't work, you may actually have a privileges issue. Use the techniques in the previous section, or the ones in Chapters 11 and 12 to regain your privileges for the file, then Trash it.

If you have multiple locked files, you can unlock them all at once with Golden Key, which you can find at **http://www.trinfinitysoftware.com**.

The second Trash-related issue occurs when you try to empty the Trash and an error message about privileges appears. This sometimes means a locked file has somehow snuck into your Trash, so the first thing to do is use File|Show Info to see if that's the case. If so, you know what to do.

But if that's not the problem, you can try a couple of other things.

The first and easiest method is to use an OS X utility such as Super Get Info or BatChmod to do the dirty work.

To use Super Get Info, launch the program, then choose Super Get Info|Empty Trash. After supplying an administrator name and password it will empty your Trash of all but the most stubborn files, even if you don't have enough privileges to delete them (so be careful).

To use BatChmod, launch the program then click its Dock icon and choose Force Empty Trash. After you supply an administrator name and password, it will empty your Trash of all but the most stubborn files, even if you don't have enough privileges to delete them (so be careful).

If neither of those programs do the trick, you can try one more thing, but it requires Unix and the Terminal. So you might want to read Chapters 10–12 first. On the other hand, this task is relatively easy to perform so you should be okay even if you've never used the Terminal before.

Here's how it goes:

1. Launch the Terminal program (/Applications/Utilities).

2. Type "cd /.Trash/" at the % prompt. (Capitalization matters and there's a period before the word "Trash.") This command changes the directory (cd) you're working with to .Trash.

3. Type "sudo chflags nouchg *" at the % prompt. (Don't capitalize anything, and put spaces after each word and before the *.) This command unsets the **nouchg** flag, which is a flag that tells the system that the file can't be modified or changed by any user.

4. Type your administrator password at the % prompt.

5. Quit Terminal.

6. Empty the Trash.

Figure 8.20 shows the whole sequence in a Terminal window, with what I typed in Steps 2, 3, and 4 highlighted.

If for some reason you still can't empty the Trash, boot into Mac OS 9, find the problem file (/Users/Home/.Trash), drag it to the OS 9 Trash icon, then choose Special|Empty Trash.

TIP

If none of these techniques worked for you, try searching your favorite software Web site (such as **www.versiontracker.com** or **www.tucows.com**) for "Trash" or "empty Trash." Maybe a new tool is available that I didn't know about when I wrote this.

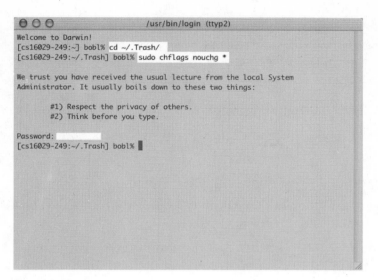

Figure 8.20
This is what the Terminal should look like if you do everything right.

When Applications Turn into Folders

Every so often your applications turn into folders. It has only happened to me once, but it's kind of scary. Fortunately, it's relatively simple to fix. Here's how:

1. Open your Preferences folder (/User/UserName/Library/Preferences).

2. Find these three files: LSClaimedTypes, LSSchemes, and LSApplications.

3. Drag them into the Trash.

4. Log out.

5. Log in.

Your applications should be back to normal.

When Good System Preference Panes Go Bad

Every so often your System Preference panes get funky. By this I mean they work when you open the System Preferences application, but don't work when you launch them any other way. I usually notice this problem when I try to launch one via LaunchBar, but this bugaboo will also manifest itself when you choose Dock Preferences from the Apple|Dock submenu. It's happened to me a couple of times, and I'm not quite sure what causes it, but I do know how to fix it.

NOTE

This technique should be familiar to you if you read the previous section called "Dealing with Documents That Launch the Wrong Program." There is a small difference, so I'll walk you through the steps.

1. Navigate to the /System/Library/PreferencePanes folder on your boot disk.

2. Select any pane and choose File|Show Info or use the keyboard shortcut (Command+I).

3. Choose Open With Application from the pop-up menu.

4. Click the icon with the little black triangle in its lower-right corner and choose Other from the menu that drops down.

NOTE

The icon may say "Not Applicable" or display an application other than System Preferences. Don't worry. That's what you're about to fix.

5. Choose Show|All Applications from the top of the Choose Other Application dialog box.

6. Choose System Preferences (it's in the Applications folder at root level on your boot disk) and click Add. The warning shown in Figure 8.21 will appear.

7. Click Continue.

And that's all there is to it.

Figure 8.21
This is exactly what you want to do, so click Continue.

Why Don't Those Services Work?

You've probably noticed the Services submenu in the Application menu of the Finder and all non-Classic programs. But if you've tried to actually use any of those services, you've probably met with disappointment, because they appear not to work. They actually do work, and are quite wonderful. That's the good news.

The bad news is that the services work only with a handful of OS X applications so far. They work automatically in programs developed using Apple's Cocoa environment, and they work in "Carbonized" programs if the developer enabled Services. Unfortunately, most developers haven't enabled them in their Carbonized applications.

Before I tell you a bit more about services, read the short sidebar that attempts to define Cocoa, Carbon, and Classic.

Cocoa, Carbon, and Classic

Here's a very short course in how programs for the Mac are made. Because I'm not a programmer, I borrowed these definitions from Apple's Developer Connection Web pages and their PDF publication, "Mac OS X: An Overview for Developers," which is why they appear in italic text.

The Cocoa application environment is designed specifically for Mac OS X–only native applications. It is composed of a set of object-oriented frameworks that support rapid development and high productivity. The Cocoa frameworks include a full-featured set of classes designed to create robust and powerful Mac OS X applications. The object-oriented design simplifies application development and debugging.

Cocoa provides developers starting new Mac OS X–only projects the fastest way to full-featured implementations. Applications from Unix and other OS platforms can also be brought to Mac OS X quickly by using Cocoa to build state-of-the-art Aqua user interfaces while retaining most existing core code.

The Carbon APIs can be used to write Mac OS X applications that also run on previous versions of the Mac OS (8.1 or later).

Carbon is designed to provide a gentle migration path for developers transitioning from Mac OS 9 to Mac OS X. As most Carbon APIs are supported on Mac OS 9, developers can enhance applications for Mac OS X while continuing to support customers who are using previous versions of Mac OS. Carbon also allows Mac developers to use the software development tools and languages they are most familiar with to develop for Mac OS X.

The Classic environment is actually a full version of Mac OS 9.1 running in a protected memory space under Mac OS X. As a result, most Mac OS 9 compatible applications will run side-by-side with Mac OS X applications. This allows users to upgrade to Mac OS X without fear of application incompatibility. Carbon is a native Mac OS X environment that allows programmers to take advantage of advanced Mac OS X features while retaining compatibility with the installed base of Macintosh computers running Mac OS 8.1 and later.

There are multiple ways to develop for Mac OS X. Individual skills, preferred languages and tools, target-user base, and time-to-market concerns will influence a developer's approach.

(continued)

The Carbon APIs are based on earlier Mac OS APIs. While Carbon allows applications to take advantage of Mac OS X features such as multiprocessing support and the Aqua user interface, Carbon is specifically designed to allow compatibility with older versions of the Mac OS.

The Cocoa application environment runs natively under Mac OS X. For those who wish to develop for Mac OS X using rapid application development (RAD) tools and object-oriented techniques, the Cocoa frameworks provide a fast and complete way to do so.

Unfortunately, there's no easy way to tell whether an application is Cocoa or Carbon, so if you pull down the Services menu and find that none of the Services are enabled, you can pretty much bet it's Carbon. Classic programs, on the other hand, are easy to identify—when you launch them, they either start up the Classic environment or launch into it if it's already running.

Some of the Cocoa programs I know of that support services are TextEdit, Mail, Stickies, Notes, Fire, OmniWeb, and ProjectBuilder. The only Carbon application I know of that supports Services is BBEdit 6.5.

NOTE

This book's Web site contains links to some useful Services. TextSoap and WordService 2.1 both let you manipulate text in a document—change case, reformat, strip line-return characters, and such. And OmniDictionary lets you select a word in services-enabled applications (or type a word) and look it up in a free, Internet dictionary. But because this is the troubleshooting chapter, I'll leave the detailed descriptions for Chapter 14.

When Really Bad Things Happen to Really Good Macs

OK, now we're in the home stretch. I've told you a lot about solving little nagging problems you might encounter with Mac OS X, but now we're going to get to the meat of the matter—what to do when your Mac is totally hosed. What follows are a bunch of different techniques to be used when different things go wrong. I'll present them in roughly the order you should consider them, but honestly, some of them will be more appropriate for certain situations than others. As you grow more accustomed to Mac OS X, you'll develop a kind of sixth sense as to which technique works best for what problem. Until then, you can try them in the order they're presented here.

NOTE

All of these techniques are nondestructive unless otherwise noted.

Before I get into the techniques, though, you can do a couple of things—before a problem occurs—to make troubleshooting easier.

If your Mac ever gets really screwed up, you will need to start up from a disk other than your usual startup disk.

The first and most important discs are the ones that came with Mac OS X (or with your Mac). Both the OS X installer CD and the OS 9 installer CD are bootable (hold down the C key at startup), and both contain software that may be helpful in resolving problems. Make sure you know where the disks are *before* disaster strikes—you're going to need them.

Another option is to partition your hard disk and have more than one volume capable of starting up your Mac, or have an external hard disk with system software installed on it. Restarting using one of these steps is somewhat faster than using the CDs but requires you to erase (reformat) your hard disk or buy a second drive. I recommend either setup highly if you can swing it.

Equally important is a backup of all your important files. Believe me when I tell you that your hard disk will someday fail. If you're vigilant about backing up, it'll only hurt a little. If you're not, you'll be very upset. I already went on and on about how important a backup is in Chapter 4, so I'll leave it at that.

Finally, having at least one third-party disk utility in your arsenal is always a good idea. I cover these in more detail later in the chapter.

Several circumstances exist that might render your Mac unusable. Some occur while you're using your Mac, some manifest themselves when you first turn on or restart your Mac, and some prevent you from even turning on your Mac. You can use most of the following techniques in any of these situations.

Let's start with what I mean by "unusable." Either:

- Your Mac stops working while you're using it. This is called "freezing," "locking up," or "crashing." Fortunately, it doesn't happen very often under OS X.

- Your Mac doesn't start up or restart.

8

How to Deal with Freezing, Locking Up, or Crashing

If your Mac freezes while you're working, the first thing to try is the Force Quit command discussed earlier.

If that doesn't work (and sometimes it doesn't), the next thing to try is to activate the Finder by clicking it, clicking its icon in the Dock, or using the Command+Tab application-switching shortcut. None of these methods may work, but it's worth a try before doing anything further. If you're able to use the Finder, (or even if you're not), choose Apple Menu|Restart.

If that doesn't work, you need to (attempt to) force your Mac to reboot. There are several ways; not all of them work every time. Here's the order in which I'd try them:

1. Use the force restart keyboard shortcut(s): Command+Option+Shift+Power key or Command+Control+Power key. If neither works, go on to Step 2.

2. Press the Power button on your Mac and hold it for at least five seconds. If this turns your computer off (which is what it's supposed to do), press the button again to restart it. If it didn't turn your Mac off, try Step 3.

3. Press the hardware reset button—a little tiny button marked with a triangle some-where on your Mac. Refer to the documentation that came with your Mac to find its location—it's different for every model and could be on the front (G3/G4), the side (iMac), the back (iBook, PowerBook), or somewhere else. If that doesn't work, try Step 4.

4. Unplug the power cord, wait a few seconds, then plug it back in.

> **TIP**
>
> In many cases, your problem will disappear spontaneously after you restart using any of these techniques. So, the first thing you should always try when your Mac or a program starts acting weird is to restart and try again. Only if the problem reoccurs do you actually have a problem. If the problem is cured by a reboot, thank your lucky stars and get back to work.

If none of these steps get you back up and running, work your way through the techniques in the upcoming section, "Troubleshooting Techniques and Tips."

If one of them does work, try whatever you were doing when your Mac froze again. If it freezes again, go through the troubleshooting steps in the upcoming "Troubleshooting Techniques and Tips" section. If everything seems to be normal, breathe a sigh of relief and get on with your work.

Different Types of Startup Failure

Before we look at specific techniques, let's look at the different kinds of startup failures and what to do when they occur.

The Flashing Question Mark

If you see a flashing question mark icon at startup, it means that your Mac can't find a valid startup disk. The first thing to try in this case is to select a valid startup disk. Here's how:

1. Boot from your Mac OS 9 CD, then use the Startup Disk control panel to select a startup disk.

2. Restart.

> If you can't get the disc tray to open so you can insert a CD to boot from, try restarting while holding down the mouse button. Continue to hold it down until either the tray slides out or you get sick of waiting.

If your problem persists, work your way through the techniques in the upcoming section, "Troubleshooting Techniques and Tips."

8

The Startup Freeze

Another startup problem you may someday encounter is when your Mac doesn't complete the startup process. By this I mean that between the time you press the Power key or button and the time the Finder's desktop appears, you crash or freeze.

In the old days, under Mac OS 9, you could hold down the Shift key to disable all extensions or control panels, which often allowed you to at least get your Mac back up and running. Mac OS X doesn't have that feature.

A startup freeze can happen for a wide variety of reasons; work your way through the techniques in the upcoming section, "Troubleshooting Techniques and Tips" to resolve it.

The Sad Mac

A sad Macintosh icon at startup usually indicates big trouble—a fatal hardware failure. You can try to work your way through the techniques in the upcoming section, "Troubleshooting Techniques and Tips" to resolve it, but chances are your Mac is going to need to be repaired by a trained professional.

The Chimes of Doom

If you hear an unusual set of tones (an arpeggio power users refer to as "the chimes of doom") or what sounds like a car crash instead of your usual melodic startup chime, it's just like the sad Mac—probably a hardware failure. Sometimes you hear the chimes of doom first, then see the sad Mac icon. Again, you can try to work your way through the techniques in the upcoming section, "Troubleshooting Techniques and Tips" to resolve it, but chances are your Mac is going to need to be repaired by a trained professional.

Black Screen

If your Mac screen stays totally black when you start up, and you don't hear any tones at all, you've probably got a hardware problem. Either that or your Mac isn't plugged into a power outlet (check the power cord and the outlet).

I know you're getting sick of hearing me say it by now, but I think this is the last time I'll have to. . . Try to work your way through the techniques in the upcoming section, "Troubleshooting Techniques and Tips" to resolve it, but chances are your Mac is going to need to be repaired by a trained professional.

Troubleshooting Techniques and Tips

First, before trying a single one of these techniques, check all your cables, including the Mac's power cord. There's nothing more embarrassing than finding out the reason you were having a problem was that the Mac wasn't plugged in.

If you have any external devices you don't need for troubleshooting, unplug them. You never know if a USB or FireWire device is at the root (pun intended) of your problem.

Finally, if you've recently installed anything—RAM, PCI card, storage device, or whatever—check to be sure that the card or RAM is seated properly in its slot, and that all internal cables are connected to what they should be connected to.

OK, let's do some troubleshooting.

Zap the PRAM

The first thing I try when I'm having serious problems is zapping my PRAM.

What is PRAM? It's the acronym for Parameter Random Access Memory. What does PRAM do? It's a small amount of memory continually powered by a lithium battery inside your Mac that retains its contents even when the computer is shut down. PRAM stores information such as background color, default video selection, network information, serial port information, and default highlight color.

Sometimes, for reasons unknown, the contents of your PRAM become corrupted (scrambled, broken, messed-up, and so on). Clearing (i.e. resetting or zapping) your Parameter RAM is relatively harmless, and can often bring the dead Mac back to life by restoring all its settings to the factory defaults, so anything you've customized (like background or highlight color) will be changed back to the way it was the day you got your Mac.

Here's how to do it:

> NOTE
>
> Apple says you may not be able to do this with some third-party keyboards. But I've used only third-party (i.e., non-Apple) keyboards for years and it's always worked for me.

1. Make sure the Caps Lock key is not pressed, then start up or restart your computer and hold down the Command, Option, P, and R keys.

2. Keep holding down the keys until you hear the startup chime three or four times. It takes a few seconds between chimes, so don't let up on the keys too soon.

3. After the third or fourth chime you can take your fingers off the keys. Your Mac should start up normally now.

Remember that zapping your PRAM resets all kinds of stuff back to the way it came from the factory. So your Time Zone and Daylight Saving Time settings will need readjusting, though the current date and time generally survive a zapping. Other settings you may need to readjust include your AppleTalk settings, keyboard and mouse settings, speaker settings, screen resolution, and/or startup disk. Some of these items may remain unchanged; others may not. I usually open System Preferences after a PRAM zap and check them all, just in case.

Check Your Disks

If PRAM zapping didn't clear up your problem, and often it doesn't, the next step is to ensure that your hard drive(s) haven't become damaged. Mac OS X uses a bunch of invisible items on your hard disk to keep track of files and folders it contains. If one or more of them becomes corrupted or damaged in any way, your Mac may malfunction.

What are these items? They have names like tree depth, header node, map node, node size, node counts, node links, indexes, siblings, and more. But that's not important. What is important is that you check them to ensure their integrity.

You can do this several different ways; each has its strengths, and none of them has much of a weakness. Sometimes one method will work when another didn't, or one will find damage another overlooked. The safest bet is to run them all.

> **NOTE**
>
> Many of the issues the following disk utilities find and repair occur after improper shutdown, forced restart, or power interruption. If any of those things happen, you might consider running one or more of them, even if things seem okay.

If you are having startup problems, Mac OS X includes a pair of tools that can examine your disk and repair most types of damage should they find it. **fsck** (File System Check) is a Unix utility that you run by typing at the command line at startup. You don't have to boot from a CD to use it. Disk Utility is a double-clickable Mac OS X application (which means that unlike **fsck**, it has a user interface), but it does require you to boot from an OS X CD-ROM to check and repair your drive.

Last but not least, several commercial utilities are available—Alsoft DiskWarrior, Norton Disk Doctor, and TechTool Pro—that not only inspect and repair your disks, but also do other useful troubleshooting/maintenance tasks.

I'll tell you all about them now.

File System Check (fsck)

Disk Utility and **fsck** are *supposed* to do the same exact thing, but at times, **fsck** may be preferred. For example:

- Your CD-ROM drive is broken or otherwise unavailable.

- Your Mac OS X CD is not handy (I warned you about this a few pages back).

- You are a Unix hound, and you like the command line.

Now, as I said, Apple implies that Disk Utility runs the same tests and repairs disks the same way as does **fsck**. But my experience has been different. Several times in the past few months, Disk Utility has given my hard disk a clean bill of health, but when I ran **fsck** immediately thereafter, it found and repaired multiple issues.

Apple says you should run the Disk Utility application on the Mac OS X CD *before* **fsck**, but I am going to go against the grain by stating that I believe your chance of success is greater if you run **fsck** first.

To run **fsck**, you first need to start up your Mac in single-user mode. Here's how:

1. Restart your Mac.

2. Immediately press and hold the Command and S keys down until you see a bunch of text begin scrolling on your screen. In a few more seconds, you'll see the Unix command-line prompt (#).

Congratulations. You're now in single-user mode. I bet you've never seen your Mac screen look like that before. (I wish I could show you a screenshot of it, but as far as I can tell, it's not possible.)

Now that you're at the # prompt, here's how to run **fsck**:

1. Type "fsck –y" (that's **fsck**-space-minus-y).

2. Press Return.

   The **fsck** utility will blast some text onto your screen. If there's damage to your disk, you'll see a message that says: ***** FILE SYSTEM WAS MODIFIED *****.

   If you see this message—and this is extremely important—repeat Steps 1 and 2 again and again until that message no longer appears. Having to run **fsck** more than once is normal, because the first run's repairs may uncover additional problems.

   When **fsck** finally reports that no problems were found, and the # prompt reappears:

3. Type "reboot".

4. Press Return.

Your Mac should proceed to start up normally to the login window or the Finder.

Disk Utility

If you have the option, you can run Disk Utility instead of **fsck**. But as I said, I've had better results with **fsck**. On the other hand, typing that Unix stuff is a little intimidating, so I can understand if you wish to avoid it. So here's how to do it using Disk Utility:

1. Insert your Mac OS X CD-ROM.

2. Restart your Mac while holding down the C key.

   This causes your Mac to boot from the disc in the CD-ROM drive (assuming it has valid startup software on it—Mac OS 9 or X will do).

3. When the first Installer screen appears, choose Installer|Open Disk Utility.

ALERT!

Do not click Continue, or you will have to quit the Installer and restart to get to Disk Utility again—it's available only from the first Installer screen.

4. Click the First Aid tab at the top of the window and select your boot disk in the disk and volume list on the left, as shown in Figure 8.22.

5. Click Repair.

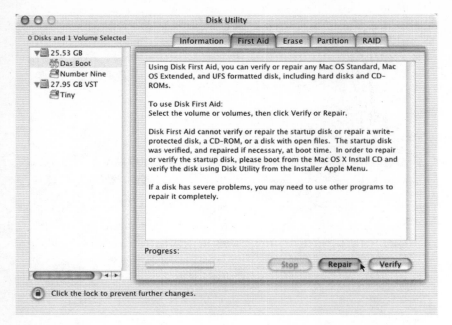

Figure 8.22
Repairing a disk with Disk Utility.

Some text will scroll in the Disk Utility window: *"Repairing disk "Das Boot." Checking HFS Plus volume, Checking Extents Overflow file, Checking Catalog file, Checking Catalog hierarchy, Checking volume bitmap, Checking volume information."*

If a problem occurs, you'll see error messages between some of this text. Read it. If it says "fixed" after the error, do Steps 4 and 5 again. If you see an error message that tells you First Aid can't fix the problem, either run **fsck** if you haven't already, or try one (or more) of the commercial utilities in the next section.

Keep repeating Steps 4 and 5 until the problems have been resolved and you see: *"The volume* YourDisk'sNameHere *appears to be OK. Repair completed."*

Choose Disk Utility|Quit Disk Utility (Command+Q), which will return you to the first Installer screen. Choose Installer|Quit Installer (Command+Q), and a window will appear with two buttons. Click Restart and your Mac should proceed to start up normally to the login window or the Finder.

If Disk Utility and/or **fsck** found errors they couldn't fix, they'll tell you so. At this point, you have two choices: You can either reformat (erase) your hard disk to fix the problems, which almost always works but destroys all your data on that disk, or you can try one of the commercial disk utilities, which can sometimes repair damage that neither Disk Utility or **fsck** could fix.

Three competing utilities—DiskWarrior, Norton Disk Doctor, and TechToolPro—each includes a component similar to Disk Utility's First Aid feature. Any or all of them can sometimes repair problems that Disk Utility or **fsck** couldn't fix. Note that I said "sometimes" because there's no guarantee they will work. Alas, unlike Disk Utility or **fsck**, none of them is free. So I can't just say, "run them." But sometimes they will save your bacon, and when they do, they're worth every penny.

Most power users have at least one or two of them. I have all three. Each has its fans and its detractors. What follows are my opinions of each, based on years of experience with all three.

DiskWarrior

Alsoft's DiskWarrior is the one I'd buy if I were only going to buy one. The other two programs have more bells and whistles, and give you more tests and functions, but DiskWarrior has saved several disks—of mine and of others I know—that no other program could resurrect.

DiskWarrior is admittedly a one-trick pony, but it does that one trick exceedingly well. The only thing this program does is repair disk damage by rebuilding your disk directory. Directory errors are the most common problems Mac OS users have with their disks; DiskWarrior eliminates almost any problem those errors might have caused, and recovers files that might have otherwise been lost or unusable.

DiskWarrior includes only one other bell (or whistle), but it's a good one: PlusOptimizer, a program that optimizes disks by defragmenting files and free space. The more fragmented a file (or disk) becomes, the slower it will be. A disk optimizer speeds up disk access; the more fragmented your disk becomes, the more benefit you'll gain by optimizing. Most power users optimize their disks several times a year and many do it much more often.

Granted, all three programs include an optimizer, but PlusOptimizer is at least as good as any of the others, and may be better.

Street price: $70 (**www.alsoft.com**).

Norton Utilities

Norton Utilities is a suite of disk utilities that solve and prevent disk problems, optimize disks, and recover deleted files. Norton SystemWorks has all of that plus Norton Antivirus, Dantz Retrospect Express for backing up files and disks (under OS 9 only when I wrote this), and Aladdin's Spring Cleaning, a program that removes old programs, preferences, and Internet clutter. It also uses a nifty "Live/Update" feature that automatically updates the programs and virus definitions via the Internet.

8

As I said, if I were only going to buy one, it'd be DiskWarrior. But Norton is a good suite of useful utilities, and because many users need an antivirus program anyway, SystemWorks is an excellent value that provides a lot of bang for your buck. If you can afford to, buy both SystemWorks and DiskWarrior. Many users, myself included, use both. If one can't fix a disk problem, the other usually can.

Street prices: Norton Utilities: $100, Norton SystemWorks: $130 (**www.norton.com**).

TechTool Pro

Micromat's TechTool Pro 3 is another all-inclusive suite of protection and diagnostic tools. Like Norton, it's a good value—it includes comprehensive diagnostic testing for your disks and many other parts of your Mac, and also offers disk repair, data recovery, optimization, and virus protection.

Micromat's other program, Drive 10, is a lot like DiskWarrior, but unlike DiskWarrior and Norton, which both require you to boot from their OS 9.2.1 CDs, Drive 10 is a Mac OS X application.

Don't read too much into that—you still have to boot from its CD to use it (as you do for all disk utilities). Frankly, I think both DiskWarrior and Norton do a better job of fixing disks.

Micromat has many fans and some users swear that their programs are better than Norton's. I'm not so sure. Over the years, I've had the most successes with DiskWarrior, followed closely by Norton. TechTool Pro has some nice features, but as a first line of defense against disk damage, I would pick either of the others over it. And Drive 10 didn't work for me the two times I've tried it, though I've seen other users rave about it saving their disks.

Still, unless you're going to spring for all three, I would recommend DiskWarrior first, Norton SystemWorks second, and TechTool Pro if you still have money to burn. I can't recommend Drive 10, at least not the two versions I've tried (1.0 and 1.0.2).

Street prices: TechTool Pro: $100, Drive 10: $70 (**www.micromat.com**).

Dealing with Preferences

If none of those disk utilities solved your problem, the next thing to consider is a corrupted (damaged) preference file or files. To understand why preference files can cause untold heartache, you need to understand what a preference file is, what it does, and how the whole preferences thing works.

Most programs have a dialog box called Preferences, which let you configure specific features of the program so that they work the way you want them to. In Figure 8.23, you

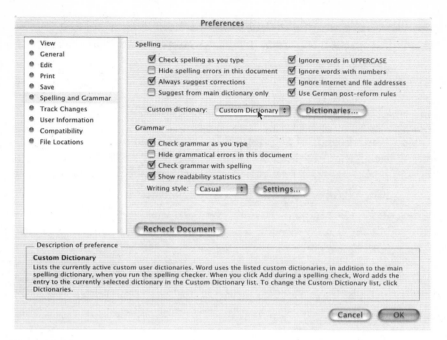

Figure 8.23
Word's Preferences dialog box has nine other panes like this; all your choices in all 10 panes are stored in Word's preference file.

can see Microsoft Word v.X's Preferences dialog box (or at least part of it—it has nine more windows like this one, each packed with different options for you to choose from).

So preferences are program options. And preference files are where programs store your choices for those options. When you quit a program, it remembers your choices by saving a (usually) small file to your hard disk. When you launch the program again, it reads this file and puts everything back the way you left it last time you used the program. It's an elegant idea, and it usually works great.

But sometimes it doesn't. If a program crashes or freezes while it's writing something to its preference file, the file may become corrupted (i.e., damaged). If you're lucky, all that will happen is that you'll have to configure all your preferences again. But if you're not so lucky, the corrupted preference file will cause all sorts of problems.

Some of the indications that you may have a corrupted preference file include the following:

- A program that "quits unexpectedly," either when you launch it, or when you perform a particular action, such as choose a particular item from a menu or open a particular dialog box.

- A program that stops acting the way it should in almost any way; for example, if you can't click a button or checkbox anymore, or a menu item that should be enabled isn't.

- A program that either freezes when you launch it, or doesn't launch when you try to launch it.

- A program that displays almost any other type of improper behavior.

Mac OS X itself stores dozens of preference files, and should one of those become damaged or corrupted, the result may be a Mac that doesn't work right. Corrupted preference files can prevent your Mac from starting up. They can cause your Mac to crash or freeze during startup. They can cause your Mac to crash or freeze when you try to use a System Preference pane. If you have items that launch automatically at startup (i.e., Login Items), a corrupted preference file can cause your Mac to lock up when those programs launch.

In a nutshell, whenever something isn't working right, the first thing to suspect is a corrupted preference file. So let's consider how to deal with preferences that go bad.

Back Up Your Preferences Folder

Even if you don't back anything else up, you should back up your Preferences folder when everything is running smoothly. You'll find it in /Users/YourName/Library; it's called Preferences.

Let me give you an example of how having a recent backup of my healthy Preferences folder saved me hours of agony.

A few days ago I turned my Mac on in the morning and went to get coffee in the kitchen, as I always do. Because I have about 10 Login Items, it takes my Mac a couple of minutes to boot, load those programs, and be ready to use. When I walked in a few minutes later, I noticed that none of my Login Items were running, and that the beach-ball cursor was still spinning. When I tried to move the mouse, nothing happened. The keyboard wasn't working either, so I couldn't Force Quit or force restart from the keyboard. So I shook my head and pressed the reset button, hoping this was just some strange one-time occurrence.

I wasn't that lucky—it happened exactly the same way three more times. I hadn't installed anything new, and I hadn't added any new Login Items lately, so I deduced that my problem was something else. I had a hunch it was a corrupted preference, so I restarted my Mac again, and forced it to boot from my other hard disk volume, Number Nine, by holding down the Option key at startup, then choosing Number Nine in the Startup Manager, as I described way back in Chapter 2.

I opened my Library folder and moved the entire Preferences folder to the desktop. Then I created a new folder in my Library and named it Preferences. I figured this would be a quick way to establish whether a corrupted preference was causing my problem. If my Mac started up from OS X now, I could pretty much bet on it; if the problem persisted in spite of the empty Preferences folder, I would have to start considering other possible causes.

So I restarted into OS X and it worked fine. I launched each of my 10 Login Items manually, and they all worked fine. "Ah ha," I exclaimed, it must have been caused by a corrupted preference file.

But I have close to 300 files in my Preferences folder. How was I going to determine which one was corrupted? The answer is, I didn't bother. Because I had backed up my Preferences folder a few days before, I merely replaced the Preferences folder in my Library with the one from my backup disc and restarted. And after that, like magic, everything was back to normal.

If I hadn't had a backup of my Preferences folder, I might have spent several hours trying to figure out exactly which file was corrupted. Or, if I didn't want to do that, I might have thrown the Preferences folder with the corrupted file in the Trash, and then spent several hours setting the preferences for 300 programs, preference panes, and utilities back the way I had them. Instead, I was up and running in less than 15 minutes.

My Mac has been running perfectly the last few days. I have not had a single crash, freeze, unexpected quit, or any other weirdness lately, so I just burned another backup copy of my Preferences folder onto a CD-RW disc and stuck it in my drawer.

If you're smart, you'll do the same immediately (assuming that your Mac is running smoothly).

If your Mac is not running perfectly, and you don't have a recent backup of your Preferences folder, here are some tips to help you determine if a preference or preferences could be the cause, and if it is, how to fix it.

Hunting Down a Corrupted Preference File

If you have configured your Mac for more than one user, try starting up using a different account. If you don't have a second account handy, skip to the next paragraph. (And when you get things working again, consider creating a "dummy" account, which you'll only use for troubleshooting, which is what I've done.) If it works, you can be relatively certain that you have a bad preference file in your Preferences folder.

If you were able to work successfully using another account, or if you don't have another account, the next thing to do is restart your Mac using an OS 9 CD as your boot disc (remember to hold down the C key). Now move the Preferences folder from your Library (/Users/YourNameHere/Library) to the desktop, then restart your Mac without holding down the C key and log back in using your usual account.

If it works now, you either need to track down the corrupted preference file or resign yourself to setting the preferences for all your programs, preference panes, and utilities again over the next few hours or days.

I have a couple of tips that can make the hunt for the corrupt preference file a lot easier. The first tip is to create a new folder on the desktop and name it something descriptive like Preferences In Quarantine. Now open the Preferences folder that contains the suspect file, choose View|As List, and click the Date Modified column header to sort the folder by modification date. You want the most recently modified preference file first, so if the top item wasn't modified today, click the column header again to reverse the sort order.

Now think back to the last time your Mac worked properly, then click the first item in the folder (which should be the most recently modified preference file), hold down the Shift key, and scroll down until you see a file with a modification date you think is before your problem started. Without releasing the Shift key, click it. That will select all the files between it and the first file in the list.

For example, if I knew that my Mac ran fine this morning, the result of those steps would look like Figure 8.24.

Now drag all those files into the Preferences In Quarantine folder and restart your Mac in OS X and log in. If things are okay, you know that one of the files in the Quarantine folder is the culprit. You can either refine your search further or trash all of them and live with the consequences. In Figure 8.24, I selected 30 items that were modified today, which means I'd have to redo the preferences for only 30 items, instead of the entire 310 items in the Preferences folder. As you can see, this option is a lot better than trashing the whole folder. So give this technique a try if you're having problems with preferences.

My second tip is a lot shorter and easier—if you're having a problem at startup, try this: Start out the same way as before, but this time just move one file—the one named "loginwindow.plist"—out of the Preferences folder, then restart from Mac OS X. If you're able to boot successfully this way, one of the items in your Login Items list has a corrupted Preference file. Just find those and trash them and you'll be fine. You will have to create your Login Items list again, but that's a small price to pay for the time you saved.

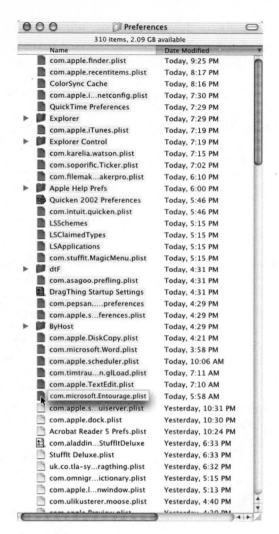

Figure 8.24
I've selected all the preference files that were modified today.

That's about it for the relatively painless stuff. If you've tried everything I've told you so far in this chapter and your Mac still won't start up properly, you have only one thing left to try, and that is . . .

Reinstalling Mac OS X

This isn't so bad. Unlike Mac OS 9 and earlier, reinstalling Mac OS X is virtually painless and fixes almost anything that couldn't be fixed by the previous techniques. Furthermore, the Mac OS X installer is smart enough to leave applications you've installed in the Applications folder alone, and to leave your Home folder intact.

Sometimes, nothing but reinstalling Mac OS X will do, and other times, reinstalling is easier than trying to figure out just what is wrong. In either case, it's quick, easy, and almost always does the trick.

That said, I urge you to back up your Home directory and anything else you couldn't bear to lose before you run the Installer. I've never lost anything and I've heard no reports from others who have lost anything by reinstalling Mac OS X, but you're better off safe than sorry.

So when do you reinstall? If you've done everything in this chapter before this section, and are still having a problem, that's one good time to give it a try.

If you ever find that you can't start up your Mac for whatever reason, that's another time you might want to give it a shot.

Finally, if you ever encounter a kernel panic—a kernel panic is a type of error that occurs when the core (kernel) of the operating system has a meltdown—reinstalling may be your only option.

If you ever encounter a kernel panic, you'll know it—your screen will fill with white text on a black background floating on top of whatever image was on the monitor before the kernel panic happened, and your mouse and keyboard will stop responding. The first time you see one it'll freak you out, so Figure 8.25 shows a picture of one.

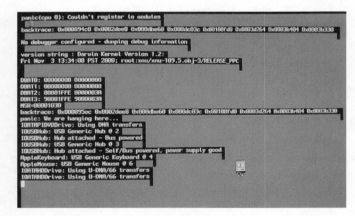

Figure 8.25
A kernel panic captured live on film.

NOTE

Of course, there's no way to take a screenshot of a kernel panic. If Mac OS X is having a meltdown, it can't be bothered with trivial pursuits like capturing a picture of itself in a compromising position. So what you're looking at is a screen shot of a photograph of a kernel panic, which I discovered while reading the Apple Tech Note on kernel panics. If you're interested, it resides at **http://docs.info.apple.com/ article.html?artnum=106227**.

I haven't experienced a kernel panic in months, and some users have never seen one in their lives. But every so often the kernel will panic when you least expect it. Now you've been forewarned.

If you ever have a kernel panic, I suggest you try restarting your Mac once or twice to see if the kernel panic comes back—they're relatively rare and are often a one-time only occurrence. On the other hand, if you get one every time you start up your Mac, reinstalling Mac OS X is the way to fix it.

The process is simple—insert your Mac OS X Install CD, restart while holding down the C key, and follow the instructions the installer provides. There's nothing unique about reinstalling—it's the same as installing. The installer program is smart enough not to kill your Home folder, and your administrator account will still be intact after installation.

ALERT!

The only thing you could possibly do to screw up the reinstall would be to erase your disk before installing. To avoid this, when you get to the Installer's Select Destination screen, whatever you do, do *not* choose the Erase Destination And Format As option. As long as you don't do that, you should be back up and running in 15 minutes or less.

8

Customizing Mac OS X

Why do we customize our Macs? Probably for the same reason dogs—well, never mind, probably just "because we can." The more you use your Mac, the more it becomes an extension of yourself. The same way we make our homes into comfortable places, we find ourselves making our Macs more comfortable. You can make your Mac look just the way you want it to look, you can make your Mac sound just the way you want it to sound, and best of all, you can make your Mac work just the way you want it to work.

The secret is to know how it's done. And that, my friends, is what you're about to learn—a bountiful abundance of ways to fine-tune your Mac to suit your every need and desire.

Apple, in its infinite wisdom, has provided a virtual smorgasbord (pun intended) of customizable components in Mac OS X. You can change the behavior and appearance of just about every facet of your operating system, and for the most part, you can do it without typing a single line of code or using a single program not provided by Apple.

But wait, there's more: Beyond the parts of Mac OS X that Apple lets you customize, you can find several tons of really cool stuff that *doesn't* come from Apple. Programmers have, since time immemorial, created useful hacks and utilities that let you customize many of the little things Apple *doesn't* let you customize. And all over the Internet, you'll find wonderful sites that allow you to download gobs of great icons, desktop pictures, sounds, and more to make your Mac even more interesting and enjoyable.

This chapter is fun. We'll start with some simple, easy tweaks you can make to the OS X to make it work the way you want, and look and feel the way you want, too, all without spending an additional cent. Then, we'll move on to more great ways to make your Mac truly yours, using some excellent third-party software I have links to at **www. boblevitus.com/xfiles.html**. And, at least in my humble opinion, that's the most fun stuff of all.

Freebies from the Big Apple

As I'm sure you're aware by now, the Finder is the heart of your Mac. You use it every time you turn on your Mac, and you probably spend as much time using the Finder as you spend using almost any other program. So most of this first section is about the many ways you can fine-tune that puppy using nothing Apple hasn't provided for free. When you're done, your Mac will act just the way you like it (and look pretty, too).

> **NOTE**
>
> Some stuff that *should* be in this chapter has already been covered. What can I say? Sometimes I get ahead of myself. So although custom icons and customizing the Dock and toolbar ought to be in this section, I already told you most of the good stuff in Chapter 2 and elsewhere. My point? I didn't want you to think I forgot these customizing tips and hints just because they're not covered in this chapter.

We're going to spend a lot of time looking at system preference panes, but before we get to them, here are some tips for using toolbars.

> **NOTE**
>
> Why stick the toolbar tips here and cover them now? Because the first tip is about the System Preferences window itself and will help make it easier to use.

Toolbar Tips

You can customize the System Preference window's toolbar the same way you customize a Finder window's toolbar. If you find yourself using the Screen Saver preference pane more often than Displays or Sound, by all means stash it in the toolbar where it'll be handy. I've replaced icons I rarely use, such as Displays and Sound (which have those nifty little system menus in the menu bar), with ones I do use frequently, such as Screen Saver, Desktop, Login, and Sharing, as you can see in Figure 9.1.

To add an icon to the toolbar, just drag it up there, as I'm doing with Startup Disk in Figure 9.1. To delete an icon from the toolbar, just drag it off and it'll disappear with a satisfying "poof."

Or, if you don't want a toolbar in your System Preferences window at all, merely hold down the Shift key and click the hide/show toolbar gumdrop in the upper-right corner. That'll get rid of that pesky toolbar until you Shift+click the gumdrop again.

Here's another little-known toolbar tip for Finder windows (I mentioned it back in Chapter 2, but it's short and well worth repeating here): You can remove those custom toolbar icons—Back, View, or the four semi-permanent icons (Computer, Home, Favorites, and Applications) without bothering with any of that Customize Toolbar stuff. To get rid of one, just press the Command key and drag the icon off the toolbar. Poof—it's gone!

Figure 9.1
Customize the System Preference toolbar with the icons you use most.

Last, but certainly not least, Apple has created a set of free AppleScripts that are incredibly useful in your toolbar but are also useful when run the usual way—by double-clicking them in a folder. They're called Toolbar Scripts, and you can download one or all of them at **www.apple.com/applescript/macosx/toolbar_scripts/**.

These are my favorites:

- *Snapshot*—May be my absolute favorite. This slick script remembers the layout of all your open windows and recalls that layout with a single click. To use it, you set up all the windows in the Finder just the way you like them, then click the script and choose either the Snapshot option to save the layout, or the Restore option to put all your windows just the way they were when you saved your snapshot. Don't miss it—try it once and you'll be hooked.

- *Stack*—Resizes and stacks all open Finder windows behind the front window. If you're a neat freak, you'll love this one, too.

- *Open Tandem Browser Windows*—My other absolute favorite. I just love it. Click it in the toolbar and it opens two new Finder windows and sets them in column view one above the other, as shown in Figure 9.2. It's perfect for finding and copying items between locations.

9

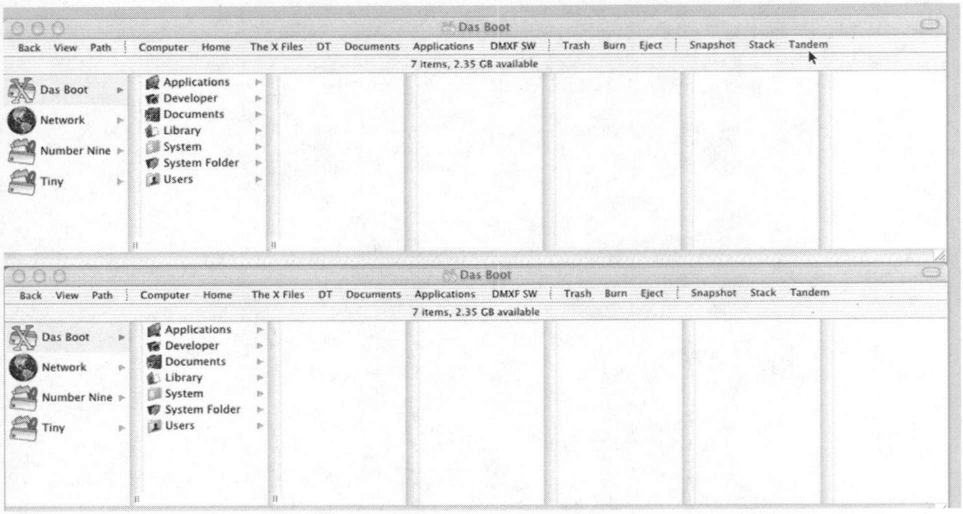

Figure 9.2
The Tandem Toolbar Script gives you two windows in column view, one above the other, like this.

- *Browse Images*—Also quite slick. It creates an HTML catalog of the images located in the folder of the frontmost window, then opens the HTML catalog in your browser. Neat!

And that's just the tip of the iceberg. You can choose among more than a dozen others, all equally impressive and capable of saving you a ton of time. You're making a mistake if you don't at least download the four I just described, but you may find that some of the others are even more useful to you. Go there. Now.

The Joy of X: System Preferences

The fastest, easiest, cheapest way to make your Mac look and work the way you want it to is to use its system preference panes to adjust things. The following sections describe some of the better and more useful adjustments you can make.

Desktop Pictures and Patterns

Even though the default "Aqua Blue" desktop picture is as beautiful as a default Mac desktop has ever been, as I told you in Chapter 2, you can change it easily. It's a cinch—here's how:

1. Launch System Preferences and click the Desktop icon.

2. Choose a collection—Apple Background Images, Nature, Abstract, Solid Colors, or Pictures—from the pop-up Collection menu.

3. Click the one you like best, and your desktop will change to that picture instantly.

But Apple includes only 45 pictures with OS X. If you want to use your own picture(s), you have two different ways of doing it.

Here's way 1:

1. Launch System Preferences and click the Desktop icon.

2. Drag any picture onto the picture well, as shown in Figure 9.3.

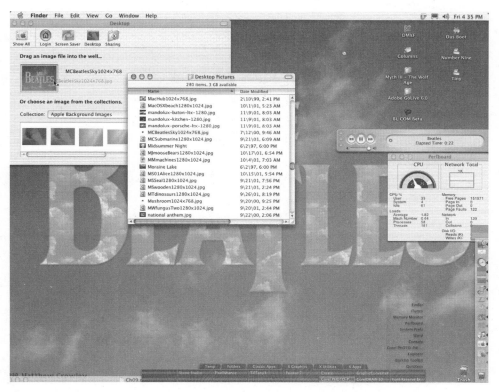

Figure 9.3
Drag any picture into the well and voilà—it's your desktop.

Way 2 may be better if you plan to change desktop pictures frequently, because it lets you access them right from the Desktop system preference pane. Here's how that's done:

1. Launch System Preferences and click the Desktop icon.

2. Choose a folder full of pictures in the Collection pop-up menu by selecting Choose Folder, as shown in Figure 9.4.

Figure 9.4
I added the folder I call "Desktop Pictures" for easy access.

Here are two tips for getting the best results from your desktop pictures:

The first is that the pictures need to be in one of the common graphics file formats, such as TIF, JPEG, or PICT, or they won't work.

NOTE

In other words, graphics saved as native Photoshop, Painter, Illustrator, or Corel PHOTO-PAINT won't work. Use File|Save As to save the file(s) in a format the desktop understands.

The second is that desktop pictures look best when they're the same size, or close to the same size, as your screen resolution. In Figure 9.3, you can see that many of my pictures have the number 1280 or 1024 in their name. That's because my preferred screen resolution is 1280×1024. If you try to use a picture that measures 400×300 pixels as a desktop picture, it's going to look jaggy and ugly.

TIP

You can use GraphicConverter, which you'll find a link for on this book's companion Web site, to resize smaller images to more closely reflect your monitor's resolution.

One last thing before we move on: If you're a fan of desktop pictures (as I am), several programs exist that will randomize and change your desktop picture automatically every startup or login. See the "Desktop Randomizer" section later in this chapter for more details.

General

The General system preference pane offers several useful adjustments, but the one that is most welcome is the Highlight Color menu, which changes the highlight color for selected text and lists. When you get to be my age, your eyes aren't as sharp as they used to be, so I prefer a highlight color that contrasts with the background a lot—more even than any of the preconfigured colors. So I choose Other from the Highlight Color menu and select a bright orange, as shown in Figure 9.5.

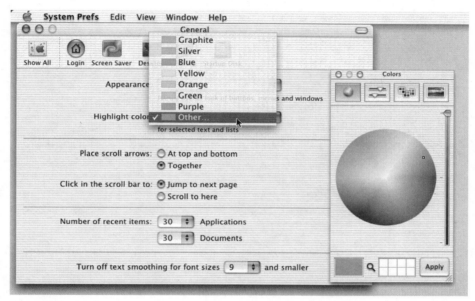

Figure 9.5
It's not easy to discern in black and white, but trust me—the color I picked from the color wheel is a very bright orange.

The result is that when I highlight text in a document or a menu, my old eyes can pick out the highlighted text a lot easier than if I use one of the colors Apple supplies.

While you're in the General system preference pane, you might want to check out all the other options—scroll arrows, scrollbars, number of recent items (I like having 30 better than the default, which is 5), and text smoothing.

NOTE

A nifty freeware system preference pane I tell you about later in the chapter, TinkerTool, gives you much better control over text smoothing than the single size menu in the General pane, so you may want to wait until you've played with TinkerTool before you diddle with text smoothing.

Login

Because I have plenty of RAM, I like to automatically open programs I know I'm going to use when I turn on or restart my Mac, so I add them to the Login Items tab in the Login system preference pane. Anything you add to this tab opens automatically each time you log in. You can even have folders open automatically, which is exactly what I'm doing in Figure 9.6—dragging the OpenMeAtLogin folder into the Login Items tab.

Figure 9.6
Adding a folder to the numerous applications that open automatically when I log in.

To make an item—document, application, or folder—open automatically when you log in, you can use either the Add button to select the file(s) you want to open, or drag the item right onto Login Items as I'm doing in Figure 9.6.

Login Items are convenient. I don't have to search for items, or wait for them to launch—everything I need is ready and waiting for me immediately after I log in.

ALERT!

Mac OS X 10.1.1 had a bug that caused the login items function to be unreliable, often crashing your Mac until you deleted one or both of your login preference files (com.apple.loginwindow.plist and loginwindow.plist). Although I'm sure the issue has been resolved by now, if you ever run into a situation where your Mac freezes or spins the rainbow beach ball cursor endlessly while it should be loading your login items, that's one way to correct the problem—boot into Mac OS 9 and then delete those two preference files. You'll have to put all your favorite programs back into Login Items unless you've got a backup of those preference files, but that's a small price to pay for getting your Mac back up and running in minutes.

Users

Here's another way to customize the Login window. You probably know that you can attach *a* picture—a dog, cat, bird, flower, cactus, or many others—to your login name, but did you know you could attach *your* picture, so your login picture actually looks like you instead of a dog, cat, bird, or whatever?

To do this little trick, open the Users system preference pane, click your username, then click the Edit User button. If you want to be a dog, cat, bird, or flower, just drag one of the supplied images below onto the Login Picture well. But if you want to use a picture of yourself, click either the Choose button to find a picture of yourself using the Open dialog box, or drag a picture of yourself from the Finder onto the Login Picture well, as I've done in Figure 9.7.

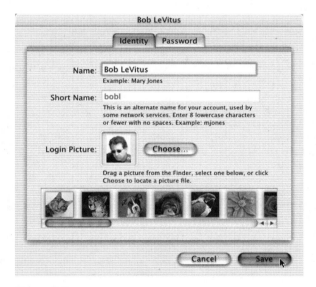

Figure 9.7
Next time I log in, my smiling face will greet me. Cute, eh?

Universal Access

If you're like me, you prefer using the keyboard whenever you can, and reaching for the mouse as infrequently as possible. And wouldn't it be nice if you could use the keyboard to choose menu and dock items?

The good news is that Apple added this capability to OS X in version 10.1, though many users didn't notice. To turn this feature on, just open the Keyboard system preference pane and click the Full Keyboard Access tab.

The bad news is that I've never gotten the hang of it and leave it turned off. It works okay for Finder menus and the Dock, but it's flaky with menus in other programs, as well as with toolbars and palettes. I do most of the things I could do with Full Keyboard Access with a macro utility called QuicKeys, which I show you in the aptly titled "QuicKeys" section toward the end of this chapter.

Speech

If you've never talked to your Mac or had your Mac talk to you, both of the following tricks are worth checking out. The Speech system preference pane is where the magic begins.

The first trick is talking to your Mac and having it recognize what you said and do what you asked it. All you need is a microphone.

If you've never tried it and you have a microphone handy, here's how. . .

First, plug in your microphone, then open the Speech system preference pane and click the Speech Recognition tab. Click the On button to turn Speech Recognition on (duh) and an unusual-looking round window (called the feedback window) will pop up on your screen, as shown in Figure 9.8.

NOTE

Click the little black arrow at the bottom of the round window and choose Open Speech Commands if you don't see the Speech Commands window.

Now press Esc and hold it down while you say, "Tell me a joke." Your Mac, believe it or not, will tell you a bad joke. You can say any of the phrases you see in the Speech Commands window and your Mac will do whatever it is you said.

TIP

Before you go any further, click the Helpful Tips button in the Speech Recognition tab of the Speech pane and read it. Now would also be a good time to open the Help Viewer and search for the words "Speakable Items."

The other speech-related trick is also pretty cool—you can have your Mac read to you in a robotic-but-nearly-human-sounding voice. This trick is turned on by default, so to see it in action, launch TextEdit (in your /Applications folder) and either type some words or paste in text from another application. Select the text you want to hear (or

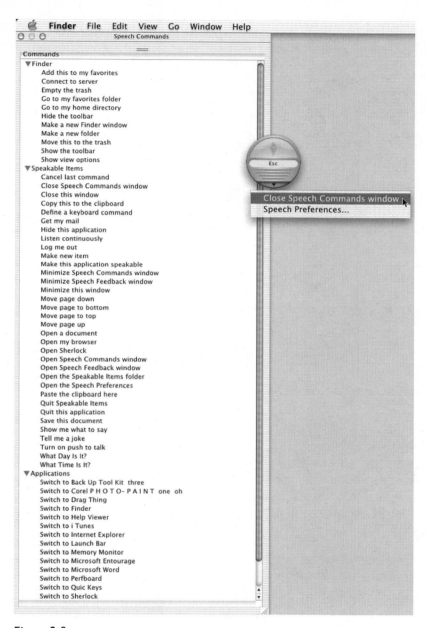

Figure 9.8
The round feedback window and Speech Commands window are the guts of your Mac's speech-recognition capabilities.

don't select any if you want to hear the whole document), then choose Edit|Speech|Start Speaking, as shown in Figure 9.9.

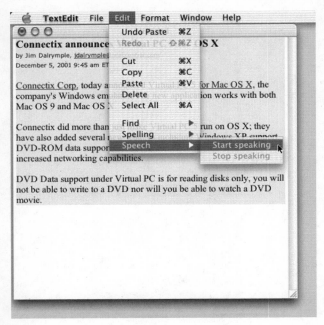

Figure 9.9
This is all it takes to have text read to you in a robotic-but-nearly-human-sounding voice.

Note two more things about this trick:

1. You can change the sound and speed of the voice in the Speech system preference pane's Text-to-Speech tab.

2. This trick works in the background (thanks to OS X's wonderful preemptive multitasking capabilities), so you can do what I do—copy a page of text from a Web site, paste it into TextEdit, then start the speaking and switch to another program. It's like listening to the radio except you get to choose exactly what you wish to hear. Neat!

I have never been able to use Speech Recognition for more than a few minutes—it's just not good enough for me, yet. But I use Text-to-Speech the way I just described fairly often, especially when I'm pressed for time and don't want to stop working just to read something. Instead, I let my Mac read it to me. It's far from perfect, but it works for me.

Sounds
Another way to customize your Mac is to change the alert sound you hear when your Mac "beeps." Just open System Preferences and click the Sound icon, then click the

Alerts tab. Click any of the sounds in the list— Basso, Bonk, Frog, Funk, Glass, Ping, Pong2003, Pop, Purr, Sosumi, Submarine, Temple, or Tink—to hear what it sounds like and/or make it your beep (alert) sound.

Whichever sound is selected when you close the Sound pane will be your alert sound. I'm partial to the gentle tones of the Purr alert but you may find you like another sound better. In the unlikely event you don't find one you like, it's fairly easy to add your own. All you need is a sound stored in the popular AIFF format, which you can download from many Web sites. I found a huge list of sites with downloadable sounds at **http://dmoz.org/Arts/Music/Sound_Files/Samples_and_Loops/**. And I found more than a dozen short AIFF files suitable for alert sounds at **www.zakcomm.com/ Gallery/noize/nhtml/sndaif.html**.

Once you have a sound or sounds in the AIFF file format, here's all you need to know to make them available in the Sound system preference pane as alerts:

1. Some AIFF files use the extension .aif (with only one "f"). You need to change it to .aiff with two "f's" or it won't work. Your Mac will ask if you're sure you want to do that when you attempt to change the file extension. You do.

2. You need to move sounds into one of OS X's Sounds folders, which you'll find in the Library folders. If you want all users to be able to use the sound, put it in the System Library folder (/System/Library/Sounds). If you want it all to yourself, put it in your Home Library folder (/*YourShortName*/Library).

NOTE

If you move the sounds into /System/Library/Sounds you'll need to read the rest of the following steps. If you move them into your own Home Library, you're done— open the Sounds system preference pane and check out your new sound.

3. The Sounds folder in the System Library is owned by root, so when you try to drag a sound into that Sounds folder, you'll get a message that says the Sounds folder can't be modified.

    You can get around this dilemma in one of two ways (actually, three if you count using Unix commands from the Terminal application, but that's the extremely hard way):

    1. Boot into OS 9. Now move the sound or sounds into the /System/ Library/Sounds folder.

    2. Or, use a program such as Super Get Info, Get Info, or Xray (all available via links at this book's Web site) to change the owner to yourself.

> **ALERT!**
>
> Don't forget—using this type of program (or Unix) to change the owner or permissions of the wrong file or folder can render OS X dead on the spot. If you're not sure how to use these programs or are not certain of what you're doing, use the method of booting into OS 9 first. And after you're done moving the sounds, you should probably change the owner back to root.

Screen Saver

The Screen Saver system preference pane lets you pick from a handful of screen savers that come with Mac OS X, some of which are even decent. But you can easily add more if you like.

You need to move any new screen saver files into one of OS X's Screen Savers folders, which you'll find in the Library folders. If you want all users to be able to use the screen saver, put it in the System Library folder (/System/Library/Sounds). If you want it all to yourself, put it in your Home Library folder (/*YourShortName*/Library).

If you move them into /System/Library/Screen Savers, you'll need to follow the steps as in the previous section for Sounds. Just replace the word "Sounds" with the words "Screen Savers."

If you move them into your own Home Library, you're done—open the Screen Savers system preference pane and check out your new screen savers.

A set of 22 of them, called epicware Mac OS X Screen Savers, is on this book's CD-ROM. That should get you started. But if you hunger for even more screen savers, lots more can be had, most of which are freeware. To download more savers, visit **www.versiontracker.com** or **www.tucows.com** (or your favorite Mac OS X–ware site) and search for "saver" in the OS X downloads section. You should find plenty of 'em.

> **ALERT!**
>
> Because they're free, and many are adapted from older Unix source code, I've found that some savers may crash when you select them in the Screen Savers system preference pane, which will make it impossible to use the Screen Savers pane again until you disable the crash-prone savers. If this happens, just remove the offending .saver file from the Screen Savers folder you put it in earlier. Now you should be able to use the Screen Saver pane again with impunity.

One other thing that you probably know already, but I'll tell you just in case: When you choose the default "basic" screen saver, your computer's name bounces around on the screen. If you don't like its name the way it appears, open the Sharing system preference pane and type a new one.

One Last Apple Goodie

Do you own any games or applications that require you to insert the CD-ROM disc before you launch them? If you do and you would like to avoid having to find and insert the CD each time you want to play, there is a way. The down side is that this method requires up to 650MB of hard disk space; the up side is that your game will run faster than ever before, because you're going to be running it from a fast hard disk instead of a slow(er) CD-ROM drive.

> **NOTE**
>
> This isn't really a customizing tip, but I couldn't find a better place for it and it's done with software that comes with OS X and won't cost you a dime, so I suppose this is as good a place as any.

This trick involves creating an "image" of the CD and saving it on your hard disk, then using the image instead of the CD in the future. Here's how it's done, step-by-step:

1. Insert the CD-ROM.

2. Open the Disk Copy application (in Applications/Utilities).

3. Choose Image|New Image from Device (or use the keyboard shortcut Command+Shift+I).

4. Select the CD-ROM in the Device Selector window, then click Image, as shown in Figure 9.10.

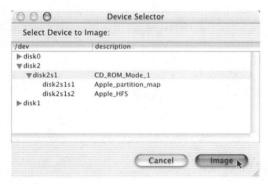

Figure 9.10
Selecting the CD-ROM in the cryptic Device Selector window.

5. Copy the name of the CD-ROM and paste it into the Save As field of the Save dialog box so the image file you're creating will have the exact same name as the actual CD it's impersonating.

6. Choose Read/Only from the Image Format menu in the Save dialog box.

7. Click Image to save the image to your hard disk, as shown in Figure 9.11.

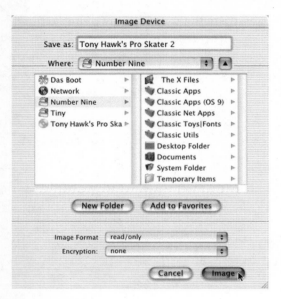

Figure 9.11
Saving the image file on Number Nine.

Now go make some coffee or something—it's going to take a while to create the image file. When it's done, Disk Copy will have a message for you saying the image file was created successfully, and you'll have a 500+MB image file (denoted by the file extension .dmg) on your hard disk.

You can eject the real CD now and put it away. You won't need it anymore. The next time you want to play the game, open the DMG file and Disk Copy will transform it into an exact replica of the original CD and mount it on your desktop, as shown in Figure 9.12. Slick, eh?

What Apple Doesn't Provide

Apple takes you a long way toward creating a desktop environment you can call your own. But lots of other tricks, techniques, and add-ons let you customize it even further. In this section, we'll look at some of the best.

New on the Menus

One of the first things Mac OS 9 users notice about Mac OS X is that the menus are different. Some users really miss the old Application menu you used to find in the

Figure 9.12
The real CD (top), the replica of it (middle), and the .DMG file that creates the replica to appear (bottom).

upper-right corner. Others don't find the Dock a suitable replacement for the good old configurable Classic Apple menu. And although both of them reappear while you're using a Classic application, for many of us, that's not enough—we want them all the time and we want them to do more. Not asking much, are we?

The following sections describe some menu enhancements that make using OS X easier, and in the case of the first two—ASM and Classic Menu—more like the Mac OS 9 menus you know and love.

ASM

ASM is an elegant reenactment of the old Classic Application menu with a bunch of additional features that enhance Mac OS X. In Figure 9.13, you can see both the ASM menu (Bob's Cool ASM), and the main tab of the ASM system preference pane.

What makes ASM better are its multiple unique options, which you'll find in the ASM system preference pane. As you can see, the Menu Bar Options tab lets you turn it on or off, choose whether a title or icon or both appear in the menu bar, set the menu width, alignment, and order, and turn those pretty drop shadows on or off.

TIP

> Speaking of shadows, those drop shadows are pretty but require a sizable amount of CPU time to redraw themselves on the fly. If your Mac is not as peppy as you'd like it to be, I suggest you turn them off in any program that lets you, or use ShadowKiller (freeware from those brilliant coders at Unsanity; you'll find a link on this book's Web site) to turn all shadows off globally. G3 users in particular may benefit from turning off all shadows. But if your G4 feels sluggish, give it a shot. It can't hurt.
>
> As always, YMMV (Your Mileage May Vary).

Anyway, getting back to ASM. Rather than explain all the other options it provides, Figures 9.14 and 9.15 show its two other system preference pane tabs—Menu Settings and Special Features.

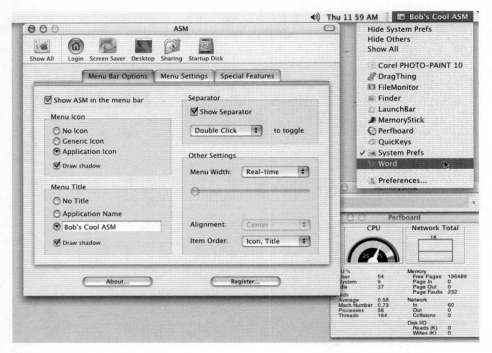

Figure 9.13
ASM is a lot like the Classic Application menu, but better.

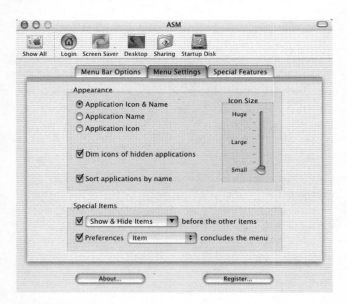

Figure 9.14
The Menu Settings tab gives you almost complete control over the ASM menu's appearance.

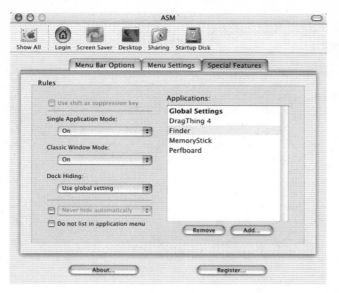

Figure 9.15
The Special Features tab lets you assign these special features both globally and on an application-by-application basis.

These pictures pretty much tell you the whole story, so I'll just explain one feature I think is way cool and leave it at that. That is the Single Application Mode, which I have enabled for the Finder. This feature hides all other applications, so whenever I'm using the Finder, all of my other applications are automatically hidden. And a checkbox prevents certain applications from hiding in Single Application Mode. So that's what I've done with Perfboard, MemoryStick, and DragThing in Figure 9.15. Now when I'm using the Finder, those three programs remain visible while all others are hidden.

I love this particular feature—it's so good that Apple should have built it into OS X. But because ASM is free, there's no reason not to give it a try. I predict you'll like it.

Classic Menu

Classic Menu works at the opposite end of the menu bar from ASM, the upper left, where it replaces the OS X Apple menu with one similar to the one you knew and loved in OS 9. Unlike OS X's static, nonconfigurable Apple menu, Classic Menu lets you put anything you like in the Apple menu.

Unlike ASM, Classic Menu is an application. When you launch it for the first time, it installs a folder called the Classic Menu Items folder in your Preferences folder. From that moment on, whatever you place in your Classic Menu Items folder appears in the Apple menu, as shown in Figure 9.16.

Figure 9.16
My Classic Menu Items folder, the Classic Menu version of the Apple Menu Items folder, and Classic Menu's simple preferences dialog box.

If I want to use one of the items in the OS X Apple menu, I press Control, then click the apple. The normal OS X Apple menu drops down instead of the Classic Menu rendition.

Between these two menu enhancements—ASM and Classic Menu—you get back most of the functionality of OS 9's menu bar, without leaving the comfort of OS X.

NOTE

You can use Classic Menu and ASM at the same time if you like them both.

One last thing before we move on. And that is: Classic Menu is not free. If you like it, pay for it. Classic Menu costs just $10 per single-CPU license. The unlicensed version is fully functional but occasionally displays a reminder to purchase a license. A package with a license for Drop Drawers X ($15 on its own) costs $20 (a 20 percent savings). Currently, you can only purchase licenses online at Sig Software's online ordering page: **http://order.kagi.com/?BX**.

I talk more about Drop Drawers X, which is also very cool, in Chapter 14.

StuffIt Deluxe Magic Menu/Contextual Menu

If you send and receive, or upload and download, files you're no doubt familiar with StuffIt, the longtime standard for compressing Macintosh files. StuffIt Expander, a free "expand only" version, has been standard equipment on every Mac for years. But not everyone is familiar with StuffIt Expander's bigger, more expensive brother, StuffIt Deluxe, a commercial suite of programs from Aladdin Systems (**www.aladdinsys.com**).

StuffIt Deluxe is a total compression and expansion solution for OS X. If you're not sure what that means, rest assured I'll talk more about StuffIt Deluxe in Chapter 14, but for now, I want to show you the feature I use most and like best—the Magic Menu. Magic Menu lets you expand, unstuff, encode, and compress any file or folder without launching a separate application. Furthermore, it works with all the popular Mac, Windows, and Unix compression file formats, including StuffIt (.sit), Self Extracting Archives (.sea), MacBinary (.bin), BinHex (.hqx), Zip (.zip), Unix Encode (.UU), Tape Archive (.tar), Unix Compress (.Z), Bzip, Gzip, and others.

Here's a quick demonstration. Say that I have a folder containing 80 items and using 20.9MB of disk space. "Stuffing" it will result in a single, much smaller file. So I select the folder and use one of the two Magic Menu menus, as shown in Figures 9.17 and 9.18.

Figure 9.17
Stuffing a folder using the Magic Menu in the menu bar.

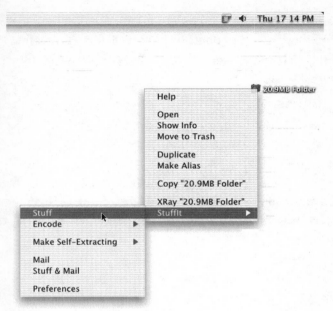

Figure 9.18
Stuffing that same folder using the contextual (Control+click) Magic Menu.

Either way the results are the same: I end up with a single StuffIt Archive file (.sit) that uses a mere 2.4MB of disk space, as shown in Figure 9.19.

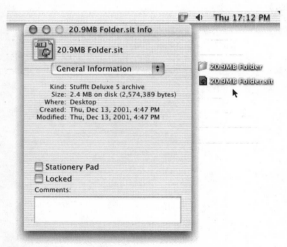

Figure 9.19
Stuffing this folder reduced its size by almost 90 percent!

As you can surmise, sending a 2.4MB file over the Internet as an email enclosure will take a lot less time than sending 80 individual files that add up to 20.9MB.

One other great feature—you can use the contextual menu to encode files in more than a dozen compressed file formats including several flavors of Zip, Tar, UU, BinHex and others, as seen in Figure 9.20.

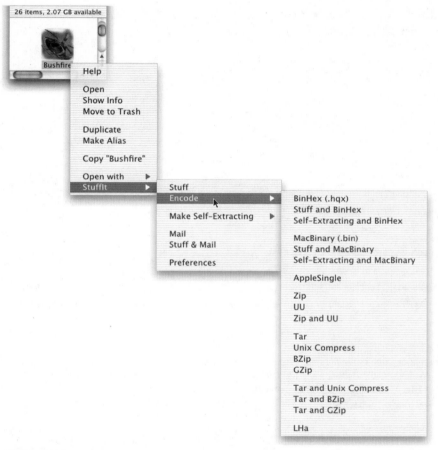

Figure 9.20
A dozen and a half compression choices ought to be enough.

And that, my friends, is the joy of Magic Menu. I can do the whole thing from either menu without launching a separate program. And although you don't always see such dramatic results (i.e., 30–60 percent reduction in size is more typical), you do almost always create smaller files.

Script Menu
One last menu before we move along: Allow me to introduce you to the versatile Script Menu menu, available from Apple at **www.apple.com/applescript/macosx/ script_menu/**.

TIP

You'll find a bunch of useful scripts to use with the Script Menu at that URL as well.

The Script Menu, like the aforementioned Toolbar Scripts, makes it easy to use AppleScripts. Just reach up to the menu bar and perform dozens of actions with the flick of a wrist, as shown in Figure 9.21.

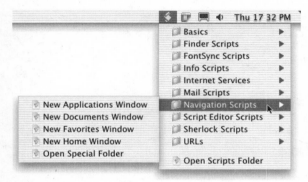

Figure 9.21
It's fast, it's convenient, it's free—it's Script Menu.

To use it, download the Script Menu (called ScriptMenu.menu) and some scripts from the Apple site I just mentioned. Then drag the ScriptMenu.menu icon onto your menu bar.

TIP

To move the Script Menu icon in your menu bar, press Command, then click the icon in your menu bar and drag it. Unfortunately, you can only drag it to the left or right of other menu bar icons; you can't drag it to the middle or the far left.

Finally, open either the root level Library folder or your home Library folder, create a folder called Scripts if one isn't there already, and put scripts or folders full of scripts in the Scripts folder. When you pull down Script Menu, you'll see the contents of that folder in the menu, as shown in Figure 9.22.

Desktop and Dock

The desktop and the Dock are two easily customized parts of Mac OS X, and you can find many third-party programs to customize them with. You'll find many more wonderful accoutrements (such as docklings, icons, and other utility programs) in Chapter 14, but for the time being, here are a pair I like a lot.

Figure 9.22
These are the items you see in the Script Menu in Figure 9.21.

NOTE

> Don't forget, as you learned in the whimsically-titled sidebar, "A Brief Iconic Diversion," way back in Chapter 2, you can also replace almost any icon with almost any other icon or picture. This is yet another way to beautify your desktop, but because I've already told you exactly how it's done, I won't waste any space on it here. You'll really appreciate them if, like me, you're not much of a graphic artist. They are some of the nicest OS X icons I've ever seen—I think you'll like 'em a lot. You'll find links to all this software on my companion Web site **www.boblevitus.com/xfiles.html**.

Desktop Randomizer

Do you like using a picture as your desktop background? Would you like to have those pictures rotated automatically and at random? Well have I got a freeware program for you: It's Desktop Randomizer, and it couldn't be easier to install and use.

NOTE

> In fact, no installation is actually necessary, and if you put Desktop Randomizer into your Login Items, you don't really use it, either—it just changes your desktop picture at random each time you log in.

Here's how it works (this will only take a second):

1. Launch Desktop Randomizer.

2. Click the Choose Folder button, as shown in Figure 9.23.

3. Navigate to a folder with more than one picture in any of the popular file formats, including TIF, GIF, and JPEG. After you select the folder in the Open File dialog box, click Choose.

4. Close Desktop Randomizer.

That's it. From now on, every time you launch the Desktop Randomizer program, a new and different picture, selected at random from the folder you specified in Step 3, will become your desktop picture.

To change the folder your desktop pictures are selected from, hold down the Option key when you launch Desktop Randomizer and the window shown in Figure 9.23 will reappear. If you don't hold down the Option key, launching Desktop Randomizer changes your desktop picture without displaying the window at all—your desktop picture just changes, right before your very eyes.

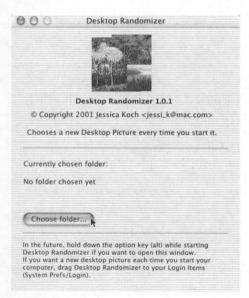

Figure 9.23
This is the whole program. Simple, eh?

If you want it to be totally automatic, just drag Desktop Randomizer onto the Login Items tab of the Login system preference pane, and every time you log in you'll be greeted by a different picture. In Figure 9.24, you can see four pictures of my desktop, snapped immediately after I launched Desktop Randomizer.

Figure 9.24
Four of my more than 200 desktop pictures.

9

> **TIP**
>
> As I said way back in Chapter 2, I find most of my desktop pictures at **www.macdesktops.com**. I make the rest of them myself, using either Photoshop or GraphicConverter.

Hats off to the lovely and talented Jessica Koch, who wrote Desktop Randomizer and gave it to the Mac community for free. It's available via the link located on the book's Web site.

NOTE

> I've never met or even talked to Jessica, but she sounds lovely in the email we exchanged. From the simple elegance of Desktop Randomizer, there's no doubt she's talented. If you use Desktop Randomizer and like it, maybe you could send her a "thank you" note via email. Her address is **jessi_k@mac.com**.

Snard

What's a Snard? The short answer is that a Snard is a dockling that makes your dock more powerful. The longer and more technically correct answer is that Snard is a multifunctional launcher. You can make it work as a system menu (you know, like Sound or Displays or Script) or as a dockling (program that lives in the dock).

Snard, made by Gideon Softworks, is way cool. It reduces dock and screen clutter by replacing lots of folders and icons with one convenient menu you access from the dock, the menu bar, or both.

But calling Snard merely a launcher is like calling Texas merely a state. It's a launcher, and much, much more. Aside from merely launching files, it can also do the following:

- Allow direct access to every system preference pane (my favorite feature by far)

- Launch Applications as an Administrator

- Perform a search locally or on the Internet, with Sherlock

- Provide custom worksets, so you can open/launch groups of programs and/or documents with one click

- Access recent items without reaching for the Apple or Go menus

You know I'm a firm believer in the old "a picture is worth a thousand words" saying, so Figure 9.25 shows the Snard dockling, Figure 9.26 shows the Snard system menu, Figure 9.27 shows Snard's direct access to the System Preferences menu, and Figure 9.28 shows Snard's easy-to-use Snard Config window, where you make the magic happen.

I will confess that I use only the dockling portion, and don't turn on either of the system menus. That's probably because the lower-right corner of the screen is where all my navigation/organization stuff resides, so that's where I want to find my Snard. But regardless of which Snard menu you use, it's a handy little program that does a lot without using a lot of screen real estate.

Figure 9.25
Snard works as a dockling (shown here displaying the System Preferences menu).

9

Figure 9.26
Snard can also work as a system menu (shown here displaying the Apps menu I made with my favorite programs in it).

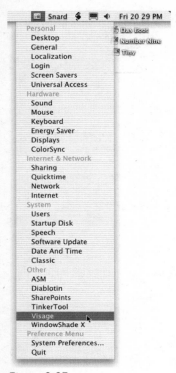

Figure 9.27
Snard has a separate direct access to System Preferences menu, if you so desire (both menus are optional).

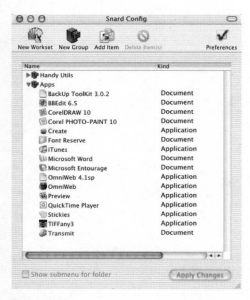

Figure 9.28
Snard is easy to configure—just drag icons onto the Snard Config window.

Click the Preferences checkmark in the Snard Config window, and you can select a new icon. You can find some nice ones at the Gideon Web site (**www.gideonsoftworks.com/snard.html**) to get you started. I downloaded a handful of them; they're shown in Figure 9.29.

Name: aqua_apple.tiff
Kind: TIFF Document
Size: 68 KB
Created: 12/7/01
Modified: 12/7/01

Name: blue.tif
Kind: Document
Size: 104 KB
Created: 12/3/01
Modified: 12/3/01

Name: sningsnang.tif
Kind: TIFF Document
Size: 36 KB
Created: 7/11/01
Modified: 7/11/01

Name: ipod_apple.tiff
Kind: TIFF Document
Size: 68 KB
Created: 12/7/01
Modified: 12/7/01

Figure 9.29
Previews of some of the Snard icons (top) and what one looks like after installing it (bottom).

Snard is fully functional shareware, but it costs only $10. If you try it and get hooked, do the right thing and send the guy his 10 bucks—he earned it. Just double-click the Register document in the Snard folder. It's fast, it's easy, and it's cheap enough to buy one for yourself and buy one for a friend. ("What did you get Bob for his birthday?" "Oh, I got him some socks and a Snard. . . .")

No Pane, No Gain (A Trio of Cool System Preference Panes)

These next three customization tools are among my favorite hacks for Mac OS X. All three are system preference panes, all three modify your Mac's appearance, and two of the three (WindowShade X and TinkerTool) add functionality as well.

I have used all three of these fine programs since the day they came out, and paid my shareware fee for the two that require it (a whopping $7 for WindowShade X, and all of $10 for Visage) within hours of trying them.

Before I go on, a small bit of history is in order. When Mac OS X first arrived on the scene, on March 24, 2001, it was only a matter of days before power users discovered that many options for the Finder, desktop, dock, fonts, and other bits and pieces of the operating system could be "tinkered" with, but Apple didn't include any software with which to do the tinkering. So if you wanted to modify these "hidden" features, you had to do it from the Terminal program's command line.

But then, programmers realized many Mac users didn't *want* to use the command line. And soon real double-clickable Mac programs appeared that let you unlock these hidden features without the muss and fuss of using Terminal.

With the introduction of Mac OS X 10.1 in October 2001, Apple opened the system preference pane architecture to third parties. Since that time, programmers have not only been able to write double-clickable programs to unlock the hidden features, they've also been able to create system preference panes with the same sorts of features.

The programs in this section are three of the finest examples of third-party system preference panes.

How to Install Third-Party System Preference Panes

Some system preference panes come with an installer (such as WindowShade X and ASM). If that's the case, use it. But when you come across a system preference pane that doesn't have an installer (such as TinkerTool and Visage), follow these simple instructions to install it.

> **NOTE**
>
> You can identify system preference pane files by their .prefPane extension—ASM.prefPane, TinkerTool.prefPane, Visage.prefPane, and so on.

To install any third-party system preference pane that doesn't have an installer:

■ Drag it into the PreferencePanes folder in /Users/*YourHome*/Library.

> **NOTE**
>
> If you don't have a PreferencePanes folder in your home library, create one now and *then* drag the .prefPane file into it. Make sure you name the folder PreferencePanes exactly as you see it here—two upper case P's and no spaces—and put it in your Library folder (i.e., not a subfolder) or it won't be recognized by OS X and your system preference panes won't work.

We'll start with the freebie, TinkerTool.

TinkerTool

Don't be misled—just because TinkerTool is free, that doesn't mean it's not worth using. It is a fine piece of work, and I've used 10 or 12 different versions of it (TinkerTool's creator, Marcel Bresink, updates it frequently to squash bugs and/or add new features), and it's always been among my favorite OS X hacks.

TinkerTool doesn't implement any features of its own. It just unlocks hidden features that Apple has built into the applications that are part of Mac OS X. In other words, all it does is turn on or off the features Apple has included but not enabled user controls for.

Here's just some of what you can do with TinkerTool without going anywhere near the command line:

- Enable or disable the Mac OS desktop

- Disable the animation effect when opening files

- Show hidden and system files in the Finder

- Control the scaling options for the Desktop background image

- Set the Dock position and pinning

- Select the Dock animation effect

- Use transparent Dock icons to mark hidden applications

- Select different styles for display of the scrollbar arrows

- Select the default fonts used in Cocoa applications

- Make your Terminal windows semi-transparent

- Control font-smoothing in all types of Mac OS X applications

NOTE

I'll leave it for you to explore most of these nifty options, but I do show you a couple I find particularly useful.

9

First and foremost, as you've seen throughout this book, I prefer my Dock to live in the bottom-right corner of the desktop. Apple allows you to choose Left, Bottom, or Right from the Dock system preference pane but doesn't let you specify exactly where you want it. TinkerTool lets you "pin" the dock to the beginning or end of each position. So mine is pinned to the end of the right position as you've seen in countless screenshots. Figure 9.30 shows TinkerTool with my Dock Options.

You may like another combination, so give them all a try.

TIP

The default Genie Minimizer Effect seems to slow down your Mac much more than either of the other effects. You should definitely give the Suck In and Scale effects a try.

The other TinkerTool option I love is the transparent Terminal window setting in the Terminal tab. I've got mine set to 35%, so I can see what's behind the Terminal window without moving or minimizing it. As you can see in Figure 9.31, Perfboard and MemoryStick can be seen right through the transparent Terminal window.

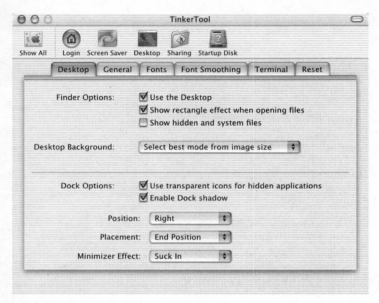

Figure 9.30
These are the Desktop settings I prefer in TinkerTool.

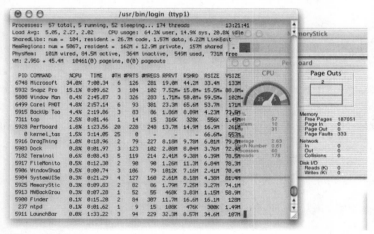

Figure 9.31
The transparent Terminal window trick is neat, don't you think?

NOTE

Some TinkerTool options require you to log out and log back in for them to take effect. If that's the case, TinkerTool will display a message at the bottom of its window saying so.

WindowShade X

When I first started using Mac OS X, I couldn't believe that Apple had removed the wonderful Windowshade feature we know and love from Mac OS 8 and 9. But they did—it was gone without a trace. Mac OS X doesn't have a hidden windowshade feature, so you can't enable windowshades from the command line or any other way. So, for many months, all I could do was gripe and moan about it.

Then one day WindowShade X appeared on **VersionTracker.com**'s Mac OS X page. I couldn't download and install it fast enough. Sure enough, it brought back all of the functionality of the old windowshade option, and even brought a new trick to the table as you'll see in a moment.

Figure 9.32 shows the WindowShade X system preference pane.

Figure 9.32
So simple but so necessary; WindowShade X makes me want to jump up and shout "hallelujah."

When I double-click any window's title bar, the window "rolls up" like a windowshade, as shown in Figure 9.33.

Figure 9.33
With apologies to Bruce Springsteen, with WindowShade X you can "roll down the windows and let the wind blow back your hair."

You have to love that. But wait, there's more! If I Control+double-click on a window's title bar, the window becomes transparent, but remains active and usable, as shown in Figure 9.34.

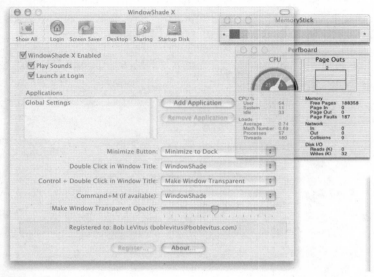

Figure 9.34
Notice how I can still see MemoryStick and Perfboard right through the System Preference window, which, incidentally, still works the same as if it were opaque.

This is very cool and is not part of the old Apple/OS 9 WindowShade.

> **NOTE**
>
> The programmers of WindowShade X, who call themselves "Unsanity," refer to WindowShade X as a "haxie," which I suppose means it's a hack for OS X. They've even gone so far as to trademark the term.

Whatever you want to call it, WindowShade X is awesome. If you liked Windowshade in OS 9, you'll send Unsanity their $7 shareware fee within a few minutes of installing it.

> **NOTE**
>
> Of course, if you don't, WindowShade X will work for only 30 minutes each time you log in before it disables itself.

I'm usually opposed to crippleware (that is, a shareware offering that doesn't provide full functionality until you pay), but in this case I don't blame Unsanity a bit. I might not have paid quite so quickly had the program continued to work for free. But, the first time I tried double-clicking a title bar and saw the "WindowShade X has disabled itself" message, I couldn't whip out my wallet fast enough.

This is one of those programs I can honestly say I would hate to be without. Thanks, Unsanity!

Visage

Let me start by saying that Visage is totally useless but so incredibly cool and fun that I paid for it the first day even though it's not crippled in any way, and the only thing you receive for paying is relief from its nag screens (and, of course, the warm, fuzzy feeling you get from doing the right thing).

Visage lets you customize the way the startup sequence for Mac OS X looks. In Mac OS 9, you could alter the startup screen by merely placing a PICT resource file in your System Folder. In Mac OS X, it's not quite so easy—changing the look of the startup sequence requires TIFF and PDF files that are exactly the right sizes, root access so you can swap your pictures for Apple's, changing the names of multiple files, and other less-than-pleasant stuff. I had done it by hand once or twice, but it wasn't fun and it took a long time to get things just the way I wanted. Visage changed all that for me.

Figures 9.35 and 9.36 show the first two tabs of the Visage system preference pane—Boot Panel and Boot Strings—respectively.

Figure 9.35
The Boot Panel tab lets you replace the boot panel you see at startup.

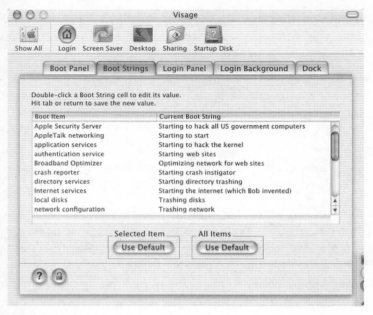

Figure 9.36
The Boot Strings tab lets you change all the text that appears below the Boot panel at startup.

So now when I start up my Mac, instead of seeing Figure 9.37, I see Figure 9.38.

Figure 9.37
A stock OS X boot panel.

Better still, all the nutty phrases you see in Figure 9.36 flash across my screen during startup, which really puzzles Mac users who aren't hip to Visage yet.

Figure 9.38
My "post-Visage" boot panel.

But wait, there's more! I also can choose a new Login Panel and Login Background, so after the boot screens disappear, instead of seeing Figure 9.39, I see Figure 9.40.

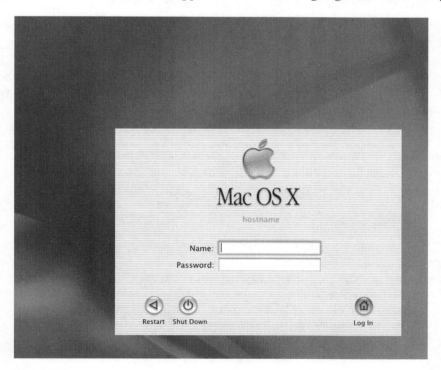

Figure 9.39
A stock OS X Login Panel and Login Background.

Figure 9.40
My "post-Visage" Login Panel and Login Background.

Finally, as Steve Jobs is wont to say, "there is one more thing. . . ." Visage also lets you modify several Dock attributes, including the "poof" animation you see when you drag an item out of the dock. Figure 9.41 shows the Dock tab with the Apple "poof" selected, and Figure 9.42 shows some of the optional poofs you can replace it with.

Okay, now for the good news (like the whole section on Visage wasn't good news): I did not create any of the graphics you see in this Visage write-up. I found every single one of them except the Login Background at a wonderful Web site called ResExcellence (**www.resexcellence.com**). Figure 9.43 shows just some of the goodies you'll discover at ResExcellence.

> **NOTE**
>
> I'd love to give credit to the artists who created the boot panels, login panels, and poofs, but after I downloaded them I tossed everything into a folder I called "stuff for Visage" and now I don't know who created what! So, let me say this to the folks who created them: Thank you, thank you, thank you!

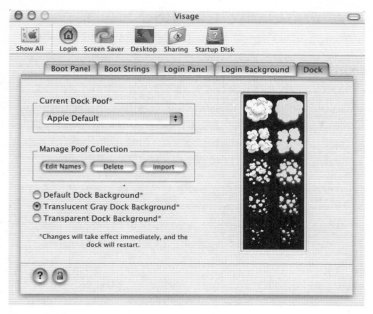

Figure 9.41
The Dock tab lets you customize the Dock.

Figure 9.42
Here are just a few of the neat "poof" replacements you can use.

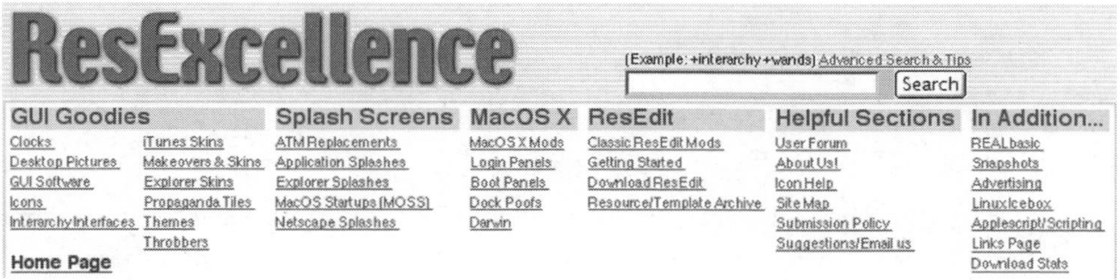

Figure 9.43
ResExcellence is the place to find boot panels, login panels, poofs, and much more.

Four More Customizations to Cherish

Here are four more customizations that fill four gaps left in Mac OS X by Apple.

QuicKeys

Although Apple has long included AppleScript with their operating systems, and AppleScript is without a doubt a robust and useful solution to automating some tasks (see Chapter 13 for the lowdown on AppleScript), the fact remains that it's still far too complicated for many users and not an appropriate solution unless you have time to invest in its fairly steep learning curve.

Frankly, I know how to use it a bit, but I rarely write scripts. If I can't find a good script written by someone else that I can fine-tune to meet my needs, I usually look for another solution. Writing an AppleScript from scratch, at least for most tasks, is beyond my purview and beyond my skill set as well.

Which is why I've been a QuicKeys fan since Mac OS 6 (a.k.a., System 6). QuicKeys, from CE Software (**www.quickeys.com**) is a macro utility that lets you perform common tasks with a single keystroke. It can do a lot of cool stuff that can't usually be done, or can't be done easily from the keyboard, and it's now available for Mac OS X!

For example, without touching the mouse, QuicKeys lets you do the following:

- Copy or move files

- Type text

- Switch, show, and hide windows and applications

- Open programs, folders, and documents

- Insert the date and time anywhere you can type

- Run Unix commands

- Shut down or restart your Mac

- Launch your browser to any Web site

- Connect to a server

- Record your mouse actions

In QuicKeys parlance, each of these things is called a "shortcut," and you can string together multiple shortcuts to make a "sequence."

As I said before, QuicKeys lets you execute your shortcuts from the keyboard, but if you're not a keyboard-oriented user, you can also execute them from a menu in either the Dock or the menu bar, from a QuicKeys toolbar, or with a timer. Figure 9.44 shows some of my shortcuts displayed in three different ways: Dock Menu (right), QuicKeys main editor window (middle), and a QuicKeys toolbar (top).

Figure 9.44
A few of my oft-used QuicKeys shortcuts seen in three places.

What do all those shortcuts do? Glad you asked—here's a quick primer:

■ *System shortcuts*—Columns and List (both triggered with Command+Option+Control+F12) perform system-related tasks. This pair of shortcuts chooses the Column or List View for the active window in the Finder. Each time I press Command+Option+Control+F12, the active window toggles between List View and Column View. So now I can view a window in my favorite view without reaching for the mouse. I use this shortcut a lot.

■ *Open items shortcuts*—(Corel, Entourage, QuicKeys, Quicken, Word, iTunes—all triggered with Command+Option+Control+function key). These open a program (or document or folder) when I press the trigger keys. If the program or document is already open, it makes that item active.

■ *Type text shortcuts*—Sig types my signature as I use it for email; pw types my administrator password for this Mac, a particularly handy shortcut; bl@bl.com types my email address. Text shortcuts are all triggered with: Command+Option+Control+letter key. So my email address is Command+Option+Control+B, my administrator password with Command+Option+Control+V (don't ask why "V"), and so on.

You might not want to do the password thing if other people use your Mac. I would never do it if I worked in an office where someone could easily figure out that Command+Option+Control+V types my administrator password. But I trust the wife and kids not to do that, so I have no problem with it. In fact, I find the shortcut extremely convenient given the number of times each day one program or another asks me to type that password.

- *Hide most*—(Command+Option+Control+H) This hides all open programs except the three I like to be able to see at all times—DragThing, PerfBoard, and MemoryStick.

To create a shortcut, you choose the individual actions from the Create menu (not shown) or click their icons on the QuicKeys Editor window's toolbar. To add another step, choose another action. Figure 9.45 shows you my Hide Most shortcut.

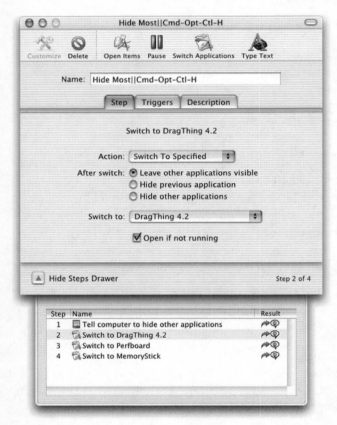

Figure 9.45
It's simple to create shortcuts that do just what you want them to.

For this shortcut, the first step is to hide all applications but the current one, then switch to Drag Thing, then, without hiding it, switch to Perfboard, and finally, without hiding Drag Thing or Perfboard, switch to Memory Stick. The end result is that everything but the program I'm using and those three other programs are hidden, all with a single keystroke.

I consider QuicKeys my "make it easier and faster" utility and before the OS X version came out, I was very depressed. But it's been out for several months now, and although it still lacks some of the features of the old QuicKeys for OS 9 (for example, it can't select a menu item; the OS 9 version can), it's rocking awesome, and I use it a million times a day.

QuicKeys is a commercial program from CE Software (**www.cesoft.com** or **www.quickeys.com**). It sells for around $60.

A shareware program called Keyboard Maestro was in beta (prerelease) testing when I was writing this chapter. Written by Michael F. Kamprath, it is similar to QuicKeys and also includes a very nice program switcher module more powerful than Apple's built-in Command+Tab. Unfortunately it was not finished when the book was. It's probably available now (by "now," I mean when you read this), so you might want to check it out at **www.KeyboardMaestro.com** or **www.versiontracker.com**, which is where I found the beta version.

PTHPasteboard

This little gem is way-cool. You know that OS X has but a single clipboard, and remembers only the very last item you copied or cut. Well, PTHPasteboard gives you as many clipboards as you like and can remember the last 10, 20, or even 30 items you cut or copied.

Just launch it and it begins doing its magic. In Figure 9.46, you can see the Pasteboard History window with the last five items I cut or copied on it.

To bring up the Pasteboard History window, click the pushpin icon in the menu bar (it's a nice shade of aqua in real life). Then, select the item you want to paste with the mouse, keyboard arrows, or by pressing the 0–9 keys.

Pressing Esc closes the Pasteboard History window without pasting.

It's simple, it's elegant, it's useful, and you sure can't beat the price—it's freeware!

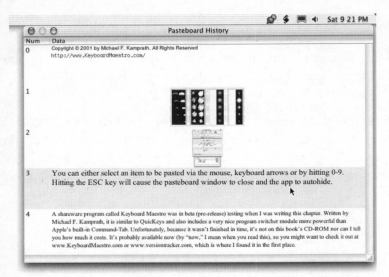

Figure 9.46
As my uncle Yogi LeVitus always says, "Thirty clipboards are better than one!"

X Font Info

If you used OS 9 or other pre-X systems, you remember how nice it was to double-click a font to display a little window showing what the font actually looks like. Apple didn't include that functionality in OS X for some unimaginable reason—when you double-click an OS X font, you see an annoying message like the one shown in Figure 9.47, instead of a little window with a typeface sample.

Figure 9.47
I hate when that happens!

So here's what to do. First, download the X Font Info program from the link at **www.boblevitus.com/xfiles.html** to your hard disk. Then, click Choose Application in the annoying message dialog box, as shown in Figure 9.47. Navigate to the copy of X Font Info you just copied to your hard disk and choose it. Presto-chango—X Font Info launches, and a little window that shows you what the font actually looks like appears, as shown in Figure 9.48.

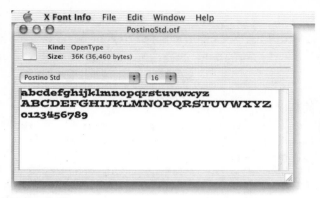

Figure 9.48
Isn't this better than Figure 9.47?

But wait, there's more. If you want a sample to open *whenever* you double-click *any* font, here is what to do:

1. Single-click on a font to select it.

2. Choose File|Show Info (or use the keyboard shortcut Command+I).

3. In the Show Info window, choose Open With Application and choose X Font Info.

4. Click Change All button, as shown in Figure 9.49.

Figure 9.49
Now all my fonts display a little window with a typeface sample when I double-click them.

NOTE

I'd like to take this opportunity to thank X Font Info's author, Vincent Jalby (**http://members.aol.com/vjalby/**) for resolving one of Apple's few unfortunate missteps in Mac OS X. And I want to thank him again for making it available as freeware! That rocks.

The Mouse That Roars

In Chapter 7, I told you about lots of hardware you can add to your Mac. What I'm not sure I stressed was that mice with more than one button and/or mice with scroll wheels are great for OS X.

> **NOTE**
>
> Why Apple continues to insist on a one-button mouse is beyond comprehension. The original reason for a single button (to keep the Mac simple) just doesn't cut it anymore. I would venture that most power users upgrade to a two or more button mouse with a scroll wheel, so Apple could cut us a break by including one or making it an option when you order your Mac. ("Would you like one button with that mouse, or two?")

Anyway, Mac OS X includes built-in support for two-button mice and scroll wheels—for these two functions, you don't need any special drivers. Just hook a mouse or trackball with those features up to an available USB port, and it'll work beautifully in the Finder and most applications. (Classic doesn't recognize the scroll wheel, at least at the time I wrote this, but that's a small price to pay.)

The right mouse button is automatically set to be a Control+click, so you can access contextual menus with it without holding down the Control key; the scroll wheel does what scroll wheels do—it scrolls pages up and down in most OS X applications, including Web browsers and Microsoft Word v.X (the two places I need it the most). And, of course, both right-clicking and scroll-wheeling work in the Finder and most Apple-provided programs as well.

Read the section on mice and trackballs in Chapter 7 again if you need to, then hustle down to the store and buy a multibutton, scroll-wheel mouse. You won't regret it.

Learning to Fish

I hope this chapter has given you a taste for customizing your OS X experience to suit your style and tastes. But I've barely scratched the surface here. Be sure to read Chapter 14, which describes most of the software at the companion Web site.

> **NOTE**
>
> A lot of the stuff you'll discover in Chapter 14 is in the same vein as the items in this chapter. I just don't have room here for any more.

But it doesn't end there, either. If you've got the customization bug, new and interesting programs are released every day.

Fishing via the Web

Here are some Web sites you can check out every now and then to see what's new:

■ www.iconfactory.com

■ www.macaddict.com/osx/

■ www.macdesktops.com

■ www.macosxhints.com

■ www.resexcellence.com

■ www.tucows.com

■ www.versiontracker.com

■ www.xicons.com

■ http://osx.hyperjeff.net/Apps/

Fishing via Email

Another excellent resource for learning how to customize your Mac are any or all of the Mac OS X discussion lists maintained by The Macintosh Guy:

■ *Mac OS X for Users*—Offers discussion, support tips, and techniques focused on the needs of end users dealing with everyday OS X issues.

■ *Mac OS X for Unix*—Offers discussion of the Unix underpinnings of Mac OS X, the command line, and discussion generally too geeky for the other lists.

■ *Mac OS X for Hardware*—Offers discussion of hardware issues on Mac OS X, including supported computers, hardware drivers, and configuration.

■ *Mac OS X for Newbies*—Offers help with installation, setup, basic finder use, and troubleshooting for novice users.

■ *Mac OS X for Servers*—Offers discussion of the built-in and third-party servers for Mac OS X.

■ *Mac OS X for Apps*—Offers discussion of the software programs for Mac OS X, native or classic, cocoa or carbon.

■ *Mac OS X for Dreams*—Offers discussion of the future of Mac OS X, including feature requests and support for Intel hardware.

In addition to these OS X lists, The Macintosh Guy (Eric Prentice, CEO of Dr. Bott, a great place to buy cool stuff like speakers, microphones, hubs, and carrying cases and other interesting hardware; **www.drbott.com**) has more than a dozen other lists—for PowerBook, iBook, G3, G4, business, home office, and so on. You'll find everything you need to know about his lists at **www.themacintoshguy.com/lists**.

Apple also has a list of email discussion lists at **http://lists.apple.com.** The Apple list includes lists that are hosted by Apple, as well as more than 100 lists hosted by others outside of Apple. You will also find an excellent section on how responsible list members should behave, with links to several good articles about how to be a good citizen (i.e., *netiquette*). If you've never taken part in an email list before, I urge you to read at least some of this before you make your first post or risk being *flamed*.

NOTE

Being flamed is what happens when you say something stupid (or something list members *think* is stupid) in a post to the list. It's not fun—you'll be heckled, razzed, and made fun of publicly by other users posting to the list. Forewarned is forearmed.

One Last Thing

The people who make the shareware and freeware mentioned in this chapter, as well as those who maintain discussion lists (better known as "list moms"), deserve recognition for their good deeds. Most of them don't do it for the money, and most of them don't even do it for the fame. They do it because they love the Macintosh. They do it because it's fun. They do it because they want to contribute to the wonderful thing we call "The Macintosh Community."

Please consider giving them the recognition they so deserve. The next time you:

■ *Find a great piece of freeware*—Drop the creators a note and let them know how much you appreciated their work.

■ *Find a great piece of shareware*—Send the programmer some money.

■ *Find an email list you enjoy*—Send the list mom a note to let her know how much you appreciate her time spent managing the list.

End of sermon.

Part III

The Power of UNIX and Applescript

More Than Enough Unix to Get By...

Beneath Mac OS X's sleek, eminently likable Aqua interface, there beats the heart of an old, established operating system known as Unix. A veritable Methuselah among operating systems, Unix has been around for more than three decades—10 years longer than the IBM PC and almost 15 years longer than the Macintosh. Unix even predates the graphic interfaces at Xerox PARC, the very interfaces that inspired (according to legend) Steve Jobs and his associates at Apple to create the Lisa and the Macintosh.

But unlike using graphical user interfaces in, for example, any version of Mac OS, you communicate with Unix by typing commands into a *command-line interface (CLI)*. A CLI, for all of you youngsters, means the operating system has no graphical elements whatsoever—no icons, no scroll bars, no menus, no mouse support—you control everything by typing text then pressing the Return or Enter key.

What Is a Unix Shell and Why Do I Need It?

This CLI is called a *Unix shell*. A wide variety of Unix shells are in common use, and many of them are included with your OS X distribution. Apple makes the shell known as **tcsh** the default; however, you could switch to shells named **sh, csh, ksh, zsh,** or **bash** with very little effort.

TIP

If you know what those are and how to use them, you probably don't need to be reading this chapter.

I'm going to limit the discussion in this chapter to the default shell, **tcsh**, not because it's better or worse than others, but rather for the sake of brevity, clarity, and sanity.

NOTE

The difference between it and other shells is roughly analogous to the differences between American English and British English—some slightly different syntax and vernacular, but the same fundamentals.

It's quite possible that you will never really *need* a Unix shell, but if you do, you'll probably need it badly. At the level of managing your system, there is nothing you can do with Aqua that you can't do in the shell, although the methods employed will likely be quite different. The converse is not true. Until someone wrote a GUI front-end, for example, the only way to specify how the Dock was to be positioned was via the command line, using a command called **defaults**.

NOTE

Apple wisely added much of this functionality to the Dock Preferences Pane in release 10.1.

Eventually, we can expect GUI front-ends to be created for virtually all command-line functionality; however, some things will almost certainly remain more convenient from the command line. For example, using a script to change all occurrences of a string in a bunch of files is more convenient than opening each file in an editor and making those changes via a find/replace dialog box.

Unix comes with a huge collection of commands; some are built into the shell, some are executable binaries, and some are scripts. In addition to all the ones you would expect—such as those to list a directory (**ls**), set the current default directory (**cd**), tell you what the current directory is (**pwd**), display a text file (**cat**), delete a file (**rm**), copy a file (**cp**), move or rename a file (**mv**), and so forth—it even includes such handy little tools as **cal**, which will print a calendar for you for any year you specify from 1 to 9999; **diff**, which will compare two files; and **crypt**, which will encrypt (encode) files.

In addition to issuing commands, a shell can run *scripts*—preconfigured sequences of commands. A script, for the most part, can do almost anything an executable Macintosh program can do. For example, when you launch the Terminal program, a couple of scripts run so that you can establish some commonly referenced shell variables. These include determining what prompt you see at the command line and what directories will be searched for commands you wish to execute (and the order in which they'll be searched).

Getting Started with Unix and Terminal

In your Utilities folder (in the Applications folder), you'll find a program called Terminal. Terminal is your window into the world of Unix.

NOTE

When you run Terminal, you are running the Unix shell **tcsh**.

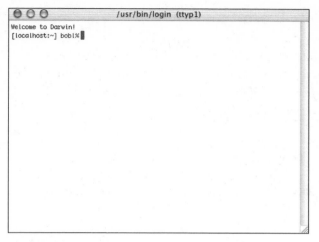

Figure 10.1
A brand-new Terminal window doesn't show you much.

When you launch Terminal, you see a near-empty window like the one in Figure 10.1. **Welcome to Darwin!** is the terminal's way of saying "hi."

> **NOTE**
>
> Darwin is the name of the open-source BSD Unix environment at the heart of Mac OS X. Although Mac OS X, with all its snazzy graphics and Mac applications, requires a G3 processor, Darwin can be downloaded from Apple's Web site and installed on almost any PowerPC-based Mac. In fact, if you have an older Mac sitting in the corner somewhere gathering dust, you could turn it into a decent Unix machine by installing Darwin. It wouldn't really be a Mac any longer, but it could be very useful as a server if you wanted to learn enough Unix.

The next line, **[localhost:~] bobl%**, is known as the Unix prompt. The current directory path is displayed in the brackets, and your (short) username is displayed before the %.

What Goes On Behind the Scenes When You Launch Terminal

The prompt, your default search paths, and so forth are established when you start a *shell* (which is what you're doing when you launch the Terminal application in OS X).

The first thing **tcsh** does is execute the commands from a number of files. It begins by executing the commands in the system files /etc/csh.cshrc and /etc/csh.login. After that, it looks for a file named .tcshrc in your home directory and, if it doesn't find it, it looks for a file named .cshrc. Following that, it will look in your home directory for .history, then .login, then .cshdirs, executing the commands each one contains.

Commonly Used Unix Commands

One particularly useful abbreviation in Unix is ~, which is a shorthand for Home directory (a.k.a. your Home folder). Typing **cd ~** will change your current directory to your Home directory. But ~ is even more flexible than that. If you were to type **cd ~newbie**, you would be switched to newbie's Home directory (assuming its privileges were set to allow you to see its contents).

> **TIP**
>
> This abbreviation also works with the Finder's Go To Folder command (which, interestingly, uses the keyboard shortcut Command+~), and in Open File "sheets" in OS X programs as well. Alas, it doesn't do anything in Open File dialog boxes in Classic programs.

You can run multiple shell sessions simultaneously just by choosing Shell|New (Command+N). You can save shell sessions, and then reopen and reuse them. You can even specify when saving them that you want them to open automatically when you start Terminal by checking the checkbox shown in Figure 10.2.

> **TIP**
>
> Saving a shell session with the commands you regularly execute is a really good idea. Because Terminal supports copy and paste, next time you can just copy the commands you need and paste them in to the Terminal window. This can eliminate typing mistakes, which in Unix can be fatal, and save you time as well as, perhaps, heartache.

As you can see in Figure 10.2, Terminal doesn't attempt to save your files in your Documents folder by default (as most applications do). Instead, it tries to put them in the Application Support folder within your Home directory's Library folder. The What To Save pop-up menu (not popped in Figure 10.2) gives you a choice of just the main (front) window or all windows.

> **NOTE**
>
> Because the **save** command isn't necessarily tied to the front window, Terminal displays a Save dialog box rather than the sheet we're accustomed to in most OS X applications.

Unix has a well-deserved reputation for being cryptic. The command names are abbreviated and most are somewhat less than straightforward—after all, **ls** for a directory list, **cat** for concatenate (which is also how you display a text file on screen), and **mv** for rename (it's really *move*, but rename is how it is most often used) are nonobvious to the casual observer. Add to this terseness the wealth of wild cards

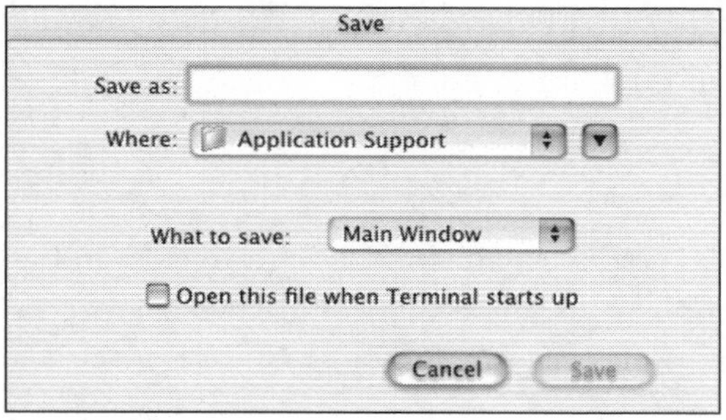

Figure 10.2
Terminal's Save dialog box is just a little different from the typical Mac OS X Save "sheet."

available to specify patterns in strings and file names, and you can do such things as obtain all the file names that have the character "e" as their third character (and only those file names) by entering:

```
ls ??e*
```

> **TIP**
>
> The asterisk (*) is the most commonly used wild card character in Unix. It means "any string of zero or more characters." Another common wild card character is the question mark (?), which matches any single character. Both are worth remembering.

The Unix term for expanding these wild-carded file name specifications is *globbing*.

Using Unix wild cards, the Terminal, and the shell's **open** command, it's relatively simple to open all the Microsoft Word documents in the current directory by typing

```
open *.doc
```

at the command line, or to open all the TIFF files in your Pictures directory using GraphicConverter by typing

```
open -a /Applications/GraphicConverter   ~/Pictures/*.tiff
```

at the command line.

One important thing you have to remember is that, unlike the Finder and the Mac OS to which you're accustomed, a Unix shell is *case-sensitive*. That means that if you capitalize a file or command name that shouldn't be capitalized, the shell won't know what to do with it.

10

You can even make the output of one command be the input to the next command via the Unix pipe character, the vertical bar (|). For example,

```
cat foo.txt | tr "[A-Z]" "[a-z]"
```

would display the contents of the file foo.txt, with all alphabetic characters in lowercase. Of course, this is a somewhat simplistic example that could have been accomplished via *input redirection* rather than piping, as follows:

```
tr "[A-Z]" "[a-z]" < foo.txt
```

The less-than sign (<) tells the shell to take its input from the file specified rather than from *standard input* (usually the keyboard). Similarly, a greater-than sign (>) tells the shell to send the output to the file specified rather than to *standard output* (usually, the Terminal window). Not surprisingly, this is called *output redirection*. Two successive greater-than signs tell the shell to append the output to the file specified.

TIP

You can execute multiple commands sequentially on a single line by separating them with semicolons.

Because Unix is a multitasking operating system, you can put commands that are going to take some time to execute into the background while you go about your business. Putting an ampersand (&) at the end of the command tells the shell to execute the command in the background. You will be notified when it completes, as shown in Figure 10.3.

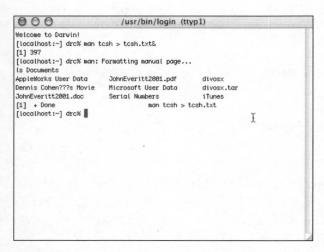

Figure 10.3
The shell lets you know when a background task completes.

> **NOTE**
>
> If you're wondering who "drc" is and what he's doing at my command-line prompt, he's Dennis R. Cohen, my friend and collaborator who wrote the first draft of this chapter. He's forgotten more about Unix than I'll ever know.

Some Other Useful Commands

You've already been introduced to some of the most important Unix commands: **cat**, **more**, **ls**, **cd**, **mv**, and **rm**, but here are some others that may come in handy:

- **man**—Displays the Unix manual page(s) for the command given as an argument.

- **head**—Displays the first 20 lines of a file (you can specify an argument to display a different number).

- **tail**—Displays the last 20 lines of a file (you can specify the number of lines here, too).

- **grep**—Searches for strings or patterns (as described in the next section).

- **find**—Locates files in your directory structure.

- **mkdir**—Creates a directory (folder).

- **rmdir**—Removes an (empty) directory (folder).

You can find a wealth of other commands by typing:

```
ls /bin /usr/bin  /usr/local/bin
```

If you really want to get deep(er) into Unix than this, the **man** command is going to be one of your best friends. Several freeware GUI utilities display man pages for you in a somewhat more familiar environment.

> **NOTE**
>
> Two of the OS X programs you can use to read man pages—**ManOpen** and **Xmanview**—are covered in great detail in Chapter 14.

These OS X programs are better than the Terminal for viewing man pages. In Terminal, you have to enter the right text command to find the syntax and options for a command. In one of these programs it's more Mac-like and a lot easier.

One last thing before we move on: To quit from a shell session, press the Unix end-of-file character, Ctrl+D. If you do this, then Quit Terminal (Terminal|Quit Terminal or Command+Q), you won't be hassled by the dialog box asking if you're really sure you want to do so.

10

> **TIP**
>
> Of course, you could click the checkbox in that dialog box and tell Terminal not to prompt you unless there are active processes, but cleaning up after yourself properly by using Ctrl+D is a good habit to get into.

Getting a Grip on grep

Regular expressions take wild cards to a whole new level. A *regular expression* is a string that represents patterns of characters by the use of *metacharacters*, which are characters such as wild cards, escape characters, grouping operators, and repetition indicators.

If you've used a text editor such as BBEdit, you've seen references to **grep**. It stands for *global regular expression print* and lies at the heart of all the regular expression handling in Unix, whether it is on the command line, in an editor, or anywhere else.

> **NOTE**
>
> Some Unix wizards swear that **grep** stands for *general regular expression parser*. So which is correct? Who knows? Frankly, it doesn't matter—**grep** is **grep**. I toss this note in only to appease Unix wizards and avoid a flood of email.

In an attempt to make **grep** a little less cryptic, Apple has included a variation of it in its Macintosh Programmers Workshop (MPW) since the late 1980s (almost all the metacharacters are different—usually, Option-key characters).

Unfortunately, the syntax of an expression is a little different depending upon whether it is being parsed on the command line or by a Unix editor program that runs in the Terminal window (such as vi or ed). As I mentioned earlier in this chapter, an asterisk stands for any string of zero or more characters. That's true on the command line. If, however, you want the same result in one of these editors, you type a period followed by an asterisk. Here, the asterisk stands for zero or more iterations and the period means any character. Are you getting confused yet? If so, don't worry—that is the normal reaction to a first exposure to **grep**.

The most basic form of a regular expression is a simple string, much like any other string you might enter into the Find box of a program's Find dialog box. To find all instances of the string "Bob" in files whose names end in .txt, you would type **grep Bob *.txt** at the shell prompt. Notice that **grep** searches are case-sensitive. In other words, the preceding search would find "Bob," but wouldn't find "bob" or "bobbin." You can use the –i switch (option) with the **grep** command to make the search case-insensitive. For example, **grep –i Bob *.txt** would find all three instances as well as "bOB" and any other variation.

You can get even fancier with expressions by using some of the wild card and pattern capabilities. For example, you could type **grep [Bb]ob** *.txt and get just the occurrences where only the case of the initial "b" was irrelevant. Typing **grep ^Bob** *.txt would produce just those instances where "Bob" appeared at the beginning of a line, and **grep Bob$** *.txt would tell you only the cases where it was at the end of a line. To find only the instances where "Bob" was followed by a single digit, you could type **grep Bob[0-9]** *.txt.

grep even lets you find instances where one of a variety of patterns is present. The following line would print all lines that contained the words "Bob," "Carol," "Ted," or "Alice:"

```
grep Bob|Carol|Ted|Alice *.txt
```

Like Unix in general, **grep** supports some special characters and combinations. For example, **\t** indicates a tab character and **\n** means a new-line character. Any time you want to treat literally a character that would otherwise be considered a wild card or special character, you precede it with a backslash. Thus, if you wanted to search for a period, you would have to "escape" it with a backslash because a period is a wild card for any single character. Likewise, if you want to search for a backslash, you would escape it by preceding it with another backslash.

Some of these special characters are called *repetition characters*. They are * (0 or more instances), + (1 or more instances), and ? (0 or 1 instance). Another special character is the caret (^), which has a different special meaning depending upon the context. If it occurs at the start of an expression (as shown a few paragraphs ago), it means to look at the text at the beginning of a line. However, if it occurs as the first character within square brackets, it means to exclude the character class enclosed. For example, **grep ^[^0-9]** *.txt would find all instances in which a numeric digit was not the first character in a line.

Okay, now how about when you want the string to match only full words? Regular expressions provide even that capability. Just enclose the expression between an escaped left-angle bracket (\<) and an escaped right-angle bracket(\>). For example, **grep \<can\>** *.txt will match only the word "can" and not "cantaloupe," "pecan," or "recant."

You can combine all of these various techniques in (virtually) unlimited variety. In keeping with Unix's (and **grep**'s) enormous versatility, you can specify the −v switch to **grep** and find all the lines that don't contain a match rather than all the lines that do contain a match.

That isn't the end of what regular expressions make possible. You can even *tag* subexpressions for reuse in some tools by enclosing them in parentheses. An example of this would be the Find–Replace dialog box in a **grep**-supporting text editor like BBEdit, shown here and in Figure 10.4:

10

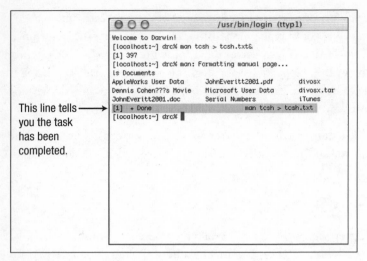

This line tells you the task has been completed.

Figure 10.4
Half-and-half: What it looks like in BBEdit's Find and Replace dialog box.

```
In the Find box: (.+)\t(.+)\t(.+)
In the Replace box: \2\t\3\t\1
```

This takes a file with three tab-delimited columns and reorders them so that the second column is now first, the third is now second, and the first is now last.

As you can see, this is significant flexibility and power compared to what we're accustomed to via the mouse when editing, but it is also extremely arcane. It's kind of like speaking in tongues, which probably goes a long way to explaining why Unix experts are often called "wizards"—they use strange incantations to do awesome things.

Shell Command-Line Editing Shortcuts

One of the really nice things about **tcsh** is that it can fill in text for you so you don't have to type everything, and you can drag items from the Finder onto the Terminal window to obtain their path. In this section, I explain a few of the handiest shortcuts available. In addition, you can edit command lines interactively using a wealth of Control-key shortcuts.

> **TIP**
>
> You can get a full list of all the shortcuts by typing **bindkey** at the command-line prompt. Many (okay, most) of these have names that are not obvious to people who haven't immersed themselves in Unix jargon, but the **tcsh man** pages have brief descriptions of what all these weird names mean. Remember, the **man** pages (although dry and jargon-filled) can be an invaluable resource.

Don't Type Full Pathnames—Use Drag and Drop

Open a Finder window and drag the icon to the Terminal window, as shown in Figure 10.5. **tcsh** will enter the full path specification for you, as shown in Figure 10.6.

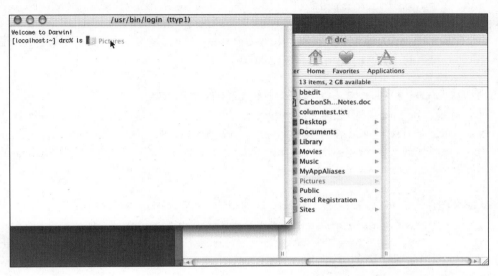

Figure 10.5
Drag an icon from the Finder into your Terminal window.

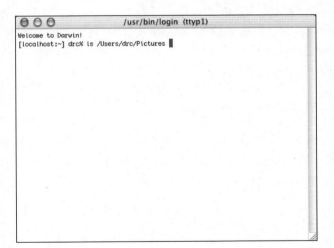

Figure 10.6
The shell will fill in the path for you.

10

When you press the Enter key, a list of the files and folders (remember, that's what the **ls** command produces) in your Pictures folder will appear in the Terminal window (not shown).

The Shell Will Also Help You with Pathnames

If you don't want to go rooting around in a Finder window to locate the file and drag it, you can have the shell help you. Enter the command name, a space, a letter or two, and press Tab. If there is only one possible completion, **tcsh** will complete the command; otherwise, the shell will tell you all the things that are available. Type another letter or two and press Tab again. Keep iterating through this until you have the full file name entered (with the shell's assistance).

You Don't Have to Retype Commands

To repeat the last command, just type two exclamation points in a row. To repeat the last command with additional arguments, type two exclamation points, a space, and the additional arguments. If you want to reinvoke the last **ls** command, but it wasn't the last command you entered, type a single exclamation point followed by **ls**.

Arrow Keys Work through Your Command History

You can press the up-arrow key to step back through the commands you've previously executed. If you step too far back, the down-arrow key will step forward through the command history. When you get to the command you want, you can execute it again or edit it in place before executing.

Unix Software You May Want to Try

Unix is the breeding ground of some of the more powerful and pervasive tools used on the Internet and in publishing. Before there was PageMaker and PostScript, Donald Knuth and his cohorts had developed TeX and Metafont. Perl, the ubiquitous tool of the Webmaster, comes from Unix. As I mentioned earlier in this chapter, **grep** (used in many powerful editors) had its origin in Unix.

Perl

Perl is actually an acronym for Practical Extraction and Report Language. Apple includes the standard BSD Unix distribution of Perl with OS X.

You'll find more than 100 Perl-related files and folders that were installed with OS X. Just follow the System/Library/Perl path on your OS X boot disk.

Although not quite so straightforward as AppleScript, Perl is even more powerful when it comes to manipulating text and files, and you can use it to invoke AppleScripts (as well as shell scripts). If you're going to use the built-in Apache Web Server that comes with OS X, you're going to need to learn more about Perl.

NOTE

Instructions on using Perl are beyond the purview of this book. If you're interested, Coriolis has several titles to help you. Check out *Perl Black Book, 2nd Edition* (by Steven Holzner; ISBN 1-58880-193-4) and/or *Perl Core Language Little Black Book* (by Steven Holzner; ISBN 1-57610-426-5).

Avi2Mov

Part of the Divx for X freeware package, this command-line tool converts DivX-encoded AVI files into QuickTime movie (MOV) files you can view in QuickTime Player. At the time I write this, Avi2Mov understands 3ivx (Microsoft's kludge variant of MPEG-4), as well as the new MPEG-4 files becoming popular in the Windows world. You can use Avi2Mov to view these files, and using Toast 5 Titanium's VideoCD compressor, you can convert them to VideoCD (MPEG-1) files. These can then be burned to VideoCDs, playable in most commercial DVD players and viewable on Macs or PCs using a VCD player program. Not only does this tool enable you to view these movies and clips, but with the addition of Toast 5 Titanium's VideoCD compressor, you can actually convert them to VideoCD (MPEG-1) files to be burned onto VideoCDs, which can be played on most commercial DVD players or viewed on a Mac or PC using a VCD player.

TIP

To find a shareware VCD player, search for "VideoCD" at your favorite software download site. (I generally use **www.versiontracker.com**, discussed in greater detail in Chapter 5.) You should find a bunch of VideoCD players you can download and experiment with. Another great Web site for budding VideoCD-makers is **www.vcdhelp.com**.

10

The GIMP

The GIMP is the GNU Image Manipulation Program. It is a freeware program often referred to as "the poor person's Photoshop." Its tool palette is shown in Figure 10.7.

Figure 10.7
The GIMP offers many of the same graphics tools as Photoshop, but for a lot less money.

The GIMP is suitable for photo retouching and editing, image creation, animated GIF creation, and other image editing chores. It supports Photoshop plug-ins, and the default installation includes many of the better plug-ins. Best of all, it's absolutely free if you're willing to download it and all the other pieces you'll need to make it work (not a particularly pleasant thought).

The GIMP is not trivial to install (or remove). In addition to the GIMP Unix application itself, you also need to install several other Unix programs to run it. At some point, a native OS X version with a "one-click installer" will probably be available, but as of this writing, there isn't one.

You can download the GIMP and all the other stuff you'll need from VersionTracker, but it's huge. The GIMP weighs in at almost 200MB, and that's without all the other supporting programs you'll also need.

Another option is to order the whole shebang on CD-ROM for around $30. For that low price, you'll receive everything you need to install and run the GIMP under OS X on a CD-ROM. The project is run by MacGIMP (**www.macgimp.com** and/or **www.macgimp.org**); the CD-ROM includes an installer that makes setup of the GIMP as easy as it's going to get—it installs everything you need at once: Free86, Oroborus, GTK, and the GIMP. Plus, the CD-ROM also includes source code, alternative window managers, font packs, and lots of documentation.

If you can't afford Photoshop, the GIMP may be just what the doctor ordered. I managed to install it from the MacGIMP CD and get it running without any trouble. Although I still prefer Photoshop, if you're on a tight budget, you can't beat the GIMP's price.

TeX

Do you ever have to write papers filled with mathematical equations, scientific formulas, or complex references? If so, TeX could well be worth learning. At least two OS X implementations (CMacTeX and OzTeX) are available, and others are sure to follow.

TIP

To find a shareware or freeware TeX program, search for "TeX" at your favorite software download site. I strongly recommend searching for the exact phrase "TeX" because if you merely search for "tex" and don't specify that you're looking for the exact phrase, you'll end up finding every program that includes the word "text," and that's a lot of programs.

VersionTracker offers "Exact Phrase" as one of its Advanced Search options, as shown in Figure 10.8; this search found four TeX programs you could download and experiment with. You'll probably find even more by the time you read this.

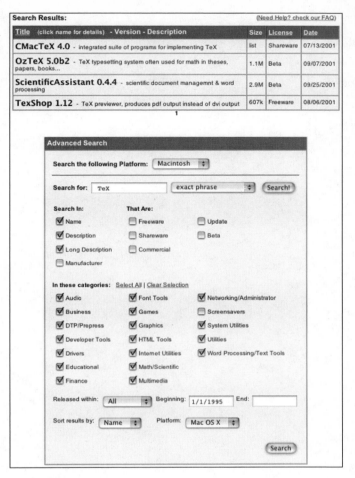

Figure 10.8
Check the Long Description check box and enclose the word "TeX" in quotes for best results.

10

More Unix for Power Users

This was an extremely difficult chapter to write. Virtually anything you can do from the command line you can also do with a double-clickable Aqua application with a real GUI (graphical user interface, which uses windows and menus instead of a command line) if one exists. And, if none exists yet, tools such as AppleScript and REALbasic (**www.realsoftware.com**) make it so easy that anyone with the desire could write one.

The techniques in this chapter demonstrate how to accomplish some common, useful tasks from the command line.

> **NOTE**
>
> Some power users, particularly those who are already familiar with Unix, actually prefer the command line even if a GUI tool already exists. So try it—you might just like it. However, if I know of an existing GUI tool that lets you do the same thing without the command line, I'll say so. If I don't know of a GUI tool and you do (or if you write one yourself), please drop me a line—I want to hear about it. I'll take a GUI over a command line any day of the week.

So let's look now at a few useful command-line techniques. But before we do that, here's an important sidebar about access privileges and the root account.

Root Access: A Necessary Evil?

When you first set up your OS X system, you create an account. That first account is always an *Administrator* account. This means that you can, by entering your password at various places (such as unlocking those little padlock icons in so many installation and preference windows and dialog boxes), do things that Mac OS X would otherwise tell you that you have insufficient privileges to accomplish. However, even in Terminal running as an admin, you can't do many things. For instance, you can't change the owner or group of a file.

But there is one account in any Unix system that can do pretty much whatever it wants, whenever it wants. That omnipotent account belongs to a user named *root*. Known also as the *super-user* or

(continued)

god account, operating as root brings with it nearly as much danger as it does power. Because root can do virtually anything, simple typos can have far-reaching effects. For example, critical files could be deleted or modified.

Running as root is obviously a dangerous thing to do, but it is sometimes necessary to have root access for specific commands. Thus was born the **sudo** (switch user and do, or super-user do) command. By entering **sudo** followed by the root-level command, you can keep running as yourself but enter specific commands as though you were root. The first time in a shell session that you invoke the **sudo** command, you will be prompted for an administrator password. Subsequent **sudo** commands in that session will not invoke a password request. Here are a couple of examples of using **sudo** (don't worry if they don't make sense yet—this is just to give you an idea of the syntax). This command will change the owner of all DOC files in the current directory to bobl:

```
sudo chown bobl *.doc
```

This command will change the mode (i.e., privileges) for all DOC files in the current directory:

```
sudo chmod 750 *.doc
```

> **NOTE**
>
> I'll talk about **chmod** again in Chapter 12, but here's what the command I just showed you means. The **750** is actually three different commands: **7** gives the owner read-write-execute privileges; **5** gives the group read-execute privileges; **0** gives everyone else no privileges; and ***.doc** means all DOC files in the current directory.

There's even a way to **sudo** from the Finder and use a double-clickable GUI program to do something that would ordinarily require root access and the command line. This method requires a shareware application known as Pseudo. With Pseudo, you can launch any OS X application with root admin privileges. I'll talk more about using it in Chapter 14.

> **NOTE**
>
> Throughout this chapter, I'm going to assume that you know to change directory (**cd**) to the appropriate directory to work on a file, or that you fully specify the file's path. Just as in the Mac GUI, where you have to traverse the directory hierarchy to specify a file's location, the command line requires you to either specify the path to the file or have it in the current working directory.
>
> Unix is also a little dense about where commands are. You either must have them in one of the directories specified in your shell **PATH** variable or, again, specify the path to them. Remember, the current directory is *not* necessarily part of your path—if you want to execute a command in your current directory, for example, **mycommand**,

you specify **./mycommand** followed by its arguments and options. Any file(s) for which you don't specify a path will be assumed to be located in your current directory or will be created in your current directory. Until and unless you **cd** to another directory, that will be your HOME directory.

Log In to a Unix Shell Instead of Aqua

If you want to feel like a true Unix geek, running at a plain terminal with white characters on a black screen, you can very simply, just be aware that none of the handy shell integration—where you can drag files onto the Terminal window, launch OS X applications, or do anything except execute Unix commands—exists when you start up in console mode. The main advantage of the plain mode of operation is speed and responsiveness because none of the overhead normally required for Mac OS X is present.

To set up your Mac to start in the Unix command=line environment, follow these steps:

1. Set your System Preferences for an Administrator account to put Other User as a choice in your Login window. You do this in the Login Window tab of Login System Preferences, as shown in Figure 11.1.

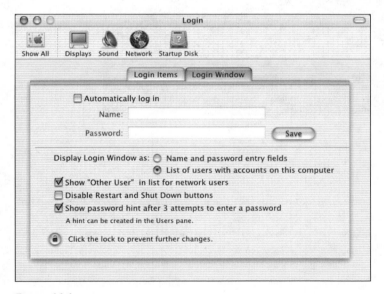

Figure 11.1
Tell OS X to offer Other User as a choice in the Login window.

2. Log out from OS X.

3. Click Other in the Login window.

4. Type ">Console" in the Name field. You don't have to type anything in the Password field. Click Login.

5. At the shell login prompt, enter the username of the account you wish to use and enter a password when prompted.

You're now in a traditional Unix command-line environment, completely divorced from the standard OS X interface and applications. Your Mac's screen is now a throwback to the dark ages, as shown in Figure 11.2.

```
Darwin/BSD (localhost) (console)

login: bob levitus
password:
Welcome to Darwin!
[localhost:~] bobl% ▮
```

Figure 11.2
I bet you've never seen your Mac look like this before!

NOTE

Sharp-eyed readers may have figured out that the picture above is a phony. Because I'm working from the shell, the screen capture tips I showed you way back in Chapter 2 don't work. Though Figure 11.2 looks pretty much like a Mac booted into the shell, I faked the whole thing in Photoshop.

To return to your Aqua Mac OS X environment, log out from the shell in one of three ways: press Ctrl+D, type "logout", or type "exit". Then, when the login prompt appears, press Ctrl+D. The usual Mac OS Login window (from Step 3) will appear. Log in the usual way.

Put Double-Scroll Arrows at Both Ends of the Scrollbars

OS X 10.1 adds an option in General System Preferences to have double-scroll arrows at the bottom of the scrollbars. As a matter of fact, that is the default setting. If you wish to enable double-scroll arrows at *both* ends of the scrollbars, start a terminal session (from an Administrator account) and type the following:

```
defaults write "Apple Global Domain" AppleScrollBarVariant DoubleBoth
```

You then need to log out and log in (or, perhaps, simply Force Quit the Finder) to see the effect. But once you've done so, you will have double-scroll arrows at both ends of your scrollbars, as shown on the right in Figure 11.3.

Figure 11.3
Choose scroll arrow placement At Top And Bottom (left) or Together (middle) in the General System Preferences pane, or enable the DoubleBoth option (right).

This method works in the Finder, Cocoa applications, and in most Carbon applications—at least those where the programmers use standard system scrollbars. To return to the traditional (arrow at either end) mode, type the following from a terminal session:

```
defaults write "Apple Global Domain" AppleScrollBarVariant Single
```

(Or you could just open the General System Preferences and check At Top And Bottom.) To place both arrows together at the bottom, type this:

```
defaults write "Apple Global Domain" AppleScrollBarVariant DoubleMax
```

(This is equivalent to clicking Together in the General System Preferences for scroll arrows.) If, for some reason, you want the arrows together at the top (or left) of the scrollbar, type the following:

```
defaults write "Apple Global Domain" AppleScrollBarVariant DoubleMin
```

11

Why Apple would choose to include some, but not all, of these features in the General System Preferences pane is a mystery to me. They hid this information in Mac OS 9 as well, and you had to use a utility that set a different appearance variation for the scrollbar proc (programmer jargon for the scrollbar control definition routines that well-behaved Mac applications called to work with scrollbars).

After I wrote this section, a most-excellent freeware utility called TinkerTool was released. It can set your scrollbar preferences (and more) without using Terminal.

> **NOTE**
>
> OS X 10.1 has a number of undocumented options like this. You'll find out about them over time as programmers and others stumble across them and figure out how to use them. So watch for new programs (or AppleScripts, or instructions for the command line) that unlock undocumented features and options. New ones are showing up all the time (at **www.versiontracker.com**, among others).

Change File Ownership, File Type, and Other Attributes

Although you can use OS X utility programs such as xFiles, Super Get Info, and many others to change file type, creator, and other attributes, sometimes doing everything from the command line is easier or more efficient.

Remember that cute little booklet that came with OS X, the one that explains how to install OS X? It also says that the Developer Tools CD is for programmers, so you may not have paid much attention to that CD. But that third CD in your OS X package includes some handy and interesting Unix commands, including a pair I find quite useful—**SetFile** and **GetFileInfo**.

> **ALERT!**
>
> You must first install the Developer Tools from the CD, then you must copy the contents of the Developer/Tools directory (which is where **GetFileInfo** and **SetFile** are installed) into a directory that is in the Unix default path (in this case, local/bin). If you don't do both things, **GetFileInfo** and **SetFile** won't work.

So first install the developer tools (if you haven't already), then launch Terminal and type "cp /Developer/Tools/* /usr/local/bin".

> **NOTE**
>
> If you're a Unix guru, you probably know at least three other ways to accomplish this. Use them if you know how, but copying the files to local/bin was the easiest way I could think of.

SetFile

I know that I receive a lot of email, and a lot of those emails include attached files. Sometimes the enclosures arrive with dates that imply the existence of time-travel. Perhaps you've had a similar experience. A simple **SetFile** command can fix those dates:

```
SetFile -d . -m. theFile
```

This command will set both the creation (-d) and modification (-m) dates of *theFile* to the current time and date. If you want to specify a time/date other than "now," use a string enclosed in quotes to specify the date and time, such as:

```
SetFile -m "09/11/2001 09:23 AM" Vizsladogs.jpg
```

to change the modification date of the file, Vizsladogs.jpg, to be 9:23 on the morning of September 11, 2001.

The –c and –t options let you set the Creator and Type information, respectively. But, the really handy option is –a. This option lets you set Finder attributes, such as whether the file is invisible, is an alias, is stationary, or is locked. Each of these (and other attributes as well) has a letter code. If that code is entered in lowercase, you're turning the attribute off, whereas uppercase turns it on. Failure to include an attribute says that you're leaving that attribute unchanged. For example,

```
SetFile -a Lv Spenser.jpg
```

will change the file Spenser.jpg to visible (if currently invisible) and will lock the file. In other words, the –a option means "change an Finder attribute," the uppercase L means "Lock," and the lowercase v means "visible" (if the file is invisible; if it's visible there will be no change.)

The flip side of **SetFile** is the **GetFileInfo** command. Using **GetFileInfo**, you can find out what the current attributes, type, and creator of a file are. Okay, I know you're thinking ahead. You can write a shell script that will compare attributes and make different changes based upon type/creator/attribute. A simple example would be to change the creator of only the Photoshop-created JPEG files in a directory to be owned by GraphicConverter:

```
foreach i (*.jpg)
    set foo = 'GetFileInfo -c $i'
    if ('expr $foo = \"8BIM\"') SetFile -c "GKON" $I
end
```

11

Of course, this could be made even more cryptic by eliminating the intermediate variable, *foo*, but what's the point?

Sherlock on Steroids

We all know Sherlock is great for finding files on your disks. And most of us also know how to use the Customization options to refine a search. But, do you know how to get Sherlock to print the results to a text file?

The answer is: You can't. Other than taking a screenshot of the Sherlock window and printing that, there's no way I know of to create a printed list of what Sherlock finds. Sherlock doesn't have a Print command, and you can only save the search criteria so you can reuse it.

You may not have noticed, but there is no Print Window command in OS X (or any other Finder Print commands). So once again, the answer is to delve into the arcane incantations of Unix, and the **find** command certainly qualifies. To find out all about the **find** command or any other Unix command, refer to its man page, as described in Chapter 10.

```
find projfolder/ -type f -name '*.doc' | sed -e 's;.*/;;' -e 's/\.doc$//' >
mydocindex.txt
```

This strange command line tells the **find** command to search starting in the directory *projfolder* (first argument) for all entries that are files (not directories, aliases, and so on; **type -f**), and whose names end in *.doc* (argument to the **−name** option). The results of this command are piped (that's the vertical bar; see Chapter 10) to the stream editor (**sed**), where the leading path information is stripped using a pair of editor substitution commands (the **−e s** arguments), leaving just the file names. Finally, the results are written to the text file **mydocindex.txt** (note the > output redirection operator; see Chapter 10 for more information).

TIP

If you don't want the leading path information stripped, remove the pipe symbol (|) and everything following up to, but not including, the redirection symbol (>).

Move Over, PGP (Pretty Good Privacy)

Apple provides OpenSSL, the cryptography package implementing the Secure Sockets Layer (SSL v2/v3) and Transport Layer Security (TLS v1) network protocols, including the cryptography standards required by these protocols. The **openssl** command gives you access to the all the encryption, decryption, and key creation capabilities.

A wide variety of ciphers is available, including (among others) Base64, Blowfish, DES, triple-DES, RC4, and RC5.

To encrypt the file confidential.doc to confidential.rc5 using the RC5 cipher, just type the following:

```
openssl rc5 -e -in confidential.doc -out confidential.rc5
```

And to decrypt confidential.rc5 back into confidential.doc, use the following syntax:

```
openssl rc5 -d -in confidential.rc5 -out confidential.doc
```

View DivX-; Files in QuickTime Player

A few years back, Microsoft hacked at the MPEG-4 draft standard, creating a private implementation known as DivX-; (yeah, even the little smiley on the end is part of the name, but that's the last time you'll see me use it). Fortunately, a small company named Jamby has developed a freeware QuickTime component based upon the ffmpeg development effort (**http://ffmpeg.sourceforge.net**). Even with that implementation QuickTime doesn't quite synchronize the audio and video correctly, so Jamby includes two Unix command-line tools with the component: Avi2Mov and getMp3. Both do what you would expect from the names. Avi2Mov takes a DivX file (DivX files have .avi file extensions) as input and separates out and synchronizes the video and audio tracks, then packages them together to create a QuickTime movie file (MOV).

getMp3 extracts the MP3 audio track into a separate file. In Figure 11.4, you'll see Avi2Mov converting a DivX file to MOV format (though the ffmpeg codec still needs to be present in your /Library/QuickTime or ~/Library/QuickTime directory). Now, you have a viewable, listenable movie file, and you can watch it in QuickTime Player.

Although what I'm about to tell you doesn't require the command line, it is nevertheless a very handy tip. If you want these (and indeed, all) digital movies to be viewable almost anywhere, you need a copy of Roxio's Toast Titanium. Not only is Toast the best CD and DVD-writing software for the Mac, but it includes a converter of its own to change movie files into MPEG-1 files, re-encode them, and multiplex them. Not only can you watch these MPEG files on virtually any computer, you can write them to VideoCDs, which you can play in most major set-top DVD players as well (mostly ones that are CD-R–compatible). This conversion process and multiplexing is not fast, though, taking 5 to 15 minutes for every minute of video on a G4 5(depending on the speed of the G4 processor).

11

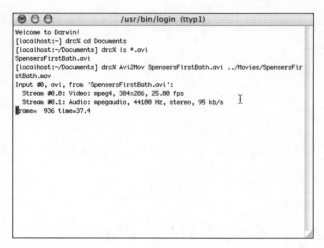

Figure 11.4
Use the freeware Avi2Mov command to make DivX movies watchable.

After writing this section I stumbled upon a double-clickable application that does the same thing (or at least it seems to). It's a freeware program called DivosX Tool. So, at least for this exercise, you now have a choice of doing it from the command line or from a GUI application. You can link to this at **www.boblevitus.com/xfiles.html**.

Exterminating the "Multiple Server" Bug

Do you use other Macs in a networked environment? If so, you may have awoken one day to find that when you opened the Connect To Server dialog box (Go|Connect To Server, or Command+K), one or more of your Macs had "multiplied."

If you see multiple entries for the same computer in your Connect To Server dialog box, as shown in Figure 11.5, you're seeing this bug, which has been in all versions of OS X to date.

It would merely be an inconvenience if all six of the entries worked. But only one of them does, and there's no way to tell which one except by trial and error.

I think this bug has to do with Dynamic Host Configuration Protocol (DHCP), the scheme used by cable or DSL modems or routers to supply an IP address to your Mac dynamically (on-the-fly). So your Mac does not have a permanent IP address.

I suspect that Connect To Server becomes confused when it sees the same Mac sporting a different IP address than yesterday or the day before. So, if you have a dial-up (modem) connection you probably won't see this bug—which is lucky 'cause it's a pain in the keister.

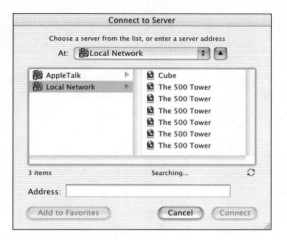

Figure 11.5
I have only one Mac named The 500 Tower, so five of the six entries on the right are bogus—caused by the "multiple server" bug.

Here's how to fix it. In Terminal, type the following:

```
cd.. <enter>
cd.. <enter>
cd var <enter>
Sudo rm slp.regfile <enter>
```

You'll be asked for your administrator password. Type it, then press Enter. Restart your Mac and things should be hunky-dory once again, as shown in Figure 11.6.

Here's a quick summary of what all that typing does: The first command, **cd..** (c-d-period-period), changes directories by moving you up one level. The second command does the same. The upshot of these first two items is that you're at the root level on your startup volume. When you type the third command, **cd var**, you're changing to the directory called *var*, which is an invisible Unix directory you can't see in the Finder. Finally, the last command deletes the file slp.regfile, which stores information about available servers.

NOTE

I say "delete" but Unix thinks of it as "remove." The **rm** command, as you probably remember, stands for "remove."

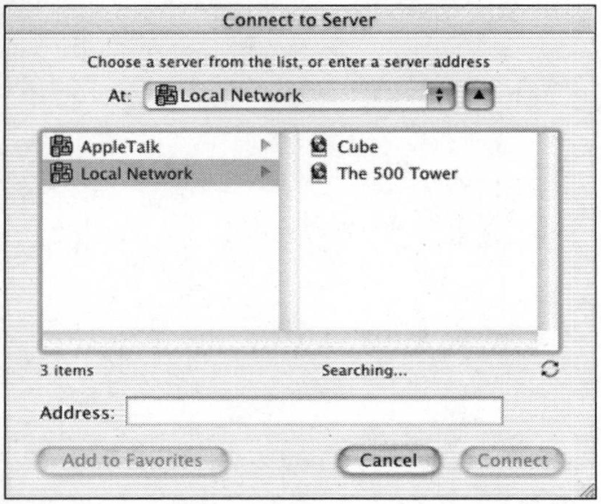

Figure 11.6
The Connect To Server dialog box after deleting the slp.regfile and restarting.

Three Ways to View Your RAM

You can find out more about what's going on with your installed RAM by using the "top" utility in the Terminal, but you also have two other ways that don't involve Unix at all. Because all three methods are covered extensively in the section, "Maximizing RAM Usage" in Chapter 7, I won't waste any more time on them here.

Users, and Groups, and NetInfo (Oh My!)

As you've probably noticed by now, most (if not all) of the old, familiar Classic (as in Mac OS 9) methods of managing your Mac have changed, primarily due to the Unix underpinnings of Mac OS X. You no longer have an inherently single-user computer which can be made to act like a multiuser computer via kludges like the Multiple Users Control Panel introduced in Mac OS 9. Today, your Mac is a multiuser computer system, even if you're the only person who ever uses it.

This chapter explains how to use the necessary tools for a multiuser computer system. As usual, we'll start off nice and easy with some background on the Unix way of sharing files, disks, and computers and the NetInfo database. Once that's out of the way, we'll move on to some tutorial material that will help you create users and groups, and show you how to manage Unix permissions using Terminal. Finally, we'll look at an easier way to do that permission thing—it'll cost you $20 but will avoid having to resort to Unix. (I think this application is worth every penny.)

What Is NetInfo Manager and What Does It Do?

Traditionally, a Unix System Administrator–type would manage a wide variety of files with cryptic names and even more cryptic formats in order to administer the users, groups, and resources of a Unix system. Many of these files are interrelated.

NetInfo is a database (called a *directory system*) that applications and the operating system can use to retrieve and store the information. NetInfo Manager, as the name implies, is a graphic interface to let you manage the services NetInfo provides. The NetInfo Manager window is shown in Figure 12.1.

I'm not going to tell you that NetInfo Manager has the most straightforward interface you're ever going to see—you'd call me a liar and never again trust my word. What I am going to tell you is that the tasks NetInfo Manager can perform are so varied and can be so complex that the interface is probably about as straightforward as it can be given the multitude of things it does.

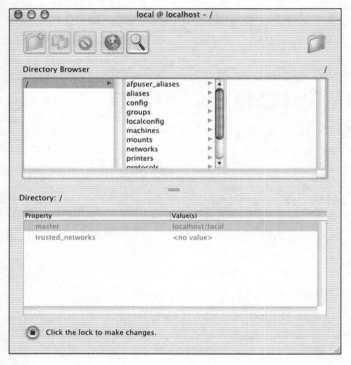

Figure 12.1
Here's what you'll see when you launch NetInfo Manager.

Here are a few of the things NetInfo Manager can do:

■ Create and manage groups of users

■ Distribute login directories to different computers or disks

■ Assign networked printers to specific domains (I'll cover domains in a minute)

The first item, creating and managing groups, is the most common NetInfo Manager use by the typical user. I'll focus on that after the following sidebar, which covers domains: what they are and why you need to know about them.

Understanding Domains

Each collection of information stored and administered in NetInfo is called a *domain*. Every Mac OS X computer has a local NetInfo domain. This local domain is the first domain checked when a login attempt is made or any other NetInfo data access is attempted.

(continued)

When you first ran the Setup program after installing Mac OS X (or the first time you booted your Mac into Mac OS X), the local NetInfo domain was created and filled with data records. Some of these records include the username and password (encrypted) you entered during the Setup process, as well as the UID (user ID number) you were assigned and the location where your user (Home) directory was created.

Generally, the local domain is the only one you will ever use. However, the real power of NetInfo is that you can create *shared domains*, allowing multiple networked computers to share administrative information. When your Mac is configured to use a shared domain, a *hierarchy* is established where requests for information will first check the local domain and then, if the information is not found there, will check the shared domain(s).

If you really want to get into this level of administration, Apple has produced a PDF document (62 pages in length), *Understanding and Using NetInfo*, which you can download from **www.apple.com/macosx/server/pdf/UnderstandingUsingNetInfo.pdf**.

NOTE

I only mentioned distributing login directories and assigning network printers earlier to give you a sense of some other things you might do with NetInfo Manager. If they're of interest to you, check out the PDF I just mentioned. But those topics are, as they say, "beyond the purview of this book." So that's the last you'll hear about them from me.

Managing Groups for File Sharing

In OS 9 and earlier, setting up and administering file sharing was somewhat tedious, but at least it was all consolidated (pretty much) in the Users & Groups Control Panel and the Sharing panel of the Get Info window. Compared to the steps necessary in Mac OS X, those days were the "good old days."

In those good old days, you assigned permissions to the items you wanted to share and those privilege settings were applicable only while sharing was on and only within the framework of file sharing.

Mac OS X changes all that. Now, *all* files and folders have owners and privileges, regardless of the state of sharing. More than that, the User & Groups Control Panel is now just the System Preferences Users pane—you have to use NetInfo to create groups and assign users to groups.

As a further complication, you can't set a folder's owner or group in the Show Info (formerly Get Info) window; you have to do that either via the command line (see Chapter 10 for a discussion of Terminal and the command line) or using some other tool that puts a graphical user interface on the **chown** and **chgrp** commands.

12

I like Brian Hill's xFiles (pronounced "ten files") utility for this; I'll show you how it works in the section called "The Slightly-More-Expensive-but-Much-More-Mac-Like-Way". There's a link to the xFiles utility at **www.boblevitus.com/xfiles.com**.

Step 1: Create Users

Before you can share with other users, you need to create user accounts for them. You create accounts from the System Preferences' Users pane, shown in Figure 12.2.

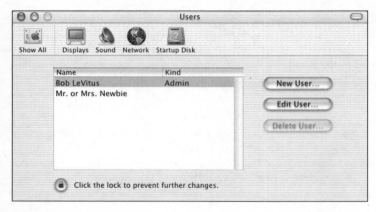

Figure 12.2
Create user accounts in the System Preferences' Users pane.

Although you don't have to be logged in using an Administrator account to create new users, you will need an Administrator account ID and password.

Unlike in Mac OS 9, where user accounts were just a way to allow someone access to certain files and folders, the user accounts in OS X that you're about to create are real user accounts. Each user will have his or her own Home directory (folder) and each will be able to log in to this computer from the keyboard or remotely. In other words, you can't share with someone unless you create a user account for him or her first. And once you've done that, the user is a full-fledged user of this particular Mac, complete with his or her own set of preferences, files, folders, and other stuff, all of which resides in his or her own personal Home folder.

To create a user, just click New User to present the New User dialog box (shown in Figure 12.3) and fill in the blanks.

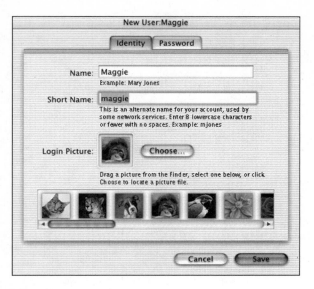

Figure 12.3
Give the account a name, a short name, and (optionally) a login picture.

NOTE

You can choose a login picture as well, though that has absolutely nothing to do with the rest of the material in this chapter.

When you've established the user's identity (and chosen a login picture if you like), click the Password tab and set up an initial password for the user. Unless you consciously wish to extend administrator privileges to the user, be sure to disable Allow User To Administer This Computer by leaving that checkbox unchecked.

Step 2: Create the Group

You use the NetInfo Manager application (located in Applications/Utilities) to create groups and to control group membership. So now it's time to open NetInfo Manager, click the padlock in the lower left-hand corner, and enter your administrator password.

TIP

If you don't unlock NetInfo Manager first, you won't be allowed to make changes.

If you click the *groups* item in the second column, you're presented with a list of all the existing groups on the local machine in the third column, as shown in Figure 12.4.

12

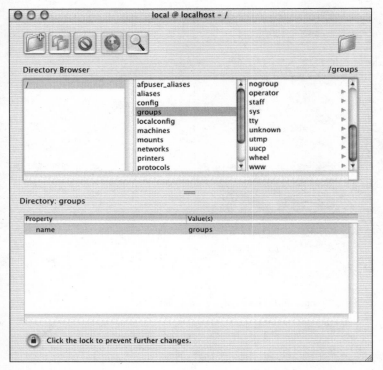

Figure 12.4
Selecting *groups* in the second column presents a list of all existing groups in the third column (what a surprise!).

Now, it's time to create our new group for file sharing. Let's call the new group "sharegroup."

The easiest way to create a new group is to duplicate an existing group and then edit the duplicate's properties. So, from the groups list (third column in Figure 12.4), select the staff group and click the Duplicate button (the one with two folders on it). NetInfo Manager will ask you if you really want to duplicate the group, so confirm that you do by clicking the Duplicate button in the alert. The properties for your new group will then appear in the bottom pane of the window, as shown in Figure 12.5. Click the name and then select the value Staff Copy so that you may edit it to say "sharegroup."

Next, you must assign the group a unique group id number (gid). This is somewhat tedious because you have to make sure the number you choose isn't already in use. I chose 333 after double-checking this.

Figure 12.5
Rename the new (just-duplicated) group in NetInfo Manager's bottom pane.

Step 3: Populate the Group

The root account was already listed as a member of the group. Leaving the Unix deity account intact never hurts because root can do anything anywhere anyhow, but we do need to add the user accounts we created for sharing purposes to this group. You add a user by choosing Directory|Insert Value (Command+Option+I), then typing the user's short name in the text box that opens (the long name won't work). Keep repeating the Insert Value operation until you've added all the users you want in this group. After doing this, you're done with NetInfo Manager, so feel free to close (Quit) it now.

Step 4: Set Permissions on the Directory to Share

The easiest (but least Mac-like) way to set permissions and the group ownership of a folder or item is from the command-line. I'll talk about this way first, and then I'll explain the much more Mac-like way.

12

The Easier-but-Less-Mac-Like-Way

Launch the Terminal application and run the command **cd** to change to the directory containing the item(s) whose sharing permissions you want to change.

> If you want to make sure that the files and directories are all there, type "ls –l" to view the contents of the directory.

To change the permissions and group ownership requires executing as root, which, of course, means using our old friend **sudo**.

OK, then. If the folder you want to share is named SharedFolder, for example, type "sudo chgrp sharegroup SharedFolder". You will be prompted for your Administrator password; enter it.

Now, if you want the sharing users to be able to read, write, and execute items in the shared folder, type "sudo chmod 770 SharedFolder".

About the 770

The **770** in the **chmod** statement is based on the octal-based numbering system Unix uses to designate permissions. Execute permission has the value 1. Write access has the value 2. Read access has the value 4. When you look at the three digits that are the results of an **ls –l** command, you will see three groups of three permissions: owner, group, and everybody (sometimes called "world"). **chmod** uses the same pattern; thus **770** means "give the owner and the group read-write-execute (4 + 2 + 1 = 7) and don't grant any access privileges to world." Similarly, a 750 would equate to read-write-execute for the owner, read-execute for the group, and no privileges for world, and would be displayed as **rwxr-x** in an **ls –l** listing.

Congratulations—you now have set up a group for sharing under OS X!

The Slightly-More-Expensive-but-Much-More-Mac-Like-Way

If you wish to avoid the command line, you can *set* privileges from the OS X Finder's Info window by choosing File|Show Info (Command+I). Unfortunately, you can't assign groups or change ownership in the Show Info window.

This is where Brian Hill's wonderful little xFiles (gee, I *really* like that name) utility comes in. xFiles is a $20 shareware utility that is worth every penny if you wish to avoid the command line. You'll find a link to this utility on this book's Web site.

NOTE

xFiles is not crippled in any way, but if you're going to use shareware like this on an ongoing basis, you should absolutely and positively pay for it. If you don't, folks like Brian won't have any incentive to keep producing such fine products. Brian is well worth supporting—he's also the author of Pseudo, another fine utility that allows you to enter root-level (**sudo**) commands without going to the command line, as well as many other handy tools for OS X. A link to Pseudo is also on this book's Web site, but I encourage you to visit Brian's Web page at **http://personalpages.tds.net/ ~brian_hill/** to check out his other fine works.

When you launch xFiles, the Change File Attributes window appears, as shown in Figure 12.6. Drag the folder whose permissions and ownership you want to change into the Change File Attributes window, and it will display the current permission, owner, and group information, as shown in Figure 12.7.

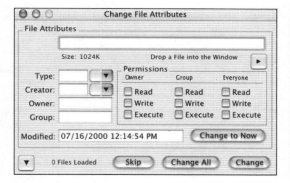

Figure 12.6
This is xFiles Change File Attributes window as it appears just after launch.

Figure 12.7
Here is what it looks like after you drag the SharedFolder folder onto the xFiles Change File Attributes window.

Change the permissions and fill in the text boxes with the new values and settings, then click Change. That's it. You're done. And all without dirtying your hands at the command line.

12

AppleScript for OS X

When Apple and Steve Jobs first unveiled the Macintosh as the "computer for the rest of us," the computer industry and the hacker and phreak communities dismissed it as a toy. They complained that the Finder and Mac programs were limited in terms of user customization and control. If you can remember back that far, Apple][and DOS computers had command lines; the Mac did not. Many DOS and Apple][programs had their own built-in programming languages; the Mac did not. In fact, it was so long ago that Bill Gates hadn't even dreamed of ripping off the Mac interface and calling it Windows, much less shipped a buggy first version of it.

In 1986, everything changed. A prerelease version (call it "buggy" or "beta") of a groundbreaking program, code-named WildCard, began making the rounds. Written by Bill Atkinson, WildCard became perhaps the hottest unreleased program of all time—bootlegged on electronic bulletin boards and passed from hand to hand on floppy disks at user group meetings and other gatherings of the faithful.

NOTE

> Atkinson, now a photographer (**www.natureimages.com**), was the genius programmer who wrote most of MacPaint and much of QuickDraw.

Even though it wasn't ready for prime time, Mac aficionados immediately saw the program's potential. Everyone who was anyone was building projects (called "stacks") with the buggy prerelease software long before Apple officially released the program under its new name, HyperCard.

What made HyperCard so special was that, in addition to the painting tools you'd expect from the Godfather of MacPaint, it was based on an easy-to-understand, English-like scripting language called HyperTalk. HyperTalk let anyone create programs ("stacks") with all the features of a real Mac program—buttons, data entry fields, menus, and more. It was a programming environment that was easy enough for even nonprogrammers to use, wrapped in a totally Mac-like interface.

When System 7 showed up in 1989, with program-to-program communication via AppleEvents, Apple dreamed up a HyperTalk-like language as a method for users to control their various applications—by sending and receiving AppleEvents.

And that's how AppleScript came to be.

What Is AppleScript and What Can It Do?

Using AppleScript (and a scriptable application, such as AppleWorks), you can do such cool things as position text along a curve within a drawing document. In fact, AppleWorks 6 shipped with a collection of AppleScripts by an Australian company called T&B—one of the scripts was the aforementioned text along a curve script.

AppleScript support has three levels (not counting None):

■ *Scriptable* applications will respond to the commands in scripts when sent by another application (such as the Script Editor, in your Applications/AppleScript folder).

■ *Recordable* applications will not only respond to scripted commands, but will let you record a sequence of operations and save that as a script in Script Editor, which you can either run at a later time or modify and then run.

■ *Attachable* applications, which you can customize by attaching scripts to specific objects in the application. For example, you can attach scripts (called Folder Actions) to folder icons in the Finder.

Apple provides a handy little editor/compiler for AppleScript, known appropriately as Script Editor. You write and edit your scripts in the Script Editor window. Script Editor will even check to make sure that what you write is legal AppleScript when you either click the Check Syntax button or save your script. See the "Good News and Bad News" section for a partial explanation of why "legal AppleScript" isn't enough to guarantee that your script does what you want done.

Using the Script Editor, you can save your script as a double-clickable application, as a *compiled script*, or as text. You already know what applications are, so I won't bore you with an explanation. A compiled script is one in which the Script Editor has checked the syntax and saved an internal representation that is independent of the language in which you created it. Compiled scripts can be run only from within Script Editor or by using Script Runner (also in your Applications/AppleScript folder). When you save as text, you can also open the script in other applications, such as your word processor. Script Editor also allows you to save applications or compiled scripts as "Run-only." This means that other people can't see what your code is when they try to open or run it from Script Editor.

Good News and Bad News

Let's start with some bad news: AppleScripts are programs, so to create your own AppleScripts that do more than just repeat actions you perform on screen requires that you do a bit of programming. Now some good news: Apple (and other folks) have made lots of fairly complex AppleScripts available for free—all you have to do is find and download them.

> **TIP**
>
> Check **www.apple.com/applescript** for links to many excellent AppleScript resources.

The first thing you have to know about programming (and computers) is that computers are *stupid*. That's right, you heard me correctly: Even your beautiful G4 Cube or powerful G4/800 dual-processor system is dumb as a stump. Although they may be totally stupid, they do offer absolute, literal, rapid, and complete obedience. When you program them, they do *exactly* what you instruct them to do, no more and no less, and they do it incredibly quickly. But, if you leave one little thing out of your program, or fail to precisely specify some object, you can be sure that the computer will also leave that little step out or get confused when it tries to do something with that object.

> **NOTE**
>
> This is how "bugs" are born ... programmers leave things out, reference objects that don't exist, reference objects incorrectly, or instruct the computer to do something it can't.

Eliminating the ambiguities is one reason that programming languages, even AppleScript, are "English-like" rather than English. AppleScript just comes closer to English than almost any other programming language (except, perhaps, the aforementioned HyperTalk).

I can't give you a complete course in AppleScript in this book. Fortunately, Apple has a very fine document available in PDF format for free, called the "AppleScript Language Guide." You can find it at **http://developer.apple.com/techpubs/macosx/Carbon/pdf/AppleScriptLanguageGuide.pdf**.

13

> **NOTE**
>
> The guide is 416 pages long and the pages are 8.5×11. In other words, it's roughly the size of *this* book. That said, if you want to learn to write AppleScripts, there's no better (or cheaper) place to start.

Creating Your First Scripts

Probably the easiest way to see what an AppleScript looks like is to open one someone else has written. Luckily, Apple provides quite a few (arranged in folders) in the Example Scripts folder. One of the simplest is the AppleScript Help script in the Basics folder, which you can see (in Script Editor) in Figure 13.1.

Figure 13.1
A very basic script to search Help Viewer's database for all references to AppleScript.

The first line tells AppleScript that you want the commands that follow to be sent to Help Viewer. The second line sends a message to Help Viewer instructing it to activate. Activate, in AppleScript parlance, means that if it is running, to bring it to the front (i.e., make it active), and if it isn't running, to launch it and bring it to the front. The third line instructs Help Viewer to search its database for all instances of the word "AppleScript." The result of clicking the Run button is the same as typing "AppleScript" in the Ask text box in Help Viewer, as shown in Figure 13.2.

The last line tells AppleScript that you're done telling Help Viewer what you want from it.

Directing where your commands are sent is fundamental to AppleScript. Going back to basics: If you don't specify to whom the commands are directed, AppleScript won't know, and you won't get the results you seek.

Your First Script

You can modify the script to search for QuickTime, AppleWorks, System Preferences, or just about any other program or technology to get a list of all that Help Viewer knows about those subjects. All you have to do is change the word "AppleScript" in the third line. Make one of the suggested changes and click Run.

Congratulations, you've just "written" your first script!

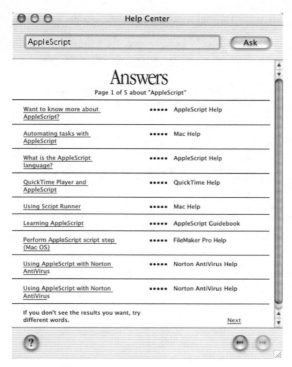

Figure 13.2
This is what happens when you run the script.

TIP

> The word you wish to search for must be contained in quotation marks. If you leave out one or both quotation marks, the script won't run. Instead, you'll see an error message about an undefined variable.

The example was trivial but it demonstrates a basic fundamental of programming—almost everything is a variation on something else. The point is that many times, if you can find a script that does something similar to what you want to do, you can make it do exactly what you want it to do by changing a word or two. The trick is knowing which word to change.

Many applications are scriptable and their number is increasing daily. For example, iTunes 1.1 (the first OS X iTunes release) was not scriptable, but iTunes 2 is almost completely scriptable.

13

NOTE

> There's a cool tip in Chapter 14's AppleWorks coverage about using a free (from Apple) iTunes AppleScript that lets you create a jewel case insert in AppleWorks, with song titles and lengths, automatically from an iTunes playlist.

How Scriptable Is Scriptable?

You can find out how scriptable an application is and what commands and objects it understands by opening the application in Script Editor. You can do this in one of two ways:

■ Choose File|Open Dictionary in Script Editor, then select the application from the Open Dictionary window shown in Figure 13.3.

Figure 13.3
Select an application from the Open Dictionary window to see what it understands.

■ Drag the application's icon onto the Script Editor icon and release it.

In either case, you'll see the dictionary window for the selected application. Figure 13.4 shows the AppleWorks dictionary. Objects appear in italics; commands appear in regular text. Boldface groups the commands and objects into categories called *suites*.

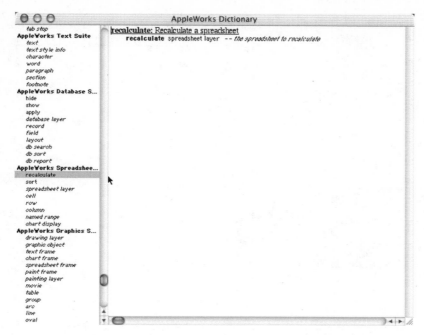

Figure 13.4
AppleWorks 6 has an extensive dictionary.

A few control statements (sometimes called *verbs*) are AppleScript-intrinsic. Two you will use often, if you proceed to write your own scripts, are **tell**, which you've already seen, and **set**, which tells AppleScript to assign a value to a variable or object.

More on Scripting

AppleScript doesn't know about colors, but it does understand arrays (lists or tables of values). Because colors on a Mac are represented by three numbers, the red, green, and blue components (RGB) that describe the color, you can write "**set orange to {65535, 13107, 0}**" and then tell AppleWorks to set the fill color of any cell in a given range containing a negative value to orange. This script and its result are shown in Figure 13.5.

A slight variation on this lets you specify that the text color be red for negative values, as shown in Figure 13.6. Notice that I omitted the cells containing non numeric entries from the test. The reason for this is that you will get an AppleScript error saying that a descriptor mismatch has occurred if you include those and don't explicitly test to make sure that you are comparing only numeric values to zero. Remember what I said about computers being very stupid and very literal?

13

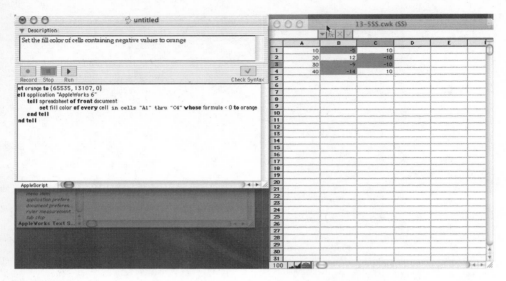

Figure 13.5
Turning negative cells orange.

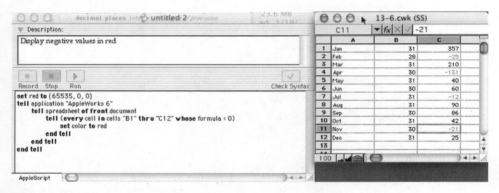

Figure 13.6
Displaying negative values in red.

AppleWorks, like BBEdit and other applications that promote the use of AppleScript, contains a Scripts menu (that's the one with the little scroll symbol just to the left of the Help menu). If you put scripts in AppleWorks' Scripts folder (in the AppleWorks Essentials folder, which you'll find in the AppleWorks application folder), they'll appear in AppleWorks' Scripts menu.

NOTE

You can also find a very useful "*AppleScript Usage Notes*" document in the Scripts Support folder of AppleWorks Essentials. This document details many useful techniques for leveraging AppleWorks' AppleScript support.

> **TIP**
>
> Some applications that support a Scripts menu prefer to store their Scripts folder in the ~/Library/Application Support folder for that application.

Okay, I'm going assume that I've scared (or confused) you enough that you'll think long and hard about writing your own scripts. But don't let that stop you from benefiting from AppleScripts others have written.

A Script Menu for All Seasons

When Mac OS 8 was just a pup, a clever programmer (and heck of a nice guy) named Leonard Rosenthol created a popular extension called OSA Menu. OSA stands for *Open Scripting Architecture*—a general framework for scripting languages. It's main function was to install a Scripts menu in OSA-compliant applications. Unfortunately, OSA Menu isn't available for Mac OS X at this time.

Fortunately, Apple liked Leonard's idea so much they created a free add-on for Mac OS X 10.1 and higher called Script Menu (**www.apple.com/applescript/macosx/script_menu/**), which allows you to invoke AppleScripts (and Perl and Shell scripts) by choosing them from a Script menu that appears in the menu bar of every Mac OS X application, regardless of whether it's scriptable. The Apple Script Menu is shown in Figure 13.7.

Figure 13.7
Choose the script you want to run from the Script menu.

Not only do you have the Script Menu, but Apple also has created a large (and growing) number of Toolbar Scripts (**www.apple.com/applescript/macosx/toolbar_scripts/**). You just drag the icons for these scripts into the toolbar of any Finder window, as shown in Figure 13.8.

13

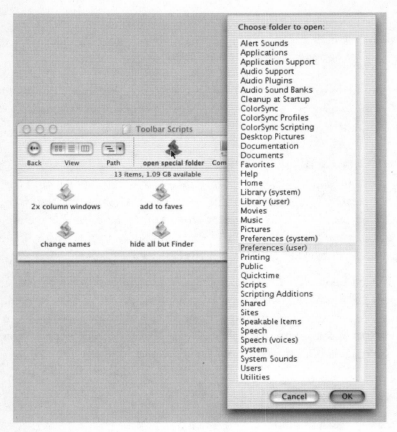

Figure 13.8
When I click the toolbar script as shown, the Choose Folder To Open dialog box appears.

These scripts operate on selected items in Finder windows or on the Finder windows themselves. Some of the included scripts give quick access to special folders or to the items you've specified as Favorites, create Web pages of selected graphics files, rotate the images in files, and tile the top two Finder windows.

Script Runner is similar to Script Menu, but the menu is now a pop-up menu in a mini-window that floats above all other windows, as shown in Figure 13.9.

Where to Learn More about Scripting

Obviously, the number one place to start looking for the latest news about AppleScript is Apple's Web site (**www.apple.com/applescript**). The Mac OS X–specific information starts at **www.apple.com/applescript/macosx/**. On these pages, you'll find links to MacScripter and other sites full of examples, tutorials, useful scripts, and utilities to use in creating and debugging your own scripts.

Figure 13.9
Script Runner—another way to run scripts stored in your Scripts folder.

Another excellent site is **www.applescriptcentral.com**, a fantastic resource when you're looking for scripts to control applications such as Entourage v.X, iTunes 2, AppleWorks 6, GraphicConverter, or other scriptable applications. Microsoft experts, in particular, have uploaded lots of useful scripts to help you get more out of Entourage and the other Office v.X applications.

Finally, the newsgroup **alt.comp.lang.applescript** is a fabulous resource. Because it's an "alt" group, not all news servers carry it. Hope that yours does, because the folks that hang out in this newsgroup are exceptionally helpful about answering your questions and sharing their techniques.

Coming Soon

Apple has announced and previewed an exciting new development environment called AppleScript Studio. Studio gives the AppleScript programmer access to all the interface elements and tools used in creating Cocoa applications.

NOTE

Reread the *"Cocoa, Carbon, and Classic"* sidebar back in Chapter 8 for the scoop on Cocoa, Carbon (and Classic) and what that whole thing is about.

Unfortunately, AppleScript Studio hasn't been available to me while I've been writing this book, so I can only go by what I've seen in demos and on Apple's Web site. If you're interested in creating double-clickable applications with the buttons, lists, sliders, toolbars, and so forth that a true Aqua application uses, you'll want to check this out.

13

Part IV

The
Cool Stuff
in the Back
of the Book

Highly Recommended Software

In the end, it's all about the software. An operating system is only as good as the stuff you run on it. So now that I've told you all I know about your operating system, it's time to switch gears and spend the remainder of the book looking at some of the wonderful "made for OS X" software you can run.

The first section covers commercial software—shrink-wrapped programs that come in a box that you buy at a store. The second section covers freeware (absolutely free) and shareware (try-before-you-buy-ware).

NOTE

In both sections, the entries appear in alphabetical order. Why? Because after racking my brain for days, I couldn't come up with a better way to organize them (i.e., utility or application; productivity or frivolity; game or puzzle; you get the point).

We've got a lot to cover here, so let's get to it!

Commercial Software Worth Paying For

Let's face it. As I write this, eight months after Mac OS X 10.0's release, there is still not nearly as much OS X software as there is Classic software. And, because it's likely to remain this way for quite some time, it's even more important for OS X users to know which programs are worth shelling out dough for and which are not.

There's not enough space here to tell you which ones are bad (that's a whole book in itself), but I will tell you about a handful of software that I have used long enough and tested hard enough to be comfortable recommending.

There's also not enough space here to provide thorough descriptions of all the things these programs can do, but I'll use a lot of pictures and tell you enough so that you at least get a feel for them. If they're something you need, rest assured that the programs I discuss in this section are indeed worth paying for.

AppleWorks

AppleWorks may be the most underrated software available for Mac OS X. That's not to say it will ever replace Microsoft Office for those who need industrial-strength applications, but for many users, AppleWorks has more than enough oomph for just about any document you care to create. And here's a little-known fact: AppleWorks now includes file translators so that you can work with Microsoft Word and Excel documents painlessly.

But it's more than just documents. In addition to its capable (and easy to use) word processing module, AppleWorks includes modules that let you create spreadsheets, paintings, drawings, presentations, and databases, plus oodles of nifty clip art.

My wife, for example, didn't want to deal with the complexity of Word even though she's got a Word expert living with her. So she creates almost everything in AppleWorks. She recently used its word processor to create a directory for my daughter's middle school—a 40+ page booklet listing more than 1,000 families. She started with the database module to sort and organize the names and other information. Then she finished it in the word processing module, and did it all without asking me for help. (Well, okay, she did ask a few questions, but only a few—and she could have done it without me if she had to.)

It won't take you long to get up and running with AppleWorks. It includes a handful of built-in assistants (see Figure 14.1) and templates, or you can start from a blank slate in any of the six modules.

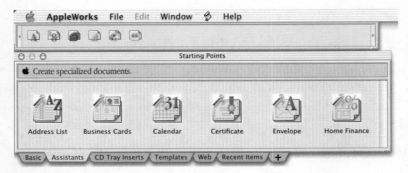

Figure 14.1
These are AppleWorks assistants which, well, assist you.

Here's how the Business Cards assistant works. Click it and the assistant window appears (top left; Figure 14.2).

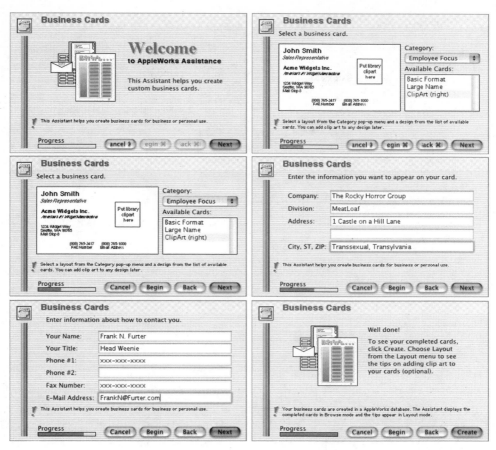

Figure 14.2
The Business Cards assistant screens from start (top left) to finish (bottom right).

Just do what the assistant asks, then click Next. When you're done, click Create and presto—you've got business cards (see Figure 14.3) ready to print on standard Avery business card stock you can buy at any decent office supply store.

The creation of the cords in Figure 14.3 took me a little more than two minutes, but that's only because I used AppleWorks way-cool Clippings to search the Web for an appropriate vampire graphic, as you can see in the lower-right portion of the figure. You see, AppleWorks not only installs more than 100 clip art images and 30 file templates on your hard disk, it also lets you search more than 25,000 high-quality photographs and vector clip art images on Apple's servers, and you can download as many of them as you like for free. Better still, you don't need to launch a Web browser, remember a URL, or decompress files—you can download the images, photos, and templates right from AppleWorks.

14

Figure 14.3
The finished business card(s). Not bad for two minutes of work, eh?

And it's not only convenient; it's easy as pie. Here's an example—the other day I wanted to design some new letterhead and wanted to use a whimsical typewriter as the artwork for it. I first searched the art that came with AppleWorks, but there were no typewriters to be found. So I clicked the Search Web Content check box, and AppleWorks found more than a dozen typewriters in its Web archive. It turned out that one of them was perfect, so I dragged it from the Clippings window into a word processor document, as shown in Figure 14.4. A minute or two later I had my letterhead completed.

Let me just show you one last thing I love about AppleWorks. It has to do with two of my other favorite pieces of Apple software, iTunes and AppleScript. Apple has created some free AppleScripts to use with iTunes. One of them automatically creates a CD insert from an iTunes playlist. I absolutely love this. Just open a CD Tray template in AppleWorks, create a playlist in iTunes, and then select the script from iTunes script menu, as shown in Figure 14.5.

In less than a minute, the insert is created for you automatically in AppleWorks. No copying, no pasting, no measuring, no muss, and no fuss. The result is shown in Figure 14.6.

Figure 14.4
AppleWorks has drag-and-drop almost everywhere. It's easy to use and fun, too.

Figure 14.5
Make your playlist, then choose this script.

14

Figure 14.6
In less than a minute, this insert was created for me automatically.

You've got to love that! I've been doing this manually for as long as I've been burning CDs, and I have to tell you, this way is *way* better.

NOTE

You can grab the entire free iTunes script collection at **www.apple.com/applescript/itunes/**.

I'd be remiss if I were to leave you with the impression that AppleWorks is perfect. It's not. It can be sluggish as all heck, even on a G4/500 like mine. And though the online help is pretty good, and the program is mostly easy to use, you'll sometimes wish it came with a printed manual. Finally, it's still got some bugs and can freeze or "quit unexpectedly," so save your work early and often.

But hey, it's a great, easy-to-use program with a low price that can't be beat. If you can't afford Microsoft Office, or don't need a program with that many bells and whistles, AppleWorks is an excellent choice.

AppleWorks Details
Company: Apple Computer, Inc.

Web: **www.apple.com.**

Street price: $80.

BBEdit
Because there's no way I could explain it as well, as eloquently, or in as few words as its developer, Bare Bones Software, here's how their Web site describes BBEdit:

BBEdit is a high-performance HTML and text editor for the Macintosh. It is designed and crafted for the editing, searching, transformation, and manipulation of text. BBEdit provides an array of general-purpose features, which are useful for a wide variety of tasks, and includes many features that have been specifically developed in response to the needs of Web authors and software developers.

Now from that description you'd think that this is a program for Web authors and programmers, but you'd be wrong. It's a program for anyone who manipulates text. And, of course, it's also the best HTML programming code editor in the world, bar none.

But what makes it really special, aside from those attributes, is the wealth of special "OS X–only" features that make it even more useful to folks like us who love and use Mac OS X.

NOTE

I should probably point out that BBEdit is not a word processor as you probably think of word processors. If you need sophisticated formatting features such as columns and tables, or need to include graphics in your text, it's not the right choice. But if you work primarily with text, it's got everything you'll ever need and more. I know many writers who use nothing but BBEdit and leave it to editors and page layout people to do that kind of stuff for them.

14

BareBones has a fully functional demo (it will expire after 25 launches, but it is otherwise identical to the retail version) of the latest (as of this moment) version which can be linked to from this book's companion Web site at **www.boblevitus.com/ xfiles.html**. I will give you a peek at a few of its niceties and some of the cool OS X– only features in a moment, but I'm going to try to limit myself to just a couple of pages.

I encourage you to try BBEdit—I know I am totally hooked and would hate not to have this versatile tool on my hard disk.

> **NOTE**
>
> If you try it and like it but can't afford it, check out the freeware program, BBEdit Lite. It has many (okay, it has "some") of the features of the retail product and won't cost you a dime. It's discussed further in the next section of this chapter, "Shareware/ Freeware."

First, here's a look at some of the killer HTML editing features, shown in Figure 14.7.

Let me try, in just a few bullet points, to show why BBEdit is the best way to edit raw HTML (i.e., you aren't using a graphical page-builder program such as HomePage, Dreamweaver, GoLive, or whatever). In addition to its complete set of HTML tools, which support all major standards, including HTML 4.01, XHTML 1.0, and WML 1.1, 1.2, and 1.3, BBEdit also lets you do the following:

- Use all the HTML Tools from a menu or palette

- Apply HTML markup from contextual menus

- Check any page or entire site for compliance with any supported standard

- Preview in any or all browsers

- Easily create file or image links using drag and drop

- Apply syntax coloring (syntax coloring preferences are shown in Figure 14.7)

- Maintain and use custom text or tags in a glossary

- Batch find and replace

- Check spelling with the built-in HTML-aware spell checker

And so much more I could fill a book (and I did once—*The Official BBEdit Book*, now out of print).

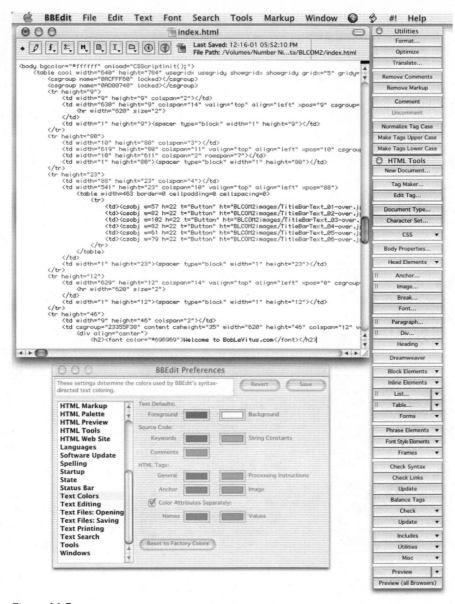

Figure 14.7
My home page as HTML, two (of the many) palettes, and a preference panel (one of many).

But wait, there's more. Forget about HTML for a moment and look at Figure 14.8, where you'll see just a fraction of BBEdit's incredible searching power, which lets you find literally anything in any pile of text regardless of its length.

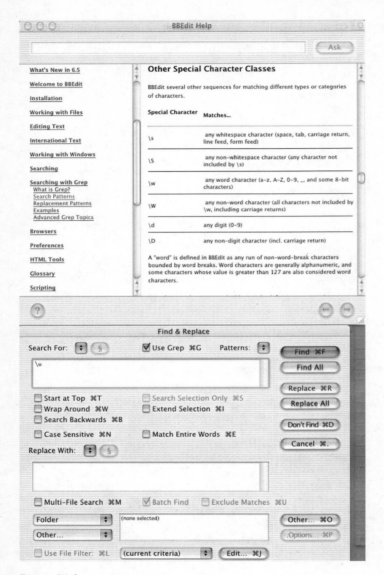

Figure 14.8
The Find & Replace dialog box (bottom) and a small fraction of the online help for it (top).

Suffice it to say there's a learning curve, but once you get the hang of it, if you can't find it with BBEdit, it doesn't exist in the text.

OK, just one more cool feature before we have to move on, and that feature is BBEdit's Shell Worksheets, which let you execute Unix commands and view their output right in BBEdit!

In Figure 14.9, I selected the Unix command **ls –l** in the top window (to list the current directory), then pressed Command+Return to issue the command. You can see the results—right there in BBEdit—in the bottom window. Very cool for editing Unix files and/or issuing the occasional Unix command without firing up the Terminal program.

Figure 14.9
It's not the Terminal; it's BBEdit pretending to be the Terminal.

14

OK, I lied. Because we're on the subject anyway, there's still one other thing worth mentioning: BBEdit has "Authenticated Saves," which is a fancy way to say it lets you modify and save files that you don't own or you don't have write permission for (as long, of course, as you can provide a correct administrator password). If you edit many Unix files (most of which you don't own or have write permission for), this trick alone may be worth the price of admission.

Last, but not least, how can you help but love a product from a company whose registered trademark is, "It doesn't suck?"

BBEdit Details
Company: Bare Bones Software.

Web: **www.barebones.com**.

Street price: $100.

A demo version of BBEdit (as well as its baby brother/sister, the freeware program BBEdit Lite) can be linked to from **www.boblevitus.com/xfiles.html**.

Conflict Catcher

Conflict Catcher is like Apple's Extensions Manager on Vitameatavegamin™, and then some.

NOTE

Yes, I really am including a program that doesn't run in OS X. If you're going to use Classic often, and especially if you don't have your disk partitioned into two or more volumes, it's worth every single penny. I'll prove it with several reasons why in a moment.

Of course, one of the things Conflict Catcher does is manage extensions and control panels—the little icons that march across the bottom of the screen or the Classic Environment Starting From "Your Disk" window when you turn on an OS 9 Macintosh or start Classic.

Extensions and control panels are necessary in OS 9; they provide things like the capability to use the Internet, CD-ROMs, or networking. But each extension or control panel you load increases the likelihood of problems, including, but not limited to, freezes, crashes, and applications that quit unexpectedly.

Conflict Catcher helps you manage extensions and control panels, but it also does a lot more:

- It includes a database with descriptions of thousands of extensions and control panels and tells you what each one is for. This is particularly convenient for figuring out which ones you can safely turn off for Classic. Better still, these database entries have built-in hotlinks to the Web, so you can easily score updated versions when you need them.

- You can switch on or off entire groups of related files with a single click, such as the various extensions required for an Apple CD-ROM drive (which, incidentally, you don't need in Classic).

- When you encounter an extension conflict, in OS 9 or Classic, Conflict Catcher automates the troubleshooting process. So even if you (like me) have hundreds of startup files, Conflict Catcher will make it a lot easier to determine which one—or ones—are causing your heartache.

- If you ever find your System Folder screwed up big time, a clean install may be the only cure. After a clean installation, Conflict Catcher's Clean Install Assistant will move your fonts, preferences, extensions, control panels, Apple menu items, and other customized components from your Previous System Folder into your freshly installed clean one in minutes.

But those features are the icing on the cake for OS X users, because these next two are worth their weight in code snippets to the busy OS X fan:

- Choose the startup set automatically based on which OS version is running. So you can create one set for Classic and another for OS 9, and never have to worry about choosing the right one before you restart or start up. It's pretty darn sweet.

- Choose the boot volume at startup.

Conflict Catcher auto-picks my Classic Set For X set if I'm booting it via Classic, and my Base Set For 9 set if I'm booting it via OS 9, as you can see in Figure 14.10.

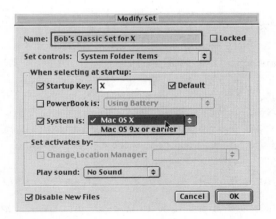

14

Figure 14.10
I'm telling Conflict Catcher to use this set if the OS is X (i.e., when being launched for use with Classic).

And the Startup menu lets you choose a boot volume before the march of icons (i.e., loading of extensions and control panels) even starts; it's shown in Figure 14.11.

Figure 14.11
Boot from any OS 9 startup disk at startup or any other time with the Startup menu.

Conflict Catcher Details

Company: Casady & Greene

Web: www.casadyg.com

Street price: $70

Microsoft Office v.X

Although I don't think much of their monopolistic business practices in the Windows world, I try not to hold it against Microsoft's Mac Business Unit or Microsoft products. The guy who builds the best mousetrap wins. And I've found, regardless of what you think of the company, in many cases the Microsoft product is by all means the "best of breed."

The Mac Business Unit—the team responsible for Office v.X—wants to build "best of breed" apps. I talk to them. They talk the talk and walk the walk. I know a bunch them and I think they "get it." I think the MBU knows what makes good Mac software good and are trying to put as much of "it" into their programs as they can.

Office v.X is the case in point. It's lots better than Office 2001 in lots of ways. Unlike some ports from OS 9, which shall, for the most part, remain nameless to protect the guilty (are you listening Canvas 8 and Corel Suite 10?), Office v.X looks and feels like a real Mac OS X app, right down to the OS X way of displaying Save dialog boxes as "sheets," which, unlike dialog boxes, are attached to a single document, which means you can continue working in another document or program, even when a Save sheet is (or 10 Save sheets are) on screen (kind of like I'm doing in Figure 14.12).

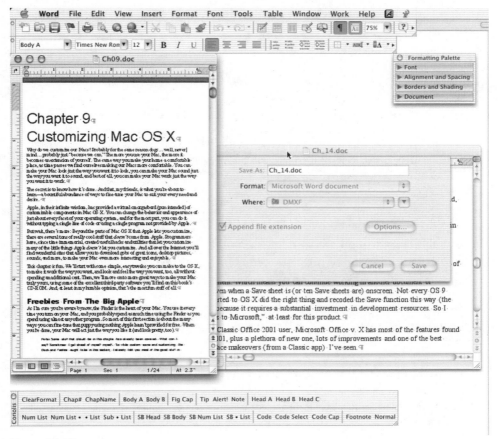

Figure 14.12
I'm working on Chapter 9 but stopped to move Chapter 14's window and Save sheet just to show that I can.

Not every OS 9 program ported to OS X did the right thing and recoded the Save function this way (the right way) because it requires a substantial investment in development resources. So I say, "cheers to Microsoft," at least for this product.

If you're a Classic Office 2001 user, Microsoft Office v.X has most of the features found in Office 2001, plus a plethora of new ones, lots of improvements, and one of the best Aqua interface makeovers (from a Classic app) I've seen.

14

New features in all the programs include over 700 new high-resolution OS X-style icons, buttons, interface elements, dialog boxes, and widgets.

> **NOTE**
>
> You can see many of these features in Figure 14.12 if you look closely.

Microsoft did the right thing with Office. It's got a real Aqua interface and for the most part feels like a real OS X program. Thankfully, it's not just a warmed-over program "quick-Carbonized™" to allow it to run in both Classic and OS X.

> **NOTE**
>
> Don't get me wrong. I'll take quick-carbonized over running something in Classic anytime. Even quick-carbonized programs take advantage of some aqua features "for free," including gumdrops widgets in the windows, and such. And they also share the OS X benefits of preemptive multitasking (though some aren't very good at it yet) and memory protection. But to me, the best developers, seeing all the great stuff OS X gives them "under the hood," spend the extra time to make their product more "Mac OS X–like," rather than just do a quick, straight Carbonization port.

Other new features shared by all the programs in Microsoft Office (except Entourage) include the Formatting Palette, a single, context-sensitive palette that takes the place of dozens (or hundreds) of different commands scattered about in dialog boxes, sheets, toolbars, and menus, kind of like what you see in Figure 14.13.

In Figure 14.13, you can see how the outline-like structure of the Formatting Palette lets you open only what you need, saving screen real estate in the process.

> **NOTE**
>
> Figure 14.13 is a fake. You wouldn't ever have five different Formatting Palettes on your screen at the same time. But because I wanted you to get a sense for how this handy little windoid can be rolled up or expanded, I used a bit of copy and paste to composite five different screenshots into one picture.

They say good help is hard to find, and it is. In other words, I wish I could tell you Office v.X's Help was better. Though the Help system in all four programs is somewhat improved (you can see the Table of Contents in Figure 14.14), it is still often obtuse and confusing. And all too often it can't help. Finally, Office hasn't included any printed documentation whatsoever in several releases.

> **NOTE**
>
> I've managed to avoid Clippy, the stupid animated help icon, so far. I know he's in there somewhere but I've turned him off permanently. I think. No, wait, is that. . . OH NO!!! Clippy makes his appearance in Figure 14.15.

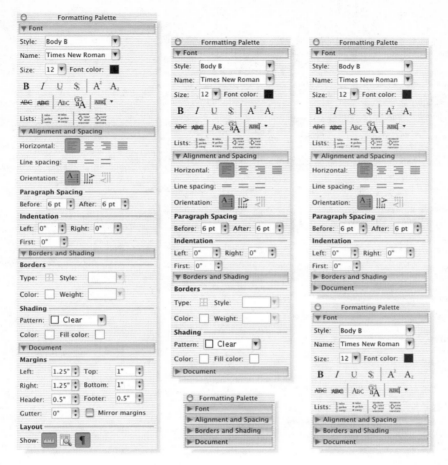

Figure 14.13
The Formatting Palette can be as small (bottom middle) or as large as you need it to be.

Here is how to turn off that annoying feature—Control+click in his face and then choose Hide Assistant. Or choose Help|Use The Office Assistant (but only if it has a check mark). In other words, the Help|Use The Office Assistant menu item is a toggle. If there's a check mark, you've chosen to use it; if there's not, you haven't. This is why you want to choose it only if there is a check mark (which will uncheck it, and turn it off).

Maybe the best new feature in the whole suite is Word's new multiple selection capability (see Figure 14.16).

14

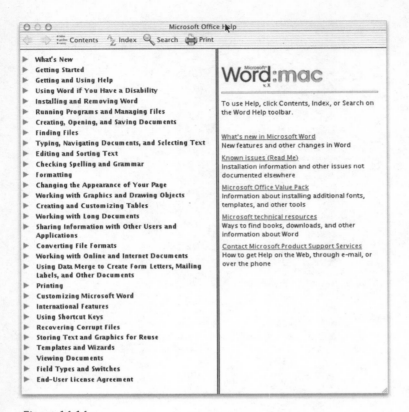

Figure 14.14
The Help system isn't perfect, but it's better than it was.

Figure 14.15
Clippy makes an unscheduled appearance.

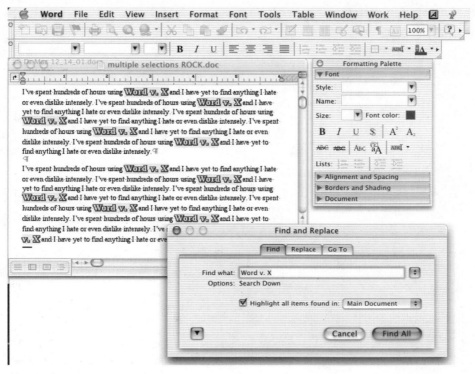

Figure 14.16
I searched for and highlighted "Word v.X" all at once, then used the Formatting Palette on every instance at once.

This is a great feature and one you'll find a million uses for once you get the hang of it.

I've spent hundreds of hours using Word v.X and I have yet to find anything I hate or even dislike intensely (OK, there's Clippy, but not much else). For me, the word processor is my main axe, the program I use by far the most every day. And Word v.X has been a pleasure.

Furthermore, Word v.X uses the same file formats as Windows Office XP/2000/97 (and Mac Office 2001), so I've had no problems exchanging hundreds of files with my Windows-using editors, nor a single issue with Word templates I created with Word 2001.

Entourage, the Office email-calendar-to-do list-event tracker-contact manager-note keeper program, is much improved as well. I keep it running 24/7 and use it quite literally for everything, as evidenced by Figure 14.17.

And I love the little reminders that pop up even when no Office programs are running—it's one of those features I can't live without. They come from the Office Notifications window, which you see in the upper-right corner of Figure 14.17. I only wish Entourage was capable of syncing with a Palm or Visor. (They say someday it will.)

14

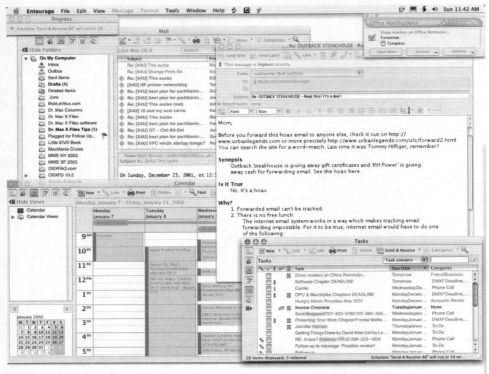

Figure 14.17
I use Entourage for appointments and events (lower-left Calendar window); deadlines, phone calls, and things to do (lower-right Tasks window); email (upper-right Re: OUTBACK window); and more.

> **NOTE**
>
> Rant on: I take issue with Microsoft requiring you to have a Microsoft .NET Passport if you wish to register online, and for not including a snail mail registration card in the box. What if I don't want a Microsoft .NET Passport? Which I don't. What if I'm not interested in even learning what one is?
>
> What were they thinking? Perhaps by the time you get it, they will have abolished that silly and self-serving requirement. But it bugged the heck out of me.

Still, I'm ready to go on the record about Word and Entourage for OS X—they are the best versions I've ever used and I've been using Office since time immemorial. I don't use Excel (spreadsheet) or PowerPoint (presentations and slide shows) enough to know if they're the best, but I will say that in my limited testing, they worked fine for my admittedly lightweight presenting and spreadsheeting needs.

Office v.X Details
Company: Microsoft Corp.

Web: **www.microsoft.com.**

Street price: $450; Upgrade price: $149.

MouseWorks for Mac OS X

MouseWorks for Mac OS X is the software that controls my Turbo Mouse Pro Wireless trackball. I talked about it at some length in Chapter 7, and there is a picture of the software and the device in Chapter 7, too. I stuck this here only because MouseWorks is good OS X software that keeps getting better (another new release came out today, making about five new releases since it shipped, each with more features and fewer bugs than the one before it).

MouseWorks for Mac OS X Details
Company: Kensington.

Web: **www.kensington.com.**

Street price: Free with mouse or trackball.

Timbuktu Pro

I talked about Timbuktu Pro at some length back in Chapter 5. Don't leave home without it.

Timbuktu Pro Details
Company: Netopia, Inc.

Web: **www.netopia.com.**

Street price: $100 per node.

More Commercial Software Worth Paying For, (I Think)

Don't get the wrong idea about these next dozen or so programs. They're all good enough that, had I only more time and pages, I could say much more. But the ones in the previous section are the ones I just absolutely and positively wouldn't want to be without. Ones I'd pay for with my own money if I had to.

But for the past three months I've spent all of my "product testing" cycles checking out the shareware and freeware links at **www.boblevitus.com/xfiles.html**. The good

14

news is that I've looked at well over 1,000 shareware and freeware programs in the past 90 days and culled out roughly 150 that I think are a cut above the rest. The bad news is that I've been derelict in the time I've spent with new commercial programs. So, although some of the programs in this section may well turn out to be "home runs," I haven't been using them enough to say for sure yet.

These are all programs that were either released during this book's gestation or programs I became familiar with only after starting this project. I'm looking forward to spending more time with all of them soon.

Anyway, I'll describe each briefly, show a picture or two, and move on.

BackUp ToolKit

I talked at length about this one way back in Chapter 4. I stuck this here just to remind you: You absolutely and positively need a backup program (or a fabulous memory). Unless you've never forgotten something important ever in your life, buy a copy of BackUp ToolKit or Retrospect immediately if not sooner.

Okay? 'Nuff said.

FWB Software. **www.fwb.com**. Street price: $40.

Corel Graphics Suite

Corel Graphics Suite includes three main applications: CorelDRAW (vector-illustration and page layout), Corel PHOTO-PAINT (image editing and painting), Corel R.A.V.E. (vector animation similar to Flash). Also in the box are: CorelTRACE (bitmap-to-vector tracing utility), Font Reserve Corel Edition (font manager for OS X), and Canto Cumulus Desktop LE (media management; the application ran only in Classic, though an OS X version may be out by the time you read this). The last two are especially useful for the 2,000 clip art images, 500 stock photos, and 2,000 fonts Corel throws in.

The Corel graphics programs have been a staple in the Windows market and were, for a while, almost as popular as Adobe's Windows offerings. But Corel's earlier efforts to capture the hearts and minds of the Mac market never really flew and Adobe's Windows apps got better and better. Today, many users remember Corel only as the company that finally put poor old WordPerfect Mac out of its misery.

But the press release for Corel Graphics Suite made it sound like the second coming of PageMaker, Photoshop, Flash, Suitcase, and a bunch of other stuff all in one box, and all optimized for Mac OS X. I requested a copy, which showed up in the middle of this book's production.

Now usually I'm superstitious about changing production software in the middle of a book. And I rarely do. But in this case, Corel PHOTO-PAINT was (and still is) the first native OS X alternative to Photoshop. And because I wanted very much not to use Classic anymore (Photoshop being my last "must-run" program without a better OS X alternative), I gave it a try. First I submitted a few test pictures, and when nobody in production complained and the soft-proofs—which are PDF files because we're a thoroughly modern publishing operation—looked great, I went ahead and used Corel PHOTO-PAINT to create and save all the graphics in this book from Chapter 8 through the end.

NOTE

I used it for everything on every graphic: cropping, compositing, adding text, adding drop-shadows, editing, and retouching. For example, look at Figure 14.13—it was created entirely in Corel PHOTO-PAINT 10, including the phony OS-X-type drop shadows. (The screenshots themselves, of course, came from SnapzPro X.)

I've barely touched CorelDRAW or any of the other stuff that came in the box. Frankly, all I know so far is how to use Corel PHOTO-PAINT to do the stuff for the book. But it wasn't half-bad. When I find some free time, I'm going to explore it further—it's got some nice features Photoshop doesn't (directly selecting and operating on several layers, directly selecting and aligning and distributing separate layers, an interactive drop shadow tool) and uses many of the same keyboard shortcuts as Photoshop. It looks like what you see in Figure 14.18.

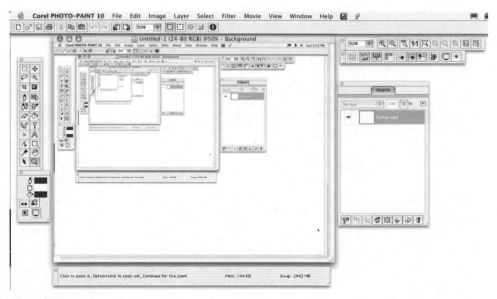

Figure 14.18
Corel PHOTO-PAINT. I dunno. It's kinda like Photoshop but not really that much like Photoshop.

14

Anyway, I don't know it well enough to recommend it wholeheartedly, yet, but I will say that PHOTO-PAINT has been fairly dependable, if not particularly speedy on my G4/500. I can't tell you any more about the other programs, but the font collection isn't bad at all, and the clip art is okay. All in all it seems like a good deal if you need OS X graphics tools and don't want to wait for (or just don't want) Photoshop for OS X.

Corel Corporation. **www.corel.com**. Street price: $500.

FileMaker Pro

The easiest-to-use relational database has been running on OS X for many months already—it was one of the first made for Mac OS X applications ever released. If you've used FileMaker before, there are no surprises. It's still the same old powerful-yet-easy-to-use database it's always been, but now it runs natively on OS X. And it's a darned nice little program if you have a lot of data to manage. I used it to manage the names and contact information for the authors of all the shareware I provide links for at my Web site, as shown in Figure 14.19.

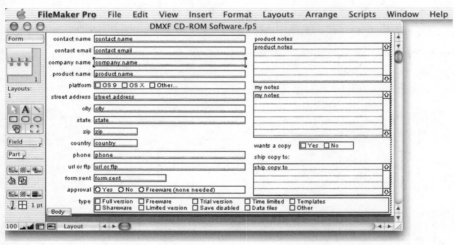

Figure 14.19
My little shareware author tracking database.

It only took me about half an hour to plan, design, and build it. And I can find any program or author now—and get a dozen little pieces of information about them—in a fraction of a second. I can also tell at a glance which authors have returned the paperwork (by the state of the Approval radio buttons).

If you have only "some" or "a little" data to manage, the database module of AppleWorks looks and acts a lot like FileMaker Pro and is just as well suited for less demanding data management tasks.

To be perfectly honest, I rarely need to use a database for my work. Most of the stuff I'd have used a database for in the old days is handled by Entourage. But when I do have a suitable project, and I do encounter a few every year, FileMaker has never let me down. I've been using it since version 1.0 and I think it's better than ever in OS X. But what do I know? I'm a just a geeky word jockey who tinkers with data every so often.

FileMaker, Inc. **www.filemaker.com**. Street price: $225.

Photoshop X

Don't I wish? It wasn't even announced (much less shipping) when I wrote this. I've tried lots of native OS X substitutes but there is nothing like Photoshop for graphical heavy lifting. By the time you read this Photoshop X should be available. I expect, given how long it's taken Adobe, that it will be superb.

Adobe. **www.adobe.com**. Street price? What can I say—it's not even announced as I type this. I guesstimate it'll sell for around $600.

Quicken 2002 Deluxe

I've used Quicken, the ubiquitous financial management/bill-paying/check-writing software, for a long time. I can't manage a checkbook manually, but since I've been using Quicken, I have rarely had a reconciliation go bad on me.

Some versions of Quicken over the years have been better than others. But there's never been a version so awful I was forced to abandon it. And fortunately, the latest version, Quicken 2002 Deluxe, has given me very little grief (albeit in limited testing) under OS X.

I really like several features:

- Annual income and expenses neatly categorized for tax reporting

- Online reconciliation (download bank statements)

- Stock portfolio tracking and graphing

- Comprehensive reporting and graphing of my income and expenses by category

- Always legible (the register in my checkbook isn't)

But my very, very favorite feature, absolutely and positively, is paying bills electronically. For less than the cost of stamps and gasoline, I am able to enter a payee into Quicken and have them paid electronically. It's so easy I have no idea why everyone doesn't do it. I don't have to remember to buy stamps. I don't forget to mail the envelope. I don't lose the envelope. I don't mix up envelopes and invoices. And I have automatic reminders in Quicken so I never forget to pay any of my regularly occurring bills. Figure 14.20 shows some of Quicken's many windows.

14

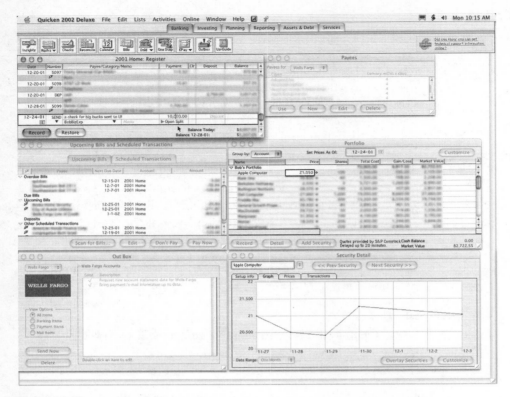

Figure 14.20
Clockwise from top right: Quicken's Payees, Portfolio, Stock Detail, Online Out Box, Upcoming Bills and Scheduled Transactions, and checkbook Register windows.

A caveat: I use Quicken only twice a month so I don't have a ton of hands-on time with it. So far it's been fine, and mostly well behaved. But it's quit unexpectedly more than once, and that worries me even though I've not lost a single transaction. So I'm not ready to give it three thumbs up just yet.

Intuit, Inc. **www.intuit.com**. Street price: $60.

QuicKeys X
A great macro utility. The only reason it's in this section is that you can do most of what it does with shareware such as Keyboard Maestro or TypeIt4Me if you like. I use Quick Keys daily and have found it robust and reliable so far. Because I covered it in full and loving detail in Chapter 9, we'll leave it at that for now.

CE Software. **www.quickeys.com**. Street price: $60.

REALbasic

I would guess that up to 25 percent of the programs I offer links to at **www. boblevitus.com/xfiles.html** were created with REALbasic from Real Software. Simply put, REALbasic is programming for non-programmers. Even I kind of understand how it works. If you've never programmed before, this is the only place to start. And even if you have, unless you've got pretty good OOP (object-oriented programming) chops, REALbasic may still be the way to go.

REALbasic is a construction kit for building powerful, fully featured, double-clickable applications for both Mac OS 9 and X, and Windows. Your programs support all the great features of the computer your application runs on, and REALbasic supports most of the high-end technologies and open standards in the industry (SQL, ODBC, Visual Basic, QuickTime, TCP/IP, and more).

And it's fun—to do much of your design work, you merely drag items from the toolbox to your project window (the Untitled window in Figure 14.21).

I'd be remiss if I didn't tell you that you'll have to write the appropriate code if you want any of the elements to actually do anything. You can see the Code Editor window for my project at the lower right in Figure 14.21. That's the kind of code you'll have to type yourself for each item you drag and drop.

You won't become a brilliant programmer overnight with REALbasic, but if you stick with it, you could very well write the next great Mac program. There's a free 30-day trial available on their Web site.

> **NOTE**
>
> There are two things I really regret not having enough time for. The first is learning to program better in REALbasic, the other is to shoot and edit more video with Final Cut Pro 3.

Real Software. **www.realbasic.com**. Street price: standard $150, pro $350.

Retrospect

I talked at length about this one way back in Chapter 4. I stuck this here only to remind you: You absolutely and positively need a backup program (or a fabulous memory). 'Nuff said.

Dantz Development. **www.dantz.com**. Street price: $150.

Stone Studio

I discovered these programs only a few weeks ago, so I've not had sufficient time to work with them all yet. But they're among the first commercial programs for OS X

14

Figure 14.21
I built this stupid dialog box in about two minutes.

written in Cocoa, which means that they use almost all of the cool OS X features and aren't available for OS 9 at all.

There are seven programs in the Stone Studio Suite:

- *Create*—A professional page layout, illustration, and Web page authoring application with many advanced features, and a surprisingly simple interface.

- *PhotoToWeb*—Turns your digital photos into Web sites for sharing with others. Advanced features include full screen slide shows, Web image preview, thumbnails, and complete control over look and feel of albums.

- *GIFfun*—Makes animated Web images via drag and drop. You can create the individual frames in Create automatically or just drag in any kind of image.

- *SliceAndDice*—Lets you turn images into clickable Web pages. Automatically add fancy JavaScript rollovers and build navigation bars for use in Create and Web pages.

- *PackUp&Go*—A shareware, open-standard file and folder compression and uncompression application. Simply drag on files to pack or unpack. Creates universally readable tar.gz and tar.Z files.

- *PStill*—An advanced PostScript distillery that turns EPS and PS files into viewable, beautiful antialiased PDFs.

- *TimeEqualsMoney*—Lets you track work sessions with full documentation and then instantly create invoices for that work. A real moneymaker for independents.

> **NOTE**
>
> These descriptions were cribbed from the Stone Design Web site, www.stone.com. Who better to describe them to you than the guy who wrote them?

Speaking of which, here's what CEO/Programmer Andrew Stone has to say about his suite: "The true power of OS X shows when you use the apps together. Drag SliceAndDice and GIFfun documents into Create to make dynamic Web pages. Use Create to make background patterns for PhotoToWeb pages. Install PStill and then drag EPS files directly in Create. Generate your Web site in Create or PhotoToWeb and drag the resulting folder into PackUp&Go to make an archive that can be easily transferred to a Web server. It's all seamless."

For a peek at Create see Figure 14.22.

Mr. Stone, who seems to be a pretty cool guy, runs a mailing list of Studio users—it's a small but vocal community that seems to like his tools a lot. And Stone is responsive to user feedback; I saw a feature request on the list turn into a full-blown feature in the next release.

Because there is a link to a full-strength demo of Stone Studio at my Web site, we'll leave it at that. But if you need a set of cool graphics tools, you have no excuse for not checking out Stone Studio—the free demos are fully functional for several weeks after you begin using them.

Stone Design. **www.stone.com**. Street price: $300.

StuffIt Deluxe

You know about SIT files and compression already. Well, you know a bit about them if you read the StuffIt Deluxe Magic Menu/Contextual Menu section in Chapter 9. And surely you've seen a small SIT file turn into a big folder full of stuff on your own computer, via the magic of the free StuffIt Expander that is included with every copy of Mac OS X.

14

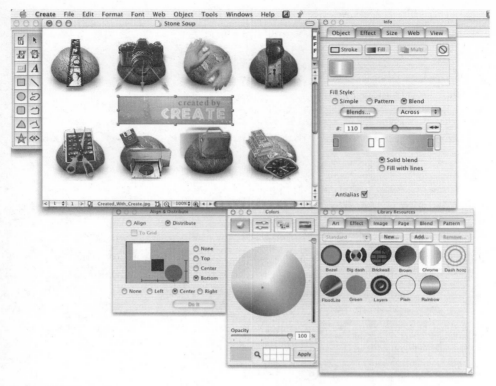

Figure 14.22
Page layout, illustration, and Web design, all in one easy-to-use program.

But what you may not know about is the granddaddy of all StuffIt products, the commercial big brother to Expander: StuffIt Deluxe. And with the 6.5 release (6.5.1 at this writing), it's actually become an exemplary OS X program with a system menu, keyboard shortcuts, and a slick contextual menu, too.

Here's just some of what StuffIt Deluxe can do for you from Aladdin Systems Web site, **www.aladdinsys.com**:

- Access any file, download, or attachment

- Send files faster over the Internet and networks

- Simple one-click Stuff and mail

- View, compress, expand, and access items within compressed files

- Quickly search for files buried deep within archives

- Encrypt files to secure sensitive data

- Scan archives to protect from viruses

- Automate all your file transfer tasks

- Magic Menu for Mac OS X

- Expand and install Palm files automatically

(Bullet list cribbed from Aladdin Systems Web site.)

I talked about Magic Menu in Chapter 9, so I won't belabor the point here. Suffice it to say it's one of my favorite parts.

Two more reasons I like StuffIt Deluxe:

One, I have a lot of files I don't need often but want to keep available on my hard disk. Stuffing the folders for some finished book projects, as shown in Figure 14.23, shrunk them by 30–75 percent!

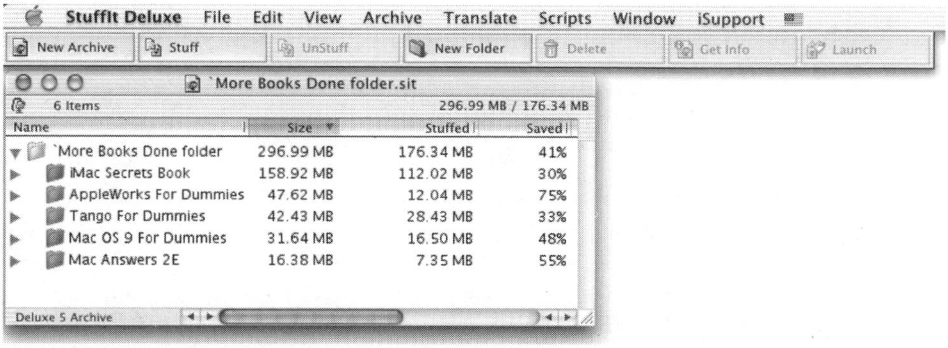

Figure 14.23
Look at how much disk space Stuffing these folders saved!

And, of course, almost anything I send as an enclosure via email, and most of what I transfer via FTP, is squished with StuffIt compression before going out onto the wire. Which leads me to reason number two. . .

Stuffit Deluxe can compress or decompress just about every file format I'm likely to encounter. (And I'm likely to encounter a lot more of 'em than you!)

Figure 14.24 shows some of the compression schemes StuffIt Deluxe can encode and decode.

14

Figure 14.24
Stuffit Deluxe can also encode and decode almost any combination of the above, too.

So, for example, a file encoded with MacBinary, StuffIt, and BinHex will expand completely and automatically, reconstituting the file(s) or folder(s) to their pristine precompression state.

I use this program a lot. But because compression and its "de," are not for everyone, it's down here instead of up there. That doesn't mean it doesn't rock, just that while it *may* rock, you may not need it.

> If you think you might need it, an in-between step is the shareware offering from Aladdin, StuffIt Lite, discussed later in this chapter. It offers some of StuffIt Deluxe's capabilities but at a greatly reduced price. (No Magic Menu, though.)

Aladdin Systems. **www.aladdinsys.com**. Street price: $75.

Virtual PC

Virtual PC 5 for Mac OS X showed up a few days ago. Virtual PC is a Mac OS X program that gives your Mac the functionality and compatibility of a Pentium PC through the magic of software emulation. In other words, VPC (what hip insiders call it) tricks your Mac into believing it's a PC equipped with the standard Intel chip set and other hardware components.

I've used previous versions of VPC, and it just plain works. I wouldn't use it to play Quake III Arena, but to run an occasional program or test HTML in different browsers—it's definitely a viable option.

I installed only Version 5, the first for OS X, a few minutes ago. So I can't tell you much yet. I will say that installation of both Windows 98 and Windows 2000 versions went smoothly, and I was able to browse the Web with both as soon as they booted for the first time (simultaneously, I might add), as shown in Figure 14.25.

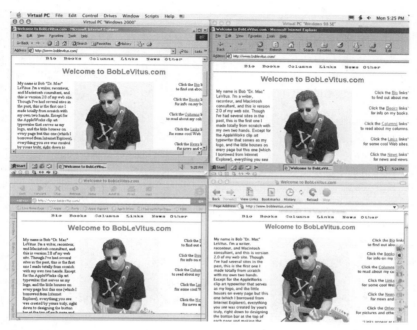

Figure 14.25
Four browsers on four operating systems on one monitor—you don't see that every day.

Clockwise from bottom left you see Microsoft Internet Explorer running under Mac OS 9 (actually Classic), Windows 2000, and Windows 98. The fourth window, at bottom right, is OmniWeb, running native in OS X.

As I said, I just installed it, so I have no idea how it works. It installs nicely enough, though. According to their Web site, here's what's new in version 5:

- Supports Mac OS 9 and Mac OS X in one application
- Multiprocessor support in Mac OS X
- Network between Virtual PCs running on the same Mac
- Undoable drive images let you to back out of any Windows session
- Full support for Windows XP Pro and Windows XP Home as guest OSes

14

- Ability to share removable media storage devices

- DVD-ROM data support for the guest OS

- Key mapping between Macintosh keyboard and standard PC keyboard

- Snappier user experience: Faster menus and faster text scrolling

Other users have been complaining (MacFixIt, MacInTouch) about the speed, and sure enough, it feels somewhat sluggish on my G4/500. Windows 2000 seems to run faster than Windows 98, but neither is what I'd call "blazing" or even "snappier." Still, it's impressive, and it does get the job done, albeit sometimes not as quickly as you'd like.

The new version supports all these flavors: Windows 95, Windows 98, Windows ME, Windows NT 4, Windows 2000 Professional, Windows XP Home, Windows XP Professional, and Linux. Some are available from Connectix as "OS Packs," and the others you can install yourself if you like.

Connectix Corporation. **www.connectix.com**. Street price: $99 (DOS), $199 (Windows 98), $249 (Windows 2000).

Shareware/Freeware

Now for the really cool stuff: shareware and freeware. Some of the best things in life really are free (or inexpensive)—this section proves it. You'll be introduced to a plethora of superb software offerings and a few that are just pretty good. There are links to more than 100 programs on the Web site for you to try.

Freeware, even badly-done-but-well-intentioned freeware, is cool. I just love a good freeware application or utility. Behind each freeware program stands a programmer (or company) that's not in it for the money. And some of the freeware is so useful and necessary, you'd probably be willing to pay for it. Some of the best and most useful programs linked from the Web site are freeware, so go for it—use them to your heart's content at no additional cost.

> **NOTE**
>
> Do me a favor: If you like one of the freeware programs a lot, send the author an email and tell him or her so.

The ones that aren't free are shareware (i.e., try-before-you-buy ware). Some of them are disabled in some way unless you pay the shareware fee. Some function for a set number of days before expiring unless you pay the shareware fee. Some are fully functional but nag you and make you wait at startup and other annoyances unless you pay the shareware fee. And some are fully functional: The authors are depending on your honesty and good character to pay them if you like the programs; the software works, and usually quite well, even if you don't pay. But you should.

The screening process was rigorous. Every day for the past four months I've gone to **www.versiontracker.com** and downloaded any and all Mac OS X freeware or shareware that sounded remotely interesting. I'd say I downloaded more than 1,200 files in all. The screening process was simple. I had a folder called "under consideration." And I used whatever was in that folder until it was either "kept" or "canned." If it was kept, it went into the X-Files Maybe folder. Hundreds of programs (names withheld to protect the guilty) were canned. But there were at least 200 "keepers," from which I selected what I hope is a balanced mix of utilities, applications, useless diversions, games, stupid Mac tricks, icons, screen savers, system preference panes, and other interesting stuff for Mac OS X. In other words, I want you to have a lot of little tastes of the best stuff.

On the Matter of Honor

I put a lot of effort into prescreening the files with links on this book's companion Web site, but it's the authors of the programs who are the real heroes in this whole deal.

Non-commercial software for Mac users has exploded since the release of Mac OS X in March 2001. For the first time in a long time, I'm seeing shareware and freeware programs so good that nothing you can buy in a box is better. In some cases, nothing even comes close.

So please, take the time to register and pay for each and every shareware program you download and continue to use regularly.

I have nothing but respect for the men and women coders of shareware and freeware for Mac OS X. I want to encourage them to grow, and prosper, and continue creating great things. So I pay for shareware I think is worth paying for, and so should you. It's the right thing to do.

Think of this section as an appetizer menu: I'll describe each dish briefly, show you a picture or two, and conclude with the fine print. One last, but very important, thing before we begin...

14

Don't Come Cryin' to Me

I beg you to back up important files before using or installing *any* new software. When you install new components or tweak existing ones, it's always possible that something will go wrong. And, of course, because we're often talking about the operating system itself, if something does go wrong, you have to fix it before you can get anything else done.

If you don't have time to deal with that, don't install the item (whatever it is) until you do. If you just gotta try it now, install it on a second Mac. It's that simple. I've tested every program with a link on the Web site and not one of them wiped out a single byte of my data. Almost all of them have received good reviews on VersionTracker, which tells me other users have not lost data (or haven't lost much).

So here's the warranty I'm offering: I don't know if any of this stuff will work on your particular Mac. I don't know if any of it will work *properly* on your particular Mac. And most of all, I have no idea whether one of these programs is going to cause an unforeseen problem, unexpected quit, kernel panic, or explosion with flames and smoke licking out of the vents on your Macintosh. I'm not putting a gun to your head; I'm not forcing you to install anything you're not prepared to install and live with the consequences of that installation, whatever they may be.

I hope throughout this book I've impressed upon you the importance of having a backup plan and multiple backups. You never know when some gremlin will stop your Mac dead in its tracks and if time is money to you (as it is to me), every hour your Mac isn't working is an hour you're not being paid for.

The point is: It is going to happen to you. The bigger point is: You cannot blame me when it does. I try hard to answer polite email, but when I get a letter that starts out, "YOU WRECKED MY HARD DISK YOU SLIMY WEASEL!!! YOU BETTER FIX IT OR ELSE," my answer is always the same, "You cannot blame me."

My own personal rule (which I'll admit I break occasionally but not often) is: When I'm working on a project "on the clock," I think long and hard about installing *any* new software on my main writing and telecommunicating Mac. For this book, I found myself breaking that rule almost daily, but I usually don't experiment on the machine I use to earn my daily bread. And you shouldn't either.

I can get back up and running after most catastrophic losses in less than two hours. But when I'm in the thick of a project with an absolute deadline, even two hours lost hurts too much. So if I have to try something new, I usually do it on another computer, or wait until I have a break in my schedule where losing a few hours to do some involuntary troubleshooting wouldn't be so painful.

We've got a lot of appetizers to look at, so let's move along.

Airburst

Airburst is a tasty piece of eye candy as well as a rollicking good game by Aaron and Adam Fothergill, a.k.a. Strange Flavour. I love these guys. They work at a game company in their native England, but in their spare time they write these killer Mac games.

Here's how they answer the age-old question, "What is Airburst?" *(From the Airburst manual.)*

It's sometime in the near future. With the TV rights to all the sports on Earth accidentally sold to a Martian megacorporation, people were a bit lost for what to watch on a Saturday afternoon.

Then someone came up with the bright idea of televising a sport that wasn't "on" Earth, but 30,000 feet above it, and the Airburst Federation was born!

To play Airburst, players wore a high altitude suit, along with a customized helmet, and sat on their Floater, a large hydrogen filled ball (gyroscopically stabilized of course) surrounded by their shield balloons. These shield balloons are also filled with hydrogen, but have much thinner skins, so can be burst by small mines, cluster bombs, and the recently discovered high-altitude woodpecker.

Because it was decided that Airburst should be a ball game, a ball was added to the mix. Not an ordinary ball, but a high-speed razor tipped steel ball, held up by a small anti-gravity field. After banging their heads together for a while, the TV companies also managed to get scientists to build Von Neumann capability into the balls, so that they could replicate themselves for "multiball" action!

It was the "high-speed razor tipped steel ball held up by a small anti-gravity field" that did it for me. I tried it. I liked it. A typical game is shown in Figure 14.26.

The game is easy to play but hard to beat. Two keys rotate your bat and a third key is used as an "action" button, firing a ball away from you if you have a sticky bat or shooting small balloon bursters if you have pop-gun ammunition.

Read the Airburst manual—it's a hoot. If you like Monty Python, you'll enjoy this. And check out their other game, Bushfire, which is also linked to at this book's Web site. I prefer Airburst, but you may not.

> **NOTE**
>
> Only two game types are available until you send the $5 registration fee. Just do it—it unlocks nine more cool game types.

14

Figure 14.26
I'm the upper-left guy with the small bat (two balloons worth).

Airburst: The Fine Print

The Mind(s) Behind: Aaron and Adam Fothergill Strange Flavour Software;

For more info: www.strangeflavour.com.

Type: Shareware.

Cost: $5.

From the Airburst Manual: To register your Strangeware game, just send either £2 (2 pounds UK sterling) or $5 (5 U.S. dollars) in cash (you remember, that stuff you used to use to pay the milkman) to the following address:

Aaron Fothergill
30 Heronsgate
Edgeware
Middlesex
HA8 7LD
United Kingdom

Simply tape two one pound coins (or 1 £2 coin) to a piece of card, stuff it in an envelope with your name and an email address and post it to us. For US$, put a $5 bill wrapped in a piece of paper in an envelope and post it to us. Remember to include your name (or the name of who you want the game registered to) and an email address where we can email you the unlock key file.

Please allow at least a week for email delivery of your key file (in the meantime get as far as you can in the Levels game so that you can gain some of the new games to play when you get your key!).

Hopefully, this system means that you don't have to part with much money or personal information, and we should be able to afford to write more games for the Mac (we're planning a few before the end of the year).

Anthology for OS X

Anthology is a collection of four classic games made over for Mac OS X.

Old-time Mac users will surely remember Daleks. There have been at least half-a-dozen renditions of it for the Mac over the years, and it's still as addictive as ever. Dalek is shown in Figure 14.27.

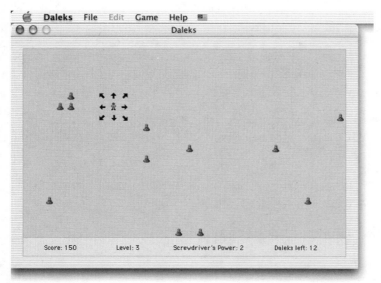

Figure 14.27
I'm the dude with the arrows around him. I want to make those other things crash into each other.

14

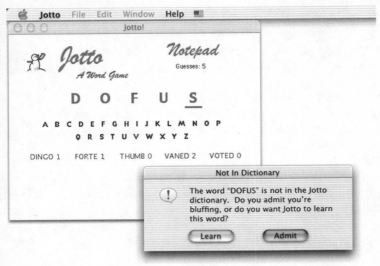

Figure 14.28
Doh! I should know that "doofus" has two "o's."

Jotto (shown in Figure 14.28) is a "guess-the-word" game. You have 10 guesses at a five- or six-letter word (your choice). The game tells you how many letters in your guess are in the word (i.e., one each for dingo and forte, two for vaned, none for thumb or voted.) Guess the word and win.

You've surely played Peg Solitaire before, the one where you have to jump one peg over another to remove the jumped peg; get to only one peg left and you win? Maybe this will refresh your memory (see Figure 14.29).

Helios Blackjack is a simple card game: Vegas-rules (mostly) blackjack. I think it's the weakest of the four, but if you're a blackjack lover, I suppose there's no such thing as a bad game of blackjack. It looks like this (see Figure 14.30).

Anthology: The Fine Print
The Mind(s) Behind: Coded by Mark Pazolli.

For more info: http://homepage.mac.com/quirinus/.

Type: Freeware.

ASM

I already raved about ASM, with three pictures (in Chapter 9; Figures 9.13, 9.14, and, 9.15), so I'll keep this short. ASM is an elegant re-enactment of the old Classic Application menu with additional features and options just for Mac OS X. It's useful, it's free . . . and it's really good.

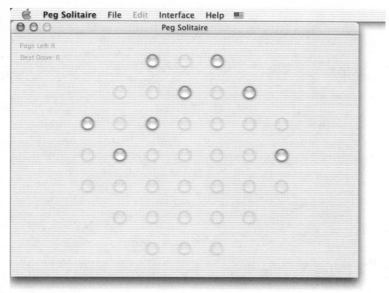

Figure 14.29
When I click the empty hole, the highlighted peg will jump to where I'm pointing, and the peg it jumped will disappear.

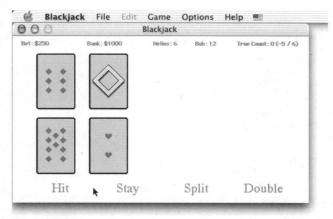

Figure 14.30
A simple game of blackjack.

ASM: The Fine Print

The Mind(s) Behind: Frank Vercruesse.

For more info: http://asm.vercruesse.de.

Type: Freeware; GNU GPL.

14

BatChmod

I talked about it in Chapter 8; now, here is the low-down. BatChmod is the freeware program that lets you diddle with the ownership and privileges for files or folders without the Terminal. BatChmod can also empty the Trash sometimes when you can't, as I demonstrated in Chapter 8.

So here's the deal. BatChmod is a great program. And it's totally free. There's no reason not to keep it handy in case you ever need it. But if you're like me, BatChmod won't be the only tool in your arsenal that does this stuff. BatChmod's author Renaud Boisjoly even says so himself in the BatChmod Docs.pdf: document:

*For a great tool to manipulate all of a file or folder's information in great detail: point your browser to **www.brockerhoff.net/** and download XRay! A fantastic tool from Rainer Brockerhoff.*

I concur. XRay is another "gotta have it" utility, which we'll get to later, toward the end of the alphabet. And I'd add Super Get Info to that list as well. All three overlap to some extent in what they do, but XRay and Super Get Info both have unique capabilities worth paying for.

Meanwhile, BatChmod looks like this (see Figure 14.31).

Figure 14.31
BatChmod is a capable little diddler with a nice price—free.

ALERT!

Programs like BatChmod can change your privileges and ownerships in ways that may adversely affect your system. In other words—don't change anything you're not sure it's okay to change. One slip of the finger and you could kill OS X deader 'n a Texas 'dillo on a median strip.

BatChmod: The Fine Print
The Mind(s) Behind: Renaud Boisjoly.

For more info: http://homepage.mac.com/arbysoft or **renaud@mac.com**.

Type: Freeware.

BBEdit Lite/BBEdit 6.5 Demo

BBEdit Lite is a free text editor for the Macintosh based on the award-winning BBEdit, which I went on and on about earlier in the chapter (see Figures 14.7, 14.8, and 14.9). Unlike a word processor, which is designed for preparing printed pages, a text editor focuses on producing, manipulating, and changing content. BBEdit Lite can manipulate text in ways that word processors generally can't.

For what it looks like see Figure 14.32.

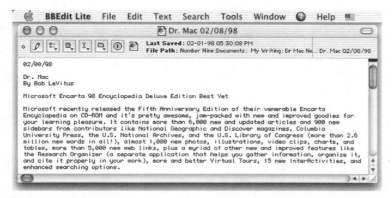

Figure 14.32
No frills. Hey, you want frills? Buy the real deal—it's got frills galore.

For a free program, it's actually pretty decent. Here's what the feature list looks like:

- Runs natively on Mac OS X (10.0 or later required); also supports Mac OS 7.5.5 and later

- Reads and writes Macintosh, DOS, and Unix line endings

- File sizes limited only by available RAM (up to 2GB Mac OS limit)

- Powerful **grep** search and replace

- Multifile search and replace (**grep** too)

- Sophisticated text transformations

14

- Numerous hard and soft wrap options

- Zap Gremlins (remove control characters)

- Case change command

- Rewrap quoted text (from email or newsgroups)

- Support for BBEdit plug-ins

- Documentation in PDF format

- Customizable key bindings

- Automated file backups

- Extensive drag & drop support

BBEdit 6.5 Demo is a copy of the BBEdit software I showed you earlier in the chapter with everything enabled so you can really give it a proper workout. It will, however, expire after being launched 25 times. After that, Bare Bones Software expects that you'll be totally hooked and will gladly order a real copy. (See Figure 14.33.)

BBEdit Lite/BBEdit 6.5 Demo: The Fine Print
The Mind(s) Behind: Bare Bones Software

For more info: www.barebones.com

Type: Freeware (BBEdit Lite); Commercial (BBEdit 6.5)

Cost: $0 (BBEdit Lite); $100 (BBEdit 6.5)

BrickHouse

BrickHouse is a firewall for Mac OS X. More technically, Mac OS X comes with a built-in firewall but Apple doesn't provide a graphical interface for configuring it. That's what BrickHouse (and Norton) do—provide an interface and services so you can use the firewall built into of every copy of OS X.

What's that you say? You're not sure if you need a firewall? In Chapter 8, I talked at some length about who needs Net security and why, and even included some URLs where you can get more information on network security and OS X.

If you do need one, BrickHouse couldn't be easier to install and configure. Figure 14.34 shows the setup assistant—four screens and you're done.

BrickHouse's configuration window is not only easy to use, it's pretty, as seen in Figure 14.35.

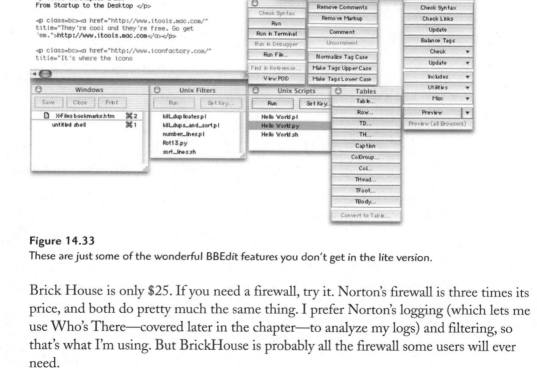

Figure 14.33
These are just some of the wonderful BBEdit features you don't get in the lite version.

Brick House is only $25. If you need a firewall, try it. Norton's firewall is three times its price, and both do pretty much the same thing. I prefer Norton's logging (which lets me use Who's There—covered later in the chapter—to analyze my logs) and filtering, so that's what I'm using. But BrickHouse is probably all the firewall some users will ever need.

14

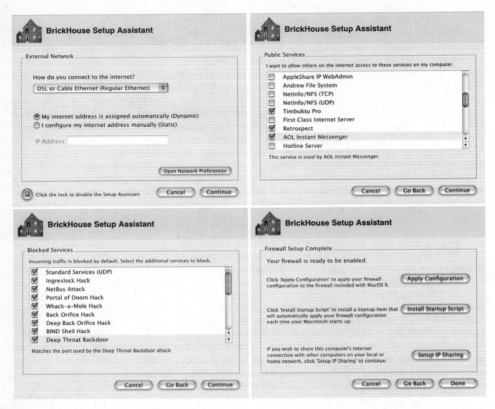

Figure 14.34
Four screens and BrickHouse is ready to be configured, to serve and protect you.

BrickHouse: The Fine Print

I've never met Brian Hill, but I do love his software (MacJanitor, Pseudo, and xFiles, all covered later in this chapter) and his sense of humor. On his Web site, he lists his contact information as follows:

> *Go to the isthmus between Lakes Mendota and Monona in Madison, Wisconsin, USA. I'm the one with the beard and ponytail.*

The Mind(s) Behind: Brian R. Hill

For more info: http://personalpages.tds.net/~brian_hill/ or brianhill@mac.com

Type: Shareware

Cost: $25 per machine

I'm of the opinion that people will either pay shareware fees, or they won't. You may use BrickHouse without registering it until you feel that it is worth $25 to you.

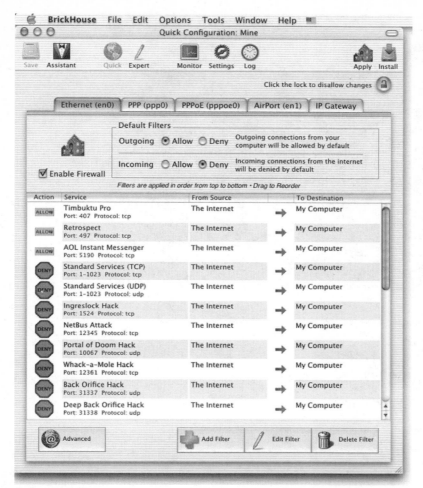

Figure 14.35
Brick House is easy to use and pretty, too—it's hard to beat that combo.

Bushfire

Bushfire is a classic (in the traditional sense) side-scrolling arcade game from those wacky Englishmen Aaron & Adam Fothergill, better known as Strange Flavour. The object is simple: Put out forest fires and don't let civilians die. Look for bonuses and get them.

You control the chopper with the arrow keys, press space to drop water and press *Z* to drop a smoke jumper. It looks like Figure 14.36.

As I said before, Airburst tickles me more than this one, but I know people who are totally hooked on Bushfire.

14

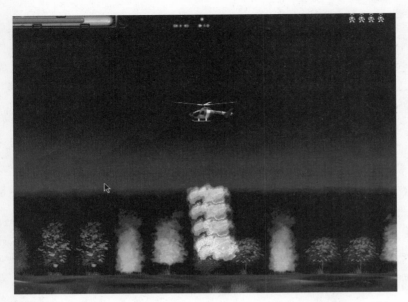

Figure 14.36
Drop some water, save some trees. It's kind of mindless but kind of fun, too.

Bushfire: The Fine Print

The Mind(s) Behind: Aaron and Adam Fothergill Strange Flavour Software;

For more info: www.strangeflavour.com

Type: Shareware

Cost: $3

From the Bushfire Manual: To register your Strangeware game, just send either £2 (2 pounds UK sterling), or $3 (3 U.S. dollars) in cash (you remember, that stuff you used to use to pay the milkman) to the following address:

Aaron Fothergill,
30 Heronsgate,
Edgeware,
Middlesex
HA8 7LD
United Kingdom

Simply tape two one pound coins (or 1 £2 coin) to a piece of card, stuff it in an envelope and post it to us. For US$, put three $1 bills wrapped in a piece of paper (no $3 bills please!) in an envelope and post it to us. We don't need your name and address, or anything worrying like that (the game is already fully featured, so we don't need to send you anything).

Hopefully, this system means that you don't have to part with much money or any personal information, and we should be able to afford to write more games for the Mac (we're planning a few before the end of the year).

We're quite prepared to accept that not everyone will register the games, but hopefully, enough will do so to make it worth our writing them.

Classic Menu

I covered this in Chapter 9, where I said, "Classic Menu replaces the OS X Apple menu with one similar to the one you knew and loved in OS 9. Unlike OS X's static, nonconfigurable Apple menu, Classic Menu lets you put anything you like in the Apple menu." There's even a picture back there (Figure 9.16).

Classic Menu: The Fine Print

The Mind(s) Behind: Sig Software

For more info: www.sigsoftware.com

Type: Shareware

Cost: Classic Menu costs just $10 per single-CPU license. The unlicensed version is fully functional but occasionally displays a reminder to purchase a license. A package with a license for Drop Drawers X ($20 on its own; and covered a few pages hence) costs $25 (a 20 percent savings). Licenses can currently be purchased only online at Sig Software's online ordering page: **http://order.kagi.com/?BX**.

Classic?

Classic? (Yes, that's it's name—Classic-question-mark) uses the Dock to let you know if Classic is running. When Classic *is* running, the icon in the Dock glows green (right dock in Figure 14.37); when Classic is *not* running, it's dimmed and gray (left dock in Figure 14.37). Hold down its Dock icon for a submenu that lets you start or stop Classic without a trip to the System Preferences app.

I don't use it now, but that's only because I so rarely fire up Classic that I don't see the need.

14

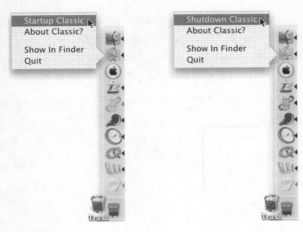

Figure 14.37
It's hard to tell here, but the one on the right is green; the one on the left is gray.

Because I haven't used it that much, and I know you may have forgotten that part back in Chapter 1 when I told you how helpful it is to RTFM, I'm going to paste a message from Classic's author, Edward O'Rourke. It's in the file entitled IMPORTANT READ THIS!.txt, which I fear you won't read:

"The last version of this application had a known memory leak. I believe the leak is fixed in this version.

Please be aware if your machine starts acting sluggish or all your RAM is used, it could be "Classic?" All you need to do is quit "Classic?" and your machine will be fine. Some times a restart may be needed but there is no permanent damage.

I have run "Classic?" for 3 days with no trouble so I don't think you should have any problems.

This is still a beta and should be treated as such. IF you find any problems, PLEASE let me know so I can fix them.

Now read the read me.

efo@mac.com"

Classic?: The Fine Print
The Mind(s) Behind: Edward O'Rourke; Jupiter Multimedia

For more info: http://jupitermultimedia.com or efo@mac.com

Type: Freeware

classihack

Back in Chapter 6 I said that classihack made Classic applications' windows "redraw one heck of a lot faster," and that it was "almost like magic."

It must have been too magical. Though it was working when I wrote Chapter 6, it's not working with Mac OS X 10.1.1 or 10.1.2. And its author Andrew Welch has taken it off his Web site and VersionTracker as well. Here's how he described the situation on the Ambrosia Web site:

"Classihack doesn't work under 10.1.1, and it looks like it never will. Classihack just turned on a hidden option, one might say. Apparently Apple doesn't like that option anymore."

It's too bad because although it looked a little strange, there was no doubt it made those windows refresh faster.

Desktop Randomizer

I showed you all there is to know about the lovely and talented Jessica Koch and her Desktop Randomizer back in Chapter 9, so I won't waste trees on it here.

Desktop Randomizer: The Fine Print
The Mind(s) Behind: Jessica Koch

For more info: jessi_k@mac.com

Type: Freeware

DivosX Tool

I'm going to let you in on a little secret. I haven't a clue about this one. It's here because I found it when I went through the first draft of Chapter 11, and it does something that Dennis R. Cohen, my friend and collaborator who wrote the first drafts of Chapters 10 through 13, had shown you how to do from the command line.

Anyway, that whole example was a Dennis invention. I don't have any of those silly DivosX files to even try this thing with.

DivosX Tool: The Fine Print
The Mind(s) Behind: Gabriel Rousseau

For more info: grousseau@mac.com

Type: Freeware; GNU GPL

14

DragThing

DragThing has probably gotten more ink in this book than any other program—I gush about it extensively in Chapters 2 and 3. Suffice it to say DragThing is one fine piece of software. Give it a try and you'll be hooked, like me.

DragThing: The Fine Print

The Mind(s) Behind: James Thomson

For more info: www.dragthing.com

Type: Shareware

Cost: $25

Drop Drawers X

I admit I don't use Drop Drawers. But that's not because it's not a great program, or because there's a feature I hate, or anything like that. I don't use it because it does almost the same thing(s) as DragThing. And after years of using DragThing, it's configured precisely the way I like it. And it would take me hours to re-create my perfect DragThing setup in Drop Drawers X.

In my opinion, the big difference is that Drop Drawers docks (which it calls "drawers") are free-form—you can drag any item (see the upcoming list of item types it will hold) onto a drawer and then move it around within the drawer. DragThing's docks have a more rigid structure—you drag things into buttons; buttons are arranged into layers.

According to the Sig Software Web site, these are some of the things you can store in a drawer:

- Aliases to frequently used files, applications, and folders

- URLs for Web sites you often visit

- Snippets of text information, such as phone numbers or passwords

- A catalog of thumbnails for image files

- AppleScripts for automating tasks

- Email addresses for individuals you often contact

- Multimedia formats, including pictures, movies, and sounds

- Styled text phrases for easy inserting into your documents

- A Trash can that acts just like the Finder's

■ Absolutely anything you can copy via the clipboard or drag and drop

■ A list of running applications (in a separate drawer; top right in Figure 14.38)

Figure 14.38 shows six different drawers.

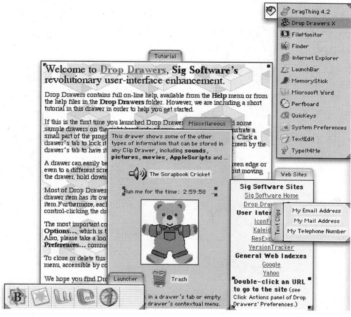

Figure 14.38
A drawer can hold text, sounds, movies, AppleScripts, pictures, and more.

You can also use information while it's in the drawer. For example, you can edit text, and you can drag icons from the desktop onto any icon in a drawer.

The floating pull-out, snap-shut drawers are kind of cool, too. And Drop Drawers works beautifully with any Mac OS application that uses drag and drop. Sig Software says it's "more than just another floating application launcher, although it fulfils all those functions too."

If I wasn't already hooked on DragThing, I'd seriously consider Drop Drawers. Heck, if I ever find myself with some spare time I may try using it instead of DragThing anyway.

Drop Drawers X: The Fine Print
The Mind(s) Behind: Sig Software

For more info: www.sigsoftware.com

Type: Shareware

Cost: $20

14

A package with a license for Classic Menu ($10) on its own (and covered a few pages previous) costs $25 (a 20 percent savings). You can currently purchase licenses online only at Sig Software's online ordering page: **http://order.kagi.com/?BX.**

Elze

Elze is a simple, free reminder program. I don't use it, but not because it's not a good program. For my way of using it, Entourage does everything Elze does and a whole lot more. But that's me. Reminders are vital to me, and I'm willing to pay more for a program with more features.

But you may not need such an elaborate and expensive reminder program. If you don't, Elze may be just the ticket. It's elegant, takes no time to learn, and it's free, too.

To create a reminder, click the Add Reminder button or use the keyboard shortcut Command+R. The Add Reminder window appears as shown in Figure 14.39.

Figure 14.39
Creating a reminder is a breeze.

Click OK. It couldn't be easier. When the reminder comes due, an alarm sounds and a little window pops to the front of your screen, as shown in Figure 14.40.

It's not fancy, and it's not feature-laden, but Elze does the job when you need to be tickled every now and then. And, of course, you can't beat the price.

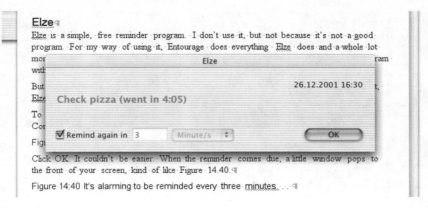

Figure 14.40
It's alarming to be reminded every three minutes.

Elze: The Fine Print
The Mind(s) Behind: GeneralOrganics

For more info: http://homepage.mac.com/generalorganics/ or generalorganics@mac.com

Type: Freeware

epicware Mac OS X Screen Savers

There's not much to say about screen savers. They're screen savers. They're free. Read the installation instructions and put them in the proper folder. You know the drill. Then, open System Preferences, choose Screen Savers, select one of your new toys, and enjoy it.

Figure 14.41 is a little collage I put together showing small previews of 15 of the most photogenic savers (snapped in the Preview window in the Screen Saver system preference pane).

epicware Mac OS X Screen Savers: The Fine Print
The Mind(s) Behind: Eric Peyton; epicware

For more info: www.epicware.com, screensavers@epicware.com, or epeyton@epicware.com.

Type: Freeware

14

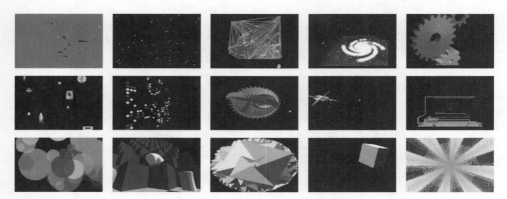

Figure 14.41
The others aren't this pretty—but these are pretty sweet, wouldn't you say?

File Buddy 7

File Buddy 7 wasn't quite done when this book was finished, so it didn't get as big a write-up as many other programs. Don't be fooled though; even without a lengthy write-up, File Buddy is a winner and can save you time and trouble in many, many common situations.

The good news is that the final (and well-tested) version became available on the SkyTag Web site (**www.skytag.com**) just as we went to press.

I would be remiss if I didn't at least tell you what FileBuddy can do. Here is a bullet list I grabbed from the SkyTag software Web site that answers that question:

- View and edit a wide range of file and folder information in the info window.

- Create droplet applications that automatically apply changes to items dropped on them, including the contents of folders.

- Find files and folders using an extensive set of search criteria. Enhance file searches with plug-ins that extend file search capabilities. Conveniently perform a wide variety of actions on found items. Make File Buddy your default file finding application using the File Buddy CP control panel.

- Modify the names of multiple files at once. For example, remove ".txt" from the names of a group of files.

- Use contextual menus to accomplish many tasks in a single step. Contextual menus are supported on all versions of the Macintosh operating system.

- Create custom icons: from PICTs on the clipboard; from other icons; for folders using a variety of templates; with blank icons; using only small icons.

- Create aliases.

- Find empty files and folders, orphaned files, duplicate files, broken aliases, and unused preference files.

- Automatically repair broken aliases.

- Rebuild the desktop file.

- Move, delete, and copy files. Even copy invisible files and use the Replace Different option to skip copying files that already exist.

- Delete data and resource forks from files.

- Erase files and unused disk space.

- Create snapshots that can be used to track the changes on a disk, such as files installed by an installer. Use snapshots to uninstall applications.

Figure 14.42 shows two File Buddy windows—a Get Info (top) and a list window (bottom).

File Buddy 7: The Fine Print
The Mind(s) Behind: Laurence Harris; SkyTag Software, Inc.

For more info: www.skytag.com

Type: Shareware

Cost: $40

FileMonitor

File Monitor is Console on steroids. I showed you how to enable crash logging in the console back in Chapter 8. If you liked that, you'll like this even better.

File Monitor allows you to monitor any number of selected files for changes, so if you want to be alerted when error messages are sent to the console, FileMonitor will bring up a window showing new input immediately, and even color code the new stuff when

14

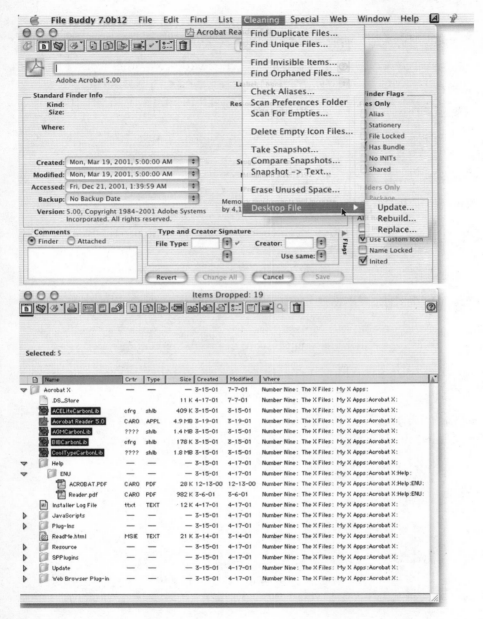

Figure 14.42
Look at all these buttons and gizmos! I'm not sure there's anything File Buddy can't do to a file.

it appears. This can be particularly useful for system administrators and software developers interested in process output or debugging information, but it can also be valuable for a curious power user who wants to know what's going on under the hood.

Here are some reasons File Monitor is better than Console:

- File Monitor can automatically display monitored files when they change, so you don't have to leave the log open all the time.

- File Monitor highlights changes in a customizable color (the default is blue).

- File Monitor remembers all your window settings between sessions.

- File Monitor offers sophisticated filtering of log files.

- File Monitor can monitor directories (mostly folders) for changes.

- File Monitor's convenient Monitors window lets you keep none, some, or all of your monitored files open.

Here's how mine looks (see Figure 14.43).

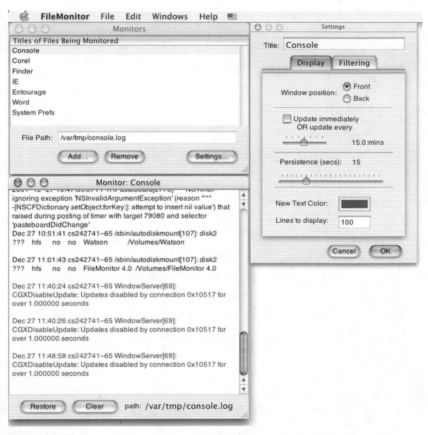

Figure 14.43
I monitor the console and five or six applications, including the Console, whose Monitor and Settings windows are shown.

File Monitor is one of my Login Items, so it's always running. When Console logs a message, I'll hear about it in 15 minutes because of the way I have its display set (see Figure 14.43). But when any of my other applications logs something, its log appears on screen as soon as it happens. If that's what you want, set the monitor to Update Immediately instead of Update Every *X* Minutes. You can set this for each log you monitor, so they don't all have to be the same.

You can also add keywords in the Filtering tab in the Settings window (not shown). Log entries that contain the keyword can either be shown or suppressed.

> **NOTE**
>
> Don't be alarmed by the number of messages you see, especially in the Console log—many or most of them aren't errors at all, they're merely "notifications." You can filter them out or learn to ignore them. Also note that it's not easy for a non-programmer to decipher most of the messages in any of the logs. You may be able to figure out what's malfunctioning by reading them—I can sometimes—but mostly they're Greek to me.

File Monitor can get annoying sometimes, and you can spend more time tweaking it than you'd probably like, but it's my "distant early warning system," and I'm going to be running it for a long, long time.

FileMonitor: The Fine Print

The Mind(s) Behind: P&L Software

For more info: info@plsys.co.uk

Type: Freeware

Fire

Here's another little freeware gem from Eric Peyton. (Remember him? From the epicware Screen Savers a few pages back?) Anyway, Fire is a universal instant messenger client you'll find quite useful if you're an instant message–type person (I'm not). Fire supports six different IM services—AIM (AOL), ICQ, IRC, JABBER, MSN, and Yahoo—and you can use them all or only one or two.

In Figure 14.44, you can see me conversing with my daughter (who is on AOL in the next room).

> **NOTE**
>
> Her name has been purposely blurred—I know what kind of people read my books, and she's only 13.

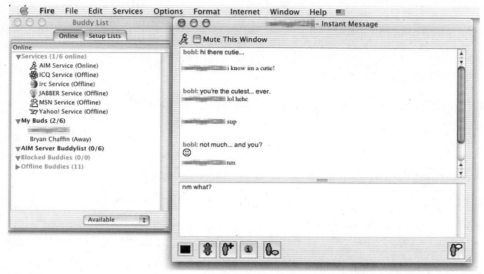

Figure 14.44
Fire: The Buddy List window (left) and a conversation between my daughter and me (right).

Sometimes this is the easiest way for me to communicate with my wife and daughter, because it's easier and faster than dialing the phone, and they're usually on AOL if they're in the house. But most of the time I don't use Fire, not because it's not a great app, but because I prefer not to be interrupted by IMs when I'm working. Still, many of my most X-savvy friends like it a lot and use it every day. If you like IMs, give it a try.

Fire: The Fine Print

The Mind(s) Behind: Eric Peyton; epicware

For more info: www.epicware.com/fire.html or epeyton@epicware.com

Type: Freeware; GNU GPL

FoldersSynchronizer X

This is a budget version of a program I do use. I use FWB's Backup Toolkit to do what FoldersSynchronizer does, which is synchronize and/or back up one folder or disk to another folder or disk. According to the readme file, here's what else FoldersSynchronizer can do:

■ FS also can backup the deleted files.

■ FS can filter the documents to copy by type, by creator, and by modification date.

14

- FS can do 16 multiple synchronizations or backups from custom lists. The user can save and load the lists.

- FS allows creating, renaming, and deleting up to eight pop-up lists for each Option area.

- FS can synchronize or back up at the time you specify in the timer list or by the timer interval.

- FS can copy invisible files and folders.

- FS can unlock the locked files, so the "exact backup" can also delete the locked files.

- FS can stop or skip or ask for further instruction, if an error occurs.

- FS can exclude, from the sync or backup, the folders and files you specify in the Excluding item list.

- FS can resolve aliases.

- FS can save detailed Log Files.

- FS can save and open "Session Files."

- FS can show the "Items to be copied" Preview List.

- FS allows drag and drop of "Session Files," "Multiple Lists Files," and source and destination folders and files.

- FS can work in background.

- FS can control the last Backup Date of the files.

- Tested on MacOS 8 and 9 and MacOS X.

- Scriptable by AppleScript.

- Registered users will receive an email on every new X.X or important release.

- Folders Synchronizer on MacOS X doesn't yet work properly with long file names (whose length is greater than 31 characters) and on Unix permission. We are working on these points.

ALERT!

Notice that last point—it's important. It means that unlike Retrospect or Backup ToolKit, you can't restore some Mac OS X files properly if you back up or synchronize them using this version. You might want to check the Softobe Web site for an update if you need that feature. (As you know, I don't. I don't back up OS X files, only data and "my stuff.")

Folder Synchronizer's main window looks like Figure 14.45.

Figure 14.45
Drag one folder or disk to the top folder, drag the other folder or disk to the bottom folder, and click Synchronize.

It's fairly simple and easy enough to use. The PDF manual isn't half bad, either.

FoldersSynchronizer: The Fine Print
The Mind(s) Behind: Softobe

For more info: www.softobe.com or info@softobe.com

Type: Shareware

Cost: $10

File Diddlers

Before I launch into my spiel about Get Info, there are at least three other programs with links on this book's Web page, with capabilities similar to Get Info—namely Super Get Info, xFiles, and XRay. I call this kind of program a "file diddler" because it lets you diddle with a file (or folder) and change permissions, flags, owners, groups, and so on.

Try them all for a while. Each is unique in its own way. Look at their differences and try to determine whether or if one or any of them could make your life better. For example, each one handles contextual menus, dock menus, system menus, and other menus a bit differently. And some can process keystrokes even when they're not running. It just depends on what you want and how much you're willing to spend. None of them costs more than $20.

I've used them all, and the remarkable thing is that they're all quite good. There isn't a single "buy this if you're only going to buy one" option. All four are worth their price. And, of course, if you want a freebie, there's BatChmod, quite capable with the added allure of being absolutely free.

14

Get Info

From the makers of Snard comes Get Info, one of the many file attribute editor programs (a.k.a. file diddlers) I provide a link for at **www.boblevitus.com/xfiles.html**.

Here's Get Info's feature list (from its release notes):

- Open multiple batch/info windows at once
- Change Unix permissions of a file or folder
- Change the Owner/Group of a file or folder
- Change Macintosh type/creator codes associated with a file
- Lock and unlock files
- Can be used as a get info helper for SNAX (**www.cocoatech.com**)
- Set user ID, set group ID on files
- Set the sticky bit on folders
- Batch mode—change attributes on multiple files/folders at once
  - Change Type/Creator
  - Permissions
  - User/group
  - Lock/unlock files
- Get Info supports authenticating as an Administrator to perform all actions
- Type and Creator favorites with built-in editor
- Recursive Owner/Group and Permission setting
- Dock menu—integrates Get Info seamlessly into the Finder
  - Copy path(s) of selected items to clipboard
  - Group selected item(s) in new folder
  - Get Info on selected item(s)
  - Batch Get Info on selected item(s)
  - Force Empty Trash
  - New Empty Batch Get Info window
  - Get Info. . .

- Services support
- Hot Key support
  - Copy paths of selected to clipboard (Apple+Shift+C)
  - Group selected in folder (Apple+Option+G)
  - Get Info on selection (Apple+Shift+I)
  - Batch Get Info on selection (Apple+Shift+B)
- External hex editor support

See Figure 14.46 for what Get Info looks like up close and personal.

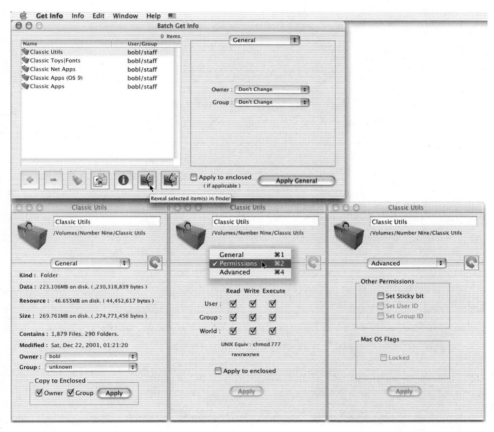

Figure 14.46
Just some of the items you can change, individually and in batches, using Get Info.

14

Figure 14.47 shows another view of Get Info, this time from its ever-so-useful Dock menu.

Figure 14.47
Select items in the Finder and Get Info on them using this handy Dock menu.

File diddlers like Get Info eliminate the need to use Terminal for permission, owner-ship, group, and other unsavory Unix-y issues. File diddlers, if they do nothing else, make changing attributes on file(s) and folder(s) a breeze.

Get Info: The Fine Print
The Mind(s) Behind: Gideon Softworks

For more info: www.gideonsoftworks.com

Type: Shareware

Cost: $10

GlLoad

GlLoad is two, two, two load meters in one—a freestanding application and a screen saver. Here's the application version (see Figure 14.48).

The glLoad application's Preferences window is shown in Figure 14.48. You can adjust the colors and display scale here.

Figure 14.49 shows the Screen Saver system preference pane with gLoad selected.

By now, I'm sure you know the drill but in case you were sleeping last time, just drag the glLoadSaver.saver icon into your Screen Savers folder (in yours or the system's Library folder).

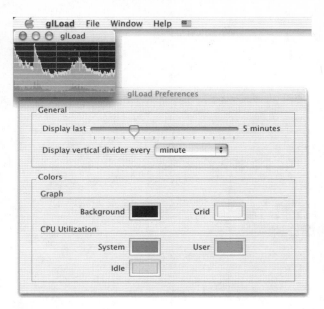

Figure 14.48
The glLoad monitor window is resizable; this is the smallest you can have it.

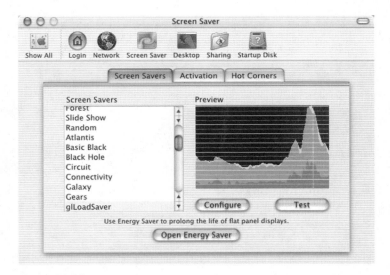

Figure 14.49
The graph fills the screen when the screen saver is invoked.

glLoad: The Fine Print

The Mind(s) Behind: Tim Trautmann

You wanna know more about the mind behind glLoad? Check out the Apple iCard
Tim sent me in Figure 14.50.

14

Figure 14.50
What kind of guy sends an iCard with a bulldog on it? I know. . . . Thanks, Tim.

For more info: www.timtrautmann.com/glLoad/

Type: Freeware

GMem!

Oh my gosh. It sounded so promising:

Wouldn't it be nice to know how much memory you're using without having to hunt for the information? How about getting notified when your used or available memory is at a specified point?

GMem!, by G-Utilities, is a nifty application that lets you keep tabs on your memory consumption. Just run it and relax! Not only that, but you won't take up extra space on your dock or your desktop, because GMem! does its reporting right on your dock in the same place as its icon!

I loved this program once. It used a colored "fill bar" in its Dock icon that changes the amount of fill depending on memory status. You could have a text display in the Dock as well as the fill bar. Or you could have both.

And oh my gosh, you could choose a specific sound for your audible alert, which you could base on your choice of active memory, used memory, or free memory. You could display in megabytes or percentages. It was so sweet.

Why am I talking in the past tense? Did GMem die when the 10.1 update came out, like classihack? Well, not exactly. But it's not feeling that great after the update, either.

The "Spew of Technicolor" Bug

There was a bug created in some programs developed in a popular software development environment that would manifest a horrid cosmetic "issue," which I came to call the "spew of technicolor" bug. You'd know a program had it because the rainbow-colored spume where most of the text in a window should have been is illegible. Sounds like a Stupid Mac Trick but it's not. And the dock icon is almost always bad (and illegible), regardless of what colors you choose in the color picker.

Anyway, the bug was fixed and most developers dealt with their spew of technicolor issue, which I understand wasn't very hard. SOT has almost died out—I haven't seen a new program with it in months.

But GMem still suffers from an extreme case of SOT that renders it near worthless to me (I'll show you in a second). And even though I sent the programmer a couple of emails asking if it was ever to be updated, I never got a reply. (His Web site is **http://g-utilities.com**; I just checked it, and it's still there and still looks the same as it did last summer.)

The issue with programs with the SOT bug is purely cosmetic, and as far as I know, the programs still work fine if you can decipher them.

Speaking of which, here's an unretouched picture of the SOT bug and how it affects GMem, in Figure 14.51.

At the bottom of Figure 14.51, you can see the icons and how hard (impossible) it is to read the text. The two Dock pictures on the bottom show GMem in its normal state.

14

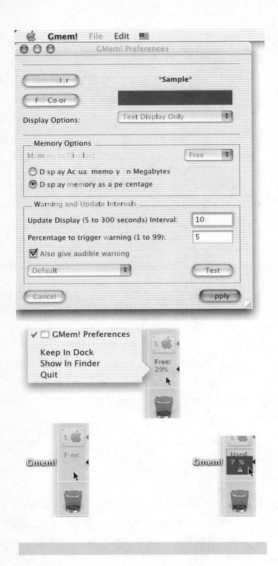

Figure 14.51
The SOT bug makes text quite hard to read (top) and plays havoc with Dock icon's display as well (bottom).

The left one is supposed to say, "Free: 29%," and the right one should say, "Used: 71%." If you think it's hard to see the numbers in that picture, you should see it in my tiny dock. Anyway, the top-middle picture of a Dock is the best of a bad bunch. It makes "Free: 29%" legible in the Dock icon, but it's only legible when I'm pressing on it. Bummer, huh?

But, if you can understand the GMem Preferences window well enough to configure it, its audible warning is still just as useful as when its text was beautiful and legible, and that's a feature I don't think I've seen in other memory programs.

> **NOTE**
>
> I know that MemoryStick has an alarm, but it's not configurable: It rings when you start having page outs and not a moment before.
>
> Don't get me wrong. That's okay, and if I only get to know one thing, page outs are that thing. But GMem let me *choose* what one thing I wanted to trigger the alarm. And so I could configure GMem to: "Ding if I get to 10 percent or less free memory remaining." Which is more useful than, "I'll ding at you, but not until all your RAM is totally used up . . . and no, there are no other options."
>
> I mean, God bless MemoryStick. I love it, and I'm using it instead of GMem right this second and have ever since I got it. But it would sure be nice to have the ability to decide what you want to be "alarmed" about rather than have it decided for you. I'm going to drop the programmer, Matt, a note. Maybe he'll do that in version 2. (Yeah, that's the spirit. A feature request! Programmers just love those.)

Anyway, I'm including GMem! here because you could still find it useful. Ugly, perhaps, but useful.

GMem!: The Fine Print
The Mind(s) Behind: Mark Boucher and G-Utilities

For more info: http://g-utilities.com

Type: Freeware

GraphicConverter

At its simplest, Thorsten Lemke's brilliant GraphicConverter program can open and save files in more different graphics file formats than you can count. And I just tried and gave up—let's just say it's a lot.

GraphicConverter can open: PICT, Startup-Screen, MacPaint, TIFF (uncompressed, packbits, CCITT3/4 and lzw), RIFF, PICS, 8BIM, 8BPS/PSD, JPEG/JFIF, GIF, PCX/SCR, GEM-IMG/-XIMG, BMP (RLE compressed BMPs also), ICO/ICN, PIC (16 bit), FLI/FLC, TGA, MSP, PIC (PC Paint), SCX (ColoRIX), SHP, WPG, PBM/PGM/PPM, CGM (only binary), SUN, RLE, XBM, PM, IFF/LBM, PAC, Degas, TINY, NeoChrome, PIC (ATARI), SPU/SPC, GEM-Metafile, Animated

14

NeoChrome, Imagic, ImageLab/Print Technic, HP-GL/2, FITS, SGI, DL, XWD, WMF, Scitex-CT, DCX, KONTRON, Lotus-PIC, Dr. Halo, GRP, VFF, Apple IIgs, AMBER, TRS-80, VB HB600, ppat, QDV, CLP, IPLab, SOFTIMAGE, GATAN, CVG, MSX, PNG, ART, RAW, PSION, SIXEL, PCD, ST-X, ALIAS pix, MAG, VITRONIC, CAM, PORST, NIF, TIM, AFP, BLD, GFX, FAX, SFW, PSION 5, BioRad, JBI, QNT, DICOM, KDC, FAXstf, CALS, Sketch, qtif, ElectricImage, X-Face, DJ1000, NASA Raster Metafile, Acorn Sprite, HSI-BUF, and FlashPix.

GraphicConverter can save as: PICT, Startup-Screen, MacPaint, TIFF (uncompressed, packbits and lzw), GIF, PCX, GEM-IMG/-XIMG, BMP, IFF/LBM, TGA, PSD, JPEG/JFIF, HP-GL/2, EPSF, Movie (QuickTime), SUN, PICS, PICT in Resource, PBM/PGM/PPM, SGI, TRS-80, ppat, SOFTIMAGE, PNG, PSION, RAW, WMF, XWD, XBM, XPM, System 7 Clip, PAC, Icon, RTF, VPB, Psion, and X-Face.

But it's much more than just a file converter. As you can see in Figure 14.52, there's a toolbox just to the right of the large image window, with all the tools you'd expect from a graphics editing program—pencil, paintbrush, magic wand, lasso, text, and such.

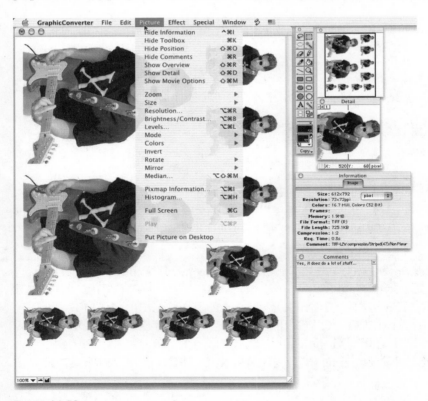

Figure 14.52
Don't let its name fool you—GraphicConverter does a lot more than just open and save graphics files.

You'll be surprised how much you can do with GraphicConverter, and how much of that has nothing to do with converting files. I know a lot of people who prefer it over almost anything else. And priced at $35, there's no question that you get a lot of program for your money.

GraphicConverter is also quite adept at batch processing—it can easily convert whole folders of graphic files from one format to another in a batch process.

There are a ton of keyboard shortcuts and keyboard modifications, including the one shown in Figure 14.53, which is my favorite and something I wish every program offered.

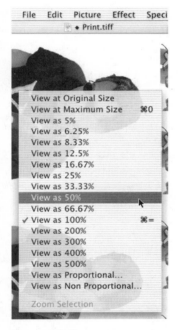

Figure 14.53
A pop-up zoom menu. Wherever your cursor is, it's there too. Slick, huh?

After gazing at that long list of file formats GraphicConverter can open and save, I was surprised to discover that it can't open a PDF file. Oh well.

But that's a mere quibble. Thorsten Lemke updates GraphicConverter often, squashing bugs and improving features. If you don't believe me, read the History file in the GraphicConverter folder.

GraphicConverter really is one of the most polished and well-maintained pieces of shareware money can buy. I have to say this, though: Photoshop Elements, the baby brother (sister) of Photoshop (Classic only right now) sells for $99. It's a wonderful

14

program, and if you're going to spend a lot of time working with graphics, it's worth every penny. But if your needs are more modest, a copy of GraphicConverter for $35 could well be all the graphics program you need.

One last thing: If you see what's in Figure 14.54, more than a few times, do the right thing and send Thorsten his $35. God knows he's earned it.

Figure 14.54
Pay the man.

GraphicConverter: The Fine Print
The Mind(s) Behind: Thorsten Lemke

For more info: www.graphicconverter.net or lemkesoft@aol.com, or support@graphicconverter.net

Type: Shareware

Cost: $35

iColumns

iColumns is a simple yet extremely addictive game. It's just another Tetris knock-off, but there is something compelling about the way it looks and feels that makes you say, "Okay, just one more game." And say it again, and again, and again.

You control the falling trippleballs (that's what I call 'em) using the J, K , L, and spacebar keys by default. The object is to get three balls in a row of the same color (a tripplepalooza), vertically, horizontally, or diagonally. When you do, those three balls disappear and everything else slides down.

Because a picture is worth lots of words in this case, I've created a little "how it works" visual, which goes by the name of Figure 14.55.

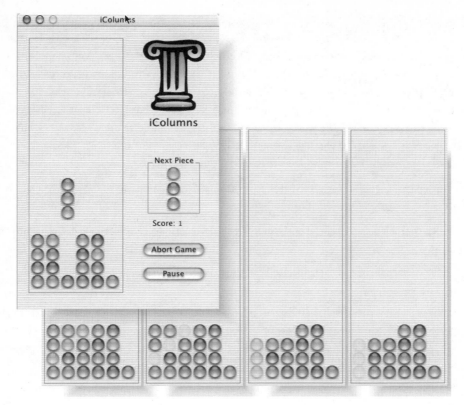

Figure 14.55
Look at the big window in front, then look at the little ones from left to right.

Here's a blow-by-blow. In the big picture of the whole game, you can see a trippleball falling towards the bottom of the window. I navigate using J, K, and L, so when the trippleball drops it create two tripplepaloozas. In the two smaller pictures on the left, you can see the red tripplepalooza (it's red, trust me) disappearing. When they disappear, all the gumdrops above them drop down to fill the holes their disappearance left. So in the two smaller pictures on the right, you see the result—the blue tripplepalooza (it's blue, trust me) also disappears.

Just play it for a few minutes, and you'll get the hang of it. I'm warning you though, it'll suck the time right out of your day if you let it.

Oh yeah, did I mention that it's free?

iColumns: The Fine Print
The Mind(s) Behind: Brian Webster

For more info: bwebster@mac.com

Type: Freeware

14

My Funny iColumns Anecdote

So I'm giving a speech at the Houston Area Apple Users Group, or HAAUG, and I am demonstrating some of my favorite OS X software for them. I have my iPod chock full of my favorite X-ware, and I decided to show iColumns, because it's totally addictive and the price—free—rocks. So I play a game up there on the big screen monitors, and as I play, I explain what I'm doing and what a wonderful thing the programmer did for us, by releasing this great game as freeware. Somebody from the audience shouts out, "If you like it so much, why don't you just tell him?" I looked at the guy who shouted, puzzled. "He's sitting right there," the guy explained.

Yes, while I was up on stage gushing about this cool little freeware game, unbeknownst to me, the guy who wrote it was sitting in the fifth row, giggling.

So I'd just like to say, "Hi again, Brian. Sorry I didn't get more time to chat at the meeting. And yes, I still play it way too often."

Icons

You must realize by now that I like icons. I told you about the sites where I found these (and indeed, almost all of my icons)—**www.iconfactory.com** and **http://xicons. macnn.com**. I have 10,000 or more of the little boogers on my hard disk, so it wasn't easy deciding which ones to direct you to. I wanted to give you a nice variety. You'll let me know if I succeed.

I ended up choosing four of my favorites. Each of these four artists have created icons I use or have used to make my desktop brighter. Each one has a different style, and each is an excellent representation of the art of icon making. So here now are four shining examples of icon art for OS X, all of which you'll find linked at **www. boblevitus.com/xfiles.html**.

The first artist I selected is Harvey Lubin of Agrapha Design. There are eight sets of Harvey's photo-realistic (or maybe they're just really little photos—I don't know) icon sets linked at the Web site. His icons are very cool—I still use the briefcase for documents folders. I get a big kick out of these.

Figure 14.56 shows most of the Agrapha icons.

The second artist is Carlos Reyes, better known as "Carlito," who created seven sets of icons—mostly storage icons like folders and disks—which you'll find a link for. His designs are simple and elegant, as you can see in Figure 14.57.

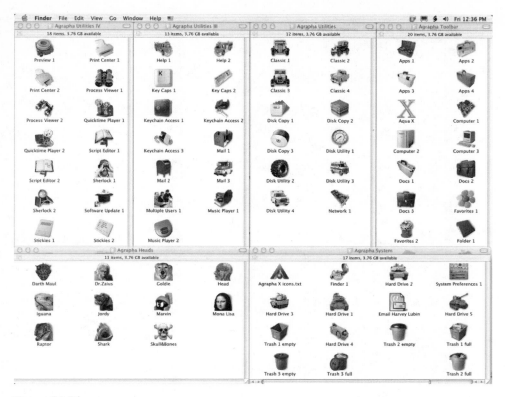

Figure 14.56
Agrapha icons are among my favorites—I've used lots of them on my hard disk, and you've no doubt seen them in screenshots throughout this book.

There's only one set—Liquid Buttons X—from the mysterious one-named, lower-cased icon artist who goes by "mendelini," but it's a big set (50 icons) and one of my favorites. His (or maybe her) surreal round icons look great in the Dock or just about anywhere.

The complete Liquid Buttons X set is in Figure 14.58.

And last, but by no means least, David Catmull is represented here by the whimsical and imaginative, hand-drawn-looking Squiver and its sequel, Squiver Hardware. I like these a lot, too; both sets are shown in Figure 14.59.

They're all beautiful, but better still, they're all free. Enjoy them.

14

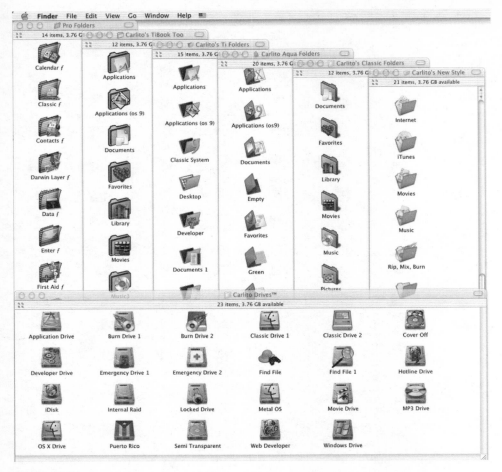

Figure 14.57
Stylish and simple, the Carlito icons are great for organizing stuff.

> NOTE
>
> You can find instructions for using icons in the *A Brief Iconic Diversion* sidebar in Chapter 2.

Icons: The Fine Print

The Mind(s) Behind: Harvey "Agrapha" Lubin, Carlos "Carlito" Reyes, mendelini, David "Squiver" Catmull

For more info: www.agrapha.com, carlito@mac.com, www.mendelini.com, and www.uncommonplace.com

Type: Freeware

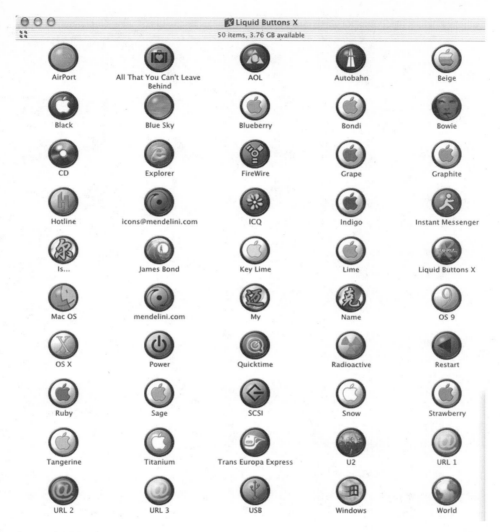

Figure 14.58
mendelini's Liquid Buttons look good enough to lick.

iTunes Tool

I mentioned this one in Chapter 5, and it's a find. I use iTunes all day long. I sometimes want to pause or switch tracks; it would be nice if I could do it without activating iTunes. And now I can. iTunes Tool is the key. It shrinks all of the iTunes controls (well, most of them) into a teeny-tiny toolbar that floats over other applications. So I can move forward or backward in my playlist, adjust the volume, see what song is playing, and pause—all from this little tiny tool.

14

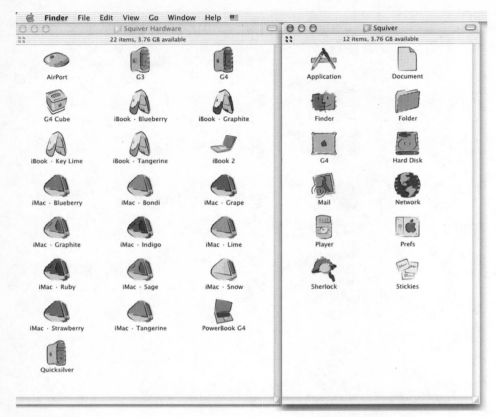

Figure 14.59
Squiver icons have a unique look and feel for icons.

In Chapter 5, I said that iTunes pop-up Dock menu has Pause/Play, Next Song, and Previous Song commands, and the title of the song, but no volume control. Then I said iTunes Tool didn't show the title of the current song but did have a volume control.

Things change. By the time I got to this section, young Chiper of ChiperSoft had released about three different updates. The one I'm writing about now, is version 1.4.3. And it does display the song titles (though the iTunes Dock icon's menu still doesn't change the volume).

TIP

> Given Chiper's penchant for updating iTT, you might want to check his Web site—it could be up to version 3-point-something by now.

I shrink the iTunes window as small as it can be and still show the song title, but it still takes up too much screen real estate. Here's proof (see Figure 14.60).

Figure 14.60
Smallest iTunes (top) vs. smallest iTunes Tool (bottom).

Furthermore, iTunes window doesn't float over other windows. And using iTunes Tool, you can shrink it as small as 30×15 pixels, as seen in the top image in Figure 14.61.

Figure 14.61
The different looks of iTunes Tool.

In the very top picture in Figure 14.61, the tool is shrunk to its smallest size possible. Below it is a shrunken tool with song title turned on. Next you see how the little tool expands when the cursor hovers over it as it is in that middle picture. Clicking the gray triangle drops down the volume control, as shown in the fourth picture. Finally, you click and hold on the rightmost icon on the tool to Quit or adjust its Preferences, which look like Figure 14.62.

iTunes Tool is free but requires an installed copy of iTunes 2.*x*.

iTunes Tool: The Fine Print
The Mind(s) Behind: Jarvis Badgley; ChiperSoft

Jarvis can be found on IRC hanging out on #macintosh, #machelp, and #realbasic on Undernet, under the nickname _Chiper_. He can also be found on AOL Instant Messenger as ChiperSoft.

14

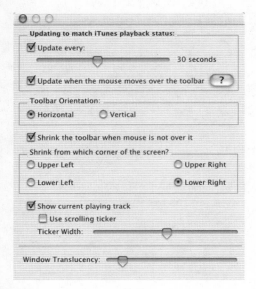

Figure 14.62
iTunes Tool's Preferences window is bigger than the whole program!

For more info: www.macatawa.org/~chiper/

Type: Freeware

JewelToy

JewelToy is a simple game played against the clock. It's as addicting at iColumns, maybe even more so. The object of JewelToy is to form vertical or horizontal lines of three or more identical gems. When you get three or more in a row, that line then disappears and all gems above fall down to take the place of the disappeared line.

To play, you click a gem, and then click any gem touching it. The two gems will then swap positions, at least in theory. The trouble is, it works only if the swap will form at least one line of three or more identical gems.

You get points and bonus time for removing lines. You get more points and more bonus time for removing longer lines. Here's what the game looks like in Figure 14.63.

> **TIP**
>
> If you don't make a move for 20 seconds the game will try to give you a hint by highlighting a gem you can move.

There's also a Free Play mode with no timer and no bonuses—the game ends only when you can make no more moves.

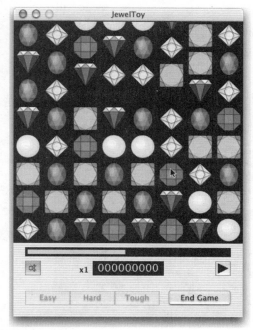

Figure 14.63
This is JewelToy—it's trickier than it looks.

NOTE

Here's a word to the wise—don't start playing this one when you've got a deadline looming.

JewelToy: The Fine Print

The Mind(s) Behind: Giles Williams

For more info: aegidian@mac.com

Type: Freeware; GNU GPL

Jiggy!

Jiggy! is a game that pits you against a clock as you assemble a jigsaw puzzle on screen. When each level starts, you see the finished puzzle for a few seconds, as shown in Figure 14.64.

Then the pieces break up and disappear from the board. Puzzle pieces then start to fall slowly down the right side of the screen. To select a piece, click it. Move it onto the puzzle board and click again to drop it. If that's the right place, it will drop in, and you'll get points, as shown in Figure 14.65.

14

Figure 14.64
A quick preview of the puzzle before the game begins.

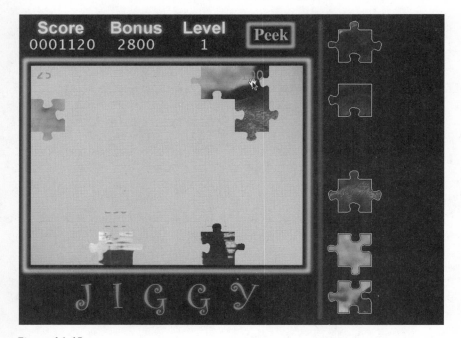

Figure 14.65
I received 100 points for the piece I just placed.

If you try to put the puzzle piece in the wrong place, you'll hear a buzz and the border of the piece will flash red. If you want to try a different piece, move the current piece you're holding to the right of the line and click to drop it. Now click any other piece.

There is enough room on the right of the line for 12 pieces. When all 12 slots are filled up and another piece tries to fall, the game ends! Kind of like Figure 14.66.

Figure 14.66
The thirteenth piece just fell so the game is over.

There are lots of ways you score and gain bonus points, but I'll leave it to you to explore them. One thing I will mention is peeking. You can click Peek to get a quick look at the finished puzzle (again), but each time you peek you lose 500 bonus points, and when you have fewer than 500 bonus points left, you can't peek anymore.

With hours of play under my belt (and the readme file to refer to), here are a few Jiggy tips:

- Pieces with one straight edge are good. They go on an edge. Pieces with two straight edges are better. They go in a corner.

- There is no penalty for trying a piece in the wrong place. So click like crazy if that's the way you like to play.

■ Peeking will cost you.

■ If you can't find a place for a piece, put it back in the pile and try a different one.

It's surprisingly addictive.

Jiggy!: The Fine Print

The Mind(s) Behind: Mark and Suellen Adams. Those names may be familiar to you if you're a gamer. Mark and Suellen are the proprietors of Westlake Interactive, one of the most prolific game software developers of Macintosh games in the world.

Don't believe me? Here are just some of the games they've developed for Macintosh: The Sims; Deus Ex; Scrabble; Unreal Tournament; Civilization: Call To Power; Total Annihilation; Railroad Tycoon II; Falcon 4.0; Tomb Raider I, II, and III; and Unreal.

Jiggy! is the game they made in their copious spare time.

For more info: MavSftWre@mac.com or **http://homepage.mac.com/MavSftWre**

Type: Shareware

Cost: $15. Payment garners you a CD with the full version of the game, including 25 new puzzles. The full version also lets you put your own pictures into the game.

LaunchBar

You're probably sick of hearing about it by now—I began talking about LaunchBar in Chapter 2 and pretty much haven't stopped. This will be the last time I'll tell you about LaunchBar.

I write a column (called "Dr. Mac," of course) for the *Houston Chronicle* and have for the past six years. Every week, for the past 200-some-odd weeks I've come up with 600 words about something to do with Macs. Having spent so much time the past few months evaluating shareware and freeware for this book, I wrote a column highlighting a few of my favorite shareware and freeware items for Mac OS X.

LaunchBar was one of them. Now you have to understand that unlike a book, in the column I had about 150 words to explain LaunchBar well enough to make someone want to try it. Which is a roundabout way of saying, if this is going to be the last time I talk about it, these are the 150 words I'd use:

I prefer using the keyboard to the mouse, which is why LaunchBar is among my favorite OS X programs. It provides lightning-fast access to my thousands of files, folders, Web bookmarks, email addresses, and applications just by typing short abbreviations. After pressing its configurable hot key (Control+spacebar), when I type "W-O," Microsoft Word launches or becomes active, when I type "C-O-R," Corel PHOTO-PAINT 10 launches or becomes active, when I type "T-M-O," The Mac Observer Web site appears in my browser, and when I type "S-H-A," a blank email message pre-addressed to Shawn King appears in Entourage.

LaunchBar uses a very powerful, adaptive abbreviation search algorithm that learns your habits. So even though the application is named "Microsoft Word," LaunchBar figured out that when I type "W-O," Word is what I want.

I rarely use the Finder anymore—LaunchBar is so much faster and easier. I love it.

Dr. Mac. Column. Copyright ©2001 Bob LeVitus. Houston Chronicle: *12-28-01.*

I got an email the day that column ran from a reader who said:

I'm not sure I would have found LaunchBar on my own. I saw it go by on VersionTracker, but it didn't tweak my interest. What a sweet hack!

If you haven't tried it, you're missing something good.

And that's the end of it. I won't talk about LaunchBar any more. But I will flash one more picture. This time I've moved LaunchBar to the bottom of my screen (I think I like this arrangement) and am using it as a program switcher (Command+R) in Figure 14.67.

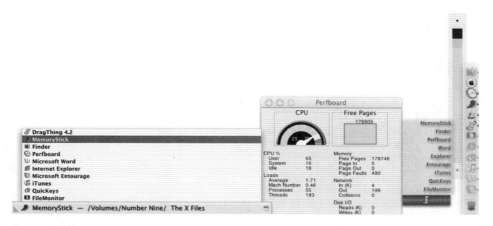

Figure 14.67
I forgot to mention that LaunchBar has a built-in application switcher. It does. This is what it looks like.

Figure 14.67 shows the way the lower-right corner of my monitor looks today. I think I like it.

14

NOTE

There are three different programs in this corner of my screen in Figure 14.67 that do program switching or choosing. On the far left, of course, is LaunchBar, which would ordinarily be hidden. But I pressed its hot key for this photo op. At the far right is the

OS X Dock, which would ordinarily be hidden, but I waved my mouse over the magic area so the Dock could be in this picture as well. Finally, there's the one that's always showing, the translucent DragThing process dock. Just under it is a dark tile that holds my main DragThing dock. It opens with a keystroke or wave of the mouse in its hot corner and holds the rest of my "stuff."

LaunchBar: The Fine Print
The Mind(s) Behind: Norbert Heger; Objective Development

For more info: **www.obdev.at**

Type: Shareware

Cost: $20

Lines

It's another "five or more balls of one color in a row" game but don't be put off by that. It's pretty and it's fun. Get five or more in a row, and the row disappears.

At the beginning of a game, five balls are on the board. You can move any ball to another cell to try to make five in a row in any direction. Figure 14.68 will give you an idea of what the colored balls and board look like.

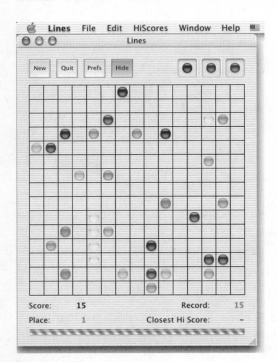

Figure 14.68
Click a ball, then click a cell. If the ball can get there, it will.

Balls try to find a free and unblocked path to the cell you click. If there is no such path, you're out of luck—balls can't jump over one another. And, just for good measure, every time you move a ball, three *more* balls fall onto the board at random places, except when you build a line. No balls fall then and five balls disappear. So making lines is what it's all about. The more balls you make disappear, the more points you get. When every cell has a ball in it, you can't move, so the game is over.

Figure 14.69 shows an example of how it works.

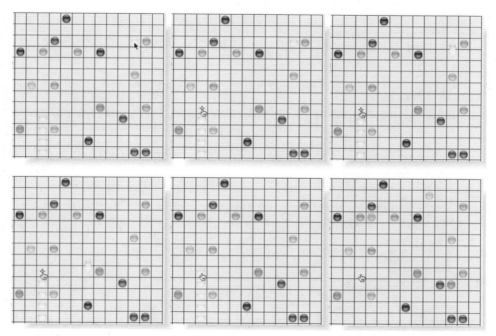

Figure 14.69
Moving a yellow ball to make five in a row.

Here's what just happened in Figure 14.69:

1. (Top left) I click the yellow ball in the upper-right quadrant of the playfield.

2. (Top center) I click the cell I want that yellow ball to move to.

3. (Top right) I watch the ball find the shortest route to where I clicked.

4. (Bottom left) The yellow ball is almost there.

5. (Bottom center) The ball arrives, and the line of five yellows in a row begins to disappear from the playfield.

6. (Bottom right) The aftermath: A playfield with five more cells than it had before.

14

The release notes, which you may not read, say there is a known problem—sometimes Lines quits unexpectedly immediately after launch. If it happens, try trashing the Lines preferences file (it's the com.brakesoff.lines.plist file in the Library/Preferences folder in your home directory) and move it to Trash. If this does not help, send Konstantin a bug report with info on your Mac and version of Mac OS X.

Lines: The Fine Print

The Mind(s) Behind: Konstantin Anoshkin

For more info: costique@mac.com

Type: Freeware

LoadInDock

Yet another nifty little CPU monitor. This one displays a graph of system usage in the Dock or in a semitransparent window. I talked about it a little back in Chapter 2. It gives me the same information as Perfboard, just displayed a different way. Both are shown in Figure 14.70.

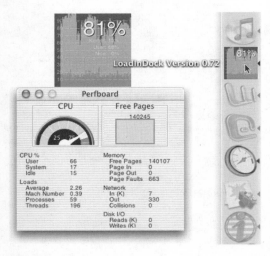

Figure 14.70
Looks like my CPU is using somewhere between 81 percent (according to LoadInDock) and 83 percent (66 + 17 = 83 percent, according to Perfboard).

The semitranslucent floating square and Dock icon with the white "81%" on them are the two different ways LoadInDock can display your CPU usage.

Here's another view of the floating window, along with LoadInDock's Preference window and its only menu (see Figure 14.71).

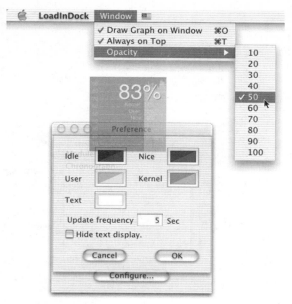

Figure 14.71
The floating window "floats" in front of any and all other windows like this.

LoadInDock: The Fine Print
The Mind(s) Behind: Takashi T. Hamada

For more info: I couldn't find any information about him or her. . .

Type: Freeware

MacArmyKnife

MacArmyKnife (MAK) is a collection of Mac mini-utilities and "things that other apps don't do."

Here's a picture of just some of its "blades," the MAK name for little utilities (see Figure 14.72).

The window in the upper-left corner is the "Dashboard" interface—click any button to launch that function. Beneath that is the File Finder, a Sherlock alternative. Below that you see the Process Options window, which governs the function of the Process Manager, at lower right.

In the lower-right corner is the Process Manager, which allows you to quit processes and get detailed process information about each item, including how much memory each is using, and what their attributes are (this information is available via the Get Info button). It's a decent substitute for Apple's Process Viewer with a few nifty features you won't find in the Apple utility, most notably the "Kill All Processes Now" options.

14

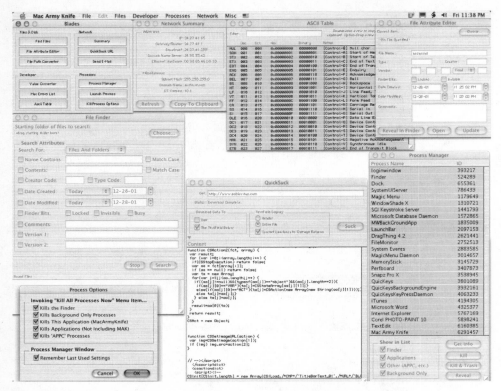

Figure 14.72
Each window is a separate utility. And there are many more than these.

There's a lot more—a Value Converter that converts any value into any other, a Macintosh System Error list, and about a dozen other little utils, including one I really like called "QuickSuck," which you can see in the lower center of Figure 14.72. It sucks the guts out of Web pages without having to use your browser or save files to disk or anything like that. The HTML in the lower part of its window is my home page, which it just sucked down for me. Slick.

Okay, most of the utilities aren't that great. Some are useful, others are not as good as something else. Is it worth $25? I couldn't tell you. If it saves your bacon someday, or you find yourself hooked on one of its "blades," then certainly so. If not, keep it around anyway, just in case. You never know when you might need one of its many tools.

On the other hand, the programmers have a great attitude (see "The Fine Print"). And they also make the excellent MP3 Rage (which you should download from their Web site if you work with MP3 files at all—it's a veritable Swiss Army Knife of MP3 utilities). MP3 Rage can edit ID3 tags; analyze MP3s and adjust their sound volume automatically to play at similar levels; export MP3 files to AIFF format for burning

CDs; play MP3 files; and catalog, organize, rename, find, and change thousands of MP3 files and their ID3 tags quickly and painlessly. And it's easy-to-use.

Mac Army Knife: The Fine Print
The Mind(s) Behind: Jason Giles, Bob Bradley; Chaotic Software

Mission Statement: *We endeavor to bring quality software solutions to Macintosh users. We believe that we should support the Macintosh platform, a computer that has pioneered new paths in the computing industry. It is a platform that is often mimicked, but never surpassed. Apple Computer has led the charge of creating and developing technologies that drive the industry, and we would like to be able to say we are contributing to that drive and success.*

If it doesn't have anything you need, then check back in a future rev, as we might have added something you need. If there is some utility-esque function that you think it's crying out for, please send us your suggestion. We can't guarantee it'll be implemented, but it can't hurt to ask!

So for gosh sake send them some money if you like their stuff. Let them know you appreciate it and them. Heck, read what they say. These guys love the Macintosh and are willing to listen to your suggestions. That's more than some commercial software vendors will do for you (okay, make that many commercial software vendors).

For more info: www.chaoticsoftware.com. To contact the authors directly, email Jason Giles at **jgiles@chaoticsoftware.com**, or Bob Bradley at **bob@chaoticsoftware.com**.

Type: Shareware

Cost: $25

MacBlox

Yet another Tetris clone. This one's not as pretty as some of the others, but it has several nice touches, it didn't use much disk space, and it's free. Plus, it was the programmer's first program done in Cocoa—you have to respect that.

Here's a peek in Figure 14.73.

One cool thing MacBlox does—mostly because it can—is to allow transparency. So if you want to play a game and watch something in a window behind it, you could. I guess. Anyway, it looks kind of neat, like Figure 14.74.

MacBlox: The Fine Print
The Mind(s) Behind: Joakim Arfvidsson

The author says: *Do send me comments (my address is at the end of the "Don't read me.rtf" file). I long for feedback. . . it would encourage me to improve the game! Tell me what you*

14

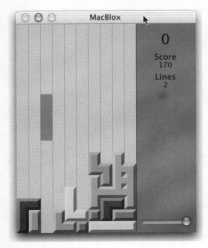

Figure 14.73
Tetris, more or less.

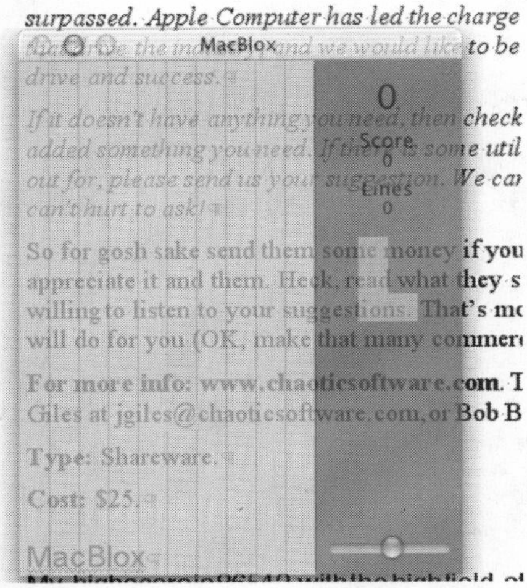

Figure 14.74
See the little knob lower right in the MacBlox window? It controls the game's transparency, so you can see through it. Or not.

think of the game and what is needed to make it better. If I haven't got anything better to do, it might just happen. Thanks!

My high score is 86,542 with the high field, standard pieces. I got to level 35. Beat that! I'm sure some of you will. Have fun.

Do correct my spelling if you find it bad. I'm from Sweden.

For more info: arfvidsson@mensa.se

Type: Freeware

Cost: Joakim says: *It's free, but don't hesitate to send something if you really want to :-)*
PayPal account is arfvidsson@mensa.se.

MacJanitor

I talked about MacJanitor in Chapter 8. It's another gem from the prolific Brian Hill,
but unlike his other programs, BrickHouse, Pseudo, and xFiles, MacJanitor is totally
free, so there's no reason not to use it if you like to turn your Mac off at night.

There's a picture of it in Chapter 8 (Figure 8.3), and it still looks like that. So instead
of a picture, here's a list of what, exactly, it does when you run its tasks (from the
"What Is It Doing?.rtf" file):

Daily Script:

- If the rwho system has been configured, clear out the old files in /var/rwho

- Clear out files old files and directories in the /tmp and /var/tmp directories

- Remove system messages older than 21 days

- If system accounting is on, process the accounting files and gather daily statistics

- Backup the NetInfo database

- Output the disk capacities and storage available

- Show which filesystems haven't had "dump" performed on them in a while (archaic)

- Show accumulated network statistics and network uptime (ruptime)

- Rotate the system.log file and restart the syslog process

- Clear out the Webserver log files older than a week

- Run the /etc/daily.local script if it exists

- Run a /etc/security check script if it exists

Weekly Script:

- If the /usr/libexec/locate.updatedb database exists, update the "locate" database

- If the /usr/libexec/makewhatis.local file exists, rebuilt the "whatis" database

- Rotate the following log files: ftp.log, lookupd.log, lpr.log, mail.log, netinfo.log

- Restart the syslog process

- Run the /etc/weekly.local script if it exists

14

Monthly Script:

- Run the login accounting process

- Rotate the wtmp log files

- Restart the syslog daemon

- Run the /etc/monthly.local script if it exists

Don't worry, I don't understand most of it, either, but Unix-heads assure me that it's good for what ails OS X, so just do it.

MacJanitor: The Fine Print

The Mind(s) Behind: Brian R. Hill

For more info: http://personalpages.tds.net/~brian_hill/ or brianhill@mac.com

Type: Freeware

ManOpen

ManOpen is a graphical interface for viewing Unix manual pages, which are discussed in Chapter 10. It's got a user interface, but it's basically a quick-and-dirty search and display program for man pages.

ManOpen is much easier (to me) than opening a man page from the command line, and much easier to use for browsing and searching long man pages (and many of them are indeed long), and also much easier if you want to print them.

Here's a side-by-side picture of both (see Figure 14.75).

You can do all (or most) of those things in Terminal. But you have to know all the proper Unix to do them. Also, ManOpen includes this deal called "an apropos interface," which lets it search the entire man page database for a word, phrase, or command, then show you a list of man pages that contain that word, phrase, or command.

Here's the bottom line: Unless you're a Unix guru, ManOpen, with its Mac interface, is what you should use for viewing, searching, and printing man pages.

ManOpen: The Fine Print
The Mind(s) Behind: Carl Lindberg

For more info: lindberg@clindberg.org

Type: Freeware

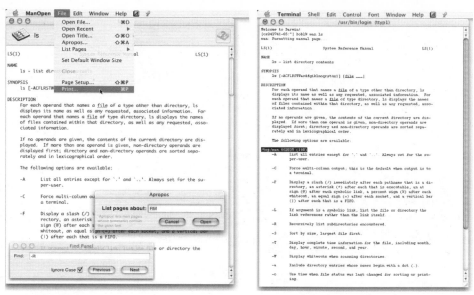

Figure 14.75
ManOpen (left) vs. Terminal (right).

Master Key

Way back in Chapter 1 I said, "If you're not typing at least 40 words per minute without looking, you're wasting time" right before my plug for this program.

Master Key is a good deal for $15 (try it for free). It has some good information about posture and finger positioning (see Figure 14.76).

It includes all types of drills, including stories and anecdotes, historical documents, and nonsense "conditioning" drills, as seen in Figure 14.77.

And, for those of you who like to track your progress, it's got plenty of historical data on your skills over time, as seen in Figure 14.78.

Because I've only used it a little (hey, I type 60+ already) I took the liberty of copying its features list right from Jay's Web site:

Key Advantages:

■ Multiple users and groups

■ Ubiquitous access to user files on an AppleShare network

■ Takes advantage of Macintosh Manager/Multiple-User preference model

■ A two-tier password system that can be turned on or off

14

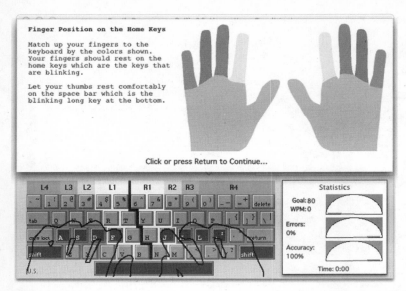

Figure 14.76
Master Key starts you out with the basics.

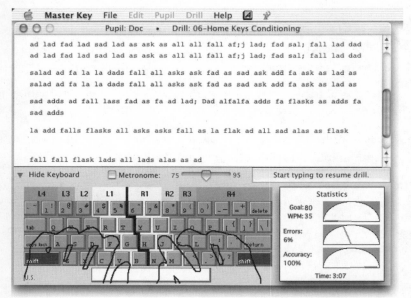

Figure 14.77
Master Key's drills are plentiful and well designed.

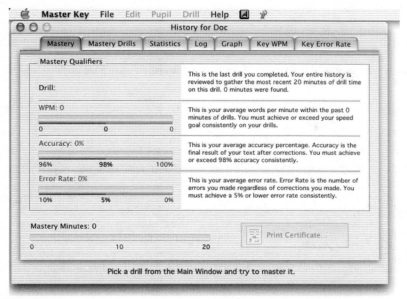

Figure 14.78
Master Key provides a plethora of historical data on your progress.

- Standard Mac OS interface elements

- Typing drills can be paused

- Deleting to previous lines

Other Key Features:

- Comprehensive individual statistics and history

- Breakdown of WPM and Error Rate for each key

- Optional timed drills

- Optional font sizes

- Mastery goal for speed and accuracy with certificate print-out

- Drills can be any plain text file

- Typing instruction tips

- Dvorak keyboarding support and drills

- International keyboard support

- Centralized settings on an AppleShare network

14

- Class Editor to change settings for groups

- Optional restrictions on pupil activities

- Optional audio feedback, which can include high-quality samples of actual type-writers

If you're not a great touch typist already, it's one of the best and most rewarding things you can do for your computer skills. So you can either use this program or a more expensive commercial one (which may not be any better, quite frankly). So just send Jay his $15 bucks, and the nag screens will stop annoying you, and you'll get lots of additional drills.

Tell him Bob sent you.

Master Key: The Fine Print
The Mind(s) Behind: Jay Lichtenauer

For more info: http://macinmind.com/ or **jay@macinmind.com**

Type: Shareware

Cost: $15

Memogram

Another memory monitoring program. Like the others, it displays all kinds of useful information about free, active, wired, and inactive pages, page-ins, page-outs, and more. Here's a look at it (see Figure 14.79).

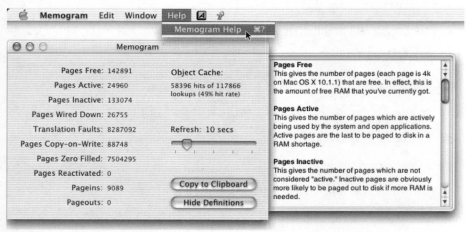

Figure 14.79
Informative, straightforward, and big.

Perhaps its most notable feature is the Help File, which appears in an oh-so-Mac OS X–like drawer, as you can see in Figure 14.79. The help text is written in English and is easy to understand. Another uniqueness is that you can copy and paste the statistics into another document—such as a spreadsheet—if you wanted to track memory patterns over time.

Memogram is a cool little tool for your toolbox—it's useful, it's free, it's small (around 200KB), and it even does at least one thing most other programs don't. There's no reason not to keep a copy on your hard disk or even use it as your main memory dingus.

> **NOTE**
>
> I don't use it. I get the same info from Perfboard and more, while using much less screen real estate. As always, your mileage may vary.

Memogram: The Fine Print

The Mind(s) Behind: Freshly Squeezed Software

For more info: www.cocoadevcentral.com/freshlysqueezed/ or freshlysqueezed@cocoadevcentral.com

Type: DonationWare (see the following)

Cost: This software is distributed as donationware, and you may use it without restriction; however, if you'd like to see its development continued, you are encouraged to make a donation to the authors. Please visit their Web site for more information on how to make a payment.

Memory Monitor

I guess this is the price of alphabetical order—you're going to hear about three of the memory dealies on the Web site in a row. That's actually good because you can compare and contrast them and pick the one or ones that you like best.

> **NOTE**
>
> I used Memory Monitor for a long time, but lately I've been using the next one we'll look at, MemoryStick, mostly because it has an alarm for pageouts that I really like.

Memory Monitor gives you a choice of two displays—a floating window graph with adjustable transparency and graph-in-the-Dock icon. Both can be seen, along with the Preferences window, in Figure 14.80.

In Figure 14.80, I included MemoryStick all the way to the left. As you can see, the two programs report pretty much the same thing.

14

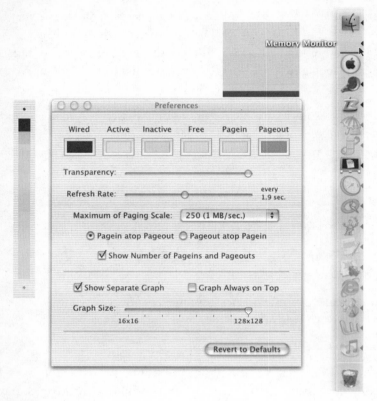

Figure 14.80
This is it—Memory Monitor and its Preferences window.

One other notable thing: Memory Monitor's help documentation is as good as you're ever going to find. If you want to really understand all this memory stuff, I implore you to read it from cover to cover. Memogram's Help is great if you're in a rush, but if you want the nitty-gritty in terms you'll understand, read MM's Help, a portion of which is shown in Figure 14.81.

Memory Monitor: The Fine Print
The Mind(s) Behind: Bernhard Baehr

For more info: http://home.t-online.de/home/bernhard.baehr/ or **bernhard.baehr@gmx.de**

Type: Freeware; GNU GPL

*Author's Acknowledgments: Memory Monitor is based on the source code of LoadInDock, a CPU load monitor application by Takashi T. Hamada, available at **www.lisai.net/ ~hamada/Acti/MacOSX/MacOSX.html**.*

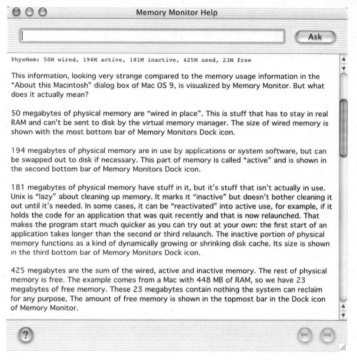

Figure 14.81
I've never seen the whole Unix memory thing explained as well as it is here.

The notes about Mac OS X memory management were taken in large parts from a newsgroup article of Rob Levandowski, posted to **comp.sys.mac.system** on March 28, 2001.

The application icon is part of the eWorld X: eHardware icon collection of The Icon Factory, **www.iconfactory.com/**.

MemoryStick

MemoryStick is what I'm using now. I like the alarm. It doesn't do much else, but it does just enough for me.

Matt Neuburg is a cool guy. He not only wrote MemoryStick and released it as freeware (read his upcoming comment about free software—he's a pistol, that Matt), but he's also a real Renaissance guy—he's the author of books about really geeky stuff like REALbasic and Frontier, he's a contributing editor for the fabulous *Tidbits* newsletter (**www.tidbits.com**), and he's an expert on ancient Greek and Latin, too.

I think Memory Stick is the cat's meow. But, having buttered him up sufficiently in that last paragraph—I want multiple, user-configurable alarms. One for page outs,

14

another for free memory below a certain number, and another for . . . well, you get the picture. And I'd like more flexibility about how the display displays. Smaller would be nice. More transparent wouldn't hurt, either.

Are you listening Matt?

One more thing: Figure 14.82 is a picture of MemoryStick in both of its possible orientations, with its Options menu (the only one with anything useful in it) showing.

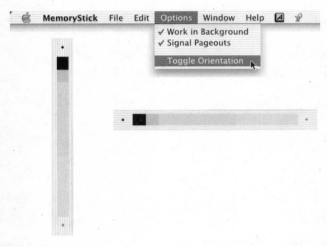

Figure 14.82
MemoryStick toggled both ways, and its Options menu.

MemoryStick: The Fine Print
The Mind(s) Behind: Matt Neuburg

For more info: www.tidbits.com/matt/

Type: Freeware

Matt says (on his Web site): *Cocoa is an application framework provided as part of Mac OS X. Apple also provides, when you buy OS X, free tools for programming Cocoa. This means it's easy to write your own Mac OS X-native applications! So naturally I've started writing some. My goal is to write freeware only. Software should be free.*

God bless him!

MouseZoom
MouseZoom is a one-trick pony—it makes your mouse faster than you can make it move using the Tracking Speed control in the Mouse system preference pane.

There are two flavors of MouseZoom:

- MouseZoom is the standalone application version. To use it, open the program, set your speed, and log out and then back in.

- MouseZoom.prefPane is the Preferences Pane version, which requires OSX 10.1. To use it, move it to the ~/Library/PreferencePanes/ folder. If you haven't already, you may have to create a PreferencePanes folder in your Home/Library folder.

  (As usual, you could also move it to /Library/PreferencePanes/ or /Network/ Library/PreferencePanes, depending on whom you want to have access to it. But if you put it in your Home, as you know, it will always be there for you).

If you've ever thought, "Gee, I wish my mouse were, say, eight times faster," well, you're going to love MouseZoom.

According to its author, Ben Hines, MouseZoom:

- *Is not a hack. It is simply sets the same setting the Apple mouse control panel does*

- *Is not a kernel extension*

- *Will not cause problems with your OS*

Note: If you set the speed in the Apple Mouse panel during the same prefs session, the displayed value in MouseZoom can get out of sync.

How does MouseZoom work? All MouseZoom does is set the com.apple.mouse.scaling parameter in the current user's .GlobalPreferences.plist file. THE ONLY THING this app does is set the SAME setting the Apple mouse control panel sets, but to higher value(s). Any bugs involved in changing this setting are not my fault, but Apple's.

Well, I suppose because you're so sure that all the bugs are Apple's and that it won't cause problems with my OS, I'll go ahead and try it. . .

It didn't do anything for me. But I'm pretty sure the MouseWorks software for my Kensington Turbo Mouse Pro trackball is already doing accelerated tracking. Meanwhile, if you look on VersionTracker, you'll see that many users love it and think it's the best thing since frozen White Castle cheeseburgers, and others can't tell if it works. It had a 4.5 (out of 5) rating when I looked, so don't hold the fact that it didn't work for me against it. It will probably work for you, and it probably isn't a hack or a kernel extension, and it probably won't cause problems with your OS, and if it does, it's Apple's fault anyway, so go ahead and try it.

14

ALERT!

I'm kidding. It's up to you. I don't want to hear about it if something goes wrong. Saying, "but you told me to try it," isn't going to make it any better. So if you're not willing to take the time to clean up whatever mess installing this thing (or any thing) could cause, don't install it!

The two versions are almost identical, as shown in Figure 14.83.

Figure 14.83
The Preference Pane version (top) and standalone program version (bottom)—take your pick; both do the same thing.

NOTE

I think in Figure 14.83 he meant "ridiculously." Extensive research has revealed that many of our best coders can't spell worth a darn, and, in fact, that's part of the reason they chose to become programmers (or doctors).

MouseZoom: The Fine Print

The Mind(s) Behind: Ben Hines

For more info: bhines@alumni.ucsd.edu

Type: Freeware

nCalc

Here's the deal: Apple was too busy to do much for the venerable old Calculator, which hasn't had a function added since its debut in 1984 or thereabouts. I wanted to include a more modern calculator for our modern operating system, one that was free; nCalc is the one I liked best. It's prettier and much more functional than the Apple Calculator app, as you can see in Figure 14.84.

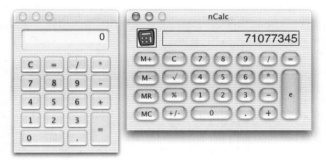

Figure 14.84
More features, and prettier too, plus a bonus.

The bonus is that if you use a PowerBook or iBook, nCalc has a special feature just for you—unlike the Apple Calculator, you can use nCalc with the embedded keypad on your keyboard without having to first press Num Lock.

Here's how nCalc's author, Russ Martin, describes his little twist:

I think that the embedded numeric keypads on Apple notebooks are extremely clever. But, I hate having to turn Num Lock (F5) on and off in order to use the embedded keypad with the calculator. I usually use the calculator to do some quick math while I'm word processing, emailing, or Web browsing. I want to be able to open the calculator, use the embedded keypad without having to remember to turn on Num Lock, and then switch back to the program I was using, again, without needing to remember to turn Num Lock back off.

So, I wrote nCalc. The "n" stands for either "Num Lock optional" or "notebook", I'm not sure which is better. So nCalc is either "Num Lock optional Calculator" or "Notebook Calculator."

Just run nCalc and then use the embedded keypad on your Apple iBook or PowerBook and forget about whether Num Lock is on or off.

Because of the way the program works, it only works with the embedded keypad of a notebook computer or the numeric keypad of a desktop computer. Don't expect the regular 1, 2, 3, 4, 5 keys to ever work, on any machine.

14

nCalc: The Fine Print
The Mind(s) Behind: Russ Martin

For more info: abecedarian@mac.com

Type: Freeware (See the following note from the author)

A word from the Author: *You are under no obligation to pay for it. However, because of the time and effort I have put into it at this point, I'm suggesting that if you like it and find that you use it on a regular basis, that you send me $5, or whatever you think it is worth, via PayPal (www.paypal.com) using the email address above.*

OmniDictionary
OmniDictionary is a Mac OS X client for network dictionary servers. There are two ways to use it. The first way is as a Service, in applications that support Services. In any that do, you can select words in documents and press Command+= to look up that word. I'm doing just that (In TextEdit) in Figure 14.85.

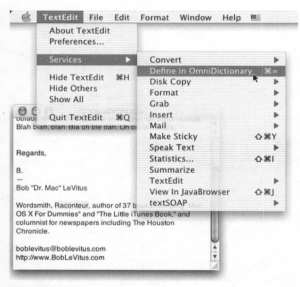

Figure 14.85
Select a word, then either choose Services | Define In OmniDictionary or use the shortcut Command+=.

The second way is to launch it as a standalone program. Type a word into the entry field, press Return, and wait a second until the definition is displayed in the definition area.

Either way you invoke it, the Dictionary program becomes active and, assuming you have an Internet connection, looks up the word at **www.dict.org**, a free dictionary server. Figure 14.86 shows what happened after Figure 14.85.

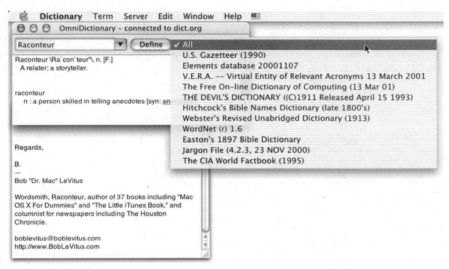

Figure 14.86
I got my definition and am showing you all the free dictionary servers OmniDictionary knows about.

In other words, if the dictionary server supports multiple dictionaries (like the one at **dict.org** does), you can select one dictionary from the pop-up menu to limit queries to that specific dictionary, or you can query all the dictionaries at once, as I've done, by choosing All.

OmniDictionary: The Fine Print

The Mind(s) Behind: The Omni Group

***Our Mission:** Make software that is useful and fun. Support other companies that are creating useful and fun software.*

For more info: www.omnigroup.com

Type: Freeware

Because OmniDictionary is simply a client for dictionary servers on the Web, you have to be connected to the Internet (or have access to a local dictionary server) in order to be able to perform lookups. Check **www.dict.org** for more information on these dictionary servers.

14

OmniDiskSweeper

The less free space you have on your hard disk, the more you'll like OmniDiskSweeper. In a nutshell, it helps you clean out deadweight from your hard disk by displaying it in a column view sorted by item size. Which makes it easy to pick out the biggest files and folders and decide how (or whether or not) to deal with them.

For example, my boot disk, Das Boot, seemed to be getting a little low on free space, with just under 2GB left. So I ran OmniDiskSweeper on it; the report it displayed is what you see in Figure 14.87.

Figure 14.87
Do I actually need 350MB of developer documentation files on my hard disk?

I decided I'd rather have a third of a gigabyte of disk space than developer docs I can reinstall from CD in 10 minutes if I ever actually need them (which is unlikely—I installed the Developer Tools just to get the goodies, not to read a bunch of programming manuals).

Anyway, I selected the /Developer/Documentation folder and then clicked Delete, as shown in Figure 14.88.

Figure 14.88
That's one way to get you to pay your $14.92.

So what did I do? I deleted the folder the old fashioned way—I dragged it to the Trash. And presto—I gained 350MB of disk space. I have to admit, if I get another big hard disk I may pay the $14.92 (I wonder how they came up with that?) just for the darned Delete button. I'm holding out until I need it more.

OmniDiskSweeper: The Fine Print
The Mind(s) Behind: The Omni Group

For more info: www.omnigroup.com

Type: TrialWare. The Delete button is deactivated unless you pay your $14.92.

Cost: $14.92

14

OmniWeb

I've already said all I have to say about OmniWeb back in Chapter 5. So give it a try. You may like it better than your current browser. I almost do.

NOTE

Just as I was putting the book to bed, OmniWeb 4.1 Beta 1 was released. Chances are you'll be able to download a recent version from the OmniGroup Web site. I tossed a link of the beta into The Bonus Round folder on the book's companion Web site. I've been using it all week, and it's pretty solid.

OmniWeb: The Fine Print

The Mind(s) Behind: The Omni Group

For more info: www.omnigroup.com

Type: Nagware

Cost: Free or $29.95

Here's its licensing information (in their words): *OmniWeb 4 for Mac OS X can be used for free, but occasionally you might get little flashes of guilt while you use it. If this overwhelms you, why not buy a license at our Web store?*

Those little flashes are the nagware dialog boxes that pop up every so often to remind you that you *could* pay the license fee if you wanted to. As you know, I like OmniWeb a lot. And I plan to pay for it just as soon as I can use it as my main browser (see the discussion in Chapter 5). But not a moment before.

By the way, besides all these nifty Cocoa apps, did you know that Omni Group was also responsible for porting such popular games as Giants: Citizen Kabuto, Oni, Quake III Arena, and Heavy Metal F.A.K.K.2 to OS X? Well they did!

Perfboard

You've heard all about this program, so I have only one thing to add—remember that column I told you about earlier in the chapter? Perfboard, like LaunchBar, was one of the utilities I described in these 125 words:

I'm a geek. What can I say? I like to know what's going on under my Mac's hood, and Perfboard provides an extensive readout of system performance data for Mac OS X including CPU load, memory statistics, network bandwidth, and disk I/O operations. Perfboard lets me know if I'm using excessive virtual memory paging, having high network activity, lacking free memory, and more.

Perfboard also provides a trend graph of any metric so I can see at a glance if a metric is degrading over time. A CPU meter graphically indicates how busy the system is as well. I've used more than a dozen different programs that do this kind of stuff but Perfboard gives me the most and best feedback, and you can't beat the price—free.

Dr. Mac. Column. Copyright ©2001 Bob LeVitus. Houston Chronicle: *12-28-01.*

PerfBoard: The Fine Print
The Mind(s) Behind: Pepsan & Associates

For more info: www.pepsan.com

Type: Freeware

PiXel Check

PiXel Check is an little one-trick pony of an application. Its single trick is to help you find bad or "dead" pixels on your LCD display(s). Here's the whole thing—the program and the preferences (see Figure 14.89).

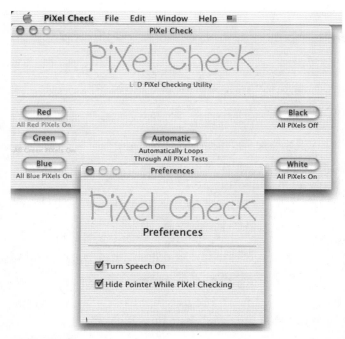

Figure 14.89
Click Automatic and look closely.

14

When you test an individual color, PiXel Check turns every pixel on the screen that color. When you use the Automatic test, PiXel Check loops through all five tests; click anywhere to advance to the next test.

The reason the tests are red, green, and blue is that each pixel on an LCD display is made up of three transistors: a red, a green, and a blue. The black and white tests activate or deactivate all red, green, and blue pixels respectively.

When any of the three colors are on screen, you should see a smooth complete coverage in that color with no black or white or other-colored pixels. White is displayed when all of the transistors are turned on; you see black if you turn all of them off.

Here's what the author says to do if you find any dead or bad pixels on your LCD:

If you should find any bad or "dead" piXels, you can try to very carefully "massage" the area of the screen where you see the bad piXel(s). Be very careful not to scratch or damage your screen!

PiXel Check: The Fine Print
The Mind(s) Behind: Michael Simmons (Mayhem!)

For more info: macguitar@mac.com

Type: Freeware

Credits: Engineering and User Interface: Michael Simmons (Mayhem!) Special thanks to Raphael Sebbe for providing the SpeechUtilities Framework.

Prefling

Prefling is a free Mac OS X dockling that lets you open individual System preference panes directly from the Dock, as shown in Figure 14.90.

And you can't beat the price—free.

To use it, put the file Prefling.dock somewhere handy, like perhaps the Dock Extras folder in your Applications folder (if you have one; if not, make one). After finding a place for it, launch it or drag its icon onto the Dock.

Okay. It's nice. It's free. It does its job, and its programmer has updated it every time an Apple change has affected it. I shouldn't complain, but I'm gonna.

Look at Snard in Figure 14.91.

Now look at Prefling in Figure 14.90 and ask yourself, "What's wrong with this picture?"

14

Figure 14.90
Prefling saves clicks and keystrokes, which makes it a very good thing.

Figure 14.91
Snard does something Prefling doesn't do.

Yup. As far as I can tell, Prefling doesn't see any of my third-party system preference panes. I have a bunch of them—ASM.prefPane, Diablotin.prefPane, MouseZoom.prefPane, SharePoints.prefPane, TinkerTool.prefPane, Visage.prefPane, and WindowShade X.prefPane. You can see them with Snard in Figure 14.91, but Prefling ignores them.

I think that Prefling displays only system preference panes in /System/Library/ PreferencePanes, but not panes stored in other Libraries. Why? Because my personal Library (/Users/bobl/Library/PreferencePanes, a.k.a. ~/Library/PreferencePanes) is where I store my third party panes. And Prefling doesn't see them, but Snard does.

Check the Web site for an update. Meanwhile, the version I used—version 1.2.2—doesn't recognize items in the ~/ Library/PreferencePanes folder.

Prefling: The Fine Print
The Mind(s) Behind: Amar Sagoo

For more info: asagoo@gmx.net or **http://homepage.mac.com/asagoo**

Type: Freeware

Print Window

In the not-so-olden days, OS 9 let you print the contents of a Finder window's list of files. Apple giveth, and Apple taketh away. There is no Print Window command in the Mac OS X Finder. Your best bet is to make a screenshot and print that picture. Or copy and paste the list from the Finder window into a document created by almost any programs. Either way, what used to be just a menu choice is now a major hassle.

Make that *was* a major hassle. Print Window is the one-trick pony that does this trick. Drag a folder or disk icon onto Print Window, as shown in Figure 14.92.

Figure 14.92
I drag The Software On The Disc icon onto the Print Window icon, and the Print Window Options dialog box appears.

After clicking a button or two, I end up with a printed page that looks very much like the mock up (created using OS X built-in Quartz Preview-in-PDF) in Figure 14.93.

Be sure and read the Read Me First file—it covers some of the details in amazing detail. It may take you longer to read it than to print a window. In any case, it's free, it's functional, and it's yet another item you can toss into your tool chest with a clear conscience.

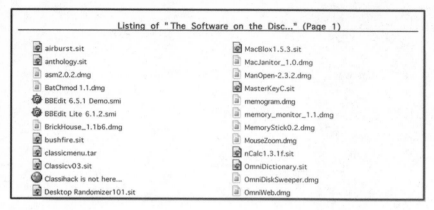

Figure 14.93
Let's see the Finder print one like this unassisted.

Print Window: The Fine Print
The Mind(s) Behind: SearchWare Solutions

For more info: www.swssoftware.com

Type: Freeware

Pseudo

Another Brian R. Hill gem, Pseudo lets you launch applications in the Finder as the System Administrator or "root." Should you need to "run an application as root," drag it onto Pseudo, type your name and password, and whammo—the program runs as root. I'm doing just that in Figure 14.94.

Pseudo also works as a service in the Services menu of other applications, but not very many OS X applications use Services. Yet. xFiles, another program written by the multitalented Mr. Hill, is one that does.

Pseudo: The Fine Print
The Mind(s) Behind: Brian R. Hill

For more info: http://personalpages.tds.net/~brian_hill or brianhill@mac.com

Type: Shareware

Cost: $15 per machine

14

Figure 14.94
I'm going to run Retrospect as root now.

Brian says: *I'm of the opinion that people will either pay shareware fees, or they won't. You may use Pseudo without registering it until you feel that it is worth $15 to you.*

If you like Pseudo, you should pay the shareware fee to help ensure future development of the product.

Please visit **http://order.kagi.com/?5MG** to register Pseudo.

PTHPasteboard

PTHPasteboard is a very cool program that gives you as many clipboards as your little heart desires. The author calls it a pasteboard buffer, and that's just what it is. What it does is store the last 20 (or 30 or 40 or however many you choose) items you cut or copied so you can paste them later. Here's a picture of the Pasteboard window and the HotKeys preferences window (see Figure 14.95).

So, to paste the words "Services menu" into the current document I would:

1. Press F2.

2. Press a hotkey to open the Pasteboard window (mine is Control+V) then press the 2 key on the keyboard.

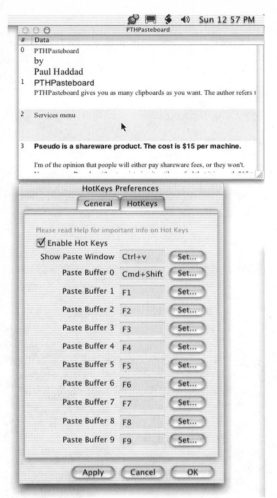

Figure 14.95
The words "Services menu" are in stored in Paste Buffer 2.

3. Click the PTHPasteboard icon in the menu bar (a push-pin) to open the Paste-board window, then click Paste Buffer 2 item in the Pasteboard window, as I'm doing in Figure 14.95.

or

1. Click the PTHPasteboard icon in the menu bar, and then use the arrow keys to select Paste Buffer 2.

You can open the Pasteboard window several ways; you can choose which item to paste several ways as well. It's really quite flexible—no matter how you work, it's there for you.

14

TIP

> You can include PTHPasteboard in your Login Items if you want it to always be there for you.

PTHPasteboard: The Fine Print

The Mind(s) Behind: Paul Haddad; PTH Consulting

For more info: www.pth.com or pthpasteboard@pth.com

Type: Freeware

You'll notice an item in the PTHPasteboard Help menu that says "Donate money for PTHPasteboard." If you like his program, Paul wouldn't mind a little donation.

PuzzleBox

This is really something, and free, too. It's a collection of 19 games for OS X, mostly puzzles. Figure 14.96 is worth a thousand words.

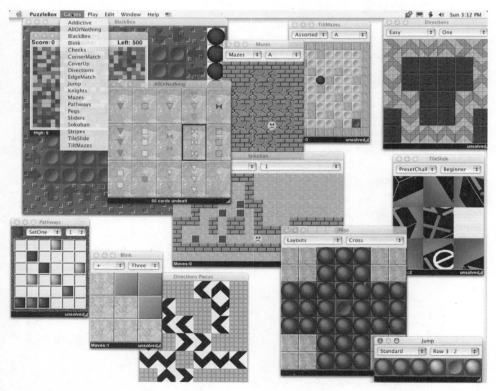

Figure 14.96
Some of the more photogenic puzzles in the PuzzleBox.

I love this guy. I could go on about this package for pages and pages, but Kevin Brain, the brains behind the whole thing, actually says it best and does it briefly and succinctly. Here's his story:

What started out as a quick Sunday afternoon project has grown into an extendable framework for building games, particularly puzzle-type games.

PuzzleBox features user-configurable graphics. The "Styles" tool not only allows you to select among the provided appearances, it also allows you to define your own, so if you don't like the look of a game, you can fix it yourself!

If you use PuzzleBox for more than a few minutes, you will probably want to extend (replace) the small included collection of images used as backgrounds for game boards. The Styles tool help explains how to do this. If you don't already have an awesome collection of background images to use, try www.ibiblio.org/propaganda.

The program also includes a tool for easily retrieving new challenges, artwork and styles, localizations, games, or new versions of the program over the Web. Share and enjoy!

If interested in creating more games or localizing the program for other languages, please contact the author. Developing new games is made easier by the existence of the common game foundation and objectware in PuzzleBox.

PuzzleBox is provided as free software.

I love this guy. I'm telling you. And some of the puzzles are pretty good, too.

Thanks again, Kevin. You rock.

PuzzleBox: The Fine Print
The Mind(s) Behind: Kevin Brain

For more info: ksbrain@visgen.com

Type: Freeware

ShadowKiller

This won't take long. Shadowkiller does one trick and one trick only: It kills all shadows in MacOS X, including window shadows, menu shadows, and so on. It's an easy trick to demonstrate, as you can see in Figure 14.97.

ShadowKiller will kill shadows while it is enabled. Once you disable it or log out or restart, the shadows reappear.

ShadowKiller is another fine "haxie" from our friends at Unsanity, makers of the deliciously delightful WindowShadeX, which you'll see soon.

14

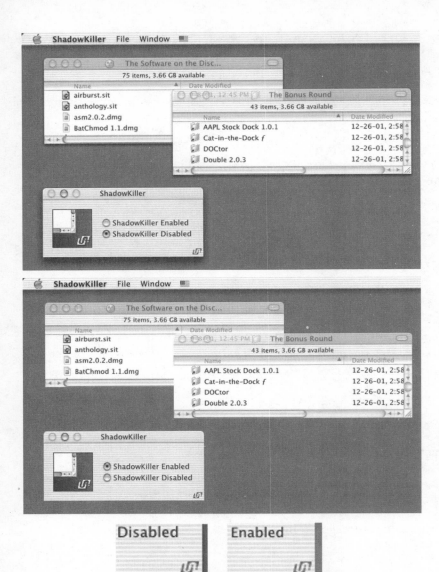

Figure 14.97
ShadowKiller disabled (top) and enabled (middle), and a 200 percent blow-up view of both (bottom).

ShadowKiller: The Fine Print

The Mind(s) Behind: Unsanity

For more info: www.unsanity.com or **unsanity@unsanity**

Type: Freeware (See the following disclaimer)

ShadowKiller relies upon some "hidden" features of MacOS X, therefore we cannot guarantee its proper operation under all MacOS X versions.

That means it may not work with Mac OS X 10.5 or whatever comes out in 2002/ 2003. It works with 10.1.2.

SharePoints

Hoo ya. SharePoints is a monster if you share files and folders, and its author, Michael Horn, is a hero to a legion of users for creating SharePoints and giving it away.

When it came time to write this book, I asked a lot of friends and colleagues to name their "must have" freeware and shareware for OS X, SharePoints was near the top of every one of them that was a file sharer.

Well, I don't do much file sharing, so although I'd heard of SharePoints, I hadn't tried it. When I looked it up on VersionTracker, it had a 4.7 (out of 5) star rating, which is excellent. And the comments were overwhelmingly positive. For example:

Wow. I did not know you could do this in OS X. I thought it was just an OS X Server thing. Very cool. It lets me run a "small" server without WO, NetBoot, and the like. Thanks mhorn.

Great GUI enhancements. . . dude, Apple should hire you!!! Five Stars for this essential application!!

Michael Horn has single-handedly made up for almost every missing network interface component in OS X. Now if he just adds a simple Users & Groups interface, he will have covered it all.

This kind of innovative software is what makes being a Mac user so great.

> **NOTE**
>
> Though I only recently tried it, I couldn't help but notice many, many revisions to SharePoints whizzing by on VersionTracker. Michael Horn likes to add new features and refine it frequently. My point is: I used version 1.6.2, but given his propensity to update SharePoints often, it could be up to version 3x-something by the time you read this. Check VersionTracker or Mr. Horn's Web site for the latest/greatest. There's also a link on this book's companion Web site.

Here are some pictures; you'll see all you can do with this little jewel. In Figure 14.98, you can see the settings for my personal server.

In Figure 14.99, you can see how easily "shares" can be set up.

14

Figure 14.98
Serving up my Big Mac with SharePoints is so easy!

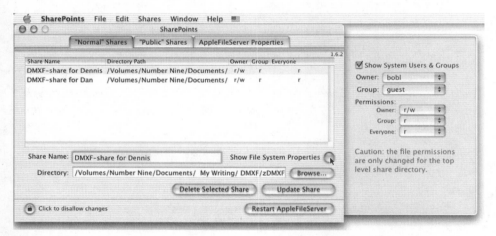

Figure 14.99
It's this simple to share a folder with Dennis and Dan.

I'll leave you with one more comment from VersionTracker:

Nice. (RTFM!)

Yes, it is nice. And yes you should definitely RTFM. You remember that phrase from Chapter 1, don't you? Read The Fine Manual. In this case, because I don't have trees to spare and won't be telling you any more about using SharePoints, you should read every word.

SharePoints: The Fine Print
The Mind(s) Behind: Michael Horn

For more info: http://homepage.mac.com/mhorn or **spamnot@mac.com**

Type: Freeware/donationware (see the following)

If you like SharePoints, please consider making a donation by going to https://www.paypal.com/xclick/business=spamnot%40mac.com&no_shipping=1&item_name=SharePoints.

Any donations that are received will be used to purchase a new PowerMac which will replace my aging Beige G3 and aid in further software development.

Snapz Pro X

Not everyone needs a screen capture utility, but if you do need to capture pictures of movies of your screen under OS X, there's really only one choice, and Snapz Pro X is it. You've heard me say it before, but every single picture in this book was captured with Snapz Pro. I used the movie capture feature like you'd use speed drive on a 35mm camera, then pick the best shot from the frames I captured. A lot of screens in this book got their start that way.

Here are a couple of shots of Snapz Pro in action. (And don't think this was easy—I had to borrow these from the Ambrosia Web site because no matter what I did, I couldn't take screenshots of my screenshot shooter! Apple's Grab utility was less than worthless. As usual.)

In Figure 14.100, you see the Snapz palette, which appears when you press the Snapz Pro hot key (I use Command+Shift+3 out of habit).

I almost always use the three capture modes on the right—Objects, Selection, and Movie—and rarely capture a whole screen. In Figure 14.101, you can see the incredibly useful Objects mode in action.

You select an object by clicking; you select a second object by Shift+clicking. You can choose to capture as many objects as there are on your screen. The dark gray areas are unselected and will not be captured.

I won't ramble on any more than that. It's great. It's worth every penny if you capture screen images.

14

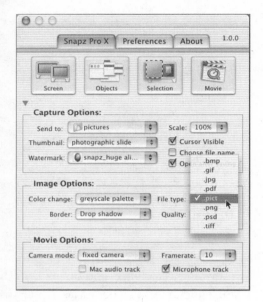

Figure 14.100
The Snapz Pro Palette, where all the action starts.

Figure 14.101
This screenshot will only contain two objects: The System Preferences window and the Dock.

Snapz Pro X: The Fine Print
The Mind(s) Behind: Ambrosia Software

For more info: www.ambrosiaSW.com

Type: Shareware

Cost: $49.00/$29.00 (see the following)

If you just want a better image capture tool, you can get that in spades with Snapz Pro X for $29. If you're into higher-end work and need movie capture, too, you can get that for $49 (you can also always upgrade to add the movie capabilities later for the difference in cost).

Snard

Right after I wrote the piece about Prefling a few pages back, I was prodded into action—I'd procrastinated about paying for it because I rationalized that I *could* use Prefling, and that even if I used Snard a while longer, something better would come along soon, and I'd pay for *that*.

But then I got to thinking—$10 for direct access to all my third-party panes? It's worth every penny. I sent Gideon Softworks $10 before I could forget.

Snard has already been covered in Chapter 2 and in Chapter 9, so I'll leave it at that and move on. But if you haven't tried it yet, you should. It's so cool.

Snard: The Fine Print
The Mind(s) Behind: Gideon Softworks

For more info: www.gideonsoftworks.com

Type: Shareware

Cost: $10

SNAX

SNAX is like the old blind men and the elephant. One might say it's kind of like ASM. Another might say it's a replacement for the Finder. Another might say it's similar to Get Info with a taste of File Buddy thrown in. And they'd all be right. SNAX is a program that pretty much defies classification.

14

Or, as the author describes it, "SNAX is a file utility similar to the Finder, but with more shortcuts and cool features."

SNAX is not meant to replace the Finder, but it does implement most of what the Finder does. It has so many features there's no way I can cover them all in any detail. I created this photo collage, which I've entitled Figure 14.102, to show some of SNAX's features, windows, menus, and preferences.

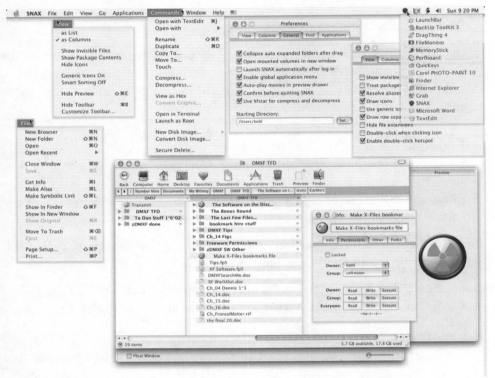

Figure 14.102
This collage shows some of SNAX's features and capabilities.

Read the SNAX Help. Choose Help|SNAX Help or use the shortcut Command+Shift+/. This is the manual. It's all the help you're going to get. On the other hand, most of SNAX is quite intuitive, so it's probably all the help you'll need as well.

I really have to move on soon, but here are a few of SNAX highlights:

- Secure delete writes a pattern over the file before actually deleting it.

- The gray band to the right of the file name is called the hotspot. Click it once and it sends a double-click. Which, at least in theory, saves 50 percent of your daily clicks!

- Its contextual menu offers more file operations than the Finder's.

- Find, which is similar to Sherlock, finds files a lot faster. And faster is better.

NOTE

> Find in SNAX uses the Unix command **locate** to do it's finding which, while making it faster, also includes some Unix-y stuff you should consider. Read the Help section about Find for more information.

- SNAX uses the Unix utility **hfstar**, a variant of **gnutar** that handles resource forks correctly, for compressing/decompressing files.

Gosh, there's so much more. You can assign any key command to almost everything in SNAX, including menu items, files, and folders. You can create and modify disk images without anything but SNAX. It can, like Pseudo, launch programs as root. And threaded file copying is faster than with the Finder.

It's a cliché, but SNAX is the Finder on megavitamins *and* steroids.

TIP

> Steve Gerhman is another developer who updates his baby often. I visited the Web site to make sure I had the latest version and, although I do (it's 1.1.9), I saw a note that a new version is coming out right away.
>
> Says Gehrman: "SNAX 1.2.0 will be released next week, so come back soon. I'm adding the ability to customize the font and color. It's going to be really cool!"
>
> So if I were you, I'd hit his site if you like what you read here. There's almost certainly a newer and more refined version waiting for you (and 1.1.9 is pretty refined itself).

SNAX: The Fine Print

The Mind(s) Behind: Steve Gehrman; CocoaTech, Inc.

For more info: www.cocoatech.com, sgehrman@cocoatech.com, support@cocoatech.com, sales@cocoatech.com, 310–472–8710

Type: Shareware

Cost: $30 or $32

Registering SNAX: *Blood sweat and tears went into the creation of SNAX. It wasn't easy, many 7 day work weeks, a few all nighters, and many hours scouring the Cocoa docs. I didn't write this to make a million bucks; my main goal was to show my support for Cocoa and OS X, and try and write something both useful and cool. So please show your support for the independent Mac OS X developer and register.*

14

Registering is both easy and painless. Go to the Web site, enter a credit card number and we send you a registration code. Enter the code and receive a huge positive boost in karma and feel good knowing that you are helping support the Macintosh community.

CocoaTech uses PayPal, SWReg, and Kagi to handle it's order processing. Paypal charges us less, so we pass those savings on to you! SWReg offers the most options for payment. Kagi is best for international customers because the order form is offered in many different languages. All three systems are safe, secure, and simple.

SpeedSearch

SpeedSearch is an application that quickly searches *inside* files for text. I love a utility that does this. In the OS 9 era, there was a wonderful little program called RetrieveIt that I loved. It did pretty much what SpeedSearch does, but the company folded long before OS X.

SpeedSearch uses lots of memory and processor power when running in the background, but it didn't disturb my work in the foreground (even more so in OS X with its preemptive multitasking than in OS 9). I'm writing this while the search I'm going to use to illustrate what it does is running in the background. I don't feel a thing.

Okay, here's the illustration (see Figure 14.103). I have more than 9,000 items in my Documents folder. I remember someone once said something funny about Guy Kawasaki in something I wrote. But I had no idea when, which folder, what year, or anything other than Guy's name.

No problem. In about three minutes, SpeedSearch had searched 9,404 files and found 31 that contained the words "Guy Kawasaki" (see Figure 14.103).

The item highlighted in Figure 14.103 sounded like it could be the one I was looking for. So I double-clicked it (see Figure 14.104).

Here's a list of SpeedSearch's features from its readme file:

■ Searches a folder hierarchy or one or more volumes.

■ Search results are displayed using the WASTE text engine.

■ Search results are limited in size only by the amount of memory given to SpeedSearch.

■ Search results are displayed in color, which is user-configurable.

■ Search results are displayed in a font and size that is user-configurable.

■ Search results can be searched for a specified string.

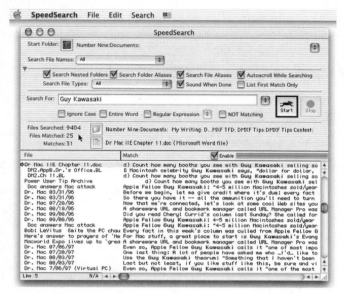

Figure 14.103
It took only a few minutes for SpeedSearch to scan 9,404 files and find 31 matches.

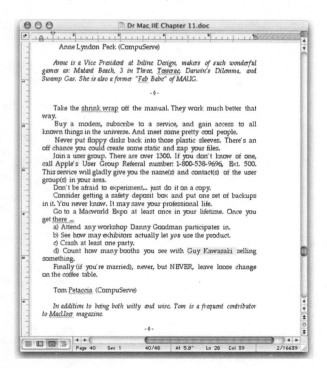

Figure 14.104
Sure enough, the story I was thinking of came from this document: Chapter 11, "What Other Power Users Think You Should Know," of *Dr. Macintosh: Second Edition*.

14

- Search results can be saved to and loaded from a file.

- Search results can be copied using the copy command or drag and drop.

- Functions such as text scrolling and window resizing remain available during a search.

- Regular expression (like **grep**) matching is available, using extended regular expressions.

- Files and folders of matches can be opened by SpeedSearch.

- Patterns can be specified to limit the search to only file names matching the patterns.

- The start folder can be set using drag and drop.

- Start folders can be added to a menu for easy access at a later time.

- Multiple search windows can be opened.

- Macintosh, DOS, and Unix file formats are handled, transparent to the user.

- Extensive Balloon Help is available for all windows.

SpeedSearch: The Fine Print
The Mind(s) Behind: Matt Brunk

For more info: www.kagi.com/brunk/ or **brunk@kagi.com**

Type: Shareware

Cost: $10

Super Get Info

With a feature set comparable to programs like Get Info, BatChmod, xRay, xFiles, and many other programs, Bare Bones Software took a different approach with its rendition, Super Get Info, which expands on the metaphor of the Show Info command in the Finder.

Here's what it does:

- Open one information window for *each* selected Finder item. The Finder has one context sensitive Show Info window.

- View and edit the Mac OS type and creator codes for a given file.

- View and edit the Unix owner, group, and permission settings for files and folders (and optionally apply these settings to enclosed items).

- Modify a file's creation and modification dates.

- Copy a file's full path name, via the Clipboard, as well as via drag and drop.

- Preview a file's contents in a bigger preview window than the Finder's column view's preview.

- Empty the Trash, even when the Finder tells you that you don't have sufficient privileges to do so. And I must say this works 99 percent of the time with Super Get Info. It's always the first one I try. And it almost always works for me.

Super Get Info: The Fine Print

The Mind(s) Behind: Bare Bones Software. "It Doesn't Suck" is a registered trademark of Bare Bones Software, Inc.

For more info: www.barebones.com

Type: Commercial. Time-limited demo (14 days) (see the following)

Cost: Super Get Info is commercial software from Bare Bones Software Inc. It costs US$20 per copy. The demo version is fully functional, but will only run for 14 days after installation. To purchase Super Get Info, choose "Purchase Super Get Info" from the Help menu in the demo version. Choosing this menu item will open your preferred Web browser, and take you to eSellerate's online store, where you can place your order. Or, visit the Bare Bones Software online store.

textSOAP

You'd never guess by its name, but textSOAP is a text cleaner-upper program. I don't know about you, but I get a lot of email. And some of it, no matter who it's from— newbie or power uber guru, needs to be cleaned up for reuse somewhere. That's what textSOAP does.

Here's the old thousand words' worth of picture. In Figure 14.105, you see some text badly in need of a cleaning.

SCRUB is almost the only part of textSOAP I use. ninety plus percent of the time a SCRUB is exactly what I need. It just works. Here's how it handled that dirty job (see Figure 14.106).

SCRUB is a multicleaner that does a bunch of different actions: It strips spaces, forwarding characters, weird characters, line feeds, and multiple paragraphs all in one shot. But the order it does them in is important, so SCRUB runs the cleaners in the proper order, which is probably why I almost always get what I want.

I don't know. It takes a certain kind of user to need one of these. If you do, this one is certainly one of the best.

14

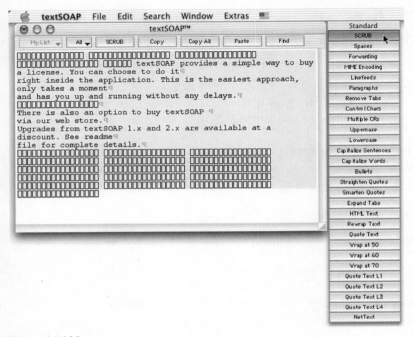

Figure 14.105
This text is dirty—I'd better give it a SCRUB.

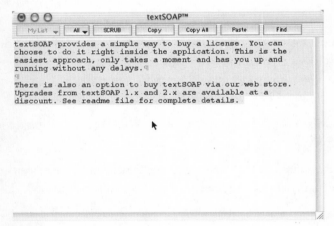

Figure 14.106
Clean and fresh without all that nasty dirtiness.

textSOAP: The Fine Print
The Mind(s) Behind: Mark Munz; Unmarked Software

For more info: www.unmarked.com or support@unmarked.com

Type: Shareware

Cost: $20

TinkerTool

I talked about this program at great length in Chapter 9. It's awesome, useful, and free. Don't miss out—give it a try.

TinkerTool: The Fine Print
The Mind(s) Behind: Marcel Bresink, Ph.D.

For more info: www.bresink.de/Downloads/TinkerTool.dmg.gz

Type: Freeware

TypeIt4Me

TypeIt4Me is a terrific time saver, too. It watches you type, and helps you do it faster and more accurately by expanding "abbreviations" into full text. For example, I've taught TypeIt4Me to replace "xf" with "Dr. Mac—The OS X Files, or, 'How to Become a Mac OS X Power User.'" The spacebar triggers the expansion, so as soon as I press the spacebar after the "f" in "xf," TypeIt4Me automatically expands it in the blink of an eye. Every time I use this particular shortcut I save at least 50 keystrokes. And I have dozens more like it. I love this thing.

Praise Break

Before I go any further, I want you to know that while it's still a beta (pre-release) under Mac OS X, TypeIt4Me has been around since 1989; it won the 1994 MacUser Shareware Award for Best Publishing Tool; Macworld magazine called it "indispensable" and a "truly wonderful shareware gizmo," and awarded it a four-star rating; and it won America Online's "The MUT 1996 Shareware Award."

This is a widely acclaimed and beloved program. Everyone who uses it loves it (and its author, Riccardo). Check this out:

"a spectacular typing-shortcut utility" and "a blessing for anyone who uses the Mac for typing"

David Pogue & Joseph Schorr
Authors

14

(continued)

"Check it out. It's one of my favorite pieces of software—I use it to input all the keywords for EvangeList."

Guy Kawasaki
Former Apple Fellow and Mac Evangelist

". . . you'll quickly become addicted . . ."

Bob LeVitus
Author

The reason I'm calling this to your attention is that the version of TypeIt4Me I used is a beta release. Riccardo says, "After six months of development and private beta testing, the OS X carbonized version of the popular abbreviation expansion utility is ready for its public debut." I've been using it for a week now, and it doesn't appear to have any showstopping bugs, but I highly recommend you visit Riccardo's Web site and grab the latest, greatest, most bug-free version. There's also a link on this book's companion Web site.

Alrighty then, here's how it works. First, you define abbreviations. You can set them up in the Edit Entries dialog (shown in Figure 14.107).

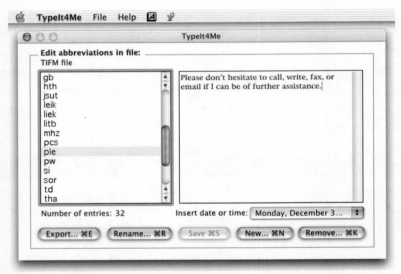

Figure 14.107
One way to create expansions.

Or you can copy the replacement text to the clipboard and choose Add An Entry from the TypeIt4Me (little juggly dude) menu, as shown in Figure 14.108.

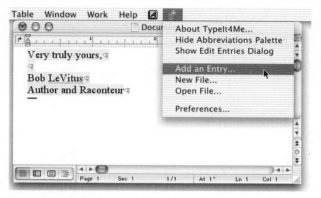

Figure 14.108
Another way to create expansions.

A dialog box appears (see Figure 14.109) so you can give this text its abbreviation.

I choose "vty," a mnemonic device for the "very truly yours" part. I click OK, and the whole thing is stored automatically. The next time I type "vty(space)," that whole chunk—four lines of text—will magically replace it.

TypeIt4Me is also great for common typos. I have it replace "hte" with "the," and "fi" with "if." Just select the mistyped word the next time you mistype it, and do the little dance in Figures 14.108 and 14.109.

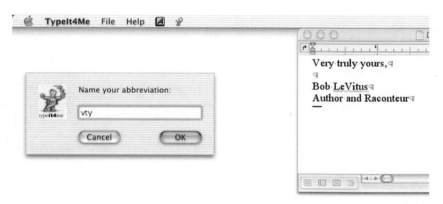

Figure 14.109
Give your text an abbreviation for its trigger.

Finally, if you can't remember all those abbreviations, if your mnemonic device is out of order, or if you just prefer menus, you can choose Show Abbreviations Palette from the TypeIt4Me menu (the one with the little juggling dude in the menu bar). The palette appears, as shown in Figure 14.110.

14

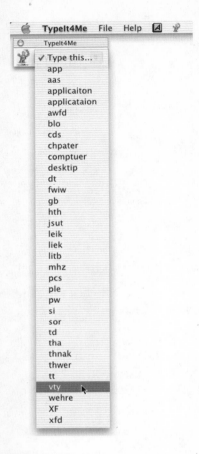

Figure 14.110
TypeIt4Me's Abbreviations palette—for the menu lover in all of us.

Can you guess what some of those expand to? Here's a translation of some of the less obvious ones:

■ **dt** inserts the current date and time: Monday, December 31, 2001; 1:57 P.M.

■ **tt** inserts the current time: 1:58 PM.

■ **app** types: application.

■ **cds** types it the proper way: CDs.

■ **gb** types the abbreviation for gigabyte the proper way: GB.

And so on. It's handy, it's useful, it saves time, it saves wear and tear on both your keyboard and your carpals. It's a bargain at $27. Buy it before Riccardo comes to his senses and starts charging what it's worth.

TypeIt4Me: The Fine Print
The Mind(s) Behind: Riccardo Ettore

For more info: www.TypeIt4Me.com or TypeIt4MeB@aol.com

Type: Shareware

Cost: $27

From the Author: *TypeIt4Me is NOT freeware. Although distributed via the shareware and demoware channels of Internet download sites, magazine or book cover-mounted floppies or CDs, user group libraries and on-line services (AOL, Compuserve, etc.), it is commercial-grade copyrighted software and carries a price of $27, 25 euro, or £16 for a single user license fee. Discounts are available for multiple user licenses.*

Please respect this distribution method in your own and other users' interest, because it allows software authors to develop reasonably priced products by avoiding the high overheads associated with more traditional forms of boxed and packaged distribution.

When you pay the license fee, you'll be emailed, faxed, or mailed a code to stop the reminders to pay which will appear frequently on your screen after the initial 30-day trial period.

URL Manager Pro

This is another one you may not have a need for, but I sure do. Because I use a bunch of different browsers, I like to have my bookmarks be portable. So I use URL Manager Pro instead of the built-in bookmark feature found in all browsers.

I said quite a bit about it in Chapter 5, but it has two features you really ought to see. The first is the Add Bookmark Here menu item, seen in Figure 14.111, which lets me add bookmarks directly into subfolders. None of my browsers will let me do that.

This means that I can organize my Mac OS X bookmarks into their proper subfolders on the fly, instead of having to open their window and "organize" them later.

The second feature is one I use every single day. It's called Read All, and it allows me to open a subfolder full of Web sites all at once, as shown in Figure 14.112.

I paid my shareware fee for URLMP a long, long time ago. It's worked well for me for many years, and I expect to use it for many more now that it's available for OS X.

14

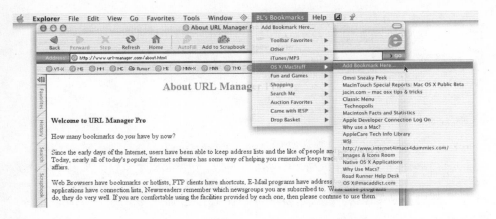

Figure 14.111
The bookmark for URL Manager Pro will appear in the OS X/MacStuff menu. Cool, eh?

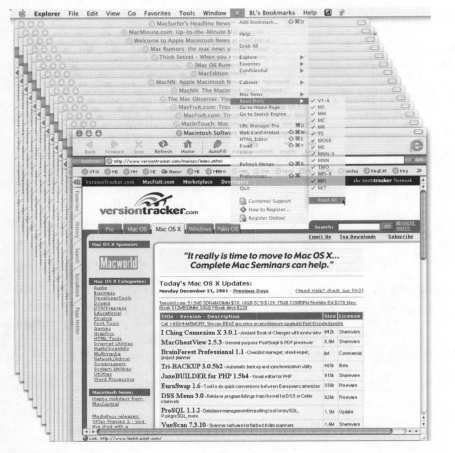

Figure 14.112
Read All gives me all the news without the wait.

URLManager Pro: The Fine Print

The Mind(s) Behind: Alco Blom

For more info: www.url-manager.com

Type: Shareware

Cost: $25 (Combination pricing as follows)

URL Manager Pro: $25

URL Manager Pro + Web Confidential: $40 (you'll find a copy of Web Confidential in The Bonus Round folder on this book's CD-ROM)

URL Manager Pro + Web Confidential (Mac + Palm): $55

URL Manager Pro Upgrade for Mac OS X: $10.95

Visage

I said it all in Chapter 9. I love Visage. I paid for Visage. If you love it, you should pay for it, too. That's all.

Visage: The Fine Print

The Mind(s) Behind: Sanity Software

For more info: Sanity@mac.com

Type: Shareware

Cost: $10 (And worth it!)

Watson

Watson is a collection of simple tools for gathering specific kinds of information on the Internet. It's also one of the slickest and most unique (not to mention useful) programs made for OS X yet.

It's kind of like Sherlock, but different. In fact, the Watson Web site refers to Watson as Sherlock's Indispensable Partner. And it's kind of like a stripped-down special-purpose Web browser. But it isn't really that either, although Watson doesn't display graphics out of context, nor does it play Flash files, and have other overhead to deal with.

I describe it as a lean, mean, information machine, designed to get you what you're looking for fast. It looks up, organizes, and displays the information you request, often querying multiple sites in the background, faster than you could type one URL in a Web browser. When I use Watson with my cable modem, I almost always start to see results pouring in within five seconds, and sometimes less.

14

Watson comes with 10 tools (modules): Movies, Flights, Images, Exchange Rates, Phone Numbers, Zip Codes, Yahoo Search, Stocks, Recipes, and eBay. The tool installer in Watson shows additional tools not yet available, including a TV Listings tool (coming soon), as well as Weather, Maps, ATMs, Horoscope, Ski Report, and Sports Score tools, all planned for the future. And a Package Tracking tool for all the major package carriers is being beta tested as I type this. It all sounds great to me.

These next three pictures illustrate what Watson does and how it does it; here are some of my favorite tools in action.

My very, very favorite tool is Movies, seen in Figure 14.113.

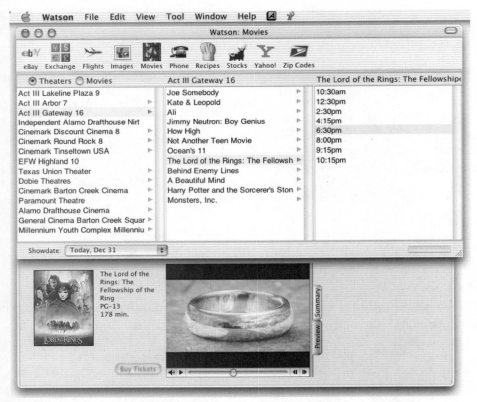

Figure 14.113
Watson knows where I live so it shows me only theaters that are nearby.

Watson gets me complete theater listings with play times, previews in QuickTime (if available), and a short written summary, all in about five seconds. The only thing missing is a "buy tickets" button, and I happen to know that Dan's working on that.

My other very favorite is Images, which lets you search for free and royalty-free images on the Internet quickly and easily, almost like AppleWorks. In Figure 14.114, I searched for Typewriters (again) and found 49 of them in about 10 seconds. I can open or save any or all of them if I like.

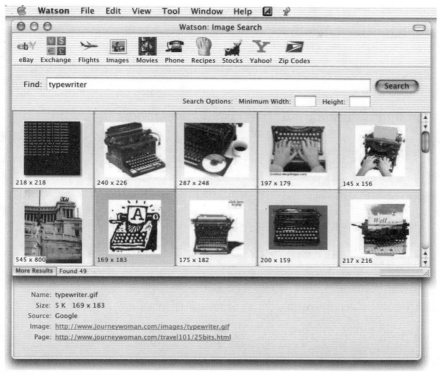

Figure 14.114
Watson makes it easy and fast to find an image on the Internet, for free (well, most of the images are).

The Stocks module is nice, tracking your portfolio and offering instant graphs for any stock. And the Phone Book module, shown in Figure 14.115, is faster and cheaper than dialing 411.

So there you have it. Watson is a tool for looking stuff up fast on the Internet. I think $29 is steep, but it's so well done, and Dan is so responsive (he's working on at least one feature I asked about) that I paid my fee the second time I used it.

14

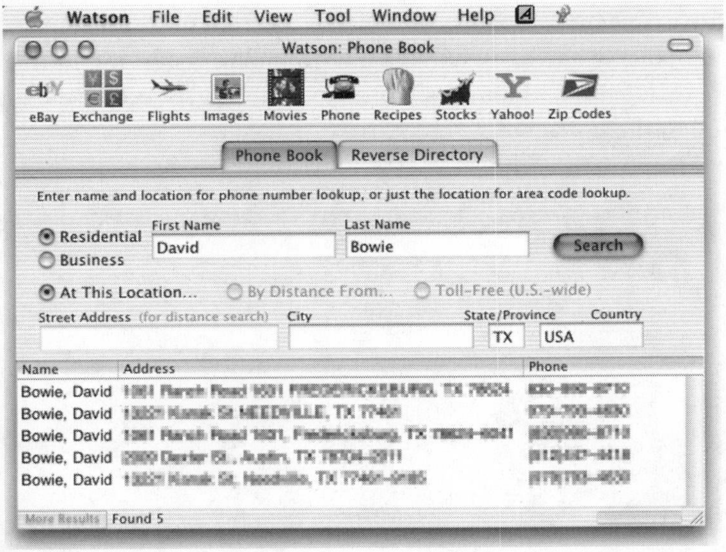

Figure 14.115
Watson found five David Bowies in Texas, but none of them would sing "Space Oddity" to me. (Addresses blurred to protect the innocent Bowies.)

Watson: The Fine Print
The Mind(s) Behind: Dan Wood

For more info: www.karelia.com/watson or watson@karelia.com

Type: Shareware

Cost: $29

Until Watson is purchased and registered, it functions as a "demo" only, limited in how long it will stay launched. Additionally, new tools cannot be downloaded in "demo" mode.

Who's There? Firewall Advisor

Who's There? Firewall Advisor, from Open Door Networks, works with your Macintosh's firewall to help you analyze and react to access attempts detected by the firewall (see Figure 14.116). Here's how it works:

First, Who's There reads the log file produced by your firewall. Then it lets you:

■ View access attempts based on several criteria, including date and risk level

■ Analyze access attempts to determine factors like risk level

■ Summarize accesses by IP address and service type (port number)

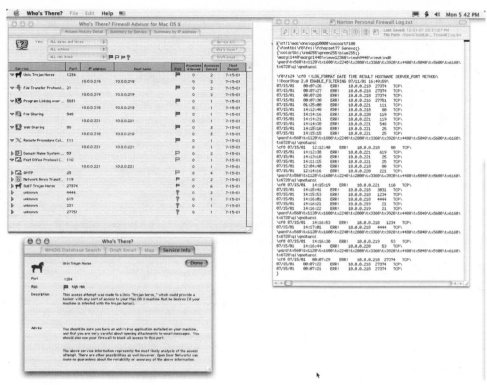

Figure 14.116
A firewall log (right) and the same data shown in Who's There's Summary By Service report (left). Which would you rather work with?

- Investigate details of the accessor's IP address, including their network's location and administrator's email address

- Draft an email to the network administrator about the access

Who's There analyzes access attempts and provides advice specific to the Mac OS X environment (Service Info tab, lower left). It can even compose an email to the appropriate postmaster(s) and paste it into your mail program.

And these guys know their stuff. Alan Oppenheimer, the founder of Open Door Networks was an 11-year Apple veteran and co-creator of the AppleTalk network system. Open Door is also the developer of Mac OS 9's TCP/IP File Sharing feature.

14

TIP

> Alan and Charles Whitaker (also from Open Door) have written the definitive book on Macintosh security: *Internet Security for Your Macintosh: A Guide for the Rest of Us* from Peachpit Press. If you're new to networking, it's an excellent place to start. It's easy to understand and will help you figure out what measures, if any, are appropriate for your situation.

If you're using a firewall, any firewall, you might enjoy using Who's There to analyze your break-in attempts and provide sensible and easy-to-understand advice.

Who's There?: The Fine Print
The Mind(s) Behind: Open Door Networks

For more info: www.opendoor.com

Type: Commercial product; time-limited demo

Cost: $49

WindowShade X

WindowShade X changed the way I use Mac OS X. But I talked about it in Chapters 3, 4, 6, and 9, so I'm not going to say much more.

I don't believe that very many programs should have been built into OS X, but WindowShade X should have. What was Apple thinking removing this great feature? Luckily, Unsanity's WindowShade X is better than even Apple's OS 9 implementation.

Just send 'em your $7 and be done with it.

WindowShade X: The Fine Print
The Mind(s) Behind: Unsanity

For more info: www.unsanity.com or unsanity@unsanity.com

Type: Shareware

Cost: $7

X Font Info

Speaking of Apple removing beloved functions from OS X, here's another one. In OS 9 (and 8 and 7 and probably 6), when you double-clicked a font, a little window opened displaying the font face so you could tell what it looked like.

In OS X, when you double-click a font, nothing happens. No application can open it. Fortunately, X Font Info can and does. It's a one-trick pony, but the trick's a good one, and the program is free.

The trick is this: X Font Info displays uninstalled fonts in their actual faces.

There are several ways to open fonts with it. The easiest perhaps is to drag one or more font files (they can be Mac OS 8/9 Font Suitcase, PC TrueType font, OpenType font, Apple's dfont) onto the X Font Info icon, as I'm doing in Figure 14.117.

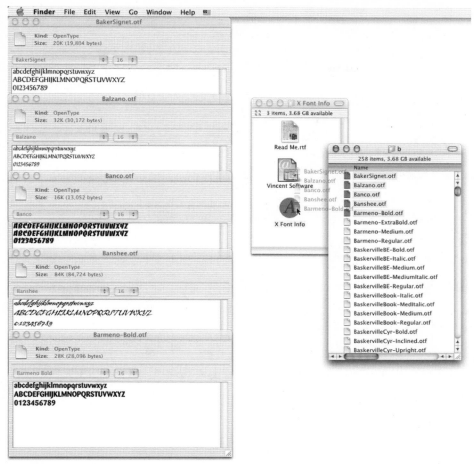

Figure 14.117
Ahhh. . . so that's what those fonts look like!

Another way is to launch X Font Info and choose File|Open to select a font or fonts to view.

But, at least in my humble opinion, the best way is to make X Font Info the default program to open fonts. To do this, click any font once to select it. Choose File|Show Info or use the shortcut Command+I. The Show Info window will appear. Choose Open With Application from the pop-up menu, then click the little black triangle to pop down the Choose An Application menu, then choose Other, as shown on the left in Figure 14.118.

Navigate to the copy of X Font Info on your hard disk and select it. Finally, click Change All to make the change apply to all fonts of this type. You may have to do this whole procedure again if you have different types of fonts on your hard disk (i.e., TrueType,

14

Figure 14.118
Here's where the work gets done.

PostScript Type 1, OpenType, etc.) You have to perform this little procedure for each type. But only once. Since I got my copy, no matter which type of font I double-click, it opens in X Font Info and shows me what it looks like, except when it doesn't.

X Font Info does not preview the following types of fonts correctly: bitmap, non-roman fonts (including Symbol and Zapf Dingbats), and fonts with the same name as a currently opened font.

X Font Info: The Fine Print

The Mind(s) Behind: Vincent Jalby

For more info: http://members.aol.com/vjalby/ or vjalby@kagi.com

Type: Freeware

xFiles

I'm going to have to use a weasel-out on this one. Although xFiles has been around as long as any of the other file-diddlers, I haven't used it much and can't really say what makes it different or better than the others, including xRay, Super Get Info, Get Info, BatChmod, and such. Read the sidebar entitled, "File Diddlers," before Get Info earlier in this chapter for the bigger picture.

According to the ReadMe.rtf file: *xFiles allows you to change the HFS+ type and creator, filename, Posix owner and group, modification date, and permissions of files you drop on it. It also includes a File List document, for easy preview, editing and modification of files located*

around your mounted drives. An HFS+ Catalog Search allows you to build File Lists based on several HFS+ criteria.

Features:

Change Posix setuid, setgid, and sticky bit.

Customizable toolbars

Reference documentation viewer using Sherlock engine.

Tip:

Although you can only drag one item into a File List at a time, if you drag a folder into the list, you can expand it to view and operate on all of its contents.

xFiles: The Fine Print
The Mind(s) Behind: Brian R. Hill

For more info: http://personalpages.tds.net/~brian_hill/ or **brianhill@mac.com**

Type: Shareware

Cost: $20 per machine

I'm of the opinion that people will either pay shareware fees, or they won't. You may use xFiles without registering it until you feel that it is worth $20 to you.

If you like xFiles, you should pay the shareware fee to help ensure future development of the product.

XRay

There are many good file diddlers, and I count XRay among the best of them. My favorite unique feature is that XRay includes a contextual menu, unlike most OS X programs (and the other diddlers, as far as I know). So I can get info on a file via XRay by Control+clicking it, as shown in Figure 14.119.

> **NOTE**
>
> I also like Super Get Info's keyboard shortcut in the Finder, which does the same thing but with keyboard commands instead of a contextual menu.

Here's the kind of information XRay provides, shown four ways in Figure 14.120.

14

Figure 14.119
XRay that folder I say.

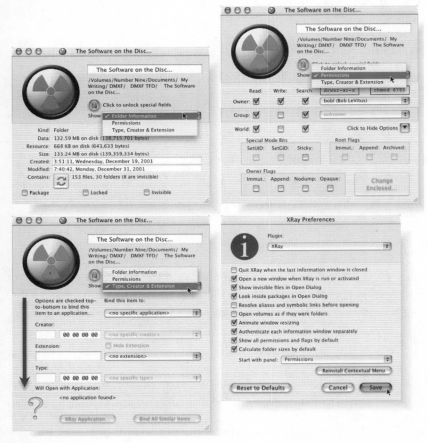

Figure 14.120
XRay lets you edit three different windows full of information about your file or folder, and offers almost infinitely configurable preferences, too.

You can XRay items by dragging them onto XRay's icon, XRay's Dock icon, or XRay's window (if it's running).

XRay also has a very fine "so you can't empty your Trash" feature, that almost always comes through when the Finder refuses because of insufficient privileges or other such nonsense.

Good stuff. And this is just the beta. I can't wait to see what it's like when it's finished.

XRay: The Fine Print
The Mind(s) Behind: Rainer Brockerhoff

For more info: www.brockerhoff.net/xray or **rainer@brockerhoff.net**

Type: Beta

Cost: This version is a beta and free, but the next one will probably be shareware.

Zingg
Rainer Brockerhoff, the mind behind XRay, just released another gem, and another great use of the contextual menu. Control+click any icon and a contextual submenu will show you every program Zingg knows about that can open that particular file. Just select any application from the list and that file will be opened by it.

Is that cool or what? Here's an example of why it is. I have configured OS X so that Corel PHOTO-PAINT opens when I double-click a TIF file. But sometimes, if PHOTO-PAINT isn't running, and I just want to look at the document, not edit it, I wish I could easily open it in Preview. Zingg is the easiest way I've found so far. I just Control+click the document, choose Preview from the menu, and the graphic opens in Preview instead of PHOTO-PAINT, which is just what I want. Figure 14.121 shows what it looks like.

I love this one. And it's free, too. Thanks, Rainer. You do beautiful work.

Zingg: The Fine Print
The Mind(s) Behind: Rainer Brockerhoff

For more info: www.brockerhoff.net/zingg or **rainer@brockerhoff.net**

Type: Freeware

14

Figure 14.121
The easy way to open a document with an application other than the one it's bonded to is with Zingg.

There Is One More Thing. . .

Bonus Round. . . where anything can happen!

Seventh Inning Stretch and a Compromise with My Editor

OK, here's the deal. We're only about two-thirds of the way through the stuff I considered "essential," and my editor informs me I'm almost out of trees. Although I've tried not to go on and on about any one program, it seems that I've gone on and on about most of them. And in hindsight, I wouldn't change a word of them.

I have roughly 50 more programs I wanted to include. My editor wants me to wrap things up in 10 or fewer pages and do it today. I want 60 more pages and another week and a half.

So here's the compromise my editor and I came up with: I get to write up the 20 I most want to tell you about regardless of how many pages it takes. But, whatever I'm going to do has to be done by tomorrow.

However, links to 40+ other programs—including great freeware and shareware such as: Cat-in-the-Dock, eBookfaces, EightBall, File Freak, FloatingNotes, Mac Uptime, Pong 2001, Reckless Drivin',

(continued)

StratWars, tuxRacer, and Youpi Key, to name just a few—are linked to from The Bonus Round folder on this book's Web site. You won't get my sparkling, wit, pernicious puns, and hands-on instructions, but at least you're getting the goodies.

Here's the final list of what the Bonus Round Folder contains:

AAPLStockDock, CatInTheDock, DOCtor, Double Folder, eBookfaces, EightBall, File Freak, FindIt, FloatingNotes, GLScreensaversGolden Key Carbon, Key Chart.pdf, Keyboard Shortcuts, LoadInDock, MacUptime, NetStatInDock, OldGlory, OmniOutliner, OmniWeb, osxguide2_11hq.pdf, Pong2001, Reckless Drivin', Sherlock Plugins, SkyFly, slashdock, SLF Helper Script, sliderz, Slides, SonOfGrok, Special Characters.pdf, Spy, StratWars, StuffIt Lite, teatimer, ThermoInDock, Ticker, tuxRacer, Typist, unlockAll, VMometer, Web Confidential, wStock, xback, Xmanview, YoupiKey, YoupiOptimizer, and Znippetizer-X.

Have fun!

14

What Other Power Users Think You Should Know about OS X

When I began to work on this book, I knew there was little chance of my remembering everything I've learned about the Mac over the past few years. So I enlisted the help of friends, acquaintances, and just about anybody with a Mac and a modem who would listen.

As I told you in Chapter 5, going online to get information is the greatest thing since sliced bread. So, because the folks who hang out on the Web are so nice and know so much, I enlisted their help.

So I issued a press release, posted some messages on some of my favorite Web sites (see Chapter 5—most of those), and announced it on my Web site. Here's what I said:

A free copy of my next book and up to 15 minutes of fame (more or less).

Thanks for taking the time to read this note.

For those of you who don't know me, my name is Bob "Dr. Mac" LeVitus. I'm a long-time Mac-head, the former Editor-in-Chief of MACazine, *a former contributing editor for the late, great* MacUser, *and the author of 37 (soon to be 38) computer books including* Dr. Macintosh, Stupid Mac Tricks, Mac OS 9 For Dummies, Mac OS X For Dummies, New and Improved Stupid Mac Tricks, AppleWorks For Dummies, *and many more.*

Long before I wrote a single book with "Stupid" or "Dummies" in its title, I wrote a book, way back in 1989, called, Dr. Macintosh: Tips, Techniques, and Advice on Mastering the Macintosh. *And that's exactly what it was— tips, techniques, and advice to help you use your Mac better, faster, and more elegantly.*

Dr. Macintosh and its sequel, Dr. Macintosh: Second Edition *were both quite popular, and I believe one of the reasons was that both books had a unique feature I've not seen in other books—a section called "What Other Power Users Think You Should Know," which was a long chapter made up entirely of tips submitted by other power users. It was, in my humble opinion, the best stuff in the book.*

And now, after an absence of 10 years, Dr. Mac is back! I'm thrilled to announce that my next book will be the long-awaited sequel to the sequel, Dr. Mac: The OS X Files (or, How to Become a Mac OS X Power User). *The book will publish in early 2002.*

Now, I need to ask for your help. I'll be the first to admit I don't know everything about OS X, and much of what I know, I learned from someone else.

So here's the deal: Send me your best power user tips, hints, undocumented shortcuts, techniques, or tutorials. If you have a favorite utility or program, submit a description of it and why it's so great, or a tip for using it. And, if your OS X desktop is way cool, send me a screenshot with a description of what makes it so special.

I'll reward you handsomely for your tips, hints, pictures, recommendations, and whatever else you care to send me. If I use your submission in the book, I will:

A. Publish your name with your tip (if you want me to), giving you at least 15 minutes of fame (give or take, depending how long it takes to read your submission).

B. Say something nice about you and your powerful Mac-ing skills.

C. Send you an autographed copy, inscribed any way you like.

So, if you've got a hot tip, cool desktop, or favorite piece of software, just send it to me at: Boblevitus@boblevitus.com.

IMPORTANT: Please include the words X-FILES TIPS in the subject line of your message (to insure that my junk mail filters don't eat your submission before I see it).

ALSO IMPORTANT: Every submission must include your mailing address (so I know where to send your book), what you would like me to inscribe in your copy (if your submission is selected for publication), and a valid email address (so I can tell you if you're a winner).

Enter as often as you like, but I can provide only one book per person, even if you have multiple submissions accepted.

The contest will end Monday, November 26th at midnight. In the case of duplicate submissions, the entry with the earliest time-stamp will get the goodies.

Thanks for your help. I appreciate it and I think readers of Dr. Mac: The OS X Files *will appreciate it even more.*

Sincerely yours,

Bob "Dr. Mac" LeVitus
boblevitus@boblevitus.com

I expected to get some good hints and tips, but I never expected the response I got—well over 200 tips and hints were submitted in the two months after I began my publicity campaign. Even after removing duplicates and stuff I'd covered elsewhere, there are still close to 200 tips in this chapter. Reading through them for the first time was fascinating. There was so much I didn't know, and so much that I'd forgotten.

This chapter is structured a little differently from the others. It contains a lot of hints and tips, organized into several categories. Each hint is credited to its author. I've added graphics anywhere I felt they were appropriate, and my comments appear in italic type to set them off from the words of others.

There are so many gems and so few clunkers, I suggest you read the whole thing, including the parts that don't interest you today. You never know when that obscure bit of Mac information will come in handy. Tuck it away for future reference.

It was hard to categorize all of this information, but I did manage to instill some sense of order. The material is broken down into three sections with three categories each:

- **Applications**
  - Finder
  - Applications
  - Classic
- **OS X**
  - Troubleshooting
  - Networking & Connectivity
  - Printing
- **Geeky Stuff**
  - Terminal/Unix
  - AppleScript
  - Potpourri

You may disagree with some of my classifications: Is that a Finder tip or an OS X tip? Shouldn't the Finder category be in the OS X section? And so on. Just so you know, I thought long and hard about each and every tip and which section and category it should go into. But many tips could fit into two or even three categories, so I put each in the place I felt was the best fit. Don't worry. Be happy. Just read them and don't worry about whether or not they're listed in the right category.

15

ALERT!

Don't blame the tip authors for the corny, pun-ridden, and alliterative headline that accompanies each tip. I wrote them all, as painful as it is to admit it. If you hate them, tell me, not the tipsters. (On the other hand, if you like them, tell your friends.)

This is by far the most useful part of the book, and it's because of all the nice folks out there who used their Internet connections to contribute to this chapter. So before we begin, I want to take a moment to again thank the members of the online community who helped out. Thanks! Your autographed copy is on the way!

NOTE

Several people submitted tips without a mailing address. If you're one of them, send me an email, and I'll see that you get your copy.

Now, on to the best advice you can get—what other power users think you should know.

Applications

This section deals with specific programs including the Finder, other programs, and Classic (yes, Classic is a program).

Finder

This first group of tips concern that always-running program you know and love and use every day, the Finder.

Finder Windows: Now Smarter Than Ever!

In the Finder, you can select a group of files. Then go open a second (or third or fourth) Finder window and navigate to where you want. When you're finished, the first window will still remember your selection. I love that!

Aaron Lynch

Isn't that sweet? And I'm pretty sure its not mentioned elsewhere in the book. Thanks, Aaron.

— ◊ —

The Scroll (Wheel) Truth

A scroll wheel, two-button mouse is a *must*! OS X supports these mice natively. One of my favorite "hidden" uses is this: If you open a Show Info window, you can use the scroll wheel to scroll through the different panes.

Small, but awesome.

Don Fuller

Figure 15.1
Each "click" of the scroll wheel selects a different pane from this menu.

You can see just what he means in Figure 15.1.

*So the first click of the scroll wheel changes the pane from General Information to Name &
Extension. The second click activates Open With Application, the third click activates
Preview, and so on. He's right—it's small, but it's great to know that Mac OS X does cool
stuff like this all by itself, without drivers or other third-party software.*

— ◊ —

A Workaround for the Missing-in-Action "Clean Up By Date" Option

OS 10.1 does not have a menu item for "Clean Up By Date" etc., that OS 9 did.
However, you can get much the same effect by going to the View Options menu
(Command+J) and clicking on Keep Arranged By Date, then clicking back on None.

James Meiss

*Good one. Make sure you click the This Window Only button (as shown in Figure 15.2), or
this little trick will affect every window in icon view (i.e., you don't want to do this globally).*

*When you're done, click the None radio button unless you want the icons to remain in
alphabetical order.*

— ◊ —

When Icons Go Wonky

There still seems to be a bug in OS 10.1 as far as changing the icons of your drives (it
apparently didn't work at all in 10.0). When you paste an icon onto a drive (Show
Info, Command+I) you sometimes get an empty icon. However, if you log out and log

15

Figure 15.2
To achieve this effect, first click the Keep Arranged By radio button, then select Name from its menu.

back in, then the icon you pasted in will appear. Lots of great OS X icons are available at **www.iconfactory.com**.

James Meiss

Hmmmm. That's happened to me. I restarted and it went away. It's nice to know that just logging out and back in will do the trick. And, of course, I agree about IconFactory. It is awesome if you like icons.

— ◊ —

How to Make Dock Magnification Usable
I don't happen to like Dock magnification much, but it is useful when you have so many things in the Dock that all your icons are super-teeny. Here's how I manage this. I set my Dock size the way I want it and then set the magnification a bit smaller. That way, I don't normally see magnification, but if my Dock gets very full, it kicks in when I need it to.

Marshall Pierce

— ◊ —

How to Find the File of Any Dock Icon

Holding down the Command key while clicking an icon in the Dock will display the item in the Finder. So, for example, if you Command+click the iTunes icon in the Dock, the folder containing iTunes will open.

Rick (no last name or mailing address)

— ◊ —

Facilitate Fast Finding with Favorites

Don't like digging through folders to get to your application or often-used items? Here's what to do: Open any Finder window (Command+N) and drag your most-used files—programs, documents, folders or whatever—to the Favorites (heart) icon on the toolbar and voila, all your often-used files or programs are in one handy location no matter where they are on the hard disk. Take it one step further and drag your Favorites folder (it's in your ~/Library) to your Dock and you have almost instant access to all your favorite (most-used) files.

Frank Farwell

And, of course, don't forget you can also access your Favorites folder from the Finder's Go menu (see Figure 15.3) or with the keyboard shortcut Command+Option+F.

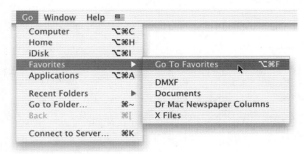

Figure 15.3
Don't forget the handy Go To Favorites menu item and keyboard shortcut.

— ◊ —

Speaking of keyboard shortcuts, here's another tip about 'em:

Edit Keyboard Shortcuts in .lproj Apps (or, ResEdit for the New Millennium)

If you want to edit keyboard shortcuts, open this file: /System/Library/CoreServices/Finder.app/Contents/Resources/English.lpro j/Localized.rsrc.

15

Inside it, you'll find a lot of gibberish, and among it, the Finder menus, like "Show Original R" *(highlighted in Figure 15.4).* You might have to search for it (BBEdit Lite works like a charm). Just change the last character (R) and voilá—you now have your own customized keyboard shortcut.

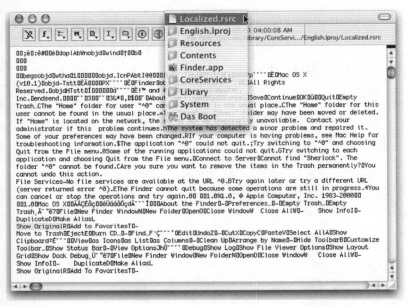

Figure 15.4
The Localized.rsrc file with the "Show Original R" item highlighted.

If you're on a foreign system, like on the German system, open the file inside your native language .proj folder. So, for example, on a German system, you would open </System/Library/CoreServices/Finder.app/Contents/Resources/German.lproj /Localized.rsrc> and look for, say, "Original zeigen R" and change the last character (R).

This also applies to other programs using .lprojs to store their interfaces.

Lucas Mathis

This one's not for the faint-of-heart. First of all, you should back up the Localized.rsrc file before you modify it, just in case. Second, you'll need to either perform this action as Root, change the permissions of the CoreServices folder so you can access it, or do the whole procedure while booted in OS 9. Otherwise, you won't be able to modify the CoreServices folder.

NOTE

I Command+click in the window's title bar to display the drop-down menu that
shows the path to this file (i.e., /System/Library/CoreServices/Finder.app/Contents/
Resources/English.lpro j/Localized.rsrc).

— ◊ —

A Flick of the Finger for Faster File Name Viewing

Here's another small tip that's sometimes useful as far as file names are concerned. If
you can't see the whole name of a file, and you don't want to wait for the yellow name
thingie to appear, move the cursor over the file name and press Option. The name will
appear instantly. Unfortunately, this works only if the window that the file is in is
activated (or, if the file is on the desktop, if no folder window is activated).

Lucas Mathis

Figure 15.5 illustrates this tip.

Figure 15.5
A long file name before pressing the Option key (top) and after (bottom).

— ◊ —

How to Shove a Document Down a Dock Icon's Throat

If you can't drag a document onto an application in the Dock because it doesn't accept
the file type/extension, press Command+Option while dragging the file to the application in the Dock to force the application to open the file.

Lucas Mathis

*I didn't know this until Lucas submitted it. It works but don't forget the warning about this
in Chapter 8: "But be careful—not all programs can open all document types. For example, if
you try to open a JPEG graphics file with Microsoft Excel (a spreadsheet), you'll end up with
a screen covered with garbage, as shown in Figure 8.13."*

15

— ◊ —

Trash in the Toolbar

What if you want to make an alias of the Trash, say, to put it onto your desktop? Seems like you can't. Well, you can make an alias of the .Trash folder in your home folder, then rename it something without a dot *(period)* at the beginning of the name and unset the invisible bit. Now you've got an alias to your home Trash (which doesn't contain *all* items that can possibly be in your Trash).

Unfortunately, that's no good, because if the Trash is empty, Mac OS X will remove the .Trash file, and you won't be able to drag files onto your alias.

You can't drag the Trash icon out of your Dock, either, but you *can* drag the little Trash icon in the Trash window out of its title bar.

Unfortunately, you can't drag that one onto the desktop either, only into the Finder window toolbar. Oh well. . . better than nothing, I guess. And you can still use third-party programs to get the desktop Trash back (not that the one in the Dock wasn't more useful anyway, I just wanted to figure out if it was possible to do it).

Lucas Mathis

Several programs can give you a Trash icon on the desktop. The one I'm using, of course, is DragThing, but there must be half a dozen others that offer this as a feature. I've also dragged a Trash to my toolbar, as shown in Figure 15.6.

Figure 15.6
How to put a Trash icon in your toolbar.

— ◊ —

Application Switching in Reverse

In the Dock, I'm sure everyone is familiar with using Command+Tab to move left to right through the Dock and the running applications.

But if you continue to hold the Command key down, and press Shift, the selector moves from right to left.

Blair Anderson

— ◊ —

Faster Way to Get to Your Invisible Folders

If you press Command+~ while a Finder window is active, you'll get a drop-down box that will allow you to enter a directory further down in the hierarchy. If you want to go more than one level down, you need to provide a full path from your starting point.

This is a great way to enter invisible folders without having to enable viewing them. Just go to the volumes and try to enter "/etc" or "/bin".

David Muszynski

Well what do you know! I showed you this (Go to Folder) in Chapter 3, but neglected to mention David's observation, which is that this may be the easiest way to make invisible folders visible (if you know their name and where they are on your hard disk). Figure 15.7 illustrates the process.

— ◊ —

The Hugely Handy "Hard-Disk-Icon-in-Dock" Trick

The handiest navigation tool I've found yet is to drag the hard drive into the documents section of the Dock. From there I can navigate the entire hard drive, five levels deep, with a Control+click (or click and hold) on the Docked icon.

Kem Tekinay

— ◊ —

Like Auto-Hide for Your Dock, Only Faster

Here's how to make your Dock pop up faster (assuming you have auto-hide of the Dock turned on).

Size the Dock from the Dock, not in Dock preferences. Place the cursor over the vertical separator between the applications section and the folders/Trash section. Hold the mouse button down, and as you move the mouse up and down, the Dock will grown and shrink in size.

15

Figure 15.7
David's way to make an *invisible* folder visible.

Now here's the tip: If you hold down the Option key when sizing, the Dock will grow
and shrink only to sizes where the icons appear in a standard size, such as 16×16 or
32×32. This prevents the screen imaging system from having to scale the icons and
the Dock will pop up and down faster.

Rusty Little

Another cool one I didn't know. Thanks, Rusty!

— ◊ —

Little Icons Are a Drag? NOT!

You can drag a file by using the little icon in the title bar of a window. It's very cool, you don't have to go back to the Finder and drag it. You work with your file, you save it, and then, for example, you need to send it to a server: You just have to drag the icon from the title bar to your FTP application.

Olivier Lebra

Oh yeah. I use that trick all the time. That little icon even has a name—it's called a "proxy." I drag proxies out of documents and folders all the time. Give it a try and try to remember it's there. It's quite useful if you remember to use it.

Commandeer These Three Command+Tab Shortcuts

I discovered that there are a couple of extensions to the Command+Tab shortcut.

You can quit a program by Command+Tabbing to it in the Dock, and, without letting go of Command, pressing Q. This is especially helpful for quitting programs in the background.

Similarly, you can Command+Tab to a program that is in the foreground, and temporarily hiding it. To accomplish this, do the same as in the preceding paragraph, but instead press H. When you let go of Command, the program will reappear. This is really nice for checking on something behind a big window.

Andrew Dunning

A Plethora of Pithy Finder Tips

Tips, tips, and more tips:

■ Command+drag to rearrange system menus or remove a system menu (by dragging it off the menu bar while holding down the Command key).

■ You can add Airport Status, Battery, Sound Volume, Displays, PPP, and PPPoE from their system preference panes.

■ You can manually add items to the menu by dragging them from /System/Library/CoreServices/Menu Extras.

■ Columns for Finder column view are resizable. Use the widget at the bottom of the column dividers. Hold down Option to resize just one column. Double-click the resize widget to auto-size the columns to fit the longest file name (and hold down Option while double-clicking to auto-resize only one column).

15

Cool! That's a new one for me (the double-clicking trick). Thanks, David.

- Hide the extension for a given file with the Hide Extension checkbox in Show Info: Name & Extension. Override the per file settings with the Show All Extensions preference in Finder Preferences.

- Use copy and paste to copy items (files, folders, and so on) between different locations (one-window copying!).

- Empty Trash: Turn off the warning in Finder Preferences. Use the Option key to bypass the warning or to delete locked items.

- Choose between Computer and Home for the default location of new windows in Finder Preferences.

- Previews in column view are disabled for items on remote volumes (afp, nfs, webdav, and so on) and for files over 500KB for performance reasons. You should still be able to preview the files in Show Info's Preview pane.

- Shift+clicking the toolbar widget in the title bar will bring up the Customize Toolbar panel.

- Desktop view options (arrangement, icon size, and so on) were relocated to View|View Options (Command+J).

- You can now find the Desktop Picture selection in System Preferences.

- To view the contents of an application package, Control+click the application icon and from the contextual menu choose Show Package Contents, and a new window will open.

David Murphy

Nice job, David. And though some of these tips appeared in earlier chapters, I left everything just as David submitted it. Maybe you missed it the first time, or David's way of saying it made more sense to you. Anyway, with luck one or more of his tips will ring your chimes.

— ◊ —

Select a Window in the Dock

Here's another OS X tip that I haven't seen documented yet: Control+click or right-click on the Dock icon for any running application and you can select a particular window rather than just the program.

James Flores

Figure 15.8
Choosing a specific window is often better than just clicking an application's icon and getting whichever window was active last.

Better still, you don't even need to hold down the Control key. If you just click an application's Dock icon for about two seconds the same thing happens. It just happens quicker if you hold down Control. The effect is shown in Figure 15.8.

How to Create and Print a Text List of Items in a Folder

If you have a folder containing, say, 147 items, and you want to create a text list of the names of those items, just select in the OS X Finder all the items at once (or choose Select All), then choose Copy 147 Items from either the Edit menu or from the contextual menu. Now open any text editor or word processor (or graphics program) and choose Paste from its Edit menu. That final action won't paste the files themselves or their icons either, of course, but just their names, thus creating your text list.

Dennis Colautti

The program Print Window will print the contents of a window, but doesn't allow you to edit the items. Dennis's way does.

Applications

This section contains tips and hints for both Apple and third-party application software.

BBEdit: Smart Open Files Trick

This applies to BBEdit 6.5 (but I'm not sure if earlier versions or BBEdit Lite do it).

When you have an open file dialog box on-screen, pressing Command+A will highlight all the files in a directory, without highlighting subdirectories (or any unopenable files at all).

Aaron Lynch

A picture is worth a thousand words, so take a gander at Figure 15.9.

15

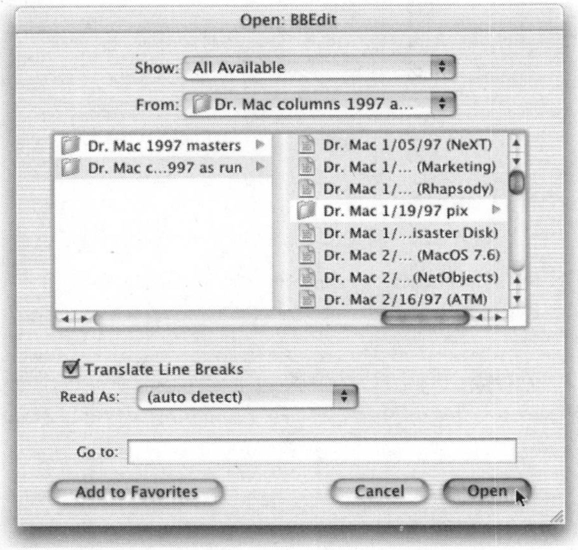

Figure 15.9
Select All (Command+A) works in BBEdit's Open File dialog box.

— ◊ —

Promoting Peace and Harmony Between iTunes X and iTunes 9

iTunes saves your playlists in a file called iTunes Library. Most people have Mac OS 9 applications and Mac OS X applications; therefore, there may be two copies of the iTunes library around, which means that changes to the library in one will not be seen in the other.

To keep the Mac OS X copy of iTunes in your Mac OS X partition and the Mac OS 9 version of iTunes in Mac OS 9 in sync, find the iTunes Library file in your Mac OS X partition (most likely in the iTunes Music folder in the Documents folder in your Home directory) and replace it with an alias to the iTunes Library on your Mac OS 9 partition.

Now when you change a playlist, add a new one, or add import new songs in either version of iTunes, both versions will reflect the change.

Sylvain F. Milet, Ph.D.

I actually went a step further. My main iTunes Music folder is in the Documents folder on my OS 9 hard disk (Number Nine). Because it had all my "stuff" in it anyway, I trashed the Documents folder in my Home directory and replaced it with an alias of the Documents folder on Number Nine. Now, both versions of iTunes use the same songs and song lists, and I have only one Documents folder to deal with.

— ◊ —

Another LaunchBar Lover

I recently discovered an extremely useful utility for OS X: LaunchBar. LaunchBar pops up when you press Command+spacebar from any application and allows you to open applications, directories, files, and bookmarks by typing their names, part of their names, or even their initials.

You select which directories you want LaunchBar to index and a combination of the types of items that should be considered within that directory (such as files, directories, and/or applications). You can even select sets of relevant file types within a particular directory by using either default configurations such as "sounds," "Office documents," "movies," and so on, or by defining your own sets of file types. LaunchBar's default behavior is to recursively index all specified directories, but this can be turned off for any given directory. LaunchBar can also parse HTML documents and extract URLs and email addresses. Thus, from the LaunchBar, you can open any of your bookmarks or start a new email to a friend.

LaunchBar has a couple of other useful features. By pressing Command+Return, a selected item is displayed in the Finder. Drag and drop is also supported if you want to open a file in an application selected in LaunchBar. Finally, LaunchBar allows you to navigate the file system by using the arrow keys. You can press right-arrow to view the contents of a selected directory or press left-arrow to view the directory containing the selected item.

All in all, a great time saver.

Michael Brunswick

LaunchBar Lover Redux

I used to be a staunch point-and-click launching-tool advocate (DragThing, DropDrawers, and so on), but in my opinion LaunchBar has them beat, hands down. I can type Command+spacebar (or Control+spacebar, or whatever you like) and LaunchBar is activated. It watches the way you abbreviate things and adjusts itself accordingly. I can type IE for Internet Explorer, OW for OmniWeb (or OMW or . . . you get the idea).

It's far superior to click-based tools in several ways:

■ It doesn't require you to set the file to show up manually (you can set LaunchBar to include any folder or file you want it to).

■ It doesn't take up any space on the screen until you invoke it.

■ It's *fast*.

15

Its catchphrase is "Keep Your Hands on the Keyboard!". When I'm typing (which is a lot of the time), I'd rather just press a key combo, type something, press Return, and get back to work than take my hands off the 'board and use the mouse to navigate through a Dock's tabs to find the thing I wanted.

It can also do lots of other stuff (app switching, folder navigation, and so on).

Marshall Pierce

I stuck these two tips in just to show that I'm not the only one who loves LaunchBar. (And there were three more submissions I didn't include, which said pretty much the same thing.)

You just gotta try LaunchBar—it's way cool.

— ◊ —

Change Button Colors in Internet Explorer

If you Control+click a button in Microsoft Internet Explorer, you can change the color scheme of all of the buttons.

Aaron Lynch

— ◊ —

A Mess o' Mail.app Tips

To display a person's picture in Mail:

1. Create a 64×64 image (TIFF or JPEG or any image type AppKit supports). The image can be bigger or smaller than 64×64, but it will be scaled to that size, so it'll look best if you get it down to 64×64 in the image editing program of your choice.

2. Name it *person's email address*.tiff. Note that it has to be suffixed with .tiff, even if it's not a TIFF file, and it will work.

3. Put it in your home directory ~/Library/Images/People/.

Now when they send you a mail, their picture shows up in upper right corner.

■ Using Option+Delete will delete a message without automatically selecting the next message.

■ Double-clicking the horizontal separator in the viewer window will automatically move the separator to the bottom. Double-clicking it again will restore it to the previous position.

■ Hold down the Command key when clicking the Mail toolbar widget to toggle between Icons & Text, Icons, and Text Only toolbars.

- You can rearrange toolbar items in Mail (or any other Cocoa apps) by holding down the Command key and dragging them around (or off the toolbar to remove them).

- To change the side of the window that the mailboxes drawer comes out from, simple drag a message towards the side of the window where you want the drawer to appear. Mail will remember this preference after you quit.

- When the horizontal separator is at the bottom of the viewer window, any messages you click on will not render and will not modify the unread state. This makes it easier to transfer or delete messages more quickly. Additionally, you can open a message from this view by double-clicking it (which presents a user interface more like Claris Emailer's, which some people prefer).

- Command+3 will copy the font style of the selected text; Command+4 will apply this style to text you select. (This actually works for all Cocoa apps, not just mail.)

- You can right-justify a signature, even though the Format menu is disabled while the signature editor is open. The trick is to create the signature in TextEdit, using the Right-Justify command in the Format|Text submenu, then copy the text and paste it into Mail's signature editor. It will remain right-justified. (Resist the temptation to apply other fancy Cocoa formatting features in TextEdit, such as ligatures or tabs. They are not supported by the text-enriched format that Mail sends, so they will get lost in transmission anyway.)

David Murphy

I'm glad David chose to submit those, because I didn't talk much about Mail (mostly because I don't use Mail—I am a satisfied Entourage user). And frankly, I don't think I knew a single one of his tips before.

— ◊ —

A Use for Classic Sherlock!

Sherlock under Mac OS X won't necessarily report the true location of files, especially if they're in hidden folders. For example, go to the Login screen, take a screenshot, then log in as your usual username. Do a Sherlock search for "Picture 1", and it should not show the file at all. If you use a Custom search for an invisible file with such a name, it will report it as being in a folder /Desktop/. However, there is no such folder.

However, a Classic Sherlock search for the same file will properly report /private/var/root/Desktop/ as the location of the Picture file. Admin users can then use the Finder's Go To Folder to get to the contents of that folder.

So, Classic Sherlock still has its uses, especially for admin and power users.

Sean McNamara

Another great tip and another one I didn't know. Nicely done, Sean.

15

— ◊ —

PTHPasteboard is Fantabulicious

Part of the reason that I spend most of my computing time in OS X, as opposed to OS 9 is a fantabulicious piece of freeware, called PTHPasteboard, developed by PTH Consulting. You can link to a download from the book's companion Web site **www.boblevitus.com/xfiles.html**.

I can't understand why Apple hasn't implemented this program's functionality into any of its operating systems. When an item is copied to the clipboard, PTHPasteboard copies it simultaneously to its *pasteboard*, which can store a number (default number is 20) of items. Then, you can—via either a menu bar icon or the Services submenu in any Cocoa application—choose which item you wish to paste into, say an AppleWorks document or Web browser address field.

In putting together this message, I copied your email address, your suggested subject line, and my desired inscription from your own Web page, one after another, without leaving the page. Then, when I saw that I had copied all that was needed, I switched to my Yahoo! Compose E-Mail page, and used PTHPasteboard to paste the afore-mentioned three items into the address field, the subject field, and the message field, respectively.

Dennis Colautti

I like it a lot, too. It's mentioned and pictured in Chapters 9 (Figure 9.46) and 14 (Figure 14.95), and, of course, there is a link on my Web site.

— ◊ —

View Microsoft Word DOC Files without Microsoft Word

Personally, I don't use Word, but lots of people send me Word-created DOC files. Now there's a freeware program available to convert them into PDFs. Get DOCtor from Stone Design at **www.stone.com**.

If you also own Stone Design's PStill, you're done. If not, you'll also need MacGhostView at **www.kiffe.com/macghostview.html**.

Just drop the PS file that DOCtor creates onto MacGhostView's macps2pdf_osx-application or Stone Design's PStill.

Lucas Mathis

You will find a link to DOCtor in the Bonus Round folder on the Web site.

Classic

This section covers tips, hints, tricks, and advice for using the Classic environment.

David Murphy

QuickLaunch Classic from the Dock

If you want a quick-launch icon for Classic in your Dock, you have one of two options:

- Open the /System/Library/CoreServices/ directory and drag the Classic Startup icon to the Dock.

- While Classic is loading, drag the Classic Startup icon from its default location to another part of the Dock. When it's finished loading, it will quit, but the icon will remain on the Dock.

Sean McNamara

A similar effect can be achieved with the freeware dockling Classic?, which has the added advantage of glowing green when Classic is running.

— ◊ —

Sharing IE Bookmarks, History, and Download History Between OS 9 and OS X

You can share bookmarks, history, and download history between Mac OS X Internet Explorer and the OS 9 version by using aliases of those Explorer files. You can choose which is the original depending on whether you already have some preferences in Classic/OS 9 Internet Explorer. If you do, you'll want to make aliases to the files in your /System Folder/Preferences/Explorer folder and place them in the Preferences folder in the Library folder in your Home directory. You can't make an alias to the Explorer preferences folder itself, but you can use aliases to some of the items in the folder.

Unfortunately, you can't share all the "application preferences" (such as AutoFill profile, location and size of cache, and so on, as defined in the Preferences dialog) as these preferences now seem to be stored in the com.apple.internetconfig.plist file in the user's preferences folder under OS X.

Sean McNamara

— ◊ —

15

Speeding the Sluggish Classic Startup

This is a modification of an old OS 9 tip for improving the speed of startup.

Sometimes when starting Classic, at the very end of the startup procedure there is a "hang" of an indeterminate time (anywhere between two seconds upward). One cause of this: OS 9 builds an index to any folder, hard drive, or server alias (or indeed any folders) that appear anywhere in the OS 9 Apple menu. This includes those found in Favorites, Recent Folders, Recent Servers, and so on.

Removing these aliases/folders will remove the hang, and speed up Classic Launch dramatically.

Michael Kaye

Excellent advice. I knew that trick for OS 9 but never thought to apply it to Classic. And you're right—it's much faster after trimming my Apple menu in my Classic System Folder.

— ◊ —

Two OS 9 System Folders Are Better Than One

My tip may be obvious, but I reckon it is something that many users might overlook when installing OS 9.

To decrease the time waiting for the Classic Environment to boot in OS X, install two copies of Mac OS 9.*x*. Ideally you should use different partitions or separate disks to make things simple. Use one system folder for the Classic boot and the other for a regular OS 9 boot.

Edit one System folder to include only the extensions and drivers you require in Classic; this means removing stuff like USB support and multiple users. With the other System folder, you can install a "regular" system for use when booting into OS 9 alone.

The only drawback of this setup is that you will end up with two preference folders, but a simple AppleScript can resolve this problem. With a little thought and making use of startup and shutdown folders in OS 9, copies of your preference folder can be synchronized, or not, depending upon whether you want to have two sets of preferences.

Steven Massey

I pretty much said the same thing back in Chapter 6, but I thought it wouldn't hurt you to hear it again—it's more convenient to have OS 9 System folders on two volumes not only for the reasons Steven outlines here, but so you can use the Option-key-at-startup trick to choose which OS you want to boot into "on the fly."

OS X

This section is chock full of tips, hints, techniques, and advice about OS X itself. There are more troubleshooting tips in the Terminal/Unix section later in the chapter, but all of those involve Terminal; none of these do.

Troubleshooting

As far as I'm concerned, you can never know too much about troubleshooting. Fortunately, this section includes many excellent troubleshooting tips and hints, and most of them are new (i.e., not covered elsewhere).

Remembering Forgotten Preference Settings

For some reason, OS X will sometimes "forget" preferences. I had an especially hard time keeping the Login preferences that specified the applications to launch at startup.

Solution:

1. Set (again) your disappearing System Preferences.

2. Quit System Preferences.

3. Go to Home/Library/Preferences and hunt for the related preference file. Note that there may be more than one (such as com.apple.loginwindow.plist and loginwindow.plist).

4. Lock these files using the Show Info window.

Note that you will need to unlock these files to make future changes to these preferences. Also, moving these items to the Trash may also solve the problem.

Tony Silva

Or, you can make a backup copy of the preference file and replace the "bad" one with that if the forgetting happens again. That way you don't have to bother with the unlocking. That's what I've been doing (as I said in Chapter 8).

— ◊ —

Restoring a Single OS X Application from Software Restore

When you install OS X, the new great and modern OS from Apple, you want everything to work fine and dandy. And it mostly does. But, sometimes along the road things can go wrong. For instance, IE will always quit unexpectedly, or something similar may happen. You try all the normal troubleshooting steps: trashing preferences, making a new user, and so on, but to no avail.

How do you then fix this?

15

In the Classic Mac OS, I would just put in my Mac OS Install CD, and reinstall the offending application or download it from the Internet. This is not the case with any application that by default is located in the /Applications/ folder.

So what can you do?

Well, you have take out the three (or four) Restore CDs and rerun the initial restore process, which reformats your hard disk before restoring. Seems like a pretty silly thing to do, just because one application is behaving badly.

Here is the ingenious how to:

1. Create a new folder (such as /Users/Shared/mosx/ or similar).

2. Copy the disc image files on each of the software Restore CDs into this folder.

3. Now mount the image, called something like PowerBook HD Disc1.img, and the three (or four) images will be mounted as one, containing all files that come with the Mac OS X installation.

4. Now you can simply drag and drop anything that has been corrupted from this image and onto the correct directory on your HD.

Tor Hildrum

One thing I should add is that you'll need about 2GB of hard disk space to pull this off. I can attest that it works—it's a big hassle, but it works.

— ◊ —

About UFS-Formatted Disks

One small tip I learned: Do not under any circumstance choose to format your separate Mac OS X partition in UFS format: On my Cube 450 MHz with over 1GB of RAM, Mac OS X (version 10.1) performed quite poorly, every installation of software was very slow, and performance overall was pathetic. I reinstalled the exact same software on an HFS+ partition and, to my surprise, Mac OS X (version 10.1) became significantly faster, installation of software completed in reasonable amount of time (minutes versus hours "optimizing the files"), and it finally became practical.

Sylvain F. Milet, Ph.D.

— ◊ —

Create a Second Admin Account/Back Up the User Folders

If you are the admin, or the only user on your computer, create a second admin account that you log in to to install new or experimental software that you're not familiar with. I do this when installing Unix/Linux packages, like xfree or Gimp. New software can make changes to your User/Library directory, and may break some things.

I created a new admin account, installed fink, xfree windows, and Gimp, and this somehow screwed up my Terminal app. I checked the Terminal app in other user accounts and my other admin account, and it was fine. So I just deleted the admin account I made the installation on, created another one and reinstalled these packages until I got it right.

Also, back up the User folders!

You can always reinstall system software and apps from CDs or downloaded installers, but the User folders often contain preferences, important docs, and data uniquely and irreplaceably created by you.

Marc Rosete

— ◊ —

Boot into 9: That's One Way Around "Not Enough Permission"
I have found a handy workaround to the frequent "Do Not Have Permission" alerts. For example, I downloaded an update to an OS X screen saver and when I attempted to trash the older version and replace it with the new one, I got an alert indicating that I did not have permission or authority to trash the file. I proceeded to reboot from 9.2.1 and then found that I could trash the old file without any alert notice. I have been running the new update to the screen saver "Old Glory" without any problem, and the earlier version has been trashed.

This doesn't say a lot for OS X security, but at least it enables you to better manage the files.

jtorren

Yes indeed. I mentioned this in Chapter 8—sometimes booting into OS 9 to do this kind of file management is the easiest way. If you're not comfortable with the command line or file diddling applications, booting into OS 9 is always an option. Just be careful. Because OS X isn't watching over your shoulder, while you're running OS 9 you could accidentally delete something vital to OS X. Forewarned is forearmed.

— ◊ —

Tons of Tips from Apple Tech Support
I have several tips for OS X. Now, let me be honest: I work for Apple Technical support.

15

If you notice that Mac OS X is hanging on the network startup, unplug the Ethernet cable. This will speed up the time out.

If Classic boots to a white screen, go into the OS 9 System Folder and trash the Classic Support and Classic Support UI. When you relaunch Classic, it will alert you that items need to be placed in the System folder, just as it did the first time you started Classic.

There seems to be some debate as to if the prefs load on login or startup. I am of the belief that they load on startup. So when trashing the prefs from the user/library, I have better luck restarting.

If you notice that your documents or music folder or one of the other folders that are in the home group, open the home folder and make a folder and name it whatever the missing folder should be. OS X will re-create that folder, icon badge and all!

What kills what? Here is a short list of what will happen if you kill certain items in TOP or Process Viewer:

- *Finder*—This is obvious. Killing this will cause the Finder to relaunch.
- *Loginwidow*—Killing this will cause the system to force quit everything and return to the login window.
- *Trubluenviroment*—This is Classic. More accurately, this is the application that runs Classic.

As a little note, you may want to use kill with caution if you have work that is unsaved.

Greg Freeman

Great stuff. Thanks, Greg. Apple's lucky to have you!

— ◊ —

Calibrate Your Screen for a Better Look
Aqua can sometimes seem very low on contrast, which makes it hard to easily discern stuff on your screen. The solution? Calibrate your screen. System Preferences|Displays|Color|Calibrate. A well-calibrated monitor can make a world of difference.

Lucas Mathis

— ◊ —

Networking & Connectivity
Here are some tips on networking and connecting to other computers.

To Connect to an NT Server

Select Go|Connect To Server. Type "smb://your_NT_username@server_name/ share_name" then click Connect.

At this time, you will be at an NT log in screen and will need to enter your NT domain name and password.

One odd observation: When running a program in Classic, the NT shares are not available.

Kathy Holton

My tech editor Brian Little, who actually knows a thing or two about NT, says I should add:

Many NT servers requires Microsoft Authentication. MS recently released their User Authentication Module for OS X. Get it at:

www.microsoft.com/mac/products/win2ksfm/default.asp

It's quite helpful on college campuses (he says, speaking from experience), where the networking people may not know where to find Microsoft's Mac stuff. Also, if your site runs Win2K servers with IP services on (which they normally are), from the Finder use Go|Connect To Server and type the server's DNS name or IP address. I can connect to our 2KB server just by typing "louise" in the dialog. Pretty swank, really.

Error –37? Blame Long File Names

Ever tried to copy files from your Mac running OS X over AppleTalk to a Mac running OS 9 and had it stop with error "-37"?

Here's the deal: Some of your files have names that are too long. While HFS+ is perfectly capable of having files with longer names and copying those files from, say, your PowerBook using FireWire target mode; copying them over a file sharing network will not work.

And here's another thing to remember: Under Mac OS X, files can be longer than they seem if you have disabled the showing of file name extensions. Some file types have really long extensions, for example text clippings—they end in ".textClipping."

(Geez, thanks for *that*, Apple! What was your argument for file name extensions again? Sharing files with people using different platforms? Yeah, I *sure* want to share my clippings with Windows users; they're so useful to them. Unfortunately, now I can't share them with other *Mac* users anymore because the long extension makes the freaking name too long! Uh. . . sorry, got a bit carried away there.)

15

So what to do? Here are three possible solutions:

- *Rename manually*—Just rename all the files that have names longer than 31 letters. (Be careful to include file name extensions if you don't show them all, and if you aren't showing them all, you probably *should* be).

- *Rename via AppleScript*—Write an AppleScript to do that task for you automatically.

    These two solutions are probably okay for most people, but they are *not* okay if your files depend on path names; say, if you're backing up your Web site. What to do then? That brings us to solution number three:

- *Stuff them*—Just drag them onto DropStuff and let it do its thang. That will also speed up the actual file transfer, because now the files are going to be smaller, especially if you're backing up lots and lots of small files.

Lucas Mathis

DropStuff is part of the StuffIt Lite package in the Bonus Round folder on the Web site.

— ◊ —

Forget AppleTalk—Share Files with TCP/IP Instead

Sometimes users have trouble setting up file sharing between just two computers where AppleTalk should work, but it sometimes does not. Here is a helpful set of settings:

- *IP address*—10.0.1.210

- *Subnet mask*—255.255.255.0

- *Router address*—10.0.1.1

These, you may notice, are the same settings as Airport; the only thing I have done is set the IP address out of the DHCP range.

On the other computer, set the IP to 10.0.1.211. Then it won't matter if AppleTalk sees the other system or not—OS X connects using TCP/IP.

Greg Freeman

Grrrr. Now he tells me. I spent an hour scouring the Internet looking for bogus IP numbers to use in a two-Mac network. Keep these numbers handy—you never know when you may need them.

I guess I should have called Apple Tech Support (where Greg works).

— ◊ —

Shut Them Out: How to Disable Guest Access

When you turn on File Sharing, Guest Access is enabled. To disallow guests from accessing it, do it the way you'd have done it in Mac OS 9. Just go to the Public Folder, Get Info (Command+I), set the privileges for Everyone to None and click Apply.

Lucas Mathis

That's cool. I never really thought about Guest Access or how to disable it. Well, now I know (and so do you).

— ◊ —

Printing

This section is about printing under OS X. A couple of these tips probably should have gone into the Terminal/Unix section, but there aren't that many printing tips so I put them here to kind of fatten up this section. (And the Terminal/Unix section is pretty fat already.)

Printing on a PostScript AppleTalk Printer from the Command Line

So you've installed OS X and decided to explore what's "underneath the hood" by opening a Terminal window to take a look at what's there. You've found or created an interesting text file (say, MyFile) and decide you'd like to print it. Sure, you could go back to the desktop and print the file from there, but is there a way to print it from the command line?

I've been a Mac user for over a decade and have never owned anything other than a Mac (plus one Mac clone), but have used many other operating systems as well. Since I first used a command-line interface, I wished I could do the same on the Mac. It's finally available, so it'd also be nice to be able to print from there as well. Here are a few tips for printing from a command prompt.

Let's say you have a PostScript AppleTalk printer somewhere on your network. You want to send your text file to the printer, but it needs to be in PostScript format. What to do?

(Before we begin, remember that everything you type at the Unix command prompt is case sensitive. Pay close attention to case when you're typing!)

Well, you could use a Unix utility called **enscript** to convert your file to PostScript and send it to a printer. If you were on a managed Unix system somewhere else, the easiest way to do this with **enscript** would be to just type the command:

```
enscript -P printername filename
```

15

replacing *printername* with the name of your printer, and *filename* with the name of the file you want to print. Well, that's easy enough.

But wait, what's the name of the printer? Are there any printers already defined in Unix? How do you define a printer in Unix? How exactly do you define an AppleTalk printer in Mac OS X Unix?

Fortunately, you don't have to figure any of this out right now. Instead, Apple has provided some utilities to help you out.

First, you can type in the command:

```
Atlookup
```

Wait a few seconds, and this command will provide you with a list of all the AppleTalk devices it can find, including your AppleTalk printer (of course, it has to be turned on and connected to the network). For more details on other things you can do with this command, you can use the **man** command to get help:

```
man atlookup
```

If you've never seen output from **man** before, this may be a frightening experience, but there's a lot of information there. Use the spacebar to page through the command description. Don't worry at this point about anything cryptic-looking; just glance at it and move on. You should be able to tell pretty easily which line describes your printer. It should look something like this:

```
ff00.5e.84 HP LaserJet 5MP:LaserJet 5P
```

It so happens that "HP LaserJet 5MP" is the name of this printer, and that's what you needed to know.

Unfortunately, that won't work with the **enscript** command because this printer is not defined in a way that is compatible with **enscript**.

Fortunately, there's another utility that will send the output from **enscript** to an AppleTalk printer: **atprint**. Use **man** to find out more about it:

```
man atprint
```

This will tell you how to use the information displayed by **atlookup** in conjunction with **atprint**, including an example at the bottom.

Now, **enscript** will convert your text file (remember, we're calling it MyFile) to PostScript, but you need to send it to **atprint** and let **atprint** send it to the AppleTalk printer. From the Unix command prompt you can send, or "pipe," the output from one program (e.g., **enscript**) to another (e.g., **atprint**). You need to use slightly different syntax with **enscript** to send the output to another program rather than a printer. Let's put it all together:

```
enscript -p- MyFile | atprint "HP LaserJet 5MP"
```

The **-p-** tells **enscript** to send the PostScript output through the pipe (|) to **atprint**, which in turn sends it to your AppleTalk printer without any additional actions on your part. You need the quotes around the printer name in this case, because it includes spaces. (Note: Here, if your file name includes spaces, it must also be enclosed in quotes. This becomes trickier with the upcoming examples, so to keep things simple, we will assume file names without spaces.)

But wait, there's more!

This is nice, but it's perhaps a bit long and difficult to remember. Solution? Make an alias for the whole line where the file name can be variable.

To define your own aliases, you need to create a file with a specific name (aliases.mine) in a specific directory (Library/init/tcsh under your home directory). If the directory (folder) doesn't already exist, you can create it in the Finder, or you can easily do it from your command line:

```
cd mkdir -p Library/init/tcsh
```

The **cd** takes you back to your home directory from wherever you happened to be. The command **mkdir -p Library/init/tcsh** will create the tcsh directory, plus Library and init if they don't already exist.

There, create a text file (pure text in Unix format—no RTF formatting or anything other than text) called aliases.mine, and put a line in it to define your alias (let's call it hpprint) that looks like this (with your own alias name and printer name instead of hpprint and HP LaserJet 5MP):

```
alias hpprint 'enscript -p- \!* | atprint "HP LaserJet 5MP"'
```

To enable that alias for use right now, **source** the file:

```
source aliases.mine
```

15

(You won't have to do this again; from now on, when you start a new Terminal window, this alias will be ready to use. The startup procedures for a Terminal window will look for alias definitions in this particular file in this subdirectory in your home directory. And remember—it's all case sensitive!)

Let's say that MyFile is in your home directory. Go back to your home directory and print it using the new alias:

```
cd hpprint MyFile
```

Voila! If all has gone well up to this point, MyFile should be printing on your printer.

But wait, there's more!

Not only can you use this alias to print files; you can also use it to print output from commands, by "piping" the command output to your alias. For example, let's say you want to print a list of file and directory names in your current directory. You can use the **ls** command with appropriate options:

```
ls -ald .* *
```

Pipe that to hpprint, and it will print on the printer instead of to the screen:

```
ls -ald .* * | hpprint
```

Finally, the **enscript** command also includes many options for formatting other than just text up and down the page. For example, the set of options **-2Gr** tells **enscript** to format the text in two columns, with a slightly fancier appearance, rotated on the page (landscape). The result is essentially two pages of text printed side by side on a single page, in an appropriately smaller font. For example:

```
enscript -2Gr -p- MyFile | atprint "HP LaserJet 5MP"
```

There are many other printing options as well. Use

```
man enscript
```

to learn more about them. And you can create a different alias for each different style of printing by following the basic directions given earlier in this section.

One word of warning—this all becomes a little more complicated if your file name has spaces in it; these details are not covered here!

Have fun!

Dave Roschke

Whew. I couldn't try all that because I don't have a networked PostScript printer handy, but I did read the man pages and it looks like Dave is spot-on.

— ◊ —

Printing the Problematic PDF

I have an OS X tip for you that involves printing problematic PDF documents, and I'd just love to get a free copy of your new book when it comes out.

I was trying to print Apple's *Understanding Using NetInfo.pdf* to do some studying, and the printer kept balking at printing page 10 (the 61 other pages printed fine). I have no idea why this happened, but I've seen many problems in the past when trying to print PDF documents, so I'm not really shocked by this (except for the fact that this is a crucial doc for many Mac OS X admins).

I tried *a lot* of different tricks to get this page to print: Acrobat Reader, Preview, Acrobat Reader in Classic, Acrobat Reader under OS 9, exporting from Preview to a TIFF/JPEG/PICT then opening it in a graphics app, and so on. The only thing that I found to work at all was this:

1. Open the PDF in Preview.

2. Go to page 10 (the page that wouldn't print) and export page 10 as a TIFF file. (By default, it will be called Page 10.)

3. Open the TIF file in Preview.

4. Select Print, then click Preview (in Preview).

5. Save the Page 10 print preview as a PDF. (It's now named, by default, Preview of Page10.)

6. Open the new PDF in Preview.

7. Print normally.

The end result is not quite as sharp a printout as all the rest of the pages, and this solution is pretty convoluted, I know, but it's the only thing I tried that worked.

I've seen PDF files before that I couldn't print at all under OS 9, and I look forward to seeing if this trick will work the next time I come across a user that has a problem printing a PDF.

Also, it still took longer than usual for the printer to deal with this print job, even though it was just one page. If you've got a better way to get this to work, please let me know!

James Flores

15

Nope. I don't. But if I ever run across a recalcitrant PDF, now I have a clue what to try. Thanks, James. Your book is in the mail.

— ◊ —

OS 9 PPD Files: We're Not Dead Yet!

Did you know you could use OS 9 PPD (PostScript Printer Description) files in OS X?

I am running a PostScript RIP on my server and can print to a Stylus Color 900 without waiting for EPSON to release drivers. All you have to do is open this path while in OS 9 or as root in OS X:

```
/System:Library:Printers:PPDs:Contents:Resources:English.lproj
```

And drop your PPD from OS 9 (System Folder/Extensions/Printer Descriptions) into it. Then, when you configure a new PostScript printer, it will automatically select the PPD you put in there (as long as it matches your printer).

This is very cool if you have a PostScript printer (or RIP) that is not directly supported by OS X.

Scot Ohl

I wish I knew that before I sold my old LaserJet. On second thought, maybe it's better this way—I replaced it with a killer Epson that has OS X support out of the box. No PostScript, but I find I don't need it much anymore, anyway. I just print from a PDF, which works great.

— ◊ —

Printing Files from the Finder

You can't print files from the Finder anymore. You can't drag them to the Print Center's icon either (at least I couldn't). But, I thought, you can still do it using AppleScript. Unfortunately, although the Finder Dictionary had a "print"-command, I could not get it to work.

So, here's a workaround. Don't tell the Finder; go directly to the program:

```
on open my_files
 ignoring application responses — so we don't get a timeout
   tell application "Microsoft Word" to print my_files
 end ignoring
end open
```

Create a script like this for each program you might want to print with and save these scripts as "Print using Word" or whatever program you're using. You could probably even check for the type/creator code or file name extension and send them to the correct program if you really wanted to. That could look something like this:

```
on open files_to_change
    repeat with a_file in files_to_change
        tell application "Finder"
            set my_creator to the creator type of a_file
            set my_type to the file type of a_file
            set my_extension to the name extension of a_file
        end tell
        ignoring application responses
            if my_creator is "MSWD" or my_extension is "doc" then
                tell application "Microsoft Word"
                    activate
                    print a_file
                end tell
            else if my_creator is "BOBO" or my_extension is "cwk" then
                tell application "AppleWorks 6"
                    activate
                    print a_file
                end tell
            else if my_type is "JPEG" or my_extension is "jpg" then
                tell application "GraphicConverter"
                    activate
                    print a_file
                end tell
            else if my_extension is "html" or my_extension is "htm" then
                tell application "iCab"
                    Activate
                    print a_file
                end tell
            else
                tell application "BBEdit 6.5"
                    activate
                    print a_file
                end tell
            end if
        end ignoring
    end repeat
end open
```

Now paste some nice printer picture on it and put it into your Dock or toolbar or wherever you want. Of course, if you want to, you can also print files using another program than they were intended to, or you can process files before printing them—

15

DOCtoring DOC files, for example, and sending them directly to the printer using the Terminal.

Isn't AppleScript great?

Lucas Mathis

Indeed it is. But if it were easier to use, came with more documentation, and any type of debugger whatsoever, it would be a lot greater.

Geeky Stuff

OK, if the last couple of tips weren't geeky enough, this last section is all geeky, all the time.

Terminal/Unix

This section is where you'll find the hardest of hardcore Terminal/Unix tips and hints.

Instant Dock Access to Removable Drives

If you want an item in your Dock that lists all removable drives (and all partitions except for the main one), launch Terminal and type:

```
ln -s /Volumes My_Volumes
```

Now go back to the Finder and drag the file /MyVolumes onto the Dock. Voilá. Personally, I think this is much more useful than showing them on the desktop, because they're always visible if you do it that way.

Lucas Mathis

That's kind of cool. I wondered how you might do that. Now I know!

A Bunch o' Terminal Tips and Tricks

Tip 1:—This is a short one, but very useful. Go to **fink.sourceforge.net** and download and install fink. This is a port of the debian dpkg manager which makes it *much* easier to do things that would otherwise be quite challenging, like compiling, configuring, and installing the Xfree86 X11 system. Fink can install all sorts of things just with the simple "fink install packagename" syntax. For instance, you can install the postcript manager/viewer Ghostscript by typing "fink install ghostscript". It will download the source, configure the build options for your computer, compile the package, and install it. Simple.

Tip 2:—Set the prompt in the Terminal. Me, I don't like seeing [localhost: ~] wyvern% as my host. I'd rather see my computer name, newton, instead of localhost. If you go and set your hostname in /etc/hostconfig, that won't do the trick. What you need to do is make a file called .tcshrc (with the period at the beginning) in your home directory (~). Here's how to do it. Open up a Terminal window and type "pico .tcshrc". Then, enter in "set prompt='[*newton*:%~] wyvern%'".

Make *newton* whatever you want. It's just the name of the computer. The %~ shows the current directory (in the tcsh shell, at least. Other shells have other syntaxes.) The space after the final % makes it so that when you type commands, they won't be squinched up to the prompt. When you have finished typing that, press Control+O to write the file (some prompts may appear at the bottom of the screen; watch there for any confirmation requests, such as asking you to press Y or Return) and then press Control+X to exit pico and get back to the prompt. Open a new Terminal window to see the changes.

Tip 3:—When you Control+click on an app in the Dock, you get a menu that includes Quit. However, if an app has frozen, Quit often won't work. You can press Option while the menu is opened to switch that to Force Quit. If that doesn't work, work fast. Though the underlying kernel and other systems are almost impenetrable, the user interface is *not*. Open up a Terminal window and type "ps -aucx | grep *application_name*". That's a pipe character, not a lowercase L or uppercase I (it's right below the delete key). It means "feed the output of ps into grep." Grep is the search tool in Unix systems. For instance, if the Finder has hung, type "ps -aucx | grep Finder".

This is what will come out.

```
wyvern 294 0.0 2.8 160512 33016 ?? S   1:27.93 Finder
```

The column headers of PS will not output, because they did not match the criteria that grep was looking for. They are, in order:

```
USER  PID %CPU %MEM   VSZ  RSS TT STAT   TIME COMMAND
```

In other words, the process that is owned by USER wyvern with PID (process ID) 294 is named Finder and is using 0% CPU and 2.8% MEM[ory]. The PID of 294 is the important thing. Type "kill 294" and that should kill it. It will restart and then you should be fine.

If that doesn't work, it's time to pull out the big guns. Type "kill -9 294". The -9 means "non-catchable, non-ignorable kill" in Unix parlance, which is an unavoidable, unblockable termination.

15

If that can't kill a process, it means the kill signal is being intercepted before the job manager can receive it. This usually means that your shell has been somehow messed up. Which leads us to our next tip. . .

Tip 4:—Always have SSH running (and an SSH client on another computer) logged in. Obviously this is valid only if you have more than one computer. Here's the benefit: Sometimes, especially when playing games that take up the whole screen, when an application locks up, it may not return you control of the mouse. If you don't have a shell logged in on another machine, you have to restart. You have no other choice because you cannot control the mouse to select which app you want to kill from the Command+Option+Esc (Force Quit) window, which very likely will pop up behind the game screen when you press that key combo anyway, because as I said, the underlying OS almost never goes down. If you are lucky and have two computers, you can simply type "ps –aucx" (use the "| grep" if you like) and look for the application that has frozen. Type "kill PID" (substituting for PID, of course) and you should be fine.

Marshall Pierce

Fantastic! Thanks, Marshall. That is some incredibly useful stuff and goes far beyond the techniques I talked about in Chapter 8. So now, if Chapter 8 doesn't fix you up, you have some more stuff to try—Marshall's stuff—before you throw your Mac out the window.

Generic Folders Got You Down? Read This:
Problem: When starting up Mac OS X, you have only generic folders in the Dock, and you can't launch any applications.

There could be three different culprits for this:

■ Corrupted LauncherServices preferences.

■ You don't have read access to your home folder.

■ The NetInfo database has been corrupted.

To start off, try getting into your home folder in the Finder. If you can do this, try trashing the following files:

■ ~/Library/Preferences/LSClaimedTypes

■ ~/Library/Preferences/LSSchemes

■ ~/Library/Preferences/LSApplications

Log out, and log back in.

If this doesn't solve the problem, you will have to get down and dirty with the command line. Hold down Command+S at startup to boot into single-user mode, then type this:

```
mount -uw /
ls -l /Users/
```

It should come up with a line like this:

```
drwxr-xr-x 18 tor staff 568 Oct 23 00:51 tor
```

If it doesn't, then type this:

```
sudo chown username /Users/username
exit
```

If the privileges are correct, then the culprit is probably the Netinfo database.

The fix would be this:

```
sudo mv /var/db/netinfo/local.nidb /var/db/netinfo/local.nidb_bak
sudo rm /var/db/.AppleSetupDone
exit
```

This will restart the machine and run the Apple Setup Assistant again; now just use the same short username as you were previously using, and everything should be fine and dandy.

Basically, how to trash the NetInfo database is valuable troubleshooting information. Also, knowledge of the LauncherServices (the aforementioned LS files) is valuable knowledge.

You can find more info about most of this stuff at **developer.apple.com**.

Tor Hildrum

Again, this is great stuff, and stuff I didn't know. Thanks, Tor. And thanks for reminding me—you should definitely back up your NetInfo database before a problem occurs—which will avoid having to use Tor's hints.

— ◊ —

15

Terminal Techniques That'll Make You Tingle to Your Toes

One thing about Terminal that tickles me pink is "drag-and-drop file paths"—dragging a file from any folder onto an open Terminal window types the file's absolute path. I use this feature, for example, with:

```
open -a application.name
```

and then I drag the file onto Terminal.

It also works to drag a folder onto an open Terminal window, making it very easy to **ls** or **cd** into a directory. I think this makes it easy for non-power users to get started with the perhaps confusing concept of Unix file paths. *(See Figure 15.10 for an illustration of how this works.)*

Another tip: To force network time sync, type this:

```
sudo ntpdate time.apple.com
```

And another: To create a symbolic link (soft link) filenameB to an existing file filenameA, type this:

```
ln -s filenameA filenameB
```

And another: **ls –F** shows and identifies items in a directory as directories, regular files, or executables.

And one last one: If you sleep or shut down overnight, you can use MacJanitor to do daily, weekly, and monthly housekeeping, or you can type this in Terminal:

```
sudo sh /etc/daily
sudo sh /etc/weekly
sudo sh /etc/monthly
```

Here's a tip that's not Terminal-related. To copy all the contents of a Mac OS X disc onto another disc so that everything still works, use Apple Software Restore (ASR). You can find ASR at **http://homepage.mac.com/dbhill/FileSharing.html**.

Two more things that I'm certain you've covered, but I just had to mention.

Control+U and Control+W are useful for deleting something that's been typed wrongly in Terminal.

For example, if I type:

```
open -a TextEdit readme
```

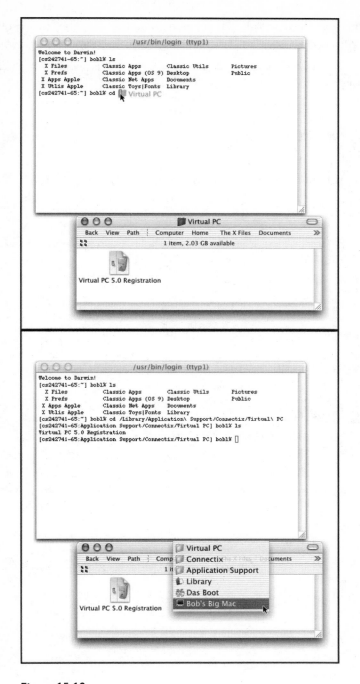

Figure 15.10
In Terminal, I typed "cd" then dragged the Virtual PC folder onto the Terminal window (top), which
changed the directory to the Virtual PC directory without my typing another keystroke (bottom).

15

without pressing Return, pressing Control+U deletes the whole line so that I can start again. And pressing Control+W deletes "readme" so that I can type another file name.

To change a file's line endings from the Mac's carriage returns to Unix line feeds, type this:

```
prompt$ perl -i.bak -1012p015e filename
```

You can use this to batch process, too.

Why would we want to do this? Well, to respond to a recent post in the x4u list, I opened an EPS file in vi. But all the lines ran together as one long line, making it impossible to read. The problem was the line endings. By changing the line endings to Unix line feeds, I could view the file in vi the way it should appear.

(By the way, just about all my tips were garnered from various lists, so you may not want to give me a book for tips I didn't come up with. Still, I wanted to share them with you.)

Did I say before that Terminal rocks? Hey, OS X rocks!

J. Thoo

You get a book. Some of those are great, and at least a couple have not been mentioned before (and the book is almost over). So thanks, J.

— ◊ —

Terminal Autocomplete Syndrome

The CLI will autocomplete file names for you. For instance, to delete a file called "ziggystardust" type "rm zi" and press Tab. The CLI will fill in the rest of the filename for you. In the event that multiple files begin with "zi", a list of them will appear, and you can continue to narrow down the list by adding characters to the command and pressing Tab. Pretty handy.

Brian Little

Brian is this book's technical editor, and since he's been such a good one I'm including his tip and sending him a free book.

— ◊ —

Ejecting a Reluctant CD or DVD

If you have a CD or DVD that is inserted, but not working or has not mounted, the command **disktool -o** will eject it.

David Cake

Bravo! I don't think I've ever seen that one before. And it will also open the CD tray when there's no CD in it, which makes it even handier. I won't forget this excellent tip—I've had it happen to me many a time, and restarting while holding down the mouse button, which was my cure, isn't a particularly elegant solution. This one is. Thanks, David.

— ◊ —

Who You Callin' a Fink?

Here is a tip about using Unix software under Mac OS X. There is a software package called fink (**http://fink.sourceforge.net**) that is ultimately invaluable if you want to take advantage of all those wonderful Unix applications and utilities.

If you've ever used Red Hat Linux, Debian Linux, or even FreeBSD, they all have a software package management system that allows you to install and uninstall apps and utilities on demand over the Internet. They will download, configure, and compile automatically. Fink gives this ability to Mac OS X. It installs in its own directory tree, so that nothing in your Mac OS X structure gets overwritten or removed. I have successfully installed XFree86 (a free implementation of the X Window System), the Gimp (free Photoshop replacement), and a myriad of development tools very easily with this tool.

Ryan J. McPherson

So here's the deal. If you've got plenty of time on your hands, using stuff like fink and XFree86, and compiling Unix apps to run on OS X is a blast. But don't be fooled. If you're not a Unix guru already, you're going to spend a lot of time tinkering with this stuff before you get it to work. If you need your Mac for other things—like earning a living—you should probably, at the very least, create a second admin account to experiment on, as suggested by Marc Rosete a few pages back.

Or better still, use a second Mac (or second hard disk) for your Unix adventuring. That way if you really mess things up, you can just reformat the disk and start over.

— ◊ —

Splitting and Reconstituting Files the Unix Way

This is a cool little trick if you want to split big files into smaller parts for removable media backup, transmission over email, or multipart download posting over the Internet.

Mac OS X comes with the command line utilities **split** and **cat**. The **split** command does exactly what it is called, and **cat** concatenates files. So, let's say that you had a 180MB MPEG file that you wanted to put on a Zip disk for backup or to show another

15

friend on his computer. Of course, the file is too big. Here is how you could split it into two parts so that it could fit on two 100MB Zip disks. Open the Terminal app in OS X and type this:

```
split -b 92m
```

(Don't forget to add a space after typing "92m".) Next, drag the file you want to split into the Terminal app window (I love this feature!). The Terminal will automatically add the path and file name. Your line should look like this:

```
split -b 92m /Users/Bob/Movies/mpegfile.mpg
```

Press Enter and **split** will go to work. It will create the files in whatever directory your Terminal was pointing to (most likely your Home directory). If you want it in a specific directory or want the files named a certain way, add a space to the preceding line and type in the directory path and file name that you want, for example:

```
split -b 92m /Users/Bob/Movies/mpegfile.mpg
/Users/Bob/Movies/mpegsplitfile.mpg
```

Remember, save to a directory that you have permission to modify (anything after **/Users/Bob/**), and don't do this in root mode or the Finder won't let you delete it later (you'll have to use **sudo rm** in Terminal to do it).

In **-b 92m**, the **-b** option specifies that you will split it according to size and the **m** after **92** stands for megabytes.

This trick is especially useful for MPEG files, because all the information required to play the movie is contained within each frame. So, for example, you could split it into 10 parts and each part would be playable (not the case though for QuickTime MOV and other file types).

As far as sending over email or posting big files as multipart downloads, the person on the other side would have to be running some sort of concatenation tool to put together the file.

This leads me to my second tip—how to put the file back together.

Let's say that you have two split files (named aa and ab, respectively). Open Terminal and type "cat". Now add a space after typing "cat" and then proceed to drag and drop the two files onto the Terminal. It should look something like this:

```
cat /Users/Bob/Movies/aa /Users/Bob/Movies/ab
```

Add a space after the last file (if the Terminal has not already done that) and type in the redirection symbol ">", add a space, and then type how you would like the concatenated file named. (The redirection symbol outputs it to a file rather than just displaying it on the Terminal. This works in any terminal program.)

It should now look something like this:

```
cat /Users/Bob/Movies/aa /Users/Bob/Movies/ab > concat.mpg
```

Press Enter and the two files are combined back into one!

Fernando Gonzalez, Jr.

Wow. That's a little more complicated than using StuffIt, but if you're doing Unix, it's the Unix way. (You're probably better off with StuffIt when dealing with other Mac users, though.)

But, for what it's worth, although StuffIt may be easier to use, it won't let you watch 10 separate pieces of an MPEG file.

— ◊ —

Unix Fun with the Login Window

You can enter the following into the username space in the login window:

```
>console
```

This allows text-only interface. (Typing "exit" after logging in successfully, or Control+D at the console login prompt brings you back to GUI.)

- *>restart*—Restarts the machine
- *>power*—Shuts the machine down
- *>exit*—Quits and restarts most processes

David Murphy

No password is needed to do any of these things, but in the case of ">console", you'll end up looking at a screen with a command prompt that looks pretty much like Terminal. At that point, you'll have to provide a username and password to use the system, or use one of the other commands in the list to get out of console mode.

*These aren't as handy as starting in single-user mode to run **fsck**, but if you're adept with Unix, they're great when you want to completely avoid the GUI (Aqua interface) and use your Mac as though it were a Unix box.*

— ◊ —

15

Pico (de Gallo): Better Than vi or emacs for Editing Text

Many Unix-heads will say you need vi or emacs to do command-line text editing, but Mac users may well find pico a better alternative. There are no special keys to go into insert mode, and common commands are shown at the bottom of the screen (including the **help** command). Pico works much more like a CLI-based Mac text editor than a CLI-based convoluted text editor (such as vi and emacs).

Just type "pico *<filename>*" at the command line—if the file exists, it's opened; if it doesn't exist, pico creates an empty file with that name.

I've never had any trouble using it, whereas I've had trouble with vi even when I have detailed instructions on how to use it.

So don't believe those Unix-heads when they say vi puts hairs on your chest—they're only there because you've pulled them out of your head trying to figure out vi!

Sean McNamara

I just hate CLI editors and pico, although perhaps better than vi or emacs, is still a command-line text tool.

I almost always use BBEdit, which is 31 tons better than any command line in the world. It can even open items inside packages, and it works like the Terminal if I need it to. I'm a Mac guy. I'll use the real Mac program with scrollbars, cut/copy/paste, a menu bar—you know, a human interface.

Here. See for yourself. All three CLI editors are pictured in Figure 15.11.

The Extension Manager Lives!!!!

That's right, the Extension Manager lives as the Kernel Extension Manager in Mac OS X.

It is certainly more complicated, less friendly, and harder to access, but it's there (in a BSD incarnation).

To look at what extensions (kernel modules or kmods) are currently loaded, go into the Terminal and get yourself into root (enabling root is another trick).

After becoming root, type "kmodstat" in the Terminal.

This will give you a listing of all the current extensions (kmods) loaded in the system.

Okay, so now that you can see them, how do you load and unload them? A more important question is, "Why would you want to if Mac OS X is suppose to do it automatically?"

Figure 15.11
Pico (top), vi (middle), and emacs (bottom). Total Yuck!

Well, the answer is simple... *because you can*! Same reason people climb mountains.

Actually, I am just kidding. There are cases in Mac OS X in which it will not load a kernel extension (KEXT), and it's containing kmod for one reason or another.

For example, let's say that your Mac stopped recognizing your Airport card. You check with kmodstat and you find that it is not loading up the following airport kmod driver:

```
com.apple.driver.AppleAirPort (1.4)
```

In the kmodstat listing, it should look something like this (although the ID will be different depending on what gets loaded first and your particular configuration):

```
40 0 0xbd22000 0x10000 0xf000 com.apple.driver.AppleAirPort (1.4) <36>
```

(**40** is the ID number, **com.apple.driver.AppleAirPort** is the driver, (**1.4**) is the version, and <**36**> is pointing to another ID number in the kmodstat listing signifying a dependency).

15

Before I go into loading extensions, I should clarify some terms.

I have used the term *kernel extensions* (*kexts*) and *kernel modules* (*kmods*) through my email. I have sometimes just used the term *extensions* interchangeably to refer to the latter.

Kexts are actually bundles (similar to applications bundles APP) in that they are actually folders containing resources, but are seen by the Finder as a single file. Kexts are located in Mac OS X in /System/Library/Extensions and have one extension .kext.

It is within these kext bundles that the actual Mach-O executable code is located (that executable binary being a kmod file).

Anyhow, for example, to load the Airport Card driver, **su** yourself to root in the Terminal and type "kextload " (don't forget to add a space after **kextload**). Now, in the Finder, go to this path: System/Library/Extensions/. Look for the kext file AppleAirPort.kext and drag into the Terminal window. It should look like this:

```
kextload /System/Library/Extensions/AppleAirPort.kext
```

Press Enter: It should now be loaded into the system, if it was not already.

To unload it, run **kmostat** first and find out what ID number has been assigned to it. Now, type "kmodunload −i ". Add a space after −**i** (**i** options specifies the id) and type in the ID number. It should look something like this:

```
kmodunload -i 58
```

Remember, if it has dependencies or another kmod depends on it, it might not unload. Also, remember that only user-space applications have memory protection. All kernel extensions reside within the same memory space, so if you mess with them or load a badly written kernel extension, it might cause you to have a kernel panic and bring down the entire system.

Fernando Gonzalez, Jr.

I admit. I didn't know most of that before. Don't know if it'll ever do me any good, but at least now I know where to find it. Well written, too. Thanks, Fernando.

— ◊ —

Terminal—We Don't Need No Stinkin' Terminal
There are two editors that contain most of the functionality of the Terminal window, being able to access the BSD layer of OS X: BBEdit 6.5 and NEdit 5.

In both programs, you can issue Terminal commands from an empty text-editing window. Type in the same text commands you'd type in Terminal; this text can be sent to OS X's BSD subsystem to execute a command.

For example, the Unix command to get a long directory listing is **ls -la**. Simply type the preceding text in a BBEdit or NEdit window.

In BBEdit, choose the **#!...Run** command. The output of the command is shown in a new document window. In NEdit, the output is appended to the command itself. This way of interacting with the BSD layer is in some ways better than the Terminal, because the command and output (at least in BBEdit's case) are in separate windows. You can easily correct errors and save every result in a text document. BBEdit even allows you to Command+drag a Finder folder or file (except a clipping) and the path to that folder or file will be entered. (This is the same as dragging a file into a Terminal window.)

In NEdit, choose Shell|Execute Command Line (or press the numeric keypad Enter key).

(Both approaches [output in a new window versus appended to the original window] have their advantages and disadvantages. BBEdit requires you to write a complete shell script. NEdit will gladly accept any text as Unix commands and try to execute it.)

Feel free to separate BBEdit/NEdit items, because most Mac users probably would not be interested in NEdit. However, I feel that next to BBEdit, NEdit is simply the most Mac-like text editor available under Unix.

You can get more information on NEdit at **www.nedit.org.** (NEdit is released under the GPL license.) NEdit requires X-Windows and the Motif or LessTif widget libraries.

Alex Morando

I included this but there are a couple of things you should know before you try it.

First, as Alex says, NEdit requires X-Windows and the Motif or LessTif widget libraries. That means you can't just download NEdit and double-click it. You need to install at least two Unix "things." So, because my rule when I'm on deadline is "no installing stuff 'til it's done," I wasn't able to try his instructions for NEdit.

Which brings me to my second thing: I couldn't get it to work the way Alex described it.

Fortunately, I'm a trained professional and I hated to throw away a perfectly good tip, just because Alex was off by a teensy bit. So I figured out why it wasn't working, and it's worth knowing.

In BBEdit, there are two things. The first is that you can't issue commands from a regular text document. You have to open a special kind of document called a "Shell Worksheet" (File|New|Shell Worksheet [(/bin/tcsh)].

15

Figure 15.12
This doesn't work.

*If you try to run **ls –la** from a regular document, you'll get an error. But if you run **ls –la** from a Shell Worksheet by choosing #! \ **Run**, you'll get the same error, as shown in Figure 15.12.*

It took a tiny bit of RTFM, but I learned that to issue a command in a Shell Worksheet you press Command+Return. That's it. It spits your long directory listing out, but not in a new window as Alex said, but right below the command, as shown in Figure 15.13.

And the moral of the story is: When in doubt, Read The Fine Manual.

— ◊ —

Several Tons of Unix from Lucas Mathis

I don't know Lucas personally, but we exchanged several emails. In the last one I told him he was only getting one book, and he could stop submitting tips if he wanted. His response was to submit the following Unix tips. Lucas submitted every tip from here to the end of this section and I want to recognize him for his gracious contributions to this effort. So, because I'm not about to put his name on the cover (though he deserves that, too), I hereby bestow upon Lucas Mathis, by the power vested in me by me, Dr. Mac's Inexorable-Raging-Thunder-Lizard-OS X-Power-User award.

(I apologize to Photoshop guru/Workshop Presenter/Writer/Editor and all around nice guy Steve Roth for ripping off his inexorable riff. I didn't make it up, but I can't think of a more appropriate name for Lucas's award.)

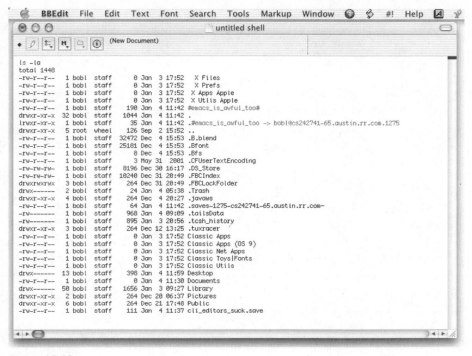

Figure 15.13
Type "ls –la" Command+Return and you'll see a long directory listing like this one.

And now, back to our regularly scheduled programming. . .

Can't Delete Folder?

If you can't delete some folder because you don't have the permission to do so, type "sudo rm –r" into your Terminal and drag the folder into the Terminal window. Then press Return, enter your root password, and it will get removed.

— ◊ —

Multiple Instances of the Same Servers in the "Connect To" Dialog Box?

If you get your own server (maybe even multiple times) in the Connect To dialog box, type this in the Terminal:

```
sudo rm /private/var/slp.regfile
```

That will fix it.

Note that this particular fix is detailed in Chapter 11, but in a slightly different fashion. I showed you the cd command because it was a chapter on Unix, and I wanted to explain what

15

each part of the command was doing. Go back and take a look—you'll see that it is merely a slightly different way of doing the same thing Lucas describes.

Unix Downloading Made Easy

To download stuff, switch to the folder you want to download to (type "cd" and drag the folder into the Terminal), then type "curl –O" (that's a big O, not a zero). Now drag the URL into the Terminal. Then press Return.

Symbolic Links: Aliases Unix-Style

Some Unix programs won't recognize Mac alias files. Instead, you can make symbolic links. How do you do that? Open the Terminal and type "cd". Then, drag the folder that you want the symbolic link to appear in onto the Terminal. Press Return and then type "ln –s". Drag the file you want to make the alias (symbolic link) of to the Terminal. Enter its name, press Return, and voilá—you've got a file that looks like an alias, but stores only the path to the original file.

This is very useful for programs like Apache, which won't recognize Mac-style alias files.

If you intend to use your Mac as a Web server, you might want to memorize this. I expect that at some point the Finder will make SymLinks as easily as it now makes Mac aliases. But until then, that's how you make a symbolic link. And trust me, if you're going to play with Unix stuff, you'll definitely want to remember this.

Is man –k Apropos?

Other Unix's have a command called **apropos**. With **apropos**, you can find commands related to a word you enter. MacOS X doesn't have **apropos**, but it does have something equal. Just use **man -k** and some word, for example, **man -k link** and you'll get a list of commands related to that word.

A related command is **whatis**. If you have a command and don't know what it does, but you don't want to wade through the whole man page, use **whatis command**.

Force Unmount—Like Force Quit, But Handier

Sometimes, you can't eject a CD or a mounted image file, even though you've made sure that everything on them is closed. You could restart your Mac to unmount everything, but then you'd have to restart all your apps, and that is annoying if you just want to swap CDs or make some mounted image go away. Try this: Make sure all apps are closed and documents saved, then open Terminal and type this:

```
sudo umount -f
```

Then drag the volume you want to unmount onto the Terminal, press Return, and enter your password.

Bravo. I needed that yesterday and knew I had seen it somewhere. Thanks for that one. I made a clipping of it and dragged it onto Znippetizer-X, a database for clippings I just started using and it's great for this. Every time I see a tip or hint I want to be able to recall someday, I select it, drag it onto the Znippetizer-X icon (a floating window that's always available), and give it a name. Check it out yourself—it's in the Bonus Round folder on this book's Web site.

— ◊ —

More Cool Unix Stuff

The **last** command shows you your last sessions. You can type "last some_other_username" to see somebody else's sessions:

```
lkm    console localhost    Fri Nov 23 21:37 still logged in
reboot  ~               Fri Nov 23 21:37
lkm    console localhost    Fri Nov 23 21:29 - crash (00:07)
```

Hmm. . . looks like MacOS X *can* crash after all.

You can see from when and for how long you were using your computer. If you have a number and a plus at the shutdown (or crash) time, it's the amount of days, like this:

```
lkm    ttyp2            Sat Nov 17 15:12 - shutdown (4+01:00)
```

Note that the last number isn't the time you stopped the session, but the time you spent in the session, so that the following line, for example, means that your session's duration was less than a minute, not that it was until 0:00:

```
lkm    ttyp2            Sun Nov 25 16:16 - 16:16 (00:00)
```

The number second to last is the time your session stopped, but it doesn't always show up, only if you've been using a Terminal window. If your Mac crashed, or you shut it down, there'll be "crash" or "shutdown" respectively instead of the time the session stopped.

The **ttyp** means that you have had some Terminal windows open. They count as their own sessions, so you can have overlapping sessions. If you have reboots in a session, it shows up on multiple lines.

15

You can use curl to download things. Just type "curl –O" and the URL (you can drag an URL from your browser to the Terminal window if you want to) to download it. Why would you want to do this? If you don't want to keep your browser running or if your browser crashes a lot, it's more convenient. It'll download the file to the directory you're currently in, which is your home directory if you haven't done anything else in that Terminal session.

However, I recommend to install wget (either get a package or compile it yourself or use fink, which is really great, by the way [**fink.sourceforge.net**].

Type "wget –c" to get the same as described previously in curl. Here's the cool thing though: If you want to download several files, put the URLs into a text file, listed sequentially (this can, but doesn't need to, be an HTML file), then type "wget -c -i mytextfile" to get all of the URLs. Oh, by the way, if you want to reissue a command—for example, if you first typed "wget -c -i mytextfil"—just press up-arrow so you see the command again, and you can fix your mistake in the file name. Press down-arrow to see the next command (if you've pressed up before). Unfortunately it won't work without pressing up before pressing down. Without this restriction, just pressing down would be a whole lot more useful!

Quick Terminal Tip

If you're in the Terminal, you can move up and copy something. No matter where the selection is, or where you scrolled to, as soon as you paste it, you'll move down to the prompt and the text will be inserted there.

Another Quick Terminal Tip

You can quit all applications by pressing Control+C, though it's not always a good idea because you won't be able to save any changes you've made.

Yet Another Quick Terminal Tip

Type "telnet towel.blinkenlights.nl" into your Terminal. Wait. Watch. It's not really a tip, but it's fun.

I had to go try it. You should too. I was going to provide a screenshot but I don't want to spoil the fun. Just do it—it's the first (and maybe the only) Stupid Unix Trick in the book.

One More Quick Terminal Tip

Enter "pwd" to see the path to where you are. Enter "open ." to open the current folder in the Finder.

Note that there's a space between open and the period. If you forget the space, it won't work.

— ◊ —

Kill Programs Using the Dock

If you can't get the graphical Force Quit dialog box to work, but you *can* use Terminal, use this technique to kill programs. First type "top | grep *MyProgram*", where *MyProgram* must be part of the name of the program you want to force quit (it's case-sensitive). You'll get something like this:

```
[localhost:~] lkm% top | grep Sweet
 7933 SweetMail  0.0% 25:59.96 7 135 250 21.6M 10.7M 26.4M 84.9M
```

The | is a pipe, which inputs the output of the first command into the second one, hence the output of **top** gets input into **grep**, which looks for the word you entered (in this case, "Sweet"). So only the line with the word in it gets displayed.

Now press Control+C to get the prompt back, and type "kill –9 [the number at the beginning of the line]".

To kill the program, in our case, you'd type "kill -9 7933".

— ◊ —

Wouldn't It Be renice (to Make a Program Run Faster)?

If a particular application is running too slow, use the **renice** command to give it more priority from the CPU. For example, say, SweetMail is running way too slow (which it isn't, but let's just assume it is for a second. I don't have Virtual PC 5 yet, but I heard it was really slow, so you might want to try this on it).

Type "top | grep SweetMail". You'll get something like this:

```
700 SweetMail  0.0% 2:44.60 6 126 215 19.4M 8.34M 24.0M 80.1M
```

Remember (or copy) the first number (700). Now type this:

```
sudo renice [speed] [my number from above]
```

Speed is a number between 20 and –20. –20 is the fastest, 20 is the slowest possible speed.

— ◊ —

15

Fun with the Terminal

Open your Terminal and type this:

```
more /usr/share/misc/flowers
more /usr/share/misc/airport
more /usr/share/misc/birthtoken
more /usr/share/misc/ascii
more /usr/share/misc/na.phone
more /usr/share/misc/zipcodes
```

There's more. To see what else is there, type this:

```
cd /usr/share/misc/
ls
```

Lucas Mathis

If you're wondering where all that stuff is coming from, it's on your hard disk in an invisible directory called usr.

Here, see for yourself in Figure 15.14.

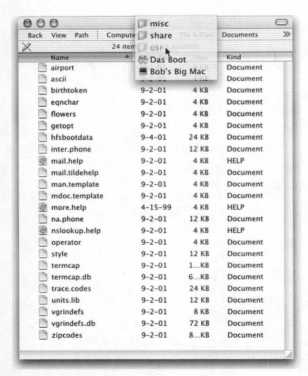

Figure 15.14
The invisible usr folder's contents.

AppleScript

Okay then, if that wasn't enough geeky code and such, here's more code for you to type, but this time they're AppleScripts.

AppleScript Menulet Lover

Well, I for one am totally in love with the AppleScript menulet. I rarely shut my TiBook down, but I often close out applications like Instant Messenger, Internet Explorer, and Entourage when I am in a non-networked location. When I first started using OS X, I would find that I'd open up IE and get distracted, and not open up Entourage or IM for a while. Adding these apps to my Login items does not serve the purpose, because I don't log out—I just close the network apps and put my Ti to sleep.

I have added a very simple AppleScript to the Script menu that activates those three programs, so I can easily open them all up as soon as I am back on a network. I saved the script as an application, with the startup screen always hidden, so I can easily run it whenever need be.

I also have a script that I downloaded somewhere that hides all open windows, and a few other little goodies that I found here and there in this menu. It isn't installed on OS X.1 by default, but it is really useful. You can download it from **www.apple.com/ applescript/macosx/script_menu/**.

By the way, I am really looking forward to the release of this book, because OS X is such new ground for me—so many of my old tricks are no longer there! As a funny aside, did you know that the related items links on the **Amazon.com** page for your book are all to Scully and Mulder X-Files merchandise?

Maia Gemmill

I love Script Menu too. I talked about it a little in Chapter 9, and you can see it in action in Figures 9.21 and 9.22.

As for the Scully and Mulder stuff, I didn't know. That's pretty funny. It says if you want to find books similar to this one, you should look in: Entertainment | Television | Shows | X-Files.

What a hoot.

— ◊ —

An Awesome Script to Replace Spring-Loaded Folders

A lot of criticism has been directed at Apple for not carrying over spring-loaded folders to Mac OS X. I find the following Apple Script (placed in the Finder toolbar) a superior approach to move multiple files/folders to a single location:

15

```
on open TheFiles
 tell application "Finder"
  activate
  try
   set MyFolder to make new folder at "Mac OS X Drive" with properties
{name:"Hold it Folder"}
  on error
   set MyFolder to "Mac OS X Drive:Hold it Folder"
  end try
  move TheFiles to MyFolder
 end tell
end open

on run
 tell application "Finder"
  activate
  set MyWindow to front Finder window
  set MyTarget to target of MyWindow
  if the folder "Mac OS X Drive:Hold it Folder" exists then
   try
    move entire contents of the folder "Mac OS X Drive:Hold it Folder" to
MyTarget
   on error
    move entire contents of the folder "Mac OS X Drive:Hold it Folder" to
MyTarget's container
   end try
   delete "Mac OS X Drive:Hold It Folder"
  else
   display dialog "No items have been selected." giving up after 2 buttons "OK"
  end if
 end tell
end run
```

After creating and saving this script as an application, place it in the Finder toolbar. Then, any files that you want to move are simply dragged onto this script. After all files to be moved have been selected, simply navigate to the destination folder and click this icon once. The source files are moved to the current path of the Finder courtesy of this script. Of course, the name and path of the temporary ("Hold it") folder is left up to the user, but basically this provides a temporary holding place for a group of files to be moved from one place to another. I think this is much better than spring-loaded folders for two reasons:

■ First, the files that you want to move to a common destination can be from various volume/folder structures.

■ Second, folder navigation with spring-loaded folders works only one way—deeper into a folder structure. Moving files from (for instance) Mac OS X Drive: The Folder to Mac OS X Drive still requires two windows to be open even if spring-loaded folders are available. With this script you should never need to open more than one window to move files from one location to another.

Frank Restly

Frank, that's a fantastic script. I mean that. I like it so much I made one for my toolbar and one for you. You'll find it in the Bonus Round folder on this book's Web site.

You can see them both in Figure 15.15.

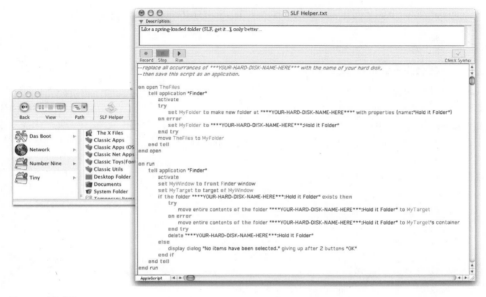

Figure 15.15
It couldn't be easier—this script is in the Bonus Round folder on this book's Web site.

*Just open the script SLF Helper.txt (SLF = spring-loaded folder), replace "***YOUR-HARD-DISK-NAME-HERE***" with the name of your hard disk, then save this script as an application. Put the script where you want it, then drag it into the toolbar. Next time you want to move or copy a file, files, or folder, give it a try. It's very, very nifty.*

This may help you think about all the little things you can do with AppleScript. Even I understand how this script worked. And even I was able to customize it enough to make it work the way I wanted it to (doh—I typed in my hard disk's name five times).

15

You have to give AppleScript a try. Download some scripts and look at them. Then customize a script someone else wrote. Start small. Don't undertake huge tasks with it. Yet. At some point (and you won't even notice it happen), you'll begin to write small scripts for yourself, or rewrite other people's scripts, or you'll even start writing big, complicated scripts.

After that you can't stop. If I ever find myself with some time on my hands, I'm going to learn how to do more with AppleScript. Speaking of which, AppleScript Studio came out just as this book went to press, and it looks interesting, if not a bit geeky for me.

One other thing: Rumor has it that Apple has heard our cries of anguish and will bring back spring-loaded folders in Mac OS X 10.2. We'll see. I hope they do. And they should just buy WindowShade X from Unsanity, too.

Anyway, give this script a shot. And thanks again for a terrific script, Frank.

Lucas Mathis Script Solution for Image Capture

There's a small problem I found with Image Capture: It doesn't set the correct file type, and unfortunately Photoshop seems to have a problem with that as it won't open any files downloaded by Image Capture. So I wrote this small AppleScript that will change the file type of files dragged on top of it to JPEG:

```
on open files_to_change
  repeat with a_file in files_to_change
    tell application "Finder" to set the file type of a_file to "JPEG"
  end repeat
end open
```

If you want to, you can also change the creator type. For example, for Photoshop, you'd write:

```
on open files_to_change
  repeat with a_file in files_to_change
    tell application "Finder"
      set the file type of a_file to "JPEG"
      set the creator type of a_file to "8BIM"
    end tell
  end repeat
end open
```

Now this script is not recursive, so you can't drag folders onto it. Just drag all your files onto it though, and it will change the file type and/or creator type to what you want.

But that's not the end of it. You probably want all files downloaded with Image Capture to have the file/creator type you want. Open Image Capture. There's an option called Automatic Task. Select Other and then chose the AppleScript you just made. From now on, Image Capture will set the correct types.

Lucas Mathis

Way cool. I don't use Image Capture much so I'm sure I'd never have even thought of it, much less figured out a workaround.

Lucas: You are a wizard, a true star (with apologies to Todd Rundgren, who named an early album "A Wizard, A True Star" a long time ago, before most of you were born).

Lucas Mathis Scripts cron Tasks

MacOS X has certain tasks scheduled to be executed automatically. Unfortunately, it uses cron for this, and the problem is that cron won't run a task if the computer wasn't running when it should have started the task. Hence you need to start them yourself from time to time.

You could do so manually using the Terminal, by typing this:

```
sudo sh "/private/etc/daily"
sudo sh "/private/etc/weekly"
sudo sh "/private/etc/monthly"
```

If you don't want to do this, you can use MacJanitor (**http://personalpages.tds.net/ ~brian_hill/macjanitor.html**).

I wrote an AppleScript so I could run these automatically at startup:

```
set my_pw to "put your password here between the quotes"
tell application "Terminal"
  do script with command "echo " & my_pw & " | sudo -S sh /private/etc/daily"
  do script with command "echo " & my_pw & " | sudo -S sh /private/etc/weekly"
  do script with command "echo " & my_pw & " | sudo -S sh /private/etc/monthly"
end tell
```

Or, because Apple's Script Menu can run shell scripts, you could probably put aliases or soft links of the shell scripts into the Script Menu (**www.apple.com/applescript/ macosx/script_menu/**).

So you don't need MacJanitor if you don't want to use it.

Lucas Mathis

15

There's no reason I can think of to not use MacJanitor, which we've talked about several times before. But this is a good example of how AppleScript can solve a problem. And if Brian hadn't written MacJanitor, this is probably how we'd all be doing it.

— ◊ —

Greg's AppleScript to Launch OS X from OS 9

I keep the script in Leonard Rosenthols' OSA Menu as a compiled script, and simply click it to boot into Mac OS X. Here's the AppleScript:

```
tell application "Startup Disk"
 activate
 set startup system folder alias to alias "Mac OS
X:System:Library:CoreServices:BootX"
end tell
tell application "Finder" to restart
```

Greg Spence

Isn't that something? Way back in Chapter 6, which I wrote long before the tips started pouring in, I talked about this script and said, "I don't remember where I got it, but I have a handy little AppleScript that changes my startup disk to OS X when I'm booted in OS 9, then restarts my Mac with OS X."

So, because Greg was the only one to submit it, I'm going to give him credit for it.

One last thing: Don't forget to change the Mac OS X *in the third line of code to your hard disk's name, or the script won't work (unless, of course, your hard disk's name actually is* Mac OS X*).*

Potpourri

Which brings us to our final section, Potpourri, which is another way of saying, "catch-all-for-tips-that-didn't-really-fit-anywhere-else."

NOTE

Then, it's off to our final chapter together, the always enjoyable, "MacStyles of the Not-So-Rich-and-Famous (Power Users)," where you'll see the Mac OS X desktops of more than a dozen different power users.

Quickie for Dragging Background Windows

Here's a quickie. Holding down Command and dragging background windows works almost universally. With live dragging, it's also a lot more useful. I often use this to shuffle a window around until I can minimize it into the Dock.

Marshall Pierce

I mentioned it in Chapter 2, but it's something I use a lot, so it's worth repeating. Thanks, Marshall.

— ◊ —

They Should Have Called It TimBukFree :-)

I think that you ought to plug AT&T Research's VNC program. The OS X server is available at **www.osxvnc.com** and is called "OSXVNC". The client I like is called VNCThing.

It is quite similar to Timbuktu. It works over IP only (not on AppleTalk networks), and is limited in certain scopes. However, it does work on just about any platform, and is, best of all, free!

You'll find VNCThing at **www.webthing.net/vncthing/**. The main VNC Site is at **www.uk.research.att.com/vnc/**. You can download servers and clients for any number of platforms there.

I currently use it to control a Windows 98 machine that runs a barcode system at the other end of our large building. No more walking back and forth for me!

Tom Rymes

Coolness. You just can't beat free. If I didn't have my free reviewer's copy of Timbuktu Pro that I'm real happy with I'd certainly try it. (What can I say? It's a tough job, but somebody has to do it!)

— ◊ —

Security Tip

In Classic Mac OS, Multiple Users was fairly secure. You would need to use a CD to boot from to bypass it. In Mac OS X, you don't need a CD to bypass login security, as long as you can reboot a Mac OS X machine, you can simply "root" it. Either by trashing the NetInfo database, or by **sudo passwd root** and so on.

So, how can you 100 percent secure your machine?

You can set a firmware password, which means that you need the firmware password to even be able to boot the machine.

This might not seem like a Mac OS X tip, but I believe it to be an important one, because you can root Mac OS X in less two minutes.

To set a firmware password, do the following:

Hold down Command+Option+O+F on boot. You should boot into Open Firmware. Type "Password" and press Enter. Here, you need to enter the firmware password.

Dr. Mac: The OS X Files

Then type "setenv security-mode full" and press Enter. They type "reset-all" and press Enter.

Your machine will now restart, booting straight into Open Firmware, and it will continue doing that on each boot.

To start up the machine, you need to type "Mac-boot" and press Enter and then the password you previously set.

P.S.: You have to do this each time you boot. But your machine should now be fairly secure to hands-on access hackers.

Tor Hildrum

When Tor submitted that tip, his way was the only way. But in December, 2001, Apple released a program that lets you do the Open Firmware password setting Tor just described using a slick Aqua application instead of the command line. Figure 15.16 shows what you see when you start up a Mac with an Open Firmware password.

Figure 15.16
The Startup Manager with Open Firmware password enabled.

So you can't even get past this point, long before the Mac OS X splash screen, unless you have the OF password.

*You really ought to read the Apple KnowledgeBase article about this before you decide whether it's right for you. It's at **http://kbase.info.apple.com/** and is called "Mac OS X 10.1: How to Set up Open Firmware Password Protection." Search for Article ID: 106482.*

Then, there's the Open Firmware Password program, as seen in Figure 15.17.

*To read the Apple KnowledgeBase article about this and download the program, go to: **http://kbase.info.apple.com/** and search for Article ID: 120095, which is called "Open Firmware Password 1.0.2: Information and Download."*

— ◊ —

How to Move Your Home to a New Neighborhood (i.e., Another Volume or Disk)

For people using beige G3s or earlier (unsupported machines), the partition holding OS X must begin and end within the first 8GB. Assuming that you put OS X, the

Figure 15.17
No offense, Tor, but I'd rather do it with this Open Firmware Password program from Apple.

classic System folder, and all your applications on that same partition, there's not a lot of space left for a few home folders with all the documents, email, Web pages, iTunes library, photos, and so on that most of us generate. The other option, having a collection of folders on a second partition, leaves a lot to be desired, because the OS and applications expect a lot of files to be in very specific places.

A better option is to just move your home folder onto a different partition. Apple conveniently includes the tool that allows you to do this in its Utilities folder: NetInfo Manager.

We'll assume we've got a second partition named NewHome, and that your short username is JayT.

Do the following:

1. Make a folder at the base level of the partition NewHome named JayT.

2. Open NetInfo Manager.

3. Click the lock in the lower-left corner to allow Administrator access.

4. In the Directory Browser pane on top, select Users from the level below "/".

5. Select the user JayT.

   The bottom pane should now list the details on JayT.

6. Scroll down to view Home. Select the Home line, and then double-click in the Value(s) column to allow editing (it should say "/Users/JayT").

7. Change the value from "/Users/JayT" to "/Volumes/NewHome/JayT".

8. Press Return.

9. Press Command+S to save.

15

10. In the Finder, copy all the contents of your existing home folder to the new one.

11. Log out and log back in.

Your new home folder should now be in effect. To test this, use the Finder's Go menu to go to your home folder, then check its path by Command+clicking the folder name in the title bar. You can then go to your previous home folder and delete its contents to free up some space.

Note that I didn't use spaces when I was naming these folders. Mostly, using names with spaces won't cause a problem. If, however, you plan to spend a lot of time mucking around with the Unix portion of OS X, some of that software will freak out. If you're not sure whether you'll take this step, it's always safest to plan ahead and be cautious now.

Although I haven't tested it, this should even allow you to have your home partition on a portable disk (think FireWire hard drive), and move it from between two computers that you've configured this way. Just make sure the disk is present when you boot up.

Cheers,

Jay Timmer

I like it! I have been thinking about moving my home to another disk to free up space on Das Boot (I'm down to 1.5GB, which isn't that much). I may just give it a try as soon as I've got a free minute.

— ◊ —

PDF—Pretty Darn Fantastic

I've been a Mac user for 12 years and although I am not a Power User, I'm a Power User Wannabe.

So, picture my moment of epiphany when I realized that having the ability to convert documents to PDF easily (and freely) solved 99 percent of my compatibility issues with other (PC) platforms! Woohoo!

Virtually everything you do in OS X can be saved as a PDF file in Mac OS X. Documents, Web pages, even screen captures! With all formatting intact and all graphics included. Sweet.

Under the Print Menu, pull down to Output Options on the pop-up menu and choose PDF. Save to the desktop. Then later, just send them as attachments. Every PC I've ever laid hands on has the free Acrobat Reader on it. Cool.

(Some background. . .)

Most documents that I send to others are read-only, and are not meant to be edited—things like resumes, letters, flyers, and invoices for contract services. I like to think that I represent an average ordinary computer user, because documents that I produce do not get much more complicated than that.

For my resumes and letters, I use AppleWorks. For invoices I'm using the same five-year-old version of QuickBooks Pro. I first discovered this amazing Mac feat late in life and under OS 8.6. A quiet, little shareware program by James Walker called PrintToPDF (**www.jwwalker.com**) installs in your Extensions folder as a "printer" extension. It appears in your Chooser window and plays nice with your system because nothing loads upon startup, minimizing Extension conflicts.

So, by the time OS X came out, I was actively seeking this very same feature. Lo and behold, they added it natively. (Apologies to Mr. Walker, but a nod of appreciation as well.)

I've seen some progressive attorneys from California maintaining lots of legal documents, evidence, exhibits, and the like as PDFs on their laptops. So, when a Mac user like myself can finally relate to a corporate Windows user, it's a beautiful thing.

Now my desktop is pock-marked with PDFs. PDF is my new file format of choice!

Michael Labay

The more I use them, the more I like them. And it is nice to have it right there in the Print dialog box, as shown in Figure 15.18.

The results can be seen in Figure 15.19.

— ◊ —

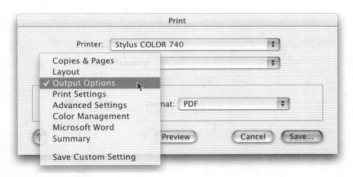

Figure 15.18
The Output Options pane of the Print dialog box.

15

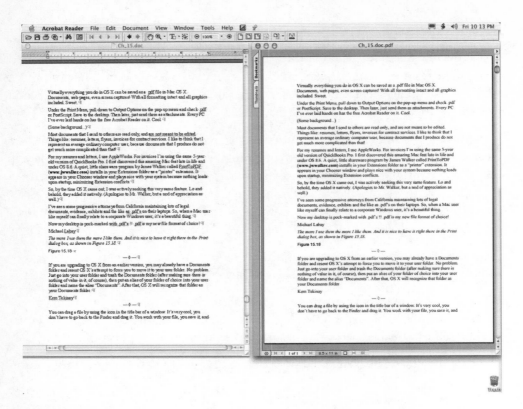

Figure 15.19
The one on the left is the document being edited in Microsoft Word; the one on the right is the PDF I just printed of it, displayed in Acrobat Reader.

How to Put Your Documents Folder Anywhere You Want It

If you are upgrading to OS X from an earlier version, you may already have a Documents folder and resent OS X's attempt to force you to move it to your Users/Home folder. No problem. Just go into your User folder and trash the Documents folder (after making sure there is nothing of value in it, of course), then put an alias of your folder of choice into your Home folder and name the alias "Documents". After that, OS X will recognize that folder (the one the alias points to) as your Documents folder.

Kem Tekinay

Yup. I said something similar before when we were talking about sharing an iTunes music library. My Documents folder actually resides on Number Nine—the Documents folder you see in my Home directory on Das Boot is merely an alias of the real Documents folder on Number Nine.

— ◊ —

File Sharing with a FireWire Cable? You Bet!

You can link two Macs together with a FireWire cable. This technique, called Target Disk Mode, is usually used between a laptop and a desktop Mac, but any FireWire Mac can be the target.

Here's how to do it:

1. Turn off the target Mac.

2. Connect your Mac to the target Mac with a FireWire cable.

3. Hold down the T key and power up the target Mac. It starts up in Target Disk Mode, and its drives and volumes automatically mount on your Mac.

Olivier Lebra

I don't think this particular procedure has been mentioned yet, and I probably should have included it somewhere. I use it all the time. Oh well, it's certainly a useful thing to know. So thanks for thinking of it for this section, Olivier. Someday someone is going to say to you, "Your tip was a lifesaver for me."

— ◊ —

Typing Funny Characters with the Option Key

In Classic applications, enter an accented character in a text box of any sort (Save dialog, document, Web browser URL line, and so on) by Option+typing the character for which the accent mark is assigned in Key Caps and then the vowel (or N for Ò), and you get what you asked for.

However, notice that in Cocoa applications, when you Option+type the key with the accent assigned, you get the desired accent character highlighted orange, confirming your selection. Then type the letter to appear underneath it. Those who type other languages using English characters (like French and Spanish) will like the reminder of the accent they are typing before they type it.

Classic apps never make any visible movement until the second character is typed. This is just one more Mac OS X nicety that shows the user what is happening before it happens. (Carbon apps go a similar direction as Cocoa by showing the accent and an ellipsis [AppleWorks Save dialog] or zigzag [Finder Show Info window] character below it.)

Ben Rosenthal

Yup. Another reason OS X is such a sweet OS. Little touches like that abound. Thanks for pointing that one out—I don't think I'd ever noticed it before.

— ◊ —

15

Use Multiple User Accounts to Save Your Marriage!

While the Multiple User aspect of OS X can be helpful for those in a lab, workstation, or gigantic family setting, it can also be a crucial and effective way of saving a two-person relationship. One particular preference owners of Apple portables should note is the setting that makes tapping a clicking action. My wife and I have two very different philosophies on this, and whenever one of us uses our iBook, it is inevitably set on the opposite preference. The answer? Multiple Users, and now my wife has a zoo picture she took of a camel pop-up as her desktop picture, the Dock set on the left with her work document folder waiting there, and she can tap and click to her heart's content.

Dean & Corri Browell

Ha. That's cute. My solution was equally effective but much more expensive. I bought the wives and kids each their own iMac. It was expensive but worth it—I don't have to deal with peanut butter and pancake syrup on my input devices anymore, and I don't have to bother with multiple accounts on my Mac (except for my four or five different ones I use for different purposes).

Type and Creator Codes: They're Back

I actually found this in *MWJ* (which is a tip all by itself, actually): **www.macjournals.com.**

In MacOS 9, you could use ResEdit to change type and creator of files. Nowadays, in MacOS X, there are files that don't have their type and creator code set and that you can't change with ResEdit, because they're bundles, which means that they're actually folders showing up in the Finder as files. If you want to change the type and creator codes of these files, proceed accordingly:

1. Control+click the bundle and select Show Package Contents.

2. Open the Contents folder.

3. Open the PkgInfo file in a text editor (if the file is owned by root, you might have to use BBEdit [which can edit root files]. Or, if you don't have BBEdit, open the Terminal, type "sudo pico", drag the file into the Terminal window, press Return, enter your password, edit the file, exit with Control+X, press Y, and press Return).

4. Now that you've opened the file, you'll see something like "BNDL????". The first four letters are the file type; the second, the file creator. Change them to whatever you want and save the file. That's it.

If the Finder doesn't recognize the changes, trash the Launch Services databases (in ~/ Library/Preferences/, the files called LSApplications, LSClaimedTypes, and

LSSchemes). This is actually another tip by itself too: If you have problems that you'd normally solve by rebuilding the desktop file in OS 9, just do this in OS X.

In *MWJ*, they actually described the tip because they thought it would solve the iDVD-problem where Preference Panes showed up as iDVD files and launched iDVD instead of System Preferences.

If *that* happens to you, just change type and creator code of system preference panes (you can find the preinstalled ones in /System/Library/PreferencePanes) to BNDL and sprf. That should solve the problem.

Lucas Mathis

Lucas, you amaze me. I really like that comparison of rebuilding the OS 9 desktop to trashing the three "LS" files. I never thought of it that way, but it's a good way to describe when you should probably give the LS-trash thing a shot. Thanks.

Also, I feel terrible about not having mentioned MWJ *before. They should have been raved about several times by now, and I completely omitted them. I'll try to make it up here because* MWJ *(and its sister publication,* MDJ*) are the only Mac publications I feel are worth paying for. Each issue provides news, information, opinions, products, and perhaps the most insightful analysis in the industry. Plus, Matt (the editor) injects a healthy dose of skepticism into every page.*

I look forward to MacJournal. *When I see one in my in box I sometimes save it for later, as a reward or treat for finishing some other task. It's that good.*

So please, go to the MacJournal *Web site and check them out. There's usually a "try it free for X days" deal going on. Take them up on it, and you'll almost certainly be willing to pay their reasonable subscription fee to get this caliber of news, not available elsewhere, sent to your email box regularly.*

— ◊ —

Lucas Gets Rid of That Pesky Internet Explorer Once and for All

If the Mac keeps changing your default browser to Internet Explorer, rename it. Go to the Applications folder and rename Internet Explorer to something like "Explorer." Now the Mac won't find it anymore, and you can keep the browser you actually specified as the default one. Which is iCab, in my case.

Lucas Mathis

— ◊ —

15

What Has 66 Pages of OS X Tips and Hints, But Isn't This Book?

A shareware guidebook has been released for Mac OS X, from Rob at **http://macosxhints.com/** (which is a great Web site for the technical side of OS X). You can also get it here: **http://homepage.mac.com/rgriff/osxguide2.html**.

It is a 66-page PDF chocked full of OS X hints, tips, and general information.

And it is the best type of shareware: inexpensive ($10, $5 for students), and you pay for it only after you've read it and decided it is worth the asking price.

Go get it!

Jim Krenz

He's right. I just downloaded it and it's very, very nice. If you've enjoyed this book so far, you'll love this PDF. Rob has done an awesome job with it. In fact, I liked it so much, I just contacted Rob and got his permission to include it on the Web site. You'll find it in the Bonus Round folder; it's called osxguide2_11hq.pdf. If you like it, do send him his $5 or $10 bucks. I just took a two-minute break and sent him mine—he earned it, big time.

— ◊ —

Backup Home Alone

A tip on backing up: Only back up the Home folder and any applications that were downloaded that are self-containing. They are self-containing if you dragged one icon from a CD or disk image. Trying to back up the entire drive is pointless and will cause more troubles down the road.

Greg Freeman

Yes, indeed. Unless you're using a program that lets you restore a fully-bootable drive, it's senseless to back up most of the OS X files. So design your backup strategy around backing up the most important things as often as possible, and other stuff as your time and schedule permit. Finally, try to determine how much downtime you could withstand and factor that in to what you back up and how often you back it up.

— ◊ —

Three Lists Contributed by a Genuine Rocket Scientist!

Looking forward to your new book—I have been writing an internal OS X guide for our NASA customers (we are the IT contractor for several NASA sites) and with apologies to your fine work *Mac OS X for Dummies*, I have titled my book *OS X for Rocket Scientists*. In producing this book, I created a couple of lists that you may be able to modify and reformat for your new book or combine with other user tips. I have attached the Word files—feel free to use whatever might be helpful—there are no copyright issues.

Nick Van Valkenburgh

Modify my eye. They're fine and with the print-to-PDF trick Michael Labay submitted a few pages back, it was no trouble at all to save them as PDFs and put them in the Bonus Round folder on this book's Web site. The three files are called: Special Characters.pdf, Key Chart.pdf, and Keyboard Shortcuts.pdf. They're all pictured in Figure 15.20.

Stash 'em on your hard disk somewhere—they don't take up much space. Someday any or all of them could come in very handy.

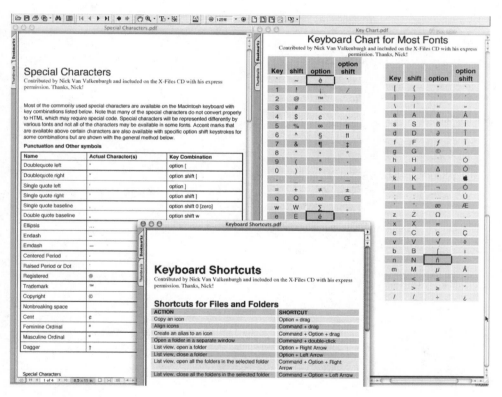

Figure 15.20
Here's a peek at Nick the rocket scientist's three lists.

15

MacStyles of the Not-So-Rich-and-Famous (Power Users)

If you haven't heard me say it before, I'm saying it now—everyone develops their own style with the Macintosh over time. The longer you use your Mac, the more likely you are to add those touches that make your Mac uniquely your own. I'm always fascinated at the way other people set up their work environment, and I thought you might be, too. So I asked some people I knew and some people I didn't know if they'd let me take my readers (that's you) on a little tour of their desktops. Believe it or not, a few actually agreed.

As in Chapter 15, my comments appear in italic type, *like this*.

So without further ado, here are a baker's dozen—desktops of the not-so-rich-and-famous.

Joe Zobkiw

The desktop pattern originally came from an old iTunes visual effect. I doctored it up in Photoshop to make it more desk-toppy (see Figure 16.1).

I run Terminal mainly to handle some telnet and FTP work I do remotely. Adium is simply the best AIM client for OS X—bar none.

iTunes is playing an ambient mix of a piece of music composed and performed by drummer Jeff Dopko and myself.

Sound Studio is being used to preview a vocal track for the tune, playing over top of the music playing via iTunes.

And lastly, in the foreground, Project Builder is currently being used to review some sample Cocoa source code for another project in the works.

Other third-party Mac OS X necessities include: BBEdit (Web and development work), Interarchy (FTP), Entourage (mail and calendar), OmniWeb (Web), and Snapz Pro X (screen shots).

Figure 16.1
Joe Zobkiw's desktop. I think his Dock is about to overheat.

Mac OS X really lets you not only multitask but to work smarter. When I first started using it, I was a bit leery that I could become fluent, but it didn't take long to realize that it not only thrust the doors open, it threw them right off the hinges!

Nicely put, Joe. Right off the hinges. . . . I like it.

Now look at Joe's Dock. He's giving his a real workout. Maybe he'd like DragThing or DropDrawers.

Anyway, Joe is one of the users I know. We worked together at a startup called **notHarvard.com** *a few years back—I was the Dean of Technology and Joe was a technology professor, who taught online courses about programming. Quite well, I might add. Anyway, thanks for sharing Joe, I enjoyed it.*

Aaron Lynch

Aaron Lynch didn't send any text with his desktop. But it's a nice contrast to most of the others you'll see—it's uncluttered and clean-looking (see Figure 16.2).

The icons are from a collection called Egypticus, which you can download from **www.xicons.com** *and is shown in Figure 16.3.*

16

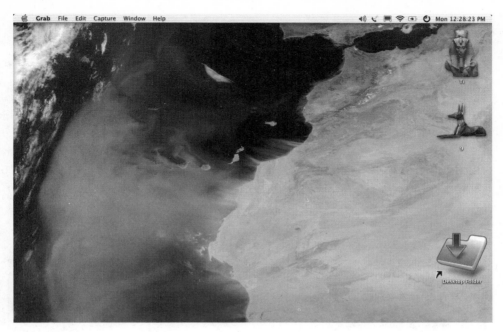

Figure 16.2
Aaron Lynch's desktop. I love those geographically correct (it looks like) Egyptian-themed icons.

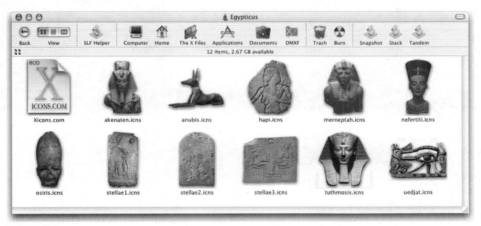

Figure 16.3
Egypticus icon collection. Gorgeous, isn't it?

Jonathan Gurule

Having heard about your contest for submissions. I decided to submit my desktop. Why? I think it's cool and original.

I combined two of my loves—the Mac and Star Wars—into one desktop picture that I made. I found a real cool picture of prototype idea for a Pod Racer. Pod Racers, by the way, were used in the movie *Star Wars: Phantom Menace*. So when I found the picture, I thought "what better idea than to make it look like an Apple product?". So I created my own slogan for the iPod racer: "1,000 miles in 5 minutes," as you can see in Figure 16.4.

Figure 16.4
Jonathan Gurule's desktop.

Now for the icons in the desktop: Starting from the left is the Finder. Microsoft Entourage for the red mailbox. Microsoft Internet Explorer is the blue globe. America Online Instant Messenger is represented by the yellow figure. AppleWorks 6.2 is shown with a Mac Genius atom; since with AppleWorks you can create, it only made sense to me to use the atom for AppleWorks. Next is a Fender guitar for iTunes. Adobe Photoshop is the last icon in the applications portion of the Dock. Past the applications is my hard drive icon, for which I am using a Pod Racer icon. The next

16

icon is for the Applications folder. The final icon, located next to the Trash can, is my own home folder. The Autobots icon is from the animated TV show *Transformers*.

I have changed all of the icons, because one of the great things about the Mac OS is that you can change the icons to make the Mac fit your personality.

Thank you for viewing and reading my submission. May you have the best success possible with your book.

And thank you, Jonathan. I love what you've done with the place. This is exactly what I meant by people making their Mac their own. I'd venture that nobody has a desktop quite like this. And that's a good thing.

Shawn King

By way of background, I'm a huge fan of old and classic movies and their posters. As OS X desktop pictures preferences is incredibly inadequate, I use the excellent little piece of shareware called SwitchPic (**http://homepage.mac.com/maceuph/apps/SwitchPic/index.html**) to randomly select pictures from a poster collection I've amassed. Other-wise, my desktop is rather boring (see Figure 16.5). I'm still experimenting with layouts and such under X. I haven't found one I like as much as my old OS 9 setup.

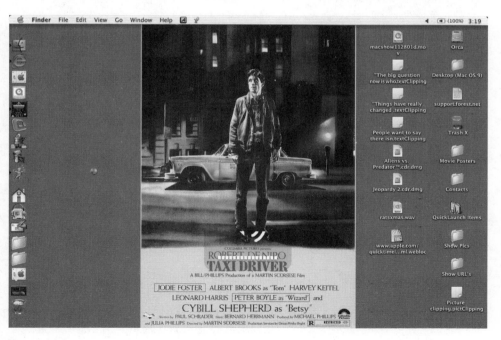

Figure 16.5
Shawn King's desktop. What're you looking at? You looking at me?

That's my buddy Shawn King's desktop. If you're not hip to Shawn's act, he's the host of an Internet talk radio show—The Mac Show Live. All the cool people I know listen to it. And, in fact, I was on it just last week (see Figure 16.6).

Figure 16.6
MacShowLive's Web page promoting my big appearance in January and a glimpse of Shawn.

You should definitely have that nose looked at, Shawn. I'm a doctor. I know these things.

OK, I'm not really a doctor, but I do play one in books and magazines. And your nose isn't that bad.

Here's my real diagnosis:

You seem to be suffering from a serious case of iconeverywhereitis. That means you sure have a lot of icons on your desktop. I think you need a dose of DragThing or DropDrawers.

And those clippings all over the place—aach. I'm recommending a round of Znippetizer-X therapy. It's a clippings database that stores and organizes your clips. Just drag text onto the

*Zxnippy floating windoid and later you can organize, sort, search, and edit them. It's neat. It's available via a link at **www.boblevitus.com/xfiles.html**, as are DragThing and DropDrawers.*

Jason Whong

The background photo is one I intentionally took with a shallow depth of field, so the icons would stand out better (see Figure 16.7). I got the rice bowl icon from **www.iconfactory.com**. iTunes is playing in the bottom-right corner. I use large icons because their size forces me to keep the desktop uncluttered, and because I like their look. I use normal-sized icons for windows.

Figure 16.7
Jason Whong's desktop. I dunno about those huge, honkin' icons, though.

I installed Apple's Script Menu specifically because I was tired of not being able to quickly launch my Calculator and Stickies. Looking for them in the Dock was too much trouble when I had six or seven programs running at once, and the Dock's hierarchical menus were too slow for me.

Writing simple AppleScripts to launch these handy apps took only a minute, and it's almost like having my Apple menu back again! (See Figure 16.8.)

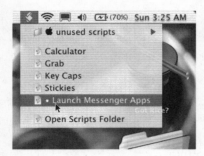

Figure 16.8
I think we have a consensus about Script Menu—it rocks!

I admit it—I turned Dock magnification all the way up because it's a conversation starter (see Figure 16.9). It actually makes the Dock harder to use when I drag something to the trash, but it's worth it to see people drop their jaws whenever I take the iBook out on the town.

Figure 16.9
Jason showing off: "My Dock's more magnified than your Dock."

Jason Whong is well-known to gaming fans as "the boy who ate the bugs at Macworld Expo." You see, he used to work for Andrew Welch at Ambrosia. One day he was quoted saying he would eat a bug for every bug that shipped in an Ambrosia game before the next Macworld. And, at the next Macworld, he dutifully ate more than one bug on more than one day. I was there. I actually saw several rather nasty-looking bugs enter his maw.

He's also a frequent contributor to MacAddict, writing mostly about digital cinema.

Thanks again for the desktop pix, Jason. Keep in touch.

> **NOTE**
>
> Speaking of Ambrosia Software, I should probably mention that, in addition to making the stellar screen-capture utility Snapz Pro X, they also make a bunch of cool and addictive Mac games, many of which now run under OS X. You can find them at **www.ambrosiaSW.com**.

Alex Morando

Here's my desktop for inclusion into your OS X book (see Figure 16.10). I thought this one might illustrate how many OS 9 GUI features can be duplicated in OS X, including WindowShade X, tabbed folders (DropDrawers), a Control Strip (DragThing), an application switcher (ASM) on the upper-right corner, not to mention OS X features like a nontiling background (Finder window in lower-left corner), heavy use of docklings and menu items, and transparent elements (DragThing Dock, OS X Dock, and the Terminal).

How can I tell? Look at all the cool software he's running to make his environment responsive to his needs.

I never thought about using both DropDrawers and DragThing together at the same time, but really, why not? It's not like I'm going to run out of RAM with 1.25GB in this Mac.

Thanks, Alex. I hope you find some stuff you like using the links on this book's Web site—it has a lot of really great offerings; I hope at least a few of them are new to you. Check out Watson. Also FruitMenu. If you want your Apple menu back, as Jason wished a page or so ago, FruitMenu has your name all over it. I'll tell you more at the end of this chapter before I say so long for the last time.

Figure 16.10
Alex Morando's desktop. Here's a man who gets more out of his Mac.

Bill Loritz

When I switched to OS X, I decided to clean up my desktop and just keep my most used folders there and keep everything else in the Dock (see Figure 16.11). I put an alias of the desktop in the Dock so I could get to those folders when other programs cover them up. The folder in the Dock with the apple on it is my replacement for the Apple menu. Other than that I have not done much with it, but then again, that's why I need your new book. Good luck.

I have good news for you, Bill—you're getting a copy of this book with my compliments and thanks.

I'm happy you sent your desktop. I suspect plenty of readers' desktops look more like yours than Alex's or mine. That's the beauty of the Macintosh way. You're clean, functional desktop works great, but you say you "need my new book." And now, as we near the end, I hope the book has delivered what you wanted. I hope I've empowered you, at least just a little. As I've said so many times, I'd rather not just give you the fish, I'd much rather teach you to fish. I hope I've been successful. Drop me a line and let me know. And thanks again, Bill.

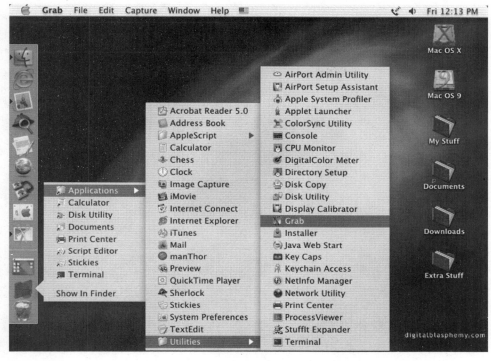

Figure 16.11
Bill Loritz's desktop. It's a lean, clean, mean-but-functional machine.

Jaime Romero

An easy way to organize your apps is to set up a separate applications folder in the Applications folder, and place aliases of the application (or the actual app) in that folder—that way it is easier to get to. For example, when FileMaker installs, it places the folder in the applications folder and then within that folder is the FileMaker application.

Furthermore, I have that second Applications folder in my Dock for even faster access (see Figure 16.12).

I like it. I do pretty much the same thing, and my structure for folders is remarkably similar to yours. But I use DragThing instead of a folder full of aliases. I know I'm beginning to sound like a broken record or a paid shill—and I'm neither one—but all these desktops cry out to me, "This person would benefit from DragThing." I can't help it.

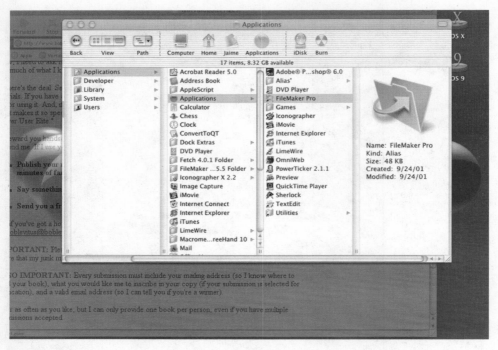

Figure 16.12
Jaime Romero's desktop. Well, most of his desktop anyway.

Paul Sahner

Here are some of the various programs I use (and can be seen in Figure 16.13):

- *ASM*—A carbon app that resides in the System Preferences. It brings back the old Mac OS 9–like Application Switcher.

- *iTunes Tool*—A small app with no Dock icon. It's a floating window that allows you to control iTunes.

- *TinkerTool*—Allows you to turn on the hidden parts of OS X. In this screen shot, I used it to move the Dock to the top of the screen.

- *Window Shade X*—This Application brings back the window shade effect in OS X. It overrides the Dock. In this screenshot, I used it to make windows transparent instead of minimized.

Figure 16.13
Paul Sahner's desktop. I absolutely love it. Period.

Also in this screen shot:

■ In the menu bar, I have two clocks—one digital, one analog, I learned about this hack from an article on **www.resexcellence.com**.

■ I hacked the look of iTunes using ResEdit and a package of images from **www.resexcellence.com**.

■ I added images to the backgrounds of my more commonly used folders.

■ I use custom icons to make my desktop more my own.

■ Using QuickTime Pro, I am able to download my favorite QT movies from the Internet.

Way, way cool. Looks like I'm going to have to pick yours as the one closest to my heart. As you've probably figured out by now, a link to every program he mentioned is included on this book's companion Web site, and received more than a little coverage. I couldn't agree more with your tastes, Paul. I hope you enjoy the book.

George Guerrette

I'm a big fan of that glassy trip His Jobsness is into, although I favor Graphite to Stoplights. So, my desktop picture (chosen randomly, thanks to RandomDesktop) is part of a nice collection I culled from a site with beautifully deep glassy pics (and some goofy stuff, too), called Rampant Mac (**http://home.att.net/~s.a.chitwood/**). (See Figure 16.14.)

I have always been frustrated by Apple's ridiculous limitation within the Apple Menu to allow the user to go only five folders deep. In OS 9 and earlier, I used BeHierarchic to assert my will to swim deep into my folders. Sadly, Apple maintained their rigid rules for the Dock. After searching high and low on the Net, I found the one and only software that does the same job as BeHierarchic. It's called piDock. It's popped open at the root of my drives at the bottom-right. A lovely bonus with piDock is that it has an option to show glassy bubbles gently floating up from its base. As I have my Dock oriented vertically on the right of my monitor, I also positioned piDock in the same place, stretching it all the

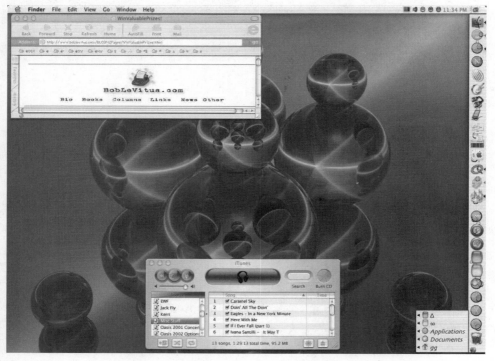

Figure 16.14
George Guerrette's desktop. Pretty, pretty, pretty. And big, too.

16

way up from the bottom. With the Dock set to a translucent background, these bubbles gently rise up behind my (yet more) transparent, glassy Dock icons (most of which are the handiwork of **http://homepage.mac.com/patrick9/Eye9ddd.html** and some found at **http://xicons.macnn.com/**.

The more colorful menu bar controls at upper right are from menustrip. And iTunes is hacked with a file I got at **www.resexcellence.com**.

Now, for my next trick, I have found a great way to organize favorites in Internet Explorer, and without additional software.

You can create folders in the Toolbar Favorites folder itself (which resides within the Favorites window). Name these folders by the categories of favorites you tend to collect. These folders will now appear in your toolbar! As you surf the Web, you can drag URL addresses from both the Address field of a browser window, as well as dragging links embedded within a Web page directly to any of the folders. When you want to use a favorite from a folder, click-hold on a folder and it will drop down for you, just like the Apple Menu does. It's too easy!

To allow for more space on the toolbar for a lot of folders, use short forms for folder names, or even alternate font characters to denote their contents.

If you want to rearrange the order of the folders in the toolbar, there's no need to go through the Organize Favorites menu command. With a browser window open, hold the Command key while dragging a folder around the toolbar to reposition it.

Also, if you want to clean up the contents of a folder, there's no need to use the Favorites menu for this, either. Command+click the folder and it will open up right in front of you.

This has to be the coolest "hidden feature" of Internet Explorer (see Figure 16.15). I don't know if it works with Netscape.

I hope these offerings rate.

Yes sir, George. You're a winner. Thanks for the snapshots.

I've never heard of piDock before, but it looks interesting. I'll have to give it a whirl. Thanks! And I love those colored System menu replacements, which you readers will just have to imagine. They look way cool in color.

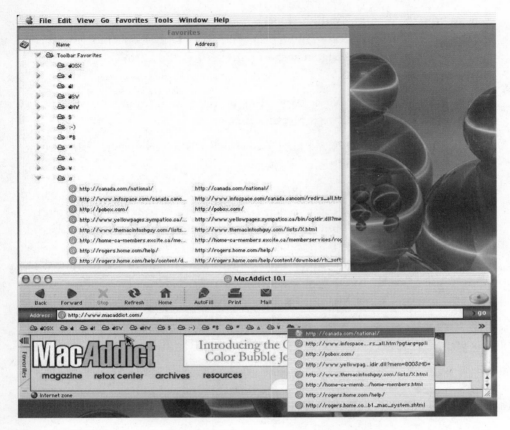

Figure 16.15
George Guerrette's Internet Explorer discovery.

Richard Krutina

In Figure 16.16, find ye a picture of my desktop—just because you asked for it.

Giffin Scientific is my company; picture was composed in Bryce (duh). Ah, and therein lies another tip, which I admittedly scammed from Macfixit: Fire up Terminal and type in "**defaults write NSGlobalDomain AppleScreenShotFormat JPEG**" because TIFF is just a silly waste of space.

NOTE

Bryce is a very cool program for creating three-dimensional landscapes and animations. It's too much fun for me to keep on my hard disk. It's worse than even JewelToy or Columns.

Figure 16.16
Richard Krutina's desktop. Yeah, those Bryce-scapes all have a certain look to them.

The Terminal tip Richard just gave you will change OS X's screen shot format from TIFF to JPEG. Because, as Richard says, "TIFF is just a silly waste of space." The production department might have something to say about that, but because I use Snapz Pro X to do screen shots, I can pick from half a dozen file formats.

Anyway, if you do use the built-in screen grabbing shortcuts, Richard's tip should save you some disk space.

Bob "Dr. Mac" LeVitus

OK, last but not least, here's mine (see Figure 16.17).

From the bottom of the Dock (see if you can spot them on screen) we have: Corel PHOTO-PAINT, QuicKeys (don't bother looking—it's hidden), Microsoft Word, File Monitor, DragThing, LaunchBar, BackupToolKit (35 percent of the way through a backup in the background, I see), Perfboard, and MemoryStick, which is almost full.

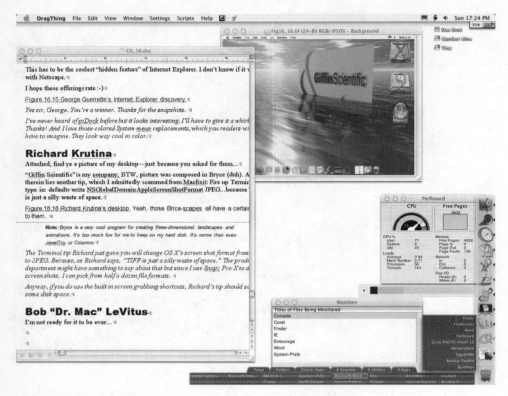

Figure 16.17
A typical setup for me.

Notably missing from Figure 16.17: Snard (I don't know where it went but it's back now), iTunes (I quit because it seemed to be responsible for all that RAM and CPU abuse I was taking), and two other things.

The first program I mentioned earlier, and it's a Chapter 16 exclusive, you won't hear about anywhere else in the book. But I've been using it since it came out and I've already coughed up my whopping $7 shareware fee for it. May I present FruitMenu, another awesome Unsanity haxie (see Figure 16.18).

FruitMenu is configurable, hierarchical, and customizable—you can even change the name of an item in the menu. The FruitMenu Items folder, which you can see below the menu in Figure 16.18, is the Apple Menu Items folder of yore. It's so sweet having an Apple menu you can mess with again. Unsanity got my $7 the second day and deserve every penny. Go try it. They're at **www.unsanity.com**. There's also a link on the book's companion Web site.

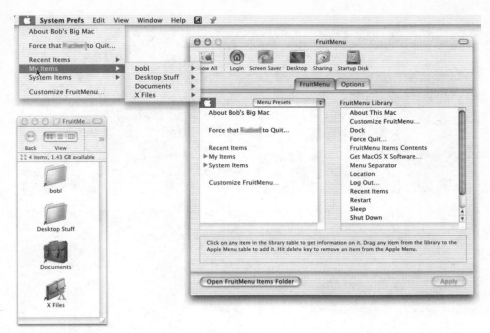

Figure 16.18
FruitMenu lets you configure the Apple menu any way you choose.

I did say that there were two things. Here's the second: My desktop is not white. I know it looks white in most of the screen shots you've seen so far in this book. And it has been white. For you, gentle reader. Apple's given us beautiful drop shadows that enhance your perception of windows on the screen. So I set mine to white at the beginning of the book process so the shadows would always be as clear as they could be. And when they weren't, I faked them with Corel PHOTO-PAINT's interactive drop shadow tool.

Anyway, here's the last picture of the book—four typical desktops you would ordinarily see instead of plain, functional, boring old white (see Figure 16.19).

Three of the four came from **www.macdesktops.com**; the other (blue gas flame, top left) came from **www.mandolux.com**.

And that's how it ends.

Almost. I'm not quite ready for it to be over yet. I've had more fun writing this book than I've had writing any of the previous 37. I hope you've had as much fun reading it as I have had writing it.

Figure 16.19
Here are four desktops I like. Imagine you've been seeing them where all the white-as-snow white has been.

Oh, one last thing: If you liked it, tell your friends. If you didn't like it, tell me (and please try to be specific—just telling me you didn't like it isn't going to help me make it better for the second edition).

And please, don't forget to write. I want to hear about your adventures, your favorite new shareware program, Web sites you recommend, or whatever.

Until next time. . .

Bob LeVitus
Writer and Raconteur
boblevitus@boblevitus.com
February, 2002

Index